THE MERCHANTS OF SIBERIA

THE MERCHANTS
OF SIBERIA

TRADE IN EARLY MODERN EURASIA

ERIKA MONAHAN

CORNELL UNIVERSITY PRESS
Ithaca and London

Copyright © 2016 by Cornell University

All rights reserved. Except for brief quotations in a review,
this book, or parts thereof, must not be reproduced in any
form without permission in writing from the publisher.
For information, address Cornell University Press, Sage
House, 512 East State Street, Ithaca, New York 14850.

First published 2016 by Cornell University Press

Printed in the United States of America

Library of Congress Cataloging-in-Publication Data

Names: Monahan, Erika, author.
Title: The merchants of Siberia : trade in early modern
    Eurasia / Erika Monahan.
Description: Ithaca : Cornell University Press, 2016. |
    Includes bibliographical references and index.
Identifiers: LCCN 2015041817 | ISBN 9780801454073
    (cloth : alk. paper)
Subjects: LCSH: Merchants—Russia (Federation)—
    Siberia—History—17th century. | Merchants—Russia
    (Federation)—Siberia—History—18th century. |
    Siberia (Russia)—Commerce—History—17th century. |
    Siberia (Russia)—Commerce—History—18th century.
Classification: LCC HF3630.2.Z8 S5256 2016 | DDC
    382.0957—dc23
LC record available at http://lccn.loc.gov/2015041817

Cornell University Press strives to use environmentally
responsible suppliers and materials to the fullest extent
possible in the publishing of its books. Such materials
include vegetable-based, low-VOC inks and acid-free
papers that are recycled, totally chlorine-free, or partly
composed of nonwood fibers. For further information,
visit our website at www.cornellpress.cornell.edu.

Cloth printing   10 9 8 7 6 5 4 3 2 1

For Seth

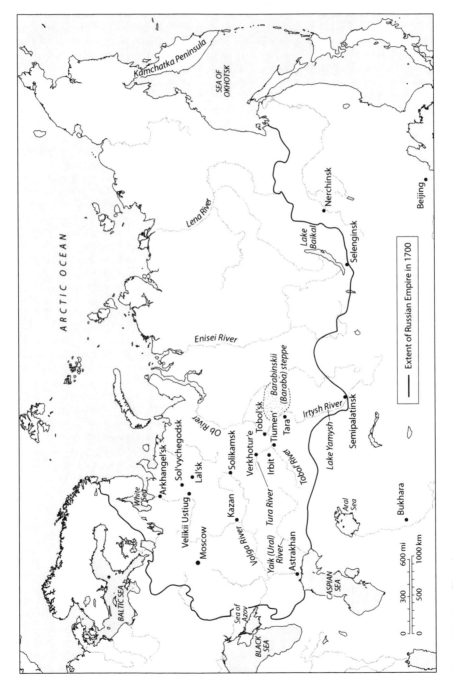

FIGURE 0.1 Map of Eurasia.

CONTENTS

ILLUSTRATIONS

GLOSSARY

dan′ tribute payment imposed by Kievan princes. The term was retained when it was transformed to a regular tax in Old Russia.

desiataia one-tenth tax rate

dvatsataia one-twentieth tax rate

gost′ / gosti (pl.) merchant who holds the highest rank, granted individually by the tsar and bestowing privileges and obligations

gostinii dvor the marketplace

gostinia sotnia the Merchant Hundred, the second tier of privileged merchantry

iam a station in the state porter system

iarlyk permission to collect tribute for the Mongol khan

iasak a Turkic word for fur tribute extracted from indigenous peoples of Siberia

kitaika very thin fabric; it could be made from cotton or silk

kormlenie literally, "feeding." This was the system whereby Kievan and Rus′ government officials extracted their personal remuneration from their juridical populations. It was formally abolished in 1555 but did not disappear immediately from Russian administrative culture.

kupchina state merchant

lavki trading shop

myt, the mytnaia tax levy associated with the transport of goods

obrok a term referring to various tax obligations to state, including rent payments on land or trading shops in the state marketplace

Oprichnina Ivan IV's secret police (1564–72)

podvod a kind of subsidy

polka a portion of a shop; literally, a shelf

posad merchant and artisan quarters of Russian territories

prikazy government departments

prikazchik agent

promyshlenniki fur entrepreneurs

raznochinets a person of no fixed social rank

rublevaia poshlina the ruble tax, the keystone of indirect tax collection in Russia

sukonnaia sotnia the Woolen Clothiers' Hundred, the third tier of privileged merchantry

tamozhnia the Russian customs administration: the government institution responsible for regulation and taxation of goods moved within the territory of the Russian Empire and across international borders. It derives from the Turkic word "tamga" which under Mongol rule meant "a stamp" indicating that a certain fee pertaining to commercial activity had been paid.

tiaglo direct tax paid in money or in-kind by townsmen and peasants in Russia in the fifteenth to eighteenth centuries

tseloval'nik auxiliary customs official

ushkuiniki fur trappers and traders of Novgorod in the fourteenth to fifteenth centuries

voevoda / voevody (pl.) military governor

ABBREVIATIONS

AI   *Akty istoricheskie sobrannye i izdannye arkheograficheskoi komissieiu.* 5 vols. St. Petersburg, 1841–42.

DAI   *Dopolnenie k aktam istoricheskim.* 12 vols. St. Petersburg, 1846–72.

Golikova, PKK Golikova, N. B. *Privilegirovannye kupecheskie korporatsii Rossii XVI–pervoi chetverti XVIII v.* vol. 1. Moscow, 1998.

MIUTTSSR   *Materialy po istorii Uzbekskoi, Tadzhikskoi i Turkmenskoi SSR.* Vyp. 3. Ed. A. N. Samoilovich. Pt. 1, *Torgovlia s Moskovskim gosudartsvom i mezhdunarodnoe polozhenie Srednei Azii v 16–17 v.* Leningrad, 1932.

Miller, IS   Miller, G. F. *Istoriia Sibiri.* 3 vols. 2nd ed. Moscow, 1999–2005.

NT   Bakhrushin, S. V. *Nauchnye trudy.* 4 vols. Moscow, 1952–59.

PSZ   *Polnoe sobranie zakonov Rossiiskoi imperii.* 40 vols. with 5 additional vols. of indices. St. Petersburg, 1838.

RIB   *Russkaia istoricheskaia biblioteka.* 39 vols. St. Petersburg and Leningrad, 1872–1929.

RKO   Demidova, N. F., and V. S. Miasnikov, comp. *Russko-Kitaiskie otnosheniia v XVII veke v dvukh tomakh.* 2 vols. Ed. S. L. Tikhvinskii. Moscow, 1969–72.

RMO   Slesarchuk, G. I., et al. *Russko-Mongol'skikh otnoshenii, 1607–1691.* 4 vols. Moscow, 1959–2000.

TKSG   *Tamozhennye knigi Sibirskikh gorodov,* 4 vols. Ed. D. Ia. Rezun. Novosibirsk, 1997–2001.

Introduction

Merchant Adventurer, and free of Russia

—epitaph on the tombstone of Richard Chamberlain, d. 1562

That Indian marveled immensely that nowhere [in Russia] does anyone instigate any sort of abuse against him.

—Foreign Office report of interview with Indian merchant S. Kedekov, 17 c.

Richard Chamberlain was an ironmonger, alderman, and merchant. He was a charter member of the Company of Merchant Adventurers to New Lands, the precursor to The Russia Company which, formed in 1555, was the major first trading company of the early modern era. When he was laid to rest beside his first wife in the graveyard of St. Olave parish in London's Old Jewry neighborhood in 1566, the epitaph on Chamberlain's gravestone read "Merchant Adventurer, and free of Russia."[1] With this phrase, he may have been fashioning himself a freeman with rights to trade in Russia, an interesting choice since this usage was one that neither The Russia Company nor the sixteenth-century Russian government embraced. Encountering this epitaph, however, I heard a different voice. Having myself struggled to do business in the newly opened Russia in the 1990s—an exercise in chronic perplexity and frustration that no amount of diligence could fully shake—my sympathies went out to this man. In the phrase "free of Russia" I heard Chamberlain, with a sigh of exhausted deliverance that transcends measures of success or failure, announcing to posterity that he no longer had to toil in the Russian business climate. He had had enough.[2] If this was the sentiment he sought to convey, Chamberlain was

---

1. Willan, *Muscovy Merchants*, 86–87. The Russia Company is also known as The Muscovy Company.
2. I thank Greg Afinogenov for bringing this to my attention.

not alone in feeling "worked over" by doing business in Russia. Numerous sources bemoan the venial officials, untrustworthy partners, harrowing
logistical challenges, cold, distance, amorphous regulatory environment, and
language and cultural barriers that added to the difficulties of plying one's
wares in Russia. It was true for foreigners and nationals alike. Even the most
privileged Russian merchants faced competition from both ends of the social
spectrum. More than a few entrepreneurial peasants from the Russian north
began in petty trade and rose to become formidable merchants. While they
were still lowly, they sometimes acted as desired functionaries for many foreign merchants, which their Russian betters worried would undermine their
competitive advantage. The highest, too, engaged in entrepreneurial commerce: Boyar Prince Boris Ivanovich Morozov, brother-in-law to the tsar,
was heavily involved in two of Muscovy's most important export industries,
leather and potash.[3] Doing business in Muscovy was tough going.

   And yet the stone-etched epitaph of this English entrepreneur does not
account for the range of perspectives on commerce in early modern Russia.
Incidentally, as an Englishman in the Russia of Ivan IV, Chamberlain traded
absolutely tax free, a perk even the most privileged Russian merchants did
not enjoy. It was certainly not a privilege the Indian expatriate merchant S.
Kedekov enjoyed. In fact, as a temporary resident in Astrakhan, Kedekov paid
one of the highest tax rates in Russia, and yet he "absolutely marveled" at
the propitious trading climate he found there. In stark contrast to the conditions in Persia, nowhere in Russia, he reported, "not in Astrakhan or Kazan
did anyone do any sort of offense to him and they let him trade freely, they
levied taxes 'straight,' and released him everywhere he went without any sort
of delay."[4] Granted that this Indian's praise, coming to us from a report in the
Foreign Office, is cause for skepticism. The merchant may have had reasons
for gilding his experiences to the secretary who interviewed him, but we
should not a priori conjecture that the secretary sugarcoated his account,
because how then would we explain the voluminous complaints of abuse
that such secretaries did record into the historical record?

   The point is that Kedekov's is not the sort of perspective that prevails
in historiography about commerce in Russia, where typically the state is
portrayed as abusive and the merchants dishonest, and both display copious
doses of incompetence. But this Indian's perspective deserves attention, for
Kedekov was not alone. Whether the commercial environment was indeed

   3. Geiman, "O khoziastve boiarina B. I. Morozova," in Geiman, *Khoziaistvo krupnogo feodala-
krepostnika XVII v.*, 1:lxxiii–lxxvii.
   4. Golikova, *Ocherki po istorii gorodov*, 161. All translations my own unless otherwise noted.

so sanguine or at least the profits outweighed the hassles of trading there, the fact is that thousands of merchants came to early modern Russia to trade. Thousands immigrated to the Russian Empire from the Near and Middle East and Central Asia and India (but not China) during the seventeenth and eighteenth centuries. In the 1730s when the German academician G. F. Müller interviewed descendants of émigrés from Bukhara, he received similar answers: their predecessors had immigrated to Siberia for the favorable trading environment. Could it be that relative to economies eastward, Moscow was a benign environment, and relative to economies westward, the Muscovite commercial realm was chaotic and corrupt? Such a position (which would problematically reify Orientalist tropes about East and West) falters when we consider that almost 1,400 Western Europeans also took up extended residence in Russia in the seventeenth century. Some European merchant families were active in Russia for nearly all of the seventeenth century; 50 English, Dutch, and German merchants made Russia their physical and spiritual homeland by converting to Orthodoxy.[5] Further, Richard Chamberlain was a first-generation member of the Muscovy Company, to whom Ivan IV granted generous conditions for the sake of English arms and an (unrealized) alliance. Not to discount a dying man's last word to posterity, but under the Romanovs, English merchants would know tougher times in Russia than Chamberlain faced. And yet still they came.

These conflicting perspectives point to this book's purpose: to describe the business climate and illuminate commercial life in early modern Russia. The above anecdotes refer to foreign merchants whose commercial interests brought them to Russia temporarily. Certainly we could stand to know more about the thousands of merchants who fit that category. We know even less, however, about merchants who were subjects of the tsar. This book is about them. Of course, one book cannot begin to narrate the history of all such merchants in premodern Russia, especially given Johann de Rodes's declaration that everyone in Russia traded. "Everyone," he wrote, "from the very highest to the very lowest, is occupied with and thinks only about how he could, either here or there, seek and get some sort of profit."[6] And so this book focuses on merchants who traded in the various wares that brought merchants from both East and West to Russia in the region that constituted

---

5. Demkin, *Zapadnoevropeiskie kuptsy i ikh prikazchiki*, 11; Zakharov, "Torgovlia zapadnoevropeiskikh kuptsov v Rossii," 177–214. According to Maria S. Arel, thirty-eight "Moscow foreigners," European merchants who had converted to Orthodoxy, lived in Moscow in the first half of the seventeenth century. See Arel, "Masters in Their Own House," 407.

6. Kurts, *Sostoianie Rossii*, 149.

the state's largest territorial acquisition in the seventeenth century. This book is about the merchants of Siberia—the practices they developed, the strategies they employed in dealing with the state, and the niches they occupied with their friends, families, and competitors in the Siberian borderland.

Merchants of Siberia

The commercial scene in Siberia was surprisingly diverse for an ordered hierarchical society such as Muscovy. A striking heterogeneity among the trading population is borne out in the "meticulously" kept pages of Siberian customs books, where it becomes immediately apparent that merchants shared the market with soldiers, women, Cossacks, butchers, Tatars, and to a lesser extent, administrators and natives.[7] The Russian merchants this book focuses on were what are known as privileged merchants. They belonged to one of three groups which existed very roughly from the late sixteenth century to the 1720s and whose membership was designated by the state. The three categories of privileged merchants in Muscovy were: gost', Merchant Hundred (*gostinia sotnia*), and Woolen Clothiers' Hundred (*sukonnaia sotnia*). The merchants were almost always Russians.

Before proceeding, a brief discussion considering the origins, privileges, and obligations of the privileged merchant corporations is in order. Fixing the origins and meaning of these statuses is complicated because all of them (*gosti, gostinye sotni, sukonnye sotni*) existed organically before they were formal corporations whose membership was determined by the Muscovite state. For example, two types of gosti simultaneously existed in sixteenth-century Muscovy: those whose status derived from the grand prince in Moscow and those whose status did not. Further, not only did their privileges evolve but, unsurprisingly in an empire of "separate deals," gost' privileges could also vary according to charter. Common early privileges included freedom from quartering troops, permission to privately distill alcohol, and the right to have one's legal cases heard in the court in Moscow. In general one can say that the privileges became more uniform and expanded across the seventeenth century. By 1648 gosti were free from paying the tiaglo tax in Moscow, although gosti appear to have enjoyed tax privileges before official charters indicate that they did.[8] Generally, gosti did pay customs duties on goods they traded.

Reflective of the affinitive, personal culture of Muscovite politics, each gost' was issued an individual charter document from the tsar, but there was

---

7. Kurts, *Sochinenie Kil'burgera*, 88.
8. DAI 3, no. 44, pp. 150–51 (August 26, 1648).

no founding charter document of the corporation itself. Granted, when they were operating privately gosti appear much like influential merchants in other early modern states without an incorporated status obliging them to state service. When in state service, gosti can be functionally compared with ad hoc commercial envoys from other countries: merchants sent on behalf of the king or khan. Their state service most typically consisted of manning state bureaucratic apparatus related to commercial and fiscal matters, or acting as factors of the tsar. Duties could extend to other areas as well, such as overseeing construction projects or fulfilling diplomatic missions abroad. This was an exclusive group. From 1613–1725 the number of gosti at any given time ranged from ten (in 1725) to 61 (in 1687), but the average was about thirty-two.[9]

If the gosti were the generals in executing Russia's commercial projects, the second-tier merchants, the Merchant Hundred, were a commercial corps intended to be ready to execute those duties deemed to advance the empire's fiscal health. Unlike the more exclusive gosti corporation, the Merchant Hundred and Woolen Clothiers' Hundreds corporations consisted of several hundred merchants at a time. Membership was hereditary and extended to all close male relatives (brothers, sons, nephews).[10] The Woolen Clothiers' Hundred corporation is much less visible in state documents. While the Woolen Clothiers' Hundred is specifically mentioned in some documents, such as a decree by Tsar Fëdor in 1681, many state documents that do mention the Merchant Hundred corporation do not mention the Woolen Clothiers' Hundred.[11] That the dishonor fine for a "big" merchant of the Woolen Clothiers' Hundred was equivalent to the dishonor fine of a middle" merchant of the Merchant Hundred suggests their lower status.[12] Presumably their commercial niche pertained to woolens and they shared similar service duties with the members of the Merchant Hundred, such as serving in the Siberian Office.[13] At some point in the late seventeenth century, the Woolen Clothiers' were subsumed into the Merchant Hundred.[14] Since merchants of the Woolen Clothiers' Hundred were virtually absent from Siberian trade, they receive no further attention in this book. Gosti and merchants of the Merchant Hundred fulfilled state duties and pursued their own interests when not in state service, and to some extent, in the margins of state service.

9. Golikova, PKK, 113, 148, 171, 206.
10. Solov'eva and Volodikhin, Sostav privilegirovannogo kupechestva Rossii, 3.
11. PSZ 2, no. 864, pp. 307–310 (May 3, 1681).
12. Smirnov, "Posadskie liudi Moskovskago gosudarstva," 91.
13. Ogloblin, Obozrenie, 4: 81.
14. Kotilaine, Russia's Foreign Trade, 203.

I am unaware of a formal meeting of the gosti corporation, although there has to have been some coordination among themselves, for gosti determined who would man which customs office with rare interference from the tsar.[15]

As with any project, the framing entails gains and losses. The purpose here is to write neither an economic nor a microhistory. I rely on existing scholarship to present an overview of the former, a component as essential as it is incomplete. In order to accomplish the latter, this book would pay much more attention to Cossacks, soldiers, peasants, and tribute payers. Thus my analysis of juridically designated merchants will not generate a complete picture of commerce in Siberia. But it can illuminate the social history of merchants in Russia and demonstrate how trade and state building interacted in an early modern borderland. In Siberia, the history of merchants also includes Bukharans, Muslim merchants who had emigrated to Siberia from Central Asia and were rewarded by the Russian state with privileges, although they were not one of the three privileged groups discussed above. This book attempts to show a textured picture of commercial life in Siberia, depicting everyday choices and challenges, and the ways that state administrators could help or hinder merchant interests. Such an approach is valuable because although in theory the state was disposed to facilitate (and tax) merchant activity, in practice the center's control over its borderland administration was hedged by distance and long-standing traditions of self-enrichment that preceded a salaried bureaucracy.

In these pages we will follow family commercial enterprises, sometimes across several generations. Although the concept of "family enterprise" is quite familiar in business history, the methodology used here is different. Histories of family businesses are often based on careful study of a business archive. Those internal records are then contextualized into the broader surroundings. But in the case of the enterprises of the Shababin family or the Russian merchants studied here, there is no family archive.[16] The reconstruction presented here is the result of moments in which members of the family interacted with the state. Imagine, for example, a history of the Fuggers or Rockefellers in which all the information came not from centrally located records of the business but rather the study of state records in which permits recorded, taxes paid, fines paid, and applications for permits, visas, and

---

15. Merzon, *Tamozhennye knigi*.

16. The only surviving merchant family archives that I am aware of prior to the eighteenth century are of the Stroganov and Pankrat'ev families. Sources do not afford the production of works such as Emma Rothschild's *The Inner Life of Empire* (Princeton, NJ, 2011) and *The Self-Perception of Early Modern Capitalists*, ed. Margaret C. Jacob and Catherine Secretan (NY, 2008).

so on were the extent of the information. Without the luxury of centrally located institutional records, illuminating the history of multigenerational family businesses is obviously more challenging. Historians from other fields occasionally comment on the heavily statist approach of Russian historiography, evidently without appreciating that this is not a deliberate choice of the researcher but a function of extant sources. This history is just such a case.

Situating the Merchants of Siberia

The annexation of Siberia began in the late sixteenth century and was superficially accomplished in under seventy-five years, although the Russian state would face real challenges to its sovereignty there into the late eighteenth century. Doing business in and across vast continental spaces in which the Russian state was just extending its hegemony engendered its own dynamics, and so the story of the merchants of Siberia cannot be told without attention to the state and empire building amid which they operated. This, then, is also a history of Siberia, of the borderland spaces the state sought to control and of the merchants who inhabited them. Siberia immediately evokes associations of exile and fur, but the history of Siberia told here is that of an empire learning to function.

Long before the Industrial Revolution catalyzed "economic growth" into its iconic role as the heartbeat of political economy, another kind of revolution had taken place. States had evolved and developed as entities that did more than mobilize military action, although military capability remained the germ and driving force behind the innovations alluded to here. As states developed from "domain states" to "tax states," administrative evolution was driven by the recognition that the effectiveness of the state's regulation, mediation, and participation in commerce in large measure determined its fiscal well-being.[17] In Russia, where somewhere between one- and two-thirds of state revenue was generated through customs—the taxation of commodities bought and sold—this was especially true. Finally, these important processes of state building took place in the presence of empire building. If it was once thought that states got their house in order before venturing out into the world, such a model does not withstand close scrutiny. It certainly does not in Russia.

Further, the story of the merchants of Siberia cannot be told without consideration of the larger context of the expanding world economy, in which Russia became more connected to the Far East and more integrated into an increasingly dynamic world economy. A defining feature of the early

17. Glete, *War and the State*; Bonney, *Rise of the Fiscal State*; Brewer, *Sinews of Power*, 25–134.

modern period is that the cross-cultural interactions that had been taking place for centuries gained a new impetus, increased in scale, and found themselves the objects of political scrutiny in ways that were new. As Martha C. Howell has put it, "Between 1300 and 1600 commerce left the margins of the European economy where it had been confined for centuries."[18] By "left the margins," she means that the fruits of long-distance trade were no longer confined to elite courts and the relatively few merchants and factors who supplied such needs and wants.[19] This is not to say a peasant or humble townsman never possessed a swatch of silk in the medieval period, but the products of long-distance exchange came to touch more germanely the lives of people everywhere. Sugar from the Caribbean, calico and cottons from India, medicinal rhubarb and tea from China, woolens from England, or fur pelts from the Great Lakes or Siberia became objects known to those not counted among the elites. Russia participated in these global developments even as its particularities make its history unique. This, then, is a history of family fortunes and imperial fortunes intertwined. Parts 1 and 2 are largely devoted to describing and explaining the institutional, social, and physical environments in which merchants operated. Without establishing concretely the linkages between them, it aims to make readers aware of the local, imperial, and global dynamics that affected life for the merchants of Siberia.

Amid such heady geopolitical dynamics and metastructural shifts in political economy, people were getting on with the business of living and trading. Although merchants are present throughout, they take center stage in part 3. Chapter 6 traces the history of the Filat'ev family, who rose to the pinnacle of Muscovy's commercial world on their endeavors in Siberian and China trade. Chapter 7 traces the history of a Bukharan family of Muslim merchants who emigrated to Tiumen' from Central Asia and prospered as merchants and occasional state servitors, retaining their Muslim faith all the while for well over a century. Chapter 8 delves further down into commercial hierarchies to highlight the history of one family, the Noritsyns, who never rose to prominence but were near ubiquitous in the networks of privileged merchants and in their own right in Siberian trade. It also features merchants from the Merchant Hundred who were particularly involved in the China trade.

---

18. Howell, *Commerce before Capitalism*, 1.

19. Long-distance trade was not entirely in luxury goods even in ancient times. Grain and dried fish traveled long distances, often as ballast in ships. But in the early modern period, more people began to participate in commercial exchange that encompassed greater distances. De Vries, "Connecting Europe and Asia," 35–105, esp. 91–92.

Examining the history of all of these merchants at the local level illustrates the pragmatism of the Russian Empire. This is particularly true for the
Bukharans, whose history also adds considerably to the history of Islam in
the empire. With the "imperial turn" of the 1990s, postcolonial approaches
became de rigeur, as Russianists rushed to close the gap between themselves
and other European scholars. Subjugated peoples, accommodation, and resistance received tremendous attention; indigenous intellectual elites received
particular consideration.[20] In the post-Soviet world nationalities studies
exploded.[21] Questions concerning Islam in the Russian Empire received
ultimate pride of place as scholars moved to write the history of Russia's
periphery, which is where the majority of its Muslims resided. The events
of 9/11, the Chechen wars, the rise of Tatar nationalism, and demographic
projections of Muslims outpacing Russians in Russia in the coming century
further conspired to bring the history of Muslims to the forefront. As is the
case with most post-Soviet merchant scholarship, the overwhelming majority
is contemporary in focus.[22] Further, it has largely focused on issues of identity, with scholars debating the extent to which Islamic experience can be
represented by state archives, etc.[23] As a result of this "overwhelmingly cultural" emphasis, "twenty years after serious research on 19th-century Central
Asia began in the West, we are still stuck with a Soviet-era narrative when it
comes to understanding social and economic change in the tsarist period,"
writes Alexander Morrison.[24]

Working in a time and place where the details of personal life and men-
talities are largely hidden from the historian has made the cultural history
of seventeenth-century Russian merchants I would like to write essentially
impossible. Where I have discovered such details, I have incorporated them
in the hope that readers who have struggled with similar absences will grant

---

20. Morrison, "Pleasures and Pitfalls of Colonial Comparisons," 918–20.

21. There was certainly an awareness of Muslims in the Russian Empire during the Soviet
period. Invaluable document collections on Central Asia were published (MUITTSSR, RMO). In
Western scholarship, Edward L. Keenan engaged the confessional complexity of Muscovy in his
dissertation, "Muscovy and Kazan', 1445–1552: A Study in Steppe Politics," (Ph.D. dissertation,
Harvard University, 1965). Donald Ostrowski's *Muscovy and the Mongols*, underway long before 1991,
addressed the legacy of the Mongol yoke in Russian history with nuance that anticipated the post-
Soviet blossoming of scholarship on Islam in Russian history.

22. Most of this work focuses geographically on the Caucasus or Volga Tatars and chronologically on the nineteenth century and later. My work extends and responds to scholarship by the
historians Lantzeff, Fisher, Pierce, and Hittle, who wrote several decades ago. Forsyth's 1992 history
of native peoples of Siberia is an exception.

23. See Stephen Kotkin, "Mongol Commonwealth?" for a plea that scholarship move beyond
identity. See the "Ex Tempore: Orientalism and Russia" debate in *Kritika* (2000).

24. Morrison, "Pleasures and Pitfalls of Colonial Comparisons," 933.

indulgence. Where sources prompt, the book reaches beyond commercial life to consider matters of confession: to explore, for example, Siberian Bukharans' engagement in proselytization or religious education among the Tatar population. Commerce and confession were, after all, fellow travelers. If this creates thematic dissonance for the reader, let it serve as a reminder that merchants were not solely economic actors and life was hardly neatly compartmentalized. Priests and mullas accompanied the caravans that traversed Eurasia and merchants invoked God's favor in all things.

Imperial Russian and Soviet Historiographical Contours

My central focus on commerce in the Russian Empire differs from a preponderance of inquiry on early modern Russia that has focused on the nature of the Russian state and its relationship to society. Marshall Poe showed in "*A People Born to Slavery*" that Muscovite political culture was not the original concern of its earliest European chroniclers, but from the sixteenth century it did become the central concern (Herberstein, Fletcher, etc.), which set the scholarly agenda for centuries to come (although it need not have—these writers were no less interested in Muscovy's economy). The state (and its relation to society) was of supreme importance to the first generations of Russian professional historians, whose statist, Marxist, and populist sympathies imprinted their work. Richard Pipes was proceeding along a well-trodden path of inquiry when he revived debates about the nature of the Russian state with his patrimonial model. In passionate, authoritative prose Pipes described a state in which the tsar owned all and there was no freedom.[25] The work of scholars such as Edward Keenan and those who have been called the Harvard School have shown that Pipes's model of despotism was a fiction. Keenan proposed that the Muscovite tsar operated under tremendous constraints and that hardball politics trumped theocratic principles among Muscovite elites; a "fictional subservience to an autocratic tsar" belied that the tsars were in fact "hostages—(herein the true secret) of an oligarchy of boyar clans."[26] Late-twentieth-century scholars have aptly attenuated the picture, skeptically interrogating the hostile pronouncements of early modern commentators to produce a more nuanced, analytically and empirically robust vision of Muscovite political culture in which consensus politics were the norm and interactions between state and society were in many ways reciprocal and

---

25. Pipes, *Russia under the Old Regime.*
26. Keenan, "Muscovite Political Folkways," 145, 132.

intimate.[27] Their work has incorporated a much richer picture of society into its assessment of the Muscovite state. In examining the relationship of the state to society, legal and political rights have been the main concerns.[28]

Meanwhile, and perhaps of greater import for this book, Pipes's chapters describing Russia as poor—poor soil, poor weather, poor agricultural yields, poorly fed livestock, poor peasants—were standard reading among a generation that was not directly focused on the economy.[29] Jerome Blum's *Lord and Peasant*, Arcadius Kahan on the eighteenth century, more recently Jarmo Kotilaine on the seventeenth century, and Robert Jones, *Bread upon the Waters: The St. Petersburg Grain Trade and the Russian Economy, 1703–1811*, are exceptions to a Western corpus of scholarship in which political economy has not been a priority.[30] With the exception of Kotilaine, these works too perpetuated images of Russian poverty and backwardness.[31] Remarks such as Nicolaas Witsen's: "They consider that Siberia, especially the southern part, is one of the most blessedly endowed parts of the world. In the meadows are many livestock, in the woods many wild animals and birds. The rivers are rich with the very best fish," found little traction in scholarship on Russia.[32] Consequently, Pipes's image of skinny cows (destitute compared with the dairy farms of pastoral Europe), the English traveler Giles Fletcher's likening the essential dynamic of the Muscovite economy to a lemon being squeezed, and assumptions about Russian poverty as a consequence of a dysfunctional economy seem to have been internalized. Yet, in addition to the vibrant trade world described herein, other bits of accumulated and emerging evidence—such as attempts to tally the funds Russia devoted to ransom or calculate the costs of armies fielded, accounts that marvel at the wealth of Muscovy and the lifespan and hardiness of its subjects—suggest that Russia's

---

27. Kollmann, "Concept of Political Culture in Russian History," 89–104; Rowland, "Did Muscovite Literary Ideology Place Limits?" 125–55; Poe, "The Truth about Muscovy"; Kivelson, "On Words, Sources, Meanings." Poe argues against what he calls the "Harvard School" view of Kollmann, Kivelson, etc. Martin, *A Bride for the Tsar*.

28. Kollmann, *Crime and Punishment*; Kollmann, *By Honor Bound*; Baron and Kollmann, *Religion and Culture*; Kivelson, *Autocracy in the Provinces*; Kivelson, "Muscovite 'Citizenship,'" 465–89; Kivelson, *Cartographies of Tsardom*; Ostrowski, "Façade of Legitimacy," 534–63.

29. Another influential piece that emphasizes Muscovy's poor physical endowment is Keenan, "Muscovite Political Folkways," 115–81, esp. 121.

30. Blum, *Lord and Peasant*; Kahan, *Plow*; Kotilaine, "Quantifying Arkhangel'sk's Exports," 276–92; Kotilaine, "Competing Claims," 279–311; Kotilaine, "Mercantilism in Pre-Petrine Russia," 137–66; Kotilaine, *Russia's Foreign Trade*; Jones, *Bread upon the Waters*. See also Hellie, *Economy and Material Culture of Muscovy*; and Arel, "Arkhangel'sk Trade," 167–93.

31. For a seminal formulation see lectures 3 and 4 in Gerschenkron, *Europe in the Russian Mirror*.

32. Witsen, *Severnaia i Vostochnaia Tartariia*, 2: 1019.

poverty is an assumption that bears revisiting. That wealth was unevenly distributed goes without saying, but how unique was Russia in this regard?[33]

While twentieth-century Western scholars debated the nature of the state, the historiographical traditions in late imperial and Soviet Russia had peculiarities of its own. When history became a profession proper in the nineteenth century, Russia was out in front, and not only in the Russian context. The Russian historian Paul Vinogradoff revolutionized the understanding of medieval England while M. I. Rostovtzeff made no less seminal contributions to the study of the ancient world.[34] V. O. Kliuchevskii, a giant in the field of Russian history, and other Russian historians were innovative leaders of social history.[35] Whereas other national traditions were writing more strictly political histories, Kliuchevskii delved into lower layers of society, striving to characterize the personality and life of the Russian peasant and soldier as richly as the machinations of dynastic politics. Such fruitful approaches owed much to the particular milieu of imperial Russia. The intelligentsia was stridently attuned to the consequential power of the state. Socialist and Marxist sympathies among nineteenth-century Russian intellectuals made them sensitive to the ways in which subjects' lives were shaped and ordered by the state and by their material conditions.[36] Whereas such sensitivities to statist and socialist frameworks supplied a certain comparative advantage to nineteenth-century Russian historians, it proved itself too much of a good thing in the Soviet era. Strident Marxist mandates ravaged Russian historical traditions. History writing gave way to crude materialist interpretations, inevitably bounded by pronouncements from Lenin or Stalin, both of whose names trumped alphabetical order in the indices of Soviet historiography. After the terrors of the 1930s purges, some historians sought refuge in quantification and annotation. Some bolder historians went so far as to couch perceptibly opposite analyses in safe state-sanctioned rhetoric. It made for some puzzling publications.[37]

---

33. Hellie, "Great Wealth in Muscovy," 226–70.

34. Vinogradoff, *Villainage in England*; Rostovtzeff, *Social and Economic History of the Roman Empire*; Rostovtzeff, *Social and Economic History of the Hellenistic World*.

35. The economist M. I. Tugan-Buranovsky (1865–1919) was a political Marxist who sought to combine Kantian ethics with a materialist approach. The progression of his thinking seemed to presage the direction of the Frankfurt School decades later. See Barnett, "Tugan-Buranovsky," 79–101. S. F. Platonov, E. D. Stashevskii, P. N. Miliukov, and Iu. V. Got'e, about whom one can elaborate in this vein.

36. Emmons, "Kliuchevsky and His Pupils," 118–45; Sanders, *Historiography of Imperial Russia*.

37. See Cherepnin, "I. V. Stalin o russkom feodalizme," 3–18. This article epitomizes the disturbing episode in which experts turned sycophants to Stalin's theories. Cherepnin sidestepped interpretive hazards by stringing quotes by J. V. Stalin together on p. 13.

The stakes for Soviet Marxist historians were high. The legitimacy of the Bolshevik revolution depended on it. In some minds, the Russian revolution had abrogated any possibility of commanding Marxist legitimacy by not having an appreciable proletariat to, according to Marxist theory, effect revolution. But Bolsheviks were never ones to let the facts get in the way of destiny. Intellectual salvation of the revolutionary project could be had if it could be shown that Russia had a capitalistic economy. Thus Soviet historians poured their energy into showing that the Russian economy had developed sufficiently to merit a Marxist revolution—this meant demonstrating developed manufacturing and a unified national market. This priority obtained in Siberian historiography as well, where historians sought out price correlations that would demonstrate an all-Russian market.[38] Theoretical mandates such as Stalinist anticosmopolitanism muddied the waters of impressive empirical research and made Soviet conclusions hard to trust. Soviet works that make broad claims are often based on a surprisingly narrow body of sources, such as Kafengauz's valuable *Ocherki vnutrennego rynka Rossii pervoi poloviny XVIII veka* (Essays on the internal market of Russia in the first half of the eighteenth century), based on close study of thirteen customs books, a small fraction of the number that would constitute a complete sample.[39] Another consequence: Soviet works maintained an intensely Russian focus. The intention was not to assess Russia's place in the world or to compare Russia with other countries (comments by eighteenth- and nineteenth-century intellectuals referring to Siberia as "our Peru," "our Mexico" notwithstanding[40]), but rather to evaluate Russia's status in relation to a theoretical model of development.

Lastly, if there was no return to the Silver Age, there was a silver lining among some of the travesties of Soviet historiographical scholarship. More attention was paid than in the West to peasant concerns and uprisings. A relative abundance of source studies and document publications provided a wealth of material to historians outside of Russia; indeed, such publications provided the evidentiary base of many studies, since archival access for Americans was heavily restricted. But this silver lining stopped at the boundary of entrepreneurship. Although Russian imperial and Soviet historiography made profound achievements in innovating social history, it was

---

38. For one among countless examples, see Vilkov and Preobrazhenskii, *Ocherki sotsial'no-ekonomicheskogo razvitiia Sibiri*, 1. He goes on to detail chronology by industry: salt, 1640s; metal, 1660s; leather and wine, late seventeenth/early eighteenth century.

39. Kafengauz, *Ocherki vnutrennego rynka Rossii.*

40. See Bassin, "Geographies of Imperial Identity," 48.

not inclined to explicate the social history of entrepreneurs, an endeavor that could imply toxic bourgeois sympathies. Insofar as merchants were conduits to commodities, they were unavoidable detritus of the past, but the individual merchant was not a subject of focus.[41]

While Soviets were busily describing the creation of the all-Russian market,[42] Cold War Western scholars were writing the history of the failure of capitalism.[43] Samuel H. Baron's unequalled (by Western historians) contribution has left the field remarkably enlightened. To his credit, Baron pioneered the path of merchant histories when others were uninterested: what the English-speaking world understood of the early modern merchant class in Russia was predominantly the result of Baron's work. Moreover, with his attention to the history of capitalism, merchant culture, and knowledge transmission, Baron's intellectual agenda has proven ahead of its time. Yet his important work also contributed to the entrenchment of what is commonly known as the "failure narrative" of Russian history. According to Baron, it was mostly a throttling state, but also a backward, risk-averse, dysfunctional merchant culture, that accounts for the "failure" of capitalism to develop in Russia.[44] Merchants' "failure to assimilate the dynamic spirit, accumulated experience, and methods of Western commerce condemned Russia to continued backwardness."[45]

In 1980, Paul Bushkovitch published *The Merchants of Moscow, 1580–1650*, in which he challenged the conclusions of Baron and his predecessors. Recognizing that there is no productive telling of the history of merchants without a sense of the economic context in which they existed, Bushkovitch strove to make comprehensive sense, from frustratingly fragmentary evidence, of the political economy of Muscovy in the late sixteenth and seventeenth centuries. As a result, in his monograph the merchants themselves get lost behind the economic history. Although Bushkovitch was criticized

---

41. Rare exceptions include Bakhrushin, "Torgi gostia Nikitina v Sibiri i Kitae" NT 3/1 (Nikitin), Bazilievich, *Krupnoe torgovoe predpriiatie* (Bosov and Pankratev), and work by Aleksandrov. For more on Soviet work about merchants, see Monahan, "Trade and Empire," 32–38, 81–85.

42. Bakhrushin, "Ocherki po istorii remesla . . . k voprosu o predposylkakh vserossiiskogo rynka)," in NT 1:23–236; Kafengauz, *Ocherki vnutrennego rynka Rossii*; Preobrazhenskii and Tikhonov, "Itogi izucheniia nachal'nogo etapa skladyvaniia vserossiiskogo rynka," 80–109; Tikhonov, "Problema formirovaniia vserossiiskogo rynka," 200–223; Ustiugov, "Ekonomicheskoe razvitie russkogo gosudarstva," 18–74; Mironov, *Vnutrennii rynok Rossii*.

43. Baron, "Weber Thesis and the Failure of Capitalist Development," in *Muscovite Russia*, 321–36; Gerschenkron, "Russia," 119–51; Kahan, *Plow*. Baron agreed that the all-Russian market was created in the seventeenth century.

44. Baron, "Entrepreneurs and Entrepreneurship," in *Explorations*, 27–58.

45. Baron, "Muscovy Company, Muscovite Merchants and Reciprocity," in *Muscovite Russia*, 155.

for this deficit, it is telling that few have revisited this important subject in subsequent decades. The title of this book, *The Merchants of Siberia*, gestures to Bushkovitch's contribution and continues his project of revising the failure narrative. The book's structure derives from complete sympathy with his view that the context is essential to reaching any understanding of the merchants themselves, hence the first five chapters, with a simultaneous attempt to come even closer to describing the lives of merchants.

Post-Soviet Scholarship

The demise of the Soviet Union freed Soviet scholars from obligatory Marxist frameworks. Westerners, never bound by the ideological mandates that constrained Soviet scholars, enjoyed vastly expanded research horizons. It comes as no surprise that the history of merchants became an important historical agenda. Using far more prevalent nineteenth-century sources, scholars have done much in the post-Soviet period to write the history of merchants in Russia. Siberia has seen a flourishing of scholarship.[46] The vast majority of this work deals with the late imperial period and is written in a triumphalist mode, as Russians seek, understandably, to rehabilitate a maligned class. In the 1990s, when many were optimistic that Russia was moving toward a market (not overmanaged) economy, this seemed like a natural search for a usable past.

What Russian work on the early modern period lacks in quantity it makes up in quality. N. B. Golikova (1914–2008) has made the most important contribution to the field, painstakingly reconstructing the membership of the privileged merchant classes of *gost'*, the highest-ranking merchant status, attained through a personal charter granted by the tsar, and *gostinia sotnia*, the next highest rank.[47] *Privilegirovannye kupecheskie korporatsii Rossii XVI–pervoi chetverti XVIII v.* is more encyclopedic than monographic, producing a study that on the strength of empirical facts suggests qualitatively new interpretations of the privileged Russian merchant classes.[48] Her second volume, published posthumously, explores the place of privileged merchants in Russian

---

46. Little recent work addresses the social and cultural side of Siberian economic life in the early modern period. The economic history that exists largely keeps to analyses of commodities and prices. Historians that have focused on Siberian social life have largely emphasized the military and administrative populations. Anthropologists have given indigenous populations more attention than have historians.

47. The third privileged rank, *sukonnye sotni*, is not investigated in detail by Golikova or Baron. This group seems to have been incorporated into the *gostinye sotni* in the late seventeenth century.

48. Golikova, *Privilegirovannye kupecheskie korporatsii* (hereafter **PKK**).

society.[49] Her quantitative analysis follows in large measure questions as laid out by Samuel H. Baron: Who were the gosti? Who was promoted into the gost' ranks (new men or already privileged families)? How long did privileged families last? Golikova's students, L. A. Timoshina and N. V. Kozlova, have produced valuable work on early modern merchants as well.[50] V. B. Perkhavko, T. A. Lapteva, and T. B. Solov'eva have added considerably to our knowledge about Russian merchants in the early modern period.[51] Far less work has been done outside of Russia. One study, David Ransel's *A Russian Merchant's Tale*, and some articles have been published in English on eighteenth-century merchants.[52] With few exceptions, the focus of recent work on merchants is strictly Russian.[53] Moreover, the failure narrative, despite Paul Bushkovitch's intervention, continues to carry much weight.

My work joins the vibrant world of post-Soviet history writing. In sum, this book makes two basic interventions in Russian historiography. First, it seeks to overturn Samuel Baron's conclusions that the state placed an effective straightjacket on economic growth. Second, the interpretation of Russian merchants as particularly passive and risk averse requires revision. In describing Russian merchants as such, Baron drew directly on the assessments of two hostile seventeenth-century commentators, the Swedish diplomat Johann Kilburger and the Muscovite dissident Grigorii Kotoshikhin. Their accounts were likewise embraced by the imperial Russian historian S. M. Solov'ev, who lived through the years when the Westernizer-Slavophile debate reached a crescendo. Thus Western and Russian historiography similarly propagated a distortingly insular, to say nothing of uncharitable, view of Russian merchants.

To the extent that these characteristics were valid, they were shared by many early modern merchants the world over. Of course Russian merchants were conservative. But the notion that risk aversion was a distinguishing particularity of Russian merchants disintegrates under a wider aperture. Normal goals were security first, status somewhere after that. Many merchants sought to escape their class if they had the opportunity to do so. Merchant aspirations to give up the vulnerability of money for the status and security of land

49. Golikova, *Privilegirovannoe kupechestvo v strukture russkogo obshchestva*, vol. 2.

50. Timoshina, *Torgovlia i predprinimatel'stvo v feodal'noi Rossii*; Timoshina, *Arkhiv gostei Pankrat'evykh*; Kozlova, *Rossiiskii absolutizm i kupechestvo v XVIII v.*; Kozlova, *Gorodskaia sem'ia XVIII veka*.

51. Solov'eva and Lapt'eva, *Privilegirovannoe kupechestvo Rossii*; Perkhavko, *Pervye kuptsy Rossiiskie*; Perkhavko, *Torgovii mir srednevekovoi Rusi*; Perkhavko, *Istoriia russkogo kupechestva*.

52. Ransel, *A Russian Merchant's Tale*; Bernstein, "Eighteenth-Century Merchant Portraits."

53. Exceptions: Demkin, *Zapadnoevropeiskie kuptsy i ikh tovary*; Demkin, *Zapadnoevropeiskie kuptsy i ikh prikazchiki*; Kotilaine, "Russian Merchant Colonies." This observation does not apply to work on foreign trade, of which there is much.

look foolish in retrospect, since we know liquidity became the ultimate mark of power. But no one operated with full information. The impulse was as true for Russian merchants who voluntarily paid fees beyond their income to retain higher guild status and have their children thereby be eligible for certain schools as it was for merchants in early modern Italy who ascended to buy estates in the hinterlands.[54] The Italian example shows that nationalist historiography has not only been hard on Russians. Italian city-states "were abandoned by their commercial elites, who, in the course of the sixteenth, seventeenth, and eighteenth centuries committed what could only [be] called 'treason.' They made no attempt to revive the commercial, financial and industrial base of their cities and retreated to the countryside as neo-noble landlords as part of a 'refeudalisation' of the Italian rural economy."[55]

Other scholarship has also recently highlighted the conservative and risk-averse nature of early modern European merchants, among whom family relations and gift economies long prevailed over "rational administration."[56] Alfred Rieber faulted Russian merchants for not valuing higher education, but *The Universal Dictionary of Trade and Commerce*, published in London in 1774, instructed that beyond arithmetic, bookkeeping, languages, and foreign history, child merchants-to-be should have no further schooling. Subjects such as "Latin, Grammar, Rhetoric, and Philosophy" were not only "useless, but also very harmful."[57] In Qing China successful salt merchants who patronized scholarship were seen as squandering the family wealth.[58] Similar findings regarding state regulation of traders suggest Muscovy was not such an outlier. Muscovy is often described as xenophobic and isolated, but the treatment of merchants from afar in Moscow was a veritable welcome wagon compared with the restrictions and scrutiny encountered by outside merchants traveling to the Massachusetts Bay Colony in the seventeenth century.[59] Of particular importance, attention to state involvement and patronage in early modern Western European economics threatens to eclipse the emphasis on supply, demand, and risk-taking spirit that, according to classical political economic theory, bequeathed Western Europe its

54. Rieber, *Merchants and Entrepreneurs*.
55. Musgrave, *Early Modern European Economy*, 114.
56. Duplessis, "Review of *The Early Modern European Economy*, by Peter Musgrave."
57. Rieber, *Merchants and Entrepreneurs*, 25; Postlethwayt, *Universal Dictionary of Trade and Commerce*, book 1, chap. 4. The guide was a translation of the French guide by Jacques Savary, *Le Parfait negociant, ou Instruction generale pour ce qui regarde le commerce des merchandises et des pays etrangeres*, which was originally published with state sponsorship in 1675.
58. Ping-ti, "Salt Merchants of Yang-chou," 130–68.
59. Bailyn, *Merchants of New England*.

special world-historical place.[60] These examples bring us to the crux of the problem with imperial and Cold War historiography on Russian merchants. Russian merchants were compared against unproductive controls. Imperial historians such as S. M. Solov'ev saw Russian merchants through the imbibed inferiority complex bequeathed by Peter the Great.[61] Cold War historians such as Baron judged Russian historians against a Weberian ideal of capitalist behavior that bore little resemblance to contemporary realities.[62]

Even as I insist on a reconsideration of commercial culture in Muscovy, I am uncomfortable with the specter of being seen as an apologist for empire: I do not see gosti as heroes to rehabilitate and I would like to think that revising Cold War stereotypes is not the most valuable contribution this work makes. Rather, its most productive contribution may come in the potential to better contextualize Russian merchants in early modern history as a step toward better integrating Russian history into the broader world-historical narrative. One recent work that takes just this approach is Boris Kagarlitsky, *Empire of the Periphery*, interpreting the history of the Russian Empire through a Marxist world-systems framework with a strong focus on commercial and economic matters.[63] Muscovy did not function in isolation from the momentous changes affecting commercial exchange from the Hudson Bay to China. Every history is unique, but especially in the early modern period, Russia's peculiarity has been overstated.

Integrating Russia in World History: History of Capitalism and Rise of the West

Meanwhile, changes no less dramatic were afoot in other fields of history that make this book relevant in its content and timely in its aspiration to situate Russia in a broader world context. The question of the rise of capitalism has long been of critical concern to important scholars.[64] The history of capitalism begins with Adam Smith, even though he himself never used the term "capitalism." Classical political economists claim Adam Smith, author

---

60. Adams, *Familial State*; Dechene, *Habitants and Merchants*, esp. 88; Braudel, *Wheels of Commerce*, 332.
61. Solov'ev, "Moskovskie kuptsy v XVII v.," 508.
62. See several articles by Samuel Baron collected in 2 Varorium volumes, *Explorations in Muscovite History and Muscovite Russia*.
63. For discussions that deliberately place Muscovy in a broader context see: Whittaker, *Russia Engages the World*; Kotilaine and Poe, "Modernization in the Early Modern Context," in Kotilaine and Poe, *Modernizing Muscovy*, 1–7; Poe, *Russian Moment in World History*; Kagarlitsky, *Empire of the Periphery*; Ostrowski, "Interconnections."
64. Smith, *Theory of Moral Sentiments* (1759) and *Wealth of Nations* (1776). Attempts to define and chronologize capitalism fill libraries.

of *An Inquiry into the Nature and Causes of the Wealth of Nations* (1776), and John Stuart Mill, author of *The Principles of Political Economy, with Some of Their Applications to Social Philosophy* (1848), as original standard-bearers of classical political economy, sometimes approximated to an advocacy of free enterprise. After all, Smith was highly critical of the mercantilist policies that classic economists associate with government intervention, and Mill, early in his career, referred to income tax as a "mild form of robbery," but removed the remark from the third edition of *Principles of Political Economy*.[65] Yet Smith and Mill were no less concerned with the economic dynamics they described than they were with the effects of markets on the social and moral fabric of individuals and society. Smith's *Theory of Moral Sentiments*, published first in 1759 and revised in 1790, explored man's inalienable stake in the interests of himself, his family, and his community.[66] For Smith, the "invisible hand," first invoked in the *Theory of Moral Sentiments*, is often taken as approval of markets and greed. The "invisible hand"—which Smith understood as men acting in their self-interest to the benefit of society at large—existed, however, within the superior constraints of ethical and moral laws. John Stuart Mill, for his part, came to advocate worker cooperatives instead of capitalist chief-worker associations for the organization of industrial capital.

The disruptions and stratification among economic actors (stratification was no longer a matter of social station) that Smith, Mill, and David Ricardo (1772–1823) observed intensified in the nineteenth century and fed the development of socialist thought. "Everything which here arouses horror and indignation is of recent origin, belongs to the industrial epoch," wrote Friedrich Engels regarding Manchester, England, in 1844.[67] For Karl Marx (1819–83), the most famous socialist theorist, the social trauma wrought by industrialization that his sponsor and collaborator Engels observed in the factories of England took center stage. Cutting his intellectual teeth in the age of Hegel, Marx developed a materialist theory of history in which material conditions determined social relations and historical change. Alienation from the value of one's labor was at the root of exploitation, which drove class struggle, the ultimate change agent in immutable stages of human history from feudalism to capitalism to socialism to communism.

The influence of Karl Marx's work on thought and political action cannot be understated. The key themes he raised, such as the role of material forces

---

65. Mill, *Principles of Political Economy*, v.2.14, http://www.econlib.org/library/Mill/mlP64.html#d8.

66. Smith, *Theory of Moral Sentiments*, part 1, chap. 1: "On Sympathy."

67. Engels, *Condition of the Working-Class*, 45, 48–53.

and social classes, effectively shaped generations of inquiry. Most, if not all, of subsequent European economic history is in a Marxist mode, a revision or modified elaboration on Marxism (Antonio Gramsci, Joseph Schumpeter, the Frankfurt School, Louis Althusser), or a liberal reaction to it (Friedrich Hayek, Milton Friedman, David Landes). Max Weber (1864–1920), author of *The Protestant Ethic and the Spirit of Capitalism* (1904–5), sympathized with many of Marx's concerns about modernity but rejected Marx's materialism and determinism. He sought the roots of capitalism in the cultural sphere of religion and ideals, unlocking the "spirit of capitalism" in a Protestant aesthetic. Alternatively, Albert Hirschman offered that pursuit of self-interest and consequent profit found legitimacy within a Catholic tradition that saw it as the lesser of other impulsive evils.[68] Still others have turned from culture to politics to locate this legitimation in the growth of absolutist monarchies that subjugated commerce to state interests, rhetorically harnessing commercial prosperity to virtue.[69] Materialists, too, have admitted that components of the superstructure require a central place in explaining capitalism. Ideology has been invoked since the influential revisionism of the Italian Marxist Antonio Gramsci (1891–1937).

In the twenty-first century, globalization confronts us at seemingly all societal layers—highly capitalized rainmakers destabilize physical markets from their keyboards with zinging cyber transactions; much farther down the wealth scale, remittances of "little people" sent across oceans to support family back home amount to massive movements of capital. Whereas many twentieth-century historians emphasized manufacture—Joseph Fuhrmann's ambitiously titled *The Origins of Capitalism in Russia* is an informative history of factories in Russia[70]—students of capitalism in the twenty-first century are more attuned to connections. Global institutions, global transfers, and "transnational" movements have captured the attention of contemporary analysts of the ever-morphing world economic order. There is much agreement that, however ill named the period is, the early modern period was the age in which the strands of global connection multiplied and thickened, long-distance trade became less exclusively luxury items and more oriented toward (proto) "mass" markets, which is not the same as saying that this is the age in which the West became the wealthiest corner of the globe.

One driving question behind all this is the problem of the rise of the West, a topic that fills libraries and remains hotly debated. Adam Smith and

68. Hirschman, *Passions and the Interests.*
69. See Takeda, *Between Commerce and Crown*, 5–7, chap. 2.
70. Fuhrmann, *Origins of Capitalism in Russia.*

Karl Marx both saw critical changes in the world economic order emerging in the sixteenth century with the establishment of New World colonies. In the 1960s Western liberal historians, rejecting the Marxist paradigm, looked to politics, declaring the "crisis of the seventeenth century" an explanation that contributed to a triumphalist Eurocentric model.[71] Expanding the post-Marxist Annales paradigm, Fernand Braudel's ambitious three-volume *Civilization and Capitalism* (1955–79) presaged importantly the need to understand metaconnections in ways that kept little people in view. Braudel (1902–85) documented global commerce, accounting for deep (environmental), middle (institutions), and surface (events) structures in an interpretation that is colorful, provocative, insightful, and anticapitalist but not Marxist. An account deeply inflected by Marxism even as it went beyond historical materialism, Immanuel Wallerstein's world-systems theory—which at the risk of oversimplification can be seen as a geographical application of Marxist class struggle—sounded a hearty critique to the triumphalist "rise of the West" narrative, although it still located the genesis of modern capitalism in the sixteenth century.

Other schools have done more to destabilize this narrative. Demonstrating that Europeans made little headway competing in, let alone controlling, Muslim-dominated Indian Ocean commerce until well into the eighteenth century, subaltern studies and world history have shown that the rise of the West was neither as meteoric nor as unique as previously understood.[72] (Such reticence to European hegemony, however, was contrasted to the domination of European *en companera* and slave-plantation systems in the New World.) Europe pulled ahead of the rest in demographic and economic indicators, not in the sixteenth century, but later, according to much less triumphant literature in which the problem of the rise of the West has been rebranded as the Great Divergence. Analyzing metrics indicative of quality of life such as life span and caloric consumption, Kenneth Pomeranz and scholars who have become known as the California School have argued that, until the nineteenth century, the continent of Europe knew a standard of living that was not appreciably superior to the standard of living in China or the Ottoman Empire.[73] Dating the material divergence between East and West continues to be debated vigorously; the respected economic historian Jan De Vries has

---

71. Trevor-Roper, *General Crisis of the Seventeenth Century*; Smith and Parker, *General Crisis of the Seventeenth Century*; De Vries, "Economic Crisis of the Seventeenth Century."

72. James Tracy, *Rise of Merchant Empires*; Tracy, *Political Economy of Merchant Empires*; Lieberman, *Beyond Binary Histories*.

73. Pomeranz, *Great Divergence*. NB: Cold War scholars of economic development engaged in debates about standard of living.

argued that the critical changes associated with the rise of the West are to be located in the seventeenth century.[74]

This range of understanding on when to date the rise of the West and the emergence of capitalist economies suggests that substantial reconsideration of just what happened during the early modern period is in order. Indeed, the work of subaltern studies has demonstrated that empirical certainties asserted in past decades are anything but assured. In earlier scholarship Western superiority was an a priori assumption rather than a concept interrogated. Indeed, to assume that absence of evidence equates to absence of activity—especially in the vast overland Eurasian trade—is no less an error than to extrapolate a norm from one piece of evidence.[75] A global perspective that does not examine just the Atlantic economy, or just the Indian Ocean sphere, for example, is in order, as is incorporation of explanations that span a matrix of economics, technological advancement, political institutions, cultural attributes, and combinations therein. For example, the problem, in De Vries's view, ties back into state institutions. His remarks on French mistreatment of its merchants, and Jack Goldstone's apologetic discussion of advanced organic societies' refusal to innovate, resonate with Russian history, wherein the state has been heavily implicated for Russia's economic deficits.[76] Yet Russia is left decidedly out of the picture of the reams of rich studies that academic presses have published on merchants and commerce in the early modern era.[77]

Also implicated in this new work is the "decline" thesis regarding overland Eurasian trade networks.[78] The classical interpretation was that the rise of maritime trading companies sounded the death toll for Eurasian trade beginning in the sixteenth century. But historians have questioned such visions: Morris Rossabi and Scott Levi have pointed to the political instability in

---

74. De Vries, "Economic Crisis of the Seventeenth Century," 189–90, 194.

75. Ben Fine calls this a "horizontal understanding." See John Brewer, "Error of Our Ways."

76. See De Vries, "Economic Crisis of the Seventeenth Century," 186; Goldstone, "Problem of the 'Early Modern' World," 249–84.

77. Kotilaine, "Review of *Tamozhennye knigi.*"

78. For the classic formulation of the decline thesis see Niels Steensgaard, *Asian Trade Revolution* (1974). It was initially published in 1973 as Carracks, *Caravans and Companies.* Steensgard's study focused on Hormuz in the Persian Gulf and diversion of the overland trade to the Levant after its conquest in 1622. From this case study, he argued for the superiority of English and Dutch maritime trading companies over peddler trade and the aristocratic and extortionist Portuguese company. Note that early reviewers found the work provocative and erudite but criticized the Eurocentricity of his approach and were not entirely persuaded by his argument. See reviews by: Simon Digby, *Bulletin of the School of Oriental and African Studies*, University of London 38, no. 1 (1975): 198–200; Fritz Lehman, *Pacific Affairs* 48, no. 3 (1975): 436–37; Briton Cooper Busch, *Middle East Journal* 29, no. 3 (1975): 367–68.

Central Asia that reoriented trade routes.[79] More germanely, sweeping conclusions have been extrapolated from narrow sources or a lack of empirical information about Eurasian trade and without fully appreciating the extent to which consumption was emerging.[80] The history of Lake Yamysh in chapter 5 offers a picture of a thriving node of inland Eurasian trade in the seventeenth century and sends the large message that Russia deserves a place in narratives of the connected world.

Thus the significance of this history reaches beyond the expansive bounds of the Russian Empire. However one characterizes the Russian state or the nature of freedom there, Russia, by dint of nothing but its geography (but for more reasons than that, as this book will show), deserves a place in narratives of early modern commercial expansion on a transimperial or global scale. This book eschews tired formulations of "Russia and the West" because there is far more to be gained by analyzing Russia in its early modern world context. In doing so, it endeavors to take a small step in the direction of better situating Russia and Siberia in the early modern world.[81] For example, Russia was notorious for bad roads, a deficit immortalized in the aphorism "Russia has two problems—roads and fools" (*V Rossii dve bedy: duraki i dorogi*).[82] But in comparative perspective, Russian roads may not have fared so badly, only in that the competition was similarly unsound. In France, "even in the eighteenth century the roads from Amiens—one of the chief industrial cities of seventeenth- and eighteenth-century France—to its port St. Valery-su-Somme were so poor that merchants frequently paid local landowners to be allowed to take their carts through the ploughed fields rather than along the main road."[83]

The question of Russian "backwardness" is effete and ill put, as is Russians' tortured wrangling with Russia's relationship to the West, but nevertheless Russian historiography has its own "divergence debate" to sort out. That is the question of when the Russian political economy diverged from the West. "The West" as a historical category, of course, is a problematic construction. Perhaps a better formulation is to ask when Russian political economic stratification diverged from societies that developed "healthy" middle classes who enjoyed material security and engagement in political process. Such big

79. Rossabi, "'Decline' of the Central Asian Caravan Trade," 351–70; Levi, "India, Russia, and the Transformation of the Central Asian Caravan Trade," 93–122.

80. For stimulating challenges to the decline thesis, see Frank, "ReOrient," 11–38.

81. See Ostrowski, "Toward the Integration of Early Modern Russia."

82. The origin of the phrase is disputed. It is attributed both to Nikolai Gogol and the historian N. M. Karamzin.

83. Musgrave, *Early Modern European Economy*, 99.

questions, of course, cannot be answered without consideration of political and cultural difference, and of political economy and commercial practice. This book, by illuminating the nature of commercial life in early modern Russia, presents one contribution to reconstructing the history of Russia's political economy and commercial culture and therefore making progress on understanding the historical problem of Russia's missing middle class. Further, arriving at good answers has been made more complicated by the fact that the Soviet experiment derailed Russia from inclusion in "normal" Western historiographical trajectories (a remarkable myopia on the part of Western scholarship, considering that a great portion of the world went socialist in the twentieth century). The rejection of traditional, universal historical trajectories has comprised a cornerstone of postmodern applications to historical study: every place is particular and Hegel is out; there is no unified historical path of development. Embracing subjectivity and fragmentation are the alternatives to being hoodwinked by pretensions to truth. These tenets of postmodern thought, however, have done little to reincorporate Russia into broader historical narratives. Indeed, a field in which the majority of sources were written by monks and government clerks holds little appeal for most cultural historians raised in a secular age.

Depending on one's perspective, the story of the rise of the West is a narrative of triumphalism or aggressive imperialism. Whether one sees the expansion of wealth, liberty, and happiness or a juggernaut of capitalist exploitation, Europeans colonized much of the New World, and where they did not settle, they infiltrated with economic might and political leverage. In the unsettled historical debates that surround these questions, Russia provides a valuable case study. Russia developed neither representative political institutions (for the most part, neither did most European countries in the early modern period) nor a voluminous literary culture. Yet for all its purported backwardness, Europeans never overtook Muscovy, although some would have liked to. During the Time of Troubles (1598–1613), a traumatic period in which Muscovy endured famine, dynastic expiry, foreign occupation, and civil war, plans to colonize Muscovy were more a fringe pipe dream than seriously on the strategy table for James I, but even that nonepisode aside, the imperialist stance that English traders took toward Muscovy is indisputable.[84] When the elite merchant Osip Nepea traveled to England as the tsar's trade representative in the 1570s, people at court found him a model of comportment, whereas Muscovy Company members accused him

---

84. Dunning, "James I," 206–26.

of untoward behavior. Evidently, his offense was seeking to negotiate equal reciprocity for Russia.[85] This episode, placed in a broader context, raises the question: What was it about Muscovy's encounter with England that produced an outcome so different from India's encounter with England, given that England demonstrated imperialist tendencies in both places? In India, with an arguably larger and more vibrant economy than Muscovy, it came to be that the entitled classes on the steamy subcontinent take afternoon tea hot with milk and speak English with a British accent. This is not the case in Russia, where tea is drunk black at every opportunity, a quotidian practice manifesting as a synecdoche to show that English imperialist impulses in both places produced quite different outcomes.

One aspect of this encounter is that Europeans failed to appreciate the geopolitical crucible from which Muscovy had emerged.[86] Perhaps in certain ways—formal education, print culture, fashion, consumption—Muscovites struck Europeans as primitive. But savvy Muscovy was not nearly as unschooled in competitive Eurasian geopolitics, covered schematically in chapter 2. Perhaps situating Russian commerce more vividly in its early modern socioeconomic context and illuminating the lives of early modern merchants in Inner Eurasia can help advance understanding about the Great Divergence. If that agenda is too ambitious, at least this book takes a step in the direction of integrating Russia into world historical narratives. I seek to contextualize the Siberian economy in the Russian, Eurasian, and expanding early modern global economies, a contribution that has remained surprisingly elusive in scholarship. On the question of Russian backwardness, I suggest that this is an issue for the later eighteenth and nineteenth centuries; in the early modern period, Russia was not such an outlier.[87]

On Empire

The imperial turn sparked much valuable work in Russian history. One productive scholarly vein has examined the people on the ground that built and participated in empires. Russian military brigades were not the only bearers of imperialism; Willard Sunderland has argued that Russian peasants have been passed over as colonizers because they hardly amassed wealth and status to be legitimately viewed as exploiters.[88] The role of merchants in Russian

---

85. Baron, "Osip Nepea and the Opening of Anglo-Russian Commercial Relations," in *Muscovite Russia.*
86. See LeDonne, *Russian Empire and the World.*
87. See for example, Kivelson, "Merciful Father, Impersonal State," 635–63.
88. Sunderland, *Taming the Wild Field,* 227.

history and expansion deserves a place in the constellation of how empires function. Indeed, Kotilaine's appellation of foreign merchants as "midwives" of empire can apply to all merchants in Siberia.[89] English-language historians have generally followed the Russian lead and mentioned the role of Russian fur entrepreneurs (*promyshlenniki*) without making further connections with the early modern world of Muscovite commerce. However, private merchants that ranged along a broad spectrum of capitalization participated in these dynamics. Whereas second-tier merchants, discussed in chapter 8, were often sent to Siberia on state-ordered business, the gosti operating in Siberia, discussed in chapter 6, did so overwhelming as part of their own personal enterprises. Where fur entrepreneurs were not merchants themselves, they invariably sold their furs to them.

Another important line of inquiry has coalesced around the question: "Was the Russian empire more pragmatically or ideologically driven?" Edward L. Keenan formulated the question in so many words in his seminal "Muscovite Political Folkways" article in which he posited a model whereby Orthodox rhetoric was checked at the door of the boyar duma. Michael Khodarkovsky, however, in *Russia's Steppe Frontier*, argued that ideology drove Russia's expansion.[90] When mastering the vast Eurasian steppe finally became a possibility, Muscovites embraced the project as something of a crusade. Brian Boeck, on the other hand, along with his mentor, Keenan, sees the growth and maintenance of the Russian Empire more pragmatically. His work on the Don Cossacks demonstrates the many times in which Moscow retreated at its southern fringe and, more significantly, accommodated non-Orthodox players. Boeck characterizes Russia as an early modern empire, not of universalizing Orthodox Russian culture but of "separate deals."[91] Thus two schools have materialized, on which Michael Khodorkovsky and Brian Boeck are on opposite sides: a pragmatic versus an ideologically driven empire.

Matthew Romaniello has productively moved toward a synthesis of the two views with *The Elusive Empire: Kazan and the Creation of the Russian Empire, 1552–1671*.[92] In some ways Romaniello approaches a return to Keenan's views—a center in which politics and religion occupied separate spheres (how unpostmodern)—but with more complexity. Romaniello argues that the empire was rhetorically and in the center ideologically strident and Orthodox, but in practice and at its fringes far more pragmatic and

---

89. Kotilaine, *Russia's Foreign Trade*.
90. Khodarkovsky, *Russia's Steppe Frontier*.
91. Boeck, *Imperial Boundaries*.
92. Romaniello, *Elusive Empire*.

accommodating. He argues that the center conceived of the Orthodox community at the fringe as within its purview and was prepared to police it, but that it was not prepared to "squander" a tenuous loyalty (or nonrebellion) on the fringe by imposing Orthodoxy (i.e., pragmatic). He shows how even the Orthodox Church was not an inveterate engine of conversion. In the interests of economic well-being monasteries in the Kazan region even defended non-Orthodox peasants against coercion by the state, a stance for which they were arguably rewarded during the explosive Stenka Razin rebellion of 1670–71. Romaniello's and Boeck's emphasis on pragmatism brings Russian scholarship in line with other recent work on early modern empires that emphasizes the extent to which empires managed politics of difference.[93]

This mix of Orthodox commitment and pragmatism is captured poignantly in a directive from Moscow to the governors of Verkhotur'e and Tobol'sk in the summer of 1700. The letter discussed fire prevention measures and instructions for reconstruction after fires. The document advised governors to take advantage of fires to rebuild burned mosques farther away from Orthodox churches. In taking such actions, the instructions directed governors to use their judgment and "take such measures not suddenly but considering the local conditions and according to appropriate events, so as to antagonize neither Russians nor foreigners [in the town]."[94] This book adds another layer to understanding Islam in the Russian Empire by examining Muslim merchants in Siberia, and it demonstrates the pragmatism that governed the Orthodox Russian government in Siberia.

Attending to governance at the center and periphery renders apparent the simultaneity of Russian state and empire building. Siberia was a borderland and remained so long into Russian domination. Scribes, merchants, lowly military men, and high officials wrote and spoke of Sibir' as territory that was different from Muscovy (*Moskovskoe gosudarstvo*); they were distinct regions between which people traveled. The creation of the Siberian Office, when it was finally separated from the Kazan Office in 1637, distinguished Siberia administratively. Yet even more significant than the particularities of the administration of Siberia as a distinct territory is how its incorporation into the Russian state was virtually indistinct from the emergence of the Russian state. "Empire" is a notoriously slippery concept to define. Defined most simply, it is a sovereignty that rules over a different people. Kenneth Pomeranz refines that definition. In his terms, empires are "polities in which leaders of one society also rule directly or indirectly over at least one other

---

93. Burbank and Cooper, *Empires in World History*; Barkey, *Empire of Difference*, 3–27.
94. *Pamiatniki sibirskoi istorii XVIII veka*, bk. 1, no. 12, 55–68, esp. 68.

society, using instruments different from (though not always more authoritarian than) those used to rule at home."[95] Technically, by this definition, Russia's relationship to Siberia fit the definition of empire. Tribute collection was a central Siberian endeavor (but tribute was also collected west of the Urals in the sixteenth century). Russia's tenuous hegemony along with chronic population deficits meant that military presence in Siberia was far more pronounced. Demographics differed, as the proportion of military men to women was more highly skewed than most of European Russia. Yet this was not a peculiarity of Siberia alone: a heavy military presence was found in many non-Siberian border towns.[96] A different property regime emerged in Siberia. Technically, Siberia did not develop with the large (and then much smaller) estates granted to the servitors of the tsar. Consequently, there was no serfdom—even though forms of slavery and unfree labor were common in Siberia—but this just meant that Siberian peasants were state peasants who paid rent (*obrok*) as state peasants in European Russia did. Although the regime differed somewhat, it operated according to existing categories.

These important differences notwithstanding, the differences between Siberia and the Russian core are more qualitative than structural. At its most basic the administrative structure was similar: rule by military governors (*voevody*). The position of governor (*voevoda*) persisted in Siberia even after it was abolished in central Russia, but the tsar implemented in Siberia what had been the norm in European Russia. Peasants paid rent to the state. Similarities are even more apparent in the commercial sphere. European Russia and Siberia were similarly laced with a network of internal customs posts, even if different rules applied to Siberia for most of the seventeenth century.[97] Thus the more salient and relevant feature of early modern Russia is that state building and empire building were not chronologically serial endeavors. The Russian state was an evolving one, developing government institutions and norms simultaneously as it expanded territory.

A quick chronological survey makes the point best. As Russia expanded into Siberia, it was already an empire and had been a growing, expanding entity for nearly two centuries. Novgorodian bands of fur entrepreneurs had been operating extractive enterprises in Siberia from at least the fourteenth century, long before the establishment of Tiumen' and Tobol'sk. The grand princes in Muscovy involved themselves in Siberian forest-steppe

---

95. Pomeranz, "Social History and World History," 87.

96. Smirnov, *Goroda Moskovskogo gosudarstva.*

97. PSZ 3, no. 1654, p. 494. The New Trade Statutes of 1667, which introduced a more unified and protectionist tax schedule, were not applied in Siberia until 1698. For most of the seventeenth century, as many as thirteen taxes could be charged at Siberian customs posts.

politics by the fifteenth century, long before making outright claims to sovereignty. Upon making sovereign claims in the late sixteenth century, Muscovy quickly established a chain of military forts that extended to the Pacific Ocean before the middle of the seventeenth century, even though it was sporadically challenged for Siberian sovereignty into the eighteenth century. From there, settlers trickled in, slowly putting foliage on the bare branches of imperial presence. These processes took place alongside the formative crises from which emerged the Russian state. To give some perspective: eight Siberian towns had been founded before the expiration of the Riurikid dynasty in 1598, and fourteen existed before the coronation of the first Romanov tsar in 1613. Moscow itself was sacked by invading Tatars in 1571, just fifteen years before the founding of Tiumen'. Siberian customs posts were operational under Boris Godunov (r. 1598–1604). Russia had established itself on the Pacific Ocean one decade before the Conciliar Law Code of 1649 became law. Amid these political developments, institutions of administration, taxation, and oversight were developing in Moscow and on the frontier simultaneously. Lessons on the frontier informed developments at the center, rather than central institutions being exported and modified on the frontier.

The experience of territorial conquest and establishing administrative apparatuses informed the center just as the center left its imprint on distant lands. Whether it was expanding with construction of a frontier line or consolidating administration, in European Russia the common denominator was the state's recognition of commerce as an essential source of revenue. Both at home and abroad, or across the Urals in the Russian case, states sought to regulate economic exchange. Trade was important as a means of channeling revenue to the state coffers and meeting the needs of the realm through the distribution of needed commodities and merchandise. Tax-generated revenue increased in proportion to increased trade flows and improved administrative efficiency. More directly, states could profit greatly through direct participation in the business of trade. In early modern Russia empire building does not look so different from state building; the two projects were inseparable.

This observation resonates beyond Siberia. As Janet Martin has observed, the nascent bureaucratic structures of the Muscovite state "developed in concert with the needs of the territorially expanding realm of Muscovy."[98] Willard Sunderland noted the same of Russian imperial administration in the eighteenth-century southern steppe, writing, "Russia's mode of power on the steppe was premised on patterns of state building and incorporation that were

---

98. Martin, *Medieval Russia*, 295.

easily as characteristic of the making of unitary states as of empires. . . . [They were always stressing] security, centralization and administrative integration rather than maintaining and exploiting a territorially distinct territory."[99] Vera Tolz, writing on nineteenth-century Russification policy, observed that the Russian state used its nation-building tools on the larger empire. "In a land-based empire such as Russia the metropole and the imperial periphery were a single geographical, and to some extent, political space."[100] John LeDonne has suggested that Russia was building a unitary state in its periphery.[101] These particular observations bring home the power in the dictum that "Britain had an empire, but Russia was an empire."[102]

My research speaks to the above observation most relevantly by highlighting the fact that Siberian commerce was an essential prong of Russian expansion, just as it was an elementary facet of Russian statehood. This book is a case study of that story of simultaneous state and empire building through the lens of merchant endeavors. It is told on the early modern Eurasian frontier through the lens of trade from the ground view, with state policy decrees in Moscow a distant background to the transactions that took place at the Siberian customs post. Revenue was revenue, and in seventeenth-century Muscovy, commercial activity was the means through which the Muscovite state sometimes generated the majority of its revenue, a trend that obtained in coming centuries. Dynamic, centralizing, and ever in need of revenue, the new Romanov dynasty was as savvy as it was innovative and continued to build on what worked for Muscovy: commerce. Thus chapters 1 and 2 argue that commerce was a crucial sector to the Russian state as part of both its very survival and as part of its imperial project. This relentless commercial aspiration was, on the ground, a hybrid of state and private initiative. No less important than state approaches were the actions of individual merchants, some of whose stories are featured in chapters 6, 7, and 8.

99. Sunderland, *Taming the Wild Field*, 227. This observation complements scholarship focusing on later periods that argues that despite the irony, given the powerful force nationalism has played in Russian and Soviet history, Russian nation building was an incomplete project. See Hosking, *Russia*; Kotkin, *Armageddon Averted*.

100. Tolz, *Russia's Own Orient*, 24.

101. LeDonne, "Building an Infrastructure of Empire," 607. Echoing that impression, one scholar has called the Habsburg realm not an empire but a "relatively confederal dynastic agglomeration." Nexon quoted in Kollmann, *Crime and Punishment*, 20.

102. Geoffrey Hosking, "The Freudian Frontier," *Times Literary Supplement*, March 10, 1995, quoted in Plokhy, *Origins of the Slavic Nations*, 250.

PART ONE

Commerce and Empire

CHAPTER 1

"For Profit and Tsar": Commerce in Early Modern Russia

> The radicalism, breadth, and volume [of the early Romanovs' economic policy] certainly got the attention of the observer of social life in the first half of the seventeenth century and forced him to think that all the country in this period was being mobilized for trade or commerce.
>
> —P. P. Smirnov, "Economicheskaia politika"

Since there's no leaving the political out of political economy, this chapter surveys the state's approach to commerce and argues that the Muscovite state consciously promoted commerce. The Muscovite state may not have promoted commerce in ways that moderns deem effective, nor that proved superior among contemporaries; nonetheless it did so according to its own understanding. Its practices were not unlike the practices of other early modern states and empires. This chapter addresses important state institutions that shaped the commercial climate in Russia: policy, customs collections, merchant corporations, and state monopolies. The latter two were means by which the state not only regulated the economy but directly participated in it as well. Before proceeding to the commercial landscape of Muscovy, some pages are devoted to situating Kievan Rus' and early modern Muscovy in their respective contexts in order to demonstrate that Muscovy was neither as isolated nor as isolationist as is sometimes portrayed; it had more in common with other early modern polities than is generally appreciated.

Beyond the East-West Binary

"Russia and the West" is a long-established binary. The metaphysical and psychological hand-wringing generated by the question of Russia's relationship to Europe has led to overlooking that Ivan IV's first requests for military aid to England sought military support against a Tatar attack.[1] Which is to say that the preoccupation with Russia's contested European identity—the "obfuscatory and unedifying East/West dichotomy," in the words of Valerie Kivelson[2]—has obscured the fact that Russia was long embedded in a geo-political context that oriented it in other directions as well. With formidable neighbors to the south, east, west, and north, early modern dynamics were never just a matter of Russia and the West.

Economic exchange prevented the Slavic principalities on the eastern edge of Europe from ever being entirely isolated from its western neighbors. Muscovite economic connections to Western Europe via the Baltic and western borders can be traced, even if they are as thin as spider webs, back to ancient times. During the Carolingian period Rus' was the main artery through which furs and Eastern goods, via the Caspian and Black Seas, reached Europe.[3] Founding Vikings moved coin and wares through the river arteries between Constantinople, rendered as Tsargrad in Slavic sources, and Reval (Scandinavian Europe) from the tenth century.[4] Novgorod grew into a busy medieval market frequented by merchants from Europe and as far as Central Asia. Its connectedness suffered, however, when Grand Prince Ivan III ejected the imperious Hansa league merchants from Novgorod in the late fifteenth century (1494).[5] Besides the Baltic exits, an overland route via Polish and German lands had long existed. In 1489 the Russian merchant Demia Frizin traveled through Lithuania with valuable pearls and carpets from the East.[6] Although these overland routes are little documented, it is speculated that they supported the highest volume of traffic because of a lack of customs regulation.[7] (The Black Sea made for an important trade point, but we leave the south out for now.)

Indeed, it was never just Russia and the West. Not only that. In the cultural-intellectual transmission whereby Russia assumed its inferior place at Europe's knee, knowledge of these connections was lost. When the first European mapmakers came to Muscovy with an interest to chart the world, a process of unknowing began. At the same time that Muscovites were re-teaching Western European mapmakers about the existence of the Aral Sea, Russians "forgot"

1. Fuhrmann, *Origins of Capitalism in Russia*. I. I. Liubimenko covered this earlier. See Valk, "Iina Ivanovna Liubimenko," 485.
2. Kivelson, "On Words, Sources, and Historical Method," 496.
3. Houtte, *An Economic History of the Low Countries*, 18.
4. Franklin and Shepard, *Emergence of Rus'*. Coins were from Frisian and Meuse towns, and perhaps other places too. Houtte, *An Economic History of the Low Countries*, 51.
5. Esper, "Russia and the Baltic," 458–62.
6. Martin, "Muscovite Travelling Merchants," 34.
7. Bushkovitch, *The Merchants of Moscow*, 87–91.

that a body of water separated Asia and North America.[8] Yuri Krizhanich, a Croatian priest exiled in Tobol'sk in the middle of the seventeenth century, reported that "this question" of whether "the Arctic and the Eastern or Chinese [oceans are] separated from one another by land which extends east from Siberia . . . was very recently resolved by soldiers from the Lena and Nerchinsk oblasts. . . . They declare that there is no land to the east, and that these seas are not divided by land, and that Siberia, the Daur and Nikan lands, and Kitai or Sina are washed on the east by one continuous ocean."[9] Yet, a half century later, the Dane Vitus Bering was charged with determining whether the continents of Asia and North America were connected. The news that the Russian Semen Dezhnev, in an exploration sponsored by the Russian merchant Vasilii Gusel'nikov, rounded the northeast coast of Eurasia in 1648 was "rediscovered" by Müller in the archive of Yakutsk in 1736.[10]

Attempts to counter the "backwardness" rap and "normalize" Russian history vis-à-vis Western traditions go as far back as the Westernizers of the nineteenth century. In 1952 R. W. Davies argued that the economic development of twelfth-century Kiev exceeded that of many European locations, including France and England.[11] "Comparative analyses traditionally have done Russian history no favors," remarked Valerie Kivelson with both humor and insight, while arguments for a less autocratic, more consensual political culture have been met with hostile rejections.[12] Implicitly or explicitly, next to early modern England and the Dutch Republic, Russia was hopelessly backward. Even scholarship insisting on the superlative particularity of England and the Netherlands as two extraordinary early modern commercial powerhouses has done little to overturn an impression of Russia's retrograde economy and culture.[13] The following discussion situates Muscovy in its global context by schematically taking inventory of its known connections with the wider world.

Reconsidering Rus' in the World

Commerce as a means of revenue and the regulation of commerce goes deep in Rus' tradition. Scandinavians who had traveled long distances in search of

---

8. See Bartol'd, *Sochineniia*, 3: 90.

9. Dmytryshyn, Crownhart-Vaughan, and Vaughan, *Russia's Conquest of Siberia*, no. 113, 1: 441.

10. Lantzeff and Pierce, *Eastward to Empire*, 190. Orlova, *Otkrytiia russkikh zemleprokhodtsev*, nos. 41, 18, pp. 167–80; Ogloblin, *Semen Dezhnev*, 1, 16.

11. Davies, "Revisions in Economic History," 116–27.

12. Kivelson, "Merciful Father, Impersonal State," 635. See exchange between Poe and Kivelson in Poe, "Truth about Muscovy," 473–99.

13. Goldstone, "Problem of the 'Early Modern' World," 263–64 (Holland), 268–75 (England).

opportunity founded the Riurikid dynasty, which ruled Russia for just over six centuries. Novgorod and Kiev emerged as trading cities, tapping into Silk Roads trades and the products of European forests, cultivating exchange with German cloth merchants and cosmopolitan Constantinople, and regulating commerce accordingly.[14] Prince Yuri Dolgorukii (1099–1157) earned his epithet "the Long Armed" for the taxes he was able to collect. Recall the Primary Chronicle's famous story of Grand Prince Vladimir, who, when considering monotheism for his state, dispatched ambassadors in all directions to learn about the religions of his neighbors. Slavic principalities fought and traded with the Bulgar kingdom founded on the Volga River in the tenth century.[15]

Political connections went hand in hand with economic ones. Medieval Riurikid princes frequently married their children to Western princes and princesses. Christian Raffensberger has shown that more than three-quarters (77%) of fifty-two known dynastic marriages were to countries west of Rus'.[16] Vladimir Monomakh took as his bride a daughter of Harold, the last Anglo-Saxon king of England, in the eleventh century.[17] Prince Daniil of Volynia and Galicia (1211–1264) made efforts to marry his children to ruling dynasties of Hungary, Austria, and Lithuania as a counterweight to Mongol power. He also established close ties with the papacy. Long-distance connections existed in other Slavic principalities in the region as well. In 1269 Novgorod concluded treaties with Gotland, Lubeck, Riga, and other German towns establishing rules governing foreign merchants' visits to Novgorod.[18]

It was Kiev's substantial diplomatic and commercial links to the wider world that led the historian V. O. Kliuchevskii to label it a "trading state" and the *Russkaia Pravda* a law code of trade capital.[19] Although the appropriate historical legacy between Kiev and Muscovy is a contested issue, these economic connections are significant for our purposes. During the appanage period (eleventh–fourteenth centuries), Rus' principalities to the north followed in Kiev's footsteps. Traffic of clerics between Moscow and Greece and Istanbul was fairly regular, and their concerns extended to commercial as well as ecclesiastical matters. Links to Istanbul were only the

---

14. Martin, *Medieval Russia*, 62–76; Franklin and Shepard, *Emergence of Rus'*.
15. Martin, *Medieval Russia*, 14–16, 68–70.
16. Raffensberger, *Reimagining Europe*, 47.
17. Davies, "Revisions in Economic History," 123.
18. Martin, *Medieval Russia*, 152, 167.
19. Kliuchevskii, *Kurs russkoi istorii*, part 2, 253–55.

most obvious way in which Moscow appropriated the historical connections of ancient Kiev.

Before Moscow reigned supreme among Slavic principalities of the European plain, its commerce was similar to neighboring regional principalities like Tver' and Riazan' and was not as important as commerce was in Novgorod and Kazan. We know little about the economy of Muscovy in the medieval period (twelfth–fifteenth centuries). Marco Polo, who never traveled to Rus', asserted that "Rosia . . . [is] not a land of trade."[20] Excavations of tenth-century camel bones around Kiev testify to connections with the East centuries before Marco Polo's adventures. The dating of deposits of Arab coins in the Baltic region suggest that eastern trade may have been cut off in the eleventh century, but in 1245 the papal legate Plano Carpini encountered Russian merchants in Urgench. And as improbable as it seems, given the problems Russia had asserting hegemony over this space even into the late eighteenth century, the tenth-century Arab writer Ibn Khaukal' referred to the Volga River as a Russian river on account of the all merchants he saw there.[21] Even if not directly, a sense of China was present as early as the thirteenth century, for the Russians referred to Beijing as Kambalyk, which had been the name of the capital city that Kubilai Khan (1215–94) relocated and renamed Peking in the thirteenth century.[22] Janet Martin tells us that Mongol conquest helped integrate Moscow into more vibrant trade networks to its south.[23] Contrary to Marco Polo's assertion, Donald Ostrowski argued that the *Pax Mongolica* facilitated trade of which the savvy Muscovites took advantage, becoming creditors to wealthy Byzantium by the end of the thirteenth century.[24] Following in the tradition of his "long-armed" ancestry, Ivan I (1288–1340) earned his nickname Kalita "money bags" for his success generating revenue as holder of the Mongol *iarlyk* (permission to collect tribute for the Mongol khan). A late-fourteenth-century chronicle describes Moscow as a city bursting with wealth and glory.[25]

Commerce—An Area of Focus for the Muscovite State

Commerce was of integral importance to the Russian state before the sixteenth-century arrival of the English, an underappreciated point in a historiography

---

20. Marco Polo, *The Book of Ser Marco Polo, the Venetian*, 2: 418.
21. Perkhavko, *Istoriia russkogo kupechestvo*, chap. 3, esp. 76, 91.
22. Kurts, *Sochinenie Kil'burgera*, 203–5.
23. Martin, "Land of Darkness and the Golden Horde," 401–21.
24. Ostrowski, *Muscovy and the Mongols*, 131.
25. Samuella Iosifovna Fingaret quoted in Andreev, *Moskva. Kupechestvo. Torgovlia*, 86.

that has focused predominantly on political culture and debated extensively
the nature of it. But when one turns one's attention to commerce, its importance to the state becomes immediately apparent.[26] Moscow's conquest of
the Russian North was motivated by a desire to tap into the fur profits
Novgorod enjoyed.[27] Commercial concerns were operative in relations with
Kazan under Vasilii III, as they were in most of Muscovy's wars. Exchange
was a fact of life during and after Mongol subjection. Muscovy, like Kiev
before it, was keen to cultivate southerly relations. And well it should: the
Mediterranean, accessed through the Black Sea, had long been the locus of
politics and of religious, cultural, economic, and technological hegemony.
Muscovy engaged in trade that moved northwest toward the Baltic and
southward toward Silk Roads termini in the Black Sea and later the Volga.

The 1453 conquest of Constantinople was a shock to Christendom but a
boost to Muscovy's prestige. In the wake of the conquest, a lively trade existed
between Muscovy and the Ottoman Empire. Janet Martin identified 220
merchants who traveled between Muscovy and Ottoman lands between1488
and 1502. In over half of these cases, merchants carried modest shipments
worth less than 50 rubles each.[28] As the Ottoman Empire extended its influence into the Black Sea region, Muscovy looked eastward to the Volga to
develop alternate trade outlets. It cultivated trade (and diplomatic) relations
with the Ottoman's rivals to the east, Persia.

From the early sixteenth century, horse trade driven from the steppe was
a major event in Moscow. In 1474 a massive caravan comprised of 600
Tatar ambassadors (*posly*) and 3,200 merchants driving about 40,000 horses
and bearing many other wares arrived in Moscow from the Great Horde.[29]
Meanwhile, goods from China were found in elite Russian households prior
to the fifteenth century.[30] No concrete evidence places Russian merchants as
far east as China in the fifteenth century, but this is largely due to the effi-
cacy of established trade networks in which Central Asian merchants acted
as middlemen. Eurasian trade was a developed world in which goods traveled
farther than their bearers.[31] But there is evidence that Russian merchants in
the fifteenth century traveled as far as India.

26. For interpretations that place commercial concerns at the center of Muscovy's expansion
in Siberia, see Janet Martin, "The Fur Trade and the Conquest of Sibir'"; Jarmo Kotilaine, *Russia's
Foreign Trade*; and Clifford Foust, "Russian Expansion to the East Through the Eighteenth Century."
27. Martin, *Treasure in the Land of Darkness*.
28. Martin, "Muscovite Travelling Merchants," 25.
29. Iskhakov and Izmailov, *Etnopoliticheskaia istoriia tatar*, 256.
30. Fekhner, *Torgovlia russkogo gosudarstva*.
31. Christian, "Silk Roads or Steppe Roads," 1–26; Hansen, *Silk Road*, 10.

Afanasii Nikitin's Journey to India

Afanasii Nikitin was a merchant whose pursuit of trade opportunities took him all the way to India during his travels from 1466 to 1474. He chronicled his journey (1466–72 or 1468–74) southward to India, where he spent nearly three years, and back to Rus', providing precious insight into the economic, political, and cultural context of an early modern Eurasian merchant.[32] Although Nikitin's account is unique among fifteenth-century Russian sources, the experience itself was probably less so since he journeyed with other Russian merchants for much of his travels.[33] Nikitin was not from Muscovy but from Tver', which at the time of Nikitin's travels was a neighboring principality, one of several that during this period were becoming subject to Muscovy. Yaroslavl' had already been absorbed into Muscovy by the time of Nikitin's departure. Rostov sold its ancestral rights to Moscow in 1474. Moscow annexed Novgorod violently in 1478, a campaign to which the sovereign Grand Prince Michael of Tver' committed troops to assist Moscow even as he moved to protect his independence by developing relations with Lithuania. Tver' was annexed in 1485, about a decade after Nikitin's death.

Nikitin's journey was shaped by the political instability and upheavals through which he passed. Nikitin traveled all the way to India not as part of prior design but because he was not allowed to return to Rus' after being captured and taken to the ruling sultan in the southern Volga region. Typical of early modern travelers' accounts, Nikitin, with a merchant's practical eye, reported the distance between towns, wares found in various markets, and customs fees. Similar to early modern envoys who were typically charged with reporting on the potential strength of neighbors and where issues of rank and protocol were integral facets of early modern culture, Nikitin described displays of military strength and ritualized entourages he observed. He also commented about food and culture. Beyond a belief in Buddha and the ubiquitous prohibition against eating beef that Nikitin understood as unifying features of Hinduism, he was fascinated by the diversity of Indian faith and customs.

Religious concerns greatly occupied Nikitin. The angst he experienced negotiating a multiconfessional world may be the most fascinating aspect of his account.[34] Nikitin worried that he had lost his faith.[35] After a book he

---

32. Lenhoff and Martin, "Torgovo-khoziaistvennii i kul'turnii kontekst 'Khozheniia za tri moria' Afanasiia Nikitina," 95–126. In English: "The Commercial and Cultural Context of *Journey Across Three Seas* of Afanasii Nikitin," 321–44.

33. Syroechkovskii, *Gosti-Surozhane*, 42–45; Crummey, *Formation of Muscovy*, 87–91.

34. Lenhoff and Martin raise this issue, which Mary Jane Maxwell explores in "Afanasii Nikitin."

35. Compare: Avvakum, "The Life of Archpriest Avvakum by Himself."

brought on his journey was stolen, he had nothing from which to read his prayers and no calendar with which to observe religious holidays. Traveling in the lands of Muslims and Hindus, he did not know when to fast for Lent or celebrate Easter. When Muslims he encountered commented that he evidently observed no faith, it sent Nikitin reeling. He began to fast with his Muslim companions and confided in his diary that he worried that he was becoming Muslim. Instrumental apostasy may not have been so rare in Eurasian commercial spaces. Sogdians, merchants of ancient and medieval Inner Eurasia, were renown for their religious flexibility.[36] In the seventeenth century other Russian ambassadors were accused of apostasy, to say nothing of the uncounted Orthodox slaves who found their way into Muslim lands. Interconfessional aspects of early modern trade are encountered again in chapter 7.

About the same time that Afanasii Nikitin was negotiating religious difference and bargaining wares on the subcontinent, Ambrogio Contarini, an ambassador from the Serene Republic of Venice who later chronicled his adventures, traveled to Persia to seek an alliance with the shah against the Ottoman Turks. On his return trip, he was kidnapped and ended up in Astrakhan. There, still several decades before Muscovy showed any pretensions to claim that Caspian port, Rus' merchants trading in the area ransomed him and brought him to the Muscovite court, where he waited until reimbursement from Venice arrived.[37] These two accounts demonstrate great breadth in Muscovy's fifteenth-century connections.

Muscovy Rising

The Muscovite princes were a dynamic group who actively consolidated wealth and power to Moscow and worked to fortify stability and exploit opportunities in all geographical directions from the fourteenth century onward. The rise of Muscovy and disintegration of the Mongol Horde overlapped in long, drawn-out processes. The Mongol yoke ended in a century-long decline from the 1360s to the mid-fifteenth century. Muscovy's ascendancy proceeded not meteorically but steadily. Ivan III (r. 1462–1505) conquered the thriving oligarchic principality of Novgorod in 1478. Arguably Moscow's first imperial conquest, this was accomplished while Moscow was still technically subordinate to the Qipchak khanate (although it had been decades since Moscow had consistently paid tribute in Sarai). Ivan III proceeded to

---

36. Foltz, *Religions of the Silk Road*.
37. Barbaro and Contarini, *Travels to Tana and Persia*.

consolidate and project Muscovite authority not only with coercion but also through marriage, international diplomacy, creation of symbolic centers, and issuance of a law code—strategies familiar to students of early modern governance in Europe. He focused his expansion efforts toward the Baltic and Silk Road/Caspian routes, important trade regions that had animated rulers in this part of the world since the period of the Vikings. Once Mongol suzerainty was eliminated, the Eurasian region faced several decades of stalemate where Muscovy along with the other successor kingdoms of the Kazan, Astrakhan, Sibir', and Crimean khanates maintained a holding pattern of sorts. Like the post-Chinggisid world in Central Asia, the Slavic principalities shared cultural and dynastic affiliations. But they often valued independence over allegiance, which made for a fragmented political landscape.

Ivan III, one of Russia's greatest state builders, sought to cultivate international commercial connections. In addition to famously marrying Sofiia Palaeologa, niece of the Byzantine emperor adopted by the pope, he sent ambassadors to Italy (1468, 1474, 1486),[38] Hungary (1482), and the Holy Roman Empire (1490). Ivan III ejected the Hansa league merchants from Novgorod in 1494. This move has been cited as an example of Muscovy's backward and isolationist nature. Given that the Hansa merchants in Novgorod operated more as a thuggish cartel than free-market proponents in fifteenth-century Novgorod, their ejection need not be seen as inimical to healthy commerce. Ivan III's action can be interpreted variously. Dovnar-Zapol'skii suggested it was retaliation for the execution of two Russian merchants in Reval.[39] Alternatively, at that moment complete subjugation of Novgorod may have been a higher priority for Ivan III than the cultivation of commerce. Or, one wonders if Hansa league members were not somehow implicated in the recent "Judaizer" episode that had recently rocked Novgorod and Moscow.[40]

Despite Ivan III's successful state building in the fifteenth century, the scaffolding of Muscovite governance remained sparse. By the end of the sixteenth century, Muscovy was the undisputed ruler among eastern Slavs but there was still very little government to speak of; the entire government may have consisted of not much more than four departments (prikazy).[41] Loyal servitors were thin on the ground and in the absence of much state bureaucracy, let alone legalized procedures, they remunerated themselves for doing

38. Noonan and Kovalev, "'The Furry 40s,'" 653.
39. Dovnar-Zapol'skii, "Torgovlia i promyshlennost'," 331.
40. See Don Ostrowski, Interconnections: Russia in World History, unpublished manuscript, chap. 4.
41. Romaniello, Elusive Empire, 55.

the tsar's bidding according to the traditional system called *kormlenie*, a word that literally means feeding. This system amounted to a laissez-faire mode of governance in that the servitor on the ground could extract whatever "the market would bear." Extortion, coercion, and force could obviously inform what the market—the local population—could bear. Squeezing a population too hard could meet with a pitchfork rebellion, but it is not taking an apologist stance to recognize that local populations in peripheral areas appreciated the defense that Russian retinues (albeit imperfectly) provided during Tatar slave raids, which southern Muscovy suffered endemically.

Ivan III's son Vasilii III (r. 1505–33) saw commerce as a component of foreign relations. His efforts to enhance nascent Moscow's regional dominance included establishing and expanding trade in Ottoman-dominated regions and, less successfully, increasing influence in the Volga region. Vasilii III sent two merchant factors (*gosti*) to Istanbul in 1515 and another in 1530.[42] These overtures succeeded in establishing direct state-trade relations, which made Vasilii III more willing to let the Muscovite-Crimean alliance deteriorate. He soon offended the Crimean khanate by withholding the generous gifts it had been his father's practice to bestow. He went to war against Crimea's ally, Lithuania. Although Vasilii seized Smolensk in 1512, prior to direct contact with the Ottoman Sultan, this action demonstrates Vasilii's interest in expanding Muscovy's commercial reach. Smolensk, located on the Dnieper River near a portage to the Western Dvina River, which flows into the Baltic (not to be confused with the Northern Dvina River, which flows into the North Sea), was an important way station on the Black Sea and Baltic trade routes. To the east, Vasilii enacted a trade embargo against the khanate of Kazan, forbidding Russian merchants from trading in Kazan and directing them to Nizhni Novgorod instead; this embargo reportedly hurt Muscovite economic interests no less than Kazan's.[43] That is, even as he effectively antagonized his neighbors (Crimea, Kazan), he took steps to fortify Muscovy's long-distance international trading position. Vasilii III cast his commercial-diplomatic net farther still, sending Russian ambassadors to the Holy Roman emperor Charles V, ruler of the largest domain on earth, in 1524 and 1527. He also received Habsburg ambassadors, one of whom was Sigmund von Herberstein, author of one of the most famous traveler accounts of sixteenth-century Muscovy.[44]

---

42. Floria, "Privilegirovannoe kupechestvo," 149.
43. Martin, *Medieval Russia*, 319–29. In "Muscovite Travelling Merchants" Martin concluded that private trade suffered as state trade increased between Russia and the Ottoman Empire.
44. Herberstein, *Notes upon Russia*.

Muscovite diplomatic relations indicate a broad geographical swath of connection. And where there was diplomacy, there was exchange. Diplomats brought "gifts" that often fulfilled commercial functions. They came with intentions to acquire certain items, whether as gifts or through purchase. Toward this end they and their retinues often transported wares to trade. Courts—and the Muscovite grand princes were no exception—conducted more formal commercial exchange, sending people to foreign lands to trade on its behalf. Depending on the reception, ambassadors might trade at court and/or local markets. Finally, private traders inevitably attached themselves to diplomatic expeditions. For Muscovy, as for much of the premodern world, significant economic exchange that was not documented by customs officials or taxed at the borders took place under the guise of diplomacy. Since commerce and politics were inextricable fellow travelers, tracking diplomatic exchanges provides valuable albeit unquantifiable information about a state's commercial relations. In fact, I suspect that the dismissal of unquantifiable data as less valuable has led to an underestimation of premodern Muscovy's commercial vitality.

Sixteenth-Century Watershed

The sixteenth century was a watershed in the history of Russia's place in the world economy for two reasons: the Muscovite state considerably increased its westward and eastward trade. In the summer of 1553 the Willoughby-Chancellor expedition, consisting of three English ships, set sail to navigate the icy waters of the northern Eurasian coast in search of a northeast passage to the riches of the Indies and "Cathay" (China). Two of the ships were sunk and one became stranded at the mouth of the Dvina River. When reports of this arrival reached Ivan IV, he ordered the ship's captain brought to Moscow. Willoughby met a watery death and Chancellor received a royal welcome in Moscow. He returned home with gifts and a promise of monopoly privileges for English merchants in Muscovy. With such happy prospects 250 English investors pooled their resources to form the Muscovy Company in 1555. Direct trade began with Russia at the English outpost situated at the mouth of the Northern Dvina. A contingent of Russian merchants returned to London with the first English merchants in 1555.[45] Although subsequent companies would enjoy more glorious fortunes and legacies, the Muscovy Company was the first joint stock company. The model came to define maritime trade in the early modern era.

---

45. Baron, "Osip Nepea and the Opening of Anglo-Russian Commercial Relations," in *Muscovite Russia*.

The English by no means comprised the whole of Muscovy's trade horizons. Ivan IV (1533–84) was even keener for commercial prospects and geopolitical opportunities than his father Vasilii III had been. In 1552, sensing political weakness, he boldly sought to command upper Volga trade with the conquest of Kazan, an event that has come to be recognized as the beginning of Russia as a multiconfessional empire. In 1567 he dispatched commercial agents to Hormuz (Persia), Antwerp (Netherlands), Tsargrad (Turkish Constantinople), Alexandria (Egypt), and Sweden.[46] Ivan IV consolidated important contacts with the Caucasus by marrying a Kabardinian princess from the Cherkasski clan.[47] Ivan received trade embassies from Iurgench and Bukhara.[48] He received embassies from Christian Georgians from the Caucasus graciously, even if he declined to deliver the concrete military aid they sought against Persian threats. The Englishman Giles Fletcher, who visited Muscovy in the late sixteenth century, reported that merchants from "Turkie, Persia, Bougharia, Georgia, Armenia, and some other of Christendome" exported furs amounting "to the value of foure or five hundred thousand rubbels, as I have heard."[49] Indeed, Ivan was negotiating a complex geopolitical landscape in which he was fighting wars to his east and west. Recall that trade in military wares was a founding component of Anglo-Russian relations.[50]

To its south, Russia's interest in securing trade routes led it to cultivate relations with both the Ottomans and the Persians. Its relationships with each in the sixteenth and seventeenth century were largely conditioned by Ottoman-Persian rivalries. Although no Ottoman caravans arrived in Moscow from 1568 to 1574, Ivan IV sent gift-laden embassies to the Turkish sultan in 1567 (as noted above) and 1570.[51] In 1590 Russian merchants returned to Moscow from the Ottoman court.[52] Safavid Iran was a mecca of early modern Eurasian culture and a producer of coveted commodities. Although politics persistently complicated economic prospects, Moscow was ever keen to cultivate trade with its Shiite neighbors, dispatching at least ten embassies

---

46. Bakhrushin, "Ivan Groznii," in NT, 2: 309–11; Martin, "Muscovite Travelling Merchants," 34; Noonan and Kovalev, "'The Furry 40s,'" 653.

47. Bushkovitch, "Princes Cherkasskii or Circassian Murzas," 9–30.

48. *Litsevoi svod*, kn. 23, 98, 101, 102.

49. Fletcher, *Of the Russe Common Wealth*, 9.

50. Bond, *Russia at the Close of the Sixteenth Century*, xiv–xx. For a suggestion that England may have instigated the arms trade, See Yakobson, "Early Anglo-Russian Relations," 600.

51. Martin, "Fur Trade and the Conquest of Sibir'," 71; Matthee, "Anti-Ottoman Politics and Transit Rights," 739–61.

52. Fekhner, *Torgovlia russkogo gosudarstva*, 67.

ѡпослѣхъ ̑иꙁбоухарѣ . Тогожемцⷶ .
прищлипослы иꙁбоухарѣ . пѣшама
рханⷮ ѡцⷬⷶбоухарсⸯⷵꙗго ишамарха
нⷪⷵслⷢⷪо . послы а̑ꙁа́мⸯ а̑ꙁпда́шихъ̑ .
с̑помнꙶнꙶсꙗ . нелюбо҇нымиⸯⷮⷱчелобⷮⷩ
емⸯ , пⷬⷪгнⷩⷳⷱидо
рогнⷪⷵⷪⷮⷷⷶⷵⷶⷣⷪⷳⷱⷮⷫ и
ѡ̑бⷬⷷⷱⷹⷶⷵ

FIGURE 1.1 Bukharan embassy to Ivan IV, autumn 1558.

Source: *Litsevoi svod*, bk. 23, 98. Courtesy: Jack Kollmann collection with permission from Akteon publishers.

to Iran from 1590 to 1626.[53] Russian merchants already resided in the Safavid Empire as the Muscovy Company tried to establish a foothold there: "Send some one hither that hath the Russe tongue, for we have need," wrote the company man Arthur Edwards in 1566.[54] The English, similarly interested in trade with Iran, sent expeditions there in 1564, 1565, 1568, 1569, and 1579.[55] As in Muscovy, the English faced Dutch competition in their efforts to cultivate favorable trade with the Safavids.

Although it is giving the English too much credit and misreading Eurasian geopolitical history to credit the English with planting the seed that grew into Muscovy's eastward expansion, it may be the case that English enthusiasm for transit to China piqued Muscovy's own interest in that direction. The Stroganovs, like northern Europeans, invested in pioneering a northeast passage to "Cathay" and, like Western Europeans, were disappointed in that endeavor.[56] From ambassadors like Anthony Jenkinson to John Merrick, the English sought transit passage that Muscovy was reluctant to grant.

The Muscovy Company was quite successful in exploiting the White Sea route in its first decades of existence. Protectionism did not seem to be Ivan IV's initial impulse. Upon the arrival of the English Ivan IV extended them substantial privileges, including tax-free trade. Yet, in the sixteenth century, Muscovy was already expanding its trade with other European countries, most notably, the Dutch. In the 1560s, a Dutch merchant ship, perhaps owned by the Antwerp émigré Giles Hooftman, happened on the bay that would become Archangel'sk while fleeing Danish pirates.[57] The English had established their operations on Rose Island at the mouth of the Northern Dvina.[58] The Dutch, over English objections, began to trade at Arkhangel'sk on the mainland. This proved a better location since it eliminated the need for ferrying from the mainland to an island port. By the 1580s, the English faced stiff competition from the Dutch, already rivals in the Baltic, North Sea, and Iran, and soon to be rivals in the Indian Ocean. Unlike the Anglo-Dutch competition in Persia, where the British supplanted the Dutch, in Muscovy the Dutch eventually prevailed over the British.[59]

---

53. Romaniello, "'In Friendship and Love,'" 113. Matthee, "Anti-Ottoman Politics and Transit Rights," 746. Martin, "Fur Trade and Conquest of Sibir'," 75, reports the first embassy to Persia as being in 1588.

54. See letters in Morgan and Coote, *Early Voyages and Travels to Russia and Persia*, 2: 384–406, quoted from 389.

55. Kagarlitsky, *Empire of the Periphery*, 83.

56. Baron, "Muscovy and the English Quest," in *Explorations in Muscovite History*.

57. Kagarlitsky, *Empire of the Periphery*, 96; Houtte, *An Economic History of the Low Countries*, 194.

58. Willan, *Early History of the Russia Company*.

59. Arel mitigates the decisiveness of the Dutch victory. See "Masters in Their Own House," 401–47.

England's exclusive privileges were short-lived. The 1555 original charter granted members of the Muscovy Company generous privileges. Those
privileges were quite soon rolled back: in 1567 the English were prohibited
from hiring Russians; a 1569 decree restricted their access to interior Russian towns.[60] The combination of native merchant lobbying and dissatisfac-
tion with England's refusal to enter a military alliance doomed the exclusive
privileges of the Muscovy Company. The Livonian War (1558–83) was
initiated by Ivan in part to promote trade interests, but dragged on for
decades until, in 1581, Sweden occupied Narva, cutting off Russia's access
to the Baltic. As Muscovy faced this pummeling against its neighbors to
the northwest, Ivan sought an alliance with England. Keen for exclusive
trade rights, England secretly sold weapons to Muscovy, but would not go
so far as to become formally embroiled in Muscovy's political quarrels. Dis-
satisfied with the refusal, in 1582–83, Russia declared its ports open to all
nations at the newly founded town of Arkhangel'sk. With the declaration
of Arkhangel'sk as an open port, exclusive English privileges were rendered
obsolete. To the English's further disadvantage, in 1584 English were denied
transit to Persia.[61]

Arkhangel'sk quickly eclipsed Rose Island and became biggest border
trade center—a distinction that lasted well into the eighteenth century when
it was supplanted by St. Petersburg.[62] The opening of Arkhangel'sk enabled
direct connections between markets that had long been aware of one another.
By the 1590s Dutch were trading in Russian commodities such as hemp,
leather, wax, fur, and caviar. In 1597 Francesco Vrins and Giacomo van
Lemens claimed to be the first to have sent ships directly from Muscovy to
Venice (embarking from Arkhangel'sk and rounding Europe via the Atlantic
Ocean), laden with hemp and hemp cables for the Arsenal. The Dutch also
drove a Russo-Venetian trade in hemp. When Italian food shortages threatened at the end of the sixteenth century, it became more attractive to produce grain than hemp in Italy, driving up the price of hemp and making it a
valuable long-distance import, which was increasingly sourced in Muscovy.
After the death of Piero Pellicorno, his heirs (the Dutch nephews Martin
Hureau and Alvise du Bois) claimed that their uncle, who had been receiving shipments of hemp, caviar, and different types of leather since at least
1597, had initiated the import of Russian commodities. Overall, the Dutch
succeeded in solidifying their middleman role with the Venetian republic,

60. Baron, "The Muscovy Company, the Muscovite Merchants," in *Muscovite Russia*, 572–74.
61. Ibid., 572.
62. Ohberg, "Russia and the World Market in the Seventeenth Century," 154, 139.

a waning commercial powerhouse. By 1607, the Venetian Board of Trade (Cinque Savi alla Mercanzia) recognized the Dutch as the middlemen who facilitated Venice's trade with northern Europe.[63] For the English and Dutch, northern Russia created one more front on which they competed for commercial supremacy. The English sent fourteen to fifteen ships annually to the northern port, but according to Jonathan Israel, the Dutch were supreme in Arkhangel'sk by 1600.[64] By no means, however, is the history of Muscovy's sixteenth-century international trade relations merely the story of English and Dutch traders vying for advantage on Russian turf.

While the English and Dutch vied for supremacy, larger drama was afoot. Chancellor arrived in Moscow just one year after Ivan IV had launched a military conquest of Kazan, fundamentally shifting relations that had been governed by negotiations and political influence in the previous century. The initial conquest, massive and brutal after decades of politicking, came in 1552. The East had been on Moscow's metaphorical radar screen long before the English came seeking passage to Cathay. Events no less consequential unfolded at the center of the Muscovite state. The sixteenth century was characterized by state expansion and centralization followed by implosion. The implosion was preceded by protracted wars, Ivan IV's bizarre *Oprichnina* (1564–72), years of crop failures, and the expiration of the Riurikid dynasty, which, taken together, inaugurated over a decade of social disruptions and civil war. Economic goals were subordinated as Muscovy struggled through this period of dynastic crises, wars, and social disruption known as the Time of Troubles (1598–1613).

Muscovy's conquests of Kazan and Astrakhan (1556) fundamentally reordered the political-economic landscape of Western Eurasia. The "discovery" of the White Sea passage by the English inaugurated a period of imperialesque pressure by the English that Muscovites managed to check, in part—but only in part—aided by the competition that other international agents of trade, like the Dutch and Swedish, exerted on the Russian scene. In the sixteenth century Muscovy not only deepened its economic relations with the West, laying the groundwork for the economic integration of the seventeenth century that has been valuably described by Jarmo Kotilaine.[65] Although one looks in vain for any coherent policy statements from the Muscovite government, in the sixteenth century one already sees

---

63. Gelder, *Library of Economic History*, 1: 73, 96, 137.
64. Israel, *Dutch Primacy*, 43–44.
65. Kotilaine, *Russia's Foreign Trade*, chap. 1.

the beginnings of an activist commercial state.[66] The Time of Troubles was a consequential rupture, but it only temporarily set back the economic activism apparent in the Muscovite state.

Activist Commercial State

Scholarship of recent decades, responding to a statist historical tradition that had emphasized a powerful, even despotic, tsar ruling over a subservient populous, has improved our understanding of Muscovite history by helping us to appreciate that the state was minimalist: it did much with little; it overreached and was chronically short of resources yet it accomplished prodigious feats in spite of those shortages.[67] When it comes to the economy in the seventeenth century and through Peter's reign, however, the state was anything but minimalist in aspiration, if not in fact. Minimalist social policies and activist commercial policies shared a common goal: military mobilization and stability. But instead of placing it outside the norm of its contemporary states, as Giles Fletcher would have had us believe, Muscovy's activist commercial policies for the most part fell within the range of standard early modern statecraft.[68]

When the Romanovs came to power, developing as an activist commercial state was a key strategy.[69] The Romanovs were innovative in many ways. They were also savvy: in a precarious situation, and where during the Time of Troubles similarly entitled boyar families had failed, they succeeded in establishing and maintaining their legitimacy. This success was not merely accidental in such a competitive political environment. When an admirer once commented on Catherine II's political success, she credited her savvy, confessing that "my orders would not be carried out unless they were the kind of orders that could be carried out . . . when I am already convinced, in advance, of general approval, I issue my orders."[70] In a similar spirit, when the early Romanovs embarked on an activist commercial strategy, they

---

66. Baron, "Ivan the Terrible, Giles Fletcher, and the Muscovite Merchantry" and "Osip Nepea," in *Muscovite Russia*. More generally, Khodarkovsky, *Russia's Steppe Frontier*, 40; and LeDonne, *Russian Empire and the World*, xv, 368, both acknowledge the lack of articulated strategy by the Russian government.

67. Kollman, "Muscovite Russia, 1450–1598," 27–54. See also Ostrowski, "Façade of Legitimacy," 534–63; Henshall, *The Myth of Absolutism*.

68. Fletcher, *Of the Russe Common Wealth*, 26–63; Baron, "The Weber Thesis and the Failure of Capitalist Development in 'Early Modern' Russia," in *Muscovite Russia*.

69. I use the term "activist" instead of "mercantilist." Mercantilism most immediately connotes specie acquisition and a positive balance of trade. Although Muscovy did enjoy a positive balance of trade in the seventeenth century, in Siberia the state was more interested in courting the regular visits of foreign merchants, who would bring goods to the Russian Empire.

70. Quoted in Ostrowski, "Façade of Legitimacy," 562.

were promoting a strategy that had considerable consensus among the ruling class. Muscovite leadership recognized the importance and potential of
commerce. This is an area of striking continuity, apparent from the fifteenth
century and persisting in the reign of Peter I, as we shall see. As such, this
interpretation departs from Michael Khodarkovsky's perspective that "unlike
medieval Europe . . . or later European colonials projects in the Americas
and Asia, which were predominantly driven by mercantilist interests, Russian
expansion in the south throughout the period was articulated by a government motivated first and foremost by geopolitical concerns, and only later
by economic and commercial interests."[71]

The Muscovite state envisioned an active role for itself as both regula-
tor of and participant in the economy. The state signaled its recognition of
the importance of commerce in a variety of ways: through its cultivation
of international trade relations, taxation policies, subsidization of commercial activities, and institution of its privileged merchant ranks, whereby the
state mobilized commercial expertise toward the generation of state revenue.
Further, the state recognized the importance of commerce through its own
participation in various markets. It did this by using privileged merchants
(although not exclusively) as commercial agents and by the institution of
various monopolies.

This activist nature of the early Romanovs has been recognized.[72] The
historian P. P. Smirnov wrote that the "radicalism, breadth, and volume
[of the early Romanovs' economic policy] certainly got the attention of the
observer of social life in the first half of the seventeenth century and forced
him to think that all the country in this period was being mobilized for trade
or commerce."[73] The imperial historian N. I. Kostomarov, the Soviet historian O. N. Vilkov, and the American historian Janet Martin all recognized
the state's efforts to cultivate trade with Central Asia, just as Clifford Foust
and Mark Bassin observed enthusiasm to develop trade with China.[74] Jarmo
Kotilaine documented Russian government efforts to develop Baltic commerce and the Smolensk hinterland (which delivered hemp and timber to
the Baltic) in the late seventeenth century.[75] Carol B. Stevens has described

---

71. Khodarkovsky, *Russia's Steppe Frontier*, 227.
72. Sergei Bogatyrev describes Muscovy as an activist state, although with a different focus. See his "Localism and Integration in Muscovy," in *Russia Takes Shape*, 103.
73. Smirnov, "Ekonomicheskaia politika v XVII v.," 404.
74. Kostomarov, *Ocherk torgovli Moskovskago gosudarstva*, 56; Vilkov, *Remeslo i torgovlia*, 170; Martin, "Fur Trade and the Conquest of Siberia," 76–77; Bassin, "Expansion and Colonialism on the Eastern Frontier," 7–10. Bassin overemphasizes the role of fur.
75. Kotilaine, "Russian Merchant Colonies in Seventeenth-Century Sweden," 97, 99.

Muscovite policy designed to channel grain in Ukraine in instrumentalist ways in the second half of the seventeenth century.[76] John LeDonne has remarked on the centrality of commercial aspirations in Peter I's policies.[77] As will be shown in chapters 2 and 3, the state was fundamentally interested in developing commerce in Siberia. Governors were in charge of tribute collection, but the state established an entire network of customs administration to generate commercial revenue.

Russian Revenues

Much of the emerging bureaucracy was centered on the maximization of revenues in order to pay for the expanding military, a phenomenon associated with what has been called the rise of the military-fiscal state. To collect customs duties (and other taxes) and regulate industries required administrative infrastructure. The prioritization is clear. Chancery documents relentlessly emphasize the need to maximize profit to the tsar's treasury. Contemporary subjects understood the state's priorities well. When servitors wanted to levy charges that would get attention, they accused one another of hurting the tsar's bottom line. As we will see, petitions to the tsar regularly use the same angle to advance their own case. When a local official jailed a Verkhotur'e peasant for resisting the appropriation of his horse—whether for legitimate service or the official's personal use was the debated point—the peasant framed his appeal in terms of the tsar's revenue. Because he was in jail during the harvest of 1655, he could not yield as much from his fields as he otherwise would have, thus his incarceration prevented him from remitting a greater portion to the tsar.[78]

In the standard parlance of the day, revenue ideally meant specie—hard currency, gold, or silver.[79] Like other early modern mercantile states, Russian administrators believed that hard currency was the kind that could truly ensure the wealth of the nation and took measures to ensure that specie filtered into—and not out of—the country. In some analyses, this precise

---

76. Stevens, "Trade and Muscovite Economic Policy toward the Ukraine," 172–85.

77. LeDonne, *Russian Empire and the World*, 23–24, 348.

78. SPbII-RAN, f. 28, op. 1, d. 706, ll. 11–13.

79. When Russian defaults on foreign debt catalyzed a financial crisis in August 1998, one of the revelations during the fallout was just how much of the Russian economy functioned by barter. From petty exchanges to factory salaries to major intrarepublic transactions, in-kind payments took place to a degree that stunned observers. That said, we need not assume continuity, for seventeenth-century Muscovy was a highly monetized economy: Kotilaine, *Russia's Foreign Trade*, 2. On Russia's modern barter economy, see LaFraniere, "Cashless Society"; Woodruff, *Money Unmade*.

aim was the essence of mercantilism.[80] Currency laws were a standard form of intervention. Edward IV made it a felony to export bullion from England.[81] France in the late fifteenth century forbade the export of money to Rome. Even Dutch authorities banned the export of silver in the 1690s, which further demonstrates that even the most laissez-faire trading republic responded to protectionist impulses.[82] The Russian state, too, did what it could to obtain specie, requiring no theoretical justification to pursue such a policy. The state needed money, the lifeblood of war. Several laws aspired to keep precious metals from exiting Russia. For example, in the 1660s, Bukharans were allowed to trade in specie but specifically prohibited from leaving the country with it. Most important, specie enters our discussion of Russian merchants because it was the thing for which the state would undermine its intention to facilitate merchant welfare. When it sold tax-farms and granted monopolies to Western European foreigners at various points in the seventeenth and early eighteenth centuries, it generally did so because that foreigner could pay in specie.[83] In other words, the desire for immediate specie could trump protectionist concerns. For example, in 1658 Tsar Aleksei Mikhailovich, conscious of the importance of the Italian market, sent a special envoy to the Grand Duke of Tuscany to negotiate an agreement whereby Tuscany was granted the monopoly on caviar imports in exchange for the payment of an annual sum of money. The Tuscan Duke, however, offered to pay only half the requested sum in cash, the rest in silk (as was common practice at Arkhangel'sk).[84] Holding out for better terms, specie-seeking Moscow negotiated with the English consul in Livorno, who set up a joint stock company, with the participation of Dutch and Italian merchants, that held the caviar contract until 1667.[85] Fiscal policy, however, was but one of the ways in which the state intervened in commerce in and across its borders.

Such attention to commercial matters is entirely unsurprising when one appreciates what a significant portion of the state's revenue derived from indirect taxes—that is, tax revenue generated from commerce. Whereas agriculture always remained the occupation of the vast majority of the population, trade and industry proceeds accounted for the most important source of state

---

80. For a recent discussion, see Findlay and O'Rourke, *Power and Plenty*, chap. 5.

81. Wilson, "Trade, Society and the State," 496–97.

82. Ibid., 505.

83. Arel, "Arkhangel'sk Trade, Empty State Coffers, and the Drive to Modernize," 186, 197; Longworth, *Alexis*, 27.

84. Kotilaine, *Russia's Foreign Trade*, 3.

85. De Divitiis, *English Merchants in 17th c. Italy*, chap. 1.

revenue in the seventeenth century.[86] Since seventeenth-century states did not have budgets, revenue is hard to quantify. Nonetheless, economic historians have surmised that in Russia a large proportion of its budget came from customs revenue.[87] For example, Novgorod and Nizhni Novgorod in the 1610s and 1620s derived one-third to two-thirds of its revenue from customs receipts alone. If duties from the state alcohol sales are included, the figures rise to two-thirds to nine-tenths of revenue.[88] In 1680 over half of the state budget derived from indirect taxes; in 1701, 40.4 percent.[89] In contrast, during this period highly commercial England generated 30–40 percent—that is, slightly less on average—of the king's revenue from indirect taxes.[90] With so much at stake, obviously commerce was a critical area of state interest.

The importance of foreign trade in the Russian economy reached unprecedented levels in the seventeenth century. Expanding European demand drove Russian development, as Muscovy was significantly drawn into an expanding European economy in the seventeenth century and that European demand drove Russian development.[91] Much of that was forest products (potash, from which navies were built, and then leather hides, furs, caviar, and items transshipped from the East). Trade especially took off in final third of the seventeenth century, such that by the end of the century, Russia was heavily integrated in the expanding European world economy, linked to colonial economies of the English and Dutch via Arkhangel'sk *and* with the Silk Roads trade through the Volga-Caspian and Siberian trade routes.

Cultivating Eastern Trade

The first Romanov tsars saw the country's trade as something to simultaneously promote and participate in toward both fiscal and instrumentalist ends. In general, more trade meant more tax revenue. According to B. G. Kurts, "India" for seventeenth-century Muscovites was the standard proxy for "riches of the East."[92] Tsar Mikhail Fëdorovich sent the merchant Fedot Afanasyev syn Kotov to India and Iran on a 1623–24 journey. By midcentury, the Romanov dynasty proactively dispatched numerous state embassies to

---

86. Ibid.

87. Kotilaine, "Mercantilism in Pre-Petrine Russia," 145; Bushkovitch, *Merchants of Moscow*, 159.

88. Kotilaine, "Mercantilism in Pre-Petrine Russia,"145. Bushkovitch, "Taxation, Tax Farming, and Merchants," 381–98.

89. Miliukov, *Gosudarstvennoe khoziaistvo Rossii*, 74, 115–17.

90. Braddick, *Nerves of State*, 49. NB: Significant portions of English customs taxes came under parliamentary control only after 1660.

91. Kotilaine, *Russia's Foreign Trade*, 2–4.

92. Kurts, *Russko-Kitaiskie snosheniia v XVI, XVII i XVIII stoletiiakh*, 10, 12fn3.

cultivate trade relations. Tsar Aleksei Mikhailovich sent a state trade embassy to India in 1646. The Kazan merchant Nikita Syroezhin and the Astrakhan merchant Vasilii Tuskhanov headed the trip, which traveled with 3,000–4,000 rubles worth of state goods (goods that they would trade on the state's behalf). In 1651 the merchants Rodion Nikitin syn Pushnikov and Ivan Derevenskii departed on another state trade embassy to India, from which only one would return in 1667.[93] A third commercial-diplomatic embassy was dispatched in 1675 to the great cotton textile producer, the Mughal Empire, which extended over the northern region of the Indian subcontinent.[94] The caravan was turned back at Kabul because of the Afghan-Mughal war. This mission was led by a Bukharan merchant, Muhammad Yusuf Qasim(ov) (aka Muhammad Islam Kasimov), a resident of the Bukharan neighborhood in Astrakhan, which was home to numerous diaspora merchant communities. The number of Indians living in Astrakhan quadrupled to over one hundred from 1647 to the 1680s. During these years, wars compromised Indians' own contact with their native land, but these expatriates managed to generate alternatives.[95]

Central Asian middlemen largely conducted Russo-Chinese trade prior to the seventeenth century.[96] Russian and Chinese merchants probably encountered each other directly in the Bukharan markets of Samarkand from at least the early fifteenth century and probably earlier.[97] Muscovy's awareness of the prospects of long-distance trade and the profit potential of facilitating it enticed the state to reach out to potential trade partners to the east. Between 1608 and 1675 Russia dispatched ten missions to China, seven of which reached China.[98] These trips require some qualification. Muscovy approached the little-known power to the east with appropriate caution. Most of these trips were not official state embassies but trips on a lesser scale. Deliberately, many of them were organized not in Moscow and headed by a high-ranking elite, but by Siberian governors and led by Cossacks. A Cossack named Ivan Petlin, who went to Beijing in 1618, led this first-known Russian trip.[99] In a 1620 missive, Moscow directed frontier servitors *not* to

93. Romaniello, "In Friendship and Love," 8.

94. In contrast to Russia, "the vast bulk of revenue of the Mughal state came from land revenue. . . . Only perhaps 5 percent came from customs revenue." Pearson, *The Portuguese in India*, 27.

95. Golikova, *Ocherki po istorii gorodov*, 160–74; Dale, *Indian Merchants and Eurasian Trade*, 78, 91–96; Romaniello, "'In Friendship and Love,'" 117.

96. Fekhner, *Torgovlia russkogo gosudarstva*.

97. Kurts, *Russko-Kitaiskie snosheniia*, 5.

98. Dmytryshyn, Crownhart-Vaughan, and Vaughan, *Russia's Conquest of Siberia*, 1: lx.

99. Demidova, *Pervye russkie diplomaty v Kitae*, 6. Although it is sometimes averred that Ivan IV sent an embassy to China (Kagarlitsky, *Empire of the Periphery*, 335 n.6.), Kurts found this to be a

engage directly with China. Proceeding cautiously, while revealing that commerce was prominent in the state's constellation of considerations, the document instructed, "not to maintain any direct contact . . . with the Chinese and Mongol empires without our permission, because these empires are too far distant for their merchants to visit our empire."[100] The state's rationale for this hedging, even if short-sighted, hinged on the state's perspective of trading potential or lack thereof.

At midcentury the state sent its first official embassy to China. It was led by a Russian nobleman (*stol'nik*), Fëdor Isakovich Baikov.[101] Baikov's arrival had been preceded by a reconnaissance mission led by Seitkul Ablin, a Bukharan merchant in state service. Whereas the Baikov mission (1653–57) foundered on diplomatic protocol, Ablin's success in trading with the Chinese prompted the Russian tsar to send him back to China on three subsequent trips, in 1658 and in 1668–72. The state dispatched a Moldovan diplomat-explorer, Nikolai Spafarii, to China in 1675. About this time private trade to China was gathering momentum. The gost' G. R. Nikitin opened up a new route through the Gobi desert in 1674. As steppe markets such as that at Lake Yamysh (chapter 5) reveal all too clearly, the state had little control over Russia-China trade. It endeavored to carve out particular markets for itself through the implementation of monopolies, such as that on rhubarb, but it in large part looked to keep channels of commerce. When the Russians and Chinese came to blows over the Amur valley, Russia was quick to cede territorial claims for the sake of regular commerce in the Treaty of Nerchinsk in 1689. When it began to organize state caravan trade, it allowed the gosti most involved in China to continue their affairs and called on other merchants to lead state caravans.

Between the riches of the Safavid, Mughal, Ming, and Russian river systems lay vast lands of forest, swamp, steppe, and desert, some of which was home to various Turkic-Mongol groups. Moscow sent numerous emissaries to the fragmented leaders of the steppe throughout the seventeenth century, including nineteen missions to the camps of the Dzhungar leader Batur Hong-taiji, who ruled between 1635 and 1653.[102] The mutual exchange between Moscow and steppe powers was so frequent that Moscow occasionally suspended the standard tax waiver for diplomats, an indication that significant commercial exchange accompanied the diplomatic mixing. Embassies went

mistake that originated with Karamzin, who misread the date of Peitlin's expedition as 1567 rather than as 1618. Kurts, *Russko-Kitaiskie snosheniia*, 20–1.

100. Dmytryshyn, Crownhart-Vaughan, and Vaughan, *Russia's Conquest of Siberia*, no. 34, 1: 99.

101. Demidova, *Pervye russkie diplomaty v Kitae*, 77–101; RKO I, nos. 85, 86.

102. Chimitdorzhiev, "Iz istorii Russko-Mongol'skikh ekonomicheskikh sviazei XVII v.," 151–56; MIUTTSSR, 64; RKO 1, no. 86, p. 217, no. 87, p. 219; Perdue, *China Marches West*, 105.

to Central Asian khanates as well.[103] These ambassadors, along with those traveling to Persia, India, and China, called on steppe leaders along the way, presenting gifts to maintain goodwill and partaking in hospitality. For example, en route to China, Ivan Petlin enjoyed hospitable accommodation from the nomadic realms, such as the Kirgiz Prince Nemei, the Mughal Altyn tsar, and the Tsaritsa Manchika in the vast Mongol lands (*shiromugal'skie zemli'*).[104] He imparted gifts in order to encourage his hosts to abstain from raiding trade caravans, a critical component to reliable and profitable Eurasian trade. As the French Jesuit Philippe Avril advised regarding travel to China via the Irtysh route, "the chief Captain of the Horde of Tartars, who have no fix'd Habitations but live after the manner of the Ancient Scythians, might, if he pleas'd secure this way, and make it safe for Travellers, which sometimes he will vouchsafe to do for the sake of some little presents."[105]

Diaspora Merchant Communities

Muscovy recognized that state trade was hardly the only channel for foreign trade. One way to increase trade was to encourage foreign merchants to the realm. Muscovy recognized that "mercurian" types—people whose greater mobility afforded them a liminal status in which they were permanent outsiders who were to certain degrees allowed "in"—would facilitate trade in the realm and toward this end sometimes granted new foreign trade partners generous tax breaks.[106] Only once relations were established and trade goods were flowing did the state become more concerned with generating revenue. It began to monitor more closely that private wares were not slipped in as diplomatic wares.[107] (Recall that much initial trade was often of a commercial-diplomatic nature and diplomatic wares were not taxed.) Second, once trade was well established, the state would begin to rescind those privileges and incrementally impose taxes. This is how it operated with Central Asian merchants and English merchants. The state well understood that there would be no tax revenue to gain if merchants did not come. By the second half of the seventeenth century, Moscow was so integrated into international trade networks that the state felt secure in instituting more comprehensive protectionist taxation. The New Trade Statute of 1667 imposed on

103. RIB 15: 1–85; Ulianitskii, "Snosheniia Rossii s Sredneiu Azieiu i Indieiu," 1–62; Romaniello, "'In Friendship and Love.'"

104. Demidova, *Pervye Russkie diplomaty v Kitae*, 56.

105. Avril, *Travels to divers Parts*, 143.

106. On "mercurian" types, see Slezkine, *The Jewish Century*, chap. 1.

107. For one of many examples, see "Nakaz Pazukhinym," in RIB, 15: 20.

foreigners higher tax rates than Russian merchants paid. Since these statutes were not applied in Siberia for several decades and exceptions were made in Astrakhan, the statutes primarily applied to European traders, whereas Central Asians, Armenians, and Indians continued to enjoy lower tax rates than Russian subjects paid. The empire extended various privileges to various people at various times, but it made sure to collect taxes.

The British of the Muscovy Company had enjoyed completely tax-free trade from 1555 to 1572, a total of seventeen years. This demonstrates typical Muscovite practice: tax-free incentives for an initial period of trade development followed by imposition of taxes. Of course there was an additional component to Anglo-Muscovite relations: Ivan IV wanted weapons, which the English could provide. In a state that recognized the importance of commerce and its potential to generate revenue, the waiving of tax obligations is an example of the state operating in an entitlement mode—resourcefully providing benefits with an alternative transaction. No less true, political strategy could always inflect economic policy. In the 1572 charter granted to the English, Ivan imposed taxes on the English at half the rate. In the 1574 charter to the Stroganovs, he reiterated that Bukharans trading in their territory must be permitted to trade tax free without hindrance. The charter stated: "if there start coming to their new places merchants from Bukhara, and from the Kazakh Horde, and from other lands with horses and all kinds of merchandise, such as do not come to Moscow, they are to trade in every kind of wares freely without duty."[108]

The state established mechanisms and devoted resources to supporting foreigner traders. Derived from Mongol practice, Muscovy established an elaborate system of way stations, manned by porters and horsemen, where travelers could refresh and change out animals. Although the restrictions on movements of foreigners in Russia are frequently observed, it is less often observed that foreign merchants who did travel through Russia generally did so at the state's expense. The state provided them resources and paid per diem for their travel in Russia. Just as the state financed its military, diplomatic, and administrative endeavors in Siberia, the state funded commercial envoys, even if the funds came sporadically, with delays and sometimes in amounts shy of those promised.[109] Illustrative of the importance Moscow assigned to commerce, the state subsidized the travel of Bukharan merchants in the realm, a courtesy Bukharan merchants came to expect, as we shall see.

---

108. Dmytryshyn, Crownhart-Vaughan, and Vaughan, *Russia's Conquest of Siberia*, no. 3, 1: 9–12 (May 30, 1574 Stroganov charter).

109. RGADA, f. 214, stb. 414, ll. 153–257.

It may be that the Russian state looked at Western European merchants through fiscal eyes only—that is, it saw the specie they could deliver. But in Siberia, Russia had a fully instrumentalist attitude toward foreign merchants. It prioritized the goods they would bring over the taxes it could collect from them. A document from Kazan illustrates how the Russian state valued the liminal social space such merchants occupied, brokering exchanges across geographical and cultural divides. In October of 1620 the governor of Kazan wrote to Moscow asking what he should do about Teziks who had come from Persia and now lived in the Tatar neighborhood. Moscow replied that Teziks should be welcomed to Kazan and treated well. They should not, however, stay more than one year at a time. They must live in the Trader's House (*Gostiniy dvor*) and should not settle in the Tatar neighborhood or become residents of the *posad* (the merchant and artisan quarter), where they would be expected to pay *posad* taxes. They should not take Tatar wives and Kazan women were not allowed to leave with them.[110] Here we see a state—ever short in human resources—that wanted these merchants from beyond to maintain a liminal status restricted to moving goods between empires. The more fully foreigners assimilated to local life in Kazan, the less likely they would be to leave. Teziks were more valuable to the Russian state as brokers of commerce than as local taxpayers. It likewise saw Bukharan merchants in Siberia as useful and did much to court them, as chapter 7 describes. This persistent cultivation of a healthy trade to support its military and civilian population pervades the history of Bukharan diaspora communities in Siberia. Subjects looked to the state to facilitate commerce; early settlers to Siberia petitioned the tsar to make traders come, and the center tried to accommodate, as discussed in chapter 2. From the Massachusetts Bay Colony to the markets of Istanbul and Beijing, this tension between regulation and support, trimming and facilitating trade, were standard for early modern regimes.[111]

That is, the state's attitude toward commerce was not only fiscal in nature; it was instrumental. Thus the state's promotion of trade in Siberia corroborates the revisionist trend that sees more strategizing in early modern economic policy. Traditional historiography has argued that economic policy, to the extent that it existed, was only there to provide cash for government's

110. Veselovskii, *Pamiatniki diplomaticheskikh i torgovykh snoshenii*, 650–54.

111. Bailyn, *Merchants of New England in the Seventeenth Century*; Yi, *Guild Dynamics in Seventeenth-Century Istanbul*, 167–68. Separate living quarters for foreigners was a common practice throughout the medieval and early modern world. See Constable, *Housing the Stranger in the Mediterranean World*. The practice came later to Moscow. See Baron, "The Origins of Moscow's Nemetskaja Sloboda," in *Muscovite Russia*.

other needs, such as fielding armies.[112] Such a position relies on the premise that early modern states should have envisioned economic growth for its own sake as good, which imposes an anachronistic vision and suggests false dichotomies with respect to state behavior.[113] More to the point, however, state actions in Siberia reveal a commercial policy that prioritized provisioning a region in which its hold and supply lines were tenuous higher than cash generation.

East–West Trade: Bridge and Gatekeeper

Muscovite governments appreciated the advantages in serving as a bridge for trade between the East and West. Throughout the sixteenth and seventeenth centuries Moscow was in constant contact with its neighbors on the steppes to its east and south. Indeed, it follows from a strategy that sought to profit from acting as a middleman fulcrum between markets of the West and East. The Muscovite state also wanted to be the gatekeeper. This is why it was so cautious about granting transit passage, and why it was so aggressive about policing the dissemination of geographical information. Moscow wanted to protect its competitive advantage.

Consistent with other early modern mercantilist empires, one way to maximize the income of specie was commonly believed to be most achievable through the maintenance of a favorable balance of trade. According to contemporary thinking, development of domestic manufactures could accomplish this. Re-export was another way. Peter's predecessors recognized the potential Russia's geographic location presented and sought to act as a bridge for the transmission of exotic products from the East to Western Europe.[114] That is, they sought not only to exploit new markets but also to profit from connecting them, an endeavor in which they faced stiff competition from maritime trading companies.

Being a middleman was a two-way street. Russians did not only shuttle Eastern goods westward. They also imported fabrics for re-export and sold "German" goods (household wares) to Central Asians. Meanwhile, another significant dynamic was afoot. Russia began to maneuver to eliminate Central Asian middlemen in Eurasian trade, roles that Bukharan merchants had held for centuries. Whereas Kagarlitsky calls Russia's role as intermediary in

---

112. Musgrave, *Early Modern European Economy*, 90.

113. LeDonne also recognized this problem in "Proconsular Ambitions on the Chinese Border," 53.

114. Kostomarov, *Ocherki torgovlia*, 56. Levi, *India Diaspora in Central Asia*, 233. The desire to connect Russia to Indian markets motivated Peter's aborted conquest of Central Asia. See Druhe, *Russo-Indian Relations*, 50.

European-Persian trade "extremely profitable," Matthew Romaniello characterizes the early modern Volga trade as a dream that never lived up to expectations.[115] They may both be right. We know much about product dynamics but far less about volume. Obviously, the volume of trade holds implications not only for understanding trade on several scales. For example, De Vries has demonstrated that Europe-Asia maritime trade flows were in volume a fraction (one-quarter to one-third) of that between Europe and the New World.[116] However, without including overland volumes in the equation, assessments can be tentative at best. The important thing is not to equate absence of documentation with absence of trade.

Two areas in which Russia achieved some success as middleman were in the silk and rhubarb trades. First, let's consider silk. The Dutch played a large role in redirecting trade away from the Levant. Much traffic in Persian silk that had been going through the Levant after the 1620s was moving through the Caspian, up to Moscow, then to Arkhangel'sk, where it boarded Dutch ships and sailed for Italy (along with caviar). The Sephardi silk broker Sebastian Pimentel reported that in 1630 only 20 percent of Dutch silk imports were arriving from the Mediterranean. This means the rest, 80 percent of Persian silk reaching the Netherlands, was arriving via other routes, including from the Dutch East India Company (Vereenigde Oostindische Compagnie, VOC) circumnavigating Africa or from Dutch merchants in Russia. According to Jonathan Israel's estimates, in 1630 four hundred bales of Persian and Armenian silk reached Western Europe via Moscow and Arkhangel'sk, eight hundred bales of silk reached Western Europe on VOC ships that departed from the Middle East, and three hundred silk bales reached Western Europe from Levant and Italy.[117] According to such figures, the preeminence of the VOC is striking: it moved over 50 percent of the silk, more than double the silk that moved through Russia. It can be easy to overlook, then, that just over one-fifth (20.9%)—a significant portion—of the silk that reached Europe traveled through Russia.

The Muscovite state similarly sought to capitalize on its access and proximity to demand with respect to the rhubarb root, a coveted medicine in early modern Europe. Beginning in the mid-seventeenth century, it restricted trade, implementing monopoly and monopsony regimes variously. Although mercantilist state attempts to cultivate medicinal rhubarb domestically proved

---

115. Kagarlitsky, *Empire of the Periphery*, 110; Romaniello, *Elusive Empire*, 15, 88–90.

116. De Vries, "Limits of Globalization," 728, 729, Table 3.

117. Israel, *Dutch Primacy in World Trade*, 153, Table 10. Total bales=1375. See Matthee, *Politics of Trade in Safavid Iran.*

unsuccessful (as they did for European botanists generally), the establishment of a quality-control system helped to ensure that Russian rhubarb garnered the highest prices in the apothecaries and markets in Europe. In the early eighteenth century, the state contracted rhubarb acquisition to Bukharan merchants.[118]

State Monopolies

Monopolies were another form of standard mercantilist fare and Muscovy behaved accordingly. In enacting monopolies, Muscovy was pursuing its fiscal needs or, writes Kotilaine, acting according to its "supply response."[119] Muscovy sold to European buyers raw and semifinished products in return for cash. Russia was already integrated into international economic dynamics and as a result had a highly monetized economy, which made its need to source bullion from foreign sources especially acute. Yet it possessed no known mineral sources at the time. (Although not for lack of trying. The Stroganov charters mandated mineral reconnaissance, an activity readily carried out in seventeenth-century Siberia.) The state's creation of several monopolies in the seventeenth century was a consequence of its quest for cash and was conceived to secure a means of obtaining foreign bullion. The Muscovite government preferred to administer monopolies itself rather than through a large trading company. On a more ad hoc basis, it would outsource the work of revenue collection and try to secure a set profit for itself by selling tax-farms, monopolies, or exclusive buying contracts to the highest bidder. Administration of the sixteen different commodities on which monopolies (potash, caviar, rhubarb, tar, etc.) were declared over the course of the seventeenth and eighteenth centuries frequently fluctuated.[120] The policy fluctuations seen with rhubarb, discussed below, were not unique. This changing and tinkering reflects a state undergoing substantial change (military, intellectual, economic, governmental) and trying hard to navigate encroaching features of modernity.

Yet the Russian state never granted anyone comprehensive monopoly rights in the Siberian territories wholesale, as Western European nations did with trading companies. The Stroganov charters remain unique events in Russian history. The state was unwilling to institute a competition-free dynamic in

---

118. For more on state efforts to profit from rhubarb, see Monahan, "Trade and Empire," chap. 9. For a broader consideration of rhubarb's use and circulation in the early modern world, see Monahan, "Locating Rhubarb." See also Foust, *Rhubarb*, chap. 3.

119. Kotilaine, *Russia's Foreign Trade*, chapter 4.

120. Kozintseva, "Uchastie kazny vo vneshnei torgovle Rossii," 267–337.

Siberia. Rather, the prompt establishment of a customs administration there showed that, to the extent the state had a vision for Siberia, it was one of state-regulated commerce. Russia made elaborate efforts to monitor and regulate the commercial activity of its subjects and the movements of its pelts. But it never tried to control the entire fur trade by declaring an outright monopoly. Although specialists such as Raymond Fisher have understood this—"The Muscovite government was jealous of the fur trade, but it was not rapacious," wrote Fisher[121]—the point has been missed in general histories, which often misrepresent the Russian fur trade as a comprehensive monopoly.[122] From the charters, to the Stroganovs, to instructions to governors, to diplomatic exchange with the Chinese Empire, an analysis of Russia's eastern expansion illustrates the extent to which the state prioritized commercial activity.

Taxation—Early Regulation

In the contemporary world, customs by definition refers to international movements, inspections, and taxes levied on people and goods moving across national borders. But in Russia, as was true for much of medieval and early modern Europe[123]—a world where identity construction was local (and religious), not national—an internal customs regime evolved where border controls existed not only between countries but between towns as well. Under the more fragmented sovereignty of the medieval period, where lords maintained roads and bridges in their particular territories, they levied taxes on the use of them. Eventually this evolved into a variety of regulations that were applied to goods as well as people. In Muscovy too, discrete principalities instituted their own regimes. That infrastructure stayed in place and was further developed as the Rus' principalities came under Moscow's control.[124]

In Kievan Rus' commercial taxes fell into two main categories. The *myt* was a levy associated with the transport of goods—tolls for using a road or bridge, and at rest stations. The Mongols imposed the *tamga*, a Turkic word from which derived the Russian word for customs: *tamozhnia*. This was a

---

121. Fisher, *Russian Fur Trade*, chap. 5, quote on 79.

122. A published textbook reads, "The state had a monopoly on fur trade." Naumov, *History of Siberia*, 227. See also Mancall, *Russia and China*, 178; Etkind, "Barrels of Fur."

123. The key difference was that regional taxation in Western Europe was imposed by guilds and/or municipalities, who sometimes had the backing of the state. In Russia, the imposition of customs duties derived from the center, which frequently channeled customs revenue to defray local state expenses.

124. On Russians customs administration: Tikhonov, "Tamozhennaia politika russkogo gosudarstva"; Razdorskii, *Torgovlia Kurska v XVII veke*, 11–57; Shumilov, *Torgovlia i tamozhenoe delo v Rossii*.

levy charged as some percentage of commercial transactions.[125] The Muscovite system of taxation drew on these basic forms as it evolved from the
eleventh to the sixteenth centuries. In 1398 Moscow Prince Vasilii Dmit-
revich and Tver' Prince Mikhail Aleksandrovich negotiated tax collection
protocols on the road between their territories.[126] Such arrangements made
for the embryonic structures of the customs system, which stayed in place as
the Rus' principalities became unified in the Muscovite state.

In the middle of the sixteenth century Ivan IV instituted important reforms.
Concomitant with the formal cancellation of the "feeding" system in the
1550s, the state began to take control of taxation via two methods: It sold
tax-farms, whereby an advance sum was paid for the right to collect particular
taxes—a model that, except for the changed faces of the collectors, probably
quite resembled traditional "feeding" on the ground. The other method was
where Moscow assigned "sworn men" to collect taxes and deliver the revenue
to Moscow. In either case it was usually middling-type merchants or artisans
that performed these tasks. Elite merchants, discussed below, served the tsar in
different capacities.[127] The *tamga* evolved into the "ruble tax" (*rublevaia poshlina*), which formed the keystone of indirect tax collection in Russia.[128] Locals,
out-of-town merchants, and foreigners were charged at differing rates, reflecting a protectionist bent before such measures came of age.[129] The various tolls
and transport taxes (of the *mytnaia* category) remained numerous. Overall, even
with the opacity of economic history, the system of indirect tax collection was
the state's biggest source of revenue, generating more income than the direct
taxes (*tiaglo*) towns paid. But the myriad charges that varied from town to town
made costs unpredictable for merchants engaging in longer-distance trade.

The Trade Statute of 1653 was enacted to correct that problem. Epitomizing in the commercial sphere the centralizing tendencies of the new
Romanov dynasty, this law sought to regularize taxation into a more uniform
system. With this reform the inconsistent collection of various taxes was
supplanted by a simplified, slightly higher tax rate.[130] The main taxes in European Russia became the ruble tax and the *mytnaia* tax. The ruble tax became
the primary customs duty (*tamozhennaia*, derived from *tamga*), set at a rate

125. Aksenov, et al., *Ekonomicheskaia istoriia Rossii* 1: 406, 2: 844.
126. Bazilevich, "K voprosu ob izuchenii tamozhennykh knig," 72.
127. Bushkovitch, "Taxing, Tax-farming, and Merchants," 381–98.
128. Merzon, *Tamozhennye knigi*, 11. Whereas the ruble tax was the mainstay of indirect taxation (i.e., taxes on purchases, as opposed to direct taxes, those levied on an individual or property) in
Central Russia, the one-tenth tax played that role in Siberia.
129. Tikhonov, "Tamozhennaia politika russkogo gosudarstva," 333–46.
130. PSZ 1, no. 107, pp. 302–5 (October 25, 1653). Bazilevich, "K voprosu ob izuchenii
tamozhennykh knig," 71–89.

of 10 deneg per ruble, or 5 percent. The *mytnaia* tax was standardized at the same rate, 5 percent, making the total general tax at 10 percent. A protectionist impulse was apparent in the 1653 statute as the state restricted inland travel of foreigners, limiting them to the border towns—Arkhangel'sk, Smolensk, Astrakhan. It called for charging slightly higher tax rates on Europeans in northern towns, but specified that trade in Astrakhan, and Greeks, Persians, and Central Asians, should be taxed as previously. Protectionist measures were expanded in the New Trade Statutes of 1667.[131]

These were the most basic developments in seventeenth-century indirect taxation. Different rules applied in Siberia. There, the 1653 Trade Statue was not implemented and the one-tenth tax remained the basic customs duty until the end of the seventeenth century.[132] Perhaps one of the most compelling points supporting the argument that promotion of commerce was important to the Muscovite state is the revenue that commerce generated. The extant records will never allow a satisfactory reconstruction, but there is broad agreement among historians that customs collections comprised the majority of state revenue—certainly more than one-half and perhaps more than two-thirds.[133] One example from a town on the way to Siberia: in 1614/15, Nizhni Novgorod collected "460 rubles in direct taxes, in contrast to a toll collection of 12,252 rubles and a tavern collection of 5,000 rubles (the latter from tax farmers)."[134]

Protectionism

Russia's policies make sense when seen within the guise of mercantilism, something other scholars have also noted in pre-Petrine Russia.[135] Nowadays

---

131. PSZ 1, no. 408, 677ff. (April 22, 1667).

132. It remains unclear if the one-tenth tax ever existed in European Russia. The one-tenth tax had ancient roots. From the eighth century it was levied around the Caspian Sea and the Byzantine emperor probably took 10% tax on goods at the Black Sea port of Cherson. See Franklin and Shepard, *Emergence of Rus'*, 10, 42. Traditionally, the tithe was a one-tenth tax that the church often levied in medieval European communities, but in Kiev and several early Rus' towns the state granted the church the revenue collected from every tenth week. See Merzon, *Tamozhennye knigi*, 11. When Muscovy expanded into Siberia, where it began collecting commercial taxes already in the sixteenth century, it replicated existing infrastructure, which led to the establishment of an internal customs regime in Siberia. It is hard to imagine where the one-tenth tax, which became standard, came from if not from European Russia.

133. Perkhavko, *Pervye kuptsy Rossiiskie*, 331. In 1679–80 revenue from customs and kabaks made up 53.5% of revenue of the Russian state: Ivantsova, et al., *Tiumenskaia tamozhnia*, 4; Bushkovitch, *The Merchants of Moscow*, 159.

134. Bushkovitch, "Taxing, Tax Farming, and Merchants," 381.

135. Kotilaine, "Mercantilism in Pre-Petrine Russia," 143–74; Arel, "The Arkhangel'sk Trade," 175–202; Bazilevich, "Elementy merkantilizma v ekonomicheskoi politike," 1–34.

scholars talk in terms of the development and/or rise of early modern capitalism rather than of mercantilism.[136] Perhaps the subsequent distancing from this original term is born from the recognition that the concept of "mercantilism," when held closely under a microscope, involves contradictory and eclectic practices with "little intellectual or logical coherence."[137] However, certain principles unite the concept of "mercantilism." In essence, it was born from a belief that trade could enrich the country faster and more effectively than could agriculture.[138] This logically led to a commitment to a favorable balance of trade because it was believed that this would maximize the amount of specie in the nation. Through the lens of these objectives, Russian state economic policy becomes more understandable and appears rather similar to other early modern empires. Protectionist laws, tax-farms, monopolies, customs duties, and recruitment of foreign expertise for domestic manufacture were all common tools of the early modern state. Simultaneously and in part in conjunction with the pursuit of these aims, governance shifted from a domain state to a bureaucratically institutionalized tax state. Depending on how fine a point one wants to put on it, discrete polities can look wildly disparate or remarkably similar. The English, Dutch, Safavid, Spanish, Portuguese, French, and Ottoman empires in some cases used similar tools to secure similar aims. As Jan De Vries explained, "By assuming more activist postures, seventeenth-century absolutist and constitutional states alike became more effective in their attempts to channel economic life to their ends."[139] Comparing Russian state building and empire building with other European empires, even perfunctorily, is instructive. Russia, with all its particularities—not least a massive geography—shared in these processes in these centuries of globalization.

Protectionist laws were a hallmark of mercantile policies. Russia proceeded proactively but its decrees and policies were no more heavy-handed than those of the highly centralized early modern France, which under Louis XI enacted protectionist trade laws from the fifteenth century.[140] Indeed, Russian policymakers may have modeled some policy after Colbert's, as transmitted to Moscow by the De Gron brothers.[141] If Moscow imposed burdensome measures on its merchants, as observers accused, it was not alone. England had

---

136. A major debate was Coleman, "Mercantilism Revisited," 773–91. For recent scholarship, see Findlay and O'Rourke, *Power and Plenty*, chap. 5; Prak, *Early Modern Capitalism*.

137. Wilson, "Trade, Society and the State," 498.

138. Ibid., 543.

139. De Vries, *Economy of Europe in an Age of Crisis*, 236.

140. Wilson, "Trade, Society and the State," 498.

141. Baklanova, "Ian de-Gron," 117; Smirnov, "Economicheskaia politika v XVII v.," 369–411.

"navigation laws"; Italian, Hanseatic, and Flemish cities all developed "navigation codes" that restricted their merchants' use of foreign shipping, often obliging them to employ a less economical option.[142] The English government, showcased as a bastion of private initiative, nonetheless pursued quite heavy-handed measures: laws forbidding the import of finished wool and the export of raw wool were in effect in the mid-fifteenth century. The Ottoman Empire undermined Turkish merchants' interests by patronizing Florentine merchants for the geopolitical sake of weakening the greater Venetian threat.[143] Even Dutch merchants, unique in their commitment to free trade (and the untimely belief that peace, not war, facilitated prosperity), were also on occasion subject to cumbersome state controls and also benefited from protectionist laws and an armed, subsidized merchant marine.

The development of a merchant marine for Russia had been a pillar of the De Gron recommendations. Aleksei Mikhailovich had initiated a sea ship-building program, which was abandoned without success.[144] Thus Russia still had no navy when a skipper from Amsterdam, interviewed by the curious Tsar Peter in 1693—as if chiding the memory of Anton Lapt'ev[145]— explained: "We take a good percent for our transport, and Russians will always be in the palm of our hands as long as we come to you on our ships and take away your wares. Whatever reciprocal agreements we establish between us, whatever price we pay for wares, it does not matter. If Russian ships brought Russian wares to us, then our profit (*barysh*) would go to them."[146]

The state enacted typically protectionist measures intended to advantage its own merchants. It restricted foreigners to trading in border towns and established the terms under which foreigners could do business. This latter matter speaks to the sway elite merchants must have held in Muscovy. By their interference, lower artisans, traders, and workers were denied opportunities that working for foreigners presented.[147] This worked to the advantage of Russian merchants, who did not have to compete for their labor, but more

---

142. Wilson, "Trade, Society and the State," 497, 505.

143. Goffmann, *The Ottoman Empire and Early Modern Europe*, 177.

144. Baron, "A. L. Ordin-Nashchokin and the Orel Affair," in *Explorations in Muscovite History*.

145. The story goes that Anton Lap'tev was a merchant from Yaroslavl' who sailed to Holland to sell his goods. Dutchmen there colluded and refused to buy his goods, no matter how steep a discount he offered. The Dutchmen then followed him to Arkhangel'sk, where they bought his higher asking price immediately, making the point that Russia should not encroach on their carriage profits. See Solov'ev, "Moskovskie kuptsy v XVII v," 515.

146. Repin, "Torgovlia Rossii s evropeiskimi stranami na otechestvennykh sudakh," 142.

147. Kotilaine, *Russia's Foreign Trade*, 206–7; Daniel, "Entrepreneurship and the Russian Textile Industry," 25; Baron, "Weber Thesis," in *Muscovite Russia*, 321–36.

important, it eliminated the competition that foreign networks, facilitated by locals, would have created.[148]

Controlling foreign access to trade opportunities that Muscovy provided was an early priority. The Muscovite government was reticent to hear numerous pleas to allow foreign merchants to use Russia as a transit route for trade with the East. They denied passage to Persian and English merchants alike, one way in which they did keep other merchants from providing additional competition to trade routes via Astrakhan and Siberia. (An exception to this was the granting of monopoly rights on the Persian shah's silk to Armenian merchants in 1667, coincident, ironically, with the issuing of the protectionist New Trade Statutes.)[149] Muscovy periodically sent diplomatic envoys to lubricate the rails of reciprocal trade and these were sometimes led by foreigners—such as the embassies led by Anthony Jenkinson, Nikolai Spafarii, Eberhard Ides, and Lorenz Lange. But the state refused to allow Western Europeans free transit through Russia to Central Asian and Middle Eastern markets. Consequently, one does not find European merchants in Siberian customs books. The only Europeans that appeared in the customs books studied were Tobol'sk exiles, and they appeared quite rarely. Anecdotal evidence suggests Russians illicitly acted as proxies for foreigners. By 1619 the state had constructed a fort along the North Sea to prevent English ships from freely trading at Mangazeia (and departing with copious fur wealth undetected by Moscow). It later mandated that foreign merchants should be constrained to carry out their business in border towns, but regularly made exceptions to this rule. Like the borders of Russia themselves, this policy was porous.

A Commercial Corps

There was nothing unique about hosting a diaspora community of foreign merchants and awarding them special trade privileges within one's empire. The feature that sets Muscovy apart from other early modern empires, even more than its contiguous colony, was its state merchant corporations. Russia was different in that it did not create large trading companies to whom monopoly powers or even administrative rights in given regions were awarded. The largest trading companies, in effect, acted like ministates. They had their own military and they dictated policies in the regions over which they presided. Thus they functioned like states. Muscovy declined to institutionalize such an entity separately. It had no large trading companies until

---

148. For an illustration of this dynamic see Kotilaine, "Artisans: The Prokofiev Family," 188–97.
149. Kotilaine, *Russia's Foreign Trade*, 458.

the middle of the eighteenth century. The difference may be explained by
the nature of the territories colonized. Whereas trading companies of Western European powers created an extractive economic system that had not
previously existed in the Americas, colonizers that ventured first into Asia,
such as Muscovy and the Portuguese, from the outset operated within an
existing framework of trade networks. The Portuguese, the first Western
European imperial power in Asia, directed its operation in Asia not through
a trading company but through a central state corporation called the Estado
da India.[150]

Muscovy did not form trading companies. It did have privileged merchant corporations. One prong of its activist stance was through the presence
of this "commercial corps." Privileged merchant corporations were not an
alternative to trading companies. Although some of the function of trading
companies and Russian merchant corporations arguably overlapped (international trade), the overlap was in theory rather than in practice. Structurally,
gosti were a sui generis entity. The functions of the gosti corporation and
trading companies in international trade shared common features (although
trading companies were appreciably more elaborate operations), but gosti
were substantially occupied by domestic duties as well.

From the sixteenth to the early eighteenth century, formal corporations of privileged merchants occupied the top of the commercial pyramid.
Late-imperial Russian historians, committed to models of universal development that defined the Western experience as normal, did the historical field
a conceptual disservice by calling Russian merchant corporations guilds.[151]
But blame does not fairly lie with nationalist historians, for the state itself
introduced the term in 1728 when it abolished the traditional privileged corporations and replaced them with a "guild" system that divided merchants
into a three-tier hierarchy. Unlike medieval craft guilds, however, the organizing principle was not a common trade; annual ruble turnover determined
a merchant's place in the hierarchy.

Guilds in medieval Europe existed in primary (agricultural, livestock),
secondary (production of crafts/industry), and service (merchants, barbers,
etc.) sectors.[152] Most Western European guilds developed around a particular
industry—baking, dying, candle-making, etc. Members of Russian merchant
corporations were not unified around any particular industry, which makes
them different from the industry-specific guilds that were most prominent

---

150. Marshall, "Europe and the Rest of the World," 229–30.
151. Mel'gunov, *Ocherki po istorii russkoi torgovli*, 210–33.
152. Ogilvie, *Institutions and European Trade*.

in Western Europe. But merchant guilds did exist in Western Europe; their history can be traced from around 1000 and they were predominantly local. This is because, in the grand scheme of things, only a small minority of merchants engaged in long-distance trade.

As was the case with guilds in general, membership in a privileged merchant corporation in Russia conferred a status that derived from state authority. Unlike most Western European merchant guilds, however, the privileged merchant corporations of Russia were not self-organized. What united them was that they had been granted this particular status by the state. The members themselves were as likely to cooperate as they were to compete with one another. At the same time, these particularities should not be taken to reify Russian commercial history as an outlier. In fact, long-distance merchant guilds evolved in ad hoc ways throughout medieval and early modern Europe. The Julfa silk merchants, an Armenian expatriate community in Persia that negotiated a monopoly on shipping silk through Russia in the seventeenth century, illustrate a more typical model for long-distance merchant guilds. But variation was the norm.

Conclusion

Stability and security always trumped economic profits and growth in Muscovite strategic thinking, as was the case for most medieval and early modern states, but, all told, Muscovy had some measure of success in its policies.[153] It maintained a positive balance of trade throughout the seventeenth century. Considering what Muscovy had to work with, it did quite well. If the East was where commercial opportunities lay, it came at a high cost. Russian geography remained an unavoidable, undiminishing challenge. Moreover, the Asian trade—with its greater travel overhead and established networks to penetrate—never enjoyed the profit margins that plantation products of the Atlantic trade returned to European colonial powers.[154] The next chapters examine Siberia and how commerce played out there. In particular, the Siberian case provides a clear example that, aside from immediate fiscal intentions, Moscow seemed to have had more subtle approaches to trade as well. Janet Martin has argued that optimizing fur supplies was a central concern in Russia's overtures to Central Asia. It wanted to find new markets for fur products to avoid the deflation that comes with oversupply.[155] In Siberia,

---

153. Childs, "Commerce and Trade," 154; Musgrave, *Early Modern European Economy*, 51–53.
154. De Vries, "Connecting Europe and Asia," 35–105.
155. Martin, "Fur Trade and the Conquest of Siberia."

Moscow behaved with an instrumentalist approach to commerce—the state recognized that vibrant trade could cover supply deficits in its Siberian colony, thereby bridging crucial gaps between the state's aspirations and logistical abilities. This perspective of Russia as an activist commercial state has been little developed in a historiography that has instead emphasized autocratic and suspicious tendencies that impeded commercial development.

CHAPTER 2

Siberia in Eurasian Context

> "We journeyed ever eastward amid native tribes and
> habitations. Much might be said of that."
>
> —Avvakum, ca. 1661–1663

Western Siberia is located in the forest-steppe
zone (alternatively referred to as the taiga-grassland zone).[1] Forests of birch,
linden, spruce, pine, poplar, and Siberian fir are punctuated by meadows or, in
some places, swamps.[2] As one moves southward, the balance shifts until large
expanses of grass dotted by occasional clusters of birch trees dominate the
landscape. This biosphere has been of formative significance for Russian history because it mediated interactions between peoples of distinct economic
lifeways. People of the forest hunted, fished, and sometimes farmed. People
of the steppe were nomads—they had pastoral diets and relied not exclusively
but mostly on trading and raiding, with more of the former.

Siberian natives consisted of various tribes who shared many cultural traits
and habits, but whose political economy varied according to the ecological
niche they occupied. Tribes in the far north followed reindeer herds. In the
Siberian forests, tribes may have herded, but hunting and fishing were main-
stays of life. These tribes varied among themselves and one finds variation
moving laterally across the continent, but in general, they were polytheistic
and adhered to shamanistic practices. Political organization was loose and

---

1. Semenova-Tian'-Shanskogo, *Rossiia*, 12. See Moon, *Russian Peasantry*, for a good description
of Siberian geography.

2. Fund, "West Siberian Broadleaf and Mixed Forests."

lateral; people lived in groups generally not too much larger than an extended family. These peoples had occupied the Eurasian landmass since ancient times, if not longer. To the south, where forest gives way to steppe (prairie, it is called in North America), culture and political economy morphed as dramatically as the landscape. Here was the land of steppe nomads, mostly on horseback, whose political economy depended on pastoral practices and commercial ways. Nomads were masters of martial skills in the saddle. But in addition to their raiding lifestyles, they also engaged in trade and even farmed a bit.[3]

Just how many people lived in preconquest Siberia and the steppes to the south remains undetermined. Imperial Russian historians reported that about two hundred thousand natives lived in Siberia prior to Russian conquest.[4] Discoveries about the devastating diseases brought to the Americas through the Columbian exchange have led to profound reinterpretation of the conquest of the Atlantic world. Such developments naturally make historians of Eurasia attentive to possible consequences of contact in other imperial conquests. The acclaimed best-seller *1491* asserts that "disease cut down native Siberians again and again," but the first evidence it marshals dates to the reign of Catherine II.[5] Russian scholars have been less assertive on public health consequences of initial Russian contact in the face of such limited details. Smallpox moved from west to east across Siberia in the 1630s.[6] Plague hit the Siberian outpost of Berezov in 1700, but systematic research on disease in Siberia remains to be done.[7] If anything, more clues exist regarding steppe peoples than the natives of the Siberian forests and taiga. Anthony Jenkinson reported that Nogais who lived east of the Volga and around the northern shores of the Caspian were decimated by civil wars, "famine, pestilence, and such plagues" in 1558. Over one hundred thousand people died, "the like plague was never seen in those parts."[8] Krizhanich wrote of the Kalmyks: "These people are extraordinarily populous, no less so than the Scythians or the Tatars. Yet the Muscovites reported that when they conquered Siberia the Kalmyks were not numerous. Perhaps there was inadequate information about them."[9] His comment intimates the shortcomings of even contemporary knowledge of this space and his "perhaps" leaves open the possibility that

3. Christian, "Silk Roads or Steppe Roads?" 1–26.
4. Glinka, *Atlas Aziatskoi Rossii*, 1: 81.
5. Mann, *1491*, 119–20.
6. Collins, "Subjugation and Settlement," 45.
7. *Pamiatniki sibirskoi istorii XVIII veka*, bk. 1, *1700–1713*, no. 31, 128–29.
8. Morgan and Coote, *Early Voyages and Travels to Russia and Persia*, 1: 52.
9. Krizhanich in Dmytryshyn, Crownhart-Vaughan, and Vaughan, *Russia's Conquest of Siberia*, no. 113, 435.

reasons other than inadequate information could account for the misreporting. In sum, precious little reliable information exists on premodern Eurasian demographics, but Siberia was not a blank slate when the Russians arrived.

Local Siberian populations endemically endured encounters with nomadic groups that migrated across the continent in waves. Many groups moved westward, such as the Huns who destabilized the northeast borders of the Roman Empire in the fifth century. In this period Turkic nomads moved northeast across the Eurasian landmass. Some left, some stayed, and these dynamics resulted in variegated mixing among migrating Turkic groups and Siberian natives. The protracted intermingling of Turkic with other indigenous peoples is born out on linguistic maps where swaths of Turkic language influence cut a northeastward path across Eurasia.[10]

Islam in Eurasia

Some of these Turks brought with them not just language but Islamic religion as well. Islam emerged as a dynamic religious and political force in the seventh century. It quickly spread beyond the Arabian peninsula, moving westward along the coast of northern Africa and into the Iberian peninsula of southern Europe. It moved northward and eastward as well. Although initially stopped by the Christian Byzantine Empire, Islam enveloped much of the Anatolian peninsula, Persian lands, and continued eastward across the steppes of Eurasia, following Nestorian Christianity and Judaism eastward all the way to China. In Eurasia, Islam's penetration was uneven. This "sweep," porous at best, was accomplished in successive cycles characterized by seasonal conquest and apostasy, as described in Narshakhi's tenth-century *History of Bukhara*.[11] The Volga Bulgars, a settled Turkic people, were a society that practiced Islam on the Eurasian steppe as early as the tenth century. Amid such protracted intermingling, not least including Turkic migrations mentioned above, fixing Islam historically among nonsedentary peoples on a map—to say nothing of mapping its germination in individual consciences—is a difficult task. What one can say is that closer to the Volga basin of the Bulgar kingdom, Islam was probably more "thoroughly" adopted by the tenth century, and of a character that scholars in Baghdad or Bukhara would have recognized. Farther northward, it is more likely that trace elements infused existing belief systems. Mongol leaders adopted Islam in the early fourteenth century, but the Kalmyks, who remained steppe dwellers, retained Buddhism.

10. Tomilov and Frank, "Ethnic Processes."
11. Frye, *History of Bukhara*; Foltz, *Religions of the Silk Road*, 89–110.

Mongols, though they could be ruthless and merciless conquerors, were not religious crusaders. Granted, when Genghis Khan conquered the city of Bukhara, he denigrated the mosque by eating in it and had horses trample the Quran under their feet, according to the account of Ebülgâzî Bahadir.[12] Genghis Khan was not interested, however, in persecuting for religious beliefs. Rather, Mongols recognized diversity as "normal and useful" and took adaptable stances toward the various religions they sheltered. They allowed the founding of an archbishopric of the Orthodox Church in Sarai, for example, and granted the Orthodox Church tax immunities.[13]

Some Chinggisid leaders went beyond tolerating confessional diversity; they were open to religious experimentation. When Temujin (the birth name of Genghis Khan) began expanding into Eurasia in the early thirteenth century, Mongols were pagans or Shamanists, or some say Buddhists, but they consciously experimented with religion and, generalizing broadly, came to adopt local religions. In the East, Kubilai married a Buddhist and raised his son in that tradition.[14] The remaining three Hordes (Chagatai, Qipchak, Il-khanid) became Islamic. Berke Khan (d. 1266), ruler of the Qipchak khanate was one of the first Mongols to personally "submit" to Islam in the middle of the thirteenth century; he was mentored by a Sufi shaykh from Bukhara.[15] Ghazan Khan (cum Sultan) of the Il-khanate (Iran) was raised a Christian but adopted Shiite Islam in 1295, which had important legacies for the region. His brother, Il-khan Oljeitu, the great-great-great-grandson of Genghis Khan, "was probably a Shamanist, a Buddhist, a Christian, and a Sunni and a Shi'i Muslim at different times in his life."[16] To the northwest, the Mongols of Sarai, the capital that Batu constructed on a channel of the lower Volga River, were converting to Islam about the same time, although they drew from a different tradition. Many of Batu's original forces had settled in Kazan quite near the Bulgar territory, which had converted to Islam early in the tenth century, decades before the Kievan prince Vladimir converted to Orthodox Christianity in 988 and had his people follow suit by mass baptism. The Mongols settling in the steppe Volga region gradually adopted the Qipchak Turkic language there and the Muslim faith.[17] In the second decade of the fourteenth century the Orthodox Slavic princes

---

12. Bahadir, *A General History of the Turks, Moguls, and Tatars*, 1: 109. Ebülgâzî Bahadir (1602–63) was Khan of Khorezm.

13. Burbank and Cooper, *Empires in World History*, 13, 107–9.

14. Morgan, *Mongols*, 40–44, 204–5; Beckwith, *Empires of the Silk Roads*, 191–94.

15. Golden, *Central Asia in World History*, 91.

16. Burbank and Cooper, *Empires in World History*, 109.

17. Morgan, *Mongols*, 141–44; Beckwith, *Empires of the Silk Roads*, 189.

delivered their tribute to Ozbek/Uzbek (ruled 1313–41), the first Muslim khan who officially proclaimed Islam the religion of the Ulus of Jochi even as he honored protections to the Orthodox Church. The khans of the Chagatai khanate, whose territory at its peak in the late thirteenth century stretched from Transoxiana north to the Altai, had officially adopted Islam by 1326.

In this same century, the mystical movement of Naqshbandiism—a variation of Sufism—emerged in the city of Bukhara. Bukhara was the preeminent cultural center of Inner Central Asia at this time and became an important center of Islamic learning as Naqshbandi scholars along with others spread their particular Islamic teachings throughout Siberia and the Caucasus in the coming centuries.[18] As Islam put down roots in cities of Eurasia, Bukhara became a symbolic center that held special importance for many Muslims in the Russian Empire. By the early modern period Islam was common even as the Eurasian steppe remained a pluralistic religious setting.[19] It is fair to say that monotheism, a defining feature of state powers of the post-ancient Western world, generally mapped less aggressively onto the worldview and political order of Eurasian nomads. The conversion of the Mongols in the early fourteenth century enhanced Islam's fortunes in Eurasia, but many other groups retained polytheistic, shamanistic, or Buddhist belief systems.

Siberia in Time

Siberia in the popular imagination is a vast, cold space that stretches across Eurasia. Over time, Siberia, mind-bending in its forlornness, has both stretched and shrunk geographically. In the nineteenth century, just as it had stretched its farthest, an administrative restructuring reduced its size significantly with the creation of the Russian Far East as an administrative region. In the period of our story, Siberia was not so large, but was growing. In the middle of the sixteenth century when the storied Ermak led his Cossack militia to conquest, Sibir' was a fairly small region (relative to the size of the Eurasian continent) referring specifically to the khanate of Sibir', one of the successor states to the Mongol Horde, which meant it traced its heritage directly to Genghis Khan. The Chinggisid dynastic principle shaped Eurasian politics long after the disintegration of the Mongol Empire.

The Chagatai Horde covering the heart of Central Asia broke up most quickly, fragmenting into the Nogai (who would migrate westward), Kazakh,

18. Bustanov, "Notes on the Yasavīya and Naqshbandīya in Western Siberia"; Frank, *Islamic Historiography and "Bulghar" Identity*, 73; Lapidus, *A History of Islamic Societies*, 342.
19. Foltz, *Religions of the Silk Road*, 90–130.

and Sibir' hordes, or khanates, by the mid-fourteenth century. Tamurlane, the brilliant general of Samarkand, briefly reconstituted much of the Mongol Empire in his reign from 1370 to 1405; of mixed Mongol descent, he was not of Genghis's line. In his wake, however, the Sheibanids, or Uzbegs, whose lineage did stem from the Chinggisid line, reconquered the heart of Tamerlane's domain.

Mongols were ousted from Baghdad in 1335.[20] Genghis Khan's line in China lasted just a few decades longer. The Bubonic Plague (1346–47) and diminished East-West trade brought about the overthrow of the Yuan dynasty by the more isolationist Ming in 1368. The overthrow of the Yuan triggered a political crisis in the long-lived ulus of Jochi, of which Russia was a part. From 1359 to 1379 a dozen different khans ruled from Sarai. Amid such high turnover, the horde fragmented into seven polities.[21] In the fifteenth century, the Qipchak khanate (which Russianists typically refer to as the Golden Horde)[22] fragmented still further as Genghis-descended khanates wrought their independence from Sarai, breaking off into the khanates of Kazan (1438), Crimea (1441), and Astrakhan (1466).

Sibir'

Borders among early modern nomads were a shifting and imprecise business. By the middle of the sixteenth century, Jochi's ulus had split up into seven different statelets, or hordes: To the north of Sarai was the khanate of Kazan. To the south lay the khanate of Astrakhan. The khanate of Sibir', which broke off from the Chagatai Horde, originally occupied the land of the more eastward steppe, but pressure from the westward migrating Nogais pushed them westward into the steppe-forest zone between the Irtysh and Tobol Rivers such that the khanate of Sibir' came to more or less abut the khanates of Kazan and Astrakhan in the second half of the fifteenth century.[23]

To many, the steppe lords of premodern Eurasia are lost to history, an oversight reified by nationalist Russian historiography that dubbed Muscovy's initial expansion the "Gathering of the Lands" and stalwartly promoted Russia as a kinder, gentler type of European power. But eschewing the gravity of Moscow's pull, one recognizes that in the wake of Mongol hegemony, other steppe rulers harbored formidable state-building aspirations. Mongols were nomads but they also built towns. Batu built Sarai, the place to which Slavic

---

20. Beckwith, *Empires of Silk Road*, 196.
21. Martin, *Medieval Russia*, 155.
22. On why the Golden Horde is an erroneous title, see Ostrowski, "Golden Horde," 571–73.
23. Frank, "The Western Steppe"; Liubavskii, *Obzor istorii russkoi kolonizatsii*, 434.

princes prostrated themselves annually in the fourteenth century. Turkic migrations from the south and the Mongol-Turkic mixing that resulted may also have given a nudge in the direction of sedentarization. The Crimean khanate is a case of a nomadic-sedentary hybrid. Tamerlane is only the best remembered of leaders who in some measure aspired to build and unite. In the early seventeenth century, Batur built a city of stone along the ancient trade route that followed the Irtysh River. Kazakh monuments on the steppe near the source of the Ishim River belie failed permanence on the steppes. Chingi-Tur was built as the capital of the khanate of Sibir' in the fourteenth century. When Tokhtamysh, the deposed (Great Horde) khan, was defeated by the new khan of Sarai in 1399, he fled to Chingi-Tur.[24] In the fifteenth century, Khan Ibak had worked to cultivate Chingi-Tur as an attractive trade center for merchants.[25] In the sixteenth century a new capital was founded, Isker, or Kashlyk, along the Tobol' River.[26]

We may add Kuchum, the khan of Sibir', to this list of ambitious early modern Eurasian rulers, who would have checked Muscovy's imperial trajectory eastward. His predecessors had been careful to keep Muscovy on their good side, asking for protection and giving tribute.[27] Kuchum, however, beat out his brother Ediger for leadership of Sibir' in 1563 and embarked on an aggrandizement project of his own. As did Muscovite grand princes, he sought to increase his tribute payers. Toward this end, in the 1570s he launched raids for slaves and tribute in the territories claimed by the Stroganovs.[28] After 1571, perhaps emboldened by reports of his ambassadors, who delivered Kuchum's final tribute to a devastated Moscow in the wake of the severe sacking by Crimean Tatars, Kuchum spurned any further rituals of subordination to Moscow that Ediger had initiated after the conquest of Kazan.[29] In 1573 the Russian emissary Tret'iak Chebukov was sent to the Kazakh Horde. En route, he was taken prisoner and killed in July 1573 by Mahmet-kula, a relative of Kuchum, an action that diplomatically amounted

---

24. Martin, *Medieval Russia*, 218. Martin says Tokhtamysh fled to Tiumen'. Frank writes that Chingi-Tur, which means ten thousand, was established as the capital in 1427. I presume he refers to its status as capital, not the establishment of the town itself. Frank, "The Western Steppe," 251.

25. Skrynnikov, *Sibirskie ekspeditsiia Ermaka*, 99; Bakhrushin, "Sibirskie sluzhilye Tatary v XVII," in NT, 3: 153–62.

26. Russians later "founded" Tiumen' in 1586 on the site of Chingi-Tur, and Tobol'sk slightly downriver from the site of Isker. G. F. Müller said the ruins of Isker were 16 km from Tobol'sk.

27. *Litsevoi svod*, kn. 23, 99, 101.

28. Dmytryshyn, Crownhart-Vaughan, and Vaughan, *Russia's Conquest of Siberia*, no. 3 (1574 charter).

29. Martin, "Fur Trade and the Conquest of Sibir'," 67.

to an act of war.[30] Kuchum came to blows with the Muscovite state in the final decades of the sixteenth century.

One facet of Kuchum's mission may have been to properly Islamicize his subjects. Like so many rulers, Kuchum had a sense of the unifying potential of monotheism and sought to make his state properly Islam. Theoretically, it was already Islamic, but Kuchum found his subjects lacking in devotion and allegedly invited religious leaders from the khanates of Bukhara and the sometimes rival Kazan (they competed for tribute payers) to convert his subjects.[31]

Enter Muscovy

In some ways the history of Russia in Siberia properly begins in the forested hinterlands of the Russian north, where the Novgorodian republic grew wealthy exploiting furs in its hinterlands and as far as the Urals. Tucked in the forests southeast of the Baltic Sea, the trading republic of Novgorod was born in the eighth century along a trade route that connected distant Byzantium and Scandinavia. Like their Viking/Varangian founders, Novgorod's rulers pragmatically practiced "entrepreneurial outreach": brute extortion, trade, gift exchange, outright raiding, or the guise of collecting *dan'* (tribute) were all used as methods. The term *dan'* is of Germanic origin. Its use by Novgorod reflects its connections to European traditions transmitted through Hansa league merchants.[32] *Ushkuiniki*, as the fur trappers and traders of Novgorod were called, raided and extorted furs from Samoyed and Vogul (and Komi) tribes in the far northern forests of Novgorod's hinterlands.[33] They traded at Itil (at the Volga-Kama confluence)[34] and with Bulgars at the seasonal fair on the Volga. They traveled beyond the Urals to extract furs, where they found themselves in the territories of post-Mongol khanates. Novgorodians referred to the people beyond the Urals as the "Iugroi."[35] Muscovy, a principality to the south, was covetous of the trade and profits that Novgorod reaped in its heyday from the thirteenth to mid-fifteenth century. In the 1470s when the ambitious grand prince of Moscow attacked and claimed Novgorod as his own, he also added to his list of official titles

30. "Torgovlia moskovskogo gosydarstva s Srednei Aziei XVI–XVII vv.," n.d., http://kungrad.com/history/doc/torg/3/.

31. Frank, "The Western Steppe," 252–53. On Kuchum's potential recruitment efforts: *Opisi tsarskogo arkhiva*, 93–94; Bustanov, "Sacred Texts of Siberian Khwaja Families," 81.

32. Moscow, with its Mongol/Asiatic orientation, followed Turkic convention and called it *iasak*.

33. Skrynnikov, *Sibirskaia ekspeditsiia Ermaka*, 98.

34. Fisher, *Russian Fur Trade*, 1.

35. Martin, *Treasure in the Land of Darkness*.

Prince Iugorskii, or Prince of the Iugroi, presaging the hegemony Moscow would strive to assert in the post-Mongol space in the coming century.

In 1552 Muscovy conquered Kazan. Kazan sits along the Volga River where the river abruptly turns southward toward the Caspian. The Volga is a shining example of a frontier space that was painstakingly transformed from frontier periphery to Russian heartland. After a brutal siege, the army of Ivan IV was still unable to capture the Muslim center and built its first Orthodox Church outside the city. Finally, the Russian retinue entered the conquered Muslim city, sprinkling holy water, according to a legend, which may be apocryphal.[36] Definitive conquest of the region would take a few more years and effective incorporation into the empire decades longer, as Matthew Romaniello has shown.[37] But none of this diminishes this historic game changer. Ivan proceeded to Astrakhan. The khanate of Astrakhan had emerged in the 1460s, another statelet born in the wake of Mongol disintegration. Small and weak, it was somewhat subordinate to its Crimean neighbors, but sparred with them as well. In the wake of the Kazan conquest, Russian forces descended the Volga and installed a pro-Moscow Astrakhanite. When the Moscow-backed leader began negotiations with the Crimean khan, however, Muscovy installed a Russian governor, formally annexing the khanate of Astrakhan in 1556.[38] These pivotal events, in which Moscow claimed sovereignty over its ex-overlords, for many marks the beginning of the history of the Russian Empire.

The khanate of Sibir', situated between the two, slightly eastward, would seem to have been next. It fits with a picture of Muscovy inexorably advancing. But it was not. Explanations why have ranged from Ivan IV's preoccupation with war on the western fronts and domestic politics, or, according to Janet Martin, that he had no intention of encroaching on the fur-rich lands east of the Urals because he feared flooding the fur markets.[39] At any rate, the question of why the khanate of Sibir', located between the khanates of Kazan and Astrakhan, was left out of these initial imperial conquests is moot because the Siberian khan, Ediger, promptly acknowledged Moscow's suzerainty. In doing so he hoped to avoid Muscovite aggression and procure support against regional rivals. Despite his preemptive machinations, Ediger was deposed in 1563 by his brother, the much less conciliatory Kuchum, who initially continued to deliver annual tribute to Moscow, but came to blows with Muscovy in the 1580s.

---

36. Lantzeff and Pierce, *Eastward to Empire*, 67. I thank Matthew Romaniello for pointing out that no evidence explicitly recalls this moment.

37. Romaniello, *Elusive Empire*.

38. Lantzeff and Pierce, *Eastward to Empire*, 69.

39. Martin, "Fur Trade and the Conquest of Sibir'," 67–79.

Russian Expansion into Siberia

The story of Russian advance into Siberia begins with the Stroganov family. Like most premodern entrepreneurial phenomena, the Stroganovs were the product of several generations of work, luck, and political connections that date back at least to the fourteenth century, when they first appear in the historical record. They contributed funds for the ransom of Tsar Vasilii II in 1445–46.[40] What is exceptional about the Stroganovs is the longevity of this family; for over four centuries they were a leading commercial family in Russia. When the Rastrelli-designed Stroganov palace, located in St. Petersburg where the Moika River crosses Nevskii Prospekt, now a popular tourist attraction, was completed in 1754, Baron Sergei Stroganov was head of a commercial/entrepreneurial (although they did not use that term then) dynasty that had been prominent and wealthy for over two centuries.[41] Their prominence attained new heights in the sixteenth century when Moscow contracted development of neighboring territories to them in an arrangement that remains unique in Russian history.

In 1558 Tsar Ivan IV issued a charter to Anika Stroganov to establish a town, invite homesteaders, and develop saltworks and mines in the "empty lands" of the Ural region surrounding the Kama River for twenty years without paying the tsar any taxes or obligations.[42] Six years later Ivan IV issued a second charter to Grigorii Stroganov authorizing further expansion. This 1564 charter came just one year after Kuchum had taken power and includes the provision that Stroganov establishments should contain a military force ("of men not under contract to the government"). Local natives complained that the Stroganovs "founded villages and settled colonists on the natives' possessions and seized the places where the natives hunted beavers and gathered honey and fished, and deprived them of the means to pay iasak [fur tribute]."[43] (Native Siberian and Uralic peoples already paid tribute, be it to Kazan, Sibir', Perm', or Novgorod.) On top of this, Kuchum's nephew Mahmet-kula effected raids into Stroganov territory against Ostiaks and others who accepted Russian rule. Thus, between the conquest of Kazan and the Stroganov incursions, the natives on either side of the Urals experienced much disruption in the second half of the

---

40. Lantzeff and Pierce, *Eastward to Empire*, 82.
41. Brumfield, *A History of Russian Architecture*, 244, 246, fig. 309.
42. Dmytryshyn, Crownhart-Vaughan, and Vaughan, *Russia's Conquest of Siberia*, no. 1, 3–6 (1558 charter).
43. Lantzeff and Pierce, *Eastward to Empire*, 86.

sixteenth century.[44] All of this was bad for business—trade, salt refining, etc., suffered. Challenges notwithstanding, the arrangement benefited the Stroganovs and the throne sufficiently so that in 1574 a similar charter was granted to Anika's sons, Iakov and Grigorii.

The 1574 charter extended the territory of the Stroganov lands eastward all the way to the Tobol' River. Citing offenses by Kuchum, the "Siberian Sultan," it also struck a new tone of aggression, instructing the Stroganovs to send a military contingent into the khanate to acquire tribute, turning Kuchum's tribute payers against him.[45] The original charter had authorized the Stroganovs to maintain defenses and protect their charter lands, but forbade them from deploying troops against the khanate of Sibir' without explicit instructions from Moscow.[46] The 1574 charter authorizes what in modern terms would be a breach of sovereignty.

It was not a Muscovite army that deposed Kuchum. Ironically, the Siberian conquest was initiated by a band of fugitive Cossacks. In 1577 Ivan sent a military expedition southward to dispel the Cossacks whose raids disrupted Volga trade and compromised Moscow's diplomatic stability in the region. Among the Cossacks who "scattered like wolves" was Ermak. He and his contingent ended up in the mercenary service of the Stroganovs. Whether the aggressive Kuchum attacked first, or whether Moscow's orders were not followed precisely, word soon reached Moscow that Ermak, a mercenary Cossack in the employ of the Stroganovs, had ousted the Siberian Sultan, Khan Kuchum, from his capital Qashliq on the Tobol' River in 1582.[47]

Although Ivan IV purportedly objected to the unauthorized provocation, he gave a generous reception to Ermak's forces in Moscow.[48] Ermak then returned to Siberia with the sanction of the tsar to advance the imperial endeavor. Not long after, however, Ermak fell victim to a fatal ruse. He received word that Kuchum, who continued to resist Russian incursion

---

44. Romaniello, *Elusive Empire*.

45. Miller, IS, vol. 1, no. 5, 332–34; English translation: Dmytryshyn, Crownhart-Vaughan, and Vaughan, *Russia's Conquest of Siberia*, no. 3, 9–12; Romaniello, *Elusive Empire*, 89.

46. Miller, IS, vol. 1, nos. 2, 5, 325–27, 332–34.

47. Some scholars call 1581 the year of conquest. Frank, "Western Steppe," 250; Armstrong, *Yermak's Campaign in Siberia*, 7, 70.

48. Miller and Pallas, *Conquest of Siberia by Chevalier Dillon*, 20; Lantzeff and Pierce, *Eastward to Empire*, 78, 90, 103; Martin, "Fur Trade and the Conquest of Siberia," 68. Although I am persuaded by Janet Martin's vision that trade was an important consideration for Ivan IV, I am skeptical of his initial opposition to the conquest. In his letter of November 16, 1581, Ivan IV chastised the Stroganovs' eastward dispatch of Ermak not because he opposed aggressive action in the region (see letters of 1572 and 1574), but because he disapproved of the Stroganovs' deployment of human resources in that particular instance—that they sent a force eastward when the situation westward, in the Perm' region, was anything but stable. See Miller, IS, vol. 1, no. 7, 335–36.

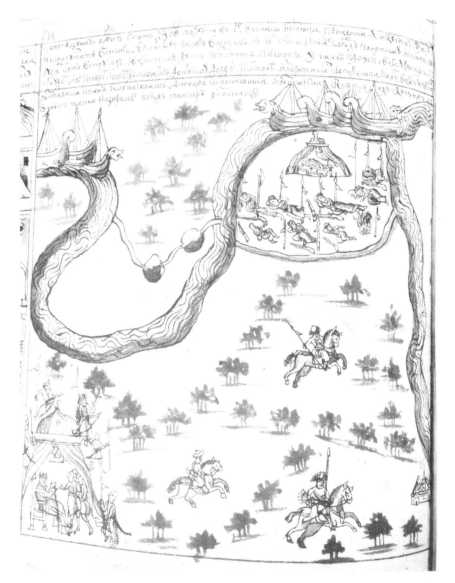

FIGURE 2.1 Image from Remezov chronicle showing canal in which Ermak and his men camped, having not found the Bukharan caravan that Kuchum was supposedly preventing from proceeding to Siberian towns to trade. Ermak died in a surprise ambush that night.
Source: Remezov chronicle, frame 98, in Guminskii, *Remezovskaia letopis'*. Courtesy "Vozrozhdenie Tobol'ska" Publishers.

although ousted from his capital of Qashliq, would not allow an approaching caravan of Bukharan merchants to proceed. After unsuccessfully seeking the caravan in order to help it, Ermak and his men camped at a cross-channel, failing to "post a strong guard, since their wits were enfeebled as the hour

of death was approaching."[49] They were attacked by Kuchum's forces during the rainy night of August 5, 1585. According to the Kungur chronicle,
Ermak drowned in a canal that he had had constructed in order to bisect a
long oxbow of the Irtysh River.[50] Legend has it he sunk in the heavy armor
that Ivan IV had gifted him.

Loath to forfeit the gains of Ermak's campaign, Moscow sent military
governors (voevody) to secure the area.[51] The Russian fort at Tiumen' (the
oldest surviving Russian-built town in Siberia) was established in 1586 on the
site of the previous Tatar town, Chingi-Tur, which Ermak had conquered.
Russians built the town square closer to the river than it had previously stood,
and faced the damage wrought by periodic river flooding. Tobol'sk, which
would become the Siberian capital, was established in 1587. Thus Russians
began establishing a network of forts that would grow into towns and stretch
across Eurasia. The annexation of Siberia had begun.

Although this narrative is widely known, it is less often observed that in
the 1558 charter to Anika Stroganov, Ivan IV instructed that basic goods
were to be available to merchants without inflating prices in the charter territory.[52] In the 1572 letter to Iakov and Grigorii Stroganov, Ivan IV instructed
that any traders arriving from Bukhara or the Kazakh Horde were to be
permitted to travel and trade at will; the Stroganovs were to levy no taxes nor
impose any burdens on them.[53] These stipulations reveal that the tsar recognized the importance of commerce for the health of the realm.

Meanwhile, as did the English and before them the Dutch in the late
sixteenth century,[54] the Stroganovs also endeavored without success to establish a northeast passage to Cathay. During the early stages of planning the
Stroganovs were, if not double-crossed, at least ill-served by a Dutch or
Flemish employee, Olivier Brunel.[55] Unsuccessful though it was, the quest
for a northeast passage illustrates that the English, Dutch, and Russians alike
competed to gain access to the goods of the Orient.

---

49. Yesipov Chronicle in Armstrong, Yermak's Campaign in Siberia, 78; Stroganov Chronicle in
Dmytryshyn, Crownhart-Vaughan, and Vaughan, Russia's Conquest of Siberia, no. 5, 21.

50. Miller and Pallas, Conquest of Siberia by Chevalier Dillon, 23. The Stroganov chronicle says
that Ermak camped at a channel that connected two parts of the river. Dmytryshyn, Crownhart-
Vaughan, and Vaughan, Russia's Conquest of Siberia, no. 5, 21.

51. Certain aspects of the Stroganov and Yesipov chronicles do not harmonize on the narrative
of Yermak's conquest and aftermath. See Armstrong, Yermak's Campaign in Siberia, chapters 20, 25,
27, 28, 30.

52. Miller, IS, vol. 1, no. 2, 327.

53. Miller, IS, vol. 1, no. 5, 334.

54. Houtte, An Economic History of the Low Countries, 198. Dutch expeditions 1593–96.

55. Baron, "Muscovy and the English Quest for a Northeastern Passage to Cathay," in Explorations in Muscovite History, 13; Dahlmann, Sibirien, 57–59.

One of the remarkable facts of Russian history is that, even as a fledg-
ling Romanov dynasty sought to establish its own legitimacy, recover from
the Time of Troubles, and contend with threats from Poles, Lithuanians,
Swedes, and Turks on its other borders throughout the seventeenth century,
it expanded rapidly to the east across the continent. The expansive territory
claimed so quickly has added to perceptions of Russian as inveterately territory hungry, but can be otherwise explained by the lack of effective resistance.
Imposing as the conquest of approximately one-sixth of the world's land
mass appears when viewed on a map, many of the peoples of the northern
Asian landmass were discrete societies that already, in some cases, paid tribute
to someone. That is not to say there was no unified resistance. A document of
1572 that records an attack on Russians by Cheremis, Ostiaks, Bashkirs, and
Buints suggests natives may have organized against encroachment.[56] Where
Russians did find challenges to their claims, contestation lasted for centuries.
Dusty tribute books in Russian archives will never tell the full story of resis-
tance by Siberian natives.

The role of rivers is often remarked on in the expansion across Eurasia. As
furs depleted it was easier to travel farther along rivers than move inland. But
rivers provide more description than explanation. Ultimately Russian rivers
flow north, and Russia's expansion was predominantly eastward. Rumors of
verdant plowable land in the distant Amur River valley may have been part of
the motivation for moving east; supplying the territory was a constant matter of concern. In an immediate sense, powers in Moscow needed revenue,
which furs generated. One historian wrote that Boris Godunov promised
one boyar, Prince Fëdor Mstislavsky, Siberia as a fiefdom for his loyalty.[57]

Nine settlements were founded by the time of Fëdor's death in 1598 (the
last of the Riurikid).[58] By 1607 five more had been established. That this
expansion took place during such dissolution at the center suggests a unity
of disposition regarding Siberia, whether Romanov or rival. Expansion then
saw a hiatus; no settlements were founded from 1607 until 1618 with the
establishment of Kuznetsk. But Mikhail Fëdorovich, the first Romanov tsar,
with his father, Filaret, advanced expansion apace. The Romanov dynasty
needed to solidify the legitimacy it had been granted after a decade of chaos.
One way to do that was by pursuing programs that enjoyed consensus. Fac-
tionalized as Moscow elites and rivals were, establishing Siberian forts does

---

56. Dmytryshyn, Crownhart-Vaughan, and Vaughan, *Russia's Conquest of Siberia*, no. 2, 7; no. 6, 25.
57. Graham, *Boris Godunof*, 22.
58. Tiumen' (1586), Tobol'sk (1587), Losva (1590), Pelym (1593), Berezov (1593), Tara (1594),
Surgut (1594), Narym (1595–96), Verkhotur'e (1598).

not appear to have been controversial. And the need for revenue was unassailable. In the next decades dozens of forts were established. Russians first reached the Pacific Ocean with a fort at the mouth of the Udsk River in 1639.

Putting Fur in Perspective

Materially inclined interpretations have long equated the Siberian project with fur. Fur was fundamental to the Siberian conquest, but it was not the whole story. In the initial stages, Siberian revenue came from furs, just as fur had been extraordinarily important to the medieval and early modern Russian economy. Furs circulated as both commodity and currency in medieval Kiev and Novgorod and then Muscovy until the fifteenth century.[59] The Siberian Office sometimes functioned as a treasury, paying in furs salaries to servants, rewards for service such as expeditions, gifts and payments to ambassadors, gifts that would be presented to foreign sovereigns, and the like. It often relied on furs as the currency with which to meet these obligations and distribute entitlements. Envy over the wealth Novgorodian *uishkoiniki* reaped acquiring furs (by various means) from natives in the fur-rich forests motivated the Moscow principality to encroach on its northern hinterlands and antagonize the trading republic.[60] Similarly, it was one of the reasons for conflict with Kazan in the sixteenth century.[61] The Russian state reaped great benefits from imposing a tribute system and taxing fur that was traded, earning fur pelts a nickname of "soft gold." Kostomarov considered fur Russia's most important commodity, a sentiment expressed in numerous foreign travelers' accounts that preceded him and echoed by historians who wrote after him.[62]

Foreigners who visited the Muscovite court associated Russia with furs. The papal legate Paulus Jociua, visiting in the reign of Vasilii III (1505–33), noted that Muscovy was blessed with "an abundance of rich furs, whose price . . . is grown to such excess, that the furs pertaining to one sort of apparel, are now sold for a thousand crowns."[63] Ranking the native commodities of the country, the Englishman Giles Fletcher designated: "First, furres of all sortes," which brought incredible sums. "Besides the great quantitie spent within the countrie (the people being clad all in furres the whole winter), there are transported out of the countrie some yeares by the marchants

---

59. Fisher, *Russian Fur Trade*, 8–9; Kotilaine, *Russia's Foreign Trade*.
60. Lantzeff and Pierce, *Eastward to Empire*.
61. Martin, *Medieval Russia*, 316.
62. Kostomarov, *Ocherki torgovli Moskovskogo gosudarstva*, 12.
63. Quoted in Martin, "Fur Trade and the Conquest of Sibir'," 69.

FIGURE 2.2 Russian Embassy of Ivan IV to the Holy Roman Emperor at Regensburg in 1576. Figs. 2.2 and 2.3 reproduce panels 2 and 3 of the 4-panel woodcut depicting the ambassadorial procession composed by eyewitness Michael Peterle (1576). Following the ambassadors shown in panel 1, panel 2 depicts an accompanying entourage of men bearing furs.

of Turkie, Persia, Bougharia, Georgia, Armenia, and some other of Christendome, to the value of foure or five hundred thousand rubbels, as I have heard of the marchants."[64] O. N. Vilkov estimated that between 1621 and 1690, over 7.2 million sables, worth 11 million rubles, were harvested from Siberia.[65] Most of those were bound for export abroad. Russia traded furs with all of its trading partners, with preferences varying by destination. The finest luxury furs were exported to the Ottomans and Venice; pelts of lesser quality were popular in China.[66]

Fur revenue brought important income to the Muscovite state. The state generated fur revenue in three ways: through tribute collections, purchase and resale, and taxation of the fur trade. As important as it was, fur revenue was but one facet of the Muscovite economy. Muscovy enjoyed a broader commercial portfolio than histories that see primarily "soft gold" suggest. Clues testifying to this are illustrated in numerous ways, including administrative practices in the Siberian Office. As indicated above, sables and other furs were often the currency of the Siberian Prikaz, but it was not rare that the items issued for these purposes were fabrics from the East (silks, cottons, etc.).

---

64. Fletcher, *Of the Russe Common Wealth*, 9.
65. Vilkov, "Pushnoi promysel v Sibiri."
66. Martin, "Fur Trade and the Conquest of Sibir'"; Kurts, *Sochinenie Kil'burgera*, 95.

FIGURE 2.3 Panel 3 depicts merchants bearing textiles, illustrating that although they receive less attention, textiles were an important aspect of Muscovite commercial diplomatic exchanges and trade. Woodcut by the eyewitness Michael Peterle (1576).

Sables were Muscovy's most important fur export among several commodities. Yet neither sables specifically nor furs generally ever ranked as Muscovy's number one export according to extant records. The Swedish diplomat Johan de Rodes ranked furs as the fifth greatest export from Arkhangel'sk in 1652 after leather hides, grains, salted fat, and potash.[67] In 1655 William Prideaux reported that sable was the third greatest export from Arkhangel'sk, after leather hides and potash.[68] (Keep in mind, since their importance was not reflected in Arkhangel'sk records, that flax and hemp were major exports that in peacetime shipped out through the Baltic.)[69]

What proportion of Russian state revenue or the Russian economy fur accounted for, no one really knows.[70] Fisher and P. N. Pavlov, authors of the

67. Kurts, *Sostoianie Rossii v 1650–1655 gg.*, 163–67.
68. Arkhangel'skii, "Diplomaticheskie agenty Kromvelia," 139–40.
69. Kotilaine, *Russia's Foreign Trade*, 248.
70. Vilkov, *Remeslo i torgovlia*, 17.

most definitive studies, are the first to acknowledge the deficits in knowledge about the fur trade and tribute.[71] Inadequacies notwithstanding, Fisher conjectured that at its peak, fur revenue may have accounted for 11 percent of the Russian state's revenue and that at the turn of the eighteenth century it probably amounted for closer to 2–3 percent of total state revenue. Vilkov's estimates were slightly higher. He proposed that fur revenue accounted for 20 percent of the Russian state budget in the 1640s and 1650s, and not less than 10 percent in the 1680s.[72] Indeed, according to Kotilaine, by the middle of the century the importance of furs had been eclipsed by *iufti* (semifinished leather hides). Fur pelts "barely exceeded 6 percent" of Arkhangel'sk exports in 1673. By the reign of Peter I, owing to fur depletion and additional competition from New World fur supplies, as well as changing tastes, that share was as low as 1–3 percent.[73] Such figures do not square with "soft gold" financing Russia's wars and wealth.

It appears that fur was never the main Russian export for the English, who came for the transit route but stayed for the forest products that came to supply the rising Royal Navy. Indeed, in 1557 the governors of the Muscovy Company wrote that sable and rich furs "be not every man's money." In 1567 they informed their agents that there had been a proclamation in England against wearing furs and that they should send no more. Significantly, this shift in fur demand left them no less interested in trade with Russia.[74] Bushkovitch noted that in the 1580s, "the extremely modest role of furs at this time is quite striking."[75] The observation fits with Janet Martin's findings that the Western European fur market was already palpably declining for Russia during Ivan IV's reign.[76] Fisher considered that "furs were the most important commodities taken out of Russia by the Dutch."[77] But Jonathan Israel found that the Dutch were no less interested in caviar and Russian leather.[78]

Early modern accounts widely acknowledged Siberia's importance as the source of the best furs.[79] Even there, however, furs were a significant portion

---

71. Fisher, *Russian Fur Trade*, 108, 116; Pavlov, *Pushnoi promysel v Sibiri*; Pavlov, *Promyslovaia kolonizatsiia Sibiri*.

72. Vilkov, "Pushnoi promysel v Sibiri."

73. Kotilaine, *Russia's Foreign Trade*, 250.

74. Delmar and Coote, *Early Voyages and Travels to Russia and Persia*, 1: lxv.

75. Bushkovitch, *The Merchants of Moscow*, 67.

76. Martin, "Muscovy's Northeastern Expansion," 459–70.

77. Fisher, *Russian Fur Trade*, 190–91.

78. Israel, *Dutch Primacy in World Trade*, 408.

79. In the sixteenth century, before they were extinct, Fletcher wrote that the best sables came from the Russian North: *Of the Russe Common Wealth*, 9. Kurts, *Sostoianie Rossii*, 161; Kurts, *Sochinenie Kil'burgera*, 36, 472.

but not the whole of what was traded. In Tara, for example, fur accounted for about 40 percent of the volume of goods traded. Leather skins, livestock, and Russian and Eastern wares account for most of the other products.[80] The discovery of Alaska extended Russian fur supplies considerably, shifting the central product from sable to sea otter pelts. Within decades of the Russian American Company's founding in 1799, however, tea, not pelts, was its number one traded commodity.[81] Eurasian trade in other commodities has been overshadowed by an emphasis on fur for much of Russian history.

The state's sights were not set exclusively on fur, but on commerce more generally. Even more to the point in making the case that Siberian commerce was important, Fisher found that the Russian state generated more revenue from taxing the fur trade—commerce—than from tribute collection.[82] For example, from 1635 to 1643 Tiumen' customs collected 21,231 rubles worth (in money and in kind) in taxes. During the same time period the administration collected 5,372 rubles worth of *iasak* tribute, roughly 25 percent of the income generated by taxing Siberian commerce.[83] Even in years when tribute collection exceeded tax collection, far more fur was leaving Siberia through private means than through the state; the tithe, as some call it, was after all a 10 percent tax.

Moscow's rapid expansion to the opposite end of Eurasia was motivated by prospects of commerce with Safavid Iran, Mughal India, China, and ancient affluent cities of the Inner Asian silk roads. Russia founded Tara in 1594, Kuznetsk in 1618, and was looking to establish a permanent fort along the Irtysh River in the 1630s, all in pursuit of eastern trade. At the same time, Russia also sought an Arctic Ocean route to the riches of Asia. The Stroganovs mounted an expedition to find a northeast passage in the 1580s, an endeavor that would be achieved by the Russian Semen Dezhnev in 1648.[84] The Russians founded places like Zashiversk (1639), Nizhne Kolymsk (1644), and Anadyrsk (1649).[85] Furthermore, Russia derived the plurality of its budget through indirect taxation on commercial transactions sooner than other purportedly more mercantile-minded Western European powers did. Tellingly, in some administrative restructuring in the 1630s, the

80. Bashkatova, "Pushnaia torgovlia goroda Tary," 87.

81. Vinkovetsky, *Russia America,* 71. Matthew Romaniello emphasizes this point in his Review of Vinkovetsky, Ilya, *Russian America: An Overseas Colony of a Continental Empire, 1804–1867,* H-empire, H-Net Reviews, June 2011, https://www.h-net.org/reviews/showrev.php?id=33342.

82. Fisher, *Russian Fur Trade,* 120–21.

83. Akishin, *Pribyl'nye dela Sibirskikh voevod,* 52.

84. Ogloblin, *Semen Dezhnev.*

85. Lantzeff and Pierce, *Eastward to Empire,* 11.

Siberian Office was temporarily subordinated to the Office of Merchant Matters, established by 1631, testifying structurally to the connection that Siberia had to trade in the state's view.[86] The Treaty of Nerchinsk of 1689 was an important moment, demonstrating that Russia prioritized commercial relations with China above the acquisition of territory in East Asia. In the late seventeenth century, the state initiated a postal service that was mostly used by private traders.[87] Thus as Muscovy established itself in Siberia, it had trade prospects very much in its sights. This has not gone entirely unnoticed by other historians, such as G. Lantzeff and R. Pierce when they noted that the "economic life of Russia took many other channels as well."[88] This interpretation does not reduce Siberian expansion to a "business enterprise," for Basil Dmytryshyn was correct in concluding that Siberian expansion "cannot be reduced to a single formula."[89] Rather, this interpretation emphasizes the important role that commerce played in the "conquest" (osvoenie)[90] and history of Siberia because that aspect has remained underdeveloped in scholarship.

Instrumentalist Approach to Commerce

Trade held another fundamental significance for empire building in Siberia: to supply Siberia with needed supplies such as textiles, livestock, and foodstuffs (dried fruit), all of which helped establish stability and ensure Moscow's hegemony. I call this an instrumentalist approach to commerce: the state was not interested in commerce solely for the revenue it could generate. Rather, it was interested in the needs that the presence of actual goods could satisfy, essentially, feeding and clothing a population, tasks for which the state took some responsibility. As Russia pushed eastward into Siberia, it faced the challenge of provisioning new territory along lengthening supply lines. Amid westward and southward entanglements, these were more than Moscow could handle. Moscow was keen for alternative ways to supply the region with necessities and believed that trade could fill the gap. The local

---

86. Perkhavko, *Pervye kuptsy Rossiiskie*, 332.

87. Ogloblin, *Obozrenie*, 4: 106.

88. Lantzeff and Pierce, *Eastward to Empire*, 226. This assessment shows evolution in Lantzeff's thinking. His 1943 monograph describes the customs administration as a means to "take from private traders the most valuable furs" since the state could not realistically exploit "Siberian fur resources in its own interests exclusively." Lantzeff, *Siberia in the Seventeenth Century*, 132–33.

89. Dmytryshyn, Crownhart-Vaughan, and Vaughan, *Russia's Conquest of Siberia*, xxxvi.

90. Instead of conquest or annexation, Russian historiography typically uses the euphemism *osvoenie*, which translates as assimilation or incorporation, to describe its establishment of empire in Siberia.

population agreed. In 1597 Baiseit Murzu and other Tiumen' residents—"all your slaves, from small to great"—appealed to the state to help alleviate their material dearth. The petition asked the tsar that permission be given to the governor Vladimir Ivanovich Bakhteiarov-Rostovskii to send an ambassador to the Bukharans and Nogai so that they might come and the land would be profitable. "No gosti nor wealthy merchants come to us in Siberia; if only merchants would come, we would all be filled and satisfied," reads the petition.[91]

In an effort to facilitate favorable trading conditions, Moscow instructed Siberian administrators to make Russian settlements attractive trade destinations for Central Asian merchants. Governors were instructed to extend protection to them, treat them kindly, and not offend or use force toward them. Visiting merchants were to be permitted to trade wherever they wanted—be it inside or outside of the city—although the governor was instructed to supervise that they did not deal in any prohibited items.[92] Finally, once Bukharan or Nogai traders had finished their business, they could depart without hindrance "so that in the future they will return with various goods to Siberian towns and trade with our Russian and serving people."[93] Facilitation of favorable trading conditions became a pillar of Siberian trade policy. An instruction dated August 31, 1596 directed the Tiumen' governor Prince Grigorii Dolgorukoi to allow Bukharan and Nogai merchants that should arrive to the town to trade tax free with the serving Russian population. The instruction explained, "Taxes are not to be taken from them [Bukharans] so that in the future it would be favorable for them to return."[94] With this decree, Moscow articulated a similar policy as that advocated in the recently expired Stroganov charter, but now the terms were slightly more restricted: Bukharans were entitled to duty-free trade with the military population. A 1607 instruction to Tiumen' regarding horse trade reiterated the principle: "but from those sold horses do not take taxes so that they do not from the start become embittered and go away from our tsarist mercy."[95] One of the primary directives to the governor of Tara, on the edge of the steppe, was to develop trade relations with Asian countries.[96] In 1607 and 1608 Moscow

91. *Sobranie gosudarstvennykh gramot i dogovorov*, 2: 129.

92. Since the marketplace of Tiumen' was not built until 1600 one can only imagine that governors were at a tremendous disadvantage in regulating the space of trade prior to its construction. Rezun and Vasilievskii, *Letopis' Sibirskikh gorodov*, 269–74.

93. Miller, IS, vol. 2, no. 4, 176–77.

94. Quoted in Ziiaev, *Ekonomicheskie sviazi Srednei Azii s Sibir'iu*, 27.

95. RMO, vol. 1, no. 3, 25. This order was likely catalyzed by a shortage. Bukharans were already being charged taxes by this time, but taxes could be suspended in periods of severe need.

96. Evseev, "Tara v svoi pervye dva stoletiia," 103.

directed Siberian governors to send servitors to Bukhara and Kalmyk lands to invite them for tax-free trade.[97]

Such policies meant that the Siberian population had a stake in trade, not least the soldiers. Trade filled a gap for the Russian military, as servicemen supplement their inadequate allowances by trading in order "to meet their own needs." Condoning such activity, the state granted a tax waiver on 50 rubles worth of trade. To the state's chagrin, however, enterprising soldiers sometimes acted as functionaries for merchants—Bukharan and Russian—operating in Siberia. They would pass off merchants' goods as their own, becoming a conduit for tax evasion. In a spate of reforms aimed at optimizing and gaining control over Siberian revenues, in 1698 the state rescinded soldiers' right to 50 rubles of tax-free trade, citing specifically that practice which deprived the state of revenue.[98] The official participation of soldiers in Siberian trade illustrates the state's struggle to construct an order in which trade served instrumentalist needs while also bringing revenue to the tsar's treasury. As the scandal at Lake Yamysh described in chapter 5 illustrates, negotiating the balance between enforcement and entitlements was not easy.

The Siberian Economy

This instrumentalist strategy brought results. More goods reached Siberia, a region in which furs, cloth, leather, livestock, horses, and household items such as pans, axes, and needles moved across micro and macro markets that overlapped and intersected. Just as merchants were not the only people trading at Siberian trading posts, furs were by far not the only products traded. Goods needed by new settlers moved eastward, passing western-bound products from the East along Siberian rivers. During the 1600s, fabrics, rugs, spices, medicines, and other Eastern products became increasingly important. Siberia was an attractive market because furs were relatively cheap and the European products Russian merchants brought were in high demand by the soldiers, settlers, Central Asians, and natives that frequented Siberian marketplaces.

The Siberian economy was important to the state for furs initially and as a conduit to trade with the East later. Russians started seeing reduced fur returns in western and central Siberia in the 1630s and 1640s. By the late seventeenth century Siberia's great fur supplies had been substantially

97. RMO I, nos. 3, 4, pp. 24–30; Evseev, "Tara v svoi pervye dva stoletiia," 104; Bashkatova, "Gorod Tara i ego torgovlia v XVII v.," 69.
98. PSZ 3, no. 1654, p. 492 (1698).

depleted, but trade with the East supplanted furs in importance for Russia's international trade. (The fur trade was not entirely gone; furs of lesser value continued to be exported to China.) Siberian trade remained voluminous, however, as Eastern trade was rapidly developing. Between 1672 and 1700 nine very large caravans arrived in Tara from the steppe.[99] According to Vilkov, author of the most authoritative study of the seventeenth-century Siberian economy, by the end of century Chinese wares accounted for more than 80 percent of all imports in terms of volume, and over 85 percent of the volume of trade conducted at Tobol'sk was in Eastern goods.[100] The historian Kopylov agreed: "In the final quarter of the seventeenth century China trade became more important than fur in the Siberian economy."[101] In 1726 Siberian goods were imported in large quantities to Moscow and the greatest number of products was from China.[102]

In the seventeenth and eighteenth centuries Russia was emerging as a world power, for whose economy transimperial trade was an important component. In the eighteenth century Russia definitively conquered its steppe enemies even as it became increasingly integrated and competitive with European powers to its west, while trade with the East was simultaneously on the increase. Even if reality fell short of outsized aspirations on this point, its position between East and West helped it garner a degree of transit trade, a fair amount of which traveled through Siberia.[103] Many Eastern goods were re-exported from Russia to the West. In the "opposite"[104] direction, many "European" goods were exported eastward. These goods were called Russian goods or German goods and they were bound for Siberia or beyond. They typically consisted of textiles, cookware such as wooden bowls and utensils or fry pans and pots with lids, locks, eyeglasses, mirrors, and ubiquitous needles with which to sew clothes or leather products. Having returned to St. Petersburg after a decade in Siberia as part of the Great Northern Expedition, Müller composed *On Trade with Siberia*, which he published in the short-lived serial *Monthly Compositions*. For Müller, Siberian trade by definition included items of Chinese, Kalmyk, Bukharan, and Mongolian origin. A designated Siberian marketplace in Moscow and the fact that merchants

99. Bashkatova "Gorod Tara i ego torgovlia v XVII v.," 69.

100. Vilkov, *Remeslo i torgovlia*, 207.

101. Kopylov, "Tamozhennaia politika v Sibiri v XVII v.," 359.

102. Kafengauz, *Ocherki vnutrennogo rynka*, 194–99.

103. Kotilaine, *Russia's Foreign Trade*, 2.

104. To suggest linearity is misleading. As Cherie Woodworth suggested, it was more a great swirling. See H-net Early Slavic discussion board, November 3, 2011, http://h-net.msu.edu/cgi-bin/logbrowse.pl?trx=vx&list=h-earlyslavic&month=1111&week=a&msg=3aZFBizPqg0tj32ewSpKOA&user=&pw=.

from European Russia kept residences in Siberian towns were concrete manifestations of his central conclusion, which has been too little appreciated, that
"Siberian trade makes up a substantial portion of Russian trade."[105]

Situating the Siberian Economy in the Russian Empire

But how important in the big picture was Siberia? In order to properly situate Siberia in the Russian Empire, we must get a sense of the Siberian role in
the Muscovite economy. What did this region do for the empire? Why did
the empire endeavor to conquer it? These questions naturally invite larger
inquiries. The remainder of this chapter attempts to assess Siberia's contribution to the Muscovite economy, first with a cursory overview of the Russian
economy and then by taking stock of the neighboring Volga region, and
indeed, of Moscow, the heart of the Russian Empire.

Russia was a reliable source for important—if not particularly glamorous—
products important to the early modern world. It was rich in forest products, skins, furs, wax, and honey. It seems that by the late sixteenth century
Muscovy was a virtual monopoly supplier of potash, hemp, and linseed for
Western Europe. Whenever Baltic exports were disrupted in the seventeenth century, prices in Amsterdam spiked.[106] In the seventeenth century
Western Europeans exported from Russia "in the main, leather, hemp, tar,
potash, salted porkfat, fish, and furs (*kozhi, pen'ku, smolu, potash, salo, rybu i
pushninu*)."[107] Indeed, as European empires took their competition to the
open seas, Muscovy benefitted because it was rich in the forest products
essential to building a navy. Fine wood such as solid oak and mast-quality
timber was exported from the Russian North (not Siberia) for shipbuilding.
Forest byproducts along with hemp and flax were even more important.
Wood materials were burned to make potash, an essential ingredient in the
pitch that sealed ship's bottoms. The ropewalks established by the English
but largely run by Russians by the 1580s supplied most of the cordage to the
English fleet that defeated the weather-cursed Spanish Armada in 1588.[108]
Indeed, "No navy could operate without flax for sailcloth, hemp for cables
and cordage, as well as pitch, tar, rosin and turpentine: over the life of the
average vessel, expenditures on such stores would exceed the costs of the

---

105. Miller, *Opisanie o Torgakh' Sibirskikh*, 2. For an exception to the general neglect see Jos
Gommans, "Review of *Indian Merchants and Eurasian Trade, 1600–1750*, by Stephen F. Dale. Cambridge, 1994." *Journal of Economic and Social History of the Orient* 40, no. 1 (1997): 142–43.

106. Ohberg, "Russia and the World Market in the Seventeenth Century," 149.

107. Demkin, *Zapadnoevropeiskie kuptsy i ikh tovary v Rossii XVII veka*, 3.

108. Fuhrmann, *Origins of Capitalism in Russia*, 46.

original hull."[109] Merchants from Reval, Riga, Danzig, Stettin, Rostock, and Lubeck made it their business to acquire forest products from Russia.

Although Muscovy does not seem to have enjoyed the domestic manufacturing might of the Chinese Empire (Ming until 1644; Manchu/Qing post-1644), it did produce key finished and semifinished products that made it an attractive trade partner. Compared with exotic spices, fabrics, and medicines, or New World fruits and vegetables, quotidian products such as leather hides can easily fly under the early modern commercial radar, but in a world before synthetic fibers, everyone needed leather sometime. Muscovy had a valuable industry in semifinished leather hides, known as *iufti*. Jarmo Kotilaine has called *iufti* Russia's undersung early modern manufactured export; he counted it as Russia's number one export in 1667.[110] Vilkov found it to be the number one commodity Russian merchants brought to sell at Lake Yamysh.[111] Chuloshnikov reported that *iufti* was the number one Russian export from Astrakhan.[112]

A salient tenet of mercantilism was that it was better to manufacture domestically. Russia is typically regarded as a country with little domestic manufacture, a weakness Peter was preoccupied with to a level of near obsession in a desire to generate domestic manufacturing. Peter's passion on the matter, and general assumptions about Russian backwardness, may have obscured a quieter reality that Muscovy did not do so badly. *Iufti* was the most profitable but not the only example of robust production and commerce. In the seventeenth century, beaver pelts were actually *imported* to Muscovy to undergo a special processing that no one else did as well as Russians.[113] Moreover, the twentieth-century disdain that made Soviet manufacturing the brunt of jokes regarding production quality (of the "We pretend to work and you pretend to pay us" variety) has been inappropriately projected back into Russian history. Russian iron production enjoyed a respectable reputation in the early modern world.[114] Adam Olearius, hardly a charitable observer, noted that Muscovites were a quick study: "They are very handy, and easily imitate any thing they see done . . . I have seen some of their carv'd works as well done as the best in Germany."[115] In 1720 a Boston newspaper

109. Price, "Map of Commerce," 841–42.
110. Kotilaine, "When the Twain Did Meet," 50.
111. Vilkov, *Remeslo i torgovlia*, 198.
112. Chuloshnikov, *MUITSSR*, 81.
113. Kurts, *Sostoianie Rossii*, 169; Fisher, *Russian Fur Trade*, 208; Crean, "Hats and the Fur Trade," 374–77.
114. Boterbloem, *Moderniser of Russia, Andrei Vinius*, 169.
115. Olearius, *Voyages and Travells of the Ambassadors*, 66.

ran a front-page story on methods of Russian tar production—not for deri-
sive purposes, but because it held that interested Bostonians had something
to learn from Russian methods.[116]

Although its products were less luxurious than Chinese, Persian, or Italian
silks, the paper-thin cotton linen of India, or the fine wools from England, the
Low Countries, and Florence, Russia traded a substantial amount of textiles.
In this age when consumerism left the courts, textiles were foremost among
consumer products for the masses.[117] From the Sahara to the Himalayas to
the Great Lakes, people needed to clothe themselves, and people in places
linked to international trade routes increasingly did so with fabrics they did
not make themselves. Textiles such as burlap, coarser cottons, and woolens
accounted for a substantial portion of the items exchanged at Russian trading
posts in Siberia. Textiles—domestic and foreign—were an important part of
the commercial mix of early modern Russia. Indeed, early modern Russia
was always more diversified than modern-day "petrostates"—the Netherlands, Middle East, and Russia, for example—whose economies were/are oil
driven to the detriment of other industries.[118]

Volga Trade: Kazan and Astrakhan

Traveling downstream along the Volga from Moscow one came to the
ancient town of Kazan, shortly before the Volga takes a hard turn southward
toward the Caspian. Kazan sat along ancient trade routes. Arab travelers
remarked on it. The Volga Bulgars oversaw Volga trade from the eleventh
century. Russians were involved in this trade from early on. Indeed, the Arab
traveler Ibn Khaukal' called the Volga a Russian river based on its active use
by Russian and other merchants traveling to Rus'.[119] A Kievan prince signed a
tenth-century trade treaty with the Bulgar kingdom.[120] Kazan was an important regional center that had a history as both rival and trading partner to
many of its neighbors in the region, including Perm', Sibir', Moscow, and,
going back further in time, the Muslim Bulgars. Moscow was intimately
involved with Kazan politically and economically from the fifteenth century. In the fifteenth century, Kazan "became a major commercial center."[121]

---

116. "Method of Preparing Tar in Russia," 1.

117. De Vries, "Connecting Europe and Asia," 35–105.

118. In 2009 mineral sales (i.e., primarily oil/gas) accounted for 69.7% of Russia's foreign
exports. *Statisticheskii ezhegodnik* (2009), 702.

119. Preobrazhenskii and Perkhavko, *Kupechestvo Rusi*, 11.

120. Rorlich, *Volga Tatars*.

121. Martin, *Medieval Russia*, 320.

By the early century, Russian merchants from Moscow, Pskov, and Novgorod operated regularly in the territory of their Muslim neighbor to the east, the khanate of Kazan, where Bulgars, Central Asians, and Cherkassy also resided.

In 1523, all Russian merchants in Kazan—all of the Russians then in Kazan, according to Kostomarov—were murdered.[122] This unfortunate event may have been a manifestation of tensions associated with Vasilii III's trade embargo against Kazan. Vasilii III tried to use embargoes on Russians trading on the Volga with Kazan as political leverage against Kazan.[123] All Russian merchants were directed to trade in Nizhni Novgorod, a Russian-built town about 390 km west of Kazan. The embargo is said to have hurt Moscow as much as it did Kazan. As was the case with Ivan III's conquest of Novgorod in the late fifteenth century, "the purpose of [Muscovy's] conflicts with Kazan' was to gain access to northeastern trade routes and assert dominion over tributaries who would supply northern luxury pelts."[124] Decades later Ivan III's grandson, Ivan IV, finally eschewed negotiated politics with Kazan and conquered the city outright, annexing it to the Russian empire.

Despite political upheaval, Russians continued to live and trade in Kazan. After Russian conquest, many residents fled from Kazan to the khanate of Sibir', delaying, but not avoiding, conquest into Russian subjecthood. The full integration of Kazan into the empire took a long time, as Matthew Romaniello has demonstrated, but just a decade after the conquest, twenty-two Russians held shops in the Kazan marketplace. Three Russians held houses there.[125] Anika Stroganov kept a household in Kazan in 1565–68.[126] The gost' Nikita Nikitnikov lived in Yaroslavl' and also maintained a house in Kazan. Both were referred to as nonlocal (*priezzhie*) gosti in the cadastral book that records their holdings. A third gost', Ivan Shukhnov of Vladimir, acquired his house by marrying the daughter of the Kazan resident Mr. Karygin.[127] In the middle of seventeenth century the same number of central Russians (twenty-two) held shops in Kazan.[128]

---

122. Kostomarov, *Ocherki torgovli Moskovskogo gosudarstva*, 10.
123. Romaniello, *Elusive Empire*, 89.
124. Martin, *Medieval Russia*, 320.
125. "Pistsovye knigi goroda Kazani," 193.
126. Golikova, PKK, 34.
127. Ibid., 34, 36. If the daughter was not Russian she would have had to convert to Orthodoxy for the marriage. Because some of these shops had been granted to the merchants by the administration, they paid no fee (*obrok*).
128. "Pistsovye knigi goroda Kazani," 197.

The destruction of the archive of Kazan means few details survive with which to reconstruct economic life. In the seventeenth century Kazan and Nizhni Novgorod were the second and fourth wealthiest towns in Russia. Both towns handled much of the traffic of Volga trade between Astrakhan and Arkhangel'sk, and both were important supply points for goods dispatched to Siberia.[129] Scholars conclude that eighteenth-century trade was even more vibrant, but without seventeenth-century records to serve as a base line, quantifying any "revival" remains elusive. Siberian customs books offer some valuable glimpses; they occasionally indicate merchants from western Siberian towns traveling to Kazan for trade and vice versa.[130] Bukharan merchants traveled from Central Asia to Kazan via the Volga and Siberia Rivers.[131]

At the serpentine delta where the Volga empties into the Caspian sits Astrakhan. The economy of Kazan was linked to Astrakhan but not exclusively so. That is, while the Volga linked Astrakhan and Kazan, and therefore presumably much trade flowed between the cities, overland routes also led to Kazan. Where the routes are not precisely known, archeological evidence testifies to their existence when the historical record does not. For example, ancient caches along the Kama, coming from China, indicate that goods moved overland across Eurasia when the Roman Republic was in formation. When William of Rubruck traveled to the Mongol court as a missionary in the thirteenth century he traveled north up the Volga to the Horde capital at Sarai and then moved east overland to the Mongol court in the Karakorum. When the Russian Army built the earliest roads in the Urals and Siberia, it was generally following preexisting paths. But much historical evidence further hints at the numerous trade routes that crisscrossed the forest and steppe in the region of the Urals-Caspian. In 1615 the tsar instructed the Kazan governor to allow a Bukharan *kupchin* (merchant) to leave "by whatever route he wants."[132] Central Asian merchants might return via the Volga or along Siberian rivers. In 1616 the khan of Khiva wrote to Moscow asking that goods that were stolen from Khivan merchants long the Iaik (now Ural) River be returned.[133] The Moldovan explorer-diplomat Spafarii, when he got to this area (just east of the Urals, heading south toward the steppe along the Ishim River) en route to China, explained that there were too many different

---

129. Fisher, *Russian Fur Trade*, 168–69.
130. RGADA, f. 214, kn. 301, ll. 10, 17, 17v, 23 (Tobol'sk customs book 1652/3); kn. 892, ll. 43, 53, 54, 113, 120 (Tobol'sk customs book 1686); GATO, f. 47, op. 1, d. 381, l. 71.
131. RGADA, f. 214, stb. 81.
132. MUITTSSR, no. 18, pp. 112–13.
133. MUITTSSR, nos. 19, 21, pp. 113–14, 116–22.

routes to detail them all, which lends us two insights: First, no route was so awesome that it became a highway. For example, travel along the Ishim was supremely arduous but the route was used because it offered decent forage for animals and was relatively secure compared with other routes. Second, that multiple routes were traveled indicates that there was substantial traffic.

Astrakhan was situated at a juncture of land-water arteries. Caravans coming across the steppe by camel could transition to boat and continue up the Volga where the several portages through the river systems would bring things to the outlets of the Baltic and North Seas. Or, from the southern shores of the Caspian goods could travel westward toward the Black Sea via routes north and south of the Caucasus Mountain, west to Aleppo and the Mediterranean coast, or southward to the Persian Gulf. Its auspicious location at a water depot of the Silk Roads would suggest the Volga-Caspian artery as the preferred route to transmit Silk Roads goods to Muscovy. Moscow recognized its significance. Russian merchants had long been aware of its significance: they visited the port long before it came under Russian sovereignty. The account of Contarini, who was "proxy ransomed" by a Russian merchant, notes other Russians in the port as well. Anthony Jenkinson, traveling through Astrakhan immediately after the Russian conquest, in 1557–59, described a moribund scene and the steppe routes connecting it to Kazan and Bukhara fraught with bandits. In 1558, Astrakhan was refounded across the river and downstream from the Tatar town. In the 1580s masonry walls replaced the wooden walls that previously protected the town. Boris Godunov commissioned the construction of a series of fortress towns (Samara, Tsaritsyn, Saratov) along the Volga to make the trade route safer.[134]

These measures reflect the state's awareness of the advantageousness of effectively projecting authority over this water route. And yet over fifty years later the Holstein ambassador Adam Olearius called the riverways about Astrakhan "the most dangerous place of any."[135] Willard Sunderland explains that the Volga steppe remained the "wild field" until massive peasant settlements under Catherine II.[136] Inference, however, might suggest Astrakhan was not such a going concern in the sixteenth century. Had it been an economic powerhouse it might have put up a stronger resistance and required a greater army to subdue it in 1556. The khanate of Astrakhan (1466–1556), in its less than century of existence, was a weak kingdom of the post-Mongol

---

134. Rowland, "Architecture and Dynasty," 38.
135. Olearius, *Voyages and Travells of the Ambassadors*, 122.
136. Sunderland, *Taming the Wild Field*.

world, one that claimed independence and based its legitimacy on Chinggisid lineage, but was a virtual pawn in the region before it was easily conquered.

When I began this book, I assumed that, compared with the trade volumes that passed through Astrakhan, Siberian trading posts saw only a fraction of the commercial traffic. The premise is of the sort that undergirds both the "decline" thesis and arguments locating the rise of the West in the establishment of maritime empires of the late fifteenth and sixteenth centuries: that water trade is more efficient than overland trade. Subaltern scholarship has challenged that assumption, as does the inexact but persuasive knowledge that numerous trade routes crisscrossed the steppe east of the Volga all the way to Siberia and Central Asia. Perhaps that instability along the Volga route boosted Siberian traffic, with merchants finding it a viable alternative for overland transport.[137] M. V. Fekhner wrote that the Volga-Caspian route became unusable to Bukharan merchants, important intermediaries of East-West trade, in the late sixteenth century as a result of fighting between Persia and the Bukharan khanate; Bukharan merchants looked for alternative westward routes, of which Siberia was one.[138] In the case of Eurasian trade, it is hard to empirically demonstrate either interpretation for lack of data. No customs books for Astrakhan from the sixteenth or seventeenth centuries survive. We do know, however, that goods were transported both overland and via the Volga and that the profiles of Russian goods exported via both routes were similar in the seventeenth century. Vilkov wrote, "The composition of Russian exports to the east via Iamyshev [sic] market was virtually identical to the export of Russian wares to the east via Astrakhan."[139]

Where we cannot quantify goods, quantifying people helps us by proxy reconstruct the commercial scene. Among the substantial construction projects Godunov sponsored were two covered Bukharan and Persian marketplaces built in Astrakhan in the 1590s. In the seventeenth century marketplaces and quarters for Armenians, Indians, Caucasians (from the Caucasus), and Tatars were established.[140] Protectionist state measures to limit inland travel of foreign merchants did not dampen Eastern enthusiasm for trade with Russia and may have been causal in Astrakhan's seventeenth-century growth. By the late seventeenth century, Astrakhan was home to thriving merchant diaspora communities.[141] Russians, Persians, Europeans, Bukharans,

137. See Baikova, *Rol' Srednei Azii v Russko-Indiiskikh torgovykh sviaziakh.*
138. Fekhner, *Torgovlia russkogo gosudarstva so stranami vostoka,* 7.
139. Vilkov, *Remeslo i torgovlia,* 199.
140. Rowland, "Architecture and Dynasty," 38; Golikova, *Ocherki po istorii gorodov Rossii,* 159–208.
141. Golikova, *Ocherki po istorii gorodov Rossii,* 159–208.

Armenians, and other merchants from the Caucasus could all be found there. In 1678–80 there were 122 townsman houses and 223 townsmen. There were "eight houses owned by chartered merchants and 6 belonging to merchants from other Russian cities."[142] Near Eastern traders learned the Russian language in Astrakhan and those wishing to study Persian or Arabic could do so at the Bukharan enclave (*dvor*).[143] But the instability of the steppe and nascent Ottoman Empire meant that Siberia was a good alternative route. The diaspora communities continued to grow during Peter's reign, despite restrictions on foreign merchants traveling to Moscow. Moreover, Indian merchants developed alternative niches when warfare prevented them from traversing Central Asia and continued to profit in their western Eurasian outpost.[144]

In the 1740s there were more than thirty privately owned ships in Astrakhan, most owned by big Russian merchants. In the early decades of the eighteenth century, silk, cotton, and other materials comprised by far the majority of imports into Astrakhan (based on records from 1733 and 1744 between 82 and 95 percent, respectively). At midcentury, it was also material—leather, wool, and other fabrics—that comprised the greatest exports from Astrakhan (~75%). The bulk of these were headed for the Caucasus and Persia. According to Iukht, about three-quarters of the Astrakhan trade was handled by Armenian and Indian merchants. Iukht argues that the Persian trade was the most significant region to government and merchants alike. Observing that private boats exceeded state boats in the Astrakhan port, he concluded that private merchants drove the majority of Astrakhan trade.[145]

In the second quarter of the eighteenth century, Russia had a negative trade balance with Persia and the Caucasus. Between 1734 and 1750 Russia exported goods worth 1,044,499 rubles and imported two and one-half times that amount, 2,658,995 rubles.[146] How much of that amount was reexported is unknown, a consideration that could significantly offset the disadvantages of this regional negative trade balance. Moreover, the activity alone reveals an active market at a time when Siberian trade was strong. A rising tide raises all ships.[147] As Kazan and Astrakhan rose in the eighteenth century, so too did many Siberian towns, to where our attention next turns.

142. Kotilaine, *Russia's Foreign Trade*, 18.
143. Savich, "Iz istorii russko-nemetskikh kul'turnykh sviazei," 250.
144. Dale, *Indian Merchants and Eurasian Trade*.
145. Iukht, "Russko-Vostochnaia torgovlia," 30, 42–56.
146. Ibid., 49–50.
147. Kotilaine makes a similar argument regarding the Arkhangel'sk and Baltic trade. Rather than "either/or" he found trade increasing at both depots. See Kotilaine, "Competing Claims," 279–311.

Conclusion: Commercially Oriented, Not Quite a Colony

In his seminal first monograph on Siberian governance, George Lantzeff wrote that the customs system was created to net any furs that might have slipped through the tribute system.[148] The tribute system delivered massive quantities of fur to the state coffers, which financed Russia's rise to imperial greatness. In that barely caricatured view, Siberia's value to the state came from fur and fur came from tribute payments. Such a description overshadows the important ways other types of trade figured in Siberia's political economy. This chapter has argued that Siberian expansion demonstrates that commerce mattered to the Russian state. The Romanov tsars of the seventeenth century were as interested in an "exit to the East" as they were a "window on the West." They sought not only to extract furs (and minerals—from the early seventeenth century the state dispatched mineral reconnaissance in Siberia) from the woodlands of Siberia but also to cultivate commercial ties in order to reap the riches of the East and capitalize as middlemen in East-West European trade. Siberia may have been "off the beaten Silk Roads" as it were, but given the instability of the seventeenth-century Volga and Caspian routes, Siberian trade routes served more than regional purposes. Tribute collection by the military was not the bulk of activity in Siberia. In general, the governor, not the customs head, was in charge of *iasak* collection.[149]

If colonies are defined by settlement, Siberia was not quite a colony; mass settlement did not occur there until the nineteenth century for various reasons. Essentially, Russia had no excess human population and the state had higher resettlement priorities.[150] Catherine II prioritized settling the Volga region and in the 1760s recruited German settlers for the purpose, a strategy that France also employed to settle its New World colony of French Guyana in 1763–65.[151] But if Siberia was not bursting with colonial settlers in the seventeenth and eighteenth century, it was more than a series of military installations and the infrastructure was more than extractive.[152] Siberia in many ways was a conduit to wealth generated by fur, Eastern wares, and the profits that European Russian towns reaped from supplying Siberian territory with needed wares.

---

148. Lantzeff himself backed off of that stance in later work.

149. The Stroganov Chronicle reports that before the tsar put governors in charge of tribute collection, the brothers Semen, Maksim, and Nikita Stroganov briefly collected tribute. Dmytryshyn, Crownhart-Vaughan, and Vaughan, *Russia's Conquest of Siberia*, no. 5, 23. NB: In eastern Siberia the customs head tended to help with *iasak* collection more.

150. Boeck, "Containment vs. Colonization," 41–60.

151. Rothschild, "A Horrible Tragedy in the French Atlantic," 67–108.

152. Michael Hittle reservedly advanced this argument in *Service City*.

It wasn't that the Russian infrastructure established some "silk road" high-way that sped from Beijing to Arkhangel'sk—the Silk Roads never worked quite like that anyway.[153] Rather, as Cherie Woodworth described, it was a "great circular churn of goods flowing into the central vortex from E, N, S, and W, changing hands and then flowing out again . . . a vast, cycli-cal sloshing back and forth of goods" that moved every which way across Eurasia.[154] For example, one can cite England's reexporting Persian silk from Arkhangel'sk,[155] a Persian merchant arriving to Arkhangel'sk on an English ship in 1689,[156] Fëdor Baikov taking rhubarb east from Tobol'sk in 1654. This swirling worked just fine for the Russian state, which understood that there was much revenue to be generated through the levying of tolls and customs. Indeed, the more significant trade may have been the local and regional trade that merchants such as those examined in the next chapters, facilitated as readily as long-distance trade. Customs revenue was important, but it was not the only thing the state sought from trade in Siberia. After all, commerce in Siberia furthered profit and the instrumentalist ends of sustain-ing Russians in the territory.

153. Hansen, *Silk Road.*

154. See post by Cherie Woodworth on H-net Early Slavic discussion board, November 3, 2011, http://h-net.msu.edu/cgi-bin/logbrowse.pl?trx=vx&list=h-earlyslavic&month=1111&week=a&msg=3aZFBizPqg0tj32ewSpKOA&user=&pw=.

155. Arel, "Masters in Their Own House," 401–47.

156. Demkin, *Zapadnoevropeiskie kuptsy i ikh tovary v Rossii XVII veka,* 88.

PART TWO

Spaces of Exchange

From Center to Periphery

The construction of symbolic centers speaks volumes about a society. A snapshot of Moscow's seventeenth-century center—much of it still preserved today—communicates important principles made manifest in the solid masonry of architecture and the organization of space. At the very heart of Moscow stood the Kremlin, home to the tsar and the seat of government, and several majestic churches.[1] The eastern gates of the Kremlin open onto Red Square, the site of much ritualized interface between tsar and people. But Red Square was established only in the latter half of the seventeenth century. When Adam Olearius visited in the 1630s, St. Basil's, with busy trading rows erected before it, was located inside Kitai gorod, Moscow's "largest and best market square in the city," in the words of Olearius.[2] That state, church, and market occupy Moscow's central space projects powerfully the organizing principles of the Russian state. The triune symbolizes that the divinely sanctioned patrimonial state, ritualized interface between state and society, and commerce form the heart of the Russian empire. This prioritization was replicated at the periphery as well in state-funded construction that functioned toward religious, state, and commercial ends: in Tiumen', the first masonry structure the state built was a

---

1. Food and weapon stores as well.
2. Olearius, *Travels of Olearius*, 114.

warehouse for money and goods on the ground floor with a church upstairs.[3] Moscow's architectural past reveals that its commerce was solid in the early modern period. In 1787 more than 80 percent of Moscow's buildings were of wooden construction, but Kitai gorod, the center of commerce, flouted that pattern. There, 148 buildings were constructed of masonry or brick, and just 7 of wood.[4]

Commerce was at the center of the Muscovite world, a fact manifested in its physical layout. The Foreign Ambassador's House, where foreign ambassadors lodged during their Moscow stay, stood three stone stories high within the walls of Kitai gorod,[5] the heart of Moscow's biggest commercial center.[6] It was no accident that the state situated ambassadorial lodgings and the busy marketplace together. It associated foreign relations with commerce, which it valued, and sought to cultivate foreign commerce. Thousands of small shops, organized according to the spatial consolidation of particular goods, be it furs, hats, or kettles, were concentrated in trading rows that few foreigners failed to note. "The Muscovite merchants' shops are all together in various streets in the inner city, known as *Kitai*, and you won't find a single cloth merchant in the goldsmiths' street, or a furrier in the shoemakers' street," noted the Italian Filippo Balatri.[7]

This is not to say that Kitai gorod was the result of deliberate planning. On the contrary, the commercial heart of Moscow was a space in which monasteries, churches, princely and merchant homes, and community baths nestled in among the trading rows. In one monastery, the humble Latin instruction that took place there was chartered as the Slavic-Latin-Greek Academy in 1682. The first printing shop in Moscow was situated in Kitai gorod before Tsar Mikhail relocated it inside the Kremlin walls. Stone shops had been built on the upper, middle, and lower trading rows in 1595.[8] In 1665 a new Merchant Court (*Gostinii Dvor*) was built of imposing brick, of symmetrical design.[9] Wealthy merchants lived in Kiati gorod. So too did boyars and

---

3. Kopylova, "K datirovke kamennogo stroitel'stva v Tiumenskom troitskom monastyre," 101–8.

4. *Istoriia Moskvy*, 1: 355.

5. On etymology: Unexpectedly, the name "Kitai gorod" does not refer to or translate as "Chinatown." *Kitai* may refer to the type of thick walls that were originally constructed around it. Another hypothesis is that it derives from the word for braided straw, of which baskets were made in which goods were sold.

6. Bondarenko, *Slovar' arkhitektorov i masterov stroitel'nogo dela*, 53. The Posol'skii Dvor (lodging for ambassadors in Kitai gorod) was different from the Posol'skii Prikaz, which was located inside the Kremlin. See Adam Olearius's description of his audience with the tsar. Olearius, *Voyages and Travells*, bk. 1, p. 18.

7. Quoted in di Salvo, "The 'Italian' Nemetskaia Sloboda," 96 n.3.

8. Bondarenko, *Slovar' arkhitektorov i masterov stroitel'nogo dela*, 35.

9. Ibid., 53.

princes. Indeed, as state functions increasingly occupied the space within the Kremlin walls, boyars and princes relocated to Kitai gorod. Olearius reported that they tended to live near the merchants, beyond "a special place where, in good weather, the Russians sit out in the open, having themselves shaved and their hair cut. . . . The place is so thickly covered with shorn hair that walking there is like walking on cushions."[10]

Kitai gorod was the site of many, but not all, of the trading rows Moscow had to offer. Like the empire itself, it expanded dramatically over the course of the seventeenth century. Commercial shops overflowed into Belii gorod; individual parish markets also took place. There was the fish market, whose stench, visitors averred, was palpable blocks away.[11] A horse market occurred on the banks of the Moscow River; nomads herded thirty thousand to forty thousand horses per year into Moscow's center. On Ivanov Square, where one procured notarial services, a slave market evolved, perhaps there because every slave purchase and indenture contract required a government document.[12] Secretaries shouted their services; they would write up the indenture (kabal'naia) document to make the transaction legitimate. Thence the saying, "To shout about all Ivanovskuiu."[13] Diverse merchants brought diverse wares to Moscow. By the mid-seventeenth century, Moscow had special accommodations (dvory) for Persian, Armenian, Swedish, Livonian, Greek, and English traders that came to Moscow.[14] Red Square now separates the Kremlin physically from Kitai gorod, but the Kremlin was intimately involved with the market on many levels. Needs of the tsar's court and stables comprised much economic activity and the legacy of neighborhoods producing particular crafts for the court and city persists in street names in central Moscow (skaternii, miasnii, etc.). The tsar was called "Chief merchant of all the Empire."[15] Moscow had its own Siberian marketplace.[16]

The earliest historical references to Moscow date to the twelfth century. Over time it became an increasingly important trade center regularly connected via trade to centers from the Baltic to the Black Sea. Moscow maintained customs agreements with several Rus' principalities before they called the Grand Prince of Moscow their sovereign. Across Rus' lands a network of trades emerged, rotating on a calendar linked to saints' days. Eventually

10. Olearius, *Travels of Olearius*, 115.
11. Goldstein, "Gastronomic Reforms under Peter the Great," 485.
12. On various forms of servitude, see Hellie, *Slavery in Russia*.
13. Mel'gunov, *Ocherki po istorii russkoi torgovli*, 177.
14. Ibid., 176, 203.
15. Collins, *The Present State of Russia*, 60.
16. Miller, *Opisanie o torgakh Sibirskikh*, 2.

fairs such as that at Blagoveshchensk monastery on the Vaga River in March, Arkhangel'sk in August, the Makariev fair on the Volga south of Nizhni Novgorod in July, and the Irbit fair in western Siberia in January became important events in Russian commercial life. Rus' lands and merchants had important links to markets such as Kazan and Astrakhan well before these towns came under Russian rule. In fact, in the early modern era, Muscovy had links to much of the known world.

Even before the watershed upheavals of the sixteenth century, Moscow made an impression as a formidable urban center. In 1517 a Polish ambassador who visited wrote that Moscow was twice as large as Florence and Prague.[17] Giles Fletcher, visiting in 1588, not two decades after a horrific sacking by Crimean Tatars, thought Moscow was larger than London.[18] Nowadays, as the headquarters of government and the financial and entertainment sectors, Moscow is, to put it in American terms, Washington, DC, New York City, and Los Angeles rolled into one. Moscow, just 0.0001 percent of Russia's territory, (problematically) accounts for an exorbitant percentage of Russia's GDP—almost 25 percent today.[19] It would be interesting to know the degree to which Moscow's relative gravity has increased or oscillated over time. In the sixteenth century it was already an impressive city, but it does not seem to have been to the exclusion of other Russian centers. Richard Chancellor, who visited Moscow in 1553, reported that Novgorod was *the* major trading city.[20] Adam Olearius, visiting in the 1630s, noted that Muscovy boasted "many large and, in their way, noble cities." He elaborated that vibrant towns and villages crisscrossed Russia, and even the Tatar lands more recently acquired boasted "good towns."[21]

Chancellor's hearsay and Fletcher's and Olearius's accounts may harmonize. After the 1571 sacking of Moscow, Ivan IV relocated many gosti from Novgorod to Moscow in an effort to rehabilitate the city. These relocations facilitated Moscow's recovery such that Fletcher saw a grand city, but, according to Floria, it hurt Novgorod's fortunes, contributing to that city's decline.[22] In addition, the opening of the White Sea trade (and only much later the founding of St. Petersburg) contributed to Novgorod's slow

---

17. Olearius, *Travels of Olearius*, 111, quoting Matthiae a Michovia.

18. Fletcher, *Of the Russe Common Wealth*.

19. In 2008 Moscow's GDP was $321 billion (http://www.ukmediacentre.pwc.com/image library/downloadMedia.ashx?MediaDetailsID=1562). In 2008 Russia's GDP was $1299.705 billion (http://www.tradingeconomics.com/charts/russia-gdp.png?s=wgdpruss).

20. Baron, "Who Were the Gosti?" in *Muscovite Russia*.

21. Olearius, *Travels of Olearius*, 110–11.

22. Floria, "Privilegirovannoe kupechestvo i gorodskaia obshchina v russkom gosudarstve," 145–61.

transition from urban commercial center to historical landmark. After all, for every gost' there were many lesser merchants prepared to take spots opportunity afforded.

Pausing in the center in a story mostly about commerce at the periphery is fitting because Moscow's vitality depended on commerce at its periphery. Moscow's structure was replicated outward toward the periphery. When one looks for the state in Siberia, one finds it, but barely. That is, sites of Russian authority were tiny islands in a vast remoteness with thin tentacles stretching outward from those islands. Think of a "Swiss cheese" empire, where the holes are the state's presence. Porous though it was, where one did find the Russian state, it consisted of military barracks, a church, and a trading square. The following chapters describe and explore the infrastructure, dynamics, and spaces of trade in Siberia.

CHAPTER 3

Spaces of Exchange: State Structures

"[That] commercial enterprise would spread widely across Siberian towns so that the Sovereign's treasury would become full."

—*Polnoe sobranie zakonov Rossiskoi imperii,* November 12, 1698

From the outset, the Muscovite government perceived Siberia as an entitlement to two kinds of wealth: wealth from furs and wealth from trade with the East. The aspiration to exploit mineral wealth was present from the first charters to the Stroganovs and throughout the seventeenth century, even if substantial mining was only realized in the eighteenth[1] and Siberian oil was discovered later, in the twentieth century. But from its first forays eastward Russians believed that the East held the promise of profitable commerce. Trade with the East could mean trade with Persia, India, Central Asia, and China. Just as the term "Orient" for Westerners had amorphous geographical bounds—Russians didn't use the term "Orient"—the term "India" in early Russian sources could encompass an area much larger, including even China.[2] Thus the story of Siberia in the seventeenth and eighteenth century is one of Russia, long embedded in the political world of the steppe, becoming more connected to the Far East and more integrated into a world economy that was increasingly dynamic and increasingly penetrating in its own right. This chapter embarks on the theme

---

1. Mineral exploitation was noted in the first charter to the Stroganovs. Remezov's "Sluzheb-naia kniga Sibiri" contains an image of silver mines in Nerchinsk from the early eighteenth century, reprinted in Semenova, *Istoriia predprinimatel'stva v Rossii,* unnumbered plate midbook. See also Kurlaev and Mankova, *Osvoenie rudnykh mestorozhdenii urala i Sibiri v XVII veke.*

2. Kurts, *Russko-Kitaiskie snosheniia,* 10, 12 fn.3.

of state building, how the Russian state created a minimalist but effective infrastructure for trade and governance in western Siberia.

Establishing Russian Rule in Western Siberia

Although we venture farther east, the primary setting for this story is western Siberia, situated to the east of the Ural Mountains in the northwestern edge of Inner Eurasia. There, the fertile steppe meadows gradually give way to mixed deciduous-coniferous forest, still free of the permafrost found in the harsher taiga to the north, as east-west rivers flow into north-flowing ones like asymmetrical ribs on a spine. At the end of the seventeenth century about 75 percent of Siberia's peasant population, which amounted to about 150,000 Russians, lived in this region.[3] As chapter 1 explained, this region had long been home to various peoples. Before Russians came along, Vogul, Ostiak, Iugra, and Samoyed natives in this region were accustomed to paying fur tribute to the Siberian Tatars and sometimes suffered from raids. Decades before Ermak's arrival, Bukharans, Muslim merchants from Central Asia, had migrated and made the flat lands along the Irtysh River and its tributaries their home. Thus Russia expanded into a pluralistic setting.

"Tatar" is an old term whose meaning has morphed over time. Medieval Europeans such as William of Rubruck and John of Plano Carpini called Mongols "Tartars," although Mongols found the name pejorative; these travelers called the space the Mongols conquered "Tartaria."[4] Russians, in yet another illustration of their position between Europe and Asia, adopted the term somewhat. Initially, all steppe peoples (this included Mongols and Turkic peoples such as Kazaks and Kirgiz) were Tatars. But as the Mongol suzerainty fragmented across the Eurasian space, by dint of closer interaction with them, Russians came to identify Mongol descendants with more specificity than did most Western Europeans. By perhaps the fifteenth century, Tatars were people that had transitioned from a nomadic to a settled life, such as Crimean Tatars, Volga Tatars, Nogais, Kazan Tatars, Bashkir Tatars, Siberian Tatars, "marsh" Tatars (Kuchum's people who fled to the swamps), and "serving" Tatars (those who had joined Russian service). Tatars who lived in the Siberian region from whom Russia collected fur tribute became known as tribute-paying Tatars (*iasachnye Tatary*). Ostiaks, Voguls, Iugras, Samoyeds,

---

3. S. N. Balandin, "Nachalno russkogo kamennogo stroitel'stva v Sibir'," in Vilkov, *Sibirskie goroda*, 174; Forsyth, *A History of the Peoples of Siberia*, 100.

4. For translations of William of Rubruck and John of Plano Carpini see Dan Waugh's Silk Roads website: http://depts.washington.edu/silkroad/texts/.

and other Siberian natives also became tribute payers (*iasachnye liudi*), but
as they tended to live in forests rather than open steppe areas and were not
descended from Genghis Khan, Russians generally did not call them Tatars.[5]

The steppe that flanked western Siberia's southern edge was home to
Mongol groups that had retained nomadic lifeways, although these people
practiced some agriculture too. Abutting Russian territory were Mongol
groups known as Kalmyks (Oriats) near Western Siberia and as Dzhungars
farther to the east. The steppe population farther to the south included
Turkic nomads such as the Kazakhs, Nogai, and Kirgiz.[6] Beyond them from
the Caspian Sea eastward were the Ottoman, Persian, Mughal (Indian),
and Chinese empires and the cities of Central Asia—all potential trading
partners for Muscovy. Moscow's influence notwithstanding, Siberia was part
of long-established trading systems. It was peripheral to Europe and to India.
At the heart of Eurasia, western Siberia was poised as a crossroads between
Russia and Asia, between East and West. Its proximity to ancient Inner
Eurasian trade routes imprinted the character of its trade. Whereas furs were
the primary products brought from eastern Siberia, western Siberian markets
from the outset were filled with a mix of furs and Eastern products from
Central Asia, Persia, India, and China.[7] So too did Moscow, almost 2,000
miles away, influence the character of early modern Siberian trade.[8] Although
this history highlights local agency on the periphery, it cannot ignore the
influence that the center exerted. Moscow issued the directives that regulated
trade; it participated in trade through caravans of the sovereign's treasury.
Even when orders were subverted, imperfectly executed, or ignored, Moscow
undeniably shaped the development of Siberian commercial life.

The earliest Siberian towns—Tiumen' (1586), Tobol'sk (1587), Tara
(1594), and Verkhotur'e (1598)—formed a nearly triangular zone in southwestern Siberia. The bulk of the archival research for this project focuses on
these four towns, most of which have been eclipsed by more modern cities. Verkhotur'e exists in the shadow of Ekaterinburg; Omsk supplanted the

---

5. Haugh, "Indigenous Political Culture and Eurasian Empire."

6. The relational fixing is intended to aid in a schematic understanding, but boundaries among
nomads were elusive. Further, so much intermixing occurred among nomads of the inner Eurasian
steppe that they are frequently referred to as Mongolic-Turkic peoples. For a description of the
peoples who lived in the western Siberian region at the time of Russian conquest, see Liubavskii,
Obzor istorii russkoi kolonizatsii, 433–35.

7. Matthew Romaniello's work showing that eastern Siberia adopted Chinese tobacco products
and methods of use and that western Siberia adopted Middle Eastern ones further illustrates how
commerce imparted different characters to western and eastern Siberia.

8. Johann Kilburger described the route from Moscow to Tobol'sk as 2,750 versts long (1,823
miles). Kurts, *Sochinenie Kil'burgera*, 203.

significance of Tara, and Tiumen' eclipsed Tobol'sk when the railroad was laid through it instead of Tobol'sk, making it the exception in that it remains an important city. Tiumen', the capital of Russia's largest province, is a modern city with Russian-style idiosyncrasies: a Gazprom glass skyscraper graces the skyline just blocks from wooden houses with outhouses and chickens in the courtyard, while downtown Tobol'sk resembles a quaint museum town. Walking down the broad avenue in Tiumen', the inexperienced can hardly distinguish a Tatar from a Slav; this city has become Russian heartland, a transformation sealed by that surreal uniformity that Soviet architecture so indelibly imposes. But it was no such thing in the seventeenth century; it was a frontier town subject to enemy attack at any moment.

Tobol'sk was built on a prominent hill at the confluence of the Tobol' and Irtysh Rivers, about 10.5 miles downstream from Kuchum's previous capital of Isker.[9] In 1621 the Siberian archiepiscopate was founded there. Tobol'sk became the administrative, economic, and cultural center of Siberia. The governorship of Tobol'sk was a powerful post to which other Siberian governors, theoretically at least, were subordinate to until administration reforms of 1736 split Siberia into two provinces.[10] Between 1639 and 1670 from one thousand to three thousand merchants traded goods worth a total annual turnover that ranged from 53,000 to 121,000 rubles, with average trading in the range of 40,000–60,000 rubles annually.[11] This made it one of the busiest commercial trading centers in the Russian empire—not as busy as Moscow, Arkhangel'sk, and Kazan, but on par with important western border towns such as Pskov and Smolensk.[12]

Tara was established along the banks of the Irtysh River about three weeks' travel upstream from Tobol'sk in 1594.[13] With this settlement, which sat along an ancient Inner Eurasian trade route, Russians pushed haltingly out of the forest zone to the edge of the Barabinskii (Baraba) steppe, which in the late sixteenth century was Kalmyk territory. More significantly, it was the region where Kuchum's descendants—who would test Russian sovereignty for the full first half of the seventeenth century[14]—had fled and congregated. It was no accident that the governor who established Tara, Prince Andrei Vasiliev

---

9. Qashliq and Sibir are alternate names for Isker.

10. Forsyth, *A History of the Peoples of Siberia*, 112. See Lantzeff, *Siberia in the Seventeenth Century*, 34–46, for a more detailed discussion of the hierarchy of Siberian towns.

11. Vilkov, "Torgovye pomeshcheniia gorodov Sibiri v XVII v.," 12.

12. Vilkov, *Remeslo i torgovlia*, 81; Kotilaine, *Russia's Foreign Trade*, 4.

13. Miller, IS no. 13, p. 347.

14. Puzanov, *Voennye faktory*, 214. State documents contain rumors of attacks in eighteen years from 1638 to 1658.

Eletskii, was a man who knew steppe warfare against nomads, having served on the southern Ukrainian frontier before being assigned to Siberia.[15] Tara had fertile soil but was not able to feed itself until the eighteenth century because nomadic threats such as periodic raids for slaves prevented reliable farming. By 1688 Tara had 5 churches and 690 houses, but mostly military servitors lived in them. In 1702 Tara still had just two registered townsmen, but Bukharan merchants and peasants composed a substantial portion of the population.[16] Despite fire prevention laws, Tara suffered major fires in 1629, 1658, 1669 (630 homes burned), 1701, and 1711.[17]

Situated at the very edge of the empire, residents tried to make Tara a proper town. In 1701 residents in Tara petitioned the tsar to authorize a clock-keeper. They explained that since Tara's founding, they had no clock, unlike other Siberian towns, and that this made many matters at the guard-house, the governor's house, in church, and in homes inconvenient. The peti-tioners had pooled their money and bought an iron clock in Tobol'sk. Now they were asking the tsar to authorize and fund the hiring of a clock-keeper. They even had a qualified Cossack candidate in mind.[18] Much ink has been spent debating whether the state or private individuals drove Siberian expan-sion. This chapter highlights the state's ambitious involvement and agrees with V. D. Puzanov, who argued that were there not military soldiers to protect them, peasants would not have ventured out to farm the steppe-forest borderlands.[19] After all, nomadic raids were not so much retaliation against territorial encroachment as a means to acquire slaves to trade. All this, how-ever, is not to adhere to a statist view of expansion. The process on the ground was symbiotic, as the petition for the clock-keeper illustrates. Gover-nors were ordered to help raise the sunken boats of merchants, and merchants sometimes supplied boats and sails to fulfill various "state" needs and man-dates. Accounting on such transactions is not clear, but in a culture where largesse, hospitality, and obligation exerted a powerful cultural force, we can imagine that an ethos of reciprocity obtained. This small incident turns our attention to another important matter: the multiconfessional nature of the Siberian borderland and, more specifically, the presence of diaspora Muslim merchants, the subjects of chapter 7. Bukharans and Tatars were among the petitioners for the clock-keeper. When the petitioning Muslims spoke of

---

15. Puzanov, *Voennye factory*, 250–51.

16. Ibid., 255.

17. Bashkatova "Gorod Tara i ego torgovlia v XVII v.," in TKSG 1:68. Vilkov, *Remeslo i torgovlia*, 186; Vilkov, "Torgovye pomeshcheniia Tobol'ska XVII veka,"

18. Ogloblin, "Bytovye cherty nachala XVIII veka," 219.

19. Puzanov, *Voennye faktory*, chap. 1.

FIGURE 3.1 The Godunov map, 1667. The earliest Russian general map of Siberia. Done under the administration of Petr Ivanovich Godunov. Notice the prominence of rivers everywhere except the dry southern steppe (the band of land across the top; south is the top of the map). This map is a visual manifestation of how rivers informed both travel through and perceptions of Eurasia.
Source: Leo Bagrow Collection, Goudonov Map, 1667, MS Russ 71 (1). Courtesy Houghton Library, Harvard University.

religious and domestic matters that would be aided with a public clock, they were likely thinking of the call to prayer.

Four years after the establishment of Tara, Verkhotur'e was founded in the Ural Mountains at the northern bend of the Tura River in 1598. It was designated as the gateway to Siberia, but never quite lived up to its name because routes to the north were more heavily traveled.[20] Early on, most Siberian fur passed through northern routes. Such patterns had begun in the

20. Fisher, *Russian Fur Trade*, 161. Semenova proposed the opposite trend, arguing that Russians first traveled to Siberia through the northerly "Cherezkammenii" route, but as the seventeenth century progressed they began to travel more regularly through the Solikamsk-Verkhotur'e-Tiumen'-Tobol'sk route. Semenova, *Istoriia predprinimatel'stva v Rossii*, 113. Such a development would fit into the argument that Eastern goods became increasingly important, that furs were not the only reason for Siberian trade. Lantzeff says all traffic went through Verkhotur'e and in his finances chapter he writes that the state decreed to close other roads in order to channel traffic to Verkhotur'e. Lantzeff, *Siberia in the Seventeenth Century*, 133; PSZ 3, no. 1518 (Sept. 21, 1695), 206–7.

days of medieval Novgorod, and the opening of the White Sea route in the middle of the sixteenth century reinforced the dynamic. The closing of trade at the mouth of the Ob River by the state in 1620, the depletion of the fine sable population surrounding Mangazeia by the 1640s, and the development of southern towns and routes accessible to the advancing eastern wall of Russian activity altered that dynamic. Around the middle of the seventeenth century probably twice as many cargo shipments still passed through the northern route as through Verkhotur'e, but trade traffic was shifting southward.[21] Eastbound traders laden with heavy wares preferred the Verkhotur'e portage, commonly referred to as the winter route, but when headed back to Russia with a lighter cargo of furs intended for sale at the Arkhangel'sk fair in August, they could manage the mountain passes of the northern "Cherz Kammenii" portage.[22] This southward shift also speaks to the importance of Eastern goods, not just furs, in Siberian commerce. By the middle of the seventeenth century Tobol'sk was the major fur center in Russia. Later, Tobol'sk was eclipsed as trade trended more along the southern borders of the Russian empire—Nerchinsk, Kiakhta, Iamysh, Irbit.

Rivers, Shapers of Empire

Rivers shaped the expansion into Siberia. Not as boundaries, but as conduits. Were it not for the extensive river system and the portages Russians developed, Siberian expansion would have proceeded differently. Rivers shaped the progress of Russians into Siberia. Rivers shaped the patterns of fur depletion. Siberian fur supplies began falling almost as soon as Russians began to exploit them. Yet, in the early waves, it was not fur populations in toto; it was the fur populations easily extracted along riverways. Moving eastward along river systems into less hunted forest banks proved a path of less resistance than moving farther inland.[23] The only other factor as significant as Siberian river systems in determining what Russian imperialism looked like was the nomadic steppe, which produced a line of Russian military forts (eventually towns) along the southern edge of Russian territorial claims. Russia expanded decidedly eastward across Siberia. It reached the Pacific in 1639, but it did not move southward into the steppe for over a century and a quarter after founding Tara in 1594.

---

21. Vilkov and Preobrazhenskii, *Ocherki sotsial'no-ekonomicheskogo razvitiia Sibiri*, 39. On southward shift: Fisher, *Russian Fur Trade*, 166, 171.

22. Bakhrushin, "Torgi gostia Nikitina," in NT, 3: 1, 250; Vilkov and Preobrazhenskii, *Ocherki sotsial'no-ekonomicheskogo razvitiia Sibiri*, 39–41, 45.

23. Fisher, *Russian Fur Trade*, 106.

Rivers made travel possible. For the most part, Siberia's main arteries, broad, not-steep riverbeds, made for gentle currents. But even they could be fickle. It took two months or more to row down the Lena River, but in favorable conditions, wrote the governor of Mangazeia in 1638, "one can sail the distance in a week."[24] It was a seasonal affair. In the spring, merchants had a window of time during which they could float goods from Verkhotur'e, the "Gateway to Siberia," down the Tura River, through the Perm' region, all the way to Tiumen'. The river ice would break up in early spring. Spring melts could make for water levels higher than comfortable, while ice chunks made river travel downright treacherous. Ice floes crushed boats, destroyed property, and claimed many lives. Yet once the winter snows melted away, the river volume quickly diminished, making rocks and river bottom more of a hazard until the river itself was actually impassable. By late summer the Tura River could be barely 3 feet deep near Tiumen'.[25] Consequently, a summer port had to be built farther up the river before reaching all the way to town.[26] Often, as along the fast-flowing upper Irtysh, trade caravans chose to follow the course of a river but proceed via land.

Rivers were the highways of Siberian trade. Even when trading parties traveled alongside instead of on the river because of too much or too little water, river courses largely determined the routes that wares traveled. Russians traveled by river in flat-bottomed boats (*doshchaniki*) that were propelled by various means. Moving downstream along wide gentle rivers could be accomplished by sail. Upstream, boats were often hauled by men walking along the shore.[27] In either direction, flat-bottomed boats required many rowers. Boat-building became an important state and private task in Siberia, but it was hard to keep up with demand. In one case servitors petitioned the tsar to protest being assigned travel in unriverworthy vessels.[28] When a contingent of the Great Northern Expedition was given a dilapidated boat they persuaded the governor to purchase them a sturdier boat from a merchant.[29] When rivers froze in the winter they could often be traveled via sledge, dogsled, or skis. Adam Olearius, traveling by sledge along the frozen Volga River, made the trip from Kazan to Moscow in just twenty days in

24. Dmytryshyn, Crownhart-Vaughan, and Vaughan, *Russia's Conquest of Siberia*, no. 53, 172.
25. Semenova-Tian'-Shanskogo, *Rossiia*, 16 : 57.
26. Kvetsinskaia, "Remesla Verkhotur'ia v XVII v.," 105.
27. Black and Buse, *G. F. Müller and Siberia*, 78.
28. Ogloblin, "Bytovye cherty nachala XVIII veka," 1.
29. Black and Buse, *G. F. Müller and Siberia*, 77.

December 1638.[30] But if rivers did not freeze solid, sledge travel overland was an alternative.

Long-distance trade often occupied more than a single season, however. Transitions from boat to a different mode of travel added much expense and logistics. Many merchants worked to move their goods through Siberia when rivers were navigable. In order to do this they had to be mindful of more than the winter freeze. By mid to late summer, the Tura River frequently ran so shallow that boats constructed in Verkhotur'e's boatyard had to be launched 40 kilometers downstream from the town in deeper water.[31] By mid to late summer the volume of the river flow dropped off significantly such that laden boats that could pass in the spring would run aground—a condition that obtained on many Siberian rivers.

Geography and climate may not have been the only reason that Verkhotur'e never quite lived up to its expected vitality as "gateway" to Siberia. It developed a reputation for corrupt and abusive leadership.[32] In 1639 the elite merchant (*gost'*) Vasilii Fedotov Gusel'nikov petitioned the tsar for permission to send his shipments via the northern route because, even if in Verkhotur'e they did not collect excessive taxes as some other places did, they made labor demands on his men that caused delay. Since the success of his caravans depended on covering certain distances via river before the rivers froze, such delays in Verkhotur'e could cause him to miss the entire trading season and sustain major losses.[33]

Along these river systems, Russians had built ten forts in Siberia by the end of the sixteenth century and continued to extend the line eastward for decades to come. A Russian detachment wintered on the Pacific Ocean as early as 1639 at a place they called Udinsk, and the first permanent Russian settlement on the Pacific, Okhotsk, was founded in 1648.[34] But Russian hegemony in Siberia was hardly a foregone conclusion. In their first two centuries of existence, these frontier towns endured their share of trial and upheaval. Even Tobol'sk and Verkhotur'e, buffered by other towns and therefore not immediately on the frontier, faced threats of attacks. A remark by Avvakum, the famous religious dissident exiled to Siberia in the 1650s, hints at the security risks. He wrote, "I was come to Tobolsk. And the folk were astonished thereat, for Bashkirs and the Tatars were scouring all Siberia. But

30. Olearius, *Voyages and Travells of the Ambassadors*, 422–23.
31. Kvetsinskaia, "Remeslo Verkhotur'ia v XVII v.," 105.
32. Ogloblin, *Obozrenie*, 1: 364–67.
33. Orlova, *Otkrytiia russkikh zemleprokhodtsev*, no. 39, 164–65.
34. Lantzeff and Pierce, *Eastward to Empire*, 10, 137.

I, trusting in Christ, went through their midst. And when I had reached Verkhoturie, Ivan Bogdanovitch, my friend, was astonished at me. 'How did you ever get through, archpriest?'"[35]

Security was tenuous, particularly for the more southerly located towns of Tiumen' and Tara.[36] Kalmyk and Bashkir forces periodically raided throughout the century, motivated by a spectrum of reasons. Russian encroachment certainly generated resentment that could elicit martial responses. In some cases Kuchumites egged them on. To some degree causes of nomadic violence were pragmatic. The "raiding and trading" of nomadic political economies converged in the slave trade. Kalmyks obtained slaves by attacking Russian villages and would then sell them either at various markets or directly back to the Russian government for ransom. Even after Kuchumites and Kalmyks were subdued, Bashkir rebellions flared in the eighteenth century.

When it confronted China in the Amur River valley, Russia pulled back, ceding territory for peace and trading relations in the 1689 Treaty of Nerchinsk. Along Siberia's southern border non-Russian nomads were a much more complicated problem. "Peace was impossible" is how Michael Khodarkovsky described the dynamic.[37] Natives, the indigenous population that in many interpretations posed no challenge, mounted serious rebellions against Russian authority. These challenges came not only from Far Eastern natives, famous for their fierce resistance to Russian rule, but also from inland and purportedly more docile tribes. Samoyeds attacked a Russian detachment bringing sable tribute to Moscow in 1641.[38] Finally, the Russian state faced serious threats to its sovereignty from within its ranks. Numerous rebellions touched Siberia, most dramatically the Pugachev rebellion of Catherine's reign. Russia faced occasional mutinies from among its own servitors in Siberia. Even when not in outright rebellion Cossack servitors in Siberia wielded important constraints over Siberian authorities.[39] Russia's hold on Siberia was tangible yet tenuous (anything but iron fisted) for centuries. There can be no understanding Siberian governance without understanding the real and sustained security threats that Siberian administrators and peasants faced.

Compared with Russia's celeritous establishment of military infrastructure across Siberia, migration and settlement into Siberia in the seventeenth

---

35. "Life of Archpriest Avvakum," 352.
36. Miller, IS, vol. 2 documents the constant security concerns in the 1620s–1640s.
37. Khodarkovsky, *Russia's Steppe Frontier*, chap. 1.
38. Bakhrushin, "Puti v Sibir' v XVI–XVII vv.," in NT, 3: 85.
39. Witzenrath, *Cossacks and the Russian Empire*.

century was unexceptional, having led some historians to characterize Siberian settlements not as towns but as military-administrative centers.[40] Although I argue that seeing Siberian towns merely as military fortification and tribute collection points fails to capture the nascent, diverse frontier society developing there, it is true that Russian migration to Siberia was paltry in the seventeenth century. The reasons were multifold. Forced migration was a well-established strategy of the Muscovite princes. "People are thrown from place to place and from province to province for colonization, and to replace [those who have departed] they send and settle others," commented one Polish observer in 1517, perhaps referring to Novgorod.[41] But there was no population surplus in seventeenth-century Muscovy. Then, in the eighteenth century, exporting settlers to the southern steppe was a higher priority. The state had longer been contending with the empty steppe region to the south; one strategy against nomadic incursion was to transform the steppe into agricultural communities, a strategy only successfully implemented in the Volga region by Catherine II.[42] As mentioned above, peasant settlers destroyed fur habitat.[43]

Some settlers did make their way voluntarily to Siberia in the seventeenth century, and some Old Believers fled to Siberia to escape persecution or find a place where they could worship as they wished, but the reasons to cross the Urals were rarely, if ever, to satisfy "wanderlust," as Baron Von Haxthausen much later posited.[44] Their reasons were pragmatic. Traditionally, farming methods made for substantial movement among Slavic peasants. In a world of marginal soil but available land, slash and burn agriculture was a common practice. Peasants would create fields by burning a forested area. The resulting ash functioned as valuable fertilizer. They would farm that area until exhausted, around a decade. The crises of the late sixteenth century precipitated many peasant desertions; some of these people headed east. After the state formally enserfed them, peasants who escaped to seek better conditions became fugitives. Some of these, too, likely sought refuge beyond the Urals, especially since the state seemed less interested in recovering escaped peasants in Siberia than it was west of the Volga.[45] After all, while the Ural

40. Hittle, *Service City.*

41. Poe, "A People Born to Slavery," 29.

42. Sunderland, *Taming the Wild Field.*

43. Fisher, *Russian Fur Trade,* 79.

44. DAI, vol. 8, no. 50, 214–26; Moon, *Russian Peasantry,* 49.

45. The Stroganov charters of 1558, 1568, and 1574 forbade the Stroganovs from accepting people registered as taxpayers in Russian towns. Miller, IS, vol. 1, nos. 2, 3, 5, 325–30, 332–34. See sections of Brian Boeck, *Imperial Boundaries,* and Matthew Romaniello, *The Elusive Empire,* for recent discussions of the treatment of escaped serfs in the Don and Kazan regions.

Mountains did rise to the mythic stature of continental divide, they were not in physical fact such great obstacles. Yet the nature of the Siberian territory made for reluctant settlement. On the one hand, once the state appreciated that the development of agriculture destroyed fur habitat and upset the tribute-paying natives, it did little to promote large-scale Siberian settlement until the nineteenth century. Second, as forest gave way to steppe, the real and sustained threat of nomadic raids deterred peasant settlement. Slavs sold well at the slave markets of Central Asia and the Ottoman Empire.

One thing more frightening than nomadic attacks may have been fire. As in many early modern towns, fire was a constant threat that punctuated the region's first century of Russian rule with sometimes devastating effect. Some fires were set deliberately, such as several self-immolations by Old Believers.[46] Tiumen' also saw its share of uprisings and rebellions. In 1670 local Cossacks were executed for involvement in the Stenka Razin uprising.[47] Out on the open steppe fire was also a fact of life. Naturally occurring burns sometimes swept across the steppe. Traveling along the Irtysh in the eighteenth century, G. F. Müller noted that distant steppe fires illuminated the night sky; it was a scene the Russian Feodor Baikov had witnessed eighty years before.[48] Not all steppe fires occurred naturally; fire was also a weapon that Russians, Kalmyks, and Tatars used against one another.[49]

Despite critical challenges, settlers did trickle in, such that the towns consisted of several hundred households by midcentury and more than double that by the end of the seventeenth century. In an age where last names were new and often indicated a person's work, names indicate that blacksmiths (Kuznetsov), saddlers (Shornikov), shoemakers (Sapozhnikov), furriers (Skorniakov), brewers (Pivovarov), butchers (Miasnikov/Miasnitskii), butter-makers (Masloboinikov), coopers (Bondarëv), bell-makers (Kolokolov), millers (Mel'nikov), pot-makers (Goncharov), icon painters (Bogomazov), carpenters (Plotnikov), and tailors (Portniagin) had made Siberian towns their homes or found their profession in Siberia. In 1701 peasants from Suzdal moved to Siberia to make their living as tailors, but found the market saturated and petitioned to move farther eastward and try Irkutsk.[50] When Semen Remezov was researching for his Siberian history in the 1680s, he consulted "old residents in inaccessible places and waterless mountains, on

46. On self-immolations: Chernyshov, *Staroobriadchestvo i staroobriadtsy zapadnoi Sibiri*, 56–86.
47. Pokrovksii, *Aktovye istochniki po istorii Rossii i Sibiri*, 1: 7–16, 147.
48. Müller, "Travels in Siberia," 80; Vilkov, *Ocherki sotsial'no-ekonomicheskogo razvitiia Sibiri*, 91.
49. Davies, *Warfare, State and Society*, 45; Miller, *Istoriia Sibiri*, 2: 124.
50. Shakherov, "Gorodskie promysly i remeslo iuzhnoi chasti vostochnoi Sibiri," 162.

the steppe and at the sea, . . . Russians of various ranks, foreigners, Bukharans, Tatars, Kalmyks, newly baptized, exiles, émigrés, and prisoners of war."[51] His list suggests both a diversity of sorts and a lack of women. Indeed, initially the Russian population was overwhelmingly military men or Cossacks, leading some historians to describe Siberia as a "military camp."[52] Moscow tried to redress the female deficit by sending eastward over a hundred maidens and widows as suitable wives early in the seventeenth century.[53] The state, on occasion, even condoned enslavement—in conflict with its own official policy—as a source of wives for men in Siberia.[54] There were never enough "imported" women to go around and local men turned to native Siberian women. Although the amount of Russian-native cohabitation is impossible to document, the emergence of the category "Sibiriak" to indicate a person with a Russian father and native mother provides strong testimony to the fact that such unions were not infrequent.

Human Resources and Politics: Inclusion and Suspicion

After the tenuous security, the other fundamental dynamic in Siberian history was the chronic deficits in human resources.[55] These shortages in people—be it women, soldiers, peasants, merchants, administrators—meant that the state did not have the luxury of exclusivity; it was forced to rely on people of questionable loyalties. In an early decree Siberian governors were instructed to treat well and incorporate into service anyone who would promise loyalty—even belligerent relatives or a track record of antistate activity would not disqualify one from Russian service. This letter from Ivan IV to the Stroganovs in 1572 conveys the lengths to which Muscovy would go to gain people:

> If among the Cheremis and Ostiaks there are some good men who might persuade their fellows to desert the insurgents and become our subjects, then spare them, do not kill them and we will show them favor.
> If some took part in rioting but now are willing to obey us and give proof of such intentions, announce to them our forgiveness and we

---

51. Bakhrushin, "Vopros o prisoedinenii Sibiri," in NT, 3: 33.
52. Lantzeff, Siberia in the Seventeenth Century, 62.
53. Khitrov, K istorii Irbitskoe iarmarki, 2.
54. A 1691 order to the Berezov governor reiterates that natives may not under any circumstances be sold as slaves. Ogloblin, "Bytovye cherty nachala XVIII veka," 1. An 1825 law directed local officials to buy native women to supply wives. Forsyth, A History of the Peoples of Siberia, 114.
55. The problem was not limited to Siberia. With an estimated population of 7 million, the Muscovite bureaucracy in the 1640s was staffed by 1,611 people. Serov, Stroiteli imperii, 11.

shall favour them. . . . They are to fight with you against traitors, and after victory they can take the property of the traitors and their wives and children as slaves. . . . If these [repentant natives] fight and acquire spoils, traitors' wives, horses, cows, and clothing, do not let anyone take it away from them.[56]

The many European prisoners of war exiled to Siberia from wars on the western front—enemies—often found themselves in positions of major responsibility in Siberian administration.[57] As was the case in Kazan, Tatars comprised much of the military force in Siberia. Sometimes they defected.[58] The Russian state was continually willing to court the loyalty of belligerent Kalmyks.[59]

In the seventeenth century Kalmyks were a near constant enemy threat and a near constant potential ally to Russian power in Siberia. The bulk of the content in Müller's magisterial *History of Siberia* deals with rumored and actual Kalmyk threats throughout the 1630s and 1640s.[60] They were diplomatically engaged, had stand offs, fought, and cooperated. The same can be said of Bashkirs and Tatars. Muscovy displayed such tolerance for suspect parties because it did not have much choice. Tatars and Bashkirs, too, were regarded with suspicion but formally welcomed into the imperial fold. As was the case with Kazan and Volga Tatars of the fifteenth and sixteenth centuries, many Siberian Tatars joined the Muscovite army. The force that repelled Kuchum in 1593 numbered more Tatars than Russians in its ranks.[61] This overlap between friend and enemy, driven by a chronic lack in human resources, characterized much of the sociopolitical dynamics in Siberia.

Bukharans were no exception. As an émigré community within the Russian Empire, they were generally regarded for their loyalty to the empire, yet they too rode that cusp between traitor and ally. The dangers of steppe travel made for unlikely bedfellows and it had to be unnerving that Bukharan caravans typically traveled with Kalmyks and could access places Russians could not. A Russian contingent explained how they could not follow the tsar's

---

56. Miller, IS, vol. 1, no. 4 (Letter of August 6, 1572), 331–32. Translation taken from Lantzeff and Pierce, *Eastward to Empire*, 87.

57. Sokolovskii, Sluzhilye "inozemtsy" v Sibiri XVII veka.

58. Miller, IS, vol. 2, no. 295, 449 (1631); no. 324, 479 (1634).

59. This pattern strongly resembles Romaniello's description of the Kazan region. See Romaniello, *Elusive Empire*, chapter 4.

60. In Krizhanich's telling, Kalmyks desired sanguine relations with Russians, but this was decades after the protracted violence documented in Miller, IS, vol. 1.

61. Lantzeff and Pierce, *Eastward to Empire*, 114. State use of foreign mercenaries was standard in the early modern period. Nearly one quarter of Britain's army was foreign in the 1690s. See Sokolovskii, *Sluzhilye "inozemtsy: v Sibiri*, 183. Romaniello, *Elusive Empire*.

orders to search for rhubarb there because it took them to hostile territory.[62] Bukharans traveled the road from Tara to Tomsk, which passed through the Baraba steppe, territory that was in practical terms off limits for Russians for much of the seventeenth century.[63] On occasion they lived for extended periods of time in the camps of hostile steppe nomads.[64] Tobol'sk had a Kalmyk guesthouse, but before it had fallen into disrepair, it had come to house transit Bukharans as much if not more than Kalmyks, who Siberians could be reluctant to welcome into their towns.[65] Expedient as it was, this Bukharan access (if not intimacy) could be unnerving for Russians. On at least two occasions, Siberian Bukharans do appear to have acted with Kalmyks against Russian state interests. In insecure moments, the posturing state threatened to consider Bukharans traveling with Kalmyk enemies as enemies, but in fact guilt by association was not a luxury people-poor Siberia could afford.[66] For example, the Bukharan Seitkul Ablin held the responsible task of heading a state embassy to China even as his brother had been imprisoned as a suspected traitor.[67] Simply put, human resource needs trumped suspicion in Siberia.[68]

Consequently, suspicion ran long and wide as the rivers of Siberia throughout the ranks of Russian government. Just as people who regularly exist in high-risk situations can appear hyperconscious about safety in quotidian situations, the Russian state, which systematically incorporated people of questionable loyalties into imperial management, was eternally suspicious.[69] Although observers of Russia from Sigismund von Herberstein in the sixteenth century to George Kennan in the twentieth have made much of suspicion as a national trait, it is helpful to ground it in the practices that evolved in a labor-strapped empire.[70] The persistent inclusion and extreme suspicion that characterized so much of Siberian life only make sense when seen through the lens of human-resource shortages.

62. RGADA, f. 1111, op. 1, d. 22, l. 49 (note from Nitsynskoi prikazchik Grigorii Barybin to Verkhotur'e voevoda, July 1652). South of the Iset River was considered off limits. This area is far west of the Baraba steppe, but only slightly west and in the general area of a trade route to Central Asia via the Ishim River.
63. TKSG, 1: 81. A Russian musketeer traded clothes in the Baraba steppe in 1674/5. TKSG 1:77.
64. RGADA, f. 214, stb. 499, ll. 210–17.
65. RGADA, f. 214, stb. 348, pt. 1, l. 60.
66. MUITTSSR, 296–99.
67. RMO, vol. 2, no. 94, 297.
68. Monahan, "Trade and Empire," 316–23.
69. For a recent case study in divided loyalties see Khodarkovsky, Bitter Choices.
70. Poe, "A People Born to Slavery."

Suspicion characterized the view from Moscow as well. The Siberian administration was an extension of central state authority. At the same time, it was both more and less: more in that governors in varying degrees found spaces to exercise independent autonomy; less in that Moscow maintained pathways to undermine governors' authority. Knowing this, Moscow was no less suspicious of its own governors. Few hierarchical structures in Muscovy were without backchannels. Just as alternative channels of hierarchy could circumvent the standard chain of command, local voices and midlevel actors could access Moscow directly via alternative pathways that could both undermine efficiency and function to check against excess.

Given distance, the tsar had limited realistic recourse to monitor the behavior of Siberian leadership. Consequently, governors could wield extraordinary power. This power typically manifested in self-enrichment and sometimes in tremendous abuse toward the local population.[71] Moscow wanted to curtail the amount of wealth bound for the tsar's treasury that was siphoned off by its servitors. More important, it recognized that populations pushed too far and squeezed too hard were more likely to rebel or flee. Moscow could "look the other way" as long as stability and profit obtained, but where governors blatantly undermined either, they courted reprisals.[72] As part of efforts to police its leadership and stability, Moscow was attuned—perhaps surprisingly so—to reports from the local populations of governor abuse. This created opportunities for locals to use the state against the governor and for the state to use locals against the governor. For example, local complaints led to the ousting of the Tiumen' governor Ivan Timofeev syn Verigin. His successor fared no better; Fëdor Ivanov syn Verigin was ousted as a result of a collective petition against him by Tiumen' residents numbering 7,166 in the same year he arrived, 1657–58.[73] In 1668 Moscow removed Governor I. I. Lodygin after receiving complaints against him.[74] These dynamics of triangulation, where the tsar relied on other voices to attempt to keep the power of the governor in check, were a consequence of a state steeped in suspicion.

Minimalist-Activist State

That the Russian state's reach exceeded its grasp can be readily demonstrated, but understanding the history of the Russian Empire in Eurasia requires

---

71. In post-Soviet scholarship, *voevoda* administration has seen a rehabilitation. For a work that celebrates *voevoda* as empire builders, see Vershinin, *Voevodskoe upravlenie*.

72. Enin, "Voevodskaia tamozhennaia poshlina v XVII v.," 248–55.

73. *Polnoe sobranie russkikh letopisei*, 36: 158–60. Vershinin, *Voevodskoe upravlenie*, 181.

74. Aleksandrov and Pokrovskii, *Vlast' i obshchestvo*, 112, 125–26.

appreciating Russia as a minimalist-activist state. The statist perspective of nineteenth-century Russian historians—that change in Russia was state driven—holds much validity in the history of Siberia. For Enlightenment-educated travelers Russia was a canvas on which to extol the lack of freedoms,[75] an attitude that manifested itself palpably in nineteenth-century interpretations emphasizing the heavy-handedness and/or incompetence of the Russian state. But state involvement could work both ways, and in Siberia's case it did. The state shouldered a considerable burden when it came to trying to ensure the Siberian population's well-being. And although outcomes such as community-wide well-being are rightfully regarded with skepticism, the level of state involvement in regional sustenance is striking.

The Muscovite state, minimalist as it was, set itself an ambitious agenda in running Siberia. The administration established forts for security; however imperfectly, it defended the Russians and natives in Siberia. It built infrastructure. The state maintained the porter system (a series of posts known as *iamy*, of which the state itself was the primary user). The state assigned work. The state mandated much of the in-migration and regulated settlement. It supplied seed and salt and grain to the region. It shipped livestock out during famine years. The state expended significant energy supplying Siberia with wine, whose distribution on holidays it regulated.[76] The state shipped out women when the deficit became painfully clear. The state regulated prices, market days, what could be sold when (no selling on Sundays or holidays, except for edible perishables),[77] and tried to guard against speculation. It waived tax obligations on multiple occasions for individuals and communities in dire straits.

As did colonizers in other places, the Russian state worked to create spaces recognizable to settlers in the Siberian wilderness. They built churches with bell towers to punctuate the landscape with Orthodoxy and create familiar sounds.[78] They passed leash laws, and although the immediate intention was to restrain dogs from hassling livestock and biting people, it is not too much of a stretch to suggest they were simultaneously striving to impose marks of civility in roughly constructed frontier towns. Sparse as its presence was, the state touched lives.

---

75. Wolff, *Inventing Eastern Europe*.

76. RGADA, f. 1111, op. 1, d. 158 (1666, 1672). On transport of wine to Siberia see: SPbII RAN, f. 28, dd. 920, 921, 928, 931 (1660 and 1661).

77. Kaplun, Kopylov, and Rozhkova, *Tiumenskii uezd v XVII–XVIII vv.*, 103.

78. The Ottoman state saw establishment and maintenance of moral order as a fundamental duty in regulating trade. See Yi, *Guild Dynamics in Seventeenth-Century Istanbul*, 167–68.

Siberian towns were governed by elite Russian nobles with military leadership in their resumes (*voevoda*).[79] Security was the governor's first obligation, one which was frequently tested in the initial decades. In maintaining security it was not sufficient to protect the fortified towns; governors also sought to protect tribute payers in the hinterland, a task they took seriously. Getting and keeping tribute payers on the books was no trivial task. Sometimes tribal groups disappeared of their own accord without a trace, eliminating substantial fur revenue for the state.[80] Consequently, the state went to great lengths to make sure nothing pushed them off the land. When Kalmyks killed, kidnapped, or scattered an entire village, governors had a hard time meeting tribute quotas.[81] Indeed, immediately after security, the collection of fur tribute (*iasak*) was the governor's highest priority.[82] However reticent it was when it came to articulating ideology, Moscow was eminently clear that it wanted fur tribute. Epitomizing this, the oldest extant document in the Tiumen' archive is a 1604 directive to find people to add to the list of tribute payers and send that to Moscow.[83]

Yet since neither security nor healthy tribute collections could be reasonably achieved without basic food stability, governors were intimately involved in the provisioning of grain to the region (grain and salt allotments were part of soldiers' salaries). In a borderland where accidents of natural and man-made provenance could lead not just to inconvenience but could jeopardize survival of entire communities, matters as basic as food were not to be left to the vicissitudes of the market. The state regulated sales, prices, and distribution of grain and sometimes livestock, ratcheting up its involvement in moments of acute crisis.[84] Grain and livestock are just two example of heavy state involvement in the economy. For the sake of maintaining staple supplies to the region, the state would readily fix prices or impose restrictions at the expense of private actors' profits. Such measures were hardly particular to peripheral regions. In the early modern world generally, from Boston to Beijing, Paris to Constantinople, one looks in vain for unregulated markets.[85]

Meanwhile, the obligations to increase fur tribute and oversee food supply created competing priorities that Siberian governors had to constantly

---

79. The term *voevoda* is translated as military governor. To be less cumbersome I translate it as governor.

80. Miller, IS, vol. 2, no. 297, 451.

81. Miller, IS, vol. 2, no. 118, 274.

82. GBUTO GATO, f. 47, d. 29, l. 1 (1646).

83. GBUTO GATO, f. 47, op. 1, d. 28, l. 1 (1604).

84. SPbII RAN, f. 28, op. 1, d. 940 (1661). Grain distribution was an important subject among Soviet historians. For a valuable English language treatment of provisioning in eastern Siberia see Gibson, *Feeding the Russian Fur Trade*.

85. For a study of grain in Paris see Kaplan, *Provisioning Paris*.

negotiate. The state wanted to develop a local grain supply, but agricultural development eliminated fur habitat. The result was a balancing act in which the state regulated and restricted settling options for the Russian peasants that the state recruited to settle in Siberia.[86] When volunteers came up short—and they did come up short—the state used exiles. When exiles still were not enough, soldiers were put to farming. Indeed, soldiers fulfilled a range of duties. Clock-keeper, smith, prison guard, boat guard, gatekeeper of the marketplace, bathhouse keeper, and man responsible for keeping the boat hulls that plied the Siberian rivers well coated in pitch were all jobs that merited a dedicated individual.[87] If another individual could not be found, a soldier would fill the job. Security, tribute collection, and food provisioning were far from the whole of Siberian governors' obligations. Siberian governors conducted their own diplomacy as they oversaw all development projects. But amid all this, a governor's overarching mission was to bring profit to the tsar's treasury. This was achieved through tribute collections and, no less important, through the cultivation of commerce. Governors were specifically directed to develop trade relations with Asian countries.[88] Toward this end, they dispatched numerous embassies inviting Asians to trade in Siberia and made conditions particularly welcome for Bukharan merchants through tax breaks and land grants, which will be discussed in chapters 7 and 8.

Before delving into the world of Siberian commerce, let us continue with this sketch of life in Siberia. Chronically short on manpower, Russians nonetheless erected homes, bathhouses, churches, monasteries, and marketplaces—construction of which was state funded—in their new Siberian settlements.[89] In time these settlements grew into genuine frontier towns where Russians, Tatars, a smattering of European exiles, and other Siberian natives lived.[90] Tiumen', Tobol'sk, Tara, and Tomsk were home to émigré communities of Bukharan merchants from Central Asia.[91]

86. Miller, IS, vol. 2, no. 357, 501, no. 386, 545.

87. Ogloblin, *Obozrenie*, 1: 291.

88. Evseev, "Tara v svoi pervye dva stoletiia," 103.

89. On marketplace construction see RGADA, f. 1111, op. 2, d. 188, ll. 31–32; d. 360, l. 1; SPbII RAN, f. 187, op. 2, d. 25, l. 1.

90. Miller, IS, vol. 2, nos. 11, 22, 93, pp. 182, 193, 255; Vilkov, *Torgovlia gorodov Sibiri kontsa 16–nachala 20 v.*

91. I have not encountered any Bukharan residents in Verkhotur'e. Godunov's 1600 *Nakaz* orders the building of a marketplace in Verkhotur'e so there would be no trading along the river, in homes, or in yurts. This suggests that either Tatars or Bukharans lived locally. Of course, Epanchin, the outpost of a previous Tatar prince, was eastward along Tura River. See Bakhrushin, "Sluzhilie tatary v XVII v.," in NT, vol. 3, pt. 2: 156.

FIGURE 3.2 Tobol'sk around the turn of the seventeenth to eighteenth century. The Bukharans tended to live in the lower town. In this drawing the Irtysh and Tobol' Rivers are improperly named; they are reversed. This image was published in the second edition of Nicolaas Witsen, *Noord en Oost Tartarye* (1705). The rivers were properly named in the artistically less accomplished drawing published in the first edition of 1692. This image was removed from the 1785 edition.
Source: Witsen, *Noord en Oost Tartarye*, 2nd ed. (1705), 2: 786. Courtesy State University Library, Göttingen, Germany.

Tobol'sk in particular boasted numerous signs of "civilization." Women's hats, children's toys, eyeglasses, mirrors, and figures for a chess game were included on registers of items transported from Tobol'sk to other Siberian towns.[92] By the end of the century there was an emerging educated class composed of people on both sides of the authorities' graces. Some Tobol'sk governors were boyars whose experiences and inclinations must have imparted a more cosmopolitan and educated atmosphere to Tobol'sk society. Governor Prince Petr Ivanovich Godunov (1667–69) tended to raise the ire of colleagues and subordinates alike, but on his initiative the first Russian map of Siberia was composed, work that would be greatly elaborated by the Tobol'sk mapmaker Semen Remezov.[93] Boyar Prince Petr Vasilievich Sheremetev

92. Vilkov, *Ocherki sotsial'no-ekonomicheskogo razvitiia Sibiri*, 68.
93. Vershinin, *Voevodskoe upravlenie v Sibiri*, 176; Bagrow, "Semyon Remezov," 111–25; Kivelson, *Cartographies*, 133.

(1676–78) embraced Western dress; when Avvakum once encountered him on the road to Kazan he scolded him for his shaven face.[94] Governor Prince Petr Semenovich Prozorovskii (1684–86) had traveled to London as a Russian diplomat before his tour in Tobol'sk.[95]

Exiled Europeans comprised part of Siberia's educated class. Yuri Krizhanich was a Croatian Catholic whose aspirations to reunite the rent Christian body resulted in a sixteen-year exile in Tobol'sk (1661–77), during which time he penned a mercantilist manifesto, *Statecraft*. Krizhanich is only among the most famous of many European exiles who lent a measure of educated culture to Siberian society. Johann Strahlenberg (1676–1747) was a Swedish officer captured in the Northern War; he spent thirteen years in Siberian exile, based on which he produced maps and a treatise of the region. Strahlenberg also copied into German *The History of Abul-Ghazi*. The book was lent to him by a Bukharan merchant in Tobol'sk.[96] Strahlenberg's writings exude a Renaissance-esque enthusiasm for knowledge about the region's ancient history—that is, the ancient graves and engravings in the region. He found in Tobol'sk companions with similar dispositions. He communicated (and competed) with other exiles in Siberia, such as Johan Gustaf Renat. Renat was a Swedish exile captured by Dzhungars, where he found himself a compatriot bride; he was allowed to repatriate to Sweden after eighteen years of service to the Dzhungar khans. Literacy was found in surprising places in Siberia. In 1674 a Verkhotur'e peasant submitted a proposal "written in his own hand" to develop a road.[97]

Simultaneous with the arrival of the state came the churches, obligatory infrastructure in an Orthodox realm. Soldiers broke ground on the Church of the All-Mighty Savior, the first Orthodox church in Siberia, even as the walls of the Kremlin fortress were being constructed.[98] In 1601 Moscow issued orders to send holy books to Verkhotur'e, build a church in Tobol'sk, and send a church bell to Pelym.[99] Monasteries took longer to establish. The first monastery in Siberia, according to Butsinskii, was built in Tara. Tiumen' got its first monastery in 1616, almost three decades after its founding and only after fourteen Russian forts and a dozen customs posts had been established.

94. Avvakum, "Life of Archpriest Avvakum," 325.

95. Vershinin, *Voevodskoe upravlenie v Sibiri*, 220–21.

96. Potanin, "O karavannoi torgovle," 72–23. Strahlenberg, *An historico-geographical description*, v. Strahlenberg's original surname was Tabert.

97. The peasant's name was Levka Babinov, perhaps a descendent of Artem Babinov, who built the first Russian road into Siberia. Skalon, *Russkie zemleprokhodsty XVII veka v Sibiri*, 237.

98. Miller, IS, vol. 1, 268. This bears a strong resemblance to the Kazan experience. See Romaniello, *Elusive Empire*.

99. Miller, IS, vol. 1, 404.

Close on the heels of the most rudimentary military structures, customs posts and market squares were built. In a typical pattern of empire building, military firepower shepherded the establishment of church and commerce.

Siberian Customs Administration

The customs post was the site and symbol of regulation. That customs posts preceded monasteries and farming suggests the importance of commerce in Siberia. It is telling that the first monastery in Siberia was built sixteen years after Siberia's first customs post was established, and by which time a dozen Russian customs posts punctuated Siberian trade routes.[100] The state built churches in Siberia but it built more customs posts. No less telling, the customs administration was not responsible for fur tribute collection (*iasak*). Taking stock of these facts points toward the argument of this chapter: commerce was a priority for the Russian state. That the labor-strapped state went to the trouble to construct and maintain an extended customs infrastructure across Siberia speaks volumes to the revenue it aspired to gain through the regulation and cultivation of commerce.

The Siberian customs administration emerged as the Muscovite state underwent one of the most severe and protracted crises in Russian history. The period from the death of Tsar Fëdor in 1598 to the establishment of the Romanov dynasty in 1613 is known as the *Smuta*, or "Time of Troubles." Severe economic dislocation plus the end of the Riurikid dynasty and foreign interventions reduced Moscow to near chaos for over a decade. Much headway had been made in the reigns of Fëdor Ivanovich and Boris Godunov. Presumably—since extant documentation precludes a clear picture—Siberian development rode that momentum into the seventeenth century.

The first Russian customs post in Siberia was established at Verkhotur'e in 1600. By 1603 customs posts had been established in Tobol'sk, Tiumen', Tara, Surgut, Berezov, and Mangazeia. The state would ultimately construct

---

100. By 1616, fourteen Siberian customs posts had been established: Tiumen' (1586), Tobol'sk (1587), Losva (1590), Pelym (1593), Berezov (1593), Tara (1594), Surgut (1594), Narym (1595/6), Verkhotur'e (1598), Turinsk (1600), Mangazei (1600/1601), Ketsk (1602), Tomsk (1604), New Mangazeia (1607). Customs books for twelve of the fourteen towns built by 1616 survive, but the earliest of these records is from 1628/29. The Siberian Office does not contain customs books for Losva or New Mangazeia at all. Regarding the other towns, evidence exists that customs collections were functioning at all towns except Ketsk and Narym before 1616. However, given their locations and dates of establishment, I am making an educated guess that Ketsk and Narym had functioning customs posts by 1616.

thirty Siberian customs posts and many more checkpoints.[101] The system operated for over a century and a half. The internal regime was officially abolished in 1753, although some posts continued to operate until the reign of Catherine II. Customs posts normally operated year round in Siberian towns. In addition, the state dispatched roving customs agents to seasonal markets such as Irbit and Lake Yamysh. Customs agents also made rounds to collect "bazaar" taxes from the boroughs (sloboda) in the district (uezd), or other places where deemed appropriate.[102] One peasant paid customs taxes at the Iset fort in 1658.[103]

Whereas the ruble tax was the mainstay of indirect taxation in Central Russia, the one-tenth tax played that role in Siberia. The one-tenth tax was the main source of the customs revenue.[104] Demonstrating that the outlines of the Siberian customs system were taking shape even before a customs system was formally established, Moscow had been collecting the one-tenth tax there since the late sixteenth century. Earliest instructions to Siberian governors, such as the instructions to Pelym in 1597, directed them to collect the one-tenth on furs and Russian goods in cash or kind.[105] Recognizing the potential of tax policy to channel trade, the state levied the one-tenth tax only on certain items and refrained from levying it on imports from Central Asia, China, India, or many goods produced in Siberia until the late seventeenth century.

In Siberia, a variety of additional taxes were levied. It varied according to location, shipment content, season, and transport methods. Generally merchants faced about half a dozen additional fees—per porter, per declaration, per cart, horn tax, bathhouse tax, etc.—although customs levies could exceed twenty different taxes.[106] These fees presumably deflected administration costs. Each individual tax was generally miniscule, but taken together may have contributed appreciably to overall revenue. For example, in

---

101. Ogloblin, Obozrenie, 2: 106–13. NB: Solikamsk, although included in this list of thirty-one locations, was not in Siberia. Also, note that the Siberian Prikaz archive references fifteen monasteries in Siberia. The list is incomplete but it is significant that more records pertain to customs than monastic administration. See Ogloblin, Obozrenie, 1: 316–17.

102. On Irbit, see Ogloblin, "Bytovye cherty," 6. On Lake Yamysh, see chapter 5.

103. SPbII RAN, f. 187, op. 2, d. 17, l. 38 (1658).

104. Merzon, Tamozhennye knigi. The historian Raymond Fisher referred to this levy as the tithe, distinguishing it from customs taxes. Insofar as tithe historically refers to a one-tenth portion of something, it is a suitable title, but the meanings of this ancient term have also extended to include annual and religious obligations, aspects that do not apply to this tax in Siberia.

105. Kopylov, "Tamozhennaia politika v Sibiri v XVII v.," 331–32. These instructions were sent from the Foreign Office, which partially administered Siberia in the late sixteenth century. Ultimately, most—but never all—of Siberian administration was consolidated in the Siberian Office.

106. Kopylov, "Tamozhennaia politika v Sibiri v XVII v.," 348–57.

September 1662, the beginning of the busy fall season, the sum of all sundry taxes collected for the month by Tiumen' customs—head tax, storage, cartage, stamp, fur, horn, stall rental, etc.—amounted to 48 rubles, 8 altyn, which was more than one-tenth the revenue for that month.[107] The total revenue collected by Tiumen' customs for the half year from September 1662 to February 1663 was at least 325 rubles.[108] At first glance it would seem that taxes were higher in Siberia, since 10 percent plus anything is more than 10 percent. But that may not have been the case. Since furs and Eastern goods faced higher assessed values in Moscow than in Siberia, the same shipment might be taxed more in Moscow than in Tobol'sk. Among other things, the content of the shipment was a variable in the overall taxes levied.

The Urals may have been an invented continental divide, but the distinction between Rus' and Sibir' was real and ubiquitous in the language of those who traversed the modest mountain range. This conceptual distinction manifested in tax policy. A merchant who paid the one-tenth in Rus' was expected to pay the one-tenth tax again in Siberia—that is, twice on the same shipment.[109] This amounted to a disincentive. If a merchant from Vologda could sell his wares in European Russia, he could avoid the Siberian tax regime altogether. And yet merchants went to Siberia anyway. Once in Siberia, the one-tenth tax—in theory—was collected just once, whereas sundry taxes were collected at every customs post. Consequently, a tremendous amount of paper and ink went toward oversight. Not only that, it was confusing. Finally, in an effort to help streamline practice in 1698, the state decreed that the one-tenth tax would only be collected at the entry/exit points of Siberia, Verkhotur'e and Nerchinsk.[110]

Because first access to the customs purse was at stake, certain bureaucratic modifications were accompanied by tension and resistance. Initially, governors were in charge of Siberian customs and soldiers were appointed to levy customs taxes and fees. By the 1620s a customs head was installed, which brought the institutional structure more in line with Central Russian towns. In 1635 the administrative structure was overhauled so that the customs head was no longer subordinate to the governor on fiscal matters but reported directly to Moscow.[111] This, along with competing priorities, chronic shortages, and

107. GBUTO GATO, f. 29, op. 1, d. 381, l. 18v. One-tenth revenue on miscellaneous market purchases was 28 altyn, which is less than 1 ruble (33 altyn = 1 ruble). See GBUTO GATO, f. 29, op. 1, d. 381, l. 18.

108. GBUTO GATO, f. 29, op. 1, d. 381.

109. Kopylov, "Tamozhennaia politika v Sibiri v XVII v.," 342.

110. PSZ, vol. 3, no. 1654, 490–517 (November 12, 1698).

111. Kopylov, "Tamozhennaia politika v Sibiri v XVII v."

complicated politics, was another one of the ongoing challenges the state negotiated as it learned (or rather, struggled) to run its empire in Siberia. The state never quite mastered the challenge of getting its servitors to toe a clean line, despite constant struggling to get its servitors not to skim off the top or squeeze those beneath them. Wrangling over reporting hierarchy and embezzlement persisted, however. In 1646 the state reissued the directive in response to privileged merchants' complaints that taxes were being demanded from them at both customs posts and outposts the governor established.[112] Where governors did obey, Moscow had few means to ensure that customs heads were righteous where governors were not. Understanding that revenue-diminishing corruption continued, in 1652 the state reversed its position and made customs heads again subordinate to governors in some matters.[113]

The state in Siberia had a canvas on which to act out economic policy. Although Russia is notorious for contradictory and irrational governance, the state maintained a course, even if it does not appear that way at first glance. The policy focused on revenue collection through taxation. Stability, however, was the higher priority. Contrary to older scholarship, which argued that early modern states had no economic policy vision, the Russian state took an instrumentalist approach to commerce in Siberia, seeing it as a means to provide basic needs.[114] In order to generate commerce that would fulfill basic regional needs, it sought to entice foreign traders to Siberia by creating a favorable trading environment and tax regime. Meanwhile, a view of human nature that recognized the power of inertia negotiated the difference between encouraging commerce and generating revenue in Muscovite economic policy. That is, initially Central Asian merchants did not pay any taxes and were subject to very few restrictions—an anomaly in the early modern world—because the state was intensely interested in making its domains an attractive trade destination. In the first charter issued to the Stroganovs in 1558 they were instructed not to tax transit merchants on goods they imported to the charter region.[115] In the 1572 renewal of the Stroganov charter, the instructions expanded to direct the Stroganovs to be kind to transit merchants, let them trade what and where they wished, and in no way hassle or impede them.[116] The instructions to Siberian governors struck a

---

112. AI, vol. 4, no. 8, 32–35 (1646).

113. Kopylov, "Tamozhennaia politika v Sibiri v XVII v."

114. For a brief discussion of the difference between early modern and modern states see Musgrave, *Early Modern European Economy*, 88–89.

115. Miller, IS, vol. 1, no. 2, 326–27.

116. Miller, IS, vol. 1, no. 5, 334.

similar tone: to Tara in February 1595[117] and Tiumen' in August 1596. This freedom was unusual, for, like other early modern regimes from Boston to Constantinople, the state worked to control where trade occurred.[118]

Once it felt that habits of trade were sufficiently established, the state moved to impose taxes. In this empire of "separate deals" the tactic played out again and again. Siberian Bukharans are just one example; their days of tax-free trade were numbered. Once the regular appearance of Central Asian merchants in Siberia was assured, the state began to ratchet back its laissez-faire policies. It decreed that all trade should take place at the marketplace, an imperative easier uttered than achieved. It soon began taxing Bukharans, albeit at a lesser rate than Siberians. By 1608 some Bukharans were paying a one-twentieth tax. If the rules changed, the state's strategy was consistent: once trade was established impose taxation and other regulations in the hopes that habit would outweigh distaste for taxes.

Siberian Bukharans did maintain certain tax privileges for the duration of the Russian Empire, however. The state, perhaps always aware of its highly limited ability to impose its will on Siberia, extended a number of tax waivers. In fact, many Siberians enjoyed tax waivers on trading. Natives did not pay taxes. Here, stability and revenue were the rationale; the state did not want to incite rebellion or hinder natives from fulfilling their most lucrative function, delivery of fur tribute to the state. Nor did clergy and monasteries pay taxes on most shipments.[119] Servitors, too, enjoyed certain waivers. Once it understood just how many soldiers moving across Siberia on this or that detail were also engaging in trade, the state tried to tap into this activity by taxing soldier trade. But here, in the face of the impossibility of enforcement, the state maneuvered to save face in its military organization. Servitor trade privileges were rescinded and then reinstated when enforcement proved impossible. In 1671 servitors were allowed to transport up to 50 rubles worth of goods for private trade tax free.[120] The privilege remained in place at the end of the century, even as the state recognized that merchants evaded taxes by using soldiers to shuttle their wares through Siberian towns.[121] In all of these waivers, the state was negotiating a balance between stability and revenue.

---

117. Miller, IS vol. 1, no. 17.
118. See Bailyn, *New England Merchants of the Seventeenth Century*; Yi, *Guild Dynamics in Seventeenth-Century Istanbul*.
119. PSZ 1, no. 81, p. 268 (1652).
120. Kopylov, "Tamozhennaia politika v Sibiri v XVII v.," 339–40.
121. PSZ, vol. 3, no. 1654, 492 (November 12, 1698).

Another area of puzzlement deals with fiscal policy, that bedrock indicator of rational governance. Money is liquid, the ultimate fungible currency.[122] Since a shortage of cash caused Moscow many problems, it is puzzling that Moscow would ever encourage barter at the expense of cash transactions, especially when Jarmo Kotilaine has argued for a high level of monetization in seventeenth-century Muscovy.[123] In Siberia, as far as the Russian state was concerned, there were more important things than money. Logistical difficulties meant that needed items became more valuable than money in Siberia. In situations where money outpaced goods, inflated prices could potentially create unrest. Finally, the state profited tremendously from its infrastructure that moved fur out of Siberia. Since the state could gain much more cash for furs in Moscow and Europe than they sold for in Siberia, furs were more valuable than cash to the state. Thus the minimalist-activist state wanted people to bring more goods, less money into Siberia. In such circumstances, it made sense for a minimalist-activist state to enact policies such as the following: (1) orders taxing import of money into Siberia, and (2) refusal to allow tribute payers to pay in cash.[124] Just as the institutional structure itself changed, laws concerning foreigners in Siberia, servitor trading, regulations on particular commodities, and cash policy evolved as Siberia developed. Decrees that Bukharan merchants dispose of their cash before leaving the empire, issued in 1673, 1678, and 1687, were consistent with mercantilist principles generally.[125]

Whatever stable vision Moscow might have had for the Siberian colony, practice was a different story. Distance, culture, and local particularities combined to ensure that decrees from Moscow were applied unevenly in the new Siberian colony. Towns varied on the discrete taxes they collected; recall, the number could range from a handful to thirty. The buyer paid some taxes, the seller others, and sometimes both paid the same taxes. In theory the one-tenth tax was collected once, but this rule, like so many, was muddied in the Siberian space by connivance and confusion alike. Requests for clarification from provincial administrators are hardly archival rarities. It is easy to see how confusion was typical: where some portion of tax was paid in kind and the composition of shipments changed as merchants traded their way across Siberia, deciphering what constituted the taxed 10 percent could

---

122. Financial innovations like the personal check and EFT remind us that currencies are invented artifacts, some of which become obsolete.

123. Kotilaine, *Russia's Foreign Trade*, 3–5.

124. PSZ, vol. 10, no. 7955, pp. 959–60 (November 20, 1739). This is a resolution whereby thirteen Buriats who requested to pay *iasak* in cash because there were no sable were ordered to pay in other pelts instead.

125. Burton, *Bukharans*, 501.

get complicated, and in some cases, state investigators determined, revenue suffered not from greed but from confusion.[126] The valuation of goods was another area for ambiguity. Indeed, Siberian commerce hinged on the steep gradient between Siberian and Moscow prices, and the valuation on a particular shipment could be a cause for debate as merchants moved through customs inspections in Eniseisk, Tobol'sk, and Verkhotur'e. Variations abound in the record, and although individuals surely maneuvered to maximize their own advantage through vagueness in the regulations, some of the confusion was likely genuine.

In the middle of the seventeenth century, Tsar Aleksei Mikhailovich's government engaged in an ambitious program of reforms—land reforms, legal reforms, tax reforms.[127] Aleksei Mikhailovich demonstrated modernizing proclivities from the outset, but riots that shook the core of government spurred sweeping changes, the most famous of which was the Conciliar Law Code (*Ulozhenie*) of 1649.[128] As was the policy in Siberia, stability and revenue were the objectives behind these reforms. Land reforms sought to reduce or eliminate lands not subject to state taxation. Numerous protectionist and modernizing tax reforms were instituted.[129] The New Statutes of 1653 sought to consolidate myriad charges into one ruble tax and eliminate the transit tax.[130] Elimination of transit taxes for travel between towns and numerous discrete local taxes under a more universal fee improved the efficiency of the internal tax system. After its issuance, Moscow ceased to send particular directives to individual Russian towns; henceforth it issued centralized orders for the entire customs administration of European Russia. In addition, the standardization to a ruble tax moved to levying taxes in cash rather than in kind. Like any early modern state, Muscovy had need of cash. But in passing the New Trade Statute for European Russia, policymakers likely had some sense that it would work. Historians have tended to explain that Moscow did not apply the 1653 Tax Statutes to Siberia because it did not want to jeopardize the high profits the territory was generating. It may be the case that policymakers did not institute the 1653 Statute in Siberia because they doubted its viability there. I suspect that the Siberian economy was a barter and in-kind economy to a greater degree, and that Moscow was

126. Kopylov, "Tamozhennaia politika v Sibiri v XVII v.," 365.

127. On land reforms see PSZ, vol. 1, no. 85 (1652 order for foreigners to sell homes in Moscow); Semenova, *Istoriia predprinimatel'stva v Rossii*, 123.

128. PSZ, vol. 1, chapters 1–25.

129. Admittedly the internal politics behind the formulation of Muscovite policy are little explored here. For examination into such questions see LeDonne, "Proconsular Ambitions"; Sokolovskii, "Reformirovanie v usloviiakh otsutstviia ratsional'noi politiki."

130. PSZ, vol. 1, no. 107, 302–5 (October 25, 1653).

content to have it remain that way: if merchants supplied needed goods to Siberia, the state did not have to—even if settlers faced the inconvenience of converting the value of a particular good into something they needed, it was their problem, not the state's. Further, because of a rising price gradient as one moved westward, the state profited more for taxes collected in kind. Where the 1653 Statute was predominantly about standardizing cash collection in Russia, the New Trade Statute of 1667 instituted protectionist measures.[131] Since it did not apply to Siberia, Bukharans were unaffected by the measures.

Although sound reasoning to refrain from implementing the Trade Statue of 1653 existed, it is worth pointing out that considering these regions separately came naturally to Muscovites. Siberia was a separate entity: documents faithfully record that people moved between Rus' and Sibir'.[132] It was only in the 1680s, during the regency of Sophia Alekseevna, that Siberian commerce reforms were instituted in Siberia. A law unifying measures (for pourable items) was issued in 1686. More significantly, a 1687 decree overhauled collections; the most significant measure here was the liquidation of the transit tax. Action for the reform may have been instigated by complaints from merchants who did business in Siberia; in 1685 and 1686 several merchants formally petitioned the tsar about improper collection of taxes and persistent abuse by Siberian administrators.[133] This meant that in Siberia myriad and variable taxes continued to be paid from town to town. Also, as stated previously, the one-tenth tax (10 percent) remained the foundational tax, whereas the 1653 law had instituted the ruble tax at 5 percent as the foundational tax.

These reforms show a state responding to known problems yet not achieving intended results. The liquidation of the transit tax in 1687 led to a marked decrease in tax revenue. The state responded with the 1693 New Trade Statute for Siberia. With this law, the state began to collect taxes on locally produced items. This was the standard strategy *writ large*. While in its infancy, the state was disinclined to tax local production in the goods-starved region. Once manufacturing—leather, soap, socks, and shoes, in particular—was established, the state, true to form, moved to garner revenue. The state did the same with foreign trade. On the first trip to Siberia, Central Asian merchants paid the traditional one-twentieth tax—which was one-half the rate that Russians and Siberian Bukharans paid—but on subsequent trips to Russia,

---

131. PSZ, vol. 1, no. 408, 677–91.

132. The administration of Siberia was mostly handled in the Office of the Palace of Kazan and the Foreign Office initially, but by the mid-seventeenth century it had been largely consolidated into the Siberian Office, which existed 1637–1710 and 1730–53, although many departments continued to have a hand in Siberian affairs.

133. Kopylov, "Tamozhennaia politika v Sibiri v XVII v.," 360–1.

the one-tenth tax would apply.[134] This move, too, was a response to the health
of foreign trade. By the end of the seventeenth century the vast majority of
goods imported to Tobol'sk—80 percent in number of declarations and up to
95 percent of volume—were of Chinese origin.[135] In the last quarter of the
seventeenth century, the state, which had long profited more from taxing the
private fur trade than from tribute collection, began to generate greater revenues from Eastern trade than from fur trade.[136] The 1693 statute, however,
engendered such resentment that, according to Kopylov, it instigated greater
evasion, which resulted in still further-diminished tax revenues.[137] And so
the state tried again. In 1698 a new customs statute regulating internal and
extra-Siberia trade was issued.[138] Essentially, this law applied the New Trade
Statute of 1667 (which reiterated the 1653 Statute) to Siberia. In doing so,
Moscow cancelled the most offensive aspects of the 1693 law; most productively, henceforth the one-tenth tax would be collected only at the border
towns of Verkhotur'e or Nerchinsk, a measure that streamlined administration even as it made the historical charting of trade dynamics less possible.[139]

Moscow never declared an outright monopoly on all furs but it did at
certain points declare monopolies on the most valuable furs. Sable harvests
peaked in the 1630s and overall Siberian fur returns began diminishing in the
first half of the seventeenth century.[140] In general, as returns diminished the
state became more proprietary, banning trade in sable, black fox, and other
types of fur in the late seventeenth century.[141] The ambiguous terms of the
changing commercial environment left room for contestation and abuse.
Whether through legitimate confusion or malfeasance, merchants bore the
brunt of inconsistent treatments. For example, in 1654–55 the merchant Ivan
Oskolov petitioned the state that his agent had paid the one-tenth tax on his
fox furs at Ilimsk only to have them confiscated in Surgut as contraband.
These sorts of incidents were not rare.[142]

Moscow was well aware for quite some time that serious problems within
its administration were negatively impacting fur revenue. Although hunting
methods were sometimes regulated to ensure reproduction in populations, the

134. Ibid., 338.
135. Vilkov, *Remeslo i torgovlia*, 207.
136. Kopylov, "Tamozhennaia politika v Sibiri v XVII v.," 359.
137. Ibid., 361–5.
138. PSZ, vol. 3, no. 1654, 490–517 (November 12, 1698).
139. Vilkov, *Ocherki razvitiia Sibiri*, 170.
140. Aleksandrov, "Rol' krupnogo kupechestva," 167; Pavlov, *Promyslovaia kolonizatsiia Sibiri*, 11.
141. Fisher, *Russian Fur Trade*, 65.
142. RGADA, f. 214, stb. 499, l. 326. The furs in question: *lisi chenko buroe beztseny.*

problem was mostly addressed as a political rather than environmental one.[143]
In 1636 Moscow wrote to the governor of Tobol'sk complaining that tribute
collections were returning furs of mediocre quality while sables and foxes of
excellent quality were for sale at the Moscow market.[144] Moscow knew that
merchants were getting to the fur supply before the state and that its own
servitors were switching out better furs for worse ones, but they did not know
how to stop it. By the end of the seventeenth century all of those problems
still obtained. Indeed, the instructions issued to Tobol'sk's new governor in
1697 repeatedly direct the governor to guard against smuggling by all people,
including its own servitors. They even go so far as to explicitly state that the
private trading of governors and their people has reduced state revenue.[145] In
this system built on still functioning traditions of "feeding" (*kormlenie*), the
boundaries between legitimate "feeding" and hurting the tsar's returns were
murky. The very same document all but admits this problem in a section providing guidelines on evaluating the performance of district bailiffs: "to take
only to fulfill their needs is acceptable, but not to get rich."[146] Government
corruption and abuse, scholars agree, worsened under the reign of Peter I.
Without going into detail, one anecdote suggests the depths of the problem.
In 1713 Peter decreed a law to reward anyone who reported on "thieves of
the people" with intentions to "harm state interests." The response was so
overwhelming that within eighteenth months the state narrowed the provisions. Whistleblowers hardly abated, however, and in 1718 the state again
revised the law to limit it specifically to "theft from the treasury."[147]

Customs Administration Personnel

Each customs post in Siberia was headed by a customs head (*golova*).[148] He
had a support staff of sworn men (*tseloval'niki*) and often a secretary. By the
1620s customs heads in busier Siberian towns like Tobol'sk were imported
from towns of the Russian North, and men from neighboring Siberian

---

143. Fisher, *Russian Fur Trade*, 105; DAI, 4: 365. Beaver and otter trapping were prohibited
around Perm' in 1635. In 1664 buying or raising fox cubs around Tobol'sk was prohibited.

144. Pavlov, *Promyslovaia kolonizatsiia Sibiri*, 11.

145. PSZ, vol. 3, no. 1594, 359 (September 1, 1697).

146. PSZ, vol. 3, no. 1594, 360: "*chem im o nuzhde mochno tol'ko byt- sitym, a ne bogatet.*"

147. Serov, *Stroiteli imperii*, 18.

148. The customs administration consisted of a customs head and assistants. Just who would be
in charge of Siberian revenues, unsurprisingly, was a contested issue. In an effort to thwart corruption
by voevody, Moscow determined in the 1630s that customs heads would report directly to Moscow.
This did not solve the corruption problems; whether it affected improvement remains open to question. See Timoshina, "Voevodskoe i tamozhennoe upravlenie v pervoi polovine XVII v.," 255–61.

towns served as support staff; Tiumen' townsmen commonly served as sworn
men locally and in Tobol'sk.[149] Typically, Verkhotur'e sourced its customs
sworn men from the northern towns of Russia, in particular from Ustiug and
Solikamsk. Sworn men in smaller towns like Tiumen' and Tara were locals.
Customs was not only staffed by outside sworn men; the town population (*posadskie liudi*) constituted an important labor pool for the government
bureaucracy. From Tiumen' alone, at least fourteen townsmen served in the
administration simultaneously. In Tiumen', one townsman served as a clerk
(*lareshnii tseloval'nik*) in the governor's office, one served with the notary, two
worked in Tiumen' customs, five townsmen served in the state distillery
operations, and two in the state grain operation.[150] Tobol'sk and Tiumen'
exchanged personnel more than any other towns in western Siberia. Two
Tiumen' townsmen served in the customs house and the trading bathhouse
in Tobol'sk. One man was deployed as assistant to the Turinsk customs head.

Privileged merchants did not serve in the customs administration in Siberia, but they did work regularly in the Siberian and Sable Offices in Moscow.
There, their jobs pertained directly to commerce; they often worked as assessors. The elite merchant (*gost'*) Ivan Klimshin headed the Siberian Office in
the early eighteenth century,[151] but privileged merchants of all ranks participated more directly in state commerce by leading state trading trips, although
this was not a task designated exclusively to privileged merchants.[152] Although
some have argued that an increasing reliance on nonprivileged merchants to
lead state trading trips presaged the demise of the privileged merchant corporations, the state employed privileged and nonprivileged merchants alike
on its commercial expeditions throughout the entire seventeenth century.[153]
Just as early modern Muscovite political leaders were not troubled by demons
of uniformity, the state was not philosophically committed to the privileged
merchant corporations; they were one of various means of conducting and
profiting from commerce.

The Russian Empire also used local Bukharans in the customs service,
capitalizing on their expertise in Eastern wares. Though very little scholarship has focused on Bukharan service in the Russian Empire, they serve as

149. GBUTO GATO, f. 47, d. 257.
150. GBUTO GATO, f. 47, op. 1, d. 264, l. 1 (no date).
151. RGADA, f. 214, op. 5, d. 841, l. 2, d. 1144, l. 1 (at least 1705–7).
152. See Ogloblin, *Obozrenie*, 4: 10–20, 61–98.
153. Examples of privileged merchants of *gostinia sotnia* making state trips: RGADA, f. 1111, op.
1, pt. 3, stb. 64.3 (1647); SPbII RAN, f. 28, op. 1, d. 863, l. 5 (1660). Examples of nonprivileged
merchants making state trips: RGADA, f. 1111, op. 1, stb. 54.5, l. 149. (A 1698 ermine-buying trip
to Irbit led by a nonprivileged merchant.)

one case study of typical imperial practice, discussed in greater detail in chapter 7. Throughout Muscovy architects, doctors, officers, soldiers, statesmen, entrepreneurs, and later academics manned the Russian ranks. Muscovy conquered Kazan with an army that contained more Tatars than Slavs.[154] It continued the practice in Siberia, where "serving Tatars" were as ubiquitous as Cossacks. Aleksei Andreevich Vinius, of Dutch-Jewish descent, headed the Siberian Office from 1697 to 1703. In Siberia, European prisoners of war often held responsible positions and foreigners led embassies to China on the tsar's behalf. Indeed, Muscovy relied so heavily on foreigners in running the empire that it is hard to see how characterizations of xenophobia have retained such interpretative purchase in Russian historiography, especially since suspicion was an ecumenical feature of Muscovite political culture.

In Tobol'sk, Tiumen', Tara, and sometimes Tomsk—the towns in which Siberian Bukharans lived—a Bukharan usually served as a customs sworn man. Bukharans seem not to have worked in eastern Siberian customs posts, which were more occupied with fur and "Russian" goods rather than Eastern ones until the last quarter of the seventeenth century. They were active in the Tiumen' customs service from at least the 1620s.[155] To take any oath before the Russian state, Bukharans "swore" by their Muslim faith.[156] It was typical imperial practice to swear by one's faith.[157] Even when the names of these Bukharan servitors slip through the cracks in historical records, their Turkic script in the pages of Russian customs books reveals their presence.

Bukharans not only fulfilled important posts as functionaries in the Siberian customs administration; they also served the Russian state as valuable cross-cultural brokers. Bukharans acted as commercial envoys on diplomatic embassies, assessors in Moscow, translators, escorts, and intelligence collectors. Their commercial activity—which Russia was keen to support—led them into "enemy" camps on a regular basis, where their liminality was valued in the same ways, even as it made Bukharans objects of suspicion.

Conclusion

Such was the setting and the structure the state established to regulate trade in Siberia, where subsistence, stability, and revenue were the state's priorities. Such prioritization, it must be acknowledged, was undergirded by

---

154. Romaniello, *Elusive Empire*.
155. Bakhrushin, "Sibirskie sluzhilye Tatary v XVII v.," in *NT*, vol. 3, pt. 2: 153–75.
156. GBUTO GATO, f. 47, op. 1, d. 271, l. 1 (1684/85).
157. Golikova, *Ocherki po istorii gorodov*, 172. See PSZ, vol. 1, *Ulozhenie*.

assumptions of entitlement—there was no discourse over the morality of expansion.[158] The Russian conquest into Siberia was a quantitative extension of long-established dynamics, not a qualitative change. A difference was that now Muscovy met with more success. But the map can be deceptive, for along the southern frontier Muscovy took much longer to succeed.

Long-distance trade and regional commerce were critical to the functioning and development of Siberia. Because the two did intersect it is hardly productive to splice which mattered more. More important is to appreciate that, amid the violent clashes that accompanied native subjugation, the state recognized the benefits of trade in providing necessities. Even as it strove to maximize profit to its own treasury, the state recognized the potential of private traders to fulfill the supply functions and provide livelihood for settlers in Siberia. Therefore, commerce was critical in its own imperial project. The state extended privileges to Muslim immigrant merchants to encourage their settlement and industry in Siberia and "looked the other way" when it felt it had to. As a result, this sparsely populated militarized zone had its share of trade and credit operations that operated locally, regionally, and in conjunction with long-distance trade. In this multiethnic, multiconfessional Siberian setting, merchant groups remained distinct yet interacted regularly with one another. The next chapter examines more closely how commerce in Siberia was practiced.

---

158. For works that insightfully analyze eighteenth-century Russian imperial ideologies see Slezkine, "Naturalists v. Nations"; Sunderland, *Taming the Wild Field*; Jones, "A 'Havoc Made among Them.'"

CHAPTER 4

Spaces of Exchange: Seen and Unseen

"Torgui pravdoiu, bol'she barysha budet." (Trade honestly,
and you'll be richer.)

—Russian saying

"Ne solgat', tak i ne prodat'." (If you don't lie, you won't
sell.)

—Russian saying

The previous chapter described the establish-
ment of Russian military power and communities in Siberia. It explained the
institutional regime and laws under which merchants operated. This chapter seeks to convey a sense of the world that merchants in Siberia experienced by visiting not only the marketplace, where many more people besides
merchants plied their wares, but also by considering the spaces merchants
inhabited—such as the pubs, guesthouses, bathhouses, and roadside checkpoints of Siberia. No less, this chapter considers the unseen aspects that were
germane to merchant life in Siberia. Despite the efforts of the Russian state
to channel all trade to the official customs posts, that goal was never achieved.
Finally, inasmuch as formal commercial transactions were not the sum of
meaningful exchange, this discussion incorporates informal channels of influence and favor that became institutionalized in the commercial landscape of
early modern Siberia. Drawing on fragmented yet revealing archival evidence, this chapter depicts exchanges that took place beyond the state's gaze.

The Commercial World of Early Modern Siberia

Goods flowed back and forth across the forests and steppes of Siberia by
various means: wagon, cart, sledge, dog sled, skis, horse, camel, boat. Activity ebbed and flowed with the seasons. The winter, despite the dangers that

extreme cold imparted, was the prime season for transport across Siberia. Sleds pulled by dogs or pushed by human strength carried goods across frozen rivers or icy ground with much less friction than wheels on a ruddy road. The sixteenth-century traveler Anthony Jenkinson explained: "In the Winter time, the people travel with sleds . . . the way being hard, and smooth with snow: the waters and rivers are all frozen, and one horse with a sled, will draw a man upon it 400 miles, in three daies; but in the summer time the way is deepe with mire and travelling is very ill. [sic]"[1] In central Moscow, logs were laid down to combat what Olearius called, in the autumn and rainy weather, "a sea of mud," but such measures were not taken throughout the countryside.[2] Indeed, in the relatively milder weather of spring and fall, mud brought overland travel to a near standstill. Russians had a name for mud season—rasputitsa. Irbit, one of western Siberia's busiest fairs, took place in January, the dead of winter.

On the open steppe, where one-way travel to China could occupy a year or more, a different calendar prevailed. And yet so many merchants were engaged in this trade in the seventeenth century that roughly twice a year, especially in the autumn, major caravans would arrive off the open steppe. Usually they went to Tobol'sk, where many merchants who had banded together for the sake of long-distance travel registered their goods as discrete individuals and got down to the business of selling and buying. The wares of these large caravans fueled the winter trade of Siberia. Many fabrics remained in Siberia to clothe the resident population, while a significant share was reexported to central Russia and beyond. Merchants from Russian towns, especially Sol'vychegodsk, Velikii Ustiug, and Lal'sk, came to Siberia once winter conditions made sledge travel convenient to trade. They brought with them Russian and European goods they had bought from local craftsmen and at the Arkhangel'sk fair in the autumn. Men involved in trapping remained in Siberia two to three years, but those who bought their furs at Siberian markets generally operated on an annual cycle. Whether merchants departed Siberia before or after the spring, mud season stymied travel (even traveling by river, portages were unavoidable), and the calendar dictated their return for the Arkhangel'sk fair in late summer.[3] Markets such as Kholmogory and Velikii Ustiug became important intermediate points for furs destined for domestic and international sale, as merchants learned that if they waited for the season's haul to arrive to Arkhangel'sk or Moscow, they

1. Morgan and Coote, Early Voyages and Travels to Russia and Persia, 1: 40.
2. Olearius, Travels of Olearius, 112.
3. Makarov, "Volostnye torzhki v Sol'vychegodskom uezde," 203–4.

would pay top dollar. In 1614 Nikita Stroganov complained, "You can't get your hands on any sable, not good, not bad . . . and those merchants who had spring sables all went to Kholmogory and traded them for German goods."[4]

The distances that Russian and Eurasian entrepreneurial operations covered were massive. Though the landscape might not betray it, Eurasian space was crisscrossed with numerous trade routes that Russian expansion intensified. Tobol'sk may have been remote to London or Amsterdam, but Remezov was not necessarily delusional putting it at the center of his map because by the reign of Aleksei Mikhailovich, Tobol'sk was not at all remote to Eurasian commerce.[5] Merchants arrived at Tobol'sk, the center of Siberian trade, from numerous markets. Despite the state's intentions that all traffic pass through Verkhotur'e, various routes led "from Rus' to Sibir'."[6] The Kazan governor in 1615 was directed to allow Bukharan merchants to return to Central Asia "by any route they please."[7] Probably a dozen routes led from Siberia to Central Asia and China.[8] From Astrakhan, merchants could travel up the Volga to Kazan and then move east, but probably more often merchants followed the Tobol' River hundreds of kilometers southwest toward its source and then traveled across the steppe through the Kalmyk Diurbet's territory (*ulus*) and the city of Iurgench across the Yaik (later Ural) River and finally reached Astrakhan. Nikolai Gavrilovich Spafarii-Milescu, an ambassador who traveled to China in Russian service in 1674, reported that there were so many variations on this route that it was impossible to describe them all.[9] Thus, from the Urals to the Yaik River, merchants might travel to the oasis towns of Inner Asia along various routes. The Ishim River, which fed into the Irtysh about equidistant between Tara and Tobol'sk, presented another route to Central Asia. This route followed the Ishim to its source in the steppe—near Astana, the capital of modern Kazakhstan—and then proceeded south through the steppe of the Kazakh horde to Bukhara.[10] This route was difficult. Ill-suited for boat travel, wagons also had a very difficult time traversing the terrain along the river, but it was used because there was food along the way for animals and it was relatively safer. But the more common Siberian route traveled by Russians and Central Asians was along

4. Bakhrushin, "Russkoe prodvizhenie za Ural," in NT, 3: 141.
5. Remezov, *Khorograficheskaia kniga*, f. 8v.; Remezov Chronicle, plate 1, in Armstrong, *Yermak's Campaign in Siberia*, 88.
6. Miller, *Opisanie o torgakh Sibirskikh*, 5–10.
7. MUITTSSR, no. 18, 112–13.
8. Agzamova, *Sredneaziatskie tsentry torgovli i puti*.
9. Spafarii, *Puteshestvie cherez Sibir'*, 18.
10. Ibid.

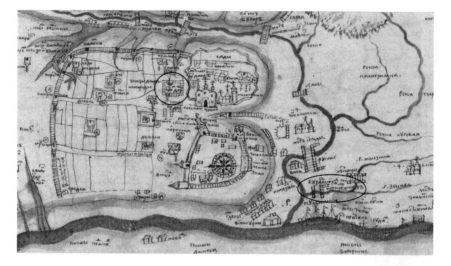

FIGURE 4.1   Map of Tobol'sk around the turn of the seventeenth to eighteenth century. The market-place in the upper town near the center of the map is circled. Bukharans tended to live in the lower town and the hinterlands. The oval in the lower right-hand section indicates the Bukharan trading rows and new converts' quarters.
Source: Leo Bagrow Collection, Remezov, *Khorograficheskaia kniga*, l. 161. MS 72 (6). Courtesy Houghton Library, Harvard University.

the length of the Irtysh River. In the second half of the seventeenth century as Russians began to trade directly with China (and perhaps as the steppe became more insecure), trade routes followed the line of Russian fortress construction, moving east via the Ob and Ket Rivers through Nerchinsk and later Kiakhta. In general, trade flows shifted eastward, "from Turkistan to Yamysh, and from Yamysh to Selenginsk and Nerchinsk," wrote Vilkov.[11] Indeed, the French Jesuit Phillipe Avril recommended the Siberian route via Nerchinsk as the best way to reach the Orient.[12]

Modernity swallowed steppe nomads. Scholars have depicted Eurasian empire building as a process whereby smaller powers were eliminated until great powers abutted each other and borderlands became borders.[13] With such a narrative it is easy to lose sight of the integral roles nomads played on the steppe. Not only did nomads participate in trade but they could also make or break trade by controlling who traversed the steppe.[14] One of

---

11. Vilkov, *Remeslo i torgovlia*, 210–11.

12. Avril, *Travels Into divers Parts of Europe and Asia*, 143–46.

13. Rieber, "Comparative Ecology of Complex frontiers," 179. William McNeill, *Europe's Steppe Frontier*, does not discuss nomads in the geopolitics of the Eurasian steppe.

14. Ziiaev, *Ekonomicheskie sviazi Srednei Azii*. On nomad participation in Eurasian horse trade see Khazeni, "Through an Ocean of Sand," 133–58.

the ways in which the Russian state tried to promote commerce in Siberia was by maintaining amicable relations with the Kalmyk and Kazakh hordes who could stymie the flow of goods on the ground. This problem was also negotiated via private means. Caravans moving across the steppe paid protection fees to nomadic escorts for safe passage across the steppe. A caravan that chose to "roll the dice" could be all but assured of more expensive losses to nomads no doubt affiliated with the refused escorts; it was as true in the eighteenth century as it had been in the seventeenth.[15]

Places of Trade: The Marketplace

Quite quickly an economic infrastructure—however inadequate and rough—grew up across Siberia. Not long after establishing fortified outposts, the state began constructing marketplaces (*gostinye dvory*). The marketplace was a compound that consisted of several structures often erected around an open space. The open space was lined with market stalls, warehouses, and, in bigger towns, stables and a guesthouse where transit merchants lodged. The centerpiece of the marketplace was the customs house, where the customs head (*tamozh-naia golova*), his assistant sworn men (*tseloval'niki*), and a secretary (*tamozhnaia pod'iach*) sat. In the customs house shipments were registered and inspected, taxes were levied, and documentation issued. Depending on the season or level of commercial activity, the customs house might operate several days a week or just a few days a month. For example, the Verkhotur'e customs post recorded 14 entries by ten individuals for the typically slow summer month of July 1704, but registered 173 entries for December of that same year.[16]

Shops or market stalls (*lavki*) were another central feature of the marketplace. The word *lavki* means benches, which describes where much premodern commerce took place. The early Medicis, famous Renaissance bankers, operated sitting at benches behind tables in the streets of Florence; the word "bank" derives from the Italian word for bench, *banco*. But by the seventeenth century in Siberia, these shops could be closed and locked with a key. At least in theory. At the Verkhotur'e marketplace in 1653 fire had badly damaged the roofs of two shops, but they remained occupied by merchants trading their wares.[17] Most shops were state owned and rented out, others

---

15. Instructions to the Russian ambassador Pazukhin in 1669 directed him not to cross the steppe from Astrakhan to Bukhara without a Kalmyk escort because they would be robbed. RIB 15: 21. Malikov, "Formation of a Borderland Culture," 41, 280–90.

16. RGADA, f. 214, op. 1, kn. 1398, ll. 224–93 (Verkhotur'e customs book, 1704–1705).

17. SPbII RAN, f. 28, op. 1, d. 555a, l. 1 (1653).

were privately owned. The same goes for warehouses. Indeed, Muscovite law insisted that merchants store their goods in warehouses, not private homes.[18] While it tried to impose the same on Siberia, many commercial goods ended up stored in church basements. In busy towns the state-constructed stalls could not meet demand and rows of privately constructed stalls extended the market space. As towns became busier and bigger, marketplaces extended beyond the market square into adjacent lanes.[19] In Tobol'sk, space was at such a premium that some striving entrepreneurs built shops atop graves.[20] The state generally tolerated such actions as long as it collected property tax (*obrok*) on the private constructions.[21] In bigger towns such as Tobol'sk, Tiumen', and Tara, the marketplace was built outside of the central fortification, but in smaller towns (and Verkhotur'e, originally) the marketplace was built within the fortress walls.[22] The Pelym market in the 1620s, for example, consisted of three state shops inside the fortress. The Moscow merchant Kondratii Stefanov Podoshevnikov regularly rented a stall for a portion of the year there at a weekly rate of 4 dengi.[23]

Devastating fires destroyed the wooden marketplaces of Siberian towns many times over. The Tobol'sk marketplace burned ten times during the seventeenth century.[24] It was not until the first decade of the eighteenth century that the first stone marketplaces were built, in Verkhotur'e and Tobol'sk. A church stood on the marketplace square in Tobol'sk. When it was destroyed by fire, merchants pooled the necessary funds to rebuild it.[25] The Petrine decree to channel stone to the construction of St. Petersburg in 1714, however, halted stone construction in Siberia and the rest of the empire.[26] There were some exceptions: a stone marketplace was built in Moscow. The Urals town of Ekaterinburg, established in 1723 and named in honor of Peter's second wife, was another exception.

Shops were owned or rented by people from a variety of ranks: out-of-town merchants, townsmen (local merchants and artisans), and other government servicemen including soldiers, Cossacks, and state porters (*iamskie*

18. PSZ, vol. 3, no. 873, 320 (1681, Instructions to Moscow Customs).
19. GBUTO GATO, f. 47, op. 1, d. 262 (1704).
20. Vilkov, "Torgovye pomeshcheniia Tobol'ska v XVII v.," 93; Vilkov, "O stroitel'stvo Tobol'ska," 74–78; GUTO GAT, f. 156, op. 1, d. 240, ll. 1–20.
21. RGADA, f. 1111, op. 1, d. 312, pt. 3, l. unknown (1688).
22. Ogloblin, *Obozrenie*, 1: 297; Vilkov, "Torgovye pomeshcheniia gorodov Sibiri," 9.
23. Ogloblin, *Obozrenie*, 1: 295.
24. Vilkov, "Torgovye pomeshcheniia Tobol'ska v XVII veka," 93.
25. GUTO GAT, f. 156, op. 1, d. 240, 20 ll. (1747).
26. Balandin, "Nachal'no russkogo kamennogo stroitel'stva v Sibir'," in Vilkov, *Sibirkie goroda*, 189.

okhotniki).[27] In Tiumen′ Cossacks sometimes owned the majority of shops.[28] In 1704 a Kalmyk man owned two shops in Tiumen′; he conducted his own trade in one and rented out the other.[29] In that same year the widow of a Tiumen′ Cossack, along with her daughters, sold their warehouse space.[30]

The Tobol′sk marketplace and customs office was located on top of the hill just outside the west wall of the fortress.[31] Despite their commercial importance, Bukharans did not own or rent shops in the official marketplace for most of the seventeenth century. This is because they had shops in the lower town, at the foot of the hill on which the fortress stood, a location that was closer to the Bukharan neighborhood and afforded much easier access to the river dock. True to form, if unconventional for early modern regimes, the state refrained from placing any restrictions on their commerce initially and for decades seems to have ignored trade in the lower town. According to its modus operandi, only once habits were in place did the state begin to impose restrictions and taxation.

By many accounts the center of trade life was in the lower town. One European exile explained that Tobol′sk Bukharans did sell imported Chinese goods in Tobol′sk's upper town marketplace. However, if they could not fetch their desired price there, they would bring the goods back to their homes in the lower town where, without walls and the strict regulation of the marketplace, they could fetch a better price.[32] A complaint from a Tobol′sk resident in 1650 may have been just the pretext to motivate the state to regulate Bukharan trade more closely. The petitioner, a frustrated competitor who paid taxes and saw fewer profits, complained that "all the real trading is done below." When Moscow insisted on trade in officially sanctioned locations, however, Tobol′sk Bukharans pushed back. They filed a petition defending trade in the lower town on practical grounds: when it rained, the mud made the steep path up the hill impassable, and when icy, it was always treacherous. The argument persuaded Moscow. Rather than police the prohibition of trade in the lower town, in 1671 Moscow ordered the construction of a second marketplace and customs post in the lower town.[33]

27. GBUTO GATO, f. 47, op. 1, d. 378, l. 1 (1658), d. 872 (1704).

28. GBUTO GATO, f. 47, op. 1, d. 3843, ll. 1–4.

29. GBUTO GATO, f. 47, op. 1, d. 262, ll. 3v–4.

30. GBUTO GATO, f. 29, op. 1, d. 39, l. 7 (1704).

31. Kabo, *Goroda zapadnoi Sibiri*, 53.

32. Account from 1666 with unknown author, in Alekseev, *Sibir′ v izvestiiakh zapadno-evropeiskikh puteshestvennikov*, 325–72, 352. This account is quoted in Burton, *Bukharans*, 515.

33. Vilkov, "Torgovye pomeshcheniia Tobol′ska v XVII veka," 93.

Table 4.1   Growth in Siberian trading venues: Number of shops and partial shops (*lavki i polki*)

TOWN	CA. 1625	MID-17C	1674	CA. 1700	1790s
Tiumen'	24[1]; 13[2]	—	—	24[3]; 40[4]; 103[5]	171[6]
Tobol'sk	29[7]	81[8]	264[9]	67[10]	309[11]

[1] Vilkov, "Torgovye pomeshcheniia gorodov Sibiri v XVII v.," 9.
[2] Kurilov, "Uchastie sluzhilykh liudei v stanovlenii g. Tiumeni kak torgovo-promyshlennogo tsentra v XVII v.," 77.
[3] Vilkov, "Torgovye pomeshcheniia gorodov Sibiri v XVII v.," 10 (1695).
[4] "Private lavki," writes Vilkov, "Tobol'sk—tsentr tamozhennye sluzhby Sibiri XVII v.," 84.
[5] Kabo, *Goroda zapadnoi Sibiri*, 78.
[6] Razgon, *Sibirskoe kupechestvo*, 151–52.
[7] Vilkov, "Torgovye pomeshcheniia gorodov Sibiri v XVII v.," 10.
[8] Vilkov, "Torgovye pomeshcheniia gorodov Sibiri v XVII v.," 11 (1640).
[9] Vilkov, "Torgovye pomeshcheniia Tobol'ska XVII," 95. V. A. Kovrigina and L. M. Marasinova, "Torgovlia, put i sredstva peredvizheniia," *Ocherki russkoi kul'tury XVII veka*, part 4, ed. A. M. Sakharov (Moscow, 1979), 127.
[10] Vilkov, "Torgovye pomeshcheniia gorodov Sibiri v XVII v.," 10 (1708).
[11] Razgon, *Sibirskoe kupechestvo*, 151–52.

The activist state took upon itself the construction of the marketplace, but with its minimal resources, projects easily fell short of full execution. In 1669, Sila Sadilov, the recently arrived customs head of Verkhotur'e, petitioned Moscow with concerns about the state of the marketplace. Construction had languished incomplete for years. On top of that, a fire ten years prior had destroyed some of the shops; they had not yet been restored, leaving merchants no place to sell their wares. Instead, they were renting shops in the local communes (*mir*), depriving the state of valuable rent revenue. Sadilov, a merchant from Ustiug who had been recruited into the job of customs head—having been discovered in an attempt to slip 44 rubles' worth of goods past Tiumen' customs seventeen years before did not disqualify him for the job[34]—had good reason to be concerned. He would be held responsible for diminished revenue on his watch, and perhaps even made to pay deficits from his own pocket, as in the case of his predecessor.[35] Sadilov implored the tsar to order the completed construction of the Verkhotur'e marketplace.[36]

Everyday Trade

The market was not only a place for trade in goods. A rare description of the Sol'vychegodsk market in the eighteenth century depicts the many tertiary functions of the market, forecasting the observations Braudel made of market

34. RGADA. f. 214, kn. 301, l. 37.
35. SPbII RAN, f. 28, op. 1, d. 898, ll. 1–3 (1660); PSZ, vol. 2, no. 679.
36. RGADA, f. 1111, op. 1, d. 150, pt. 3, ll. 430–32 (1669).

fairs in Western Europe.[37] The market was a hiring forum and social event. People hired workers to help with the harvest or haul cumbersome loads. They came in search of marriage prospects as well—and sometimes market fairs finished in weddings.[38] Fairs developed in Siberia at Irbit in January and Lake Yamysh in August. In established Siberian towns, however, the marketplace operated year round.

At the market, merchants brushed shoulders with soldiers who traded on the side; artisans such as butchers, blacksmiths, cobblers, candle-makers, and millers whose particular niches brought them to the market; peasants selling grain, land, or livestock; and occasional natives. Not only was the market scene not exclusively a merchant scene but these other market participants contributed significantly: it has been widely suggested that Russian soldiers dominated Siberian trade. Kabo called soldiers the "economic core" of Siberian town life and Vilkov found that they imported to Tiumen' three times as many Russian goods as merchants did in the middle of the seventeenth century.[39] Without assessing the veracity of that claim, the point to appreciate is that much of the trade conducted at Siberian customs posts was indeed quite small scale.[40] Pages upon pages of customs book entries record a local butcher buying one goat, someone selling one sable, a peasant selling a sack of grain or salt, a monk buying a few candles and some soap, or a Cossack selling a horse.[41]

In October 1662 Tiumen' tax revenue on fish and livestock, two important economic sectors, was 19 rubles and change.[42] Livestock (cows, goats, horses, occasionally camels) was an important part of the regional economy and in this Kalmyks played a key role, which added another reason for Russia to maintain amicable relations with them. As in many things, Bukharans served as intermediaries in the livestock trade as well. With almost two hundred fast days in the Orthodox calendar in which meat and dairy were prohibited, fish was a valuable source of protein, although early modern Russians did not eat ocean fish until Peter I encouraged the practice. Freshwater fish

37. Braudel, *Wheels of Commerce*, 2: 30.

38. Vvedenskii, *Dom Stroganovykh*, 218.

39. Kurilov, "Uchastie sluzhilykh liudei v stanovlenii g. Tiumeni," 76–86; Nikitin, "Torgi i promysly sluzhilykh liudei," 7–20; Kabo, *Goroda zapadnoi Sibiri*, 57.

40. Such an observation is consonant with much Soviet scholarship, which was at pains to privilege lower social ranks. See Shunkov, "Trudy S. V. Bakhrushina po istorii Sibiri," in NT, vol. 3: 9; Vilkov, "Tranzit'russkykh'tovarov cherez Tobol'sk," 113–26; Vilkov, *Ocherki sotsial'no-ekonomicheskogo razvitiia Sibiri*, 3–10.

41. Candles: GUTO GAT, f. 166, op. 1, d. 118, ll. 1–8 (1740s); Butcher: SPbII RAN, f. 187, op. 2, ex. 17, l. 25 (1658).

42. To be exact: 19 rubles, 13 altyn, 2 grivna. GBUTO GATO, f. 29, op. 1, d. 381, l. 28. A house or a very fine horse sold for about 5 rubles in seventeenth-century Siberia.

from Siberian rivers comprised a substantial portion of local diets and local trade. Foreign travelers complained about the odor of salted and pickled fish that wafted far beyond the rows of shops in Russian markets.[43] In Siberia fishing rights were leased to individuals of various ranks, including townsmen, tribute Tatars, and Cossacks alike.[44]

Slavery was a normal part of Siberian life—an unquestioned fate for some, a survival strategy for destitute others, and an enduring threat for natives and Russians in the borderlands. Slave raiding fed the Kalmyk economy. They would take prisoners in attacks on Russian and Tatar settlements. These victims could end up being sold in distant slave markets as far as the Ottoman Empire or sometimes Kalmyks would sell them directly back to the Russian Empire, which also suited Kalmyk political economy. Ransoming captured victims went far back in the Russian tradition, a practice mentioned in the Stoglav Council of the 1550s. Indeed, Russia even developed ransom commissions for this purpose. In 1678 one such commission ransomed seventy-seven Siberians who had been enslaved and brought to Central Asia.[45] The kidnapped included people from all ranks—peasants, soldiers, their wives and children, townspeople, religious Russian Orthodox and Tatars alike were victims of slave raiding. The fate of a lowly traded slave sometimes reflected major geopolitical upheavals. Between 1644 and 1646, Bukharan merchants, who were important middlemen in the slave trade, sold Chinese men and women in Tobol'sk.[46] This appearance of Chinese individuals in western Siberia was, to my knowledge, unprecedented. These individuals were probably victims of the war that brought the Manchu (Qing) dynasty to power. Banner (Eastern) Mongols assisted the Manchus to overthrow the Ming in 1644. These Chinese had likely been booty that the Mongols sold to Bukharan merchants, who transported them westward to Siberia.[47] Slaves were the wares those Bukharans were trading. On some occasions, however, Bukharan merchants crossing Eurasia would buy enslaved Russians and bring them to Russia, where they asked the state to reimburse them for their trouble.[48]

---

43. Goldstein, "Gastronomic Reforms under Peter the Great," 485.

44. For an example of sixty-one servitors and Cossacks cooperating to move over 200 rubles worth of fish (*osetrov, chanabyshev, i sterliadei*), see RGADA, f. 214, kn. 892, ll. 107v.–109.

45. MIUTTSSR, Appendix, Table 7. "1678. Russian captives and conditions by which they became captives . . ." Some slaves had been set free by their Bukharan owners; see: http://kungrad.com/history/doc/torg/17/.

46. MIUTTSSR, pt. 1, 380–85, Appendix, Table 1 of section 2 "Tara Customs. Import of Slaves, 1644–46."

47. I thank George Zhijan Qaio for raising this possibility to me.

48. Miller, IS, vol. 3, no. 139, 355.

The state formally prohibited the slave trade from the first half of the seventeenth century but essentially ignored its own decrees; slavery existed in Siberia well into the nineteenth century.[49] The sale of slaves is regularly recorded in the customs records of the seventeenth century, charted openly in historical documents.[50] Twenty-six individuals in 1671–72 declared to Tobol'sk customs officials slaves (*iasyry*) that they had bought not in any formal market square but along the route from Lake Yamysh.[51] Meanwhile, the state formally prohibited slave trading and simultaneously collected taxes on such transactions. In 1698 a merchant even formally protested the confiscation of his Mongol "boy."[52] In the middle of the eighteenth century slavery remained a normal institution, as documents regarding the conversion of household slaves attest.[53] In the late eighteenth century merchants still held slaves.[54] In the nineteenth century one state document condoned enslavement as a source for wives.[55]

These spheres of local petty trade and multiyear long-distance caravans shared the same spaces. Although they seemed to operate discretely, they intersected in important ways. Besides fur, livestock from the steppes went into leather manufacture, an important Russian export. Siberian Bukharans came to deftly traverse the spheres of both local and long-distance trade.

The Merchant's Life

For long-distance merchants, business was a prolonged affair whose cycles extended beyond seasons or even years. When they arrived at the customs post, caravans were inscribed into the Russian record. After all goods and people were registered and due taxes paid—the negotiations that pertained therein were not inscribed in the record—the trading began. Typically a merchant rented a trading stall for some amount of time. Some merchants owned their own trading stalls and some rented for a good portion of the year.

49. Semenova, *Istoriia predprinimatel'stva v Rossii*, 121.

50. Some examples in chronological order: RGADA, f. 214, stb. 81, ll. 39–45 (1633–35); Vilkov, *Remeslo i torgovlia*, 178 (1647/48); RGADA, f. 214, stb. 462, ll. 175–84 (1650s); GBUTO GATO, f. 47, op. 1, d. 381, ll. 95v, 98, 126 (1662/23); GBUTO GATO, f. 187, op. 1, d. 387 (1672); TKSG, 4:4, 36, 40, ff. (1672/3); GBUTO GATO, f. 187, op. 2, d. 52, l. 3 (1676); TKSG, vol. 2, 71, 74 (1697/98); RGADA, f. 1111, op. 2, d. 611, l. 174 (1699); Ogloblin, "Bytovye cherty nachala XVIII veka," 219.

51. MIUTTSSR, fig. 6, http://kungrad.com/history/doc/torg/17/. NB: *iasyr*, forced slave, is a different category than *kholop*, indentured slave.

52. Ogloblin, *Obozrenie*, 1: 172.

53. GUTO GAT, f. 156, op. 3, dd. 1987, 2092, 2241 (1780–83).

54. GBUTO GATO, f. 47, op. 1, d. 2219, ll. 1–6 (1782).

55. Forsyth, *A History of the Peoples of Siberia*, 114.

People without sufficient stock to justify rental of an entire shop could rent a portion of one, a "shelf" (*polka*). When the market was closed, a merchant would lock up his stall with a key, which could hang next to his purse on his waist belt, and leave the marketplace.[56] Although out-of-town merchants did not fund construction of churches in western Siberia, they may have visited and paid alms at one of several local churches. One stood on the market square in Tobol'sk. More evidence survives of transit merchants making their way to the local *kabak*, or pub.

The state-owned pub (*kabak*) was an important revenue source for the state and a central feature of every Siberian town and of many merchants' habits. Although high and low alike engaged in brewing spirits for domestic use, the state held a monopoly on selling them. Enforcement of this rule gives the impression of a state herding cats. Cases like the incident in which the Tiumen' townsman Andrew Reshetnikov was dragged to the governor's house, accused of possessing undeclared beer, and insisted that his wife had brewed it for their own household, are hardly rare.[57] In the spring of 1674 Vasilii Ovechkin, an out-of-town merchant, reported the following to the Tiumen' governor. He had been drinking *brag'*—Vasilii stressed that he had not paid anything for it—at the house of the infantry musketeer Silvestr Andreev. When he left and went out on the street, he was approached by the infantry musketeer Mikita Elizarov. Unmounted musketeers (*strel'tsy*) held policing functions in Siberian towns. Elizarov, according to Ovechkin, insisted that he pay him. When Vasilii refused, Elizarov assaulted him and took 2 rubles and his purse, which was hanging from his belt with his trading-stall key. Elizarov then arrested him and took him to the jail, all without justification.[58] Save for one detail, it seems that Elizarov believed Vasilii had bought alcohol illegally and he was doing his state duty in arresting him. But the musketeer's demand for money suggests the possibility that he was trying to shake down Vasilii and unjustly employed his authority and access to state resources—the keys to the jail—to advance his own interests.

Time at the pub consisted in decompression, perhaps some reconnaissance, and sharing information with other traders. It would not have involved eating unless the merchant brought his own victuals, for food was not sold in state pubs.[59] As is often the case where hard spirits are involved, situations could become volatile, and the fights, assaults, and even murders that were

---

56. GBUTO GATO, f. 47, op. 1, d. 220, l. 1.

57. GBUTO GATO, f. 47, op. 1, d. 1638, l. 2 (1700–1710), "*s pud radi svoi stvennikov*."

58. GBUTO GATO, f. 47, op. 1, d. 220, l. 1 (April 24, 1674).

59. Presentation by curator at Vodka Museum, St. Petersburg, September 2004.

captured in the historical record provide a dim glimpse of the pub as a back-drop of daily life. Violent transgressions do not provide the only glimpse: merchant bosses back in Moscow worried lest alcohol derail their agents' mission. The elite merchant Gavril Nikitin exhorted his agents in the field to keep an eye on one colleague with a reputation: "Don't let him drink!"[60]

In one recorded case an out-of-town merchant was involved in an incident of sexual assault. In November 1700, the height of the caravan season, a woman reported that she had been raped. On the night of November 19, 1700, Pelegeia Gavrilova was questioned by the Tiumen' governor Osip Iakovlevich Tukhachevskii and the secretary Timofei Posnikov. She reported that two days earlier, on November 17, in the seventh hour of the day, merchants came to her as if they wanted ale, but instead forced her into sexual sins.[61] The accused were promptly rounded up and questioned. The merchants claimed innocence. When questioned, the merchant Vasilii Ivanov syn Salamatov told the investigators that he had been somewhere else on November 17, that he had not gone to the window of Pelegeia Gavrilova and had not engaged in any sexual sin with her. He said that on November 18, the next day, he was walking on the street past Pelegeia's house when he was grabbed by the hair and dragged by force into Pelegeia's house and he, Vaska, had not gone to Pelegeia's house for any sexual sin.[62] Strikingly, Salamatov's testimony does not insist that no "sexual sin" occurred; rather, that he had not gone there with that intention. Salamatov was released from jail when some merchant colleagues posted bail for him. The outcome of the case is unknown.

Every Siberian town had a bathing house (*banya*). The state built and ran them, assigning servitors or peasants to do maintenance and keep them supplied with wood.[63] In 1657 soldiers went from the mission of transporting salt from Lake Yamysh to the task of moving two thousand rocks from Verkhotur'e to Tobol'sk for construction of a bathhouse.[64] Many privately owned bathing houses were likewise spread throughout the towns and countryside.[65] As part of fire prevention efforts, the state forbade the firing up of any bathing houses other than the trading bathhouse during summer months.[66] It is interesting to wonder how cleanliness habits, an obligatory

60. Monahan, "Gavril Romanovich Nikitin," 53.

61. GBUTO GATO, f. 47, op. 1, d. 318, l. 1. Pelegeia is described as a *privodnaia zhena*. The seventh hour in November was probably late afternoon, given the Russian manner of counting the hours from sunrise onward.

62. GBUTO GATO, f. 187, op. 1, d. 1126, l.1.

63. Ogloblin, *Obozrenie*, 1: 297 (Tara).

64. RGADA, f. 1111, op. 1, d. 30, ll. 1–4 (1657).

65. GBUTO GATO, f. 47, op. 1, d. 264, l. 1 (no date), d. 838, ll. 5–21 (1704).

66. PSZ, vol. 3, no. 1594.29, 372 (1697 *Nakaz* to Tobol'sk).

category in ethnographies of the "other," manifested in the bathhouses of Siberia, the borderlands of those cultural binaries, East and West. If Peter was right about Russia's Western heritage—that Russia was European—then the Slavs shared in a quite grubby heritage. After all, the fastidiousness of the early modern Dutch was an innovation medieval Christendom had not known.[67] Catherine of Sienna, sainted for her extraordinary holiness, was less extraordinary among Latin Christians for her refusal to bathe. Yet despite the fact that bathing *was* a tradition among Russians—the earliest chronicle describes Russians' bathhouse traditions—travel writers did not celebrate Russians for their cleanliness. The tenth-century Arab traveler Ibn Fadlan called the Rus' the "dirtiest creatures of God," a judgment repeated by several early modern travelers.[68] Early modern Europeans seemed to think, however, that Bukharans were as clean as Russians were dirty, consistently noting their cleanliness with observations consistent with other early modern characterizations of Middle Easterners and Central Asians.[69] Yet hygiene tropes collided in the Persian Shah Suleiman I's remark that Muscovites were the "Yusbecs [Uzbegs] of the Francs."[70] A bathing house, or *banya*, stood in Tobol'sk's lower town in a space inhabited by both Bukharans and Russians;[71] it is unknown if Bukharans shared the bathing house with Russians.

Hazards were a far less sanguine part of the job, and sometimes merchants trading across the continent met their deaths. In rare but frightening incidents whole parties of traveling merchants were murdered.[72] Sometimes they made their own trouble: Efim Merkurev Mezen, an agent of the Merchant Hundred merchant Vasilii Fedotov Gusel'nikov, was killed in a retaliatory attack by the Chuvansk they had raided in 1653.[73] More often, illness or accident could take merchants in the field. In 1688 a merchant from Ustiug

67. Schama, *Embarrassment of Riches*.

68. Frye, *Ibn Fadlan's Journey to Russia*, 64–65.

69. Bukharans are described as the cleanest Muslims in Frye, *History of Bukhara*, 22.

70. That is, if one elides categories of Uzbegs with Bukharans. Sir John Chardin, *Travels in Persia, 1673–1677*, 89. One seventeenth-century Italian traveler would have agreed, writing of the "uncleanly" Uzbegs: "he is most lovely who is most greasy." Levi, *India Diaspora in Central Asia*, 146. Similarly, the fifteenth-century Venetian traveler Contarini found Persian Muslims to be quite clean, as compared with many filthy Christians in eastern Europe. See Barbaro and Contarini, *Travels to Tana and Persia*, 131. For more on tropes among early modern travelers see Wolff, *Inventing Eastern Europe*.

71. See fig. 4.1, to the left of the oval.

72. Examples of merchants murdered: Lipinskii, "Rospis' komu imianem i za kakuiu vinu . . . ," 29 (1642); Burton, *Bukharans*, 510; Ogloblin, *Obozrenie*, 2: 22–23, 37 (1625); Miller IS, vol. 1, no. 4, 331 (1572).

73. DAI, vol. 4, no. 7, 20, repr. in Dmytryshyn, Crownhart-Vaughan, and Vaughan, *Russia's Conquest of Siberia*, no. 87, 322.

Velikii drowned in the Tura River. The Verkhotur'e officials issued travel documents for the deceased's father and brother to come to Verkhotur'e to claim his effects.[74] At the time the Verkhotur'e customs office was headed by a man from a long line of merchants from Velikii Ustiug; one wonders if the families knew each other.[75] When one Tiumen' townsman did not return from a trading trip, his wife was left to claim his effects and put their affairs in order.[76]

Gavril Romanovich Nikitin was an elite Russian merchant who trail-blazed direct trade with China in the 1670s. In 1695 his agent Timofei Bozhedomov died not far from Nerchinsk on a trading trip to China. But Nikitin's fortunes turned and he himself died in the intervening years between when the caravan departed and returned to Moscow. Rather than bereaved family members, creditors from Moscow met Bozhedomov's colleagues returning with his effects. Another trusted agent of Nikitin's, Vasilii Serebrianikov, had died—"did not rise," as Nikitin's letter phrased it—en route to Yakutsk in December 1694.[77] Upon his death, Serebrianikov's assistant Aleshka Nikitin was put in charge of his belongings, which included a metal-plated purse with money, documents, and icons.[78] Other effects included a Mongolian saddle and a suitcase containing a silver fur coat, a dark-green homespun coat, a fancy damask caftan (robe) with silver buttons, a short caftan, four red cotton shirts, a pair of red damask pants, two pairs of Moroccan boots (one green, one black), two pistols, some knives, and a pound of tea.[79]

Interestingly, the custodian of these effects, Aleshka Nikitin, was not Russian. He was a Mongol whom Serebrianikov had purchased as a slave when he was a little boy. He was given a Russian name, Aleshka, and his owner's boss's last name, Nikitin, when he was baptized into Orthodoxy, such that his Russian-sounding name alone would give no clue of his origins. The Eurasian steppes and forests were not densely populated, but they were diverse in ways the historical record does not always capture. In western Siberia, mosques punctuated the landscape along with Orthodox churches, though their characteristic onion domes did not share the skyline with Islamic minarets because

---

74. RGADA, f. 1111, op. 1, d. 15, l. 93 (1688).

75. RGADA, f. 214, stb. 134, l. 424; Golikova, PKK, 258, 304; Merzon and Tikhonov, *Rynok Ustiuga Velikoga*, 136; Solov'eva and Volodikhin, *Sostav privilegirovannogo kupechestva Rossii*, 36.

76. GBUTO GATO, f. 29, op. 1, d. 207, 4 ll. (Tiumen' *posad* man Vasilii Istomin, 1735–38).

77. Bakhrushin, "Torgi gostia Nikitina v Sibiri i Kitae," in NT, 3: pt. 1, 231, 235.

78. The wallet was an essential merchant's item, one of which was stolen from Nikitin's agent Boris Pikalev in 1698. RGADA, f. 214, stb. 1698, l. 32.

79. Bakhrushin, "Torgi gostia Nikitina v Sibiri i Kitae," 235.

Russian law forbade their construction. Meanwhile in the surroundings natives might turn to Shamans or the Dalai Lama for otherworldly intercessions.

As merchants in Siberian towns conducted their business and filled the remaining hours in the day, the state, in traditional fashion, sought to maintain order. When people accused others of selling stolen goods, an investigation ensued.[80] For example, in September 1700 a local Tatar found a provincial gentry man with his stolen horse, which he had bought at the market from a state porter (*iamshchik*).[81] In another case a clergyman accused a Cossack of stealing meat from his shop and then selling it. In this case the state sided with the defendant: he had taken the law into his own hands but had recouped the money that was duly owed him.[82] During a fire the goods of one merchant went missing and it was unclear if the goods had been skirted away in good-will or thievery.[83] Although keeping such crimes in check taxed the state's resources, obvious thefts only scratched the surface of challenges involved in successfully regulating Siberian commerce. The extent to which people from all ranks sought to circumvent state regulations—not least, government regulators—was a daunting and unsolved problem for the Russian Empire.

Beyond the State's Gaze

The Russian government wanted vibrant commerce across Siberia. Running a close second to that priority, the state wanted to capitalize on that commerce. Once it was comfortable that trade was reliably established, regulation became a higher priority. Optimizing revenue via taxation of trade meant controlling where and when trade took place. The state deployed various methods toward these ends. In the first place, the state decreed that merchants could trade only in the state marketplace. Bukharans were initially exempted from this requirement but, as discussed briefly in chapter 3, became increasingly subject to state scrutiny as the seventeenth century proceeded. For Russian merchants, trade anywhere beyond the state's gaze—in an individual's home, in the forest, along the river, on the road, in church—was prohibited. The state was especially concerned that merchants did not trade with tribute payers before they had submitted their tribute.[84]

80. GBUTO GATO, f. 47, d. 1634, ll. 1–6 (1676–80).
81. SPbII RAN, f. 187, op. 1, d. 1121, l. 4 (1700).
82. GBUTO GATO, f. 47, d. 1741, ll. 1–2 (1726).
83. SPbII RAN, f. 28, op. 1, karton 21, no. 37, ll. 1–9 (1674).
84. SPbII RAN, f. 28, op. 1, d. 197, ll. 1–2; AI, vol. 3, no. 184, 335–42 (1635); PSZ, vol. 3, no. 1594.21, 357 (1697); GBUTO GATO, f. 29, op. 1, d. 142, l. 17 (1750).

Unlike in central Russia, where markets tended to emerge at the doors of monasteries, in Siberia the state dictated state-built marketplaces as the locus of exchange. Such intentions did not eliminate churches from participating in commercial business. Church people would themselves own or rent shops.[85] Merchants would rely on local churches as warehouses for their goods.[86] Dmitry Konstantinov, a Greek merchant who traveled between China and Siberia, arranged with a priest to store his goods in the basement of a Tobol'sk church during his long absences.[87] The Dolmatov monastery on the Iset River was embroiled in an investigation about the clandestine local rhubarb trade.[88] In 1753 scandal erupted around Father Fëdor Rudakov for his too-close relations with local merchant(s) and the malodorous moose hides he allowed to be stored in the church.[89]

Second, controlling against trade in unauthorized, liminal spaces was an ongoing project for the Muscovite government.[90] The principle was not specific to Siberia: "Merchants must not buy or sell any kind of product on the road between customs posts," reads the Customs Statute of 1653.[91] In order to control and monitor movement, the state established checkpoints, required transit documentation, and sometimes even destroyed roads. Decrees, pleas, and warnings repeatedly implore provincial administrators to monitor passersby vigilantly and strictly and ensure that no one passed undetected through Siberian towns and checkpoints.[92] Nor was anyone to circumvent customs posts by stealth or alternative routes (*obezzhimi dorogami*) that the state knew smuggling merchants and escaped serfs alike used to avoid detection.[93] As part of monitoring movement, the state required travel documentation. As long as customs posts existed in Siberia, the state required documentation (*proezhaia vypis'*) to move commercial wares. It was not the person so much as the goods that the state was interested in monitoring. In time, the procedure

---

85. GBUTO GATO, f. 47, d. 1741, ll. 1–2 (1726).

86. GUTO GAT, f. 156, op. 1, d. 1267, ll. 1–12; RGADA, f. 214, stb. 935, l. 3.

87. RGADA, f. 214, stb. 935, l. 40.

88. Ogloblin, *Obozrenie*, 1: 202.

89. GUTO GAT, f. 156, op. 31, d. 1367, l. 32.

90. Document about all trading at gostinii dvor: SPbII RAN, f. 28, op. 1, d. 197 (1627). List of all traders passing through: SPbII RAN, f. 28, op. 1, d. 1140 (1665). Report of traders sneaking past customs post at night: SPbII RAN, f. 28, op. 1, d. 1582 (1669).

91. PSZ, vol. 1, 304. Vilkov, *Ocherki razvitiia torgovlia*, 142.

92. These were standard orders in instructions (*nakazy*) to Siberian governors and repeated frequently in state correspondence. Some examples: SPbII RAN, f. 28, op. 1, d. 863, l. 8 (1660); SPbII RAN, f. 28, op. 1, d. 1140, ll. 1–8 (1665); RGADA, f. 1111, op. 1, d. 30, ll. 249, 271 (1684); GUTO GAT, f. 156, op. 1, d. 349, l. 3 (1749); GBUTO GATO, f. 29, op. 1, d. 142, ll. 24–27 (1750).

93. SPbII RAN, f. 28, op. 1, karton 20, no. 32, l. 6 (1672); GUTO GAT, f. 156, op. 1, d. 349, ll. 1, 2, 3, 4v (1749).

became ad hominem; passports were required of people to travel at all. By the eighteenth century merchants applied for permission to travel for trade.[94]

Predictably, even with hard-to-traverse marshes and forests providing the state a helping hand, controlling movement and the location of trade with such a disadvantageous space-to-manpower ratio was impossible.[95] This was even tacitly acknowledged in official records; items that had been acquired "along the road" were repeatedly recorded in customs books.[96] A customs official explained in a June 1627 memo that Turinsk was not bringing in the revenue it needed to because merchants were bypassing Turinsk altogether. Additionally, misrepresentation was hurting revenue collection: traders, who were supposed to pay a toll of 6 deneg, were identifying themselves as vagrants (*guliashchye liudi*), who paid only a 4 deneg passage toll.[97]

Sandwiched between typical exhortations for vigilance and strictness in ensuring that Bukharan merchants and yurt Tatars did not bypass customs posts without paying the sovereign's taxes is a report intimating clandestine smuggling. On August 2, 1659, two tribute-paying Tatars came to the governor's house in Tiumen' and reported that they had seen a party of Bukharan merchants from Tobol'sk accompanied by ten porter-cooks driving seven hundred horses up the Iset River on their way to Kazan. The informants also reported that they were transporting 62 pud or just over 1,000 kg of rhubarb root with them by boat.[98] If the group was indeed driving seven hundred horses, one wonders if it was only vigilance that was in deficit. Further, that the informants knew the smugglers had 62 pud of rhubarb suggests additional elements to this story that have escaped the written record. In any case, if hundreds of horses could slip through the controls, just imagine how many more lone travelers with small but precious shipments such as Eastern medicines and gems must have evaded state authorities. Indeed, one trade attaché in Moscow reported that much rhubarb was smuggled out of Siberia in winter.[99] Another remarked that Bukharan merchants ran a massive contraband in precious stones from China.[100]

---

94. GBUTO GATO, f. 29, op. 1, d. 153, 2 ll. (1730), d. 2024 (1768); GUTO GAT, f. 156, op. 1, dd. 2361, l. 4 (1751), d. 2814, 2 ll. (1769).

95. SPbII RAN, f. 28, op. 1, d. 1582, l. 4 (1669).

96. SPbII RAN, f. 187, op. 2, d. 20, l. 114 (1662); GBUTO GATO, f. 47, op. 1, d. 381 (1662/63); MIUTTSSR, Appendix, Table 6 (1671–72). In Rus' Prince Dmitrii Mikhailovich Alachev sold wares along the road in 1643/44. RGADA, f. 214, stb. 134, l. 21. Kopylov, "Tamozhennaia politika v Sibiri," 337.

97. Miller, IS, vol. 2, no. 238, 389.

98. SPbII RAN, f. 187, op. 1, d. 184, l. 3v. 1 pud = 16.38 kg and 62 pud rhubarb = 1,015.5 kg rhubarb.

99. Kurts, *Sochinenie Kil'burgera*, 106.

100. Account from 1666 with unknown author, in Alekseev, *Sibir' v izvestiiakh zapadno-evropeiskikh puteshestvennikov*, 352. Quoted in Burton, *Bukharans*, 515.

Checkpoints were another part of the Siberian customs infrastructure, established along the roads within a few miles of towns in order to combat smuggling.[101] Some were permanent, others were established seasonally. Governors were charged with determining the most appropriate locations.[102] The point was to prevent people from stashing (*khoronit'*) their wares outside of town and then transacting deals beyond the gaze of the state, a subterfuge employed by making trades in the woods out of town or bringing their best goods into town by stealth at night.[103] Recall, where the one-tenth tax was taken in kind, merchants could increase their own profit—and hurt the tsar's—by keeping the best out of sight for inspection.[104] Sometimes a detachment of servitors would escort approaching caravans into town to prevent this. Town criers warned hinterland locals to report to authorities any passersby who tried to cache furs or contraband with them.[105] Yet, often, parties need not clandestinely sneak through the woods but could earn "unseen" passage with a bribe to the checkpoint authority.[106]

In theory checkpoint functions were confined to oversight, ensuring that passersby shipments and documentation were consistent. This was hassle enough. Merchants objected to checkpoint inspections—unpacking shipments carefully prepared for travel before the trip was finally over was a time-consuming frustration, to be repeated again shortly.[107] On top of that, each additional link in the bureaucratic chain provided opportunity for someone to profit. The Tobol'sk Tatar A. Abraimov reported that his goods were stolen from him during inspection at a checkpoint closer to Verkhotur'e.[108] Merchants complained about illegal demands, which the state warned administrators to keep in check, but the system was imperfect, which was not just a Siberian problem. After several merchant complaints, a state investigation in 1698 revealed that fourteen governors in central Russia had cooperated with one another to establish a network of personal checkpoints to extort merchants.[109] Indeed, traditions of the "feeding" system, whereby officials obtained their livelihood not directly from the state but from those over whom they had jurisdiction, lingered long in Russian

101. Miller, *Opisanie o torgakh' Sibirskikh*, 12, 25.

102. GBUTO GATO, f. 47, op. 1, d. 218, l. 1.

103. RGADA, f. 1111, op. 2, d. 188, ll. 132, 132v (1671); SPbII RAN, f. 28, op. 1, karton 20, no. 32, l. 6 (1672); Miller, *Opisanie o torgakh' Sibirskikh*, 12–13; Aleksandrov, "Narodnye vosstaniia v vostochnoi Sibiri," 162.

104. SPbII RAN, f. 28, op. 1, d. 478, l. 5 (1648).

105. AI, vol. 3, no. 184, 335 (1635).

106. RGADA, f. 1111, op. 2, d. 301, ll. 88–105.

107. RGADA, f. 1111, op. 1, stb. 304, pt. 1, l. 65 (1671).

108. RGADA, f. 1111, op. 2, d. 347, ll. 72–78.

109. Enin, "Voevodskaia tamozhennaia poshlina v XVII v.," 251

institutions. With naïveté that is almost charming, in 1664 a remote clerk wrote his superiors asking how he would survive with so little traffic through his Siberian checkpoint.[110] State orders to inspect thoroughly but not delay merchants, to not abuse passersby but neither to let any of the "tsar's profit" slip away, added to the murkiness in which provincial servitors operated.

Similarly ambiguity existed surrounding Siberia's nascent road infrastructure. When it became apparent that many merchants were traveling a new road to Berezov, the state condoned its use in 1619 and again in 1624.[111] Such permission should not be surprising in a state desiring vibrant commerce. Destroying roads, on the other hand, squarely at cross-purposes with establishing infrastructure, seems a puzzling step to take. But the specter of diminished "profit for the tsar" could push the state to do just that. Labor-strapped administrations were even directed to dig up or otherwise make unpassable unauthorized roads.[112] In 1685 Moscow ordered that the road from Siberia to the Stroganov lands be destroyed.[113] The state also ordered the road from Kazan to Tobol'sk via Kungur be closed in an effort to channel trade through Verkhotur'e.[114] In a dramatically protectionist move to close not a road but a sea route, the state famously closed the port of Mangazeia to sea traffic in 1619.[115] (Of course, the English proposal to attack Russian north coastal towns that resisted the English version of favorable trading terms seems far more dramatic in comparison.)[116]

Guarding the Guardians

In June of 1652 the merchant Misha Alartsov's silk was stolen. It turned out that the thief was a soldier apparently escorting him. The soldier confessed that he had given the silk to a state secretary, who vehemently denied having any part of the crime.[117] The case illustrates the heart of the problem: the difficulty in getting to the bottom of the crime when the guardians themselves

---

110. RGADA, f. 1111, op. 1, stb. 15, ll. 101–2 (1664).

111. Bakhrushin, "Puti v Sibir' v XVI–XVII vv.," in NT, 3: 83.

112. Fisher, Russian Fur Trade, 76; PSZ 3, no. 1654, p. 508 (November 12, 1698).

113. RGADA, f. 1111, op. 1, stb. 257, ch. 1, ll. 314–18 (1685); Fisher, Russian Fur Trade, 76. The state also wanted to prevent unwanted passage of enemy aggressors, runaway serfs.

114. Miller, Opisanie o torgakh Sibirskikh, chap. 1. The state also used these methods to control traffic to the Baltic. See Ohberg, "Russia and the World Market," 156.

115. Kabo, Goroda zapadnoi Sibiri, 88.

116. Alekseev, Sibir' v izvestiiakh zapadno-evropeiskikh puteshestvennikov, 207; Baron, "Thrust and Parry," in Explorations in Muscovite History, 19–40.

117. RGADA, f. 1111, op. 1, d. 297, pt. 1, ll. 26, 26v (1652).

were implicated. Alartsov's sack of silk was "small potatoes" compared with the commercial crime and evasion that went on.

The great volume of information so meticulously recorded in Siberian customs books can create a deceptive impression of thoroughness and seeming transparency. Customs books convey no inkling of entrepreneurial empires over which Siberian governors presided, in which they administered their designated territories as if they were their own kingdoms (*votchiny*).[118] Yet other sources do allow fragmentary glimpses of a parallel world of unofficial and illicit exchange. Despite all of the state's disincentives and efforts at oversight, smuggling was a reality. Sources contain nearly uncountable references to it. As if keeping tabs on entrepreneurs was not challenge enough, the state also had all manner of infractions to guard against from its own administrators. The enforcers themselves may have been among the most active transgressors. The state was all too aware that its own servitors might deceive it and tried to keep servitors from trading, prevent officials from abusing traders (via extortion, inappropriate valuation, stealing goods they were meant to inspect,[119] etc.), and guard against governors smuggling the wealth for the tsar's treasury out of Siberia through their family members.[120] Midcentury, in an effort to protect merchants from abuses of Siberian governors, the state released them from the jurisdiction of local Siberian administration.[121] At the end of the century, still at a loss as to what to do, the state extended the New Trade Statutes to Siberia, effectively lowering the tax rate there. With a strong suspicion that provincial servitors and merchants had teamed up on the frontier, the state, perhaps naïvely, decided to try to win the merchants into tax compliance by lowering their tax rates. All the while, with a special intensity in the last decade of the seventeenth century, Moscow officials wrote countless memos exhorting provincial administrators to monitor effectively against and not engage in any of the above, mandates whose fulfillment remained elusive.[122] The central government struggled to establish norms

118. Aleksandrov, "Narodnye vosstaniia v vostochnoi Sibiri," 255–309.

119. RGADA, f. 1111, op. 2, d. 347, ll. 72–78.

120. See Nancy Kollmann, "Corruption and Codification: Policing Officialdom in the Early Modern Russian Empire," Invited paper for the conference "Law and Transformation in the Russian and Ottoman Empires," Istanbul, June 16–19, 2005; Halperin, "Muscovy as a Hypertrophic State," 501–7.

121. Bazilevich, "Elementy merkantilizma," 9.

122. PSZ 3, no. 1443, esp. 133–40 (July 11, 1692, Instructions to Verkhotur'e customs); no. 1518, 206–7 (September 21, 1695); no. 1594, 335–75, esp. 349, 357–59 (Instructions to Tobol'sk governor, September 1, 1697); no. 1654, 508 (November 12, 1698), Kopylov, "Tamozhennaia politika v Sibiri v XVII v.," 363–68.

that were observed empire-wide[123] but, as Charles Halperin put it, by assigning governors in partnership in Siberia and keeping them on short rotations, the center in Moscow was essentially admitting defeat in its struggle to regulate the conduct of its provincial administration.[124] From small bribes to large bribes, the extortion of peasant tools and labor, embezzlement of state grains (for resale), co-optation of state boats for private use, withholding and substitution of state furs, sending family allowances twice, thrice, or by other means back to Moscow, or sending false IOUs with Russian merchants to collect in Moscow, to forging of state documentation for the dispatch of private "state" caravans to China, Siberian self-dealing took many forms.[125]

A concept of corruption was present—indeed, omnipresent—in Muscovite culture. Numerous decrees in the Conciliar Law Code of 1649 and countless decrees issued to Siberia admonish against corruption and greed. Integrity and honesty were basic criteria for the election and appointment to local posts such as sworn men; indeed, Lantzeff thought that additional appointments of sworn men in Siberia improved institutional honesty.[126] Similarly, prohibitions against hiring friends and family demonstrate that conflict of interest was an operative concept.[127] By the seventeenth century, there already existed recognition that bureaucracy could facilitate mistreatment and mask responsibility, as the plea from Bukharans who had been given the "bureaucratic run-around" for weeks demonstrated.[128]

Trading "for one's own needs" was acceptable, getting rich or harming the profit to the tsar's treasury was not. The Romanov tsars seemed to recognize the concept was unworkable, yet this recognition (or resignation) coexisted alongside long-standing and oft-repeated instructions that Siberian governors, their children, nephews, high-ranking secretaries (d'iaki), and later all servitors were not to conduct any personal trade, which included sending packages with merchants or anyone else.[129] Predictably, easier said than done. When, on a cold November day in 1667, a merchant reported that other merchants were skiing north to Mangazeia with goods for the Berezov governor in secret, Moscow summoned the informant to Moscow

---

123. Kollmann, "Corruption and Codification."

124. Halperin, "Muscovy as a Hypertrophic State," 503.

125. Demonizing provincial governors was standard operating procedure in imperial and Soviet historiography. As part of the post-Soviet quest for a past of which Russians can be proud, recent works emphasize the accomplishments and energy of frontier leaders. See Akishin and Remenev, Vlast' v Sibiri.

126. Lantzeff, Siberia in the Seventeenth Century, 117–18.

127. AI, vol. 5, 62–63.

128. RGADA, f. 214, stb. 414, l. 27 (January 1656).

129. Fisher, Russian Fur Trade, 81; PSZ, vol. 3, no. 1594.15, 349 (1697).

at once so that they could find out more.[130] It was precisely the type of smuggling the state was keen to quash. Given this state of affairs, the rare evidence of administrators trading in Siberian customs books is all the more puzzling—since it was technically prohibited, why was it officially recorded at all? A provincial administrator here, a sworn man there, or occasionally someone making a declaration on behalf of a customs head or governor, were clues to another significant aspect of Siberian trade, and/or perhaps lapses in protocol.[131] It is more common to encounter government elites involved in Siberian commerce.[132]

The career and life of the Yakutsk governor Ivan Fëdorovich Golenishchev-Kutuzov ended in disgrace and confiscation after he was found guilty of sending copious amounts of fur for his own personal enrichment to Russia with multiple merchants who passed through Yakutsk.[133] A comment by one Chinese official suggests that Siberian officials audaciously forged documents in the conduct of their own trade "on the side," offering a shadowy glimpse of the private fiefdoms historians accused Siberian governors of running. (The notorious Gagarin governors, who came into conflict with the elite Filat'ev merchants, are discussed in chapter 6.) In 1726 an official Russian state caravan was surprised to learn from Chinese officials that Chinese border control had received fifty "official" state caravans from Russia when Moscow had only dispatched a small fraction of that number.[134]

---

130. SPbII RAN, f. 28, op. 1, d. 1311, ll. 1–3 (1667).

131. RGADA, f. 214, stb. 892, l. 126 (1653); stb. 301, ll. 37, 39, 47v (1652/3); SPbII RAN, f. 187, op. 2, d. 20, ll. 17v, 32 (1661); GBUTO GATO, f. 29, op. 1, d. 134, 37 ll. (1727); TKSG, vol. 1, 52 (1675); RGADA, f. 214, stb. 755, l. 65 (1705); Bulgakov, "Torgovoe dvizhenie po Oksko-Moskovskoi rechnoi sisteme," 209.

132. Dovnar-Zapol'skii, "Torgovlia i promyshlennost'," 325. For examples of government elites involved in commerce, see Boyar Ivan Vasilievich Morozov: Merzon and Tikhonov, Rynok Ustiuga Velikogo, 571; Boyars Boris and Gleb Ivanovich Morozov: SPbII RAN, f. 28, op. 1, d. 717, l. 1; f. 187, op. 2, d. 20, l. 15; RGADA, f. 214, stb. 499, l. 328; Bakhrushin, "Torgovye krest'iane v XVII v.," in NT, 2: 125; Boyar Nikita Ivanovich Romanov: RGADA, f. 214, kn. 301, ll. 74–89v; Prince Ivan Prozorovskii: RGADA, f. 214, kn. 301, l. 71; Boyar Prince Dmitrii Mikhailovich Pozharskii: Merzon and Tikhonov, Rynok Ustiuga Velikogo, 326; Prince Iurii Ivanovich Pozharskii: TKSG, vol. 1, 1, 30, 39, 52; TKSG, vol. 3, 71; Princes Boris Aleksandrovich Repin and Mikhail Mikhailovich Saltykov: Golovachev, Tiumen' v XVII stoletii, bk. 170, 137–51; sources for chancellor (d'iak) Mikhail Erofeev: RGADA, f. 214, stb. 153, l. 233. In the southern steppe, Sunderland wrote that many Cossacks recruits were boyar trading agents who had fled under accusations of wrongdoing. Sunderland, Taming the Wild Field, 23.

133. Moiseev, ed., Vlast' v Sibiri, 196.

134. Foust, Muscovite and Mandarin, 13. This is to say nothing of the Cossacks' border trade that will never be quantified. "The Cossacks hereabouts are very rich, by reason of their traffick with China, where they are exempted from paying any custom," wrote Brand, A Journal of the Embassy to China, 59.

When servitors were not outright stealing or circumventing decreed government controls, they could profit at the expense of the people trafficking in and across Siberia. Reports of abuse by people of all ranks, from governors to customs heads to lowly administrators and other servitors abound; indeed, one would be hard pressed to study Siberian documents without encountering incidents of official abuse.[135] Privileged merchants complained against highly orchestrated, high-level abuse; in the 1640s a Siberian governor had set up his own separate checkpoints to extort goods and money from them to himself.[136] A lowly peasant complained against local bullying by the state agent at the Irbit market.[137] In another case, an indignant merchant from Ustiug reported that he had been beaten "for no reason" during inspection by the customs agent in a small borough in the Verkhotur'e district. When it turned out that his documentation was 18 rubles short of what he actually had—this could be a result of differences in valuation or of a merchant having made transactions where there was no customs official to adjust the documentation but not trying to smuggle the acquired objects—the abusive agent took a larger fine than was appropriate and would not return the merchant's transit documentation until he paid a bribe.[138] The state took such problems in stride. A dispatch to a different borough in Verkhotur'e district in 1667 denied the agent's request for more gunpowder and pork, additionally warning, almost as an aside, that if complaints against him from locals persisted, he would be beaten for his bad behavior.[139]

Informal Channels of Exchange

Merchants knew the game, of course, and had strategies for conducting their business effectively. Whereas bribes were illegal, gift giving featured heavily in commercial practice.[140] This is not surprising in a society where hospitality and obligation were important cultural norms. Gifts were due the tsar but did not stop there. Gift giving was deeply embedded in the culture and accompanied exchange relations throughout administrative levels. Although it was formally abolished in the sixteenth century, the system of "feeding" meant that practices of administrators receiving directly from those within

---

135. Some examples: SPbII RAN, f. 28, op. 1, d. 1234, ll. 3–5 (1658); d. 1086, ll. 5–6.

136. AI, vol. 4, no. 8, 32–35 (1646).

137. SPbII RAN, f. 28, op. 1, d. 706, ll. 11–13 (1657).

138. SPbII RAN, f. 28, op. 1, karton 18, no. 12, ll. 4–5 (1670).

139. SPbII RAN, f. 28, op. 1, d. 299, l. 1 (1667).

140. For a compelling discussion on gifts in early modern European commercial society, see chapter 3, "Gift Work," in Howell, *Commerce before Capitalism*, 145–207.

their administration were deeply embedded in Muscovite institutional history and continued unabated, argue historians, throughout the seventeenth century.[141] Thus archives abound with accusations of someone taking gifts that ultimately took from the tsar. For example, some on the staff of the Verkhotur'e customs in 1650 accused the customs head, Fëdor Driagin, and others, as well as their wives, of taking for themselves "gifts" (*pominka* = gift, *posuly* = bribe; the distinction could blur) of furs, fur coats, and horses at the expense of the tsar.[142]

Keeping governors on one's good side was a standard operating expense for elite merchants, as we will glimpse but not fully excavate in exploring the Filat'ev enterprises in chapter 6. This aspect of operations, of course, is most difficult to ascertain let alone analyze, given that the contested definitions of variegated gifts (*pominki, pochest', and posuly*) could function as bribes, trades, or loans, and not be recorded at all.[143] The state was not blind to these sorts of exchanges. Governors were explicitly directed—in case there was any confusion over the benign rhetoric in which imperial imposition was couched—that any gifts of furs they received were to be added to the state tribute collections.[144] Sometimes the state acted against its stated policies in an attempt to outmaneuver informal and unseen channels of exchange that reduced the tsar's profit. For example, in 1650 the gost' Vasilii Fedotov Gusel'nikov received special permission to purchase black and brown with black tint (*chernoburnii*) fox from servitors and tribute payers. The state saw the measure as a step to counter too much gifting in the provinces. "Governors and chief secretaries and various chancery officials take from us [and] from tribute payers for tribute and as gifts," read the letter from Moscow.[145] Since the state was losing good fox revenue with the status quo, it reasoned that it could generate more income by granting permission to someone who would pay duty on the fox. The other reason was that the state knew that Bukharans and Tatars and various foreigners were trading the good fox elsewhere and in secret: "the good fox show up too little in our Moscow treasury because yurt Tatars and Bukharans and various foreigners buy and sell good fox from the trapper-traders (*promyshlenniki*) and various people in other kingdoms by secret practice . . . [and] . . . various people in Siberia are selling such good pelts to Bukharans secretly, but Bukharans sell such foxes

141. Demidova, *Sluzhilaia biurokratiia*; Enin, *Voevodskoe kormlenie*.
142. SPbII RAN, f. 28, op. 1, d. 492, ll. 1–8.
143. Bakhrushin, "Torgi gostia Nikitina v Sibiri i Kitae," 248.
144. Lantzeff, *Siberia in the Seventeenth Century*, 131.
145. Orlova, *Otkrytiia russkikh zemleprokhodtsev*, no. 64, 191.

to foreigners and export [them] to other kingdoms."[146] Thus the center saw that giving this gost' the rights to vouch for a valued commodity would put someone closer to Russia's interests on the front lines of a battle that the state was losing. At any rate, the state's effort to define and eliminate inappropriate gift taking is a long and involved story interlaced with myriad issues of imperial aspirations and deficits.

Gift giving was one facet of consolidating obligations and alliances that were not only instrumental to the parties involved but also observed by a larger populace. Such connections and the perception they created could sometimes backfire, however. Take, for example, the case of the Gusel'nikov brothers. Afanasii Gusel'nikov, brother of the Vasilii mentioned above, cultivated close relations with the governor of Yakutsk, P. P. Golovin, at a cost. In July 1645 townspeople and others in Yakutsk mutinied against Golovin. Afanasii Gusel'nikov had not yet risen to the stature of gost' (he attained that status in 1658) but his brother had, and he was moving in that direction. Afanasii's close ties to the local "big man" assured that he became a target of the angry mob by association. During the uprising, prisoners from behind the jail bars shouted out, "What are we waiting for? Let's go to the governor's house and get his people and the merchants of Afanasei Fedotov and other merchants who go to the voevoda's house and [let's] beat them, and if not to death, then we will break the legs and arms of Golovin's [the governor's] people and the merchants and tie them to the guard post!"[147]

Note that spending time at the governor's house was more prolonged than delivering an envelope as an anonymous bribe, so to speak; the maintenance of amicable economic relationships—or the cultivation of trust and patronage, as it were—involved more than simple transactions of money for protection.[148] On the distant frontier, where kinship networks were stretched thin by distance, patronage was even more important.[149] As far as we know, in that instance Afanasei Fedotov's agents weathered that storm well enough, just as his brother Vasilii Skorozapis' would weather similar threats during the Moscow uprisings of 1648 when this newly minted gost''s name circulated as one of the reviled big men who should be murdered, along with the merchants Vasilii Shorin and V. I. Iur'ev. But in 1650 goods were stolen from the Gusel'nikovs in Yakutsk, which may reflect a less confrontational

146. Ibid.

147. Ibid., no. 69, 201–3.

148. For a sociological treatment of trust and patronage see Eisenstadt and Roniger, *Patrons, Clients and Friends*.

149. Hosking, "Patronage and the Russian State," 306.

manifestation of similar resentments.[150] Clearly the practices that facilitated the Gusel'nikovs' success also earned them enemies.

The calculus of when gifting and bribery did not return on the investment is not transparent and was likely not strictly numerical. Formal and informal procedures and ethos coexisted in the early modern bureaucracy.[151] Certainly there were points beyond which one would switch strategies, be it a local deciding to file a complaint or an elite merchant, instead of courting a governor, trying to confront and expose him with the help of the state. Confrontational tactics were not rare. Individual and collective petitions by merchants against abusive officials are frequently found.[152] Chapter 6 details Ostafii Filat'ev's struggles against abuse, including a confrontation with the notorious M. P. Gagarin. The point is not to lament or quantify abuse but to acknowledge, if not understand, what underlay the eruptions. An entire infrastructure of an illegal shadow collection system does not materialize out of thin air. Though extortion inarguably requires coercive practices, some measure of compliance is no less required in order for it to develop. The moments in which accusations were brought before the state were probably preceded by some sort of breakdown in the maintenance of amicable economic relations.

Conclusion

On December 30, 1699 a Russian gentryman and a serving Tatar left Tobol'sk bound for Moscow with state tribute.[153] Tatzimko Iatipov, a Tobol'sk Bukharan transporting rhubarb root, was also bound for Moscow. The plan was for the group to meet up in Verkhotur'e and proceed to Moscow together. According to standing orders for servitors and private subjects alike, they all underwent inspection in Verkhotur'e. During inspection of Iatipov's goods, the customs head Vasilii Shyshelov discovered contraband: 228 sable tails sewn into pillows for concealment. In Shyshelov's discovery we see that it takes one to know one—himself a merchant, Shyshelov spent years on the other side of the transaction at customs posts conducting his

150. Aleksandrov, "Narodnye vosstaniia v vostochnoi Sibiri," 270.

151. Sedov, "Podnosheniia v Moskovskikh prikazakh XVII v."; Bogatyrev, "Localism and Integration in Muscovy," 59–127.

152. For examples, see SPbII RAN, f. 28, op. 1, d. 1234, ll. 1–5 (1666); Orlova, *Otkrytiia russkikh zemleprokhodtsev*, no. 39, 164–65; Ogloblin, *Obozrenie*, 3: 172–74, 321–24.

153. RGADA, f. 1111, op. 1, d. 322, ll. 75, 77–78. Sobonak Avezbekaev's ethnicity is not identified in this document, but he is labeled a serving Tatar in a document from 1696. See RGADA, f. 214, op. 5, d. 841, l. 1. Elsewhere, he is called a Bukharan.

own Siberian trade.[154] During questioning, Iatipov admitted his guilt. He explained that he had bought up the sable tails piecemeal in various boroughs around Tobol'sk. He insisted that he did not set out with the intention of smuggling; he passed through the towns of Tiumen' and Turinsk without declaring them because "they never inspect Bukharans and other ranks of people."[155] By the time he reached Tobol'sk, however, the lack of oversight had piqued his desire for more of the same and Iatipov decided to try to make it out of Siberia without declaring his sable, implicitly shifting the blame onto a lax system of enforcement.[156] Unfortunately, the evidence does not reveal what consequences Iatipov faced or if his traveling companions had colluded with him.

The purported corruption of Russia is legion. It seems that, over the long term, getting by on the minimalist Muscovite state model contributed to the development of institutions and a system in which the gaps between intentions and means, entitlements and rewards, was increasingly filled with a culture that tolerated and functioned on alternative methods, transactions, and reimbursements.[157] Concepts of what constituted corruption or conflict of interest, although certainly extant, were not necessarily clear-cut. As already mentioned, traditions of "feeding" made it harder to define the border between ethical and unethical behavior.[158] Alongside the tax regime, the system of "feeding"—whereby Muscovite officials extracted their personal remuneration directly from their juridical populations—prevailed throughout the seventeenth century throughout the realm.[159] The blurriness is exacerbated by the protracted transition from a domain state to a tax state, whereby states more systematically and effectively extracted revenue from their populations for military engagements.[160] For all that modernity ushered in, it did not usher out the predominance of an affinitive culture in Russia. In Siberia and elsewhere, "one's own needs" and "best" could be slippery concepts.[161] One could pursue one's own interests once the tsar's had been

154. RGADA, f. 214, stb. 755, l. 54 (1705).

155. "*Im bukhartsom i vsiakikh chinov liudem dosmotru nekogda nebyvaet.*" Irbit apparently had a lax attitude toward enforcement. Fisher, *Russian Fur Trade*, 173.

156. RGADA, f. 1111 op. 1, d. 322, l. 75.

157. For a comparison of how such challenges were negotiated in China, see Reed, *Talons and Teeth*. I thank Matthew Sommers for this reference.

158. Enin, *Voevodskoe kormlenie*; Potter, "Payment, Gift or Bribe?"; Davies, "Politics of Give and Take," 39–67.

159. Enin, *Voevodskoe kormlenie*.

160. Glete, *War and the State*.

161. RGADA, f. 214, stb. 134, ll. 116, 194.

optimized.[162] Such standards were legitimate but vague and hard to measure, and authorities grappled to establish norms, observable to us most often in the breach. These boundaries were meaningful to contemporaries, even if not sacrosanct to all, and certainly baffling to retrospective observers.

One also might consider the assumptions brought to the question of corruption in Russian history. Whereas contemporary Americans generally take exposed corruption as indications that the system is generally working, when it comes to Russian history, the default seems to be to assume that more smuggling occurred than was captured in the historical record. Whether cynical or spot-on, such assumptions undergird one historian's assessment that what was ultimately inscribed in the customs books is not to be taken as an objective indicator of economic dynamics, but rather as a record of what state official and private actor agreed to write in the customs books.[163] One wonders what to make of entries that record contraband and fines paid according to preestablished procedure. For example, in 1704 the Tobol'sk Tatar Bakii Nazarov was discovered with undeclared red fox pelts. He paid one-tenth tax on the goods plus a fine of 10 percent of the value of the smuggled goods (2 grivny per ruble). In this case, the smuggler Nazarov paid to Verkhotur'e customs a fine of 1.6 rubles, an arguably modest punitive consequence.[164] Muller reported: "If hidden goods worth less than 200 rubles are found above the official manifest, then the merchant must apologize and pay the 1/10th tax as usual. If hidden goods worth up to 300 rubles or more are involved, then no apologizing will help and the merchant must pay double the 1/10th tax on the hidden goods."[165] Even recognizing less general access to cash, such consequences were hardly draconian. Indeed, instructions to Siberia ordered that town criers announce that death was the penalty for smuggling rhubarb. The same document, however, gives town officials different orders: to confiscate any contraband rhubarb.[166] Like a parent whose threat exceeds the punishment, this was Russian paternalism in practice.

An abstruse feature about Siberia, and perhaps Russia in general, is captured in the following saying: "The harshness of Russia's laws is softened by the nonobligatory application of them."[167] The seeming inconsistent application of rules has perplexed more than a few contemporaneous functionaries and

---

162. RKO, vol. 1, no. 87, 218–20.

163. Kraikovskii, "Torgovlia sol'iu na Russkom severe," chapter 3.

164. RGADA, f. 214, kn. 1398, l. 394v.

165. Miller, *Opisanie o torgakh' Sibirskikh*, 12–13.

166. PSZ, vol. 3, no. 1594, 373 (September 1, 1697).

167. "*Strogost' rossiiskoi zakonov smiagchaetsia neobiazatel'nostiu ikh ispolneniia.*" I thank E. V. Anisimov at the Institute of History in St. Petersburg, Russia, for sharing this with me.

historians alike. One confronts again and again in the world of commerce rules that, even in the light of day, were not quite followed: tax-free trade only for Muscovy Company members; trading only at state marketplaces; the prohibition of servitors to trade; prohibitions on the trade and transport of arms, rhubarb, and other items; and prohibitions on extortion, enslavement, and conversion are only some of the possible examples to marshal. Such practices offend one's sense of consistency, a prerequisite for a functioning bureaucracy. "A foolish consistency is the hobgoblins of little minds," Ralph Waldo Emerson famously wrote.[168] Had they stopped to think about it in those terms, early modern rulers would have invariably agreed. In an age when it was taken for granted that not all men were created equal, rulers were not bedeviled by the universalizing, rationalizing principles that have propelled bureaucracy into the modern age.[169] The Muscovite government was no different in that respect. As it set about establishing its authority in Siberia numerous priorities weighed on it; consistency was not one of them. As Brian Boeck has aptly put it, this was an empire of "separate deals."[170] In the next chapters we meet some of the merchants who navigated the seen and unseen space of Siberian commerce to make their way and turn a profit in this empire of separate deals.

---

168. Emerson, "Self-Reliance," 242.
169. See discussion of composite sovereignty in Romaniello, *Elusive Empire*, 8–11.
170. Boeck, *Imperial Boundaries*.

CHAPTER 5

Connecting Eurasian Commerce: Lake Yamysh

> "All the Countries that were formerly but confusedly known under the Name of . . . Grand Tartary, are neither so desert, nor so untill'd as people to this day imagine."
>
> —Philippe Avril, *Travels*

> "If you have nothing to tell us but that on the banks of the Oxus and the Jaxartes, one barbarian has been succeeded by another, in what respect do you benefit the public?"
>
> —Voltaire, "History," in *Philosophical Dictionary*

This chapter chronicles a space of Siberian trade that was beyond the bounds of the Russian Empire for most of our story. It is the history of Lake Yamysh, a spring-fed salt lake just east of the Irtysh River on the steppe in what is now northeastern Kazakhstan. The history of Lake Yamysh deepens our understanding of Eurasian trade in several senses. From the winding oxbows of Irtysh to the leather rolls hoisted from the backs of camels to the decks of flat-bottomed riverboats and back again, there is value in appreciating the materiality, geography, and hazards of the spaces that merchants of Siberia negotiated. Taking stock of the distance and terrain merchants traveled to reach a market that appeared and disappeared in the vast steppe brings that world closer to us. No less, this chapter offers a glimpse of the too-little documented dynamics of trade between Russians, Bukharans, Kalmyks, Kazaks, and Dzhungars—a juncture at which the (too) classically defined "settler-nomad" societies met. In doing so, this history of a steppe trading post illustrates an immutable borderland constant: the interrelated nature of violence and commerce. In this specific case, a story of *longue durée* trade intersects with the politics of post-Mongol Eurasia to bear witness to the decline of the Dzhungar state and the growth of the Russian Empire. Russia's achievement of sovereignty in this region was ultimately the result of concerted, repeated effort. The construction of a line of military forts up the Irtysh River beginning in 1715 was a project that, amid defensive, offensive, speculative, and compensatory motives, demonstrates Russia's enduring strategy of promoting commerce. Amid these political upheavals, trade at Lake Yamysh not only survived but also flourished. Lake Yamysh became the site of a thriving trade center that the Russian Empire ultimately—albeit much more slowly than it intended—incorporated into its imperial domain. This chapter tells the story of how a remote Eurasian commercial space attracted trade for its statelessness and ultimately was incorporated into the Russian Empire. Its deceptive remoteness did not inoculate it from the global economic changes afoot in the early modern period. Not only does Lake Yamysh testify to the growth in trade between Russia and China but it also presents a counterstory to the problematic commonplace that early modern overland trade declined against the competition of European maritime trade.

Along the Irtysh

The Irtysh River begins in the Altai Mountains of the Xianjing region of western China. From there this spring-fed stream trickles down, gaining speed and volume from the many mountain brooks that run into it, cutting a northwestward path toward the vast and open steppe of Inner Eurasia, a riparian oasis through Eurasian space. The Irtysh courses quickly as it descends the Altai Mountains, emerging in an epic landscape where clouds coursing across the big sky cast their shadows over forbidding snow-capped peaks and undulating grassy pastures, covering in just a few minutes distances that took early modern travelers weeks to traverse. In the upper Irtysh the fast current—sometimes a frothy white water—made river travel difficult. Seitkul Ablin, a well-traveled Bukharan merchant who led an expedition to China in the late 1660s, transitioned out of his boats and bought camels to proceed overland alongside the strong currents of the upper Irtysh.[1] The academician G. F. Müller, who visited this region in 1734 as part of the Great Northern Expedition, covered in six days what it took boats up to eighteen to travel.[2] Thus although rivers very much defined many trade routes throughout Eurasia, they sometimes directed the path that camels, carts, and horses followed without providing the actual means of travel. When the

1. RGADA, f. 214, stb. 535, l. 218. AI, vol. 5, 137–38. RMO, vol. 3, 1654–85, no. 118, 232–36 (f. 214, stb. 535, ll. 159–64, 171–75); RKO, vol. 1, no. 143, 288–93 (f. 214, stb. 535, ll. 187–203).
2. Müller, "Travels in Siberia," 81.

water was high and fast, pulling boats upstream was too dangerous or slow; when water was low in late summer, boats could not pass.[3]

About halfway through its course—near Lake Yamysh, in fact—the riverbed deepens and the Irtysh begins to meander more slowly through the long flats of the open steppe. These deeper waters are home to a variety of fish, sterlet and taimen (Siberian salmon) among them, that locals preserved with salt harvested from Lake Yamysh and depended on for sustenance. Deeper and slower, the Irtysh meanders northwestward, gaining volume as numerous rivers and brooks empty into it. A possible Tatar derivation of its name suggests just such a picture, where "Ir" means earth, and "tysh," earth-fissure or rent.[4] Gradually it leaves the open steppe and winds its way through Siberian forests. As mixed deciduous forests give way to rugged conifers of the taiga, the Irtysh empties into the Ob River. The Irtysh River is 320 miles longer than the Mississippi[5] but flows, as rivers in Siberia tend to, in the opposite direction, northward. Some have considered Siberia's northward flowing rivers a fatal flaw: an exit point on one of the planet's most forbidding environments isolated Siberia from the world economy, explaining the failure of Siberian commerce to develop. Visiting the Altai Mountains in 2000, they struck me as the most remote place I have ever been. The Russian rangers that lived on the shores of Lake Teletskoe, inaccessible by road, reported that they had walked seventy-nine days on wilderness patrol without spotting a single human footprint, let alone another person. Even to this day so much of the Irtysh's banks are empty; it is hard to imagine this remote place as an important artery of transcontinental commerce. Yet, although much of this space strikes one as unfathomably remote, this river was, for centuries on centuries, precisely that: an important artery of transcontinental commerce.[6]

Idiosyncrasies of Space: Remoteness in an Early Modern Key

Words like "remote," "vibrant," and "important" require qualification when considering premodern Eurasia. They have their place but can conjure

---

3. Vilkov, *Ocherki sotsial'no-ekonomicheskogo razvitiia Sibiri*, 86, 90.

4. Abramov, "Lake Nor-Zaisan and Its Neighbourhood," 60.

5. The Irtysh River is 2,640 miles long. The Mississippi River is 2,320 miles long. Often the length of the river systems are not mentioned in isolation but as the Missouri-Mississippi and Ob-Irtysh. Both are among the ten longest rivers in the world.

6. Other scholars have made this point regarding Central Asia and the Ferghana Valley, respectively. See Perdue, *China Marches West*, 9–11; Levi, "Ferghana Valley at the Crossroads of World History," 214.

notions that may distort as much as they describe. Understanding Eurasian space requires a different conceptual framework than does understanding the commercial port cities of northern Europe fed by hinterlands of cultivated fields, pastoral meadows, and forests.[7] For example, it is generally understood that the average peasant in premodern Europe probably lived the entirety of his or her—and women probably moved even less—days within a radius of just a few miles of his or her birthplace. Yet space must be understood differently in different times and places. While we can easily appreciate how asphalt highways and combustion engines shrink distance dramatically, circumstances other than industrialization also require a reconceptualization of space. Mountainous regions, for example, are places in which spatial units, practically speaking, are not uniform. There, vertical terrain, microclimates, and seasons may mean that covering a modest distance of just a few miles is a gargantuan task. The steppe offers a contrasting example. Properly equipped in the right conditions, nomads were highly mobile. Mongol horsemen and often their families, too, covered vast distances. They moved with seasonal cycles and geopolitical shifts. Mongol armies spanned a continent on campaign and returned seasonally to their home regions for major political events such as the selection of a new leader.

Human hands may have done little to shape the landscape in these parts but they have not been absent from this ancient trade route that followed the Irtysh River across Eurasia. Even before Russians self-consciously imprinted Orthodoxy on the spaces they occupied—with fortresses, churches, towns, monasteries, manuscript illuminations, and maps—and in spite of the claims of new discoveries declared in the publications of the Russian Geographical Society, the Irtysh River basin was not wholly unknown. Hunter-gatherers (forest dwellers, as Muscovites called them) in the cold forests of Siberia and reindeer herders of the tundra left traces with which archeologists reconstruct the footprints of their communities and burial grounds, and the remnants of small stoves, in which they worked the metals they took from the earth and shaped into tools for living.[8] Nomads generally left traces fainter still. Often their presence would be ephemeral—the trampled grass of a camp—or invisible to the untrained eye. "Pure nomadism" (that is, people always on the move) hardly existed, but even the most transitory communities sometimes left more permanent traces in special places. From a Chinese Buddhist temple at a mineral spring high in the Altai Mountains to Kazak ruins in the exposed open steppe near the source of the Ishim River, the edges

---

7. For a good introduction to nomadic commerce see Christian, "Steppe Roads or Silk Roads."
8. Müller, "Travels in Siberia," 81.

of Inner Asia, remote as they seem, were places known to and marked by people of various beliefs and lifestyles.[9]

Although the inscriptions of their presence pales in comparison to what modern civilizations leave behind, more permanent communities were built in the steppe. It is said that the Mongolian-Turkic nomads of the steppe did not sedentarize as successfully as the Chinggisid descendants of the Crimean khanate, yet Kalmyks (the name Russians gave to Torghut Mongols) built stone buildings in at least three places along the Irtysh.[10] In the mid-seventeenth century, however, Kalmyks occupied much of the middle Irtysh region, around Lake Yamysh, and the steppes south of western Siberia. Not far from Lake Yamysh, on the other side of the river, stood a tower that Russians called "Kalbasunskaia Bashnaia."[11] A couple of weeks upstream travel from Lake Yamysh, the Russians founded Semipalatinsk, which they named after the Kalmyk-built seven stone chambers—referred to as *Sedmoi Palat*[12]—that had become an eclectic manuscript depository housing texts of various regional faiths. Tsar Peter I sent a sample of Tungus texts retrieved from the ruins to Paris "to find out what they were."[13] About 66 miles upstream from the Russian fort at Ust'-Kamengorsk, there was a temple ruin known as Ablakit. In 1734 at the direction of Müller, who himself stayed behind, fearing "marauding Kirgiz-Kazakh" attacks, Russian soldiers hauled away six horse loads of manuscripts in the Tungus, Mongolian, and Kalmyk languages, adding to the seedbed of Russian Orientalist source study.[14] When Fëdor Baikov traveled up the Irtysh to China in 1654, he noted that the Kalmyk Taisha Ablai was constructing two brick palaces surrounded by walls, "Ablai's Halls," where the Bishka (Beska) rivulet empties into the Irtysh.[15]

Dzhungars, avid state builders of the seventeenth and eighteenth centuries who met their end against the Qing in 1756, did even more to inscribe permanence onto the ephemeral landscape of northern Inner Eurasia. The Dzhungars, like the Kalmyks, were one of the four tribes of western Mongols.

9. Abramov, "Lake Nor-Zaisan and Its Neighbourhood," 63. This was a spot that Chinese had long frequented, but ceased to after Russian soldiers established fishing outposts at Lake Nor-Zaisan in 1803; Bakhrushin, "Puti v Sibir v XVI–XVII vv.," in NT, 3: 93.

10. Hundreds of thousands of Kalmyks, who were Buddhist, migrated from their Mongolian ancestral lands westward to the Volga in about the 1630s, only to migrate back, in much smaller numbers, in the reign of Catherine the Great (1762–96).

11. Müller did not visit but sent a research assistant to sketch it. Müller, "Travels in Siberia," 81.

12. Chulkov, *Istoricheskoe opisanie*, 18.

13. Bell, *Travels from St. Petersburg*, 1:193. Müller, "Travels in Siberia," 81.

14. Müller, "Travels in Siberia," 82. Tungus is an Altaic language spoken by Tungusic people, who include Evenks, Manchus, and others in eastern Siberia and Manchuria.

15. Abramov, "Lake Nor-Zaisan and Its Neighbourhood," 64.

Like the Kalmyks that they supplanted in the upper Irtysh region in the seventeenth century, the Dzhungars retained Buddhism (even if Dzunghar leaders, like the Russian tsars, used Muslim emissaries to communicate with the Chinese).[16] In the same years that the first Romanov tsar was working to consolidate a new Muscovite order, Batur, the Dzhungar leader (his title, khan-taish, indicates he was not descended from the Chinggisid line), built a city on the steppe and resettled agricultural communities that seventeenth-century travelers along the Irtysh encountered.[17]

Farther upriver, well beyond any claims of Russian sovereignty, Irtysh waters fed other agricultural settlements. In the middle of the seventeenth century an embassy to China encountered three communities of farming Bukharans along the route.[18] One, referred to as "Ablaeskie farming Bukharans" because it had been settled by Taisha Ablai, was located 24.5 miles north of Semipalatinsk where the Karabuga River empties into the Irtysh. By the time Müller passed there, the settlement had been abandoned to ruins; leveled clay homes and traces of "Bukharan" irrigation systems that had once fed spring wheat and Russian vegetables were all that remained.[19] Continuing past Lake Zaisan, beyond the source of the Irtysh, and through the Khabar-Taban pass of the Mongolian Altai Mountains, travelers descended to another Bukharan farming community on the Imel' River, where they could transition from cart to camel travel as they made their way toward the Chinese Empire.[20] These communities, and the travelers who found them both vibrant and as ruins, remind us that not all Bukharans were merchants and that the steppe was not a changeless void.

Knowing the Irtysh

Rivers play standing roles in narratives of commerce, and the Irtysh River was long an important artery for the passage of commercial goods across Eurasia, but its story has been little told.[21] Merchants, who mostly traveled this route in premodern times, were generally unconcerned with aesthetic descriptions but passed on valuable practical information. Unfortunately, no

---

16. Perdue, *China Marches West*, 179.

17. Vilkov and Preobrazhenskii, *Ocherki sotsial'no-ekonomicheskogo razvitiia Sibiri*, chap. 2; Purdue, *China Marches West*.

18. Vilkov, *Ocherki sotsial'no-ekonomicheskogo razvitiia Sibiri*, 87–91.

19. Spafarii, *Puteshestvie cherez Sibir'*, 16. Black and Buse, *G. F. Müller and Siberia*, xx. Chulkov claimed these Bukharans were enslaved.

20. Vilkov, *Ocherki sotsial'no-ekonomicheskogo razvitiia Sibiri*, 87, 90.

21. An exception is Apollova, *Khoziaistvennoe osvoenie Priirtysh'ia*.

notebooks or gazetteers of merchants that frequented the Yamysh route have survived. Fortunately, the Russian government was interested in knowing the resources and routes of its peripheral borderlands and consolidating knowledge about the Irtysh region. Prince Iurii Iansheevich Suleshev, governor of Tobol'sk from 1623 to 1625, had surveys conducted for the Siberian Office describing the area population—people to be taxed—along the lower and middle Irtysh. Information about territory beyond Russian settlements came to the state from the reports submitted by all state expeditions that traveled the upper reaches and interviews consistently conducted with travelers who arrived from distant places.[22]

Surveys in the Siberian Office archive provide a fleeting sketch of the middle Irtysh region, a picture embellished by accounts of five state-sponsored travelers. Although the historian Basil Dmytryshyn emphasized the independent spirit of those who gained knowledge of the frontier, all five of these accounts were the result of expeditions commissioned by the Russian government. These expeditions catalyzed a flurry of intelligence consolidation in preparation for and debriefing after the trips.[23] Though the routes were old, writing places like Lake Yamysh into history marked a new sort of encounter for the Russian state. Where such intelligence previously was passed on orally and locally, in the seventeenth century the Muscovite government took steps to consolidate such intelligence in writing.[24] Significantly, some descriptions were penned by emissaries who themselves did not travel the entire Irtysh route they described. Having received reports that warfare made the Irtysh region unsafe, Nikolaos Spafarii followed a more northern route to China.[25] Yet he still included in his account a detailed description of the upper Irtysh, explaining that "nothing up to this very day is known of this place."[26] Although the remark hints at the "knowledge for knowledge's sake" associated with the celebrated Enlightenment, most likely he felt compelled to describe it in his report—a most pragmatic genre—because of its recognized importance as a trade route.

The earliest Russian account of the Irtysh is from Fëdor Baikov, who led a state embassy to China in 1654. Baikov could not write himself, but

22. A sampling of interviews: Pokrovskii, *Aktovye istochniki*, nos. 132, 139, 159, 160.
23. This point is nicely developed in Tolmacheva, "Early Russian Exploration and Mapping of the Chinese Frontier."
24. RGADA, f. 214, stb. 535, l. 216.
25. Milescu, *Puteshestvie chez Sibir'*, 168–69. Spafarii traveled down the Irtysh, up the Ob, then up the Ket River, via Eniseisk, finally departing Russian territory from Selengisk for the overland journey southward to China.
26. Milescu, *Puteshestvie chez Sibir'*, 14.

dictated detailed descriptions to secretaries.[27] This embassy mostly followed
the known route along the Irtysh, but in the upper Irtysh region followed
other tributary systems through the Mongolian Altai. The state sponsored
trade missions to China, led by the Tobol'sk Bukharan Seitkul Ablin, whose
reports (*stateinye spiski*) do not survive but were used by predecessors.[28] The
aforementioned Nikolaos Spafarii was a Moldovan statesman-adventurer (his
nose was removed after he ended up on the wrong end of a court intrigue)
who traveled as ambassador for Russia to China in 1674–75. He described
his route in peripatetic detail, noting villages (Russians), yurts (non-Russians),
streams, and the distances that separated each. Relying on Seitkul Ablin's
report, Spafarii notes the mosques that local Muslims had refurbished along
the Irtysh, a detail the Siberian Office surveys seem to have overlooked.[29]

For the most part, aesthetic descriptions of the Irtysh basin came later.
John Bell, an adventure-craving Scottish doctor in the Russian service who
traveled to China (1719–22) as part of Lorenz Lange's expedition, described
the Irtysh banks in pastoral terms, writing, "Between Tara and Tobolsky [sic]
are a few small towns, and many villages, inhabited by Mahometan tartars
[sic]. And the country abounds with corn, cattle, and fine pasturage."[30] In
Peter's wake, as Russia grew imperfectly into the "Western destiny" that
Peter had supposedly bequeathed it, the Great Northern Expedition (aka the
Second Kamchatka Expedition, 1734–43) was launched. If knowledge was
possession, the Russian Empire aimed with this expedition to reinforce its
Eurasian claims. Müller spent a decade documenting the history and geography of Siberia as part of this expedition. His description of the Irtysh is
even more flattering than Bell's, which is noteworthy considering that Müller
could not wait to be relieved of his Siberian assignment and return to the
city:[31] "Even though we also travelled through barren regions, I truthfully
can say that the areas along the Irtysh are among the most pleasant in Siberia. Later, we travelled through areas near the Chinese border, which were
just as beautiful. . . . We entered a paradise filled mainly with unidentified
flowering plants, a zoological garden with rare Asian animals gathered before
us, an antique museum of old heathen graves which preserved all kinds of

27. The original report (*stateinii spisok*) does not survive. Vilkov, *Ocherki sotsial'no-ekonomicheskogo razvitiia Sibiri*, chap. 2.

28. RKO, vol. 1, no. 115. *Stateinii spisok* from 1666 already lost.

29. Ogloblin, *Obozrenie*, 1: 51–64, 301–4. Ogloblin's description of these documents does not mention mosques. That is not conclusive evidence that the *dozornye knigi* don't mention them, but Ogloblin tended to note things like that.

30. Bell, *Travels from St. Petersburg*, vol. 1, chap. 2.

31. Andreev, "Trudy G. F. Millera o Sibiri," 73.

curiosities."[32] Although one might expect such observations from educated Enlightenment elites with cultivated sensibilities of the sublime, Spafarii's more practical account also includes the occasional mention of beautiful mountains, forests, and lakes.[33] Such remarks destabilize notions of Siberian landscapes as barren and forbidding.

Lake Yamysh dents the steppe about midway along the length of the Irtysh River. The lake itself was located a little over 3 miles east of the river, so it was not immediately visible, but it emanated an inexplicable smell of violets detectable from a distance and a rose-colored look that Müller said reflected into the sky above. Either of these features may have clued passersby on the river to the salt treasures that sank to the lake's bottom. There is no "discovery" of Lake Yamysh that we can mark in time. Archeological evidence reveals that goods were trafficked all the way across Eurasia via the Irtysh-Kama river system while the Roman Republic was just forming in the sixth century BCE.[34] And it was probably long before that that geologic forces deposited sodium chloride to form the mineral brew that made this landlocked lake a treasure of salt production. Since ancient times various peoples of Siberia frequented this salt lake, hauling away the mineral treasure to preserve their fish and game. It appears on Chinese maps from the thirteenth century.[35] The Turkic root of the name itself, *Iam/Yam*—a word Russians adopted—suggests that Lake Yamysh had probably been a way station on Mongol postal routes centuries ago.[36] Before Lake Yamysh supplied salt to Tobol'sk, it supplied it to Kuchum's capital of Isker. The lake was prominently depicted on the very first Russian map of Siberia, the Godunov map, drawn in 1667 (see fig. 3.1). Semen Remezov gave the lake elaborate attention in his cartographical sketchbook of the late seventeenth century, illustrating the military encampment and salt harvest from the raspberry-colored lake (fig. 5.1).

This salt lake became not just a way station but also a place of exchange. Merchant caravans traveling down the Irtysh River could water at the fresh spring-fed lake near Lake Yamysh well before they left the steppe behind for Siberian forests, where they went in search of furs. Nomads would bring livestock and slaves to sell for products shuttled by merchant caravans. Thus

32. Müller, "Travels in Siberia," 79.

33. Spafarii, *Puteshestvie cherez Sibir'*, 13–17.

34. Bakhrushin, "Puti v Sibir v XVI-XVII vv.," 3: 93.

35. "Ot Yamysheva—k slave."

36. Chulkov reported that Kalmyks called the lake Yamysh; Russians referred to it as Yamyshev. When national boundaries were drawn on Russian Turkestan, Lake Yamyshev fell within Kazakhstan. In the post-Soviet period, the lake has been renamed Lake Kalatuz, which means "much salt" in the Kazakh language.

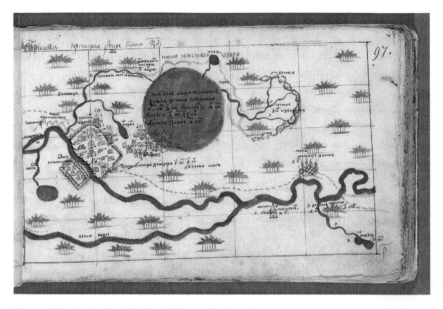

FIGURE 5.1   Landmarks of the Irtysh River: Lake Yamysh.
Source: Leo Bagrow Collection, Remezov, *Khorograficheskaia kniga*, l.97. MS 72 (6) Courtesy Houghton Library, Harvard University.

this confluence of merchants and nomads created a market that left its own ephemeral traces. One seventeenth-century account describes Lake Yamysh as a market in which people would gather by the thousands to trade once a year and then vanish, leaving the shores of Lake Yamysh as deserted as before.[37] When this market began, we cannot say—Russian merchants that traveled the Irtysh in the middle of the sixteenth century knew of it[38]—but we can say it grew significantly in the seventeenth century.

Commerce and Conflict in a Steppe Borderland

By the second half of the seventeenth century Russia had effected a remarkable recovery—after decades of crisis, the Romanov dynasty had established its legitimacy, consolidated state authority, and expanded its power. To be sure, this involved weathering severe challenges such as the riots of 1648. But the subsequent Conciliar Law Code of 1649 facilitated stability. As Russia was asserting its authority in the center, it simultaneously was extending its claims in its eastern periphery. Traveling in the late years of Tsar Aleksei

37. Spafarii, *Puteshestvie cherez Sibir'*, 17.
38. Kamenetskii and Rezun, "Ozero Iamysh kak zona," 32.

Mikhailovich's reign, Spafarii reported that Tatars in the Baraba steppe region had previously paid tribute to the Kalmyk Taisha Ablai, but now paid tribute only to the Russian tsar.[39]

Building the Russian Empire was a long, slow process, as Matthew Romaniello has demonstrated in his excellent study on Kazan.[40] The impressive speed with which Russians reached the Pacific Coast—establishing a camp at Udsk on the Sea of Okhotsk in 1639—can overshadow the fact that the empire building in southern Siberia was a creepingly slow endeavor. The lower Ob-Irtysh (in northern Siberia) was under Russian control by the first decade of the seventeenth century,[41] but the upper reaches that cut through the southern steppe on their way toward their sources in the Altai Mountains would remain contested for more than a century to come. The southernmost settlement of Tara was founded in 1594 but remained a vulnerable fringe of the Russian Empire until the eighteenth century; Omsk, the next permanent Russian town that extended into the steppe, was established only in 1716.[42] Tiumen' was established in 1586, but in 1652 servitors refused orders to dig up rhubarb along the Iset River, not at all far south from Tiumen', because Kalmyks reigned there.[43] The Baraba steppe Tatars may have paid tribute only to the Russian tsar by the 1670s, but it would be many decades before merchants could confidently take the month-long trip from Tara to Tomsk across the Baraba steppe.[44] As will be discussed below, almost a century passed between Russia's first interest in possessing the territory of Lake Yamysh, which lies at the south of the Baraba steppe, and when it successfully established a fort there.

Why the long hiatus? Nomadic groups that dominated the southern steppes of the Eurasian plain prevented the Russian state from achieving uncontested authority both on the steppe and even in forested areas of Russian settlement. Kalmyk threats were a chronic challenge for administrators in western Siberia in the 1630s and 1640s. Rumors and intelligence about, preparations for, or reactions to Kalmyk attacks overwhelm the extant sources from this period. Kalmyks kidnapped settlers, Russian and non-Russian alike; they drove farmers off their fields and drove tribute payers out of the area. Tara, located on the most fertile land in Siberia and at the edge of Russian territorial claims, did not succeed in establishing agricultural self-sufficiency

---

39. Spafarii, *Puteshestvie cherez Sibir'*, 17.

40. Romaniello, *Elusive Empire*.

41. Lantzeff and Pierce, *Eastward to Empire*, 127.

42. The Om fortress was relocated slightly in 1768.

43. RGADA, f. 1111, op. 1, stb. 22, l. 49.

44. Pokrovskii, *Akotvoye istochniki*, no. 115, 164. For instability on the Baraba steppe in the 1640s see RMO, vol. 3, 1654–85, no. 94, 297–312.

for all of the seventeenth century because constant raiding drove farmers off the land.[45]

But to see nomads exclusively as obstacles to empire explains little and distorts an understanding of empire at the periphery, for nomads were key participants in steppe commerce.[46] Warlike conditions, severe weather, food needs, and a burgeoning Siberian leather industry kept demand high. Nomads, especially Kalmyks, were the primary suppliers of livestock that was essential to farming, travel, and warfare, key ingredients of empire building.[47] Commerce was germane to the Russian expansion in Siberia. At the same time, settlers and natives, whom the Muscovite state sought to protect, were chronic targets for nomadic raids. Nomads, then, were integral to the maintenance of this economy, even as their own political economy of raiding and trading, to leave steppe geopolitics entirely aside, threatened chronically to destabilize the system. Simply put, they both threatened trade and were essential participants in it.[48] Therefore the Muscovite state had to be savvy; it was reluctant to stoke Kalmyk anger and it was too steeped in the politics of the Mongol and post-Mongol world to brand these nomads unequivocal enemies.[49] The state sought rather to achieve good relations with steppe nomads so that Russians could grow food, collect fur tribute, and benefit from Inner Eurasian commerce. This is why steppe politics and commerce are characterized by seemingly simultaneous conflict, cooperation, and accommodation. Lake Yamysh is one place where these dynamics played out. The essential commerce at the empire's steppe periphery took place against a backdrop of violence barely held at bay by a mixture of coercion, weapons, and mutual interest. In this sense, Lake Yamysh offers a case study of the interrelated nature of commerce and war on the steppe.

Salt and Politics at Lake Yamysh

The earliest mention of Lake Yamysh in Russian state documents is found in the instructions sent to the commander of the newly established fortress of

---

45. Miller, IS, vol. 2, nos. 307, 309, 371, pp. 462–64, 466, 521; Puzanov, *Voennye factory*, 266–68.

46. I use a general term here because the dominant groups in southern Siberia changed over the course of the seventeenth century even as this dynamic persisted.

47. Vilkov, *Ocherki sotsial'no-ekonomicheskogo razvitiia Sibiri*, 106, 186. See also Gommans, "Horse Trade in Eighteenth-Century South Asia," 228–50; Levi, "India, Russia, and the Eighteenth-Century Transformation of the Central Asian Caravan Trade," 100–102.

48. This dynamic contributed to Khodarkovsky's formulation of "why peace was impossible." See *Russia's Steppe Frontier*, chapter 1.

49. On Russian-steppe relations: Khodarkovsky, *Where Two Worlds Met*; Khodarkovsky, *Russia's Steppe Frontier*, chapters 1, 3.

Tara in 1594.[50] He was directed to send a detachment of musketeers (strel'tsy) and Tatars about 575 miles up the Irtysh River to a salt lake that Kalmyks called Yamysh to procure salt.[51] It was to become a nearly annual endeavor for Siberian servitors.

There were other salt sources in the vicinity that could be relied on.[52] In addition to the great distance, the few miles' trip between the lake and the river complicated logistics, to say nothing of chronic security threats. But Lake Yamysh became the most popular source because of the seemingly endless supply of high-quality salt it yielded. "The salt is of the best quality and will always be plentiful," wrote Müller.[53] Countless salt springs fed the oblong lake that Müller measured as 3 versts, 300 faden long and 2 versts, 350 faden wide (2.33 miles x 1.73 miles). The water was so clear that one could see to the bottom of the fairly shallow lake throughout. The warmth of the steppe sun caused mineral salt to crystallize on the water's surface and then sink slowly to the lake bottom—Müller recorded how he laid on the shore and watched the forming crystals drop slowly to the lake bottom—where it formed a thick crust. Harvesting involved breaking chunks of this crust off from the shallow lake's floor. The salinity was so high that minutes after breaking off a piece salt would again fill in the gap that had been left. Indeed, soldiers would amuse themselves by throwing crosses and other wooden figures into the lake, only to find them fully salt encrusted a few hours later.[54] The salt was so pure and white that additional processing was unnecessary—"the finest salt of Spain or France has nothing on it," wrote M. D. Chulkov proudly in Catherine's Enlightenment Russia.[55] And so Russians regularly made the trip—two months travel from Tobol'sk through hostile territory—to get salt.

Salt extraction expeditions were labor intensive in a manpower-scarce borderland. But salt was an essential ingredient to food preservation, a technique that made long Siberian winters survivable, and the processing of leather hides, an active industry in western Siberia.[56] Many men were deployed to build the flat-bottomed boats that floated the river and to participate in the expeditions. The need for a large security contingent added considerably to

---

50. Miller, IS, vol. 1, no. 13, 352.

51. Chulkov, Istoricheskoe opisanie, 73, 436, 525. Chulkov reports the distance from Tara to Yamyshevsk as 708 versts. 1 versta = 0.92 miles in the seventeenth century, which would make the distance about 651 miles (575 miles is the mileage according to Google maps).

52. AI, vol. 5, no. 288, 520–32; 1751 document offers inventory of salt lakes: http://www.vostlit.info/Texts/Dokumenty/M.Asien/XVIII/1740-1760/Potanin_G_N/101-120/116.htm.

53. Müller, "Travels in Siberia," 81.

54. Chulkov, Istoricheskoe opisanie, 525–26.

55. Ibid., 436.

56. Vilkov, Remeslo i torgovlia, 31.

FIGURE 5.2   Detail of salt harvesting from Lake Yamysh.
Source: Leo Bagrow Collection, Remezov, *Khorograficheskaia kniga*, l.97. MS 72 (6) Courtesy Houghton Library,
Harvard University.

the requirements. Not including boat rowers and pullers, Russian expeditions
to Lake Yamysh consisted of around 150–600 men.[57] Sails could sometimes
be used, but not as consistently as on the Ob because of the winding path
the central Irtysh cut—boats would sometimes end the day quite near where
they had started on account of the river's bends.[58] These boats were typically
rowed or pulled by men along the shore for a trip that took about eight
weeks from Tobol'sk. Traveling with the current made the return trip a few
weeks shorter.[59]

Before Russia had claimed the territory of Lake Yamysh, Lake Yamysh had
entered what Russia perceived as its sphere of interest, although it did not put
it in those terms in the seventeenth century. That said, Russian military access
to Lake Yamysh was entirely impeded in some years. In 1611 the Tobol'sk
governor wrote that "in Tobol'sk there is no salt and from Tara salt has not
been sent for two years because Kalmyks have taken the lake."[60] Peter Perdue writes that Russian settlers arrived at Lake Yamysh in 1613, presumably
adducing a Cossack camp to which Müller referred.[61] At any rate, Russian

57. Kamenetskii and Rezun, "Ozero Iamysh kak zona," 33; Puzanov, *Voennye factory*, 211, 218.
58. GBUTO GATO, f. 47, op. 1, d. 256, l. 1. (In June 1671 a boat having used sails arrived at
Tiumen' from Yamysh.) See also Müller, "Travels in Siberia," 78.
59. Spafarii, *Puteshestvie cherez Sibir'*, 17.
60. Kamenetskii and Rezun, "Ozero Iamysh kak zona," 33. The remark implies that in 1609 a
salt expedition took place.
61. Perdue, *China Marches West*, 107.

caravans traveled in the spring and the market occurred in late summer–fall. Thus, even if they were not permanent residents, Russians could be found at the lake several months out of the year.[62] A 1624–25 Tobol'sk census reported that Tobol'sk customs sent two Bukharans a year as sworn men to Lake Yamysh.[63] In 1626 and 1634 the state dispatched a survey expedition to determine the best site on which to build a Russian fort. In an assessment perhaps short sighted from an entrepreneurial perspective, but making plain nomads' crucial role in steppe commerce, the report discouraged establishing a permanent fort because Kalmyks did not come with livestock reliably every year.[64] There was plenty of fresh water and some pasture, but a lack of woods would make construction difficult. As it was, each year Russia rebuilt a temporary fortress (*ostrog*) to hold hundreds of men.[65] Perhaps they brought wood ballast on the boats that returned to Tobol'sk loaded with salt; on occasion they obtained wood by dismantling some of the boats on which they had arrived.[66] Spafarii was perhaps unaware of these previous discussions nearly half a century later when he advised, "one could build a fort in that place by the river Irtysh or near the lake."[67]

The idea of building a permanent fort was tabled, but expeditions took place most years. In 1634 an army of two thousand threatening Kalmyks delayed the Russian salt procurement. The Russian brigade buckled down in their makeshift fortress until the Kalmyk army moved on.[68] In a classic "middle ground" sense, both parties could damage the other side but neither was powerful enough to wield authority unchallenged.[69] Both parties wanted salt and trade. In 1635 Russians and Mongols negotiated a diplomatic solution; salt extraction and trade were carried out peaceably enough.[70] In some years Russian access was completely blocked.[71] The Russians continued to mount salt expeditions accompanied by military contingents of several hundred men

---

62. Spafarii, who did not travel up the Irtysh, noted that crops grow well around Lake Yamysh, which implies someone was farming in the vicinity.

63. RGADA, f. 214, stb. 81, l. 65.

64. RIB, vol. 8, 335–43, 376–78; Bakhrushin, "Voevody Tobol'skogo razriada v XVII v.," in NT, 3: 257. http://www.vostlit.info/Texts/Dokumenty/China/XVII/1600-1620/Mezd_otn_centr_azii/1-20/17.htm (1626 document). Kamenetskii and Rezun, "Ozero Iamysh kak zona," 31–33.

65. Miller, IS, vol. 2, no. 324, 479.

66. Chulkov, *Istoricheskoe opisanie*, 436.

67. Spafarii, *Puteshestvie chez Sibir'*, 17.

68. Miller, IS, vol. 2, no. 324, 479.

69. White, *Middle Ground*.

70. Perdue, *China Marches West*, 107.

71. Access seems to have been blocked or severely impeded in the following years: 1609, 1610, around 1621, and some of the years in 1688–96 and 1752–60 owing to Qing-Dzhungar wars. Bukharans reported not trading there in 1691: DAI, vol. 10, no. 80, 369.

and fighting could ensue, such as in 1673 when Kalmyks attacked at Lake Yamysh. Seven Russians were killed, but when the dust settled trade proceeded.[72] In 1696 the leader of the Russian expedition was killed during the salt expeditions. A subsequent letter from Moscow warned to make sure soldiers, not workers, handled security.[73]

Under the best circumstances, conditions were tense. Yuri Krizhanich was a Catholic Croatian priest who spent fifteen years in exile in Tobol'sk (1661–76) as a result of his enthusiastic hopes to reunite the separated Christian churches. In his "History of Siberia" Krizhanich described the scene: "When Muscovites reached this place they produce a volley of guns, and reload them anew; they then fire from arquebuses. Having saluted the Taisha in this way, Muscovites give hostages, and having received the same from the Kalmyks, on the same day erect on the bank a defense on which they put guns to have protection in case of a breach of faith. Having extracted salt from the lake, they loaded the boats with it, and then begin to trade."[74] The *amanat* system of hostage taking helped "keep the peace" by raising the stakes of violence for both parties. The expedition of 1638, a year in which at least 180 Siberian soldiers conducted a successful salt harvest, reveals this enduring practice in action.[75] On this occasion, at the Kalmyks' request, a Tobol'sk Bukharan accompanying the expedition was sent to Kalmyk ulus with the intention that he would escort a Kalmyk embassy to Tobol'sk at a future date. Thirteen years prior, in 1625, an entire caravan of Tobol'sk Bukharans had been murdered by the Kalmyks with whom they traveled.[76] These murders, which would have taken his acquaintances if not his own relations, were on this Tobol'sk Bukharan's mind as he was dispatched to the Kalmyk camp in the service of the tsar. In 1640 Ul'ian Remezov, father of the famous Siberian mapmaker Semen Remezov, was part of a mission that brought gifts from the tsar to the Kalmyk group camped at Lake Yamysh.[77] One wonders if he might have come close to being detained as a hostage. In 1690–91 Russians took hostage one Kildei Murza, and perhaps his wife, at Lake Yamysh. Instead of returning them at the end of trading, however, Kildei remained in Russian custody until he accompanied a Russian embassy

72. Kamenetskii and Rezun, "Ozero Iamysh kak zona," 35.

73. AI, vol. 5, no. 288, 520–32.

74. Quoted in Kabo, *Goroda zapadnoi Sibiri*, 69; Kamenetskii and Rezun, "Ozero Iamysh kak zona," 33. Alternative translation: Dmytryshyn, Crownhart-Vaughan, and Vaughan, *Russia's Conquest of Siberia*, no. 113, 437.

75. Puzanov, *Voennye factory*, 218, 237.

76. Ogloblin, *Obozrenie*, 2: 22–23, 37; Burton, *Bukharans*, 510.

77. Bagrow, "Semyon Remezov," 112.

back to the Kazakh horde in 1693.[78] Permanent hostages continued to be a feature of Yamyshevsk trade in the middle of the eighteenth century.[79]

This 1638 expedition reveals another salient feature of steppe politics. Russian access to Lake Yamysh was a negotiated process in which Russians sought to maximize their use of "soft" power. The Russian party sent messengers to various Kalmyk camps inviting them to Lake Yamysh for trade, diplomacy, and to hire livestock to shuttle salt from the lake to the river. That they informed multiple camps shows that they had some sense of the fragmentary political landscape of the steppe, yet inter-Kalmyk politics remained a moving and problematic target. During discussions with at least half a dozen Kalmyk nobles (*taishi*), the Russian emissary raised the issue of kidnapped subjects: the tsar wanted them returned. One Kalmyk noble, Talai, explained that he was about to go to war with one of his brothers and could not return the prisoners, but once he had made peace with his brother, who had the hostages, he would send them to Tobol'sk.[80] The fragmented nature of the Kalmyk political order made it harder for Russians to effectively strategize and negotiate. Distinguishing between good faith and subterfuge was anyone's guess. It was not just a question of whether to take explanations such as Talai's above as genuine or guileful. Highly conciliatory actions were likely to offend rival interests and/or potentially put Russia in the position of appearing a pawn in steppe politics. But Russia tried to get it right. Again and again, Moscow reiterated the need for good relations and current intelligence on the region.[81] These details illustrate that under the best circumstances, salt harvesting and trade was a tense affair. Such was the nature of steppe engagement.

Russians at the Yamysh Market

The value of Lake Yamysh's salt, precious as it was, was eclipsed by the market that developed there over the course of the seventeenth century. Like Tobol'sk, Lake Yamysh was not remote in Eurasian commerce; this market became an important regional event. Fixing the origins of the market is difficult to determine, but by the middle of the seventeenth century it had become a reliable institution around which nomads and merchants planned. Krizhanich's description continued:

---

78. DAI, vol. 10, no. 80.13, 375. On hostage taking: Khodarkovsky, *Russia's Steppe Frontier*, 22.
79. 79 Struve and Potanin, "Poezdka po vostochnoomy Tarbagatiu," 478–79.
80. Miller, IS, vol. 2, no. 378, 527–28.
81. Many such details can be found in documents. See Foust, *Muscovite and Mandarin*, 16.

Having extracted salt from the lake, they loaded the boats with it, and then begin to trade, since at these fairs, money is not in use. Muscovites bring with them goods of all kinds. Kalmyks offer in exchange horned cattle and beasts of burden, their sweets and Chinese tobacco; they also sell slaves—their own cousins, their children. Finally, the ships loaded with salt and trade completed, both sides exchange hostages.[82]

Spafarii described the scene in his account:

When the Russians collect salt from the lake there is a market. And many thousands of people come—Kalmyks and Bukharans and Tatars—and trade with the Russians. They sell horses and slaves and other Chinese wares. And they hold that market for two or three weeks, and Russians, having collected salt and traded, return to Tobol'sk, and the Kalmyks and others [return] to their uluses, and the place is left empty again.[83]

The Yamysh fair would begin around the Feast of the Immaculate Conception in the middle of August and last for two to three weeks. Although Russians were important agents in developing Yamysh trade, it was the commercial cycle more than the Orthodox calendar that determined the timing of the Yamysh market. Large caravans tended to come in from the steppe in autumn, which naturally placed them at Yamysh around August.

Livestock, fabrics, and slaves were the main products Russians bought or exchanged for leather, furs, and "Russian goods" at Lake Yamysh.[84] Kalmyks drove livestock—horses, camels, sheep, goats—to the lake and traded for Russian items as well as for tobacco.[85] Fabrics made up the bulk in nearly every caravan arriving from the east, but even herein the variety was enormous, from thick, coarse cottons to the finest Chinese silks, in all manner of colors. Livestock, dried fruits (raisins, dates), roots such as rhubarb and ginseng, slaves, Indian spices, Chinese tea, sometimes precious gems, paper, and ivory, were some of the goods that weighed Russian flat-bottomed river boats down as they sat low in the water on the return journey downstream. Merchants from the east, meanwhile, departed with furs, leather hides, English wool, fry pans, axes, utensils, mirrors, nails, needles, thread, knit socks, boots, and occasionally

---

82. Quoted in Kabo, *Goroda zapadnoi Sibiri*, 69; Kamenetskii and Rezun, "Ozero Iamysh kak zona," 33. Alternative translation: Dmytryshyn, Crownhart-Vaughan, and Vaughan, *Russia's Conquest of Siberia*, no. 113, 437.

83. Spafarii, *Puteshestvie chez Sibir'*, 17.

84. In Siberia, items imported from Western Europe and brought via Rus', such as mirrors, eyeglasses, needles, and English woolens, were referred to as "Russian" goods.

85. Chimitdorzhiev, "Iz istorii Russko-Mongol'skikh ekonomicheskikh sviazei," 153. On early modern tobacco trade see Romaniello, "Through the Filter of Tobacco."

clocks or mirrors fixed to the backs of camels and horses for the overland portion of the journey.

The slave trade deserves more consideration than it has received. Krizhanich's remark carries opprobrium. But indeed, in some cases people did choose to sell their own family into slavery. For subsistence communities it could serve as a survival strategy in straitened times. In 1701, in the wake of bad harvests and Kalmyk attacks that had brought him and his family to the brink, a Tatar near Tara sought permission—which was denied—to sell his daughter so that she might have a better chance at survival.[86]

Servitors and Cossacks involved in salt extraction also played significant roles in Siberian trade and were probably the majority of Russians at Lake Yamysh. In 1673 Cossacks, Tatars, and Siberian and transit Bukharans rode the boats downstream to Tara together after trading at Lake Yamysh.[87] Russian merchants—privileged (*gosti* and *gostinye sotni*) and nonprivileged alike—frequented Lake Yamysh as well. Though Russian merchants did not turn up at Yamysh in numbers as great as Russian servitors, the volume of trade they generated was not less significant. Merchants in European Russia could learn about Lake Yamysh through various channels. Their agents knew the landscape well, often traveling in cooperation with state servitors. Or they could connect with informed people in Moscow, as Siberian-stationed government servitors cycled in and out of the capital, such as the cartographer Semen Remezov. During his time in Moscow, the Bukharan Seitkul Ablin, who at one point commissioned a *doshchanik* (flat-bottomed wooden riverboat) to transport goods to Lake Yamysh, interacted with powerful elites.[88] At one point he took a loan from the Boyar Boris Ivanovich Morozov or his widow.[89] Elite merchants interested in developing their eastern trade could certainly have and probably did seek out experienced men like Ablin. In 1668 at least half a dozen merchants from Rus' traded at Lake Yamysh.[90] In 1685 almost fifty Russian merchants were reported to have traveled all the way to Lake Yamysh.[91] The Filat'ev agent Dmitrii Konstantinov was there in 1685 and 1686 too, along with another privileged merchant of the second rank.[92] A Russian merchant from Yaroslavl' traded at Lake Yamysh in 1705.[93]

---

86. Ogloblin, "Bytovye cherty nachala XVIII veka," 3–7.
87. TKSG, vol. 1, 75.
88. Bakhrushin, "Sibir i Sredniaia Aziia," in NT, 4: 210.
89. Tomsinskii, *Khoziaistvo Boiarina B. I. Morozova XVII v.*, chap. 1, 251.
90. RMO, vol. 3, 233.
91. RGADA, f. 214, stb. 935, l. 18.
92. RGADA, f. 214, stb. 892, l. 44.
93. RGADA, f. 214, op. 5, d. 841, l. 4.

But the merchants who turned out at Lake Yamysh in the greatest numbers were likely Bukharans from Siberia and Central Asia.

Revenue beyond Russia's Border

Salt was the original draw, but the Lake Yamysh market subsequently developed as a space, even amid the state's operations, free from the state's regulation, at least initially. True to form, the Muscovite state saw opportunity for revenue generation in the Yamysh trade and soon sought to both regulate trade at Lake Yamysh and participate in it. At some point the state began sending customs clerks from Tobol'sk to Lake Yamysh during the market to tax the trade that occurred there. As mentioned earlier, as early as 1624–25 Tobol'sk customs sent two Bukharans a year as sworn men to Lake Yamysh.[94] It may be that, at first, customs clerks accompanied the expeditions to take inventory of the salt harvested (state salt would not be subject to tax).[95] It is not clear if they collected taxes in the early stages, but in the resource-strapped periphery I am skeptical that they would have committed servitors *not* to collect revenue. Since no seventeenth-century customs books from Lake Yamysh survive, knowledge about activity there can only be gained second- and thirdhand, such as merchants declaring in Tobol'sk, Tiumen', Tomsk, or Tara customs records that they had come via Lake Yamysh and paid taxes there. In a customs book from Tara for 1674–75 several entries follow a similar formula: "and with him was released their harvest (*promyslu*) from Lake Yamysh, 1,100 pud by the customs clerks' estimate, and Tara customs recorded a valuation of 44 rubles."[96] Such language indicates a customs official was on-site inventorying salt harvests, but does not confirm that taxes were levied. Another entry from the same customs book does specify that taxes were collected at Lake Yamysh, making the earliest evidence I have located for tax collection at Lake Yamysh date to 1673–74. A Cossack departed Tara for Tobol'sk carrying fabrics on behalf of his father-in-law. Taxes were not collected on some of the fabrics because they had been traded for Russian

---

94. RGADA, f. 214, stb. 81, l. 65.

95. It is mildly puzzling that someone from the Customs Office rather than the Governor's Office would oversee such record keeping. After all, customs officers in western Siberia generally did not participate in fur tribute collection, which was the purview of the *voevoda*. Customs clerks did tend to assist more in tribute collection in eastern Siberia. Timoshina, "Voevodskoe i tamozhennoe upravlenie," 255–61.

96. TKSG, vol. 1, 75.

goods on which the one-tenth tax had been paid at Lake Yamysh in 1673/74 (7182). Other declarations indicate the same.[97]

In contrast to the picture Krizhanich painted above—of a lake deserted soon after the state salt boats departed—Russian customs officials apparently remained at Lake Yamysh collecting taxes into the autumn: on October 25, 1674 a caravan arrived at Tara that had paid Russian customs at Yamysh.[98] Yet just one week earlier a caravan had arrived to Tara from Yamysh, on which taxes were levied—one-tenth tax on the Siberians' goods and the one-twentieth tax on the transit Bukharans' goods—which suggests inconsistent inspections and/or collections.[99] Indeed, available evidence suggests inconsistency. A Tobol'sk customs book from 1686–87 (7195) indicates that taxes on people coming via Lake Yamysh were adjusted in cases where taxes had been paid at Lake Yamysh. For example, in 1684–85 (7193) the Tobol'sk Bukharan Menglish Ianmurzin had paid tax on fabrics and paper he purchased there.[100] Merchants undergoing customs inspection in Tobol'sk in 1686 reported that they had paid the one-tenth tax at Lake Yamysh in 1685–86 (7194).[101] Presumably the Russian state collected revenue relatively consistently henceforth, notwithstanding geopolitical disruptions. Russian customs collections seemed to stabilize in the eighteenth century. In 1701 the customs official who traveled to Irbit to collect taxes (a similar arrangement to Lake Yamysh) collected 3,029 rubles in taxes.[102] In 1703 about 3,000 rubles in taxes were collected on 19,043 rubles worth of goods declared at Lake Yamysh.[103] This was as much revenue for the Russian state as collections from the very popular Irbit market held in January in far western Siberia.[104]

Scandal

In the 1650s–1660s Yamysh was the most intensively traveled trade route connecting Russia to Central and Eastern Asia. State caravans had been going to Yamysh since at least 1655, and came to account for a substantial proportion of trade flow there.[105] By the last third of the seventeenth century, Lake Yamysh had become a place where state and private (legal and illegal) trade

97. Ibid.
98. TKSG, vol. 1, 81.
99. TKSG, vol. 1, 73–74 (Tara Customs book, 1674/75).
100. RGADA, f. 214, kn. 892, l. 18.
101. RGADA, f. 214, kn. 892, l. 106.
102. See Ogloblin, "Bytovye cherty nachala XVIII veka."
103. Vilkov, Remeslo i torgovlia, 207.
104. Ogloblin, "Bytovye cherty nachala XVIII veka."
105. Vilkov, Remeslo i torgovlia, chap. 2.

coexisted in parallel, but with overlap. As Russians extended their presence there, they did so with all the imperfections typical of peripheral outposts—venal officials and merchants, trading servitors, and local leverage that cannot be discounted despite proscriptions from the center. In other words, the tension that surrounded exchange at Lake Yamysh was not exclusively cross-cultural, as the following episode illustrates.

In January 1685 a caravan of the "tsar's treasury" (state goods) arrived at Lake Yamysh. It was led by two Tobol'sk locals, the provincial gentryman Fëdor Shulgin and the Bukharan merchant Seidiash Kulmametev, and consisted of 73 (or maybe 273) men heavily laden with tsarist furs. There they met transit Bukharans (i.e., Central Asian, as opposed to Siberian Bukharans) who had arrived with a caravan of Eastern fabrics and goods to trade.[106] Kulmametev was responsible for negotiating the sale of the tsar's goods, but no deal was struck. As others waited, he reported that the Bukharans were offering terms that went from unacceptable to worse with each passing day.

Impatience grew. The situation became contentious. Things deteriorated at the top first, with the two servitors in charge, Shulgin and Kulmametev, hurling reciprocal accusations at each other. The Russian accused the Bukharan of doing his own trading on the side at the expense of the state; Shulgin alleged that Kulmametev had traded his own goods before the tsar's. He accused the Bukharan of traitorous behavior—a vague but dangerous charge—and stealing. Shulgin further accused Kulmametev, helped by other Bukharans, relatives, and Cossacks, of smuggling salt and other goods onto his own boat and the state boat bound for Tobol'sk. Then, without declaring his salt at customs, he had it secretly distributed among yurts in nearby settlements.[107] Shulgin implicated Kulmametev's son and associates, including a Russian "sworn man," Ivan Pestriakov, in the wrongdoing. Apparently Kulmametev's son and Pestriakov were caught with Bukharan wares before they had been allowed to acquire them; the son and Pestriakov had forced their way past the guards in order to haul wares to the Bukharans' caravan.[108] Kulmametev retaliated with similar accusations against Shulgin, but went further. He charged that Shulgin slandered him in calling him a traitor and a thief. He accused Shulgin of misusing the labor of state servitors. Finally,

---

106. RGADA, f. 214, stb. 935, ll. 63, 103. At two points in the file, it notes not 73 but 273 people in the embassy.

107. Ibid., l. 122. He levied these charges in his *stateinii spisok*, the report submitted by Fëdor Shulgin after the expedition.

108. RGADA, f. 214, stb. 935, l. 2.

in his most serious accusation, Kulmametev accused Shulgin of harming the state treasury by thwarting the decent deals that he had struck.[109]

The scandal between Shulgin and Kulmametev was not the only conflict brewing at this frontier outpost. The servitors were becoming restless. They also wanted to trade, but were allowed to do so only after the state trading was completed. In their frustration they approached Shulgin "with mutinous shouts" (*buntom i krykom*). Not surprisingly, Shulgin reacted strongly to the servitors' insubordination. Along with his accusations against Kulmametev, Shulgin charged the servitors of mutinous behavior. They reciprocated by escalating their rhetorical stance—accusing Shulgin of myriad abuses and wrongdoing. The unpopular Shulgin admitted to beating one soldier on the name day of Tsar Ioann Alekseevich, but insisted that the victim had deserved it.[110]

One of the servitors' complaints involved a man named Dmitrii Konstantinov, referred to as a "Greek."[111] They pressured—even threatened—Shulgin to release Konstantinov to China.[112] According to Shulgin, Kulmametev had attempted to strike a deal with Konstantinov, who had arrived at Lake Yamysh from China without proper transit documentation (*proezzhaia gramota*) from the Russian authorities. The servitors anticipated that once the state contract was cinched with Konstantinov, he would be gone and they could begin to trade. Thus they lobbied for his release to China. However, following his orders, Shulgin had all the Greek's wares confiscated and sent to Tobol'sk. Konstantinov, for his part, claimed to have done the same before. On a previous trip he had stored his goods in a monastery near Tobol'sk while attending to other business. In this incident, Konstantinov revealed no affiliation with the elite merchants the Filat'ev brothers, the subject of chapter 6, but has been documented in other cases as their agent. The historian Vilkov speculated that gost' Ostafii Filat'ev may have used his influence to keep Konstantinov out of trouble, given his lack of documentation, which, by the way, became a problem only *after* the deal fell through.

It is unclear why the Bukharan negotiations stalled. The head of the Bukharan caravan, Iuge, blamed Kulmametev for the impasse, declaring that "such an example of so willfully dictating price is unthinkable."[113] The

109. Ibid., l. 122.
110. Ibid., l. 14.
111. The label "Greek" in early modern Russia referred to an Orthodox non-Russian, perhaps from the Black Sea region, Ottoman Empire, Balkans, or Greece proper (though not necessarily).
112. RGADA, f. 214, stb. 935, l. 2.
113. Ibid., l. 123. "*A takova de obraztsa ne byvaet shto v nevoliu tovaram tsena postavit.*" Fëdor, two days before departing, sent two messengers to the head of the Bukharan contingent to inquire about the dealings with Kulmametev.

subsequent investigation revealed that about 150 men were aware that Iuge had made that remark, a tidbit that may say more about gossip than truth.[114] What is striking is how attuned these servitors were to the status of state trading in this militarized market setting where supply and demand explain but a small part of the complicated dynamics this episode exposes. Moscow, predictably, ordered an investigation. The investigators cast a wide net, questioning over a hundred servitors from various Siberian posts, Cossacks, Kalmyks, and merchants, in order to produce a document even longer (144 pages) that, unfortunately, contains no resolution. Nonetheless, this story epitomizes the challenges and diversity of frontier commerce.

First, we encounter a range of characters—including monastery peasants, foreign smugglers, Russian traders, state officials, resident and transit Bukharans, and a range of state servitors (soldiers, Cossacks, bureaucrats)—on the early modern Siberian frontier in a highly charged web of cross-cultural, cross-station, militarized-cum-market commerce—legal, illegal, private, and state. The state trade of caravans of furs and precious fabrics had little in common with the subsistence trade that several of the servitors here desired and relied on.[115] Yet these different types of trade occupied the same spaces, involved some of the same actors, and affected one another. Entrepreneurial, subsistence, state, and private trade influenced, overlapped, and competed with one another for transactions. The relationship was not simply oppositional, but might be described as competitively symbiotic.

Second, this episode exposes the not only contested but also instrumental nature of frontier commerce. At this distant outpost the gaps between state aspirations and the imposition of authority are writ large. The state could turn a blind eye to bending the rules for the sake of results, but if some ineffable tipping point was crossed, the project devolved into scandal—the result of a precarious calculus of interests, results, circumstances, and proscription gone wrong. But it was not just a matter of turning a blind eye to certain transactions. The scandal at Lake Yamysh—through the soldiers' insistence on their need to trade—demonstrates the important gap that trade filled: soldiers traded to supplement their allowances in order "to meet their own needs," a phrase as vague to us as it was legitimate to the actors in seventeenth-century Siberia. Fëdor Shulgin and Seidiash Kulmametev were not newcomers to frontier commerce. They both would have known the rules in this dynamic, which heightens the mystery over why this trip devolved into scandal.

114. Ibid., l. 123.
115. On composition of trade: Vilkov, *Remeslo i torgovlia*, chap. 3.

Permanent Customs at Yamyshevsk

The Russian state established a permanent customs post at Yamyshevsk and Semipalatinsk in 1730.[116] By this time, rules of the customs regime had changed, resulting in a different institutional landscape than what we surveyed at the establishment of the Siberian customs system in the early seventeenth century. In 1687 the state eliminated the passage tax and several other smaller fees in an effort to streamline collections. In 1693 the New Trade Statute for Siberia made the Trade Statute of 1653 applicable in Siberia, with the result that Bukharans felt some of the protectionist measures they had been spared for nearly half a century.[117] A major change came in 1698. In an attempt to avoid chronic tussles over improper collection of the one-tenth tax—in theory, the tax was collected only once—the state limited collection of the one-tenth tax to Verkhotur'e or Nerchinsk, the two major entry and exit points to Siberia. Essentially, this reform gutted the rationale of an internal customs regime (fees and other taxes continued to be collected at other posts), although it continued to officially exist until 1753.[118] The internal customs regime's elimination was declared in late 1753, effective in European Russia in 1754. Although dismantling of Siberian customs posts lagged behind European Russia, Yamyshevsk and Semipalatinsk were fairly promptly, in 1755, designated as international trading posts.[119] With the 1754 reforms, Yamyshevsk and Semipalatinsk were recognized as customs posts along the international border—that is, their raison d'être obtained. However, with this reform Semipalatinsk, which had attracted more settlement as a result of its nearby mines, became the more major post. From their establishment until midcentury Yamyshevsk generated more customs revenue than Semipalatinsk. After 1754, however, Semipalatinsk revenues surpassed those of Yamyshevsk, and the gap grew throughout the second half of the century.[120] That is, Yamyshevsk's declining revenues is a reflection of administrative changes and does not indicate an overall decline in trade. Rather, Eurasian trade increased across the eighteenth century.[121]

---

116. In March 1730 the Tobol'sk Bukharan Shaim Shamurzin declared a shipment of goods with "customs documentation" that had been issued at Semipalatinsk. GBUTO GATO, f. 29, op. 1, d. 153, 2 ll. Struve and Potanin, "Poezdka po vostochnoomy Tarbagatiu," 523.

117. Vilkov, *Remeslo i torgovlia*, 9. See AI, vol. 5, 473 for a reminder to Nerchinsk voevoda in 1697 that Bukharans should in fact pay the one-tenth tax.

118. Kopylov, "Tamozhennaia politika v Sibiri v XVII v.," 368.

119. Customs collections had existed at these posts since 1730 or 1731. What changed was the status.

120. Ziiaev, *Ekonomicheskie sviazy*, 99.

121. Aksenov et al., *Ekonomicheskaia istoriia Rossiia*, 2: 847–48; Kahan, *Plow, the Hammer and the Knout*, 100, 215–31; Levi, *India Diaspora in Central Asia*, 239; Levi, "India, Russia, and the Eighteenth-Century Transformation of the Central Asian Caravan Trade," 524.

Ultimately, Nerchinsk briefly and then Kiakhta in a more sustained way did eclipse Lake Yamysh as depots for Russian trade with China.[122] But it did not happen immediately. Yamysh trade was at its most vibrant in the last third of the seventeenth century and remained strong into the middle of the eighteenth century. For example, the Dutchman Eberhard Ides, on his 1692–95 embassy, noted that Tiumen' Bukharans "drive a great trade up the Rhitisch or Irtis [River], into the Kalmakian territories and carry their goods to China. And if it were safe to travel the Kalmakian country, the most expeditious way to China would be to pass the Jamuschowa oserz, or Jamuschian Lake [sic]."[123] That he considered the Yamysh route the most desirable route reveals something of the important place this riverine commercial highway continued to hold even after alternative routes were well established. The greatest known Yamysh customs revenues were collected around the turn of the century: nearly 3,000 rubles in 1703. This level puts it at approximately the level of customs revenue of Novgorod and Pskov.[124] Owing to a lack of sources, it is unknown if revenue continued to climb from 1703 to 1730.

Eurasian Trade: Shifting, Growing

Lake Yamysh became an important way station of Russia-China trade. The trade outpost shortened the distance one needed to travel to obtain goods from distant places, as goods from Russia, Western Europe, China, and Central Asia, as well as livestock, converged at this lake on the Eurasian plain. Just how much contact Russians had with "Chinese" is unclear.[125] From the middle of the seventeenth century Cossacks in the Amur region had considerable interaction of a commercial and martial nature with Chinese. Unlike Bukharans, Indians, Persians, "Greeks," Armenians, and the nations of northern Europe, Chinese merchants seem not to have come to the Russian Empire to trade.[126] Since so little documentation of trade at Lake Yamysh exists, I have not been able to determine if Chinese merchants ever frequented the market at Lake Yamysh, but with Bukharans as able intermediaries in the Sino-Russian trade, their merchandise moved across the continent anyway.

---

122. Vilkov, *Remeslo i torgovlia*, 211.
123. Ides, *Three Years Travels*, 11.
124. Vilkov, *Remeslo i torgovlia*, 200; See Kotilaine, *Russia's Foreign Trade*, 227, 448.
125. "Chinese" as an essentialized category in the early modern era is problematic. But since it is a category Russians—attuned to the multiple identities that inhabited the borderlands they occupied—used, I appropriate their terms.
126. Perdue also includes Mongols as trade intermediaries. See *China Marches West*, 143, 205.

The sustained vitality of not only the Yamysh trade gestures toward a larger picture of the political economy of early modern Eurasian trade. Tobol'sk's apparently diminished traffic in the final quarter of the seventeenth century was a consequence of both new regulations and market dynamics, not of declining Siberian trade. Trade was shifting as a result of the growing popularity of the Irbit and Yamysh (and later, Orenburg) markets, which skirted the southern periphery of the Russian Empire. Irbit, established in the 1630s, was even closer to Rus' than was Tiumen', and by the end of the seventeenth century had become a popular alternative to Tobol'sk. It burgeoned as a market over the same time that Yamysh did. Vilkov suggested, and my research corroborates, that merchants began to circumvent Tobol'sk altogether, skirting the southern periphery of Siberia, traveling from Yamysh to Tara to Tiumen', and then heading southwest to the Irbit market.[127] For example, in 1704 merchants traveled from Yamysh to Tiumen'. A customs book survives for Tobol'sk from that year, but does not indicate that those merchants proceeded to Tobol'sk.[128] Despite this competition from other depots, Tobol'sk remained the primary trade center of Siberia for most of the seventeenth century.[129] Keep in mind as well that tax changes contributed to decreases in revenue. According to A. N. Kopylov, the elimination of the transit tax in 1687 reduced overall revenue. The state's corrective regulation in 1693 spurred tax evasion, resulting in further diminished revenue that is not the result of diminished trade.[130]

In the eighteenth century, Tobol'sk's relative importance declined as alternative trading markets at Kiakhta and Orenburg developed. And yet in the 1760s Tobol'sk's registered foreign trade turnover in ruble values was still more than double Kiakhta's.[131] Overall, eighteenth-century Russian trade increased tremendously. Russian exports were 3.6 million rubles in 1710 and 100 million rubles in 1799.[132] Siberian trade contributed substantially to this dramatic increase. China trade grew dramatically, channeled by treaty

127. For example, customs books from 1704 fix people coming from Yamysh in Tiumen', but not in Tobol'sk. See RGADA, f. 214, stb. 1376, ll. 1035–59 (Tobol'sk, 1704); GBUTO GATO, f. 29, op. 1, d. 29, ll. 1–12; d. 36, l. 16; d. 39, ll. 1–9 (Tiumen', 1704). Vilkov, Remeslo i torgovlia, 186, 172. From 1672 to 1700, nine caravans from Central Asia arrived at Tara. Evseev, "Tara v svoi pervye dva stoletiia," 105; Ziiaev, Ekonomicheskie sviazy, 50.

128. Tiumen': GBUTO GATO, f. 29, op. 1, d. 29, ll. 1–12; d. 36, l. 16; d. 39, ll. 1–9. Tobol'sk: RGADA, f. 214, stb. 1376, ll. 1035–59. A lack of extant customs books prohibit systematic testing of this hypothesis.

129. Ziiaev, Ekonomicheskie sviazy, 83.

130. Kopylov, "Tamozhennaia politika v Sibiri v XVII v.," 363–65.

131. Razgon, Sibirskoe kupechestvo, 185, Table 38. Turnover: Tobol'sk: 76,700 rubles; Kiakhta: 33,200 rubles. Irkutsk had the highest turnover: 115,700 rubles.

132. Aksenov, Ekonomicheskaia istoriia Rossii, 1: 403.

agreement via the new trading post at Kiakhta.[133] Trade with Central Asia also increased as trade routes shifted northward to accommodate local instabilities.[134] In the sense that a rising tide raises all ships, the sustained importance of Tobol'sk amid the growth of markets in Irbit, Orenburg, Nerchinsk, and Kiakhta markets suggests a vibrancy in early modern Eurasian trade. As we saw above, the story at Yamysh supports a similar interpretation.

Yamysh retained importance not only because it was an alternative route to China. China was not the only game in town. The Irtysh line offered a well-trodden route to China and better access to the important centers of Central Asia. This became particularly important when tensions with Persia made it look like Caspian Sea routes would be impeded, and after the Bekkevich crisis. Further, Yamysh was not just a way station en route to China or Inner Asia. The route also became important for the commerce it generated in Siberia. Merchants who made the trip enjoyed advanced buying opportunities. The Tiumen' Bukharan Mamshenii Minlik, who in 1733 declared a shipment of fabric and furs that he had imported via Lake Yamysh and intended to disperse to various Siberian towns, was following a trade pattern typical of many Siberian Bukharans.[135] This dynamic actually hurt Tobol'sk, as Bukharans would leave Yamysh and head to the markets of towns like Tomsk, Kuznetsk, and Eniseisk.[136]

Extending Empire: The Irtysh Line

Russian involvement at Yamysh was long-standing, but "possession" remained outside its purview—Soviet literature calling the Yamysh market "on the border" (*pogranichnii*) in the seventeenth century was an exaggeration.[137] That changed with the construction of the Irtysh line, a major geopolitical advance by Russia from 1715 to the 1720s. By 1760 G. F. Müller could triumphantly narrate: "At the start of the current century all the land between the Ob and Irtysh from the mouth of the River Om were still filled with nomads of the Kalmyk ulusi. . . . All that is now finished. The steppe between the Ob and Irtysh has been cleaned of unknown (*chuzhikh*) peoples, and in place of that has been filled with many Russian settlers; there have been established

133. On Kiakhta: Sladkovskii, *History of Economic Relations*, 53; Foust, *Muscovite and Mandarin*, 47.
134. Rossabi, "'Decline' of the Central Asian Caravan Trade," 351–70; Levi, "India, Russia, and the Eighteenth-Century Transformation."
135. GBUTO GATO, f. 29, op. 1, d. 186, l. 1.
136. Ziiaev, *Ekonomicheskie sviazy*, 87–88.
137. Kurilov, "Uchastie sluzhilykh liudei," 81.

rich silver and copper mines. . . . All this should be credited to the newly constructed forts along the Irtysh River."[138]

In 1713 Governor Gagarin reported on rumored deposits of lucrative gold dust in the riverbeds of Central Asia. According to Müller, on May 22, 1714, Tsar Peter, about to depart for battle with the Swedish fleet, hastily dispatched an order to pursue the matter: "Build a town [gorod] at Lake Yamysh. If you can, and building a fort upriver, search farther up that river, as far as boats can pass. From that place, go by foot to the town of Erkent, and try to take that city. For this, get 2,000 men, or as you need, 1,500. Also, get a few Swedes, for three years, who know something about engineering and artillery. Also, someone who knows, even a little, about minerals, and a few officers, but not more than three."[139] In October 1715, a Russian military contingent led by Lieutenant Bucholz dismantled three of the boats on which they had arrived to build a fort near Lake Yamsyh. In February 1716 the fort was razed by Dzhungars. Sometimes Dzhungars sought Russian protection, but having made a temporary peace with the Qing, the Dzunghar leader Tsewang Araptan felt no need to cultivate Russian goodwill against the empire on their other flank, goes one version. Another is that a subordinate acted against Tsewang Araptan's orders.[140] The retreating Russian army built the fortress of Omsk between Tara and Yamysh in 1716. Peter applied persistence in this case: Yamshevskaia fort, as it became known, was rebuilt in 1718, followed by Biysk, Semipalatinsk, and Ust'-Kamenogorsk in 1720.[141] By the middle of the eighteenth century, the Irtysh line consisted of five forts, ten outposts, twenty-nine redoubts, and thirty-five beacon points that stretched 888 versts (817 miles).[142] The promises of gold did not materialize, but with this series of forts Russia's fortifications no longer skirted the forest-steppe border as had the previous Siberian towns. The Russian Empire had laid claim to the steppe.

Why the Russian Empire decided to advance the Irtysh line beginning in 1715 is complicated. Geopolitics, of course, played a role. Developments in this region cannot be properly explained without reference to the rise and fall of the Dzhungars in the seventeenth and eighteenth centuries. Muscovy's

138. Miller, "Izvestie o pesoshnom zolote v Bukharii."

139. Ibid., 480.

140. Foust, *Muscovite and Mandarin*, 17.

141. See Bakhrushin, "Russkoe prodvizhenie za Ural," in *NT*, 3: 137–62; Donnelly, *Russian Conquest of Bashkiria*, 40. On fort construction in 1715: *Pamiatniki Sibirskoi istorii XVIII veka*, bk. 2, no. 39, 138–41.

142. Ziiaev, *Ekonomicheskie sviazy*, 83–84. LeDonne, "Building an Infrastructure," 581–608. For a detailed description of Irtysh and subsequent Siberian lines see Muratova, "Na strazhe rubezhei Sibiri."

attempts to put relations with steppe nomads on as good a footing as possible so as to facilitate trade threatened the Russo-China trade because China was upset by any moves perceived as Russia aiding or abetting the Dzhungars. Hindsight is not 20/20 when it comes to the early modern steppe. In retrospect, few appreciate that the Dzhungars were a major steppe power—Peter Perdue justifiably calls them an empire—that posed a major challenge to the new Qing dynasty.[143] Indeed, the Dzhungaria matter spurned China out of its aloof diplomatic stance. At a time when much of the world courted China for access, China sent its first diplomatic missions in modern times to Torguts and Russia, seeking to secure help or at least noninterference against the Dzhungars. In some sense, it is remarkable that Russia-China trade increased in spite of Manchu-Dzhungar wars. This was a major, protracted conflict between committed rivals and involved significant Eurasian trade routes; the wars constituted a real imposition Eurasian trade. Russia, for its part, most interested in securing stable trade with all as it simultaneously pursued mining development, found itself pulled between possibility and pragmatism in a dynamic in which neutrality proved impossible.[144]

The advance along the Irtysh follows patterns seen elsewhere in the Russian Empire. Defensive lines had a long history at Muscovy's edges. The Abatis line, completed in the sixteenth century, defended Russians against Crimean Tatars. It consisted of a series of constructed mounds, ditches, log barricades, and watchtowers. Like the Great Wall of China, it began as a series of discrete defensive posts that were eventually united. It was followed by the more southerly Belgorod line in the 1630s, a massive state-building project that extended Muscovite sovereignty toward the Black Sea steppe.[145] In the wake of the conquest of Kazan, defensive lines running from the Volga directly westward south of Kazan were constructed.[146] About 40 miles south the Simbirsk line, another such defensive line, was built in the 1630s.[147]

Military presence was a prerequisite to Russian steppe farming, for settled populations solidify territorial hegemony in ways that military outposts cannot. Recognizing this, Müller recommended to Empress Elizabeth mandatory serf resettlement along the Irtysh (and the Amur) to secure Russian sovereignty against Chinese advancement.[148] Elizabeth did not implement

---

143. Perdue, *China Marches West.*

144. This interpretation draws largely on Foust, *Muscovite and Mandarin,* 34, 44, 61–66, esp. 236.

145. Davies, *Warfare, State and Society,* Abatis line: chap. 2, Belgorod line: chap. 3.

146. Romaniello, *Elusive Empire,* 10, 39.

147. Simbirsk is a little over 60 versts (= ~ 40 miles) south of Tetiushii, the eastern point of the Arzamas line. Murchison, *Geology of Russia in Europe,* 244.

148. Müller, "Travels in Siberia," 21.

the recommendation, but Catherine II would institute just such a program along the Volga, a history that has been well told by Willard Sunderland.[149] But the establishment of mining in the Altai Mountains by the Demidovs in the 1720s to some degree accomplished the same, precipitating a Russian influx farther up the Irtysh than Russians had heretofore settled.[150]

This is not the place to fully analyze the motivations behind the construction of the Irtysh line. They were complicated. Geopolitical and economic concerns interacted and could even elide, such as when it came to sourcing weapons-critical minerals, which Russians were keen to exploit in the Altai Mountains. Moreover, the Dzhungars were not the only players in the region. According to Stephen Kotkin, the Russians were able to advance along the Irtysh only after the forced departure of Kirgiz from the region in 1703.[151] From the Treaty of Nerchinsk in 1689 through the Treaty of Kiakhta in 1727, Russia's first priority was securing trade, whereas China's first priority was securing its free hand to act against the Dzhungars. "To assuage fears of Manchus with regard to Russian role in Dzhungaria, Izmailov was to assure them that Russian ostrogs along Irtysh were nothing more than a fulcrum directed against the Dzhungars—not a prelude to offensive action against Manchu armies."[152] Yet Russia must too have been wary of the westward-looking Qing, and it was hard for a defensive pragmatism not to give way to opportunism as the last Dzhungar leader succumbed to smallpox in Tobol'sk in 1757, bringing the once-great steppe empire to its categorical end.[153]

Taking all of these considerations and consequences together, construction of the Irtysh line is not best understood as a military advance or a knee-jerk reaction to access fabled gold dust. It was an attempt to cultivate reliable trade routes with Central Asia and beyond.[154] Peter saw great profit and potential in trade with India and the Orient. The Caspian was one way through which to access this trade, and Peter made overtures in that direction that did not succeed.[155] With prospects in the Caspian diminishing, Peter redirected to push into the Siberian steppe with the intention of improving alternative

149. Sunderland, *Taming the Wild Field*.
150. Bakhrushin, "Russkoe prodvizhenie za Ural," 3: 159.
151. Kotkin, "Defining Territories and Empires." Bakhrushin, "Eniseiskie Kirgizy v XVII v.," in NT, 3: 176–224.
152. Foust, *Muscovite and Mandarin*, 19.
153. Ibid., 251–68.
154. Ziiaev, *Ekonomicheskye sviazy*, 81, 94; LeDonne, "Building an Infrastructure," 581–608; Kozlova, *Rossiiskii absoliutizm i kupechestvo v XVIII veke*, 178; Malikov, "Formation of a Borderland Culture," 309–17; Kilian, "Allies and Adversaries," 242.
155. Anisimov, *Reforms of Peter the Great*, 144–66.

access to Central Asia. The gruesome end of the failed Bekovich-Cherkasski expedition in 1717 provided additional stimulus to the advance up the Irtysh that had faltered in its first phase. In the coming years, Russians capitalized on their logistical (not military, emphasized Puzanov) prowess to build a series of forts up the Irtysh River into the heart of the Eurasian steppe.[156]

Conclusion

In the intervening century between when Russia considered establishing itself at Lake Yamysh and actually did so, Lake Yamysh was hardly a remote place. In 1744, 565 Bukharan merchants passed through Yamysh in the months of January and December alone. On one day in March 1745, 150 or so Bukharans departed from Yamysh in a single day.[157] In 1749 Yamyshevsk customs collected 3,378 rubles, 88 kopeks in customs taxes, a number that would soon dramatically and permanently decrease owing to changes in Russian customs law, even as trade at Yamysh continued. In the middle of the eighteenth century, Yamysh was the most heavily fortified post on the Irtysh line (only Kuznetsk had more men in all of Siberia).[158] It had a full customs staff (minus accountant) of inspectors and assessors. For all the innovation the Irtysh outpost saw, traditional aspects of steppe politics and Muscovite customs endured: the *amanat* system remained a cornerstone of security maintenance, and a merchant from Tara petitioned the tsar to be released from his duty of tax collection at Lake Yamysh.[159] The Russian Empire grew "slowly, unevenly" as well as "in fits and bounds."[160] As in other stories of imperial borderlands, Lake Yamysh's incorporation into the Russian Empire did not happen quickly or automatically. It was slow, contested, and ultimately the result of investment of imperial resources. Lake Yamysh illustrates all of that—the latently violent nature of steppe trade and the slow expansion of the Russian Empire against a steppe backdrop in which nomadic players, all but erased from the remote regions they once dominated, were formidable actors in their time, all amid an enduring tendency of people to trade in spite of obstacles and an early modern increase in Eurasian trade along the Irtysh River.

---

156. LeDonne, "Building an Infrastructure," 585.
157. Ziiaev, *Ekonomicheskye sviazy*, 84, 77, 88. On January 24, 1747, 117 transit Bukharans left Yamysh for Central Asia.
158. Muratova, "Na strazhe rubezhei Sibiri," 32–46.
159. Evseev, "Tara v svoi pervye dva stoletiia," 102.
160. Romaniello, *The Elusive Empire*, 6, 82; Foust, "Russian Expansion to the East," 469–79.

PART THREE

The Merchants
of Siberia

Previous chapters discussed the political economy of early modern Russia and explored the geographical and cultural spaces in which trade took place, from Moscow's Kitai gorod to remote Siberian customs posts to seasonal markets of the Eurasian steppe. Part 3 brings us closer to the people that inhabited that commercial world through a reconstruction of selected family enterprises. The selection of merchants featured here was largely informed by sources. The families demonstrate tenacity; they appear at various customs posts through the years and the generations, leaving sufficient evidential crumbs to begin to sketch the lines of their careers. Yet there were dozens more families who could have sufficed. These merchants were not alone.

Not all of the merchants of Siberia lived in Siberia. As we will see, most of the Russian merchants—privileged and nonprivileged alike—organized operations from European Russia. They or their agents might spend years at a time in Siberia, but they called towns in European Russia home. In addition to these merchants (and the soldiers who are little accounted for in this story), émigrés from Central Asia settled in western Siberia—Bukharans, as they are called in the sources—account for a significant amount of commercial activity in Siberia.

In the next chapters, we follow the story of the Filat'ev merchants, one of the wealthiest and most prominent families involved in the Siberian trade in the seventeenth century. We follow the story of the Shababin family, Bukharan merchants who lived in Tiumen'. Bukharans, although not formally members of Russia's privileged merchants ranks, enjoyed a privileged status in Siberia. Consequently, they were not only conduits of commerce but also integral components of the social fabric of early modern western Siberia. The final chapter delves into the lives of merchants of arguably lesser status.

In all of their stories, certain features repeat: cooperation with family, stints of state service, an ecumenical potpourri of Eurasian trade goods, and a reliance on multiple people in the long chain of transactional links between buying here and selling there. Some of these merchants knew one another, quite well even. Others were strangers. But whether they cooperated or competed, these merchants' paths crisscrossed as they navigated overlapping spaces of trade in early modern Eurasia.

CHAPTER 6

Early Modern Elites: The Filat'ev Family

> In short—he has everything necessary for a richly
> endowed home: beautiful chairs and tables, paintings,
> carpets, wardrobes, silver items, etc. He treated us to
> various beverages, as well as cucumbers, melons, squash,
> nuts and dried apples, all of it served on beautiful silver,
> very clean. Nothing was in deficit.
>
> —Nicolaas Witsen on his visit in a gost' household
> (1665)

As the seventeenth century and his own long career drew to an end, the merchant Ostafii Filat'ev, one of the wealthiest merchants in Muscovy, marked his devotion and success in stone by building the Church of St. Nicholas of the Big Cross, so called for the seven-foot-tall wooden cross that stood as a reliquary inside the church.[1] In doing so, he followed a long tradition whereby successful merchants of Rus' marked their piety and good fortune publicly with the construction of churches.[2] The church was built within the walls of Kitai gorod, on Il'inka Street, near

---

1. 1 arshin = 2 1/3 feet. 3 arshins = 7 feet high. I thank Michael Flier for sharing information about the reliquary inside the church. See West and Petrov, *Merchant Moscow*, 72 fig.5.1.

2. Moscow gosti built a wooden church for the John Chrysostom monastery near the Moscow *posad* around 1413. Ivan III rebuilt it as a stone church to celebrate the conquest of Novgorod in 1479 (Zabelin, *Istoriia goroda Moskvy*, 286; Syroechkovskii, *Gosti-Surozhane*, 39). In the 1480s a Moscow gost', Vasilii Bobr—who, one surmises from his name, made his money in beaver pelts—built a brick church to St. Varvara, from whence came the name Varvarka Street that runs close to Red Square today (Zabelin, *Istoriia goroda Moskvy*, 287). Moscow and Novgorod gosti jointly financed the construction of a stone church to Saints Boris and Gleb in Novgorod in 1536 (Bakhrushin, "Moskva kak remeslennii i torgovii tsentr," in NT, 1: 160). In the seventeenth century, the gosti Nikitnikov, Bosov, and Olisov built churches in Moscow and/or their hometowns (Preobrazhenskii and Perkhavko, *Kupechestvo Rusi*, 158, 161–62). The Usov-Grudtsyn, Nikitnikov, Kirillov, and Sveteshnikov families had private chapels in their homes (Timoshina, *Arkhiv gostei Pankrat'evykh*, 15; Perkhavko, *Pervye kuptsy Rossiiskie*, 370). On early building in northern Rus' see Miller, "Monumental Building," 360–90.

FIGURE 6.1   Church of St. Nicholas of the Big Cross, Kitai gorod, Moscow. Painting by Feodor Dietz (1813–70).

the Gate of St. Elijah (Il'inski) in the 1680s. The commanding profile the structure cut with its Polish baroque façade—imitative of the style employed by the royal dynasty on the Archangel Cathedral in the Kremlin[3]—made it one of Moscow's prominent landmarks until it was razed in 1933.[4]

The location of the church was symbolically fitting: Kitai gorod was the commercial heart of the Russian Empire. But it was practical, too: furs and silks, from whence the Filat'ev fortune derived, sold along Il'inka Street. The Filat'evs, whose Moscow residence was just around the corner, stored wares in the church basement.[5] That the Filat'evs chose to advertise their devotion and success by constructing this church in Moscow is unsurprising, since in a certain sense all roads lead to Moscow and gosti generally managed their multifaceted affairs from the empire's center.

But St. Nicholas of the Big Cross was funded with the profits from Siberian trade. In the seventeenth century about a third of the gosti (a number

---

3. Bondarenko, *Slovar' arkhitektorov i masterov*, 54.

4. Sytin, *Iz istorii Moskovskikh ulits*, 100.

5. This was common practice. The Filat'ev agent Dmitrii Konstantinov stored items in a Tobol'sk church basement when he went to east to trade. See GUTO GAT, f. 156, op. 1, d. 1267.

that could range from around ten to twenty men), dozens of Merchant Hundred merchants, and hundreds of nonprivileged merchants—mostly from the Russian North—had some involvement in Siberian trade. About half a dozen gosti were heavily involved in Siberian trade.[6] Of these, the Filat'evs had the most extensive and successful operations. Furs likely drew the Filat'evs into the region initially, but by the end of the seventeenth century, they were heavily invested in the quickly growing China trade. Typical of many gosti families, their success developed gradually over several generations. The first Filat'ev traded in the early years of the Romanov dynasty and the family gradually worked its way up the economic scale and closer to elite court circles. By the end of the century, the Filat'evs were one of Russia's wealthiest trading dynasties. They owned a grand masonry house in Moscow and kept several shops and warehouses there and throughout the empire. Managing their multifaceted commercial enterprises involved vigilance, risk, and political acumen. In addition to organizing complex operations conducted by an extensive human network in challenging and changing conditions that stretched thousands of miles, negotiating relations with government officials at the center and along the routes their people traveled was essential to long-term success.

Early Filat'evs

The first Filat'ev to enter into the privileged ranks of Muscovite merchants was Vasilii Ivanovich Filat'ev, who was granted membership in the Merchant Hundred sometime between 1600 and 1620, and was counted among the deceased in 1632.[7] Since surviving gosti charters frequently invoke the service of one's predecessors in the bestowal of privileged rank, and rising to privileged status was typically a multigenerational affair, one cannot help but wonder about the career and contributions of Vasilii Ivanovich's father. Unfortunately, we do not know. In 1626 the tsar ordered the selection of forty sables (1 *sorok*) worth 300 rubles by a master from the furrier's trading row. Ivan Filat'ev, from Novgorod, was selected for the job.[8] Novgorod, having pioneered fur exploitation of the northeastern hinterlands, was home to many savvy fur traders. Although we can speculate that this fur procurer of 1626 might have been his father, we do not know. Although Filat'ev was a rare surname in the seventeenth century, Ivan was the most popular name,

---

6. Monahan, "Trade and Empire," ch. 4.
7. Golikova, PKK, 242.
8. Ogloblin, *Obozrenie*, 4: 85.

identifying roughly 10 percent of the male population in seventeenth-century Russia.[9] Moreover, V. B. Perkhavko reports that the Filat'ev merchant family originated in Arkhangel'sk, and S. B. Veselovskii wrote that the Filatov [sic] family had resettled from Novgorod in the sixteenth century, whereas the 1626 fur procurer was from Novgorod.[10] In any case, we can reasonably speculate that Vasilii Ivanovich Filat'ev, who became the first Filat'ev to be included in the ranks of Muscovy's privileged merchantry, was the son of a man from the Russian North who knew something about trade and furs.

Indeed, traders from the Russian North were well represented among the privileged merchant ranks. In fact, the majority of merchants who crossed the Urals to trade in Siberia hailed from northern Russian towns such as Velikii Ustiug, Yaroslavl', Sol'vychegodsk, and Lal'sk. By 1630 Velikii Ustiug, which enjoyed strategic access to major trade arteries, had over two hundred trade shops and warehouses to hold goods transported to and from Siberia by merchants.[11] The region has been credited with a special industriousness and even, owing to relative administrative neglect from Moscow, a "shade of democratic nature."[12] Even before the sixteenth-century contact that led to the port at the mouth of the Dvina (eventually Arkhangel'sk), the English base in Kholmogory, and the establishment of manufacturing ropewalks that supplied most of the cordage to the English fleet, the region could already boast a discernable commercial vibrancy, evidenced by a bustling trade-craft economy and the fourteenth-century Novgorod churches testifying to the commercial success of merchants vying for heavenly rewards.[13]

Vasilii Ivanovich Filat'ev evidently had three sons, Bogdan, Ivan, and Iakov, who continued the trajectory of successful commerce that led to their father's capture in the historical record of privileged ranks. Of the brothers, Bogdan Filat'ev left the most traces in the historical record. He made his name and money in Siberian furs and set himself up in Moscow, a typical move for successful merchants. He was admitted to the Merchant Hundred in 1621, a

---

9. Kaiser, "Naming Cultures in Early Modern Russia," 276–83. Another complication regarding surnames is that sometimes documents record a surname and sometimes a patronymic (i.e., Filatov = "son of Filat"). It is not always apparent which is the case. In general, someone of lower rank would be recorded by name and patronymic, no surname.

10. Sytin, *Iz istorii Moskovskikh ulits*, 99; Perkhavko, *Istoriia russkogo kupechestva*, 227; Veselovskii, *Trudy po istochnikovedeniiu*, 32.

11. Platonov, *Ocherki po istorii Smuty*, 11, 4–7. Ustiug was near the mouth of the Iug River. The Iug River flowed into the Sukhona, which joined the Vychegda and then North Dvina, a major commercial artery.

12. Platonov, *Ocherki po istorii Smuty*, 4–7, 18; Spock, "Parfiev Family," 233–35.

13. Fuhrmann, *Origins of Capitalism in Russia*, 46.

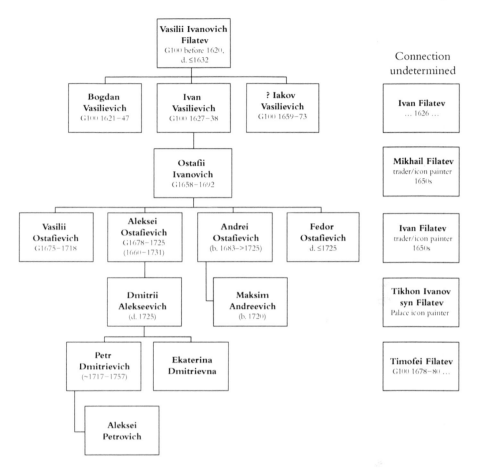

FIGURE 6.2   The Filat'ev family tree, with Filat'evs of potential relation shown to the right.

status he would hold until his death in 1647.[14] Bogdan's career was steeped in
trade and service. In 1630–31 he was head of the Sable Office in Moscow.[15]
When his term expired, he remained in Moscow and continued to be active
in trade with the Russian North. His "men" declared money and/or furs at
Vologda customs four times in the autumn and winter of 1634–35.[16] The
declarations of money in September were probably in the wake of selling
furs brought from Siberia (or bought up in northern towns) at the annual
Arkhangel'sk fair. Afterward, one of Bogdan Filat'ev's men traveled back
to Moscow with several other Moscow merchants, including an agent of a

14. Solov'eva and Volodikhin, *Sostav privilegirovannogo kupechestva*, 36; Golikova, PKK, 252.

15. Ogloblin, *Obozrenie*, 4: 80.

16. Merzon and Tikhonov, *Rynok Ustiuga Velikogo*, 325; Volkov, *Tamozhennaia kniga goroda Vologdy*, 30.

Filat'ev rival, Moscow merchant Daniil Grigorievich Pankrat'ev, who would attain gost' status in 1642.[17] In 1635 Bogdan purchased 1,100 rubles worth of furs in Sol'vychegodsk, which amounted to about one-quarter of the fur bought there that year.[18] Perhaps therein were some of the 9,000 rubles worth of treasury furs that he delivered to the court in Warsaw in late 1636.[19] In 1641–42 (7150) Bogdan Filat'ev again headed the Sable Office.[20] He died in 1647, a success in all matters but one: he did not have an heir. Fortunately for the continuity of the family fortune, his brother Ivan did.

Bogdan's brother, Ivan Vasilievich Filat'ev, was a member of the Merchant Hundred from 1627 to 1638. His later admission illustrates that although in some moments Merchant Hundred status seemed to extend automatically to immediate family members, this was not at all times the case. His later admission to privileged ranks and earlier disappearance (1638) suggest that he was a younger brother and that his life may have been cut short by some unrecorded illness or accident. Bogdan and Ivan seem to have had another much younger brother, Iakov. Whereas Bogdan's visible career lasted from 1621 to 1647, Iakov Vasilievich held privileged merchant status from 1659 to 1673.[21] The spread in time over their trade activities suggests that Bogdan Vasilievich and Iakov Vasilievich were born of different mothers.

When the Moscow merchant Iakov Vasilievich Filat'ev was inducted into privileged ranks, Bogdan and Ivan had long since disappeared from the historical record, yet only one year earlier his (presumed) nephew, Ostafii Ivanovich Filat'ev, had been elevated to the status of gost'. One wonders if Iakov's promotion, which came approximately a year after he inherited a portion of the estate of the wealthy gost' Semen Stoianov, had anything to do with that inheritance.[22] Stoianov's will names Iakov simply as a relative, leaving open the question of whether blood, marriage, or adoption united the Filat'evs with this important Novgorod merchant family. Like the Stoianovs, Iakov Filat'ev engaged extensively in trade with Sweden. In the 1660s and 1670s Iakov or his agents traveled to Sweden to trade on various occasions; the last mention we have of him in the historical record is of a trade mission

---

17. Golikova, PKK, 99. Daniil Pankrat'ev was a gost' from 1642 to 1654, perhaps a plague victim.

18. Bushkovitch, *Merchants of Moscow*, 113; Merzon, *Tamozhennye knigi*, 55. Merzon calls Bogdan a gost'. Bushkovitch refers to him as a Merchant Hundred.

19. Kotilaine, *Russia's Foreign Trade*, 416.

20. Ogloblin, *Obozrenie*, 4: 85.

21. Baron wrote that he was a gost' in 1662. Golikova reported him only as a member of the Merchant Hundred from 1659 to 1673. Baron, "Who Were the Gosti?" in *Muscovite Russia*, 27; Golikova, PKK, 312.

22. Golikova, PKK, 100. Mikliaev may also have been related to Stoianov.

gone awry in the mid-1670s, perhaps due to losses at sea.[23] Unlike the affairs of Iakov Vasilievich, a great deal is known about the career of his nephew, Ostafii Ivanovich. His career reveals strategies and practices that made for tremendous success in a competitive environment where patronage, connections, and luck were no less important than execution.

Ostafii Ivanovich Filat'ev

Ostafii Filat'ev inherited the wealth of his uncle Bogdan Filat'ev and expanded his trade operations.[24] He began his career heavily involved in Siberian furs and later expanded his trade in Eastern goods, as did several of his merchant contemporaries. The Merchant Hundred, even in family dynasties, was the feeder pool from which gosti were drawn—a form of "paying dues," although only a small fraction of the Merchant Hundred ever attained gost' status. But Ostafii Filat'ev apparently bypassed this rite of passage. He attained gost' status in 1658, though no document records him as a member of the Merchant Hundred.[25] Perhaps Ostafii was promoted directly to gost' because in 1658 the gost' ranks remained depleted after the plague. Indeed, it probably did not hurt Filat'ev fortunes that merchants from two other prominent gost' families who were extremely active in Siberia at mid-century, the Bosovs and the Gusel'nikovs, had succumbed to the plague.[26]

Well before he enjoyed the status of privileged merchant, Ostafii Filat'ev displayed the types of behavior that help account for his success. In 1646/47, not long after his uncle Bogdan's death, Ostafii brought a shipment with a declared value of 3,614 rubles through the Berezov customs.[27] Although this was a large shipment for an inexperienced merchant, the second quarter of the seventeenth century was a moment when big shipments worth several thousand rubles regularly traversed the Urals; private shipments with over 3,000 rubles in declared value became less common in the second half of the seventeenth century, though they still existed. While still a young merchant in 1647/48, Ostafii Filat'ev successfully lobbied against abuse by the customs head in Eniseisk, the same town about which fellow gost' V. F. Gusel'nikov

23. Davydov, *Russko-Shvedskie ekonomicheskie otnosheniia*, nos. 207 (June 29, 1673), 230 (Sept. 7, 1676).

24. Golikova, PKK, 130.

25. Although Golikova wrote that German Sudovshchikov was the only exception, one or both of Ostafii Filat'ev's sons may have possibly been exceptions as well since no evidence explicitly situates them in the Merchant Hundred corporation.

26. Golikova, PKK, 98, 104.

27. Semenova, *Istoriia predprinimatel'stva v Rossii*, 115.

complained years before. In this case, the state responded by assigning a clerk to guard against abuses.[28] Given Ostafii's youth, and that official abuses persisted, we must attribute a certain canniness to successful challenges against servitor abuse.

By midcentury the Filat'evs were among the most prominent merchants engaged in the well-established Siberian fur market. They maintained a winter camp in distant Mangazeia "beyond the mouth of the Enisei River," from which they organized their own trapper-trader brigades (*promyshlenniki*) to source furs.[29] They also bought furs at important markets such as Sol'vychegodsk.[30] According to one historian, in the second half of the seventeenth century the Filat'evs consistently bought up at least one-quarter of the fur market and sometimes between 42 and 100 percent. Even as furs in western Siberia declined, the Filat'evs succeeded in acquiring substantial furs: in 1693 Ostafii Filat'ev's helpers declared 10 sorok (four hundred pelts) of sable in Nerchinsk.[31]

To be sure, the Filat'evs held a commanding position, but they were not the only privileged merchants making big money in Siberia. At midcentury two merchant families, both of whom also hailed from the Russian North, were even more active than the Filat'evs in Siberian trade. These were Kirill Bosov (Merchant Hundred, 1622–46; Gost', 1646–54) and the Gusel'nikov brothers. Kirill Bosov's agents appeared in customs books throughout Siberia almost every year from 1637 to the early 1650s. One Bosov agent, who traveled to Siberia at least five times between 1640 and 1654, returned from Siberia in 1654 with ten thousand squirrel pelts bound for Arkhangel'sk.[32] In that same year, however, Kirill Bosov's career was cut short when he died from plague. Kirill's son Ivan, who had been old enough to make trips to Arkhangel'sk on his father's behalf, also died around 1654, probably, like his father, a plague victim.

The Gusel'nikov brothers—Vasilii (Merchant Hundred, 1630–48; Gost', 1648–54) and Afanasii (Merchant Hundred, 1630–58; Gost', 1658–81) Fedotov Gusel'nikov—were even more active in Siberia in the 1640s, dealing in furs, fishing, and metals.[33] Vasilii became known by the nickname

28. RGADA, f. 214, stb. 153, l. 343.

29. Aleksandrov, "Russko-kitaiskaia torgovlia," 433.

30. Merzon, *Tamozhennye knigi*, 55 (Sol'vychegodsk, 1647).

31. Aleksandrov, "Russko-kitaiskaia torgovlia," 433.

32. RGADA, f. 214, kn. 301, ll. 83v, 85v, 89, 92, 95, 99v; Bazilevich, *Krupnoe torgovoe predpriiatie*, 9, 23.

33. Golikova, PKK, 255; RGADA, f. 214, kn. 301, ll. 51v, 72v, 73 (1652); GBUTO GATO, f. 47, op. 1, d. 1774 (1656–60), l. 83; Orlova, *Otkrytiia russkikh zemleprokhodtsev*, nos. 51, 72, pp. 176–77, 209; DAI, vol. 3, no. 9.

(prozvishche) Skoraia Zapis'—fast writer—quite possibly for his writing skills.[34] Enterprising and resourceful, Vasilii looked to the state to protect his interests. In 1632 he petitioned that he was wrongly paying local taxes both in his hometown of Ustiug and Moscow.[35] On a different occasion he complained to Moscow that the Obdor customs post extracted taxes that other Siberian customs posts did not. He further explained that he sent his men via the northern route of Kamen' because, in Verkhotur'e, even when they did not overcharge taxes as in Obdor, they made labor demands that delayed his men, which, with the coming ice, could cause them to miss the whole season.[36] In 1641 he petitioned the state against Eniseisk officials who arbitrarily commandeered the boats and horses of a party of over thirty men led by his nephew. The administrator in Moscow, having reviewed Gusel'nikov's petition, wrote authoritatively across the document that the Eniseisk administrators were not to hurt Gusel'nikov's enterprise—a concrete and quotidian illustration of this monograph's larger argument that the state intended to help, not hinder, commerce.[37] There's "many a slip between the cup and the lip," however, and Vasilii Gusel'nikov continued to fight similar battles. Six years later, Moscow again instructed Eniseisk officials to avoid antagonizing Gusel'nikov's agents.[38] Also in 1647, Vasilii petitioned the tsar concerning abuse by Verkhotur'e officials.[39]

As cumbersome as petitioning the state about abuses was, we can surmise that Gusel'nikov appealed to the state repeatedly because he found it a worthwhile means to protect his interests. Far more than complaining to Moscow, Gusel'nikov spent his time organizing commercial endeavors. In 1639 he served as the customs head in Yaroslavl', which prevented him from dispatching a party of agents and promyshlenniki to Siberia.[40] But otherwise the Gusel'nikovs regularly dispatched agents to Siberia. By the middle of the seventeenth century, V. F. Gusel'nikov had at least fifteen agents in Siberia; he rented four shops in Yakutsk and one in Tobol'sk for the entire summer.[41] Further, Gusel'nikov invested in exploring unchartered territory. He helped

34. *Polnoe sobranie russkikh letopisei*, 37: 140. His brother Afanasii was sometimes called Zapis'.
35. Orlova, *Otkrytiia russkikh zemleprokhodtsev*, no. 38, 161–63.
36. Ibid., no. 39, 164–65.
37. Ibid., no. 41, 167–68.
38. Ibid., no. 52, 177. The letter references the 1641 petition.
39. AI, vol. 3, no. 229; Semenova, *Istoriia predprinimatel'stva v Rossii*, 121.
40. Orlova, *Otkrytiia russkikh zemleprokhodtsev*, no. 41, 167–68.
41. RGADA, f. 214, kn. 301, l. 66. Vasilii Fedotov's agent Maksim Fedotov, likely a relative, managed a trading stall for him in Tobol'sk from September through December 1652. Orlova, *Otkrytiia russkikh zemleprokhodtsev*, no. 60, 186–88.

fund the expedition of Semen Dezhnev to explore the northern coast.[42] Dezhnev rounded the northeastern tip of Eurasia almost a century before Bering's second expedition.

The Gusel'nikovs' energetic defense of their interests and successful currying of state favor—recall that in 1650 Gusel'nikov received special permission to trade in forbidden fox pelts[43]—contributed to their success. Vasilii attained gost' status in 1648 and his brother Afanasii entered this privileged rank one decade later, in 1658. As noted in chapter 4, despite their favored status (or because of it), these brothers were objects of public opprobrium when tensions flashed in 1645 in Siberia and 1648 in Moscow. Vasilii Fedotov Gusel'nikov died in 1654, not at the hands of an angry mob but from plague, along with Kirill Bosov.[44] Like other successful merchants, the Gusel'nikovs patronized the church. In 1668 Afanasii donated funds for the construction of a masonry church in Velikii Ustiug in memory of his brother, Vasilii.[45]

Although the Bosovs and Gusel'nikovs were more active than the Filat'evs in Siberia at midcentury, the Filat'evs ultimately left the strongest legacy in Siberian customs books, for traces of Bosov and Gusel'nikov merchants in Siberian customs books abruptly ceased when both succumbed to the plague that hit Moscow in the summer of 1654. The tsar, at the Smolensk front when the outbreak began, ordered aggressive monitoring of the crisis. The royal family was removed from Moscow. Additional checkpoints to enter and exit the city were established and heavily guarded. Dispatches brought to the tsar were held above a flame for disinfection before being copied onto clean paper that was then transmitted to the tsar. Property and homes of victims were burned. In defiance of Orthodox rules, the state ordered that the dead be buried without a ritual changing of clothes. Despite strong quarantine measures, when the epidemic was declared over in December 1656, untold thousands had died: some estimates say sixty thousand people whereas others conclude well over half a population of approximately two hundred thousand perished.[46] In the Siberian Office alone plague took the lives of nine out of seventeen of the clerks (pod'iachi) in 1654.[47]

The plague took a stiff toll on the gosti. In addition to Bosov, his son, and Vasilii Gusel'nikov, the male line of the Nikitnikov merchant family

42. Orlova, Otkrytiia russkikh zmleprokhodtsev, nos. 51, 72, pp. 176–77, 209.
43. Orlova, Otkrytiia russkikh zemleprokhodtsev, no. 64, 191.
44. Golikova, PKK, 98, 103, 141.
45. Polnoe sobranie russkikh letopisei, 37: 140.
46. Melikishvili gives a figure of 200,000 in "Genesis of the Anti-Plague System," 21. Levin, "Plague deniers."
47. Golikova, Privilegirovannoe kupechestvo v structure russkogo obshchestvo, 254.

expired at the hand of the plague in 1654.[48] Two other gosti died in 1654 and four more in 1655.[49] Causes of death in some cases are uncertain but this loss of eight men from the gosti ranks in two years—from twenty-nine gosti in 1653 to twenty-one in 1655, or 28 percent of the corporation—was the most dramatic depletion of gosti ranks from 1636 to 1725.[50] Although it is impossible to calculate overall mortality for Moscow, complete records survive for twenty elite households, four monasteries, and fifteen artisanal neighborhoods, and they show that elites suffered steep mortality: "of 6,801 inhabitants before the plague, only 1,160 were left alive towards the end of the outbreak—that is, a death rate of 83%. Boyars' household had a slightly higher rate than average—85% deaths." Records from Moscow's hinterland of twenty-four towns reported a death rate of 54%.[51] Despite their wealth and status, early modern elites could do little to isolate themselves from the health risks that threatened society at large.

In the midst of tragedy in Moscow, which evidently left the Filat'evs more or less unscathed, one Filat'ev found valuable work. In the autumn of 1654, as the death toll crept higher and Patriarch Nikon quarantined himself "in the mountains and forests, . . . in rain and snow, living in a tent, keeping away from all people, with no consolation but a fire," an icon painter-merchant named Ivan Filat'ev and his colleagues were commissioned to paint Patriarch Nikon's Church of the Three Hierarchs.[52] Three years later, in January 1657, someone bought from Filat'ev twenty icons of the Mother of God of Vladimir for the "blessing" of Patriarch Nikon.[53] That fall, on a cold November day when Patriarch Nikon said the service in the Dormition Cathedral in green Sunday vestments, Mikhail Filat'ev, a merchant (torgovii chelovek) sold ten more icons of the Mother of God of Vladimir for Nikon's "blessing."[54] Presumably, Ivan and Mikhail Filat'ev, small merchants in the icon row in Moscow's market, were related to each other and possibly to the Filat'evs, who by this time were well established among Moscow's merchant elite.

---

48. Golikova, PKK, 249, 145.

49. Golikova, PKK, 98, 104, 210–11. Gosti V. I. Iur'ev and D. G. Pankrat'ev died in 1654. The Nikitinikov family, which produced three gosti in the first half of the seventeenth century, died out in 1654.

50. Golikova, PKK, 113, 148, 171, 199. From 1710 to 1711 the corporation lost seven members, from thirty-two to twenty-five, which is a 21.8% reduction. From 1634 to 1636 the corporation went from twenty-seven to eighteen, a 33.3% reduction. From 1678 to 1679 the corporation went from fifty-four to forty-seven, a loss of seven men that amounted to a 12.9% reduction.

51. Levin, "Plague deniers."

52. Sevast'ianova, Materialy k "Letopisi," 90.

53. Ibid., 144.

54. Ibid., 162.

As part of that merchant elite, Ostafii Filat'ev directed affairs of his numerous agents, dependents, and employees in Siberia and other far-flung regions from Moscow. In an early modern world where favor and patronage were also critical to success, generally speaking, these assets were best cultivated at the center. State service was a central ethos to Muscovite society long before Peter declared himself "the first servant of the state." The state required service from all social groups and merchants were no exception. Gosti and merchants of the Merchant Hundred formally served the state in various capacities, as discussed in chapter 1. One component of service was consultation. Ivan IV famously told Anthony Jenkinson in an interview, "Wee knowe that Marchants matters are to bee heard, for that they are the stay of our princely treasures."[55] The Romanov dynasty took this to heart. The state repeatedly invited input from its merchants on commerce-related matters. Further, personal acquaintance with and access to the realm's highest officials carried obvious advantages. When Sir Donald Mackenzie Wallace (1841–1919) disparaged Russian merchants who strived to entertain political officials in their homes as guests, he was missing the precious capital won—in Russia, as in his own country—by cultivating political connections.[56] As the pace at which Russia became integrated with European economies quickened in the seventeenth century, it was particularly important to be in Moscow, for concomitant with this development, over thirteen hundred European merchants—who appreciated the importance of political patronage—came to Moscow in search of markets and profit. In this regard, the Romanovs negotiated a balance. In step with other protectionist-mercantilist early modern states, they recognized—in theory—that the realm was likely to benefit if its own merchants did well. In immediate practice, Western European merchants often offered enticements, such as specie, access to commodities and foreign markets, expertise,[57] etc., that were immediately attractive to the Russian government. On occasion the state made deals with foreign merchants that Russian merchants perceived as detrimental to their own interests. Therefore elite Russian merchants were keen to maintain access to court in order to protect their interests.[58]

---

55. Morgan and Coote, *Early Voyages and Travels to Russia and Persia*, 2: 312.

56. Wallace, *Russia*, 186.

57. Two court doctors, Oster von Rosenberge and Samuel Collins, seem to have been recruited to the Muscovite court by the foreign merchants John Hebdon and von Horn, respectively. See Unkovskaia, *Brief Lives*, 23, 25.

58. Indeed, this issue has been the most considered aspect in historiography on Muscovite merchants.

Competition for court favor was by no means the only reason it paid to maintain proximity to the center. Residing at length in one's hometown could have bad consequences. Gost' Olisov, from Kazan, in 1704 testified to the costs of being out of Moscow at tax assessment time: "And in past years when tax levies were determined in Moscow for the *gosti*, the *gost'*-assessors without adjusting my tax to that of my fellow *gosti*, in my absence, imposed a heavy tax upon me—one hundred and thirty rubles at each collection, and such collections occur twice or more each year."[59] Indeed, one of the "services" Filat'ev said he provided was to help advocate for his governor-patron in Siberia and bolster his reputation in the center.

In the highly consultative Muscovite political culture, the tsar sought gosti consultation on relevant matters, and the Filat'evs were part of this exclusive group who had the tsar's ear. In 1660 the tsar ordered reports collected from merchants on the grain trade—he was concerned that the price of grain was so high. It was a key issue on which to have a voice, especially since merchants, including the Ushakov brothers, discussed in chapter 8, were implicated in illicit speculation.[60] In 1662 Ostafii Filat'ev was among the merchants who submitted a collective report to the tsar.[61] As mentioned above, Ostafii was called on to assess the value of Eastern goods in Moscow in 1668.[62] In 1672 he was one of the gosti involved in drafting a response to the tsar regarding the effects of the Armenian trade monopoly.[63] Similarly, in 1676 he signed the gosti opinion on the Dutch ambassador Kondratii von Klenk's proposal to secure a contract for silk transit trade.[64] In 1677 he served as sable assessor in the Siberian Office.[65] In 1684 Ostafii's son, Aleksei, along with other merchants gave testimony to the head of the Siberian Office, Prince Ivan Borisovich Repnin (1617–97), regarding their labor-recruitment practices in Siberia. Sympathetic to their perspectives, Repnin instructed Siberian governors to maintain the status quo rather than introduce new procedures.[66] In 1685 Vasilii and Aleksei were among gosti who sounded a protectionist note when consulted on granting Indian merchants from Astrakhan access to the Moscow market.[67]

59. "Gost' Afanasii Olisov's Reply to the Government Inquiry of 1704," repr. as appendix in Baron, "The Fate of the *Gosti*," in *Muscovite Russia*.

60. Semenova, *Istoriia predprinimatel'stva v Rossii*, 138.

61. Ibid.; Preobrazhenskii and Perkhavko, *Kupechestvo Rusi*, 151.

62. RMO, vol. 3, no. 92, 196.

63. SGGD, vol. 4, no. 81, pp. 277–79.

64. *Armiano-russkie otnosheniia v XVII veke*, no. 37, pp. 129–42.

65. Aksenov, *Genealogiia moskovskogo kupechestva*, 42.

66. Semenova, *Istoriia predprinimatel'stva v Rossii*, 146.

67. *Russko-Indiiskie otnosheniia v XVII veke*, no. 225.VII, pp. 330–33.

Ever balancing myriad goals and interests, the state was responsive to merchant concerns, often citing them in the issuance of commercial decrees. For example, it cited specific complaints by Filat'ev in issuing clarification on the protocol for taking transit taxes in 1683.[68] Merchants expected this type of assistance and looked to the state to help safeguard their interests. From the court in Moscow, merchants would seek to mobilize the tentacles of the state when their men in the field went missing or to combat the ill effects of alcohol.[69] The gosti G. R. Nikitin and Nadei Sveteshnikov appealed to the tsar for Siberian administrators' help in keeping agents who drank in check and on task.[70] Frustrated by losses from alcohol-induced hooliganism in Siberian towns, the merchants O. Filat'ev, S. Luzin, and G. R. Nikitin collectively lobbied the tsar to close down illegal pubs in Siberia.[71] Along with sobriety, good bosses were concerned with their agents' quotidian health. And well they should be. Stripped to its most basic element, getting goods from A to B was the key to success in premodern trade and this endeavor depended inexorably on the agents in the field. Several petitions from gosti to the Siberian Prikaz request permission to send their agents in Siberia honey or molasses, which were antiscorbutics.[72]

China Trade

The Filat'evs were well positioned to exploit Siberian furs. But as fur supplies declined rapidly, there was a widespread recognition that goods of the East could bring fortune to the successful merchants. The Filat'evs were pioneers in the China trade. They dealt in both luxury and everyday goods. Ostafii sold 40 percent of the paper, probably imported from China, required for a printing of the book *Ermologiia* at the most competitive rate to Moscow's printing office in 1682.[73] The Filat'evs also traded in Chinese silks. In the eighteenth century, they domestically produced this valuable commodity, running a silk factory in St. Petersburg. Meanwhile, in the seventeenth century several Russian merchants endeavored to "get in on" the emerging markets as merchants from Western Europe waited eagerly at Russia's depot

68. PSZ, vol. 2, no. 1015 (May 26, 1683).

69. Examples include petitions from the gosti Nadei Svetshnikov, Vasilii Usov, Vasilii Gusel'nikov, and Mikhail Erofeev. See RGADA, f. 214, stb. 53, l. 771; stb. 153, ll. 233–41; Orlova, *Otkrytiia russkikh zemleprokhodtsev*, no. 65, 192–93; Ogloblin, *Obozrenie*, 3: 151.

70. RGADA, f. 214, stb. 1128, l. 109 (1681–83); Ogloblin, *Obozrenie*, 3: 153, 233.

71. Semenova, *Istoriia predprinimatel'stva v Rossii*, 168.

72. Aleksandrov, "Narodnye vosstaniia," 179.

73. Pozdeeva, et al., *Moskovskii pechatnii dvor*, 448. May 7191 sale of 86 stop paper x 27 altyn/ stop = 66 rubles, 22 altyn. I thank Valerii Perkhavko for sharing this reference with me.

Table 6.1   Filat'ev Chinese imports via Nerchinsk, 1690–94

YEAR	FILAT'EV IMPORTS (RUBLES)	TOTAL GOSTI IMPORTS (RUBLES)	FILAT'EV TRADE AS % OF GOSTI IMPORTS
1690	4,728r	9,954r	47.5%
1692	5,803r	12,473r	46.5%
1693	8,060r	8,060r	100%
1693 (via Naum)	7,734r	15,987r	48%
1694	2,239r	2,239r	100%

Source: Aleksandrov, "Russko-kitaiskaia torgovlia," 455.

cities to fill their boats and deliver Eastern goods to populations westward, increasingly with money to spend. Additionally, however meager the new Siberian population remained, it required supplies. Premodern long-distance trade is typically associated with luxury items, but livestock, dried fruit and nuts, and nonluxury textiles constituted a substantial portion of the goods that merchants of Siberia moved across Eurasia.

Typical of early modern Eurasian trade, we do not know as much as we would like about the goods traded; we know more about the routes followed. Just as sometimes Filat'ev men would cross the Urals via Kamen' to the north, and sometimes they would pass at Verkhotur'e, they reached China via various routes as well. The Filat'evs' first forays into China were probably via the more established Lake Yamysh route along the Irtysh River. They were instrumental in pioneering a new route to China directly across the Gobi desert. In 1674, their agent Gavril Romanov Nikitin was the first known Russian to lead a caravan all the way to China, forging a new route that headed directly south, boldly crossing the Gobi desert, whereas caravans had typically skirted the southwestern edge.[74] Yet the Filat'evs continued to use the Yamysh route even after Nikitin opened up the Gobi route. This was a wise strategy, for steppe security was never a guarantee. Although violence seems to have been in some ways a handmaiden of steppe trade, Dzhungar warfare seems to have reached a virulent enough stage in 1691 that it shut down trade. Bukharan merchants reported that there was no trade at Yamysh that year.[75] Fortunately, they had developed other options. In the 1690s, the Filat'evs successfully organized several caravans to China along a more easterly route that departed from Nerchinsk. On one, they escorted an Orthodox mission seeking to establish itself in Peking.[76] Presuming that

---

74. Monahan, "Gavril Romanovich Nikitin," 48; Ustiugov, Nauchnoe nasledie, 60.

75. DAI, vol. 10, no. 80, 369. Vilkov says that virtually no Chinese goods made it to Yamysh because of war with the Mongols from 1688 to 1696. Vilkov, Remeslo i torgovlia, 199.

76. Widmer, Russian Ecclestastical [sic] Mission in Peking, 28.

the escort implied some level of sponsorship, one wonders if they may have
been motivated not only by faith but also by a desire to enhance their leverage in China.

Filat'ev's involvement in Chinese trade via Siberia earned him a reputation as an expert on Eastern goods. When a Russian embassy to nearby
Kalmyk leaders returned to Tobol'sk bearing Kalmyk gifts for the tsar in
the winter of 1668, Ostafii Filat'ev was summoned to assess the value of the
items, illustrating not only another way in which gosti served the state but
also Filat'ev's perceived expertise in Eastern goods.[77] Two decades later his
engagement in Eastern trade had deepened. Every autumn, Eastern goods
disbursed throughout and across Siberia as great caravans arrived from the
Eurasian steppe to the depots of Siberian customs posts. The fair at Lake
Yamysh in August-September was one space in which goods were exchanged
and reconfigured in sacks and sledges that took them to their next point
of inspection or exchange. In October 1686 three different Filat'ev agents
passed through Tobol'sk with one sledge each laden with goods.[78] Since they
were not unpacked, the first two shipments were not inventoried, but the
third and largest declaration was. This inventory reveals the wealth of Eastern
goods Filat'ev's agents were transporting across Eurasia. Filat'ev's man, Dmitrii Konstantinov, a "Greek" from Tsar'grad (Constantinople), declared three
sledges worth of Chinese fabrics, tea, and Bukharan wares in Tobol'sk.[79] At
the time of his declaration Konstantinov's goods were appraised at a slightly
lesser value without specifying that he had sold some off, leaving one to
wonder what transpired. In any case, no one-tenth tax was collected because
Konstantinov had acquired these goods out on the steppe in exchange for
Russian goods on which one-tenth tax had already been paid.[80]

Dmitrii Konstantinov had first appeared in Ostafii Filat'ev's employ over
a decade earlier, on May 13, 1673, with a label of "the boss's man." He had
assisted the agent Gavril Romanov (the future gost' G. R. Nikitin) with a
shipment traveling by boat through Tiumen'.[81] He was not the only "Greek"
in this region. G. R. Nikitin employed a Greek, Nikolai Ivanov Grechenin,
who brought precious jewels from China through Tobol'sk in 1694 without
declaring them at customs.[82] The Filat'evs had Greek agents that based themselves at length among Kalmyks in the steppe and conducted China trade

77. 77RMO, vol. 3, no. 92, 196.

78. RGADA, f. 214, kn. 892, l. 56 (1686/7).

79. Aleksandrov and Chistiakova, "K voprosu o tamozhennoi politike v Sibiri," 137–38.

80. RGADA, f. 214, kn. 892, ll. 44v, 45, 56.

81. TKSG, vol. 4: 57.

82. Aleksandrov, "Russko-kitaiskaia torgovlia," 452.

from there. In the spring of 1700 an interpreter was dispatched to the Kirgiz to negotiate in response to a series of recent attacks. He returned to Tomsk with an enthusiastic letter from Greeks and Russians there, inviting more to come to trade: "Come to us, people, with wares; now we have many wares, not like it was before, but very good wares. This time in China we traded, not as previously, [but] according to our own desires we chose in the rows and in the shops, there were no delays of any kind. . . . Whoever is desirous, tell each other to come to us to trade."[83]

The year before Konstantinov's 1686 declaration in Tobol'sk, he had gotten in trouble with authorities for his affairs in China, as chapter 5 discussed. The Conciliar Law Code of 1649 stipulated "visa" requirements for most cross-border travel. That is, anyone seeking to travel abroad had to apply for a "passage document" from the tsar if in Moscow or the local governor if in the provinces. People were permitted to travel to countries with whom Russia was at peace for trade or other purposes, excluding betrayal (izmena) or other evil matters (likhago dela). The stipulation was relaxed for the western border region, where people were not to be punished for travel without a passage document because there they lived so adjacently (smezhno) with German and Lithuanian people.[84] At the other end of its domain, where increasing contacts were increasing tensions amid countless unknowns, the state was unwilling to take such a liberal approach to cross-border travel. In 1672 the state had issued an order forbidding Russian traders to travel specifically to China without a transit visa issued by the Siberian Office. The order was repeated in 1678, reflecting not only the sustained troubled relations that prevailed until the Nerchinsk Peace in 1689 but also that merchants were passing from Russia into China without transit visas. Meanwhile, as discussed in chapter 5, Lake Yamysh trade flourished as merchants and nomads from the West, East, and South met at the interstices of empire. At Lake Yamysh merchants could exchange Eastern wares for Russian goods and, restocked, head out for China again. According to Vilkov, this was Dmitrii Konstantinovich's [sic] function from 1679 to 1685. When Konstantinov did get in trouble with the authorities in 1685, it was Ostafii Filat'ev's influence that got him off the hook.[85] Given that Konstantinov worked for Ostafii Filat'ev before and after the 1685 incident—in 1673 and again in 1686—Vilkov's interpretation seems valid.

83. *Pamiatniki sibirskoi istorii XVIII veka*, bk. 1, *1700–1713*, no. 13 (May 1700), 68, 73–74.

84. PSZ, vol. 1, no. 1, chap. 6, p. 8.

85. Vilkov, *Remeslo i torgovlia*, 201. See RGADA, f. 214, stb. 935.

Inside the Filat'ev Network

The Filat'evs' enterprises reveal the movement of voluminous, variegated wares into and out of Siberia, as well as the storage, distributions, and dispersal of shipments to different Siberian markets.[86] That is, as with the Shababin family (chapter 7), we observe the coexistence of local and long-distance trade. These movements were effected by a vast commercial network of agents, workers, shop managers, etc., onto which customs books provide a valuable window. Over a dozen different agents or "men" made declarations on Ostafii Filat'ev's behalf from 1661 to 1688.[87] This number does not include numerous shopkeepers and other helpers whom Filat'ev or his men also employed to execute trade operations. The appearances of Filat'ev's agents at Siberian customs posts reveal the kinship patterns so typical of early modern trade networks. Agents recruited their relatives to help them in their endeavors. At least two father-son teams operated within the Filat'ev network.[88] When agents did not have an eligible son, brother, nephew, or cousin to travel with and assist them, they could compensate with adoption. Filat'ev's agent Andrei Edomskoi bought himself a five-year-old boy near Nerchinsk in 1699. Upon assuring authorities that the boy was a captured hostage and not a future tribute payer, Edomskoi took the boy for his own, having him baptized with the Christian name Grigorii Ivanov.[89]

The knowledge that underlings in the network passed between one another was invaluable. Although successful bosses worked hard to assiduously monitor affairs in the field, countless decisions small and large had to be made that contributed to the success or failure of each trade caravan or season. Agents were the organizations' indispensable front men who dealt with administrators on the ground. When the state warehouses in Verkhotur'e, inadequately

---

86. For more details on Filat'ev Siberian operations see Monahan, "Trade and Empire," 143–46.

87. The RGADA archival description (opis') notes that in 1671 a charter grant was issued to Gost' Ostafii Filat'ev. See RGADA, f. 1111, op. 1, pt. 4, stb. 190, ll. 104–5. I read the opis', not the document itself, and so rely on Golikova's reporting that Ostafii Filat'ev was granted gost' status in 1658. Filat'ev agents: Sava Bushkovskii (RGADA, f. 1111, op. 1, d. 187, l. 124 (May 1680)); Elfim Petrov (RGADA, f. 1111, op. 1, d. 187, l. 124 (May 1680)); Afanasii Iakimov (RGADA, f. 214, kn. 892, l. 155v (May 1687)); Grigorii Mikhailov Kochetov (RGADA, f. 214, stb. 1128, ll. 64, 100); Fëdor Grigoriev syn Kochetov (RGADA, f. 214, stb. 1128, l. 35); Andrei Kazanin (RGADA, f. 214, stb. 1128, l. 90); Maksim Protasov (RGADA, f. 214, stb. 1128, l. 90); Filat'ev "men": Grigorii Filotpov (RGADA, f. 1111, op. 1, d. 187, l. 124 (May 1680)); Boris Prokopev (RGADA, f. 214, kn. 892, l. 155v (May 1687)); Grishka Fëdorov plus unnamed man (Ogloblin, Obozrenie, 2: 49); Petr Ivanov syn, RGADA, Biblioteka moskovskoi sinodal'noi tipografii/staropechatnye knigi (BMST/SPK), "Apostol," no. 8, ll. 1–6.

88. RGADA, f. 214, stb. 1128, ll. 35, 64, 100 (after G. R. Nikitin's death).

89. RGADA, f. 1111, op. 2, d. 611, l. 174.

repaired after a fire years ago, were riddled with holes that allowed the elements to seep onto goods, Filat'ev's agent made arrangements with a local
priest to store Filat'ev's wares in a church basement in 1678. When the
gost' Luzin heard about this solution, he directed his agent to do the same.[90]
Filat'ev valued agents who wisely parlayed resources. In 1664 Ostafii's agent
Rodion Shchepetkin sold a boat (koch—a single-masted, single-decked sailing and rowing boat) to the administration in Yakutsk. Unfortunately for the
administration, for the next three years it sat there unused and unmaintained,
until deemed not river worthy in an inventory taken in 1667/8.[91] But the
loss was not on Filat'ev's books, so to speak. Contemplating the incident
gestures toward the importance of procuring, maintaining, disposing of, and
translating assets into working capital—an objective made all the more challenging in a resource-strapped Siberia. In such straitened circumstances, the
transmission of institutional knowledge was especially critical. Administrators likewise tapped the expertise of agents in the field. Just as privileged
merchants were called on to assess the value of the commodities in which
they traded, administrators in Siberia would call on network agents to do the
same. In March 1690 agents of O. I. Filat'ev, S. A. Luzin, and now gost' G. R.
Nikitin—all traveling together—were called on to assess the value of Eastern
fabrics and furs that would be presented to a local Kalmyk khan as gifts.[92]
In one case Siberian authorities called on Filat'ev's shop manager to sign the
report for an explorer in Russian service who could not write.[93]

In addition to the agents, porters, and shopkeepers in the field, the Filat'evs
maintained a substantial household in Moscow. The Noritsyn family were
among the father-son teams in the employ of the Filat'evs. In 1682, three men
(or boys) of the Noritsyn family were living in Ostafii's Filat'ev's household
in Moscow. Having fallen on hard times, they had moved into the household
to pay off their debt.[94] We will learn more of this family in chapter 8.

The seasonal and regional dynamics of trade meant that merchants frequently traveled together, which made for deliberate as well as coincidental
proximity. When the Filat'evs and Pankrat'evs or their affiliates appeared
simultaneously at customs posts even as they were engaged in a bitter property dispute, it may have been coincidental. Often, however, proximity was
deliberate, even if in an ad hoc way. In January 1662 Filat'ev's agents paid

90. RGADA, f. 1111, op. 2, d. 259, l. 147. This is the petition from the agent in 1677/78.
91. Orlova, Otkrytiia russkikh zemleprokhodtsev, no. 181, 467.
92. RMO, vol. 4, no. 98, 261.
93. RMO, vol. 4, no. 106, 273.
94. I. S. Ponomarev, Istoriia goroda Lal'ska Vologodskoi gubernii. I thank Yulia Strazdyn' of the Lal'sk
Historical-Regional museum for sharing this information with me.

taxes jointly with Ortelle Ivanov, the agent of Kozma Kondrat'ev, a Merchant Hundred merchant, on two sleds and three porters when they arrived at Tiumen' customs coming from Verkhotur'e.[95] Incidentally, Filat'ev's agent on this trade trip, Prokofii Fëdorov, may have been the same Prokopii [*sic*] Fëdorov, a trader from Vologda, who had had annual turnovers of 488 rubles in 1633–34 and 432 rubles in 1634–35 in Ustiug.[96] After all, merchants' agents sometimes operated independently.[97]

These seemingly random details illustrate the fluidity that marked the commercial world of early modern Russia. Beneath each dynasty and amid their networks, uncounted individuals followed their own trajectories. Although Samuel Baron, Wallace Daniel, and Jarmo Kotilaine have maintained that elite merchants contributed to the stifling of an emerging merchant middle class, we see here striking examples of privileged merchants whose successful careers were launched in the employ of other privileged merchants. Gavrilo Romanov syn Nikitin, one of the most successful gosti of the late seventeenth century, got his start working for the Filat'evs.[98] Once Nikitin ascended to privileged status, he remained on good terms with the Filat'evs; they cooperated extensively in the Siberian and China trade. Customs books reveal another such potential example. In 1672–73 the Filat'evs' employed a certain Ivan Grigor'ev. A man named Ivan Grigor'ev from the Meshanskii borough of Moscow was a member of the Merchant Hundred from 1678 to 1684.[99] Perhaps this is also a case of a merchant—Ivan Grigor'ev—operating both independently and in the employ of a larger merchant. Yet although the timing fits, where roughly 10 percent of the male population was named Ivan and 3.5 percent Grigorii, Ivan Grigor'ev is too common a name to conclude without corroborating evidence that both merchants were the same Ivan Grigor'ev.[100] Thus it is unknown if we are glimpsing an agent who progressed to privileged ranks. Nonetheless, despite the preponderance of kin as an organizing principle in early modern commerce, there were exceptions in which capable people not related to the boss advanced.

One need not only consider advancement to privileged status. In the summer of 1700, Peter Ivanov, a "man" of Vasilii and Aleksei Filat'ev, donated

95. S PbII RAN, f. 187, op. 2, d. 20, l. 29 (Book of Tiumen' customs head Tret'iak Shtil'nikov, 1661).

96. Merzon and Tikhonov, *Rynok Ustiuga Velikogo*, 254, 300.

97. Examples of this are found in the Pankrat'ev and Shababin operations. Bakhrushin, "Agenty russkikh torgovykh liudei XVII v.," in NT, 2: 134–53.

98. See Monahan, "Gavrilo Romanovich Nikitin: A Merchant Portrait," 47–56; Bakhrushin, "Torgi gostia Nikitina v Sibiri i Kitae," in NT, 3: pt. 1.

99. Golikova, PKK, 341, 370.

100. Kaiser, "Naming Cultures in Early Modern Russia," 276–83.

a copy of the 1606 print edition the *Apostol*, a book comprising the Acts of the Apostles and the Epistles, to a church in Kaluga in the memory of Ostafii (Evstefei) and his parents.[101] Print editions of the *Apostol*, which was the very first book printed in Muscovy in 1564 and went through twenty different print runs in the seventeenth century, were more expensive than manuscript versions.[102] That this agent possessed such a valuable item suggests substantial means. Recall too, the sumptuous clothes and fine pistols that belonged to an agent of the gost' G. R. Niktin.[103] All this is not to suggest that Russian elite merchants were somehow a more nurturing brand of capitalist—nothing of the sort, for I find no quibble with Braudel's assertion that true capitalists seek to eliminate competition.[104] These examples, however, complicate the existing picture.

Russia's privileged merchants have been called corporations, which reflects foremost a tradition of applying Western categories whether they fit or not. If corporation implies some pangroup cooperation among all group members, the gosti were not that. Formally, the special status of the gosti derived from the tsar's charter, and their obligations were to him, not each other. The *gostinia sotnia* was an even larger, more diffuse group. But cooperation among privileged merchants did take place. It could be informal, ad hoc, and perhaps single transaction, but it is also clear that other cooperation was deliberate and sustained, such as in the case of the Filat'ev and Luzin families in Siberia. The Filat'evs got into Siberian trade over a decade before Andrei or Semen Ostafeev Luzin traded there, but from the 1670s to 1690s the Filat'evs and Luzins cooperated in a veritable Siberian partnership. Each tended to have his own agent—that is, they did not share a single agent, as others did—but they clearly traveled together.

Theirs was not the only visible partnership by major Moscow merchants. The gosti Vasilii G. Shorin and Semen F. Zadorin teamed up actively for Siberian endeavors until Zadorin passed away in 1665.[105] Both Shorin and Zadorin were invested in commerce at various ends of the empire, including the Caspian-Persian trades. Their affairs were so intertwined that they

---

101. RGADA, BMST/SPK, no. 8, ll. 1–6. I thank Valerii Perkhavko and Evgenii Rychalovskii for help in obtaining this evidence.

102. "Celebrating the 450th anniversary of the Printing of the 'Apostol' of Ivan Fedorov and Petr Mstislavets," Exhibit at the Russian State library, Moscow, Russia. March 13–April 1, 2014. http://www.rsl.ru/ru/s7/s381/2014/apostol.

103. Monahan, "Gavril Romanovich Nikitin," 54.

104. Braudel, *Wheels of Commerce*. See Curto and Molho, "Commercial Networks in the Early Modern World," 1.

105. Vasilii G. Shorin was a G100, 1626–41; Gost', 1641–80. Semen F. Zadorin, G100 1646–51; Gost', 1651–55.

shared agents—that is, in Siberia, four different men declared themselves at customs as an agent of both "gost' Vasilii Shorin and gost' Semen Zadorin."[106] Their cooperation was not limited to Siberia. V. G. Shorin and S. F. Zadorin had a joint leather manufactory in Yaroslavl', which they sold in 1662.[107] When Zadorin sold his shops in Nizhni Novgorod, Shorin financed the purchasers.[108] Like other Muscovite elites, they solidified their business relations through marriage. Zadorin married Vasilii Shorin's sister.[109]

Sixteen gosti or their representatives appeared trading on their own accounts in Siberian customs books from 1640 to 1728.[110] Of these sixteen, nearly half were repeatedly active. Among these were the Bosovs and Gusel'nikovs, whose Siberian operations essentially ceased with their 1654 deaths. The remaining most active merchants were Filat'ev, Luzin, Shorin, and Zadorin. Filat'ev-Luzin and Shorin-Zadorin were partnerships. It is not apparent however, that these partnerships perceived each other in wholly competitive terms. That is, their agents appear at the same customs posts in close chronological proximity to each other. Moreover, marital bonds, too, joined these families. Afanasii Luzin had two daughters. One married gost' Mikhail Shorin, the other a Filat'ev.[111]

Keeping governors on one's good side was a standard operating expense for elite merchants, yet quantifying this aspect of operations eludes us. The historian V. A. Aleksandrov wrote in passing of Filat'ev's economic relationships with Siberian governors. Ostafii Filat'ev maintained regular written correspondence of an "amicable economic" nature with the Yakutsk governor Ivan Fëdorovich Golenishchev-Kutuzov, whose career and life ended in disgrace and confiscation after he was found guilty of sending copious amounts of fur for his own personal enrichment to Russia with multiple traders who passed through Yakutsk.[112] As part of the maintenance of amicable economic relations between gost' and governor—and perhaps here it is more precise to speak in terms of favors than of gifts—Filat'ev lent money to the governor's people who came to Moscow for wares; he would buy up wares according to a list sent by the governor, and, according to Aleksandrov, could act as an advocate for a Siberian governor to the tsar in Moscow, as

106. RGADA, f. 214, kn. 301, l. 83v, 85, 93 [Tobol'sk TK 1652/53].

107. Orekhov, "Tovarnoe proizvodstvo i naemnii trud v promyshlennosti," 90.

108. RGADA, f. 214, stb 806, l. 54.

109. Golikova, PKK, 131.

110. Monahan, "Trade and Empire," 120.

111. Kozlova, "Dukhovnye gostei," 190, 192.

112. Moiseev, *Vlast' v Sibiri*, 196. When I. F. Golenishchev-Kutuzov died in 1666, his son took his place as Yakutsk governor. Aleksandrov and Pokrovskii, *Vlast' i obshchestvo*, 113.

the right reputation with the right people was indispensable to a successful career. The savvy operator needed advocates at the center when stationed far at the periphery, and so Filat'ev assured his patron in Siberia that he would make Golenishchev-Kutuzov's "mercy" and "honorable service" known to those at court.[113] In return, Filat'ev reminded the governor that he expected reciprocal favors. For example, one letter advised the governor to advance Filat'ev's agent, Gavril Romanov, whatever money he might request in writing and that repayment would await him in Moscow.[114]

As we saw in chapter 4, there was a certain calculus involved in negotiating the balance between appealing to the law and strategizing to circumvent it in advancing one's interests. After maintaining evidently good relations with I. F. Golenishchev-Kutuzov, Filat'ev's rapport with Siberian administrators degenerated under the Gagarins.[115] Ostafii Filat'ev perhaps had more courage than clout when he petitioned the tsar complaining of abuse by the Eniseisk customs head Vasilii Buriakov in 1647–48, for he was then still early in his career. But the reputation of his uncle Bogdan was apparently valuable enough, for the tsar granted Filat'ev's request to assign a clerk to Eniseisk customs to guard against abuses.[116]

Property and 'Salt Wars'

As Siberian trade brought wealth to the Filat'ev family, they invested in property. In 1638 Ivan Vasili'evich Filat'ev with his son Ostafii had a home in White town (*Belyi gorod*) a crescent-shaped neighborhood that hugged the Kremlin and Kitai-gorod from the north. By 1675 Ostafii had relocated to a large estate in the southern part of Kitai gorod. In 1695, Ostafii's sons owned three properties in the neighborhood, in addition to the Church of St. Nicholas the family had built.[117] By the beginning of the eighteenth century, the family owned more property than any other gosti: 113 properties

113. Aleksandrov and Pokrovskii, *Vlast' i obshchestvo*, 137.

114. Ibid., 137–40. Also mentioned here are other traders with whom the Yakutsk governor had dealings, including Oskolkov and P. Shul'gin.

115. In the 1690s the Gagarins ruled eastern Siberia. Ivan Mikhailovich Gagarin was *voevoda* in Yakutsk, Ivan Petrovich—Irkutsk, and Matevei Petrovich—Nerchinsk. Matevei Petrovich was executed for his abuses in 1721. He may or may not have been the most egregious abuser; an investigation concluded that between 1694 and 1697, the Yakutsk governors I.M. Gagarin and M.A. Arsen'ev pocketed from servitors almost 17,000 rubles. The Gagarins had a deeper history in Siberia. Prince G. I. Gagarin had died while governor of Tobol'sk between 1615 and 1620. His son, D. G. Gagarin, took his father's place. Aleksandrov and Pokrovskii, *Vlast' i obshchestvo*, 113, 136, 139.

116. RGADA, f. 214, stb. 153, l. 343.

117. Shakhova, "Dvory torgovykh liudei," 408–9.

(*dvory*).[118] They owned or rented many shops in Moscow and Siberia.[119] Property acquisition, however, did not always proceed uncontentiously.

Typical of Muscovy's greatest families in the seventeenth century, the Filat'evs invested in saltworks. (Indeed, the houses owned by gosti in Solikamsk reads like a who's who list among elite merchants.[120]) Presumably, the investments were worth their while, because their saltworks brought them much trouble. In 1672 Ostafii Filat'ev purchased properties in salt-rich Seregov, near Solikamsk, the traditional Pankrat'ev domains. Displeased with the encroachment, the Pankrat'evs sought to oust the rivals from the start, which led to a protracted property disputes.[121] In a testimony taken when the matter had already become acrimonious, a local elder reported that on some night, "my brother and someone else, having drunken themselves drunk (*napivsia p'iani*), gave the agent of Ostafii Filat'ev" the deed to land in his [the elder's] name that he actually had no right to sell because that piece of land had been sold years previously to Daniil G. Pankrat'ev.[122] Despite such dubious origins—if this testimony was true—the Filat'evs did not relent. In December 1683, Ostafii's son, Vasilii, traveled to Seregov himself. He bought up properties during his visit and spent much time drinking with local peasants. I suspect that Vasilii bought the drinks, for, according to Pankrat'ev's agent, those who had sold land to Filat'ev then sent petitions against the Pankrat'evs to Moscow.[123] In fact, conditions only got worse and in 1684 workers from the rival saltworks in Seregov came to blows. The Pankrat'evs accused the Filat'evs of sending their people into the area to turn the townspeople against them.[124] Indeed, according to Ustiugov, workers fled Pankrat'ev's enterprises to join the Filat'evs, suggesting that the Filat'evs had the better reputation with the workers.[125]

---

118. Semenova, *Istoriia predprinimatel'stva v Rossii*, 142. Ten of forty-three gosti were counted as major property holders in the early eighteenth century. Cf. Golikova's much lesser late-seventeenth-century assessments. Golikova, "Formy zamlevladeniia i zemlopol'zovaniia gostei i gostinoi sotni," 26–45.

119. RGADA, f. 214, stb. 1398, l. 298v.

120. Ustiugov, *Solevarennaia promyshlennost'*, 145.

121. Timoshina, *Arkhiv gostei Pankrat'evykh*, nos. 18, 20, 32, 39, 44, 63, 73, 86, 91, 93, 98, 115, 120.

122. Ibid., no. 18, p. 43. NB: The heading of document no. 18 indicates that the drunken (illegitimate) transaction occurred in 1654. However, the document nowhere reveals that. Further, the document refers to Ostafii as a gost', a status he attained only in 1658. The document refers to D. G. Pankrat'ev as a d'iak. Pankrat'ev in 1654 went from being a gost' to being a d'iak. Golikova, PKK, 251.

123. Timoshina, *Arkhiv gostei Pankrat'evykh*, nos. 86, 91, p. 115.

124. Ibid.

125. Ustiugov, *Solevarennaia promyshlennost'*, 267.

The Filat'evs main saltworks, however, were located farther east. In 1680 Ostafii Filat'ev bought a property along the Lenva River (which empties into the Kama River on the western side of the Urals) with two salt boilers from the widow of a gost' for 1,800 rubles. In the course of expanding this property, Filat'ev found himself embroiled in a second property dispute as a result of him and gost' G. F. Shustov being sold the same parcel of land by different sellers. In a petition dated May 25, 1685 Ostafii Filat'ev said of Shustov, "jealous of my enterprise, they endeavor through various means to push me out of that enterprise." After a lengthy case, in which both sides were deemed to have a legitimate claim, the property was divided, but being on the same territory, something of a "partnership" resulted, which Filat'ev's sons took over after Ostafii passed away in 1692. By the mid-1690s there were forty-four salt boilers, twelve of which belonged to the Filat'evs. In addition to the home they, along with so many other merchants–cum–salt entrepreneurs, owned in Solikamsk, the Filat'evs had a masonry built house there, which is probably where ambassador Ides visited en route to China.[126] At their enterprise's peak, the Filat'ev-Shustovs paid over 10,000 rubles in customs taxes on the nearly two million pud of salt they produced annually. Advertising the service they performed, in 1695 Filat'ev and Shustov wrote to the tsars, "Sovereigns, [previously] our salt enterprises were not here and salt was expensive; but when we built our enterprises, and started boiling salt, the price of salt fell."[127]

The Stroganovs, the other great salt producers in the region, did not like the low prices or the competition and herein began the Filat'evs' third great salt controversy. In September 1695 Grigorii Dmitrievich Stroganov brought a case of dubious merit claiming the territory was historically his. The Stroganovs succeeded in having a surveyor friendly to themselves assigned to the case, despite Ostafii Filat'ev's formal protest. Tsar Peter decreed the land was the Stroganovs in February 1697. Locally, the heavy-handed methods of the land grab were so objectionable—before the Stroganovs succeeded in "legally" wresting the property, they had their people blockade access to the Filat'ev-Shustov saltworks, effectively shutting down the operation that carried the majority of the tax burden for the local population—that the community (posad) vociferously protested against the governor, who was married to a Stroganov. For their pains, the same month that Peter formally granted the land to the Stroganovs, fifteen townsmen, including the community elder (starost') with their wives and children were deported to Azov for lifetime service. Two years later, when all hope of appeal was lost, the

126. Ibid., 145; Tsypushtanov, "Istoriia Levninskoi tserkvi," n.p.
127. Ustiugov, *Solevarennaia promyshlennost'*, 29, 114–15.

Filat'evs and Shustovs signed an agreement acknowledging the outcome. The Stroganovs, for their part, promptly ceded the saltworks to the Moscow entrepreneur-financier, Gerasim V. Bel'skii, to cover a 6,000-ruble debt to him.[128] Interestingly, the Noritsyns, discussed in chapter 8, at various points worked for and were wards of both the Bel'skii and the Filat'ev families.

Despite the challenges the salt industry presented, in other spheres the Filat'evs were otherwise doing quite well. Called upon to shoulder additional financial burdens of military campaigns, the tsars traditionally thanked the gosti for their loyal support following wars and moments of great trial.[129] Upon signing the Eternal Peace Treaty of 1686 with Poland, Regent Sophia rewarded gosti who, "not begrudging their possessions, gave of their trade enterprises and paid taxes" with land and money. In this unique gesture motivated by Sophia's desire to retain her hold on power, Ostafii Filat'ev and his oldest son Vasilii each received 85 rubles and land. Aleksei received 80 rubles and land in the Rostov district, property that would be developed as a silk manufactory.[130]

Ostafii Filat'ev's success was neither meteoric nor entirely self-made but it was impressive. He inherited a family fortune and grew it. While continuing to invest heavily and profit from his Siberian endeavors, he expanded operations into China, a niche that his sons continued to pioneer. Published sources reveal a family whose affairs extended to Persia, the Caucasus, and Ukraine and western Russia as well.[131] As is to be expected of a merchant buying up Eastern and Siberian wares in the seventeenth century, Arkhangel'sk figured in the commercial spaces they frequented. In the 1680s, the august years of a remarkable career that stretched half a century—his name appears in evidence from 1646 and in Siberian customs books from 1690—Ostafii Filat'ev initiated construction of the Church of St. Nicholas of the Big Cross, which stood for centuries as a stone marker of the success—and devotion to God and state—of this merchant dynasty. In May 1692 Ostafii Ivanovich Filat'ev was interred there with the Patriarch Adrian presiding.[132] Among Ostafii Filat'ev's impressive accomplishments is that his two eldest sons (he had four) were made gosti during his lifetime.

---

128. Ibid., 115–22.

129. DAI 3, no. 44, 150–15 (August 26, 1648); PSZ 2, no. 864, 307–10 (Tsar Fëdor praising merchants after concluding Treaty of Bakchisarai in 1681 which ended the Russo-Turkish War).

130. PSZ, vol. 2, no. 1233, 846 (Jan. 17, 1687); Golikova, "Formy zemlevladeniia," 35.

131. *Armiano-Russkie otnosheniia v XVII veke*, no. 41 (1676). PSZ, vol. 2, no. 1015 (May 26, 1683); *Prodolzhenie drevnei rossiiskoi vivliofiki*, 1: 178; Kotilaine, *Russia's Foreign Trade*, 465. That the Filat'evs had one agent from Kaluga, southwest of Moscow, suggests operations that extended in that direction. RGADA, BMST/SPK, no. 8, ll. 1–6 ("Apostol").

132. Akel'ev, Evgenii. *Povsednevnaia zhizn' vorovskogo mira Moskvy*, chapter 2.

The Next Filat 'ev Generation: Vasilii and Aleksei Ostafievich

A merchant attained gost' status based on an opaque combination of merit, service—the merit and service of one's father was taken into account, although these prerequisites were not necessarily sufficient to guarantee gost' status—connections, and state needs. It usually required holding lesser office previously, coming personally to the tsar's attention, and most likely, enjoying advocates in high places. Although the majority of gosti were relatives of gosti, it was unusual for two sons to attain equal status with a living father and to become gosti without passing through the Merchant Hundred corporation, making Aleksei and Vasilii Ostafievich's early elevation to this status another indication of their father's success.

Ostafii's eldest son Vasilii was made a gost' in 1675, the penultimate year of Tsar Aleksei Mikhailovich's reign. His younger brother Aleksei was just twenty-eight years old in 1678 when he was elevated from the Merchant Hundred corporation to gost' status in 1678. Tsar Fëdor Mikhailovich's salubrious disposition toward merchants, plus vibrant growth in the China trade, may explain the anomaly of having two sons made gosti with a living father still a gost'.[133] The Filat'ev sons inherited a healthy enterprise. In 1678 a tax assessment of 1,250 rubles was levied on Ostafii's four sons.[134] Remarkably, Ostafii had remained engaged in the family enterprises until near the very end of life; his (i.e., not his sons') agents appeared in Siberia in 1690 and reported turnover of 16,000 rubles at Arkhangel'sk that same year; his business partner Semen Luzin had 8,400 rubles worth of turnover at Arkhangel'sk in 1690. In 1689 O. Filat'ev and S. Luzin dispatched agents to China for trade, so substantial capital was in circulation there as well.[135]

The two eldest brothers, Vasilii and Aleksei, managed the family business together. Although they both were involved in the saltworks and in the Siberian and China trade, Vasilii seems to have been more engaged in the former, and Aleksei, the latter. Recall that it was Vasilii who was drinking with peasants in Seregov in 1683, and Vasilii signed the map that the Filat'evs submitted in 1696 protesting the Stroganov's land grab.[136]

Vasilii served as head of the Big Customs Office in Moscow in 1687.[137] Around the turn of the century he served in the Siberian Office and was

---

133. The reviled Chistoi, who stacked the gosti ranks with three of his sons, was beaten to death by an angry crowd.

134. Akel'ev, *Povsednevnaia zhizn' vorovskogo mira*, chapter 2.

135. Aleksandrov, "Russko-kitaiskaia torgovlia," 436; Kotilaine, *Russia's Foreign Trade*, 490–91.

136. Ustiugov, *Solevarennaia promyshlennost'*, 316.

137. *Armiano-Russkie otnosheniia v XVII veke*, nos. 66–68, pp. 184–91.

called upon to assess the value of Chinese goods in 1702.[138] While in Moscow, he purchased Siberian and Chinese goods directly from the Siberian Office, presumably not for state business—as his great uncle Bogdan had bought up furs on the tsar's behalf and sold them as the tsar's factor at the court in Warsaw[139]—but for his own commercial ends. Vasilii was among the buyers when G. R. Nikitin's confiscated wares were auctioned off by the state in 1699.[140] G. R. Nikitin was arrested on August 30, 1698 for "disrespectful remarks about Tsar Peter and his favorite, Menshikov, criticizing state affairs." Unluckily, this was just days after Peter had returned to Russia to deal with the strel'tsy revolt, a moment when Peter was heavily preoccupied and ill-disposed to treat behaviors that smacked of disloyalty mercifully. The elderly merchant died in prison just weeks later on September 18, 1698.[141] One wonders if Vasilii Ostafievich Filat'ev felt a sense of irony at buying up the wares of a ruined man whose career his father had launched.[142] They had continued to cooperate over the years and in the wake of Nikitin's ruin, the Filat'evs employed people from his network.[143]

Vasilii's younger brother Aleksei was highly visible in the Siberian and Chinese trade. Agents working in the name of Aleksei Ostafievich or Ostafii appeared frequently whereas Vasilii's agents appeared just once in the Siberian customs books I studied, and that was en route to China in the 1690s.[144] Both sons were involved in this core aspect of the family business. Vasilii delivered furs to the state treasury shortly before 1680/81.[145] They both actively corresponded with their agents and people in the field. Under the leadership of A. A. Vinius the Siberian Office initiated a new postal service in 1696. The inaugural order directs that "it is ordered (for trading people) for their needs and expansion of their trade and for the increase in taxes, to send to Siberia and other places their letters to agents and other people along with special packages of their people." The Filat'evs took advantage of the new service. Vasilii and Aleksei jointly dispatched eight letters addressed to their Siberian

---

138. RGADA, f. 214, op. 5, d. 1495, l. 15; Lapt'eva and Solov'eva, *F. Lefort*, 392.

139. Bogdan bought furs in Sol'vychegodsk and went to Warsaw with furs the next year for the tsar.

140. RGADA, f. 214, stb. 1698, l. 78.

141. Bakhrushin, "Torgi gostia Nikitina v Sibiri i Kitae," 3:226; Monahan, "Gavril Romanovich Nikitin," 54–55.

142. RGADA, f. 214, op. 5, d. 1495, l. 15.

143. RGADA, f. 214, stb. 1398, l. 298v. This Iakov was likely related to the deceased Gavril Romanov Nikitin, suggesting that after G. R. Nikitin's ignominious death his relatives returned to the more secure employ of the established Filat'evs.

144. RGADA, f. 1111, op. 2, d. 599, l. 11.

145. Ogloblin, *Obozrenie*, 4: 10.

agents. As in modern postal system, the fee was assessed by weight. Instead of a specific address of delivery, however, the Filat'ev brothers attached a cover letter directing state servitors to deliver the letters "wherever they find them."[146]

Aleksei also spent time at the Lenva saltworks. When the Russian state caravan led by the Dutchman Eberhard Ides passed through Solikamsk en route to China in 1692, Aleksei Filat'ev entertained the party in their home there. Adam Brand, a German in the party who chronicled the journey described how Ambassador Ides and most of the retinue were invited to "the countryhouse" "of a certain Muscovian gentleman, one of the tsar's factors, Alexi Astaffi Philatoff [sic]." The house was located 20 miles from Solok [sic] [Solikamsk] near a large saltworks where, according to Brand, the tsar employed over 20,000 workers.[147] There, the members of the embassy "were entertained with a very nice dinner, and pass'd the Day very merrily." If Brand learned during his stay that Aleksei's father had been laid to rest one year ago that month, or of the impending battles over saltworks with their neighbors, he makes no mention of it. What Brand's reporting does convey is Aleksei Ostafievich's enthusiasm for boats. The Filat'evs were involved in a project close to the heart of Tsar Peter I: boat building. One catches a fleeting glimpse of Aleksei Filat'ev's personality—that of an ambitious Russian entrepreneur poised to exploit a still new possession—through Adam Brand's diary. Baron wrote that Peter, with his maritime fascinations and aspirations, coerced reluctant gosti into boat-building works for which they had insufficient passion and expertise.[148] Yet Brand's description of Aleksei Filat'ev proudly displaying his own boat-building yard to the traveler suggests genuine enthusiasm for his operation. Filat'ev showed Brand two large boats that he had had constructed "at his own cost" to transport salt. Aleksei had the party watch, wrote Brand, "to make us eye-witnesses of the manner of convoying these ships, and what Order and Discipline there was observed among them. Each of the vessels had five hundred men on board who were to labour without intermission at the oars, relieving each other at certain and convenient times under the command of several officers."[149] This exchange occurred in 1692, years before sharing Peter's love of boats became a sine qua non of political favor. Perhaps it was Filat'ev's enthusiasm for boat building that caught Peter's attention. Peter was certainly impressed by Aleksei

---

146. Ibid., 4: 106.
147. Brand, *A Journal of the Embassy to China*, 18–19. Brand was referring to the nearby state-owned Zyrianskie saltworks.
148. Baron, "Fate of the *Gosti*," 496–501.
149. Brand, *A Journal of the Embassy to China*, 18.

Filat'ev's familiarity with other innovations little known in Russia at the time, probably imported from Western Europe. In a letter to the Arkhangel'sk governor in 1693, Peter instructed him to procure some "small organs" of the type that Aleksei Filat'ev had shown him.[150]

By the 1690s the Filat'evs were seasoned businessmen and had learned key survival lessons from their father. Filat'ev knew what it took to get on in Siberia and he knew he was choosing a more serious battle when he went up against M. P. Gagarin, the powerful and notoriously corrupt Siberian governor, for wrongly confiscating 4,480 rubles from his agents in 1694.[151] One wonders if Gagarin's abuses alone were enough to merit Filat'ev's shift in tactics—his strategy heretofore was to "get on" with Siberian governors. Or could it have been that Filat'ev hoped to neutralize what he saw as competition in the China trade—a niche he was innovatively working to develop? In such a contest Filat'ev encountered more than one formidable incumbent. The Irkutsk governor I. P. Gagarin and his brother, the Nerchinsk governor M. P. Gagarin, both specialized in the China trade alongside their state duties, which made them competitors with gosti trying to cultivate the same trade—competitors with military means and state authority at their disposal.

Filat'ev was not the only merchant who had problems with Gagarin. The lower-ranked Merchant Hundred merchant G. Grigor'ev petitioned the tsar about M. P. Gagarin wrongfully taking 425 rubles worth of Chinese wares from him.[152] Ultimately, Gagarin's abuses and abuse of people with influence of their own became too flagrant to ignore. Peter's desire to demonstrate Russia's powerful transformation was manifest in his readiness to make an example of those who flouted his vision of an empire of honest, obedient servitors. This sealed Gagarin's fate. After a long investigation and reinstatement followed by a final indictment, he was executed by hanging in 1721.[153] The dramatic execution was one of several theatrical public capital punishments Peter staged during his reign, as was the case of a nobleman executed for taking a 5-ruble bribe in 1701.[154] Amid Peter's anticorruption pageantry, his most trusted associate, Alexander Danilovich Menshikov, amassed an unfathomable fortune on the bribes that bought his favor and went unpunished during Peter's lifetime.

---

150. Baron, "Fate of the Gosti," in *Muscovite Russia*, 500.
151. Aleksandrov and Pokrovskii, *Vlast' i obshchestvo*, 140.
152. Ibid.
153. Miller, IS, vol. 2: 104; Akishin and Remenov, *Vlast' v Sibiri*, 201–3; Serov, *Stroiteli imperii*, 225.
154. Serov, *Prokuratora Petra I*, 13. For more on Gagarin's execution and Peter's "spectacles of suffering" see Kollmann, *Crime and Punishment*, 403–15.

Filat'evs in the Petrine Era

According to A. I. Aksenov, the first decade of the eighteenth century began a precipitous decline whereby the Filat'evs sank into financial ignominy. In 1705 the assessed tax burden on the Filat'evs was reduced to 860 rubles in response to their own petition in which they cited losses in salt and sable revenue, as well as damages from a fire, for their diminished circumstances. In 1711 their assessed burden was reduced again.[155] These facts constituted the main evidence for Aksenov's assertion of their demise; he reasoned that losses in salt income, the government's increased regulation of sable, and a certain "sitting on one's laurels," created difficulties from which the Filat'evs did not recover.

This interpretation coincides with Samuel Baron's assessment that the gosti were a decrepit corporation for whom Peter had little patience.[156] To be sure, only three new gosti appointments were made after 1700 and the gost' corporation as a juridical entity was eliminated in 1728. It is worth distinguishing content from form, however. If Peter decided to overhaul the structure of a previously existing commercial corps, it does not necessarily mean he was personally inimical to the individuals of those ranks. Certainly, the case of the Filat'ev gosti in the Petrine period suggests that they not only continued as a successful merchant family but that they even enjoyed a measure of Peter's personal favor.

One wonders if the reduced tax burdens of 1705 and 1711 might reflect political favor more than loss, because other evidence suggests that these merchants remained enviably successful during the Petrine era. In 1710 Aleksei Filat'ev had a trade volume of 10–15,000 rubles at Arkhangel'sk.[157] A 1710 register of collections shows the Filat'evs paid orders of magnitude above other merchants. In this same register, the second and third biggest contributors, Shustov and Luzin, respectively, were allies and partners with the Filat'evs.[158] Indeed, it was probably in the second decade of the 1700s that Filat'ev and Luzin deepened their partnership by marrying their children: Ostafii's son Aleksei married Semen Luzin's daughter, Anna.[159] Ostafii's brother, Vasilii, married Praskovaia Mikhailova, the widow of the gost' Kirill

---

155. Kozlova, *Gorodskaia sem'ia*, 521.

156. Baron, "The Fate of the Gosti," in *Muscovite Russia*; Aksenov, *Genealogiia moskovskogo kupechestva*, 42–45.

157. Baron, "Fate of the Gosti," in *Muscovite Russia*, 493, Table 2.

158. Ibid., 489.

159. Kozlova, "Dukhovnye gostei Mikhaila Shorina," 192, 196–97; Kozlova, "Na ch'ei opeke," 349–58.

Iakovlevich Laboznev, further illustrating how elite merchant families solidified relations through marriage.[160]

Despite being on the losing side of Peter's decision on the Lenva saltworks in 1697, the Filat'evs remained in Peter's good favor. Returning from Lithuania in the spring of 1708, Peter sent ahead a list of individuals to summon for a "drunken assembly." Aleksei O. Filat'ev was included in the list.[161] On the same day that Peter invited Aleksei to join his drunken revelry, he wrote another letter identifying the need to generate cash and find a good merchant who could sell a large shipment of Russian leather hides (*iufti*) to foreigners.[162] In a place and age where politics were personal, this was probably not coincidental: Peter recognized commerce as a means to achieving state ends, and merchants like Aleksei Filat'ev as the vehicles of commerce.

Aleksei's success is in part attributable to his savvy in managing influence with the court. In the wake of Russia's defeat at the Battle of Narva in 1700, he donated 10,000 rubles to Tsar Peter. The generous donation probably accounted for a significant portion of the Filat'ev turnover. The Filat'ev brothers quite likely were among the merchants who funded construction of triumphal arches built to celebrate Peter's campaigns.[163] If Aleksei's intention was to distinguish himself before the tsar, he succeeded, and in 1714 was instructed to move to St. Petersburg. Although Peter required several nobles to relocate to St. Petersburg in its founding decades, Filat'ev was one of only two gosti instructed to do so.[164] Filat'ev curried favor in less fiscal ways as well. In 1717 a grandson was born to him and christened Peter, a name that does not appear previously in the family genealogy.

Aleksei Filat'ev's career, of course, involved state service. He gave consultative testimony in Moscow in 1684. He served as the head of customs in Kholmogory in 1690 and the major port of Arkhangel'sk in 1694.[165] In 1701 he worked as a collector of state revenues.[166] In 1711 he was called to St. Petersburg to consult on commercial treaties with England and Holland.[167] In 1712, he was appointed to a committee tasked with improving

160. "Will of Vasilii Filat'ev," in Kozlova, *Gorodskaia semia*, no. 3, 198. Fedotov-Chekhovskii, *Akty otnosiashchiesia do grazhdanskoi raspravy*, no. 110, 1: 382.

161. Hughes, *Russia in the Age of Peter the Great*, 253.

162. *Pis'ma i bumagi Imperatora Petra Velikago*, vol. 7, no. 2298, p. 91 (6 March 1708).

163. Ageeva, "Kupechestvo i sotsial'naia prazdnichnaia kul'tura," 24–42.

164. Baron, "Fate of the Gosti," 493, 499, 508.

165. Semenova, *Istoriia predprinimatel'stva v Rossii*, 146; Bulatov, et. al., *Istoriia Arkhangel'skoi tamozhni*, 19 Golikova, *Privilegirovannoe kupechestvo v structure russkogo obshchestva*, 180.

166. *Pisma i bumagi Imperatora Petra Velikago*, no. 1475, 4: 494 (Resolution on report of F. A. Golovin, March 29, 1701); Baron, "Fate of the Gosti," 508.

167. Baron, "Fate of the Gosti," 508.

trade conditions.[168] Citing the example of neighboring Sweden, the committee's first recommendation was to eliminate internal customs. Since customs revenue remained Russia's biggest source of income, the idea found no political traction for four decades—elimination of internal customs was finally decreed in 1753, but it did not apply immediately to Siberia.[169] Otherwise, little of the committee's activities are known, but its creation in 1712, even before major central reforms, shows that healthy commerce was a central component in Peter's reformist vision. In 1727 Aleksei again participated in an advisory committee on customs reforms.[170]

Aleksei's later career offers some insight into an elite merchant's attitudes about the state's proper role in commerce. When Peter's government proposed to tax-farm out trade with China (which at that point was an imperfectly enforced state monopoly), Aleksei Filat'ev was part of a committee that concluded that it would be impossible to organize a sufficiently capitalized company without government support. At the very least, we see that this corporation expected the government to finance major investments. Government involvement in large undertakings was the norm. That elite merchants advocated another entity to underwrite their risks was a rational and standard business strategy, not the reflection of a slavish, hyperconservative business culture. If Russian merchants got cold feet at the prospect of putting up significant capital for uncertain results, they were not alone: Massachusetts merchants declined to establish a bank in the 1680s for the same reason.[171]

Alternatively, perhaps it was not necessarily a risk-averse conservatism but a sense of current commercial trends that contributed to their reluctance to promote a trading company. Peter was enamored with Western ways of doing things. Observing that the great maritime powers were organized in trading companies, he wanted to follow this model. But as with the calendar—Peter adopted the Julian calendar when the Gregorian calendar was already the way of the European future—he sometimes grasped at obsolete trends despite forward-looking intentions. In the early eighteenth century the now traditional trading company model was in decline. The profit margins of the Dutch East India Trading Company had already waned to modest levels after lucrative profits in its initial decades.[172] Meanwhile, the English were abandoning the exclusivity of the trading company for "national" protectionist

168. Kozlova, *Rossiiskii absoliutizm i kupechestvo*, 46.
169. PSZ, vol. 13, no. 10.164 (December 20, 1753). Siberian customs would remain.
170. Kozlova, *Rossiiskii absoliutizm i kupechestvo*, 46–47, 191.
171. Bailyn, *New England Merchants of the Seventeenth Century*, 185.
172. De Vries, "Connecting Europe and Asia," 88–91.

legislation already in the late seventeenth century.[173] In a world where "free trade" was attaining rhetorical pride of place, trading companies—which by definition constructed monopolistic regimes—were logically passé. But the English were second to none in the idiosyncratic application of the concept "free trade."[174] The start of the eighteenth century was not the twilight of trading companies—indeed, the English East India Company's most profitable days were still ahead—but it was a lull in their luster.

One can only speculate as to just why Aleksei Filat'ev and his colleagues were reluctant to embrace a trading company model for China. Arriving at such a speculation involves considering the extent to which these Russian merchants had their finger on the pulse of international commerce: one with access to court life would have rubbed shoulders with ambassadors and foreigners with detailed knowledge about their respective national projects. Perhaps Filat'ev and his peers heard tell of the difficulties trading companies faced. Or it may well be that they saw the China trade ripe with unrealized potential and already too big to contain to one institution. Perhaps the most logical explanation is that the Filat'evs, even as they would likely have been strong contenders to win a tax-farm bid, preferred the China trade as it was. They were happy to have the assistance of a responsive government, but did not want the commitments and risk of collective investment beyond their control.

Culture, Class: On the Question of Gosti Status

As the elite of elite merchants, the Filat'evs adopted certain habits that reflected their wealth and status. The above description of Adam Brand is rare and restrained, but it, along with other such glimpses into the gost' at home, suggests a world of refinement and affluence. For example, when Nicolaas Witsen visited as a guest in the home of Averkii Kirillov, a contemporary of Aleksei Filat'ev's, he described an opulent household:

> He lives in a beautiful building; it's a large and beautiful masonry house with a top [floor][175]of wood. In the courtyard he has his own church and bell tower, richly decorated, a beautiful house and garden. The conditions inside the house are no worse, in the windows

173. See Veluwenkamp and Veenstra, "Early Modern English Merchant Colonies," 11–31; De Vries, "Economic Crisis of the Seventeenth Century," 188.

174. Pettigrew, "Free to Enslave," 3–38.

175. Drawings indicate that it was not just the roof but a top floor of wood was constructed atop the masonry building of seventeenth-century merchant homes in Pskov. See Arshakuni, "Pamiatniki 3-ogo perioda razvitiia arkhitektury zhilykh zdanii XVII veka."

[is] German etched glass. In short—he has everything necessary for a richly endowed home: beautiful chairs and tables, paintings, carpets, wardrobes, silver items, etc. He treated us to various beverages, as well as cucumbers, melons, squash, nuts and dried apples, all of it served on beautiful silver, very clean. Nothing was in deficit. . . . All his servants wore identical outfits, which was not the case even in the Tsar's household. He treated us very hospitably. . . .[176]

Kirillov, a rare case of a gost' who had successfully jettisoned his station and been promoted to the rank of secretary in the tsar's council (dumnii d'iak), may have felt particular pressure to communicate his raised status by appropriating the material culture of the elite. But Kirillov's opulence was not anomalous. Although the difference between a provincial estate and a Moscow household may have been great, we can imagine that the Filat'evs' standard of living resembled that of their peer, Kirillov.

Describing Moscow, Olearius grouped boyars and rich merchants together as the few people who lived in masonry rather than log houses.[177] The Filat'evs had a large masonry home in the Kitai gorod neighborhood. Like the Kirillov home, the Filat'evs' Moscow residence originally had a wooden roof. The roof burned in a fire in 1675, however, and by 1754 a metal roof, an expensive rarity for the time, covered the house. The Filat'ev residence stood in a large lot between Old Square (Staraia Ploshad') and Ipat'evskii Lane, in the heart of Moscow.[178] Then, as now, this was prime real estate. Of 324 privileged merchants registered in Moscow at the start of the eighteenth century, only 21 lived in Kitai gorod.[179] They had prestigious neighbors. Not far away was Vasilii Shorin's childhood home, which Peter I deemed fine enough to give it as a reward to the Moldavian prince Kantemir in 1711.[180] Also nearby was the home of gost' G. L. Nikitnikov, which Archdeacon Paul of Aleppo, Syria noted was larger than those of heads of state ministries.[181] The Filat'evs' neighbor to the north in the eighteenth century was the statesmen A. D. Tatishchev, and to the south, the distinguished Stroganovs, with whom their proximity in Solikamsk had ended so unhappily.[182]

176. Witsen, Puteshestvie v Moskoviiu, 161.
177. Olearius, Voyages and Travells, 65. The Russian word is kamennyi, which indicates brick covered in stucco (masonry), most typically, or brick. There were few stone structures built in Muscovy. I thank David Ransel for this information.
178. Shakhova, "Dvory torgovykh liudei," 408–11.
179. Zaozerskaia, "Stat'i. Moskovskii posad," 21–22.
180. Baron, "Vasilii Shorin," in Muscovite Russia, 508.
181. Perkhavko, Pervye kuptsy Rossiiskie, 370.
182. Shakhova, "Dvory torgovykh liudei," 410.

Glimpses of gost' lifestyles brings us directly to the question of gosti culture, or *mentalités*.[183] The historian Boris Floria posed the question: In which social sphere did these elite entrepreneurs-cum-bureaucrats reside?[184] Were gosti of high social status? Although gosti families did not appear in the Velvet Book (*Barkhatnaia kniga*) or bear coats of arms, coveted status markers of Muscovite nobility, in other ways it is clear that they enjoyed elite status. Legally, they were due a 50-ruble fine for dishonor; this was the fine due a boyar.[185] They were listed in the chronicles right after princes and boyars. They participated in state ceremonies; their place in highly symbolic processionals demonstrated visually for all viewers, literate and illiterate alike, their high place in society. Although their commercial operations differed in scale more than in essence from lesser merchant counterparts, they belonged to the sphere of Muscovy's elite whose lives were distinguished by a more elaborate and well-endowed material culture consisting of masonry homes, lavish furnishings, and fine clothes (although for state ceremonies, gosti would be issued vestments from the court).

Administratively, in some roles gosti functioned as peers of Muscovite nobles. N. F. Demidova found that "Of 50 people appointed directly as chancery secretaries in the seventeenth century . . . eight [came] from the ranks of gosti."[186] Although it would be naïve to suggest equivalence—the dynamics of Muscovite political culture were too opaque to be wholly revealed through bureaucratic status—that boyars and gosti occupied the same roles in the administration of state departments such as the Siberian and Sable Office and cooperated on organization objectives had to have had some leveling effect. In the event that it did not, merchant wealth gained them access to the tsar. From the Stroganov contribution to ransoming Vasilii in the early sixteenth century to Aleksei Filat'ev's donation of 10,000 rubles to Peter I, Muscovy was a world where money talked. Given sufficient wealth, gosti owned extensive properties and even serfs (although the Filat'evs were exceptional in the property they owned).[187]

183. Chartier, "*Histoire des mentalités*," 54–58. On gost' culture see: Preobrazhenskii and Perkhavko, *Kupechestvo Rusi*, 179.

184. Floria, "Review of N. B. Golikova," 181.

185. In two cases merchants were designated the special privilege of being due a fine of 100 rubles for dishonor: (1) the Stroganovs and (2) Thomas Kellerman. Smirnov, "Posadskie liudi," 91; Baron, "Who Were the Gosti?" in *Muscovite Russia*, 20.

186. Demidova, "Biurokratizatsii gosudarstvennogo apparata," 218; Bakhrushin, "Moskovskoe," in *NT*, 2: 84–89.

187. PSZ, vol. 1, no. 1, chapter 17, article 45; Golikova, "Formy zamlevladeniia i zemlopol'zovaniia gostei i gostinoi sotni," 26–45.

It has been widely observed that premodern merchants who obtained sufficient means often sought to jettison their class by buying offices and land in pursuit of noble status.[188] The many gosti who went on to become chancery secretaries (*d'iaki*) in Moscow invite inquiry into the matrix of opportunities in commerce and government that shaped such aspirations. In fourteen documented cases gosti or members of the Merchant Hundred went on to become chancery secretaries (*d'iaki*).[189] The gosti Nazar Chistii and Averkii Stepanovich Kirillov (gost', 1659–76) ascended from gost' rank to the even higher status of secretary of the tsar's council.[190]

If that political trajectory was not the norm, when seeking gosti intellectual life, one is most immediately confronted with ubiquitous markers of religious devotion—in the books they owned, the monastic donations they gifted, and the churches they constructed. The Stroganov library consisted of about two thousand volumes, the majority of which were religious texts. When Nikita Grigorievich Stroganov traveled, he reportedly did so with twenty to twenty-five books from the family library.[191] What we know of Ostafii Filat'ev's book collection also conveys religious devotion. They both owned *Peleia*, a religious work. The gost' Ostafii Filat'ev purchased a copy of the *Prologa* from the Moscow Printing Office in the summer of 1662, a book that cost about 40 copper rubles.[192] (Incidentally, Boyar Ivan Andreevich Miloslavskii bought the same book just one day before, and Andrei Vinius, the day after.) The Filat'evs and Stroganovs were in a small category of elite merchants, but they were not alone in owning books. L. A. Timoshina found that seventy-five families of privileged merchants purchased books from the Printing Office.[193] The Iudins and Gur'evs, elite merchants who succeeded in jettisoning their class and becoming gentry, owned copies of the *Domostroi*, a sixteenth-century household manual.[194] Many privileged merchants could

---

188. Curto and Molho, "Commercial Networks in the Early Modern World," 82; Brunelle, *Merchants of Rouen*, 139; De Vries, "Economic Crisis of the Seventeenth Century," 172; Mahan, *Influence of Sea Power on History*, 54; Kozlova, *Rossiiskii absoliutizm i kupechestvo*, 139.

189. See Golikova, PKK, 87, 98, 103, 124, 290, 316; Golikova, "Chislennost', sostav i istochniki popolneniia gostei," 112 fn.86, 120; Baron, "Who Were the Gosti?" 34; Veselovskii, *D'iaki i pod'iachie*, 176.

190. Golikova, PKK, 124; Baron, "Vasilii Shorin," 524. Nazar Chistii became gost' in 1620/21. By 1647 he was a *dumnii d'iak*. He soon after met a brutal death when he was dragged from his hiding place in his home underneath a slab of smoked salted pork fat (*kopchienoe salo*) into the street and beaten to death by an angry mob in the Moscow uprising of 1648. Perkhavko, *Pervye kuptsy Rossiiskie*, 371.

191. Perkhavko, *Pervye kuptsy rossiiskie*, 379.

192. Pozdeeva et al., *Moskovskii pechatnii dvor*, 398. Inflation due to the state's adulteration of currency with copper makes it hard to gauge prices in the early 1660s.

193. Perkhavko, *Pervye kuptsy rossiiskie*, 379.

194. Pouncy, *Domostroi*, 11 fn.15.

write. One hundred and sixty different merchants signed their names to collective petitions to Aleksei Mikhailovich in 1646.[195] In an analysis of records from the Moscow Printing House, Pozdeeva determined that merchants and members of the lower classes bought 1,092 out of 2,316 printed copies of the *Book of Hours* (*Chasovnik*) in the 1640s; and that for the 1646–1649 print runs, merchants purchased 15 percent of copies of the *Instructional Psalm book* (*Uchebnaia Psaltir'*) sold in Moscow, compared to 8 percent purchased by elites.[196]

Peter Mikliaev was a gost' from Novgorod. Adam Olearius described him as an "intelligent and knowledgeable" man who, for all his perspicacity, was no less keen to explain the symbolism of the making of the Orthodox sign of the cross.[197] This is not to say Muscovite merchants were devoid of the intellectual ambitions that are seen as markers of enlightened civility. Peter Mikliaev sought out Adam Olearius to tutor his son in Latin and German. Subsequently, Mikliaev's career took him both East and West. In 1660 he traveled to Holland and Holstein on the tsar's behalf. Meanwhile, he followed economic opportunity in relocating eastward to Kazan.[198] The merchant Grigorii Bokov sent his son to the Slavic-Greek-Latin Academy that opened in 1687. The celebrated Russian poet Silvester (Semen) Medvedev was the son of a Kursk merchant.[199] What needs to be included in this discussion is a consideration of just how intellectually ambitious merchants from Western Europe were. Indeed, Nicolaas Witsen, director of the Dutch East India Company, avid collector and author of *Noord en Oost Tartarye*, was a paragon of enlightened refinement. Yet his Renaissance-like curiosity was not typical of merchant stock, something he himself complained of in a letter to a friend: "You ask about the scholarly love of knowledge in connection with the East-India [Company]? No, Sir, they seek only money, and not science there, which is as you know, a shame."[200] *The Universal Dictionary of Trade and Commerce*, published in London in 1774, instructed that beyond arithmetic, bookkeeping, languages, and foreign history, child merchants-to-be should have no further schooling. Subjects such as "Latin, Grammar, Rhetoric, and Philosophy" were not only "useless, but also very harmful."[201]

---

195. Perkhavko, *Pervye kuptsy rossiiskie*, 379.

196. Pozdeeva, "The Activity of the Moscow Printing House," 54.

197. Olearius, *Travels of Olearius*, 175, 195, 293.

198. Ibid.

199. Perkhavko, *Pervye kuptsy Rossiiskie*, 379.

200. Kirpichnikov, *Rossii v XVII v.*, 13

201. Postlethwayt, *Universal Dictionary of Trade and Commerce*, bk. 1, chap. 4. The guide was a translation from the French guide by Jacques Savary, *Le Parfait negociant, ou Instruction generale pour ce qui regarde le commerce des merchandises et des pays etrangeres*, which had been originally published with state sponsorship in 1675.

In Qing China successful salt merchants who patronized scholarship were seen as squandering the family wealth.[202]

The participation of some gosti, along with some boyars, in Western cultural innovations of the seventeenth century consolidates their associations with Muscovy's highest elite. The Vologda gost' Gavril Martynovich Fetiev's household held Eastern carpets, German leather upholstered chairs, and a hanging wall mirror beside a family icon. Fetiev—one of the first known Russians to sit for a portrait in 1683—had a large wardrobe and eyeglasses, and decorations of gold, silver, pearl, emerald, and ruby graced the family inventory. He kept parrots and canaries, revealing that the Russian elite shared in the consumption of exotica that denoted high class in Western Europe.[203] Boyars and gosti were among the first Russians to sit for portraits in the seventeenth century. Experimenting with portraiture is hardly a step the most conservative elements of seventeenth-century Muscovite society would take. In a world where religious material and royalty were all that was fit for the canvas, the vanity implied was potentially scandalous.

Perhaps as frequently as gosti built masonry houses in Moscow, they sponsored construction of churches, public acts of piety both with a long tradition in Russian mercantile culture and befitting nobility.[204] As we have seen, gosti took pride in affluent homes and refined hospitality. On some occasions, gosti married into boyar families.[205] Tellingly, along with despised boyars, gosti were occasionally targets in mass protests that erupted into riots.[206] Yet gosti were not boyars—they were located farther down in the hierarchy, as their position in state ceremonies recorded in documents explicitly illustrates. And their assimilation of elite material culture was not without tension. Fletcher reported that when gosti wives adopted the fashion of pearl embroidery on their fur caps, boyar wives reacted by seeking still different styles to maintain their distinctions from trading types.[207]

Adam Olearius, Holstein ambassador to the tsar, described the gosti as "imposing old men with long gray beards" when he proceeded past them to approach the tsar's chamber.[208] Samuel Collins remarked that Tsar Aleksei

---

202. Ping-ti, "Salt Merchants of Yang-chou," 130–68.

203. Perkhavko, *Istoriia russkogo kupechestvo*, 226, 372. Perkhavko notes that he did not have many books.

204. Perkhavko, "Pervye moskovskie kuptsy," 4–6.

205. Ibid.

206. See Golikova, PKK, 275; Perrie, "Popular Revolts," 604, 612; Baron, "Who Were the Gosti?" in *Muscovite Russia*, 35.

207. Fletcher, *Of the Russe Common Wealth*, 149.

208. Olearius, *Travels of Olearius*, 62.

Mikhailovich consulted with men who were 120 years old "and delight[ed] to hear them tell what pass'd in his Ancestors time."[209] Perhaps these observations about august leadership should suggest, not gerontocracy, but more in the way of vitality. Examining the long careers of the three Filat'ev gosti, one might conclude that, notwithstanding the health advantages a life of affluence afforded—warm clothes, adequate food, sound housing—the Filat'evs were blessed with good genes. Ostafii was an active merchant for half a century. He held the rank of gost' for thirty-seven years, his son Aleksei for forty-seven, and Vasilii for forty-three. These long spans do not even cover their entire careers, for most merchants worked some amount of time before gaining admission to the privileged ranks. Given their father's success and prominence, it is likely that Aleksei and Vasilii were promoted to gost' rank while still young men. But their longevity was not unique. When Tsar Peter admiringly told the gost' Mikhail Evreinov, "You know your business, old man," he was being literal; gosti lived a long time.[210] In the sample I studied, elite Russian merchants' careers often lasted four decades.[211] Olearius, hardly a charitable observer, reported, "The Muscovites are of a healthy and strong constitution, long liv'd and seldom sick; which when they are, their ordinary remedies, even in burning Feavers, is only Garlick and strong-waters."[212] The Scottish doctor Samuel Collins described Russian children as "commonly strong and hardy."[213] Where lifespan is such a standard indicator of civilizational development, this is an important revelation for early modern Russian history (to say nothing of the disturbing fact that the average male lifespan in contemporary Russia has dipped to levels of third-world countries).[214] To the extent that health indicators such as life span are accepted markers of progress and well-being in a society, these findings undermine assertions of Russian backwardness, or at least beg clarification of what is meant by backwardness.

---

209. Collins, *The Present State of Russia*, 124.

210. Baron, "The Fate of the Gosti," 508.

211. Drawing on the sample of sixteen gosti who operated in Siberia, if we discount the careers of Kirill Bosov and Vasilii F. Gusel'nikov, which were cut short by plague, and that of Dmitrii Danilov, which remains obscure, the average career length of these thirteen gosti was just over forty-two years. Even if we exclude from our sample Andrei Luzin, whose extraordinary career span of seventy-five years begs credibility, the average career span still averages at just over forty years. For an analysis of boyar ages that offers a similar picture of longevity, see Kollmann, *Kinship and Politics*, Appendix 1, pp. 191–8.

212. Olearius, *Voyages and Travells*, 67.

213. Collins, *The Present State of Russia*, 13.

214. Feshbach, "A Country on the Verge"; "Booze Blamed for Early Deaths of Young Men."

Post-Petrine Filat'ev Fortunes

The Filat'evs continued as merchant-entrepreneurs in post-Petrine Russia. The last Filat'ev gost' outlived the gost' system. The categories of privileged merchantry—gost' and Merchant Hundred—were eliminated in 1728 and replaced with a tiered guild system whereby trade revenue determined one's status.[215] Indeed, the elimination of a juridical category did not mean the elimination of entrepreneurialism. Aleksei Ostafievich Filat'ev, like his father before him, had a long and successful career as a gost'. His older brother, the gost' Vasilii, had died in 1718; his younger brother Fëdor, who had not been a privileged merchant, had passed away by 1725. His wife, Anna Semenova passed away in the summer of 1730. In September 1731 Aleksei had his will drawn up and by December 1731, the last Filat'ev gost' had passed away at the age of 71.

Aleksei Ostafievich Filat'ev and his wife Anna Semenovna had only one son, Dmitrii, who predeceased them both in 1725. Before his death Dmitrii had reached adulthood, married a wealthy merchant's daughter, who bore him a son. Therefore, Aleksei Ostafievich bequeathed his estate to his grandson Peter Dmitrievich. According to the will, Peter's mother was welcome to live in the Filat'ev house on Kitai gorod with her children Peter and Ekaterina, and be provided for, so long as she did not remarry. The will exhorted her in-laws to discourage her remarriage; if she did remarry, she would receive 500 rubles, have to leave the house, and would have no other claims on Filat'ev property. At the time of Aleksei's death, Peter was thirteen or fourteen years old. His grandfather considered, nonetheless, that he was fit to take part in management of the family enterprises. Although Peter Dmitrievich was barely a teenager, Aleksei named no formal guardian; in fact he specifically instructed Peter not to abrogate decision making to others. At the same time, Peter Dmitrievich could take no decisions without consultation with relatives, in-laws, and the trusted friends named in the will, first among these Aleksei's only surviving brother, Peter's uncle Andrei. Thus his will reveals Aleksei's patriarchal ethos and final effort to channel family wealth in his wake. Further, and contrary to assertions about merchants seeking to flee their social station, Aleksei Ostafievich, who himself married the daughter of a gost', in strong language advised Peter to seek a wife not among the nobility but from the merchant class.[216]

---

215. PSZ, vol. 8, no. 5300, 61–62 (June 30, 1728).

216. Kozlova, "Dukhovnye gostei," 188–203; See also Kozlova, Gorodskaia sem'ia XVIII veka, 25, 124–27, 521–23; Kozlova, "Na ch'ei opeke," 344.

Various documents label Peter Dmitrievich Filat'ev variously as Member of the Merchant Hundred, a gost', and bearing the idiosyncratic label "grandson of a gost'" (*gostinii vnuk*) elsewhere, testifying to the vestiges of the old order in a transforming world.[217] Unlike his grandfather, he eschewed participation in consultative bodies aimed at steering the political economy of Russia,[218] but he maintained his status as a merchant—of the first guild, in the postgosti world, as it were. The family hard largely divested from saltworks by this time; instead Peter developed a silk factory on his estate in Rostov district. By 1753 he had established an extensive silk production and dyeing operation, powered by a rural labor force of nearly 1,000 people.[219] The serfs and household dependents who populated the many villages and estates of the Filat'evs are beyond the purview of our study. We will, however, mention one dependent, who became so famous his reputation lived on in popular Russian culture. Ivan Osip was born a serf on Aleksei Filat'ev's Rostov property in 1722. When Aleksei Filat'ev passed away in 1731, Peter Dmitrievich transferred Ivan Osip to Moscow. There, the provincial peasant fell into a world of crime, becoming known as Van'ka Kain, a Russian criminal so notorious that songs were sung about him in his own lifetime, a popular story chronicled his misdeeds, and his superlative infamy was immortalized with its own entry in V. I. Dal''s *Thick Dictionary of the Living Russian Language* (*Tolkovii slovar' zhivogo russkogo iazyka*): Van'ka Kain: soubriquet of seasoned brawlers (*prozvishche otboinyx buianov*).[220] His testimony, granted, that of a miscreant, depicts Peter Dmitrievich as a strict master who beat his deviant servants and kept Ivan Osip cum Van'ka Kain chained without food in the courtyard after his first attempt to run away.[221]

Peter Dmitrievich's lifestyle bore the trappings of the eighteenth-century elite and he was counted among the "fat cats" of Moscow's business elite.[222] No longer beholden to the sumptuary laws that forbade non-noble wealthy in his great-grandfather's day from driving carriages drawn by many horses, he had a carriage house in the Filat'ev courtyard in which a chained bear was said to guard the entrance.[223] Of the nearly fifty serfs and workers who

217. Akel'ev, *Povsednevnaia zhizn' vorovskogo mira*, n.p. see fn 224.

218. Kozlova, *Rossiiskii absolutizm i kupechestvo*, 138; Golikova, PKK, 201.

219. Liubomirov, *Ocherki po istorii russkoi promyshlennosti*, 112, 570; Aksenov, *Genealogiia moskovskogo kupechestva*, 42.

220. Akel'eva, *Povsednevnaia zhizn' vorovskogo mira Moskvy*, 1; Dahl', *Tolkovii slovar'*, 1: 166. I thank Natalia V. Kozlova for sharing this information with me.

221. Akel'ev, *Povsednevnaia zhizn' vorovskogo mira*, n.p. see fn 237.

222. Miroshchenko, "Kuptsy-staroobriadtsy v gorodakh Evropeiskoi Rossii," 35.

223. PSZ, vol. 2, no. 906, p. 367 (December 28, 1681); Shakhova, "Dvory torgovykh liudei," 414.

lived at the Kitai gorod estate, one woman was dedicated to preparing coffee for him. In 1756 Peter accused one household girl of using witchcraft to do him ill: she was caught salting his daily coffee. While we cannot of course know Peter Dmitrievich though these ephemeral glimpses of disgruntled dependents, they do, to say nothing of the dozen of serfs that fled Peter's properties during his tenure, perhaps suggest that his grandfather's warning in his last will and testament for Peter to treat servants mildly was more than formulaic rhetoric.[224]

In 1754 Peter Dmitrievich engaged in negotiations about selling his Moscow estate to the Confiscation chancery, but no deal was struck. The estate passed to his son Aleksei Petrovich Filat'ev. In 1756 Aleksei Petrovich, the great-great-grandson of Ostafii Filat'ev, became a military man in Empress Elizabeth Petrovna's army, abandoning the family's merchant status.[225] Little is known of his career, including if the translation from French into Russian of *1,001 Nights: Arabian Tales* (*Tiasicha i odna noch': skazki Arabskie*) published by the Imperial Press of Moscow University in twelve volumes from 1763–1774 was his work. The year the final volume was published, the Filat'ev house on Ipat'evskii Lane was sold for 6,000 rubles.[226] The next time the family name Filat'ev surfaced in the historical record it was in association with military distinction.

It is beyond the scope of this study to follow the family fortunes farther. But perhaps one remark underscores the impact and reputation this family enjoyed, and some eighteenth-century difficulties they faced. In the eighteenth century, the Imperial Academy of Sciences reissued the Sudebnik law code composed under Tsar Ivan IV in 1550. Vasilii Nikitich Tatishchev (1686–1750), a nobleman who bridged the worlds of high-ranking government servitor and scholar, and is perhaps best remembered for popularizing the notion that the Ural Mountains divided Europe and Asia, composed the annotations. In a footnote to a statute about commercial fraud, Tatishchev wrote:

> The gost' Filat'ev dispatched his agent (*prikashchik*) to China, having supplied him with much desired wares. The agent, knowing the craftiness and deception of Chinese, negotiated with just such a crook, so that the Chinaman would sell him the fabric [*kitaika* = simple cotton fabric from China] as inexpensively as he could. That Chinese man,

224. Akel'ev, *Povsednevnaia zhizn' vorovskogo mira*, n.p. see fns 211, 223, 227, 237.
225. Golikova, PKK, 201.
226. Shakhova, "Dvory torgovykh liudei," 414.

having made wooden blocks, and having wrapped up each in two good pieces of fabric, in fact gave him fabric worth a third of the price in comparison to the genuine. When the agent arrived in Moscow and presented the wares to Filat'ev, he [Filat'ev], having cut the fabric, found a few bales (*tiukov*) [of fabric] that were very good and for a price not all that expensive, settled up generously with the agent and sent him on, hoping for great profits. And when Filat'ev, sold [the wares] to Ukrainian merchants, they, having taken a few bales, discovered this swindle because of which Filat'ev was destroyed, suffering over 50,000 rubles in losses.[227]

The gost' Filat'ev was only mentioned in a footnote, to be sure, but that the author presumed the Filat'ev name sufficiently recognizable to his readership suggests a degree of celebrity that comes with status. If we are to believe Tatishchev, this passage also narrates the family's exit from the elite commercial stage. But Tatishchev may not have had all his facts straight, for the Filat'evs still owned and operated a silk factory—one of thirty-seven in Russia—in 1760. In addition to silk production, a cottage industry in their villages dyed silk and other fabrics.[228] If true, however, this anecdote reminds us that even seasoned merchants could fall victim to old hoaxes—adulterating a shipment's quality by intermixing cheaper wares is an ancient fraud—or of the difficulties in securing reliable help when managing a commercial network across a vast empire.

Conclusion

Through individual chutzpah, state favor, managerial stability, and favorable market opportunities, the Filat'evs rose to prominence in the seventeenth century on a multifaceted commercial portfolio punctuated by government service. The Filat'ev gosti stood at the head of an elaborate commercial network comprised of kin and nonkin support that engaged in various types of trade—diversified and niche specific, regional and transimperial, as well as running production facilities such as saltworks and silk manufactory. This incomplete portrait of the Filat'ev family reveals several features common to the histories of other gost' families. First, the Filat'ev family originated in the Russian north, as did the Bosov, Gusel'nikov, Nikitin, Zadorin, and many

227. *Prodolzhenie drevnei fossiiskoi vivliofiki* 1: 177–78. I thank Michael Flier and Paul Bushkovitch for help with this translation.
228. Liubomirov, *Ocherki po istorii russkoi promyshlennosti*, 112, 117, 570.

other merchant families. Second, in typical fashion, the Filat'ev network was largely kin based. Yet the Filat'ev enterprises served as the incubator for G. R. Nikitin, who went on to become a prominent gost'; this exception to the rule challenges interpretations that elite merchants only quashed lesser ones, and alerts us to understudied trajectories of Muscovite commercial life. Third, merchants that rose to the highest ranks of Moscow society rarely did so in one generation, and the Filat'evs were no exception. Of the seven generations reconstructed here, six ended their careers as merchants.

The first Filat'ev entered the privileged ranks at a moment when the Muscovite state was intensively reconstructing. Exceptionally, two brothers were promoted to gost' rank during their father Ostafii's lifetime. This occurred at a moment of significant state expansion from which the Filat'evs deftly benefitted. Over the course of the seventeenth century, three men from this family achieved the highest merchant status of gost', an extremely exclusive status. Among these exceptional ranks, however, the Filat'evs were not so exceptional. From 1600 to 1725, fifty-three families produced more than one gost'. Of these, thirty-six families—more than half—produced two or three.[229] Finally, typical of merchants involved in the Siberian trade, they dealt in Eastern products, mostly textiles, no less than in Siberian furs. Perhaps most important, during this period it is telling that the wealthiest—the elite of the elite—made their money in Siberia. They took advantage of the developing state infrastructure to extract furs and push forward commercial exchange with Asia. Even as they retained features of Muscovite conservatism typically imputed to merchants, the Filat'evs engaged in transformation, innovations, and in some degrees, the conspicuous consumption typical of the elite. The history of the Filat'ev family invites us to revisit traditional historiography regarding Russian merchants, a discussion taken up in the conclusion. In the meantime, the next chapter examines a merchant family of different origins, ethnicity, and religion, but that, in common with the Filat'evs, made its fortunes in Siberian and China trade.

---

229. Golikova, PKK, 208–13.

CHAPTER 7

Commerce and Confession:
The Shababin Family

"If only merchants would come, then we all would be
satisfied and full."

—written to Tsar Fëdor Ioannovich, 1597

In 1657, as a reward for his service and "for
leaving Bukhara," the tsar granted the Bukharan merchant Shaba Seitov
3 square miles (715 desiatiny = 1,930.5 acres) of land on the north bank of
the Tura River, across from Tiumen', the town Russians "founded" in 1586
on the site of the Tatar town Chingi-tur.[1] Shaba Seitov became the first
patriarch of what became known as the Shababin family in Russia. This land
grant occurred in the same decade as the centralizing reforms that marked
the early years of Tsar Aleksei Mikhailovich's reign. The Muscovite state
effected land reforms through coerced property divestment (think eminent
domain). If foreigners wished to keep their property, they were pressured to
convert to Orthodoxy. This policy has prompted historians to describe Muscovite society as xenophobic.[2] Yet, far from Moscow on the Siberian frontier,
the state was courting Muslim merchants into its service and granting them
land. The Shababin family, who benefitted from this largesse, would retain
this land and their Muslim identity as subjects in good standing for over a
century to come.

---

1. GBUTO GATO, f. 47, op. 1, d. 2228, l. 1. 1 *desiatina* = 2.7 acres.
2. Baron, "The Origins of Seventeenth-Century Moscow's Nemeskaja Sloboda," in *Muscovite Russia*, 1–17.

This chapter recounts the history of the Shababins, a Bukharan family that put down roots in Siberia as the Russian state did the same.[3] This transgenerational portrait of the Shababins depicts a thriving commercial network.[4] Trade was the family's mainstay but the Shababins also farmed and by the beginning of the eighteenth century ran a thriving tannery. Their trading practices, which operated at both long-distance and regional scales, will look familiar to students of early modern merchants. For example, trading was a family affair. Second, contrary to the much-discredited decline thesis, which posited that the onset of transoceanic trade spelled the death knell for overland Eurasian trade, the Siberian trading posts the Shababins frequented reveal that overland Eurasian trade continued throughout the early modern era.[5]

The value of chronicling this family's history extends beyond offering a perspective on local political economy in the context of global economic change. It offers a glimpse of empire building in action. Reconstructing the Shababins' enterprises reveals how Bukharans maintained an integrated yet distinct identity within a Russian Empire keen for their presence. At the very least, this glimpse into a Muslim community on the periphery gives lie to pronouncements that "the suppression of Islam, accompanied by coercive Christianization and Russification, were always central to Moscow's policy of integrating non-Russian territories."[6] On the contrary, because the Muscovite government recognized that these Muslim merchants facilitated vital commerce, it did much to encourage and accommodate Muslim merchants in Siberia. The history of Siberian Bukharans demonstrates the degree to which the state's trade policies conditioned life on the Siberian frontier. Siberian Bukharans shared space, occupations, livelihoods, and service with Russians, Tatars, and other native Siberians. They became Russian subjects yet maintained relationships with kin from their distant homeland. Their lives afford the opportunity to observe cross-cultural and cross-confessional

---

3. The only works that focus on this family are by Vera P. Kiueva, "Ispol'zovanie genealogicheskikh dannykh pri izuchenii sotsial'noi istorii"; Kiueva, "Bukhartsy v sisteme ekonomicheskikh otnoshenii sibirskogo goroda," 70–72. I am grateful to Vera Kiueva for her generous help in this research.

4. Following non-elite family lines across generations before last names became fixed is an elusive endeavor. A history of property holdings compiled in the reign of Catherine II (GBUTO GATO, f. 47, op. 1, d. 2228) definitively links the Shababin family through six generations.

5. The classic statement: Steensgaard, *Asian Trade Revolution of the Seventeenth Century*. Challenges: Rossabi, "'Decline' of the Central Asian Caravan Trade," 351–70; Levi, "India, Russia, and the Eighteenth-Century Transformation," 93–122.

6. See Pilkington and Yemelianova, *Islam in Post-Soviet Russia*, 6, 23. Although scholarship has overturned such conceptions, the notion remains typical even of scholarly works that give superficial attention to earlier centuries.

intersections in a Eurasia where the Russian presence was considerable but not hegemonic.

Finally, theirs is not just a story of Muslims in the Russian Empire, but reflects the longer and larger story of Islam in Eurasia. Western Siberia was the site of various waves of Islamicization that date from pre-Mongol conquest to the present day.[7] Bukharan communities in western Siberia, among whom varieties of Naqshbandi Sufism were most prevalent in the early modern period, linked themselves to and derived prestige from historical and sacred ancestries of both Chinggis Khan and the Prophet. Indeed, the names of Shababin family members reveal that they positioned themselves within a prestigious Sayyid lineage.[8] These sacred genealogies, fragmented, mysterious remnants that embody myth and aspiration along with historical information, are invaluable sources for recovering something of the *mentalitié* of Muslim merchants who migrated across Eurasia in the early modern period. These, along with extant nineteenth-century sketches of the mosques in Medina and Mecca, the Quran, and even older texts in Tatar, Arabic, Farsi, and Turkic discovered in western Siberian manuscript collections, only begin to hint at the cultural vectors that tied the region to the larger Afro-Eurasian ecumene. These artifacts date physically from the eighteenth century but are manifestations of oral and written traditions that date much farther back in time.[9]

The Shababins' story is exceptional but not unique.[10] The family's first three generations engaged in state service, either as commercial envoys or employees in the customs administration. Overall, however, the family seems to have devoted more energy to its private enterprises, a strategy that served them well, for they increased their landholdings substantially through purchases over the course of the seventeenth century. They benefited from state

---

7. Excavations revealing funeral customs associated with twelfth-century Samarkand suggest Islamization pre-Mongol conquest. See Bustanov, *Book Culture of Siberian Muslims*, 84, on modern Salafi missionaries, see 184.

8. Sayyid lineage linked itself to the Prophet. Khwaja lineage was also a prestigious identity that some Bukharans, including apparently the Shababins, claimed. E-mail correspondence with Alfrid Bustanov, February 20, 2013.

9. Bustanov, *Book Culture of Siberian Muslims*, 86–182. Many manuscripts are undated. Bustanov dates one manuscript (no. 29, 127–28), a dogmatic text in Arabic produced in Bukhara, to the seventeenth century, nine manuscripts date to eighteenth century, sixteen to nineteenth century, fourteen to the twentieth century, and two are unknown.

10. See Bustanov, "Sacred Genealogies and Transnational Contacts of Muslims of Northern Eurasia"; Bustanov, "Sacred Texts of Siberian Khwaja Families," 70–99; Bustanov and Korusenko, "Genealogy of the Siberian Bukharians," 97–105; Bustanov and Korusenko, "Famil'naia khronika sibirskikh saiidov," 45–61; Korusenko, "Sibirskie Bukhartsy v XVII–XIX vv.," 88–97. See Monahan, "Trade and Empire," chap. 7, for portraits of Seitkul Ablin and Seidiash Kulmametev. On Sabanak Kulmametev, who appears numerous times in Siberian customs books, see I. V., "K istorii o Sabanake Kul'mameteve."

privilege but sustained themselves sufficiently through trade, husbandry, and leather manufacture to weather later revocations of state privilege. By the mid-eighteenth century, the fourth-generation family head, Seit Shabin syn Shababin, held more shops in the Tiumen' marketplace than any other individual and was a local leader in his community. By Catherine the Great's reign, the Shababins may have been the largest Bukharan landowners in Tiumen' and the Shababin yurt numbered over one hundred healthy males.[11]

Bukharans like Shaba Seitov who migrated to Siberia in the seventeenth century arrived at a place whose population, though sparse, was remarkably diverse. There were Russians both Orthodox and schismatic (in what became known as the Old Belief). From the shamanist and animist traditions among natives such as Voguls and Ostiaks, to the Lamaism of the Kalmyks, to the Tatars of both pagan and Muslim persuasions, not to mention previously settled Bukharan diaspora merchants steeped in still different Islamic traditions, Siberia was a multiethnic pastiche of various religious commitments.

In this diverse confessional space, the Orthodox Russian state tread carefully. It imposed Orthodoxy on the landscape with its architecture, replicated ritual processions, and saw itself as the keepers of the Orthodox flock, but it did not push hard to impose Orthodoxy on non-Russians in Siberia.[12] Rather, Bukharans were a normal part of Siberian communities and Islam was a normal part of the Siberian landscape. Even if minarets were forbidden to punctuate the skyline above Siberian mosques, Bukharans traveling through Siberia felt no need to conceal from Russian authorities that they were traveling for religious purposes.[13] Indeed, Islam was even integrated into the institutional life of the Russian state. When a Bukharan gave his testimony to Russian authorities, he took an oath according to his Muslim (*Bursurmanaskii*) faith.[14] Two Tobol'sk governors were of Muslim heritage. Iurii Iansheevich Suleshev (1623–25) was of noble Crimean Tatar heritage and raised Muslim.[15] Prince Mikhail Iakovlevich Cherkasskii (1697–1711) was the son of a Kabardinian prince who had been baptized into Orthodoxy.[16] Mikhail Cherkasskii's son was later governor of all Siberia. There were dozens of mosques in Tobol'sk district alone. In some villages Muslims

11. GBUTO GATO, f. 47, op. 1, d. 2228, ll. 4, 16 (Survey of iurt property, Tiumen', late eighteenth century).

12. On efforts of the Muscovite state to create its empire as a physical and spiritual Orthodox space, see Rowland, "Did Muscovite Literary Ideology Place Limits on the Power of the Tsar?" 125–55; Kivelson, *Cartographies of Tsardom*; Romaniello, "Secular Conquests, Sacred Spaces."

13. RGADA, f. 214, stb. 301, ll. 67–71.

14. GBUTO GATO, f. 47, op. 1, d. 271, l. 1.

15. Bakhrushin, "Voevody Tobol'skogo razriada v XVII v.," in NT, 3: pt. 1, 266.

16. Bushkovitch, "Princes Cherkasskii or Circassian Murzas," 16.

mimicked the Slavic practice of having separate structures for summer and winter worship.[17] The Dutchman Eberhard Ides, who led an embassy to China on behalf of the Russian state in the 1690s, visited a mosque in Tobol'sk. His description conveys a sense of the rhythms, sights, and sounds of Islam in everyday Siberian life:

> Their metchets, called by other authors mosques, or churches, had large windows round them, all which were set open: the floor was covered with Tapistry besides which there was no other ornament. All persons at their entrance leave their shoes or slippers at the door, and set themselves down in rows, with their legs under them: the chief priest sat there in a white calico habit, and a white Turkish Turbant on his head. Then I observed one behind the people cry with a hoarse loud voice and after he had said something to them, they all fell on their knees; then the priest uttered some words and afterwards cried out, "Alla, Alla Mahomet," which the whole assembly roared out after him, three times successively, prostrating themselves to the ground: This done, the priest looked into both his hands as tho' he designed to read something there and repeated Alla, Alla Mahomet: Then he looked first over his right shoulder, then over his left, which all the people did after him and so the short devotion was ended. The Mufti or chief priest is an Arabian, whome they so highly reverence that for his sake they very much esteem any person that can either read or write the Arabick language. This priest invited us to his house, which was near the metchet, and treated us with a dish of tea.[18]

Thus, although mushroom domes topped with the three-barred Orthodox cross come to mind when one pictures a Russian skyline, the daily chorus of prostration to Allah was no less a fixture of the everyday soundscape in early modern Siberia.

Who Were Bukharans in Siberia

When, why, and even whence Bukharans came are matters of some contention. In the sixteenth century Bukharans frequented the Volga marketplaces of Kazan, Astrakhan, and the Kama region chartered to the Stroganovs.[19]

---

17. Frank, *Islamic Historiography and "Bulghar" Identity*, 29.

18. Ides, *Three Years Travels from Moscow Overland to China*, 13.

19. "Pistsovye knigi goroda Kazani, 1565–68 i 1646 g.," 72–201. Bukharan merchants traded in Nizhni Novgorod in the fourteenth century, but they had probably traveled all the way from Central Asia. Ulianitskii, *Snosheniia Rossii s Sredneiu Azieiu i Indieiu*, 6.

They first settled in the Siberian khanate probably during the reign of Khan Kuchum, who invited Bukharan missionaries to bring Islam to his tributaries.[20] After the Russian conquest, Moscow authorities proved no less welcoming. In 1596 Bukharans who had fled Chingi-Tur during the chaos wrought by Ermak petitioned the tsar to resume residence in Tiumen'. The state approved their request and designated the northern bank of the Tura River across from the Russian posad Tiumen' as the Bukharan neighborhood (*Bukharskaia sloboda*) where Bukharans could live and trade.[21] The Shababins' first property was in this area.

Indeed, the Russian state desired Bukharan settlement. As it began advancing into Siberia, the state recognized that Bukharan merchants plying wares and moving caravans over the Eurasian steppe could help to offset the challenge of lengthening supply lines and critical deficits. And so, from the time of the Stroganovs' first charter in 1558 onward, facilitation of favorable trading conditions became a pillar of Siberian trade policy. The state insisted that Bukharan merchants be welcomed and treated well.[22] They were "to trade in every kind of ware freely without duty"[23] and be allowed to come and go freely, unhassled. "Taxes are not to be taken from them [Bukharans] so that in the future it would be favorable for them to return."[24] Once habits were established, Moscow was happy to roll back privileges in order to generate revenue through taxation, but in the beginning the priority was simply to get them there.[25] In a letter dated November 3, 1644 Tsar Mikhail Fëdorovich summarized the aims that underlay the state's approach to Bukharans: "We

---

20. Radlov reported this. Bartol'd distanced himself from it. Recent work accepts this was a real historical event. See Frank, "Western Steppe," 252–53. For references in Russian archives to correspondence between Abdullah II and Kuchum, see Schmidt, *Opisi tsarskogo arkhiva XVI v.*, 94; Bustanov, "Sacred Texts of Siberian Khwaja Families," 81; Ziiaev, *Ekonomicheskie sviazi Srednei Azii s Sibir'iu*, 22, cites a Russian copy of a letter (in RGADA, f. 131, op. 1, d. 1, f. 3 (1598)) written in the 1570s by Khan Abdullah of Bukhara to Kuchum mentioning his request for Bukharan scholars. Sacred genealogies of Siberian Bukharans are rooted in a union between descendants of the Prophet via Saint Sayyid Ata (thereby rooting legitimacy in Islamic heritage) and a daughter of Kuchum (thereby rooting legitimacy in Chinggisid heritage).

21. Miller, *Istoriia Sibiri*, no. 4, 2: 176–77. The decree is dated August 31, 1596. Chingi or Chingi-Tur on the Tura River (now near Tiumen') was the Taybugha capital of the Siberian khanate, founded by a Shibanid in 1423 but came to be occupied by the rival Taybughid (non-Chinggisid) dynasty. Mamet, a Taybughid, established the new capital of Sibir (referred to as Isker in Russian sources), slightly south from Tobol'sk on the Irtysh River sometime after 1493. According to the Kungur Chronicle, this is the city Ermak conquered.

22. Miller, IS, vol. 1, no. 2, 325–28 (1558 charter); no. 17, 357 (1594 Instructions to Tara).

23. Miller, IS, vol. 1, nos. 2–5, 325–35 for charters (1558, 1568, 1574) and 1572 letter to the Stroganovs.

24. Quoted in Ziiaev, *Ekonomicheskie sviazi Srednei Azii s Sibir'iu*, 27.

25. Rezun and Vasilievskii, *Letopis' sibirskikh gorodov*, 272. Barring periods of severe need in which tax collection was suspended, Bukharans were already being taxed by 1607. RMO, vol. 1, no. 3, 25.

have granted Bukharans who have migrated to Tobol'sk to not be registered in or taxed as posad people, and from the farmland they have taken from Tatars, to not collect grain allotment, so that seeing this, other Bukharans and foreigners would come to live in Tobol'sk; and those Bukharans [should] trade among all the Russian towns and not be treated poorly and except for criminal and debt matters, not be tried in court."[26]

Tsar Peter I upheld his father's and grandfather's policy of Bukharan privileges in order to promote settlement: "so that others in the future will have the desire to emigrate and take [Russian] subjecthood."[27] In general the policy worked. Though these communities initially numbered in the tens, Bukharan immigrants gradually trickled into the welcoming empire. They lived in several settlements called yurts around the Tura, Tobol', and Irtysh Rivers and in the forests between Tobol'sk and Tiumen'. By the end of the seventeenth century, there were Bukharan communities in Tobol'sk, Tiumen', Tara, and as far eastward as Tomsk, probably totaling over three thousand Bukharan men.[28] In the 1730s descendants of early Bukharan émigrés explained to the German academician G. F. Müller: "In distant years past, our great-grandfathers and grandfathers and relatives, hearing that there was free acceptance and especially abundant mercy to foreign émigrés in the Great Russian kingdom . . . leaving our fatherland, relatives, and homes, left with our households to the Great Russian autocratic province with other Bukharans voluntarily to become subjects in Siberian towns."[29]

These memories, filtered through time and the pen of a foreigner with imperialist proclivities (Müller advocated the taking of the Amur valley and advancing up the Irtysh River), should naturally be approached with skepticism. But we need not rely solely on Müller for impressions that the Muscovite state cultivated a welcoming environment for Bukharan settlers. In the late eighteenth century émigrés from Tashkent petitioned the Russian government for permission to settle in Siberia, citing the favorable conditions they witnessed there.[30] The ethnographer Johann Gottlieb Georgi wrote in

26. Quoted in Korusenko, "Sibirskie bukhartsy: dinamika, chislennosti, i rasselenie (XVII–XX vv.)," 486. S.K. gives date as 1645, which is an error if the date Nov 3, 7153 is correct.

27. Korusenko, "Sibirskie Bukhartsy," 488.

28. GBUTO GATO, f. 47, op. 1, d. 2228, ll. 1–16; RGADA, f. 214, stb. 81, ll. 60–61; Bakhrushin, "Sibir' i Srednaia Aziia v XVI–XVII vv.," in NT, 4: 208; Chimitdorzhiev, Rossiia i Mongolia, 198; Butsinskii, Zaselenie Sibiri, 1: 111. Bukharans may have lived in Kuznetsk and Kazan.

29. Ziiaev, Uzbeki v Sibiri, 18–19. Decline in Bukhara under the Ashtarkhanid dynasty in the early eighteenth century may have helped to persuade Central Asians that the Russian Empire was a land of benevolence and opportunity. Frank, Bukhara and the Muslims of Russia, 3–5.

30. Ziiaev, Uzbeki v Sibiri, 19; Kiueva, "Mekhanizm priniatiia rossiiskogo poddanstva vykhodtsami iz Srednei Azii," 64.

1775 that more than twenty thousand Bukharan males lived in the whole of the Russian Empire and that "the empire is daily receiving supplies of new subjects from it [Bougharia—*sic*]."[31]

Bukharans acquired land and made their homes in Siberia. East of the original Bukharan neighborhood in Tiumen', a settlement grew up that became known as Embaevskie yurts. Embaevo today is a village suburb located about 20 kilometers east of Tiumen'.[32] An early map of the region depicts a special pasture just for mares next to Embaevskii yurt, clueing us in to the *kumys* (fermented mare's milk) and horsemeat that comprised much of their diet. As culinary traditions persisted, the different climate and ecology of Siberia dictated certain adjustments. For example, Bukharan immigrants quickly abandoned the traditional practice of living in mud homes.[33] They adjusted to life in Siberia and made Siberia their home, contributing to the Russia's imperial project as they did so. By the 1620s Bukharans were working in the Russian customs service and there was at least one mosque in Tiumen'.[34]

Bukharans contributed in important ways to the Siberian economy and to the local community as respected subjects who simultaneously served the Russian state and advocated for their own interests. They looked to the tsar as both sovereign and protector. Like Russian nobles and soldiers, they received land for service. Muscovy's suzerainty in Siberia and the tsar's generous solicitations provided commercial opportunities on which Bukharans capitalized. Although Bukharans were never included in privileged corporations with Russian (and a handful of European) merchants, in Siberia Bukharans enjoyed certain privileges and a better tax status than local Russian merchants. Similar to Russian nobility, Bukharan families in Siberia derived their prestige from noble and sacred lineages passed down from one generation to the next.[35] Bukharans in Siberia not only retained their Muslim faith but may also have promoted Islam among Siberian Tatars—activities that the Orthodox state, whose hold at the edge of empire was tenuous at best, largely ignored. Indeed, in Brian Boeck's view of Muscovy as an "empire of separate deals," the Bukharans got a good one.[36]

---

31. Georgi, *Russia*, 2: 127, 129.

32. Today Embaevo is rendered with an "m," where there is an "n" in early modern documents.

33. Bakieva and Kvashnin, "Nekotorye osobennosti traditsionnoi kul'tury," 225–29.

34. RGADA, f. 214, stb. 81, l. 65; Rezun and Vasil'evskii, *Letopis' sibirskikh gorodov*, 269–74; Bakhrushin, "Sibirskie sluzhilye Tatary v XVII v.," in NT, 3: 165.

35. Bustanov, "Sacred Texts of Siberian Khwaja Families," 70–99; Bustanov and Korusenko, "Genealogy of the Siberian Bukharians," 97–105.

36. Boeck, *Imperial Boundaries*, 246.

Yet whatever privileges and cultural forms Bukharans may have shared with Russian nobles, they were not nobles in the eyes of the Russian state.[37] They remained distinct and did not intermarry with Russians, unlike some elite Tatars and the noble Cherkasski clan from the Caucasus region. Bukharan yurts were subject to their own internal hierarchies of local governance on most matters.[38] That the yurt was a juridical, not strictly geographical, designation is reflected in property records showing that Bukharans of one yurt owned properties throughout the region.[39] The seventeenth-century Croatian exile Yuri Krizhanich (exiled in Tobol'sk from about 1661 to 1675) reported as much, describing Bukharans as a community set apart. He wrote, "They live in towns surrounded by walls, and have their own Tsar (Uzbek)."[40]

Just where Bukharans actually came from is unclear. Scholars consistently recite that the label "Bukharan" did not necessarily mean "from Bukhara" but was a catch-all for people from across Central Asia. Admittedly, at its apogee in the late sixteenth century the Bukharan khanate had covered most of Inner Central Asia, but many peoples besides Bukharans lived there: Turkmen, Uzbeks, Karakalpaki, Tadzhiks, and Uighurs. Whereas early modern Western Europeans tended to lump Central Asians together under the catch-all "Tatar," Russian administrators for the most part were more discerning of Eurasian identities. In Muscovy the Foreign Office kept separate archives for the khanates of Khiva and Bukhara. A Tiumen' payroll book from 1626–27 lists several men due compensation under the heading "serving Tatars." They include: one Tabynets, one Sart, and two Bukharans.[41] Only rarely did Russian scribes list "Bukharan" as a subcategory of Tatar; usually they were distinct. Even so, such specificity could mislead. That one important Bukharan family in Tara traced its origins to Urgench in Khorezm suggests that the question of "Bukharan" as signifier remains unresolved.[42] Part of the explanation may lie in Soucet's assertion that the cultural and architectural investments in the city of Bukhara during the long rule of Khan

---

37. Typically, Bukharan petitions self-identify as "orphan" (*sirota*) of the tsar, whereas military elites (and those in immediate service in some cases) typically addressed themselves to the tsar as "slave" (*kholop*). Also, Bukharans were often named according to the *syn* (as opposed to—*vich*) patronymic: Ivan Fëdorov syn Shmakov in the case of a lower-class person; and Ivan Fëdorovich Shmakov for a man of higher status.

38. Yurt residents sometimes owned land not adjacent to the yurt itself. GBUTO GATO, f. 47, op. 1, d. 2228.

39. GBUTO GATO, f. 47, op. 1, d. 2228.

40. Yuri Krizhanich, "History of Siberia," 560.

41. Bakhrushin, "Sibirskie sluzhilye Tatary v XVII v.," 3: 165. Sart can be understood as Uzbeg, according to Bartol'd.

42. Allen Frank wrote that this family was originally from Bukhara and had moved to Urgench before migrating to Siberia. Frank, *Bukhara and the Muslims of Russia*, chap. 2.

Abdalaziz (r. 1645–81) made it the cultural center of Central Asia, such that "the outside world came to think of Central Asia as Bukhara."[43]

In moving to a new empire, Siberian Bukharans did not sever ties to their native Central Asian homes. Rather, their new Siberian communities functioned as caravanserai, nodes where caravans of their compatriots could rest and provision themselves. But late in Tsar Aleksei Mikhailovich's reign, Siberian Bukharans sought to shift the burden of provisioning more squarely on the shoulders of the Russian state. In 1670–71 Seidiash Kulmametev, a prominent Tobol'sk Bukharan merchant, spearheaded a collective petition to the tsar in which Tobol'sk Bukharans complained about having to feed and house Bukharan and Kalmyk embassies since the Kalmyk House, which had previously housed visiting embassies, had fallen into disrepair.[44] The burden, Kulmametev explained, caused "great crowding and destruction to [their] homes."[45] This incident has been used to argue for a loosening of ties between transit and Siberian Bukharans, but we could instead see it as Siberian Bukharans advocating for their associates by lobbying the state to provide accommodations similar to those found in the funded caravanserai or funduq that punctuated trade routes throughout early modern Eurasia. The Russian state responded to its subjects' plea. On February 22, 1671, the tsar ordered that a new ambassador's house be built and that Bukharans would no longer have to house transit embassies.[46] Details of the project's realization are unclear; in the 1730s, G. F. Müller reported that the Kalmyk House had burned long ago.[47]

Siberian Bukharans consistently transported and purchased wares on behalf of transit Bukharans throughout the seventeenth century. Beyond the obvious commercial ties, attachments to their homeland were symbiotic and sentimental, and were not necessarily static. Bukharans from the khanate surely brought news of relatives and friends left behind. If Bukharans in Siberia could not get certain traditional medicinal plants to grow for them in Siberia, they sent for some from Central Asia, exchanges that may have turned on the capital of commodities, cash, or friendship.[48] Last names of transit and Siberian Bukharans were often the same. The case of an arranged marriage, in which a woman came from the Bukharan khanate to marry a Siberian Bukharan in 1722, shows that kin contacts between expatriate

43. Soucek, *History of Inner Asia*, 177–78.
44. RGADA, f. 214, stb. 348, pt. 1, l. 60.
45. RGADA, f. 214, stb. 348, pt. 1, ll. 59, 61.
46. RGADA, f. 214, stb. 348, pt. 1, ll. 60, 61v.
47. Miller, *Opisanie o torgakh' Sibirskikh*, 11.
48. Bakieva and Kvashnin, "Nekotorye osobennosti traditsionnoi kul'tury," 226.

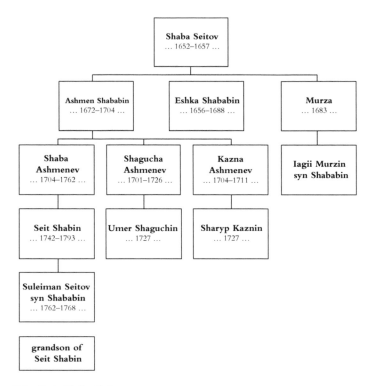

FIGURE 7.1   Shababin family tree.

Bukharans and the homeland persisted into the last years of Peter's reign at least, several generations since the first Bukharans settled in Tiumen'.[49] Russian sources distinguish between Bukharan settlers and those who came and went with the caravans. Those who had emigrated were called yurt Bukharans, whereas those who came from Central Asia were listed as transit Bukharans.[50] Transit Bukharans would sometimes reside for months in the Bukharan yurts of western Siberia.

Tatars also resided in the Bukharan yurts (the first having been resettled to Tiumen''s original Bukharan yurt from Chingi-Tur in 1609).[51] Tatars were Turkic speakers and some, in theory, were Muslim.[52] Tatars themselves were not of one social class: some, like Kuchum, traced noble lineages, whereas others came from long lines of lowly tribute payers. Relations between Tatars

49. GBUTO GATO, f. 181, op. 1, d. 8, ll. 50–52.

50. RGADA, f. 214, stb. 81, l. 60.

51. Evgenii Arsiukhin, "Sibirskoe khanstvo: Tëmnaia istoriia," http://archeologia.narod.ru/tum/tum.htm, accessed July 1, 2011.

52. Frank, "Western Steppe," 252.

and Bukharans is a more complicated subject than we can explore in depth here, but a few comments should help briefly sketch the landscape in which the Shababins lived. Whereas some Bukharan immigrants in the early seventeenth century reportedly lived off the generosity of local Tatars, by the end of the seventeenth century one commonly encounters relationships of dependency in which Bukharans were sponsors and Tatars dependents, as discussed below. Despite comingling in yurts and sharing communal property as well as the Turkic language and (supposedly) Islamic faith, Tatars and Bukharans remained distinct. They intermarried little and observed different burial rites.[53] With rare exceptions, Tatar and Bukharan remained distinct categories in the notations of Russian record keepers and remained so until the twentieth century when administrative reforms conflated them into one tax category.[54]

Generation 1: Shaba Seitov (1652–57)

As the new Romanov dynasty extended a network of forts eastward across Eurasia, and just one year before Ostafii Filat'ev attained gost' status, the first patriarch of the Shababin family, Shaba Seitov, settled in Tiumen', Siberia. Rewarded with land for his service and "for leaving Bukhara," his homeland, he was not the first Bukharan to settle there.[55] Others—quite likely a mix of kin and business connections in Tiumen'—already lived in Siberia.[56] Just why Shaba Seitov chose Tiumen' could be better understood. Was the assassination of Abdullah II, the Shibanid khan (d. 1598?) a destabilizing event? Hundreds reportedly migrated from Bukhara to Urgench in the early seventeenth century as a result of the change in the course of the Amu River;[57] might some have relocated to Siberia as well? Or does intensifying commercial exchange between Russia and the khanates of Central Asia, as part of global economic growth or Russian expansion, account for the diaspora? In

53. Bakieva and Kvashnin, "Nekotorye osobennosti traditsionnoi kul'tury," 225–29. Georgi, *Russia*, 2: 151.

54. This is according to Bakieva and Kvashin, "Nekotorye osobennosti traditsionnoi kul'tury," 225–29; *Vestnik IRGO* 23 (1858): 143, lists "Tatars and Bukharans" but counts them together in a demographic table from 1854. Bukharans called Tatars in Russian documents: RGADA, f. 214, kn. 301, l. 70.

55. GBUTO GATO, f. 47, op. 1, d. 2228, l. 1.

56. GBUTO GATO, f. 47, op. 1, d. 38, l. 3 (1643); RGADA, f. 214, stb. 81, l. 65; RGADA, f. 214, kn. 301, l. 67; Miller, *IS*, vol. 2, no. 4, 176–77; Bakhrushin, "Sibir' i Sredniaia Aziia," 4: 195; Rezun and Vasil'evskii, *Letopis' sibirskikh gorodov*, 269–74.

57. Bartol'd, *Sochineniia*, vol. 3, *Raboty po istoricheskoi geografii*, 85–90.

all likelihood, Shaba Seitov perceived opportunity in the favored status the Russian Empire promised.

Religious considerations as well may have informed Shaba Seitov's decision to settle in Tiumen'. An unusual customs book from December 1652— unusual because it records people traveling even without goods to trade—provides clues to the kin and confessional ties that linked Bukharans in Siberia. On December 4, 1652 the Tobol'sk yurt Bukharan Shikh Shikhov, who had returned from the Kalmyk steppe less than three weeks earlier, embarked on a trip to Tara with his wife.[58] On December 22 the Tobol'sk yurt Bukharan Seit Seitov (note he has the same name as the aforementioned transit Bukharan, and same last name as Shaba Seitov, first patriarch of the Shababin clan in Siberia) declared that he was en route to Tiumen' to pray and see relatives. On December 23 the "Tobol'sk yurt Tatarin" Seit Seitov set out for Tara to pray and give his daughter in marriage (*on edet na Taru po svoei vere pomolittsa i docherishko svoe zamuzh vedat*).[59] If customs posts had regularly recorded passersby who were not transporting trade goods, we would have more evidence with which to map piety and networks of Bukharans in Siberia. At the very least, these travels reveal that Bukharans maintained ties with kin in Central Asia and practiced their faith openly in Siberia. On December 16, 1652, the transit Bukharan Seleiko Acheev and his wife left Tobol'sk to visit relatives in Tara. On December 1, 1652, a transit Bukharan named Seitko Seitov left Tobol'sk for Tiumen' in order "to pray according to his faith and to see his relatives" (*on edet na Tiumen' po svoe i vere pomolittsa i s rodimtsami svoimi povidattsa*).[60] Quite likely he was on his way to visit—perhaps winter with—his émigré kinsman Shaba Seitov, who at that moment was returning from China with valuable goods from the East, including rhubarb.

Most likely, it was Shaba Seitov's expertise in the rhubarb trade that attracted the tsar's attention and ultimately earned him a generous land grant. Shaba Seitov first appears in Russian historical records in 1652 as a free agent, a merchant moving exotic products vast distances across Eurasia and probably calling Siberia home. In the 1650s he traveled between Siberia and eastern destinations of Kalmykia, Bukhara, and China.[61] We don't know how many times Shaba traversed the Eurasian continent on such trips:

58. RGADA, f. 214, kn. 301, ll. 15, 67. On the Shikhov family see Bustanov, "Sacred Genealogies and Transnational Contacts of Muslims of Northern Eurasia."

59. RGADA, f. 214, kn. 301, l. 70.

60. RGADA, f. 214, kn. 301, l. 67.

61. SPbII RAN, f. 187, op. 1, d. 126, l. 1; RGADA, f. 214, stb. 414, l. 61.

the Tobol'sk Bukharan Seitkul Ablin, with whom Shaba Seitov traveled in 1652/53, made at least four trips to China in the second half of the seventeenth century. A nearly contemporary Bukharan merchant in Astrakhan told a French diplomat he had traveled to Beijing four times.[62]

Fabrics such as silk were the counterpart staple to Siberian furs, but in Shaba Seitov's travels to the Far East rhubarb ranked high on his list of commodities. Knowledge of rhubarb's medicinal value was ancient, and as knowledge of the Far East and consumer spending in apothecaries throughout Europe accelerated demand for the medicinal root, the rhubarb trade became an increasingly lucrative endeavor. Seeking to channel profits to state coffers, Muscovy restricted the rhubarb trade in 1652.[63] Prior to the dispatch of expeditions to Lake Yamysh, Siberian town criers were ordered to cry that rhubarb must not be smuggled on pain of death . . . and that any illicit rhubarb discovered would be confiscated.[64] Shaba Seitov first learned of the new regulations on a cold day at the customs post in January 1653. Returning to Tiumen' with several sacks laden with rhubarb root,[65] the caravan party found that there was only one buyer: the state.[66] Probably disappointed by the price the state would pay, they may have been puzzled by what happened next. After taking an oath by their Muslim faith, the traders were questioned by the Tiumen' governor Ivan T. Verigin. Acting on orders from Moscow, Verigin wanted to know how the Bukharans procured, treated, and transported their rhubarb.[67] Moscow had recently begun experimenting with a program of native rhubarb exploitation, but the product was not selling. Suspecting that poor handling and improper transport of the medicinal root might be the problem, the administration sought answers from those with experience.

Obviously impressed with their knowledge, Russian officials then recruited Shaba Seitov and his son, Eshka Shababin, to procure rhubarb for the state. Direct private trade between Russians and China is generally considered to have begun in 1674 with the gost' G. R. Nikitin's pathbreaking trip across the Gobi desert, but Russia had sent several commercial caravans to China prior to that. In addition to the two expeditions to China led by Russians

62. Burton, *Bukharans*, 407.

63. On rhubarb see Monahan, "Trade and Empire," 351–78; Monahan, "Regulating Virtue and Vice"; Monahan, "Locating Rhubarb."

64. PSZ, vol. 3, no. 1594, 373 (September 1, 1697, Nakaz to Tobol'sk). The language suggests the state was well aware it would not execute for rhubarb smuggling.

65. SPbII RAN, f. 187, op. 1, d. 126, l. 1.

66. RGADA, f. 214, op. 3, stb. 414, ll. 1–5.

67. SPbII RAN, f. 187, op. 1, d. 126, l. 1.

(Peitlin in 1618, Baikov in 1654), Bukharan merchants, long-established intermediaries of long-distance Eurasian trade, led several commercial trips on behalf of the tsar in the second half of the seventeenth century. Shaba Seitov was one such Bukharan. When he next traveled to China, he went on behalf of the Russian tsar in search of rhubarb. Upon his return in the fall of 1655, Shaba Seitov proceeded to Moscow to receive payment for his service. There, in January 1656, he and the Tiumen' musketeer Boris Malyshev petitioned for and were granted reimbursement and payment for their service.[68]

Other details of this trip—such as payment of taxes on his own stocks of personal rhubarb and lack of a label identifying him in the service of the state—suggest a personal initiative.[69] Given the distances involved and the state's limited means to effect otherwise, it is unsurprising that merchants recruited for these trips conducted their own business alongside that of the tsar. As we saw in chapter 5, such practices were accepted, provided that state profits came first. Indeed, Shaba kept his family enterprise in motion even as he fulfilled state obligations, for several months later in the fall of 1656 his son, Eshka Shababin, returned home to Siberia from China with rhubarb.[70]

The settling of accounts at the conclusion of this trip reveals significant aspects of state affairs in Siberia. Alongside its military and administrative activities, the Muscovite state also financed commercial endeavors. Even when the funds came sporadically, with delays and sometimes in amounts shy of those promised,[71] what deserves pause is that Moscow subsidized not only the movements of its own factors but also those of transit Bukharan merchants. The state subsidized travel according to specific per diem rates that varied according to station.[72] Merchants (owners of the goods) were issued higher reimbursements than support staff such as porter-cooks (*kashevary*).[73] There was some confusion regarding who was who—and therefore, the appropriate level of subsidy—on this trip in 1656. Seitov and Malyshev were asked to clarify their status. Upon confirmation that they were indeed the owners of the rhubarb they had brought, officials ordered that they receive an

68. RGADA, f. 214, stb. 499, l. 171.

69. RGADA, f. 214, stb. 414, ll. 61, 63, 93, 98. Seitov seems to have moved among discrete parties of Bukharans in the same time frame, suggestive of a monitoring or escort role. For concurring remarks about blurry lines between state and private trade, see Kotilaine, *Russia's Foreign Trade*, 455.

70. RGADA, f. 214, stb. 414, l. 58. The brief time separating arrivals of father and son suggests his son stayed behind a bit longer for some reason.

71. RGADA, f. 214, stb. 499, ll. 153–257.

72. China also issued per diem subsidies to foreign merchants. See Sukharov, *Skazaniia russkago naroda*, 2: bk. 8, 130.

73. For food subsidy rates see RGADA, f. 214, stb. 499, l. 159.

allowance according to the per diem rates due a merchant.[74] Other Central Asian merchants from the caravan, however, were listed as porter-cooks and issued lower subsidies accordingly. According to them, this "mistake" had occurred previously. These transit Bukharans, although neither subjects of the tsar nor residents of the realm, knew they were entitled to more, and this time looked to Tsar Aleksei to right the wrong:

> Your orphans of Bukharan lands, Kochatka Sareev, Atliashka Medeleev, Turmametko Tiulmametev, Ziumatko Karmyshev appeal to you. We, orphans, and ours, left our land with rhubarb to you, Sovereign, to Moscow with our colleagues and according to your Sovereign order, to our colleagues your Sovereign grant of food and *vykhod* and *sukhna* was issued. But the *provincial governor* wrote us as porters, but we are not porters. We ourselves are the owners and now for the third year are dying of hunger and before our brothers we are humiliated. Merciful Sovereign Tsar Great Prince Alexei Mikhailovich Autocrat of all Great, Little, and White Rus', grant to us, your orphans, your Tsarist grant of food and *vykhod* and *sukhna* in accordance with what our brothers, our colleagues [receive] so that we, before them and in the end will not waste away and perish. Sovereign Tsar, have mercy and grant this.[75]

The state adjusted their compensation upward. Whether they themselves had mastered the customary rhetoric for such appeals or the recording secretaries ensured their plea adhered to rhetorical norms, these visitors sought the tsar's help in the same personal and deprecating language as would the subjects of the realm. Those in direct service to the tsar referred to themselves as "slave" in petitions; "orphan" is the term used by everyone else except clergy.[76]

Finally, this 1656 trip underscores rhubarb's importance to the state treasury, but taken in context, tells us something more. Shaba Seitov's expertise in rhubarb is likely the immediate catalyst that got him recruited to act as a factor for the tsar. But the state could commission Bukharan merchants as factors without them living in Siberia; rhubarb was only one facet of a larger strategy that constituted an instrumentalist approach to supplying Siberia. That Shaba Seitov's commercial services led to a substantial land grant in Siberia demonstrates that the state wanted Bukharans to settle there. The Orthodox Church did not share the state's enthusiasm for Bukharan

---

74. RGADA, f. 214, stb. 499, ll. 109–11.
75. RGADA, f. 214, stb. 499, l. 108.
76. See Poe, "What Did Russians Mean?" 585–608; Kivelson, "Muscovite 'Citizenship,'" 465–89.

settlement. Although most Bukharans lived in yurts, the segregation was not absolute. A Russian widow named Daria living in Tobol'sk's Bukharan neighborhood during Peter's reign was not the sole example.[77] Chancery records reveal that Bukharan and Russian homes were sometimes located quite close to each other. By the time Müller visited in the 1730s he noted that the neighborhood on the northern bank of the Tura River near Tiumen' was a mix of Russians, Bukharans, and Tatars.[78] The close proximity of Christians and Muslims disturbed church officials. In 1653/54, shortly after Seit Seitov informed Russian officials that he was planning to pray with relatives according to his faith, and about the time that Shaba Seitov was being recruited to procure rhubarb for the tsar, Simeon, the archbishop of Tobol'sk and Siberia, voiced his alarm to pious Tsar Aleksei Mikhailovich. "In the lower part of Tobol'sk the homes of Russian people and Tatars and Bukharans are all mixed together," he wrote. "While Christians are fasting, those unfaithful ones are having their weddings and big celebrations, and that they live mixed with Russian households, Russians are badly influenced in a variety of ways."[79] "Such impure living, Sovereign, is found nowhere else in Russian towns as it is in Tobol'sk," though he did not fail to note that near Tiumen' Tatars lived in neighborhoods along with Christians.[80] Simeon concluded, "It is impossible to tolerate such mixed living."[81]

Almost a decade later the local widow Evdokiia sounded a similar note. In May 1662 fire ripped through the lower town of Tobol'sk, destroying many shops, warehouses, and homes, including the home of the Bukharan Seitkul Ablin.[82] Evdokiia declared that she had had a vision in which God informed her he was punishing the community for singing a Latin service for mass (reference to Nikonian reforms) and for the fact that Tatars and Russians were living together in sin.[83] Except for this vision—with its varied sources of disgruntlement (it was, after all, amid Nikon's controversial

---

77. GUTO GAT, f. 156, op. 1, d. 874, l. 1.

78. Müller, "Travels in Siberia," in Black, Buse, and Moessner, *G. F. Müller and Siberia, 1733–1743*, 75.

79. RGADA, f. 214, stb. 462, ll. 236–37. Published in Romodanovskaia and Zhuravel', *Literaturnye pamiatniki Tobol'skogo Arkhiereiskogo*, 308.

80. "Neizvestnii," in Alekseev, *Sibir' v izvestiiakh zapadno-evropeiskikh*, 331.

81. Ibid. Note that Russians in Kholmogory levied similar complaints against the Dutch Protestant Michael Meier in 1663. See Orlenko, *Vykhodtsy iz zapadnoi Evropy v Rossii XVII veka*, 113–14.

82. For Ablin this was part of a string of bad luck; he'd been robbed returning from China just two months earlier. Fortunately, his connections allowed him to take a loan from as illustrious a figure as Boyar B. I. Morozov. See Tomsinskii, *Khoziaistvo krupnogo feodala-krepostnika*, vyp. 1, *Khoziaistvo Boiarina B. I. Morozova XVII v.*, 251.

83. RGADA, f. 214, stb. 582, ll. 20–24, www.vostlit.info/Texts/Dokumenty/Russ/XVII/1660-1680/Sibirsk_videnija/text.htm.

church reforms)—lay residents did not formally complain about proximity to Bukharans. It was church officials who were most bothered by "mixed living." To be sure, the historical record captured tensions, property disputes, and outright conflict.[84] Voluntary demarcations and distance were most certainly upheld. Yet at the marketplace Christians and Muslims held shop side by side. In the customs service they were forced into proximity, not just in daily work but on prolonged state trips as well.[85] Indeed, the overriding impression is that a tolerable coexistence prevailed on the Siberian frontier, resembling perhaps what Francesca Trivellato has called "communitarian cosmopolitanism."[86]

Bukharan communities became a fixture that caught the attention of early modern visitors to Siberia. Whereas most colonial narratives tell the story in which the imperial powers rule over less civilized natives, Bukharans were a diaspora community arguably more sophisticated than the imperial authority. In contrast to widespread characterizations of the "barbarous" Rus', from the corpus of early modern European traveler accounts—as problematic as they are seductive—an idealized Central Asian "other" emerges.[87] Writers consistently noted the wealth of Siberian Bukharans. A European officer exiled in Tobol'sk wrote in 1666 that Tobol'sk Bukharans lived far better than the local Tartars: "These wealthy people, they live in wonderfully constructed wooden homes, with large windows and doors in the German style. Their rooms are decorated with beautiful carved stucco work and expensive Chinese carpets; they live cleanly and tidily, dressing in beautiful clothes."[88] Krizhanich reported that during his stay a Bukharan who died was buried with 8,000 rubles in gold. (When musketeers [strel'tsy] from Moscow tried to dig up the grave, they were knouted for their crime.)[89] Travelers noted that

---

84. In addition to those mentioned: In 1670 Ermamet Tachkalov spearheaded a collective petition to protest that certain Russians were denying Bukharans and Tatars access to a local spring. SPbII RAN, f. 187, op. 1, d. 348, l. 1. On October 2, 1725, the retired Cossack Nikifor Viazmin accused the Bukharan Shadru Utiakov and his friend of assaulting and robbing him on September 13, 1725. Viazmin had been inspecting his fields along the Estru River when Shadra Utiakov approached, grabbed him by the head, knocked him to the ground, and began beating him. Shadru robbed him, including his silver cross worth 3.5 rubles. GBUTO GATO, f. 47, d. 1744, l. 12v.

85. For an imagined state trip see Monahan, "Uraisko Kaibulin," 222–32.

86. Trivellato, Familiarity of Strangers, chap. 3.

87. Poe, "A People Born to Slavery."

88. Anonymous, in Alekseev, Sibir' v izvestiiakh zapadno-evropeiskikh, 352.

89. Krizhanich, in Alekseev, Sibir' v izvestiiakh zapadno-evropeiskikh, 562. In 1662 a Tatar and a Russian were beaten for grave-robbing. Miller, Istoriia Sibiri, 1: 480. Grave digging occurred often enough that the Siberian governor Prince A. M. Cherkasskii asked if he was allowed to purchase for the state gold that had been dug from graves. Chulkov, Istoricheskoe opisanie, 258. Müller robbed graves to collect ethnographic artifacts. See Black and Buse, G. F. Müller and Siberia, 79, 83.

Bukharans were neat, educated, peaceable people.[90] Perhaps most remarkably, Bukharans are often described as honest—not a descriptor typically attached to merchants.[91]

Ides observed that Bukharans greatly esteemed anyone who could read or write the Arabic language.[92] The Swedish exile Tabbert visited the home of a Tobol'sk Bukharan merchant and noted that his texts included the Chronicle of Abul'gazi, a copy of a Gospel, and a book about astronomy that said the earth had existed 620,000 years prior to the birth of Adam.[93] One of Tobol'sk's brightest minds, Semen Remezov, consulted at length with local Bukharans and Tatars in writing his chronicle and probably his geographies, which record sacred Islamic sites, as well.[94] Nicolaas Witsen reported that Bukharans conducted "Arab" schools long before Russians established any such institutions.[95] Johann Gottlieb Georgi, an eighteenth-century ethnographer, attributed the uniformly fine qualities of

---

90. The Bukharan khanate covered the territory of what is now much of Uzbekistan. Allowing for fluidity in labeling, if one were to equate Uzbegs with Bukharans, cleanliness tropes collide in Persian Shah Suleiman I's remark that Muscovites are the "Yusbecs [Uzbegs] of the Francs." Chardin explained that the shah "thereby intimated, That as among the Mahometans, there is no Nation so nasty, so meanly educated, nor so Clownish as the Yusbecs, (who are the Tartars along the River Oxus) so among Europeans, there was not any that equal'd the Muscovites in those foul Qualities." Chardin, *Travels in Persia*, 89. One seventeenth-century Italian traveler would have agreed regarding the "uncleanly" Uzbegs, writing: "he is most lovely who is most greasy." Levi, *India Diaspora in Central Asia*, 146. Similarly, the fifteenth-century Venetian traveler Contarini found Persian Muslims to be quite clean, as compared to many filthy Christians in eastern Europe. See Barbaro, *Travels to Tana and Persia*. For more on tropes among early modern travelers see Wolff, *Inventing Eastern Europe*.

91. Witsen (and others) made such remarks. Witsen discussed the possibility that Bukharans were descended from Jews in his *Noord en Oost Tartarye*. See Witsen, *Severnaia i vostochnaia Tatariia*, 1: 461. One exception to this tendency was Krizhanich, who wrote that Bukharans could in "remarkable ways deceive the inexperienced or incautious buyer" of gems. He related one story in which a German soldier in Tobol'sk bought diamonds from a Bukharan, then invited Asbakeia, a prominent Tobol'sk Bukharan, to his house to inspect his purchase. Taking a ring off his finger, Asbakeia removed a small diamond from inside it, with which he scratched the purchased gems and told the soldier that he had purchased glass. The duped soldier brought suit against the seller but remained unsatisfied since the gem-selling Bukharan accused the soldier himself of replacing the good gems with false ones and bringing a false accusation. Krizhanich, in Alekseev, *Sibir' v izvestiiakh zapadno-evropeiskikh*, 561. If this story, for which Krizhanich's account is the only evidence, occurred, that one Bukharan served as an arbiter of truth and the accused Bukharan stood his ground to levy a counterclaim conveys a stature for Siberian Bukharans that state documents largely corroborate.

92. Ides, *Three Years Travel*, 13.

93. Potanin, "O karavannoi torgovle," 72–73. On Strahlenberg see Bustanov, *Book Culture of Siberian Muslims*, 17.

94. Frank, *Siberian Chronicles*, 5; Bakhrushin, "Sibir' i Srednaia Aziia," 4: 208; Bustanov and Belich, "Sviazi arkheologii i etnografii," 211–16.

95. Frank, *Siberian Chronicles*, 5; Bakhrushin, "Sibir' i Srednaia Aziia," 4: 208. Witsen traveled to Moscow, but only vicariously to Siberia. He voraciously collected others' accounts and information of "Tartary," which he published under the name *Noord en Oost Tartarye*.

Siberian Bukharans—"plain good sense, uprightness, and modesty; [they] are laborious, sober and cleanly"—to their "well-conducted" schools.[96]

Travelers found Bukharans as clean as Russians were dirty, and an attractive counter to Russian ugliness. "They like cleanness," wrote Nicolaas Witsen of Bukharans, in contrast to the dirty, unhygienic table habits and bad manners he described at the house of a petty Russian merchant.[97] "They are of tall height with a beautiful face; they don't busy themselves with war, theft, or disruption," wrote Krizhanich.[98] Adam Brand, a German who accompanied Ides to China, noted their cosmopolitan nature: "they are much more civilized than any of the other Tartars, by reason of their frequent conversation with strangers."[99] "They eat better food and in a more cleanly manner than the other Mohammedans," wrote another ethnographer.[100] This observation—of Central Asian émigrés gone north—is especially intriguing juxtaposed with an observation of Central Asian émigrés—presumably of the same people—gone south. The Italian Niccolao Manucci traveled in Mughal India in the seventeenth century, where a community of émigré Bukharans also resided. Manucci was repulsed by the eating habits of Uzbeks (i.e., Bukharans) he witnessed there: "It was disgusting to see how these Uzbak nobles ate, smearing their hands, lips, and faces with grease while eating, they having neither forks nor spoons. . . . Mahomedans are accustomed after eating to wash their hands with pea-flour to remove grease, and most carefully clean their moustaches. But the Uzbak nobles do not stand on such ceremony. When they have done eating, they lick their fingers, so as not to lose a grain of rice; they rub one hand against the other to warm the fat, and then pass both hands over face, moustaches, and beard. . . . The conversation hardly gets beyond talk of fat, with complaints that in the Mogul territory they cannot get anything fat to eat, and that the pulaos are deficient in butter."[101]

Even granting that such descriptions had as much to do with foreigners' opinions about the Russians in their midst, Bukharans in Siberia conducted successful enterprises, possessed some functional literacy, were deemed trustworthy in commercial and legal matters, and voiced their concerns to the state with expectations of satisfaction.

---

96. Georgi, *Russia*, 2: 149.

97. Bukharans: Witsen, *Severnaia i vostochnaia Tatariia*, 2: 949. Russians: Witsen, *Puteshestvie v Moskoviiu*, 75.

98. Krizhanich, in Alekseev, *Sibir' v izvestiiakh zapadno-evropeiskikh*, 560.

99. Brand, *A Journal of the Embassy to China*, 29.

100. Georgi, *Russia*, 2: 142.

101. Levi, *India Diaspora in Central Asia*, 146.

Generation 2: Ashmen Shababin (1672–1704)

Shababin fortunes flourished in the next generation. Eshka Shababin, who traveled to China for rhubarb in 1656, may have been the oldest son, yet his younger brother Ashmen Shababin headed the family enterprise in the final quarter of the seventeenth century.[102] Not only were Bukharan merchants lifelines to much-needed trade but they also served the Russian state directly in myriad ways: as factors for the tsar, as we saw with Ashmen's father, Shaba Seitov; as translators and in diplomatic roles, as was the case with his father's traveling companion, the Tobol'sk Bukharan Seitkul Ablin;[103] and in state customs service as assessors and officials. It was in this capacity that Ashmen Shababin served the tsar, as an auxiliary customs official (tseloval'nik) in Tobol'sk in 1672–73. The role was filled annually by a Bukharan chosen from among his Bukharan peers.[104]

Ashmen's state service record, however, pales in comparison with the success of his family's trade enterprises. Ashmen Shababin's career reveals a trading enterprise focused not only on long-distance trade of exotic goods but also one in which a network of actors circulated both exotic and quotidian goods to the surrounding Siberian region, a feature that became even more prominent in the next generation. For example, on April 3, 1676, Ashmen and the Bukharan Kolesko Ovsov departed Tiumen' bound for Ufa with two sacks of goods to trade.[105] At Irbit customs in January 1704, Ashmen declared a shipment of Russian goods he had bought in Kazan. His shipment included paper, wax, boots, dishes, frying pans, spoons, knitted socks, mittens, and gloves worth 92 rubles.[106] That spring, on May 22, 1704, Ashmen Shababin along with his kinsman the Tiumen' Bukharan Matiiar Dosaev

---

102. An early death does not seem to explain the potentially older brother's absence from the family enterprises from 1658 to 1685 when he collected sixteen horses from a local monastery (SPbII RAN, f. 187, op. 1, d. 785, l. 1). The only other evidence of Eshka is from 1688 when he and Ashmen each bought a horse from a local Tiumen' peasant (SPbII RAN, f. 187, op. 2, d. 80, l. 5v; Ziiaev, *Ekonomicheskie sviazy*, 66). Whether he was overseeing leather manufacture in Tiumen', manning a shop in Beijing, or studying at a madrasa in Bukhara during this documentary hiatus is unknown.

103. For more on Seitkul Ablin see Kurts, *Russko-Kitaiskie snosheniia*, 32–33; Demidova and Miasnikov, *Pervye Russkie diplomaty*, 89–94; Filippov, "Novye dannye o posol'stve Seitkula Ablina," 135–36. Bukharan doing diplomatic work, 1622: Miller, IS, vol. 2, no. 205, 354–55.

104. On Bukharan service see: RGADA, f. 214, stb. 81, ll. 36, 65. TKSG, vol. 4, 27. The publication, which is riddled with inconsistent spellings, lists Ishmeniasha Babin [*sic*] as *tseloval'nik* at Tiumen' customs in 1672/73. This was Ashmen Shababin.

105. SPbII RAN, f. 187, op. 2, d. 52, l. 1. Elsewhere Ashmen Shababin appears with the first names Usman and Osmanko. This entry reads Osmanko. I think they are all the same person.

106. RGADA, f. 214, kn. 1398, l. 434v.

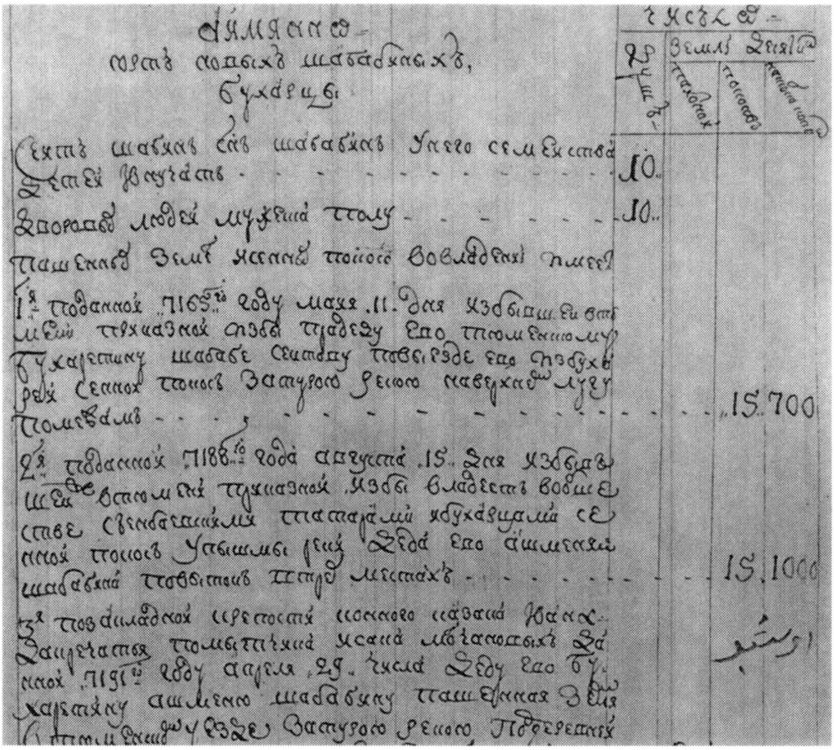

FIGURE 7.2 Detail of survey recounting Shababin property acquisitions.
Source: GBUTO GATO, f. 47, op. 1, d. 2228, l. 1. Courtesy GBUTO GATO.

dispatched a shipment of wax with the infantry Cossack Mikhail Maslian.[107] Throughout this generation and the next, Ashmen Shababin and Matiiar Dosaev and their children cooperated frequently on trade ventures.

Ashmen Shababin extended the family landholdings considerably.[108] Like his father, he was granted additional lands for state service. On August 15, 1680 the Tiumen' Governor's Office (Prikaznaia izba) granted Ashmen 1,015 desiatiny, or 2,740 acres, to be held in common with Tatars and Bukharans from Embaevskii yurt. The land was located about 40 kilometers east of Tiumen', in three different places along the Pyshma River.[109] About

---

107. GBUTO GATO, f. 29, d. 139, l. 7.

108. On Bukharan landholding see RGADA, f. 214, stb. 925, ll. 59–64v; stb. 81, ll. 50–61, esp. 59; GBUTO GATO, f. 47, op. 1, d. 2228, ll. 1–8; Korusenko, "Zemlevladenie i zemlepol'zovanie Bukhartsev v Sibiri," 98–102.

109. The Pyshma River runs roughly parallel to the Tura just south of it. It turns north and joins the Tura shortly before the confluence of the Tura and Tobol Rivers. GBUTO GATO, f. 47, op. 1, d. 2228, l. 1.

40 acres (15 desiatiny) was hay land; the vast majority neither hay nor tilled land, probably forest, swamp, or other marginal grazing land.

On May 21, 1685 the Tiumen' Office issued land directly to Ashmen Shababin. This property, 548 acres (203 desiatiny) on the north bank of the Tura River, was closer to his father's original grant. The land was also next to the Orthodox cemetery west of Tiumen' (see fig. 7.3). Evidently, as had been the case with Archbishop Simeon's objections in the 1650s, the issue of the close proximity of Christians and Muslims remained most bothersome to the church. That same autumn Metropolitan Pavel complained to the state about the dangers Muslims posed to the Christian faithful. In a letter dated November 13, 1685, he accused Muslims in Tobol'sk of standing by disrespectfully in hats and harassing newly baptized Christians during processions of holy icons and blessing of the waters, of drinking on fast days, and even of trying to seduce Christians into their Muslim faith.[110] He asked the church to relocate Bukharans farther from Christians and Christian churches.[111] Standing their ground in typical fashion, local Bukharans dismissed the charges as lies, insisting that they were not disrespectful and had never harassed converts to Christianity.[112] They implored Tsars Ioann and Peter to "not believe the groundless letter of Metropolitan Pavel, so that from his groundless driving out and accusation (*izgoni i oglasheniia naprasno*), they would not suffer and die."[113]

Moscow did not answer quickly. That it took Moscow nine months to respond suggests that the leadership felt itself torn between priorities. The tsar was the divinely appointed protector of Russian Orthodoxy, but the Tatar and Bukharan populations had existed in mixed communities with Russians in western Siberia for decades. More germanely, Muslim though they were, Bukharans performed important intelligence, administrative, and commercial functions and enjoyed historical privileges that had been consistently reaffirmed since the reign of Tsar Ivan IV.[114] In this case, the state did not do Pavel's bidding. In fact, in its 1686 reply Moscow did not even address the accusations that Muslims were trying to spread Islam. It did, however, reiterate procedures for converting to Orthodoxy. All conversion must be voluntary. Before the church could baptize, converts must submit a

110. PSZ, vol. 3, no. 1594, 355 (September 1, 1697 Tobol'sk instructions to M. I. Cherkasskii). Metropolitan Pavel's reminder that he had been twice ordered to promote conversion suggests he had received little institutional support in this endeavor.
111. PSZ, vol. 4, no. 1946, 226 (October 11, 1703).
112. Ibid., 226–27. See chapter 4 for controversy about the marketplace in Tobol'sk's lower town.
113. PSZ, vol. 3, no. 1594, 355 (September 1, 1697, Tobol'sk instructions to M. I. Cherkasskii).
114. PSZ, vol. 3, no. 1209, 816 (September 17, 1686).

petition to the Governor's Office, which must investigate to ensure that the desire was legitimate and voluntary. Tellingly, a one-month waiting period was required for "foreigners" (*inozemtsy*) who were dependents of any kind (referring to slaves or household members of Tatars and Bukharans), but no waiting period was required in the case of tribute-paying Siberians.[115] This measure was an effort to avoid antagonizing the Muslim population. The issue of contentious proximity did not go away completely, however, as we shall see.[116]

Such tensions did not prevent Ashmen Shababin from gaining property near a Christian cemetery or from further enhancing his family's assets. He acquired real estate on four other occasions. One transaction—foreclosure on an unpaid loan—brought the family its first designated farmland. In a cash-poor environment lacking institutionalized banks, merchants, or any individuals with fungible capital, regularly acted as creditors. The Shababins were not exceptional in this regard; property records show that several other Bukharans acquired land this way.[117] In 1683 two brothers, the mounted Cossack Ivan and the falconer (*krechat'ia pomytchika*) Isak Savast'ianovy Molchanov, leveraged 67.5 acres (25 desiatiny) of farmland on the north side of Tura near Erovskii village as collateral on a 15-ruble loan.[118] Four years later the brothers had not paid off the land and in 1687 they officially renounced their ownership in the presence of Tiumen' authorities.[119] Eight decades later, however, this land became a point of contention when descendants of the Molchanovs renewed their claim in the 1760s.[120] By this time Ashmen Shababin had long since passed; the legal wrangling was left to his grandson, Seit Shabin. Why Sergeant Major (*vakhmister*) Fëdor Molchanov disputed the transfer in 1764, so many years post facto, remains unknown.[121] If nothing else, the incident underscores that memory mattered: the acts of predecessors retained importance for Bukharans and Russians alike in these Siberian communities.

In the summer of 1698 the newly arrived Tobol'sk governor Prince M. I. Cherkasskii added some adjacent land to Shababin's holdings. It is unclear why the local Tobol'sk government awarded land to this Bukharan from

---

115. PSZ, vol. 3, no. 1594, 355–56 (September 1, 1697).

116. Ibid.

117. GBUTO GATO, f. 47, op. 1, d. 2228, l. 3–8v.

118. GBUTO GATO, f. 47, op. 1, d. 2228, l. 1; Trofimova, *Tiumenskaia delovaia pis'mennost'*, bk. 1, 29.

119. Trofimova, *Tiumenskaia delovaia pis'mennost'*, bk. 1, 29.

120. Ibid., 21, 29, 30, 36.

121. Ibid., nos. 34–42, pp. 29–30.

Tiumen', and especially curious since just months earlier, in March 1698, Prince Cherkasskii had been ordered to conduct a thorough survey of Bukharan landowning in response to concerns that they owned too much and paid too little in taxes.[122] Ashmen Shababin purchased additional parcels of land from local Tatars, a total of 4,413 acres, 850 acres of which was held in common with Embaevskii yurt residents. In short, Shababin increased the family's landholdings many times over. Excluding the 3,590.5 acres held in common, he acquired 4,179 acres (1,548 desiatiny) of land. Added to his father's original grant, by 1704 the family holdings amounted to 6,109.5 acres, about 9.5 square miles.[123]

In addition to his landholdings, Ashmen Shababin owned at least ten Tatar and Kalmyk slaves. On the night of June 16, 1689, about ten of Shababin's slaves allegedly tried to drive off some communally owned horses and then beat a local man named Ivan who happened to witness their midnight raid.[124] Although the details of the incident remain murky, it demonstrates that though Siberia is said to have been a land without serfdom, slaveholding was common, both lifetime (*iasyr*) or indentured (*kholop*). Captive slaves frequently appear in customs books as wares Bukharans traded.[125] Yuri Krizhanich estimated that every Muscovite in Siberia owned at least one.[126] Despite the accusation against the apparent hooliganism of his household in 1689, Ashmen Shababin remained a respected community member.

As upstanding subjects, Bukharans regularly stood in as guarantors of surety bonds, a common practice in early modern Russia that reflects the communal nature of justice and governance.[127] Only community members deemed trustworthy and solvent (with means to pay fines or account for another's debts should the person in question fail to appear) could act as guarantors on behalf of another. On March 26, 1700, Ashmen Shababin signed a surety bond on behalf of the Tatar woman Kuchuike Kutagulova. In doing so, Shababin guaranteed that she would appear at the Governor's House when summoned in the ongoing investigation (*rozysk*) or he would

---

122. PSZ, vol. 3, no. 1626, 446–47 (March 28, 1698).
123. GBUTO GATO, f. 47, op. 1, d. 2228, l. 1
124. GBUTO GATO, f. 47, d. 301, l. 1.
125. Bakhrushin, "Sibir' i Srednaia Aziia," 4: 210; Ulianitskii, *Snosheniia Rossii s Srednei Azieiu*, 6; RGADA, f. 214, stb. 462, ll. 175–78; RGADA, f. 214, stb. 81, l. 39; SPbII RAN, f. 187, op. 2, d. 521; f. 187, op. 1, d. 387 (1672); TKSG, vol. 4, 36, 40; vol. 1, 51; GBUTO GATO, f. 47, op. 1, d. 381; MIUTTSSR, 380–85; Vilkov, *Remeslo i torgovlia*, 178.
126. Krizhanich, "On the History of Siberia," in Dmytryshyn, Crownhart-Vaughan, and Vaughan, *Russia's Conquest of Siberia*, no. 113, 347.
127. On surety bonds see Szeftel, "History of Suretyship in Old Russian Law," 844–45.

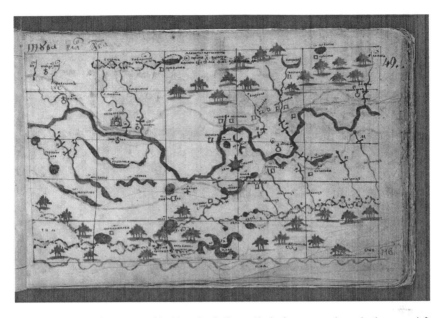

FIGURE 7.3 Map of Tiumen' and its hinterland. Tiumen' is the large town shown in the upper left quadrant along the Tura River. The first Shababin property, granted in 1657, was about 3 square miles on the north side of the Tura River across from Tiumen'. The property (not indicated specifically on this map) is located below Tiumen' here because north is at the bottom on this map.
Source: Remezov, *Khorograficheskaia kniga*, l. 49, Leo Bagrow Collection, MS 72 (6). Courtesy Houghton Library, Harvard University.

face a penalty.[128] On September 7, 1701, Matiiar Dosaev, a close associate and perhaps relative of the Shababins, signed as guarantor so that a Tatar woman, Momychka (Malychka), daughter of Karsakov from the Governor's House, could be released until her summons.[129] Such practices were typical and illustrate how the state looked to the Bukharan community as competent actors in the maintenance of community life.

The state called on them in other ways as well. In 1600 the Tiumen' governor entrusted Bukharans to conduct an investigation over a case involving the massacre of horses and destruction of small wares.[130] In 1700, a full century later, when a Russian and a Tatar disputed the rightful ownership of a horse, the animal in question was put in the custody of Ashmen Shababin until the dispute could be settled.[131] The 1700 case was an unusual one.

---

128. GBUTO GATO, f. 45, d. 2, l. 5v (*Kniga poruchnykh zapisei i rospisei*, 15 ll.).

129. SPbII RAN, f. 187, op. 1, d. 1156, l. 1. These three poruka documents release individuals from different places: from jail (*iz-za reshetki*), from the guard or Sheriff's cell (*iz pristava*), from the Governor's House (*iz prikaznoi izby*).

130. Miller, IS, vol. 2, no. 48, 221.

131. SPbII RAN, f. 187, op. 1, d. 1121, l. 4.

A horse had been stolen from a Tiumen' Tatar. The thief then disguised himself and sold the horse to the Tiumen' provincial nobleman (*boiarskii syn*) Ivan Grigor'ev syn Shishkin. Thus the Tatar and Shishkin both had defensible claims. By putting the horse in Ashmen Shababin's custody while the case was pending, the state demonstrated its perception of Shababin not as an untrustworthy foreigner whose heterodoxy or ethnic allegiances might compromise justice but as a subject whose respectability and dependability could help keep the peace.[132] In the next generation the Shababin and Shishkin families had close ties: Osip Shishkin, a relative of I. G. Shishkin, would prove to be the most useful trading agent of Ashmen Shababin's son, Shaba Ashmenev. One wonders if the Shababin and the Shishkin families were already acquainted or if this incident began what became a long relationship.

Accommodating Islam, Seeking Revenue

Bukharans' respected position did not prevent the state from increasing their tax obligations, however. When it extended the 1653 Tax Statute to Siberia in 1693, the state obligated Bukharans to some of the same protectionist statutes Europeans had faced for decades. Around this time Bukharans were made to pay the one-tenth tax rate; only transit Bukharans on their first trip to Russian lands could enjoy the reduced one-twentieth tax rate.[133] In 1698 Moscow decreed that Bukharans who lived in the town posad pay *obrok*, a proposal Bukharans had successfully lobbied against in the past.[134] In taking such measures, the pragmatic state took pains to stress that Bukharans "had it good" in the Russian Empire: "and in your own Muslim countries it is not possible that immigrants enjoy such freedom without paying tribute, and own land, and trade freely; even His Great Sovereign's natural Russian people do not enjoy such freedoms and advantages (*legosti*)."[135]

These measures characteristic of a revenue-hungry state notwithstanding, the state continued to recognize the valuable roles Bukharans played and protected them, even from the church. In 1703 the Siberian Office in Moscow again refused church pressure for forced relocation. Bukharans were to be allowed to remain where they had been so that undue difficulties would not be created for them.[136] In a nod to the church, Moscow directed that

132. SPbII RAN, f. 187, op. 1, d. 1121, ll. 1–15.
133. PSZ, vol. 3, no. 1474.13, 160–61 (August 30, 1693).
134. RGADA, f. 214, stb. 81, ll. 36, 37; PSZ, vol. 3, no. 1626, 446–47; Burton, *Bukharans*, 535.
135. PSZ, vol. 3, no. 1626, 446–47 (March 28, 1698).
136. PSZ, vol. 4, no. 1946, 226 (October 11, 1703).

longtime Bukharan and Tatar residents who lived among Russians and near churches be summoned to the Governor's House and reminded to behave respectfully, without shouting out their own prayers, laughing, beguiling, or roistering during Orthodox services, on threat of being placed "in disgrace" (*v opale*)—a temporary punishment to which errant nobility could also be subjected.[137] *In the future*, directed Moscow, mosques should be built far from churches, so that no kinds of shouts (*kriky*) or chanted prayers would be audible near the churches of God from which church bells chimed. But the significant point is that mosques were to be built. With characteristic Muscovite savvy, the center directed local governors to use their judgment in order to effect such changes without igniting local protest. Moscow suggested that the occasion of fires, inevitable with Siberia's wooden infrastructure, were good opportunities to peaceably relocate mosques.[138] The Orthodox Christian tsardom certainly grounded its internal legitimacy on its divine mandate, but however sympathetic to church concerns it may have been, it supported the status quo on the ground, which in Siberia was multiethnic and multiconfessional.

In signing surety bonds for Tatars, Ashmen Shababin underscores a dependency dynamic among non-Russian subjects that historians do not yet understand fully.[139] Siberian Bukharans often stood as guarantors for Tatars in matters of collective surety, or surety bonds, Tatars were often slaves in Bukharan households, and Tatars frequently assisted Bukharans in their commercial endeavors. These dependent relationships may have reflected more than purely economic interests. Siberian customs books and petitions contain a surprising number of individual Tatar signatures in Chagatai Turkic, revealing a rudimentary literacy among some Siberian Tatars in subordinate relations to Bukharans.[140]

This evidence of Tatar writing caught the attention of a Tobol'sk governor as well, who commented on the large numbers of literate Bukharans and Tatars in a report to Moscow.[141] As arguably the most educated Siberians, with their own established schools, Bukharans likely taught Tatars to read, not just for the sake of accounts and profits but so that they might read the

137. Ibid.

138. *Pamiatniki sibiriskoi istorii XVIII veka*, bk. 1, no. 12, 67; Pokrovskii, *Aktovye istochniki*, vol. 1 (bk. 3, *Opis' spiskam Tobol'skago arkhiva*), no. 55, 179–81.

139. Willard Sunderland has exhorted scholars to explore relations among imperial communities. Willard Sunderland, "Empire in Boris Mironov's Sotsial'naia Istoriia Rossii," 578.

140. I am grateful to Kavous Barghi in the Middle Eastern Studies department of Green Library at Stanford University for his assistance in interpreting Turkic writing in several documents.

141. Bakhrushin, "Sibir' i Srednaia Aziia," 4: 212. That Russian administrators had not previously observed this about Tatars suggests an increase in the numbers of literate Tatars.

Quran.[142] Islamization and literacy were fellow travelers.[143] Passing through Tobol'sk in 1692, Ides noted, "The Tartars that live round Tobol'ska [sic], for several miles are all Mahometans."[144] The observation is revealing, for it suggests that not all the Tatars he encountered in Siberia were Muslim, though at least in theory they should have been, having converted in earlier waves of Islamization. Yet there was something about the Tatars living near Tobol'sk, with its established Bukharan community, that caused Ides to note in particular that they were Muslims. This muted evidence may serve to corroborate Pavel's accusations about Muslims trying to "seduce" others to their faith.[145] Although the state did not respond to this part of Pavel's 1685 petition, there probably was substance to his charge that Tobol'sk Bukharans were proselytizing. It makes sense that this learned religious community, which self-consciously preserved and transmitted its faith through the generations and linked itself to the broader world of Islam, would have worked to gain new believers.[146] After all, Islam, like Christianity, is a proselytizing faith often spread by merchants, and Siberia was no exception.[147] Indeed, a common denominator in narratives of Islamization in the Volga-Urals region and the Siberian forest-steppe is that these histories implicate Bukharan merchants as missionaries.[148]

---

142. Whereas Bukharans had established schools in mosques, private tutoring was as much educational infrastructure as existed for Russians until Cherkasski established two schools in Tobol'sk beginning in 1701 (according to Witsen, *Severnaia i vostochnaia Tatariia*, 2: 947). It taught Slavic grammar, Latin, arithmetic, geometry, fortification, and artillery affairs to the children of Tobol'sk nobles and gentrymen (Akishin and Remenev, *Vlast' v Sibiri*, 181). A. A. Vinius, head of the Siberian Office 1695–1703, facilitated export of grammar books to Siberia (Kopylov, "Domashnee i shkol'noe obrazovanie v Sibiri," 87). Prior to that, Russians were left to hire tutors. Fëdor Driagin, a townsman from Ustiug who worked as a Pankrat'ev agent in the 1620s–30s, was customs head in Verkhotur'e in 1648 (Timoshina, *Arkhiv gostei Pankrat'evykh*, 13). Driagin hired a person of unfixed social rank (*guliashchii chelovek*) to tutor his four children in reading, writing, and singing of church prayers (SPbII RAN, f. 28, op. 1, d. 492, l. 20).

143. According to Frank, Siberian Tatars had their own established histories dating from around the tenth century, which were first written down in the seventeenth century, coinciding with the period of economic growth and Bukharan efflorescence in Siberia.

144. Ides, *Three Years Travel*, 12.

145. See Katanov, "O religioznykh voinakh uchenikov sheikha Bagauddina," 133–46; Rakhimov, *Astana v istorii Sibirskikh Tatar*, esp. 4–7; Bustanov, "Sufiiskie legendy ob islamizatsii Sibiri," 33–78, esp. 44–50, 59. Other historians have remarked on this. Potanin, "O karavannoi torgovle"; Bakhrushin, "Sibir' i Sredniaia Aziia," 4: 212; Burton, *Bukharans*, 502.

146. Usmanov and Shaikhiev, "Obraztsy tatarskikh narodno-kraevedcheskikh sochinenii," 85–102; Seleznev et al., *Kul't sviatykh v sibirskom Islame*.

147. An introduction to this topic: Bentley, *Old World Encounters*; Risso, *Merchants and Faith*.

148. *Polnoe sobranie russkikh letopisei: Sibirskie letopisi*, 319; Frank, "Western Steppe," 253; Frank, *Siberian Chronicles*, 18–20, 63; Burton, *Bukharans*, 557. Lantzeff and Pierce, *Eastward to Empire*, 100.

Of course, any conversion efforts by Muslims would have been clandestine and most likely focused on the non-Russian population. The penalty for trying to convert a Russian away from Orthodoxy, according to the 1649 Conciliar Law Code, was execution by burning in an open wooden cage.[149] The 1649 Code left ambiguous, however, the policy for proselytizing among non-Orthodox—pagans, for example, of which there were many in Siberia. Instructions sent to Siberian governors in 1728 clarified the point, taking aim directly at Muslim proselytization: "Insofar as in the Russian Empire many subjects are people of other faiths (inovertsy), namely: Mordvins, Chuvash, Cheremis, Ostiaks, Voguls, Lopars [Saami], and others, from which peoples it is known that Muslims convert to their faith, and circumcise, this the governor and voevoda must keep close watch over and not allow under any circumstances. If there are found such Muslims or other non-Orthodox who secretly or openly turn to their own faith and circumcise anyone of the peoples of the Russian Empire (Rossiiskikh narodov), those should be arrested and investigated and punished accordingly as per chapter 22, article 24 of the Ulozhenie—namely, execution by merciless burning."[150]

Despite the threat of such punishment, accusations of Muslim proselytization became more explicit in coming decades. Müller reported that Tatars around Tomsk had been converted to Islam in 1714.[151] He wrote in his notebooks, "I shall not discuss whether conversion from the Mohammedan to Christian religion is a rarity all over. Their clergy are no less zealous in converting other non-Christian and non-Mohammedan peoples than ours and often have converted heathens before the Russians could . . . this despite the fact that proselytizing by Mohammedans among heathen peoples in Russia has always been severely forbidden."[152] In 1751 Metropolitan Silvester blamed the Islamization of Baraba Tatars on Tara Bukharans who traveled there as missionaries.[153] In 1763 the Senate in St. Petersburg discussed that Muslims were actively gaining converts in Siberia.[154] This all suggests that Siberian Muslims may have been more enthusiastic than has heretofore been recognized in claiming souls for Allah. That they could get away with it—consonant with so much scholarship stressing the limits of central authority's effective reach—suggests that the Orthodox Christian tsardom of Muscovy lacked the will and/or means to actively instill Orthodox

149. PSZ, vol. 1, no. 1, 156 (Ulozhenie, chap. 22, article 24). Kollmann, Crime and Punishment, 352.

150. PSZ, vol. 8, no. 5333.19, 100 (September 12, 1728).

151. Frank, Bukhara and the Muslims of Russia, 50.

152. Black and Buse, G. F. Müller and Siberia, 69.

153. Frank, "Varieties of Islamicization," 252; Frank, Bukhara and the Muslims of Russia, 50.

154. Andrievich, Sibir' v tsarstvovanie imperatritsy Ekateriny II, 99.

8

CHAPTER 7

ideology in the hearts and minds of its new subjects at the outer reaches of the empire.

Generation 3: Shaba Ashmenev (1704–62)

Good material fortune, despite policies that increased Muslims' tax obligations, appears to have continued to favor the family in the next generation. As with monarchs, so too with family dynasties: stability helps. Shaba Ashmenev, the third-generation patriarch, had a long career and life, appearing in historical records from 1704 to 1762.[155] He inherited his father's place as head of the family network and traded as his father and grandfather had, only even more actively. He led the most dynamic and busiest commercial enterprise yet in his family's history, veritably dominating several Tiumen' customs books. Though he may have been the oldest, since he assumed the lead role, it is unclear whether the Shababins practiced primogeniture, ultimogeniture, or partible inheritance and how succession norms applied to commercial operations. According to steppe customs, for example, political authority passed to the most able eligible heir and property passed to the youngest son by the principal wife.[156]

Shaba accompanied his father on a trip to Kazan in 1704, returning to Tiumen' in advance of his father with writing paper, wax, and goat hides worth 163 rubles that he had bought in Kazan.[157] By this time he was already mature enough to be entrusted with wares on a journey of almost 900 miles and to operate in a management capacity, for in that same year he sent a shipment of wares off to Ufa in the care of the Tiumen' Bukharan Memetma Maschitovtsa.[158] Yet he cannot have been too old, for his career continued another half century. Indeed, since we hear no more of his father Ashmen Shababin after 1704, Shaba Ashmenev likely assumed leadership of the

---

155. GBUTO GATO, f. 47, op. 1, d. 2228, l. 1v. On comparisons of merchant longevity see Bushkovitch, *Merchants of Moscow*, 15. Shaba Ashmenev's name is recorded variously. In some state documents he is recorded as Shaba Ashmenev Shababin (see GBUTO GATO, f. 47, op. 1, d. 1763, printed in Trofimova, *Pamiatniki Tiumenskoi delovoi pis'mennosti*, bk. 2, no. 338). In most customs records he is recorded as Shaba Ashmenev, which differs from the form by which his father's and son's names were typically recorded. As recorded in Russian customs books by Russian administrators, the names of the five generations under scrutiny go as follows: Seitov—Shababin—Ashmenev—Shabin—Shababin. One hypothesis: Shababin was the last name of the first generation born in Siberia and it seems to get definitively adopted as a surname only by the fourth generation.
156. Fletcher, "Mongols," 17.
157. RGADA, f. 214, kn. 1398, l. 405.
158. GBUTO GATO, f. 29, d. 40, l. 4 (here his name was written Shabu).

family business about that time. He last appears in customs records in 1748.[159] Six year later in 1752 he acquired land from a local peasant but thereafter disappears from historical records.[160]

Typical of early modern commerce, trade was a family affair. Shaba Ashmenev had at least three brothers; at least two of them participated in the family trade. The Shababin brothers Shaba, Shagucha, and Kazna each had at least one son, and these sons participated in trade. They also engaged other relatives to help in the family commerce. Three of Shaba's nephews—Bakhmuto, Askar Margalin, and Umer Shaguchin—carried shipments on his behalf in 1726, 1727, and 1735, respectively.[161] The precise nature of the relationships and the ways profits were divided are unclear. Lower down in the network, family members cooperated among themselves. In November 1727 the Tiumen' yurt Bukharan Umer Shaguchin carried goods to Krasnoiarsk on behalf of his cousin Sharyp Kaznin.[162] In the spring of 1728 Ashmenev's nephew, the Tiumen' Bukharan Marmut Margalin, and the Tiumen' townsman Osip Shishkin (the relative if not son of Ivan Shishkin, mentioned above) cooperated on a trade venture in which they dispatched Askar Margalin to Siberian towns and newly christened Yekaterinburg to sell a consignment of eight thousand squirrel and one hundred ermine furs that they had imported.[163] The day after dispatching that shipment, Osip Shishkin was back at Tiumen' customs selling 1,000 arshin of canvas he had bought from the Russian merchant Sava Orlov in Irbit. Orlov, who had come from west of the Urals, then proceeded to Tobol'sk with the canvas he bought in Tiumen'; he would be back in Tiumen' a month later.[164] As we saw in the Filat'ev network, cooperation was not confined exclusively to family members. In May 1727 a Moscow merchant transported goods on Shaba Ashmenev's behalf.[165] In June 1727 the nephew Umer Shaguchin carried wares to Tobol'sk on behalf of a Tiumen' townsman.[166] And let us not forget the interaction that comes at the level of straight transaction, such as that same summer when Osip Shishkin sold 30 pud of wax to a merchant

---

159. GBUTO GATO, f. 29, op. 1, d. 308. l. 2. I thank Vera Kiueva for this reference.
160. GBUTO GATO, f. 47, op. 1, d. 2228, l. 2. As we saw with the Filat'evs, these wealthy merchants had long careers. Ermamet Tachkalov, a kinsman of Shaba Ashmenev's, had a similarly long career.
161. SPbII RAN, f. 187, op. 1, d. 1233, ll. 1, 1v; GBUTO GATO, f. 29, d. 134, l. 35; d. 166, l. 9.
162. GBUTO GATO, f. 29, op. 1, d. 134, ll. 21, 38; GBUTO GATO, f. 29, op. 1, d. 166, l. 9.
163. GBUTO GATO, f. 29, d. 134, l. 21. Yekaterinburg was founded in 1723 and named after Peter I's second wife, Catherine I.
164. GBUTO GATO, f. 29, d. 134, l. 21. 1 arshin = 28 in. = 71 cm.
165. GBUTO GATO, f. 29, op. 1, d. 134, l. 25v.
166. GBUTO GATO, f. 29, op. 1, d. 134, l. 30.

from the northern Russian town of Lal'sk, who then set off for Tobol'sk with it.[167]

These movements offer insight not only into the dynamics and contours of the family network but also provide a vantage point to observe macro developments in Eurasian commerce. Initially, the Tiumen'-based Shababins traversed vast distances from China all the way to Moscow, engaging in long-distance caravan trade throughout the period studied here. The autumn caravans arriving to Siberia from the steppe were an important part of their business cycle. Once Russian merchants began traveling directly to China, Bukharans faced new competition. We lack data to closely analyze their operations, but we can say that Eastern (Chinese, Central Asian, and Indian) goods remained important. Eastern goods were probably a substantial enough part of the business that Shaba Ashmenev kept someone in his network semipermanently in eastern Siberia. In the early 1730s his nephew Umer Shaguchin (the son of his brother Shagucha) arrived in Irkutsk laden with wares from China.[168] There, he transferred the wares to Shaba Ashmenev's Russian agent, Afanasei Afanas'ev syn Shmakov, who brought the shipment back to Tiumen'. Presumably, from Irkutsk Umer Shaguchin deployed again to China. He had advanced from shuttling other traders' regional consignments in the 1720s to working the family's China operations in the 1730s.

Illustrative of adaptation to the changing geography of trade, Shababin activities became increasingly engaged in the acquisition and distribution of all manner of goods throughout the towns and hinterland villages of Siberia.[169] By the reign of Empress Elizabeth, the Shababins oriented their activities to newer trade centers such as Kiakhta. But it was not just a matter of operating at the fringes of Siberia to acquire Eastern goods—be it at Tara, Lake Yamysh, Kiakhta, or Nerchinsk. "Russian" goods were an important part of the equation and the Irbit fair, a fair in the Urals region established in the 1630s, became an important place to source them. Irbit grew into the largest market fair in western Siberia in the late seventeenth century and figured prominently in Shababin operations. They acquired "Russian" goods not only for long-haul trade. They also distributed these wares throughout Siberia, enhancing their significance in the economic life of Siberia.[170]

---

167. GBUTO GATO, f. 29, op. 1, d. 134, l. 26.

168. GBUTO GATO, f. 29, op. 1, d. 166, l. 9.

169. DAI, vol. 11, 235–38. The Bukharan caravan traveled to Irkutsk. DAI, vol. 4, 352. Bukharans in Tomsk.

170. In the strange mix of Marxist-nationalist thinking that characterized much Soviet writing, bourgeois historians were excoriated for exaggerating the significance of the Bukharans' role in the Siberian economy. See Vilkov, *Remeslo i torgovlia*, 9–15.

Whereas long-distance merchants could be gone for years at a time, and in some years caravans might not come at all, Shaba Ashmenev's regional trade operations turned on an annual cycle. Customs records from consecutive years reveal that he went to the Irbit market in January to buy Russian goods, which would then be sold throughout Siberia to Russian settlers as well as to natives becoming accustomed to Western products.[171] For example, in the winter of 1726, Shaba Ashmenev bought linen (*kholsta*), wax, and gunpowder worth over 100 rubles at Irbit. He returned to Tiumen' and over the course of the year dispersed these goods in several batches for resale to various towns in Siberia with his various agents, workers, and relatives. First, he sent his nephew Sharyp Kaznin (Karipym) to Tobol'sk with 1,000 arshin of canvas (*kholsta khrushchu*)—the entire quantity he'd purchased in Irbit just weeks before. Two weeks later Shaba dispatched part of the shipment to be sold by his nephew Bakhmuto in various district villages. That spring Shaba dispatched an even larger shipment of fabric—taken from his warehouse or from other trips or transactions, since he had already dispatched the 1,000 arshin he had bought in Irbit in January—with his agent Osip Shishkin and his nephew Askar.[172] Shaba Ashmenev followed the same routine again next year, buying up many goods at the Irbit fair in 1727.[173] Again, over the next months his agents, nephews, and workers took parts of the shipment to other towns in Siberia to sell. In 1727, Shaba Ashmenev or someone in his employ made declarations at Tiumen' customs twenty-one times. Eleven times Shaba Ashmenev himself declared leather he had purchased or money he was taking to the Irbit market to purchase Russian goods. In his last entry of the year, on December 31, 1727, Shaba Ashmenev left Tiumen' bound for Irbit with substantial money and furs; the yearly trade cycle was about to begin again.

The patterns observed here conform to Braudel's observations on early modern trade in Europe: it lacked specialization. Merchants traded in local goods even as they brought their particular goods from afar.[174] Eastern goods remained a core niche of the Shababins' enterprise. We do know that some Shababins traveled the massive distance from Beijing to Moscow, yet the regional patterns observed conform to Valerie Hansen's conclusions about the Silk Roads trade: "Most travelers moved on smaller circuits, traveling a few hundred miles (around 500 km) between their hometown and the next

171. SPbII RAN, f. 187, op. 1, d. 1233, l. 1.
172. SPbII RAN, f. 187, op. 1, d. 1233, ll. 1–1v.
173. GBUTO GATO, f. 29, op. 1, d. 134, l. 1.
174. Braudel, *Wheels of Commerce*, 225.

oasis and no further. Because goods were traded locally and passed through many hands, much of the Silk Road trade was a trickle trade."[175]

With this book's focus on commerce, it is important to keep in mind that lack of specialization extended to the political economy of the Bukharan community as a whole; trade was not their sole endeavor. "They . . . live by trade and land-owning (agriculture, husbandry)," noted Krizhanich.[176] Siberian Bukharans kept herds and farmed to feed themselves, inside and outside of the Russian Empire. It may have been that the merchants who transported raisins, apricots, nuts, and Bukharan onions to Siberia were involved in their production as well.[177] In Tiumen' the Shababins developed a profitable tanning manufactory, which in the early eighteenth century was run by Shaba's brother, Kazna Ashmenev.[178] His appearances at customs, for which he signed his own declarations, involved leather hides and livestock animals.[179] The leather manufacture, which could produce four hundred to five hundred skins a year, was one of two (of a total sixty-two) owned by Bukharans in Tobol'sk province in the first half of the eighteenth century.[180]

Among the tax privileges that Siberia Bukharans enjoyed was the waiver of tributary land rent (obrok). Policymakers justified this waiver on the assumption that Siberian Bukharans practiced agriculture and husbandry only for subsistence purposes, posing no competition in agricultural commodities markets. Some of their neighbors resented the privilege, and the Bukharans' husbandry remained a long-standing source of tension. Although Siberia is virtually synonymous with abundant space, between marshes, nomads, proximity to rivers, and land arable enough to feed oneself, good land came at a premium. In 1643 several Tiumen' residents, a group consisting of mounted musketeers, Cossacks, state porters (iamshchiki), townsmen and peasants, asked the tsar to grant them lands surrounding Lake Andreev (located on the outskirts of contemporary Tiumen'). In response, several Tatars and one Tiumen' trading Bukharan petitioned that the land was theirs. They testified

---

175. Hansen, *Silk Road*, 10.

176. Krizhanich, in Alekseev, *Sibir' v izvestiiakh zapadno-evropeiskikh*, 560. Characterizations of Uzbeks (Bukharans) in Mughal India are inverted, where they were stereotyped as unclean and untrustworthy. See Levi, *India Diaspora in Central Asia*, 146.

177. These food items appear occasionally in Russian customs books. On observations about farming Bukharans, see RGADA, f. 214, stb. 535, l. 218; Milescu, *Puteshestvie chez Sibir'*, 16; Black and Buse. G. F. Müller and Siberia, 81; Balkashina, "Torgovoe dvizhenie," 1–32, esp. 2; Georgi, *Russia*, 2: 135. The parasitic diseases Gottlieb described compromise an otherwise idyllic picture.

178. GBUTO GATO, f. 29. op. 1, d. 30, 54, 73, 157, 186. I thank Vera Kiueva for these references.

179. GBUTO GATO, f. 29, d. 66, l. 8.

180. Razgon, *Sibirskoe kupechestvo*, 526, 535.

that their fathers from long ago had possessed pasturelands around Lake Andreev that the tsar had granted to them, but now other Tiumen' residents were claiming the land for themselves. They beseeched Tsar Mikhail Fëdorovich to affirm their claims, lest ambitious neighbors dispute them.[181] In the wake of that dispute, Russian locals charged that Bukharans produced at levels beyond subsistence, which put the locals at a disadvantage. Bukharans vigorously defended their privileges in a 1644 petition insisting that they farmed only for subsistence, not for sale.[182] It was a line local Bukharans had used before and would use again. In the 1624–25 survey, Bukharans reported that "they feed [themselves] by fishing . . . and livestock . . . and owing to their poverty . . . plant just a few rows of various grains."[183] In the next generation, Kazna's nephew, Seit Shabin syn Shababin, remained sensitive to the tension. In a late-eighteenth-century property survey, Seit Shabin's testimony stressed the subsistence nature of their holdings, explaining that "on all the aforementioned land, given to his great-grandfather, grandfather, and his father and to him" the tilled and hay lands were each for the purpose of feeding his family and his household people. He maintained that the land also fed the workers of their leather factory, who did not buy food from the Shababins but evidently farmed the land themselves.[184]

About the career of another brother of Shaba and Kazan, less is known. Shagucha Ashmenev paid one-tenth tax in Tiumen' on goods he bought in Ufa in 1701, but otherwise appears little in customs records.[185] When Russian officials rendered the name "Shagucha" in customs records, they were hearing what other Bukharans understood as "Shah Khwaja."[186] The moniker Shah Khwaja denoted connection to sacred genealogies of earlier Bukharan missionaries, suggesting the Shababin family enjoyed a position of prestige among their own. It may be that Shagucha was so little seen at the customs posts because he occupied himself with less worldly matters. Not that spiritual vocations precluded commercial activity: mullas regularly accompanied the caravans that crisscrossed Eurasia. Whatever the reason for his rare appearances in historical records, the archive is not entirely silent on Shagucha Ashmenev. A quarter of a century after he declared the shipment from Ufa, his yurt was the scene of a violent conflict between Bukharans. On June 27, 1726, the Tiumen' Embaevskii yurt Bukharan Sharyp Ashirepov

---

181. GBUTO GATO, f. 47, op. 1, d. 38, l. 3 (1643).
182. RGADA, f. 214, stb. 134, l. 196.
183. RGADA, f. 214, stb. 81, l. 63.
184. GBUTO GATO, f. 47, op. 1, d. 2228, l. 2.
185. GBUTO GATO, f. 47, op. 1, d. 5, l. 3v. I thank Vera Kiueva for this reference.
186. I thank Alfrid Bustanov for bringing this to my attention.

filed the following petition in the Tiumen' Judicial Chancery: on the previous night (June 26–27), Sharyp had gone to help Shagucha Ashmenev (although his testimony does not indicate why). There he found two other Bukharans, Reshit and Mamesherit Mershenev. For "no apparent reason," Reshit attacked Sharyp, beat him up, "dishonored him," and tore his shirt.[187]

Whereas evidence situates his father and grandfather in tsarist service, we have no record of Shaba Ashmenev serving the Russian state, which, at least, granted him no land. Nonetheless, he did modestly increase the family landholdings by 888 acres (329 desiatiny) through direct purchase and when lendees defaulted on loans in which land was the collateral. He almost doubled the family's plowed farmland, adding about 65 acres (24 desiatiny). He acquired 5 desiatiny of arable land below Erovskii village from the Tiumen' Bukharan Ermamet Epshanov in June 1741. This land appears to have been mortgaged to him. In 1751–52 he bought land on the north side of the Tura, three versts from the town of Tiumen', from Petr Ognev, a *raznochinets* (people of various ranks).[188] This land had previously been the site of Russian settlement that had relocated to the other side of the river.[189] In the spring of 1744 Ashmenev bought 40.5 acres—27 acres farmland and 13.5 acres pastureland—from a new convert to Christianity, Fëdor Matigorov. His baptismal name was probably taken from his spiritual sponsor, so his identity is shrouded from us, although we can be confident the seller was a non-Russian property owner. The lands were located near Embaevskii yurt and on an island in Lake Andreev.[190] Both areas had been the subjects of property disputes in the previous century.[191] Shaba Ashmenev bought not only land but people as well. In 1724 he purchased a man named Baramchuga from the Tiumen' servitor Bikina Tokchurin.[192] That man would later prove to be a headache for Shaba's son, Seit.

This third generation of Shababins lived at a time when the state was curtailing its willingness to accommodate Muslim elites. Peter I did commission the first translation of the Quran, but he also introduced decrees that made it more difficult to maintain one's Muslim identity and advance in Russian

187. GBUTO GATO, f. 181, op. 1, d. 52, l. 1. Note a non-Russian subject invoking the concept of "honor," which was germane to social praxis in early modern Russia. See Kollmann, *By Honor Bound*.

188. GBUTO GATO, f. 47, op. 1, d. 2228, l. 1v. *Raznochinets* was an eclectic category referring to someone "of various ranks."

189. Trofimova, *Pamiatniki Tiumenskoi delovoi pis'mennosti*, bk. 2, no. 133, 256–57.

190. GBUTO GATO, f. 47, op. 1, d. 2228, l. 2v.

191. GBUTO GATO, f. 47, op. 1, d. 38, l. 1 (1643).

192. GBUTO GATO, f. 47, op. 1, d. 1763, l. 85, repr. in Trofimova, *Pamiatniki Tiumenskoi delovoi pis'mennosti*, bk. 2, no. 338, 519.

imperial society, made it more difficult to construct mosques, promoted (ironically) conversion campaigns, and punished apostasy from Orthodoxy.[193] Whereas Russia had previously encouraged conversion with the carrot of reward, under Peter the state turned more coercive as servitors who did not convert were threatened with the stick of property confiscation.[194]

On the ground in Tiumen', however, Shababin fortunes continued to rise. The Shababins proved adept at maintaining a distinct yet sufficiently integrated existence. Customs records suggest increasing commercial cooperation between Bukharans and Russians and/or Cossacks. In 1704 the Tiumen' Bukharans Matiiar Dosaev and Ashmen Shababin (Shaba's father) teamed up to employ a Cossack to transport a shipment of wax to Tobol'sk for them.[195] The Shababin agents, Shishkin and Shmakov, may have been Russian. Matiiar Dosaev, a relative of the Shababins, was proactive at crossing cultural boundaries. In 1704 he and a Tiumen' townsman cooperated on the sale of some horses to a local cleric.[196] Dosaev jointly rented shop space (*polka*) in the Tiumen' marketplace with a local Cossack.[197] Such cross-cultural cooperation is found in other families as well. In 1704 the Tiumen' Bukharan Iurmart Babashev carried to Ufa a parcel of Eastern fabrics on behalf of a Tiumen' Cossack who had acquired the fabrics at Lake Yamysh the previous year.[198] In 1744 the Tatar (or Bukharan) Izmail Akhmetev left his wares in the charge of the Tobol'sk townsman V. Medovshchikov.[199] On January 6, 1728, Mikhailo Iakovlev Kornilov, son of the Tobol'sk townsman Iakov Kornilov, declared an exotic shipment of taffeta, other fabrics, some money, and 5 pud of walrus tusk.[200] He was accompanied by his workers (*rabotniki*), who included the Tobol'sk Bukharan Mosei Naurusov and Fëdor Irmakov.[201] This example not only reveals a Bukharan and a Russian side by side as hired laborers but it also introduces the term *rabotnik*, which one does not encounter in Siberian customs books before Peter I's reign. The trend revealed itself in Shababin family dealings in 1768 when Suleiman Seitov syn

193. Arapov, *Islam v Rossiiskoi imperii*, 26–40. On Peter's ironic promotion of conversion campaigns see Slezkine, "Savage Christians or Unorthodox Russians," 15–32.

194. Hamamoto, "Conversion of Muslim Elites." This policy relaxed in 1730s and 1740s.

195. GBUTO GATO, f. 47, op. 1, d. 39, l. 7.

196. GBUTO GATO, f. 29, op. 1, d. 38, l. 1.

197. Golovachev, *Tiumen' v XVII veke*, 70.

198. GBUTO GATO, f. 29, op. 1, d. 36, l. 3v (1704).

199. GUTO GAT, f. 156, op. 1, d. 149, ll. 1–15.

200. 1 pud = 16.38 kg.

201. GBUTO GATO, f. 29, d. 139, l. 1. In this book, dates appear out of order in the entries. Dates precede January 10–2 entries, January 10–3 entries, followed by an entry date June 15 (ll. 9v–11v).

Shababin, a fifth-generation Siberian, departed with his household person (slave) and a Bukharan worker to Kiakhta to trade.[202]

If a precept against antagonizing Siberian Muslims had long animated directives from the center, it vanished under Empress Elizabeth (1741–61). The Office of New Convert Affairs (Kontora Novokreshchenykh Del), created especially for the project of conversion at the beginning of Elizabeth's reign, launched an aggressive campaign to bring pagans and Muslims to Orthodoxy.[203] Conditions worsened for many Muslims in the Russian Empire. Mosques were destroyed and baptisms were often coerced, sometimes brutally, even if the degree of coercion in Siberia was less than that in the Volga region. The Siberian Office, recognizing the important role Siberia's Muslims played in regional commerce both as merchants and customs administrators, was reluctant to take steps that might disrupt commerce. Orders to implement mandatory conversion met with foot-dragging. The Tobol'sk governor requested clarification of his instructions multiple times before finally carrying out the Office of New Convert Affairs' program and destroying seventy-five mosques in the Tobol'sk region in 1745.[204]

Coincident with the conversion campaign of the Office of New Convert Affairs, the first reports of Bukharans converting to Orthodoxy emerge in the 1740s. In 1744 Shababin bought land from Fëdor Matigorov, a yurt resident who had been baptized into Orthodoxy.[205] In 1751 in what seems to have been a voluntary baptism, a Tobol'sk Bukharan who had converted to Orthodoxy and taken the name Afanasii Grigor'ev syn sought permission to travel to Moscow to pay homage to the Miracle Worker, Saint Dmitrii of Rostov. One cannot help but wonder if there is a syncretistic element to the desire of this converted Muslim to make a pilgrimage to holy Moscow. Tobol'sk was home to a shrine of the Muslim saint Aq Khoja, which was the object of regional pilgrimage for devout Muslims.[206] Although nothing directly suggests these conversions were coerced, in 1751 the Bukharan Murata Kutumov along with other Bukharans and Tatars in Tobol'sk protested baptism against their will.[207] Little is known of the Shababins during

202. GBUTO GATO, f. 29, d. 2024, l. 1.
203. Frank, *Islamic Historiography and "Bulghar" Identity*, 29. For a revisionist perspective see Werth, "Coercion and Conversion," 543–69.
204. Frank, *Islamic Historiography and "Bulghar" Identity*, 29. On conversion see Khodarkovsky, "'Ignoble Savages and Unfaithful Subjects,'" 9–26.
205. GBUTO GATO, f. 47, op. 1, d. 2228, l. 1v.
206. Frank, *Islamic Historiography and "Bulghar" Identity*, 2, 115, 117.
207. GUTO GAT, f. 156, op. 1, d. 772, ll. 1–69. GUTO GAT, f. 661, op. 1, d. 10, ll. 1–5 is an *ukaz* from Anna Ioannovna about not baptizing Persians by force. GUTO GAT, f. 156, op. 1, d. 772, l. 8 is a 1693 edict saying not to baptize anyone against their will.

Сибирской Бухаръ.
Ein Sibirischer Buchar.
Un Bouchar de Siberie.

FIGURE 7.4 Drawing of a Siberian Bukharan from the study of Johann Gottlieb Georgi (1729–1802). Georgi traveled through Siberia in 1770–74, during the adulthood of Seit Shabin syn Shababin.
Source: Georgi, *Russia*, plate. Courtesy New York Public Library.

Empress Elizabeth's reign. The hiatus of information may well be an accident of the archive: no Tiumen' customs books survive for the 1740s.[208] Instead, we learn something of Shababin affairs from reports that household slaves and dependents fled the Shababin household for monasteries seeking baptism, as we will see below.

Generation 4: Seit Shabin Syn Shababin (1742–1793)

The picture of the family's fortunes that reemerges in the reign of Catherine II, amid a general economic boom for Russia, indicates that they continued to do well. Shaba Ashmenev's son, Seit Shabin (1760s) led the diversified family businesses in the fourth generation.[209] He increased the family property considerably and served a term as elder (*starshina*) of the Bukharan yurts in the Tiumen' hinterland. His life was not without friction, both in the household and in local politics, but he appears to have maintained good relations with the state.

Trade remained a cornerstone of the family's political economy. Only four Bukharans owned trade stalls in the Tiumen' marketplace in the 1760s, but Seit Shabin owned more trade stalls than any other individual in Tiumen', Bukhara, or Russia.[210] In 1766 Seit Shabin syn Shababin purchased a shop adjacent to one he already owned from the Tiumen' townsman Stepan Bolshoi Afanas'ev syn Stukalov for 5 rubles.[211] Stepan Bolshoi's father, Afanasei Stukalov, had worked for the Shababins. Stukalov is not formally referred to as a Shababin agent in customs books, but he traveled with some of their shipments in 1727 and sometimes moved his own shipments. On one occasion he recruited Osip Shishkin to carry a consignment on his behalf and another time carried a consignment for a local soldier.[212] One wonders if the shop sale was the result of a downturn in Stukalov fortunes. Afanasei had died in 1763. That autumn (October) his two sons, Stepan

---

208. Ogloblin, *Obozrenie*, 2: appendix 85.

209. The form of his name, Seit Shabin *syn* Shababin, lends some insight into his status. Use of a name, patronymic, and family name was reserved for people of moderately high status. The use of the suffix *-vich* at the end of the father's name instead of *syn* was reserved for someone of even higher status. Thus, it seems that the Shababin family patriarch was respected as a community leader but his status was not so exalted as to afford him a patronymic ending in *-vich*.

210. GBUTO GATO, f. 47, op. 1, d. 1877.

211. Trofimova, *Pamiatniki Tiumenskoi delovoi pis'mennosti*, bk. 2, no. 89, 197–98 (repr. of GBUTO GATO, f. 45, op. 1, d. 86, l. 8–8v).

212. GBUTO GATO, f. 29, d. 134, l. 19v.

Big and Stepan Little,[213] requested that the authorities return to them their father's inventoried goods, which suggests that Afanasei had shared a fate that all long-distance merchants risked: he died on the road.[214] Although they requested the goods in the autumn of 1763, they were not issued to the older son until April 1764.[215] A month before that, in March 1764, Stepan sold his mill to a Tiumen' *raznochinets*.[216] Two years later, the sons sold their father's shop to his former employer.

Seit Shabin made significant additions to the family property. In 1763 he acquired land from local Tatars.[217] In 1765 he bought land from a local Bukharan.[218] In 1775 the state granted him plowland that had been abandoned by a Kalmyk émigré. In 1776 he purchased land and livestock from a local Russian.[219] In all, Seit Shabin acquired a total of 4,616 (1,710 desiatiny = 7.2 square miles) of land. Additionally, he owned 423 desiatiny of land in common with his nephew. As noted above, Seit was careful to stress that these holdings provided subsistence for the household and workers. It may have been for the purpose of feeding his household and workers that Shabin acquired fishing rights in a local stream and lake from a local Tatar in 1774. Two decades later, in 1793, an elderly Seit Shabin would contract a fifteen-year lease of those fishing rights to a local Tiumen' merchant.[220]

All told, the Shababins were the most propertied Bukharans in the Tiumen' region when this survey was composed in the late eighteenth century. Of 654 counted Bukharan males in the Tiumen' region, 114 were from the Shababin yurt, making it only the third most populous Bukharan settlement. Yet the Shababin yurt, in which residence was not limited to members of the Shababin clan, owned 27.5 percent of the total land registered to Bukharans—11,101 desiatiny.[221] Of the 40,300 desiatiny of land registered to Bukharans in the eleven yurts in the Tiumen' region, the Shababins owned, either directly or

---

213. Such naming would occur when children were born around the same time in different years because children were typically named after the saint whose day was nearest.

214. Trofimova, *Tiumenskoi delovoi pis'mennosti*, bk. 1, 15.

215. Ibid., 19.

216. Ibid., 18.

217. GBUTO GATO, f. 47, op. 1, d. 2228, l. 1v. June 15, 1763 he purchased 20 desiatiny of pasture and 1,500 desiatiny of land near a brook that runs into Lake Andreevskoe from the Tiumen' Tatars Kuchka and Mulai Emanaev.

218. GBUTO GATO, f. 47, op. 1, d. 2228, l. 1v. September 17, 1765 he bought 162 desiatiny of plowland and pasture on the north side of the Tura River from the Tiumen' Bukharan Isz Ermametev.

219. GBUTO GATO, f. 47, op. 1, d. 2228, l. 2. June 15, 1776 he bought 18 desiatiny of plowland near Kazarovskii yurt from the petty artisan/trader (*meshchanin*) Peter Prasolov.

220. Razgon, *Sibirskoe kupechestvo*, 508.

221. GBUTO GATO, f. 47, op. 1, d. 2228, ll. 4, 16.

in common, 6,055 desiatiny, or 15 percent of the land, making the Shababin family by far the largest Bukharan property holders in Tiumen'.

Contested Conversions

In Catherinian Russia the Siberian frontier had changed substantially from that to which the first Shababin had arrived over a century before. A growing economy, increased borderlands settlement, Enlightenment ideas, protonationalism, a more extensive (although perennially inadequate, as state documents reveal) imperial administration, diminution of church clout in state matters, and an imperial court in which high-stakes identity politics seeped out to the far reaches of empire all contributed to a changed landscape. These developments were eventually felt in distant Siberia where conversion politics came to the fore in the Shababin household.

In December 1763 Seit Shabin appealed to the state concerning converts from his household. He reported four incidents in which his household serfs had run away and sought refuge in monasteries where they asked to be baptized into Christianity.[222] What mix of material, religious, defensive, or other concerns motivated their flight remains a matter of speculation, but the incidents had not been handled according to Russian law and Seit Shabin knew it.

The first incident occurred in 1734—during the reign of Anna Ioannovna (1730–40)—when a household man that Seit himself had bought from the Tobol'sk Bukharan Kazym Baganokov escaped to a local monastery and declared his desire to convert to Orthodoxy. Sometime in the 1750s Baramchuga, a household man purchased by Seit Shabin's father, ran away to the Troitskii monastery, where he was taken in and promptly baptized, which "freed" him from Shababin, since the Russian state forbade Muslims from holding Christian slaves. Then in 1758 it happened again. Koendar Sagandykov, whom Seit had inherited from his father, ran away to the Troitskii monastery and was baptized. This time, however, he had taken with him goods stolen from Seit Shabin's household. Yet Governor Mikhail Khakholev with his secretary Iakov Nesterov issued permission for the baptism the very day the request was received from the monastery. This violated conversion procedures articulated by Moscow in the 1680s, which stipulated a thirty-day waiting period and vetting by the administration. Seit pointed out that by neither observing the proscribed waiting period nor informing him, both the Governor's Office and Troitskii monastery had disobeyed the rules set by

---

222. GBUTO GATO, f. 47, op. 1, d. 1763, ll. 85–86 (repr. in Trofimova, *Pamiatniki Tiumenskoi delovoi pis'mennosti*, bk. 2, no. 121).

Moscow. Of special concern, the 1680s procedures demanded that would-be converts did not steal property from the owners. Yet that is exactly what had happened and Seit was concerned about the precedent the Governor's Office had set. "Because of that," Seit lamented in his complaint, "our remaining household people, seeing the previous runaways, having stolen property and nothing happened to them for it."[223] The incident repeated. On a summer's night in July 1762 a woman named Kyzbaza, along with her young daughter Iakshibak, stole a substantial amount of property and ran off to the Troitskii monastery, where they were baptized. Seit and his son Suleiman reported the stolen property multiple times, but Governor Mikhail Polstovalov and the secretary Iakov Nesterov took no action; adding offense to injury, they issued the runaways an even larger state subsidy.

Seit Shabin's report is specifically aimed at the Tiumen' administration under two consecutive governors who "effect nothing toward our preservation, only [advance] our destruction." Previously, he points out in a 1754 missive, the provincial administration had followed the procedures proscribed by the center. He continued, "I am now in no small danger, so as on me, so as on my house and on my wife and children. Those household people could do such evil, or even worse, and murder." Overwrought or not, his sense of injury is palpable. "If any of those of my household people voluntarily, without stealing my property, should wish to be baptized into the Christian Orthodox faith and take the holy baptism, in that, I, your slave, have no opposition and make no sort of obstacle to," but the disregard of official procedure and unrequited theft were too much for him.[224]

Seit Shabin's timing suggests that his ear was somewhat close to the ground on political matters. Catherine II became empress in July 1762. Her reign marked a sea change in confessional policy from that of Elizaveta Petrovna. That Seit Shabin filed his petition in 1763 raises the question of how quickly Catherine made her intentions known and how quickly such information spread through the empire. Seit Shabin had evidently filed no complaints at the time of the defections in 1734 and the 1750s. Under Elizabeth, such complaints would likely have found little sympathy. Evidently hints of the new empress's stance had reached Siberia, since Seit deemed it worth his while to formally complain in the wake of the 1762 runaway. The political center was far away, but imperial policy had made itself known on the frontier.

223. PSZ, vol. 3, no. 1594, 355–56.
224. GBUTO GATO, f. 47, op. 1, d. 1763, l. 85v (repr. in Trofimova, *Pamiatniki Tiumenskoi delovoi pis'mennosti*, bk. 2, no. 121).

If the above complaint depicts Shabin's relations with local authorities as what we might call icy, other evidence suggests a more amicable rapport. According to Razgon, in 1774 it was due to Shabin's good favor with the state that Tiumen' officials registered the fishing rights intended as collateral on a 110-ruble loan as "eternal ownership."[225] In July 1775 the Tiumen' chancery issued Seit Shabin 10 desiatiny of plowland that had been abandoned by a Kalmyk émigré.[226]

In his petition, Seit insisted that he would not impede a householder desiring baptism. This raises the question of Seit Shabin's spirituality. Where on the vast spectrum and vectors of Islamic waves that ebbed and flowed across Eurasia in the early modern period might we situate his beliefs and practices? To what extent did he adhere to the Naqshbandi teachings that emanated from Bukhara and seems to have been prevalent in western Siberia? We cannot answer these questions in any depth, but that he named his son Suleiman suggests he was not interested in assimilating Russianness. An incident in 1769 offers another vague clue.

As elder (*starshina*), it was his job to report disputes in the Tatar Bukharan community to Russian authorities.[227] Oversight of religious practice was also a component of the job. Near harvest time in 1769, Seit Shababin reported that a leader (*abyz* = priest) in the Turaevskii yurt had been negligent in failing to take action against the practices of one Mulla Murtaz who, according to Seit Shabin, conducted the service improperly and was but "a nominal Muslim (*munafik*), which was worse than being an idol-worshipper."[228] There is no direct evidence that Seit Shababin played any direct role in the proselytizing activities that the governor of Siberia noted in 1767, but his reporting of Mulla Murtaz suggests that Seit Shabin was hardly complacent when it came to matters of spiritual practice.[229]

Generation 5: Suleiman Seitov Syn Shababin (1762–1768)

The family remained a prominent merchant presence in Tiumen' during Catherine II's reign. Seit Shabin had more than one son and grandchildren,

---

225. Razgon, *Sibirskoe kupechestvo*, 508.
226. GBUTO GATO, f. 47, op. 1, d. 2228, l. 2.
227. Trofimova, *Tiumenskaia delovaia pis'mennost'*, bk. 1, 44, 51; Trofimova, *Pamiatniki Tiumenskoi delovoi pis'mennosti*, bk. 2, no. 41, 102–3.
228. Trofimova, *Pamiatniki Tiumenskoi delovoi pis'mennosti*, bk. 2, no. 41, 102–3.
229. Andrievich, *Sibir' v tsarstvovanie imperatritsy Ekateriny II*, 98. See PSZ, vol. 18, no. 13,336 (August 20, 1767).

but his son Suleiman is the only one of his direct progeny about whom we have specific information. After over a century of living in Tiumen' as prominent community members and sometimes servitors in Russian state institutions, the Shababin family did not assimilate Russian names, but strongly signaled a non-Russian identity in their name choices. Suleiman Seitov syn Shababin (1763–70s), by now a fifth-generation Siberian, dutifully did his father's bidding in appealing to the state regarding the matter of runaways. He also traveled for trade. In the fall of 1763 Suleiman and a relative requested passports for four of his workers to spend the winter season trading on his behalf in the district of Orenburg.[230]

In late August 1768 Suleiman Seitov syn Shababin departed with his household person (slave) and Bukharan worker to Kiakhta for trade.[231] The documents (passports) and the destinations (Orenburg, Kiakhta) had changed, as had the Siberian topography: Russian forts now dotted the Irtysh River and Tara had a peasant population that could till the fertile soil on the edge of the steppe without such acute danger of Kalmyk raids. But amid these new manifestations of Russian imperialism, Suleiman Shababin continued to oversee a trade network from the family's base in Tiumen', a practice his great-great-grandfather had begun over a century earlier.

Conclusion

The history of the Shababin family from the Muscovy of Tsar Aleksei Mikhailovich to the empire of Catherine II testifies both to the endurance of this family and to the opportunities present in Russian Siberia before, during, and after Peter I's reign. The state's policies toward Muslims varied according to different contexts across space and time. The Shababins' story is not one of being co-opted into the Russian elite and assimilating Orthodox identity, as in the case of some Muslims of Kazan or the Crimea, nor of overt resistance and protracted warfare, in the Caucasus—narratives which are beyond the scope of our story.

While our knowledge of the earliest incorporation of Muslims into the Muscovite state is confined to the elite ranks, where assimilation hinged on military and political allegiance, this case study presents a different model.[232]

---

230. Trofimova, *Pamiatniki Tiumenskoi delovoi pis'mennosti*, bk. 2, no. 279, 451–52 (repr. of GBUTO GATO, f. 47, op. 1, d. 5248, l. 1).

231. GBUTO GATO, f. 47, op. 1, d. 2024, l. 1.

232. Lenhoff, "Rus-Tatar Princely Marriages," 23–24; Martin, "Muscovite Frontier Policy," 169–79; Bushkovitch, "Princes Cherkasskii or Circassian Murzas"; Romaniello *Elusive Empire*; Hamomoto, "Conversion of Muslim Elites."

The courting of non-elite Muslims such as the Shababins was motivated in the first place by pragmatic, economic objectives. Although security was always a matter of critical concern for Russian imperial administrators and extended, of course, to Siberia, the merchant Muslims of Siberia experienced more accommodation and privilege than Muslims of the Caucasus and Volga regions. Thus the history of the Shababins and other Bukharans in Siberia illustrates the accommodations the Russian state was prepared to make. Bukharans were integrated into the Siberian community where they enjoyed positions of respect as they both pursued their private endeavors and/or served the state. All the while, they retained a distinct identity, prompting one late-eighteenth-century ethnographer to write, "Wherever they are found they stand by one another, and make one common cause, by which means they always preserve their national character."[233] Certainly more pragmatic than cosmopolitan, the Russian state in the early modern period was hardly an assimilationist enterprise. Such findings are familiar to students of early modern empire: Russian scholars have increasingly recognized that the empire, which drew legitimacy and prestige from its foundational Orthodox credentials, simultaneously courted and extended significant privileges to Muslim merchants in its domains; in Russia as elsewhere, empire was the management of difference.[234]

This history is instructive not only regarding imperial subjects in the early modern Russian Empire but also as a case study of a mercantile Muslim diaspora community. Again, in the broadest strokes, there are no surprises here. First, their history depicts a significant and enduring kin-based commercial enterprise that operated on both long-distance and regional scales. Second, in contrast to the standard narrative of trade in the early modern era, which long averred that the rise of long-distance maritime travel sounded the death knell of overland Eurasian trade, this study resonates with work that challenges the decline thesis.[235] Third, trade and religion were fellow travelers. Siberian Bukharans linked themselves to the broader world of Islam with its history, its heroes, and distant centers of learning. They celebrated and propagated these links with family genealogies that traced their lineages back to the Prophet via his daughter Fatima; by transmitting and connecting their heritage to the sacred history of the Islamization of Siberia, conversion narratives in which Bukharan missionaries were the bearers of Islam;

233. Gottlieb, *Russia*, 2: 149.
234. Burbank and Cooper, *Empires in World History*, 1–22.
235. For a good summary of the "decline thesis" see articles by Scott Levi and Morris Rossabi in *India and Central Asia*.

and through the maintenance and incorporation of sacred shrines into their spiritual traditions.[236] Such shrines made sacred history local to the riparian landscapes of the forest-steppe they inhabited, rendering their homes part of Dar al-Islam (Abode of Islam). My sources—primarily state documents of an administrative and economic nature—give up little of the inner lives and religious practices of Siberian Bukharans. But they do, in spite of themselves, transmit more than matters of economy and administration. Though muted and tangential—naming practices, taking a Muslim oath, the customs book that records a Muslim traveling to family to pray, complaints about forced conversions, and hearsay of proselytization efforts—state documents gesture toward the religious worldview that animated the lives of Bukharans in Siberia, a worldview that motivated them to not only transmit but also spread their faith. As bearers of commerce and religion in the Russian Empire, these Muslim merchants shared a great deal with their contemporary merchant-missionaries across the premodern Afro-Eurasian world.

---

236. Narratives of the Islamization of Siberia chronicle that the learned missionaries from Central Asia who "opened the region" sometimes suffered a martyr's fate. These martyrs' graves became sacred sites that have been maintained by families with esteemed lineages whose roles as shrine keepers added to their prestige. See Bustanov, "Sacred Texts of Siberian Khwaja Families; Bustanov, "Sufiiskie legendy ob islamizatsii Sibiri"; Bustanov, *Book Culture of Siberian Muslims*. For a reproduction and translation of one narrative from the Tiumen' region, see Bustanov, Appendix 3: "Rukopis' iz derevni Karagai Vagaiskogo raiona Tiumneskoi oblasti," in Seleznev, et al., *Kul't sviatykh v sibirskom Islame*, 193–206.

CHAPTER 8

Middling Merchants

> In general one can say, that in the typical case profit
> greatly outweighs loss and so consequently, the Russian
> merchants always get other profit from Siberian trade.
>
> —G. F. Müller, *Istoriia Sibiri*

> The complexity of enterprise required significant cash
> resources and organization, and assessing seventeenth-
> century Siberian documents confirms that entrepre-
> neurial movements to the east were far more organized
> than is typically assumed.
>
> —S. V. Bakhrushin, *Nauchnye trudy*

It was a busy season at the Tiumen' customs
post in the winter of 1661/62. A steady stream of local and regional people
registered their small consignments with the customs head Tretiak Shtil'nikov.
Two recent Orthodox converts from Kazan, a Cossack, a porter in the state
iam system, a Tatar servitor, and a Tiumen' artisan by the name of Onisimko
Avvakumov (although it is not established that he was related to Russia's most
famous religious dissident) brought the odd sack of grain, a goat, a slab of
salted lard (*sala*), various varieties of salted fish from local rivers, a few pelts, or
other goods to exchange. A local widow bought a horse, as did a passerby on
behalf of the governor of Eniseisk. A handful of peasants—one from a nearby
monastery, a Kirgiz, humble farmer-artisans from the exalted estates of Boyar
Boris Ivanovich Morozov and Fëdor Stroganov—added to the activity among
the trading rows encased in snow and ice. Their consignments appeared meager compared with the many dozens of laden sleds that agents of Moscow's
commercial elite were bringing to the Tiumen' customs posts. Agents of the
gosti Vasilii Shorin, Afanasii Gusel'nikov, Semen Zadorin, and Ostafii Filat'ev
all made appearances, as well as several other merchants of the Merchant
Hundred and Wooliers' corporation. In all, ten privileged merchants or their
agents did business at Tiumen' customs in December and January 1661/62.[1]

---

1. SPbII RAN, f. 187, op. 2, d. 20, ll. 1–33 (Tiumen' customs book, 1661–1662).

Among these most petty and more illustrious consignments were other merchants that did not bear a privileged rank but were more than moonlighting dabblers when it came to Siberian commerce. On January 5, alongside the agent of the Moscow gost' Semen Zadorin, Iakov Mikiforov, the agent of a newly minted Merchant Hundred merchant, Andrei Gostev, declared his bosses wares. Iakov's nine-year-old son, Spirka—of whom we will hear more below—was helping him at the customs post that day. On January 14, after three privileged merchants registered their wares, half a dozen men from the small town of Lal'sk stepped up to the customs head to declare their sleds laden with goods either made by the hand of local artisans or that they had bought up at the late summer fair in Arkhangel'sk and Kol'mogory. This chapter, loosely construed, is about them—the lowest rank of privileged merchants and the upper eschelons of trading men who, although not of privileged rank, were substantial merchants in their own right. It is the closest we come to telling the stories of the all but nameless merchants who nonetheless helped shape consequential trends in the early modern Eurasian trade. Through the lens of a few merchants of Siberia, of what might be called the middling merchant group, this chapter considers another level of early modern Siberian commerce.

The Missing Research on the Missing Middle Class

From the sixteenth to the early eighteenth century formal corporations of privileged merchants occupied the top of the commercial pyramid in Muscovy. At the very pinnacle stood the small and most exclusive group of privileged merchants, the gosti. From 1600 to 1728, most of the corporation's formal existence, Russian tsars bestowed this distinction on 152 merchants. Below the gosti were the second and third tiers of the privileged merchant corporations, the Merchant Hundred (*gostinia sotnia*) and the Woolen Clothiers' Hundred (*sukonnaia sotnia*), characterized by fewer privileges and larger membership.[2] Most merchants who attained gosti status passed through the Merchant Hundred beforehand. Golikova documented over 2,700 merchants and artisans (and just a few women) who passed through its ranks from the sixteenth to eighteenth centuries, as opposed to several hundred total gosti.[3]

2. The Woolen Clothiers' Hundred (*sukonnye sotni*) receive no specific attention here because they appeared so little in Siberia. One theory is that *sukonniki* of the Woolen Clothiers' Hundred originally indicated merchants who dealt in trade with the west and Europe. In the last quarter of the seventeenth century the Woolen Clothiers' Hundred was subsumed into the Merchant Hundred. See Perkhavko, *Pervye kuptsy Rossiiskie*, 328.

3. Golikova, PKK, 297, 381, 443. On women: Perkhavko, "Kupchikhi depetrovskoi Rossii," 148–51.

For a scholarship in which so much explanatory power hinges on the "missing middle class," it is puzzling (or perhaps telling) that the most extensive work to date on this group is three chapters in N. B. Golikova's study.[4] The paucity of research on the Merchant Hundred calls out for correction. A new encounter with Russia's missing middle class is overdue. Beyond the fact that there was something of a middling class, paying attention to the merchants who relocated to Siberia because of the new opportunities they perceived there suggests the increasing integration of Siberia into the Russian Empire. Among the new opportunities was the developing trade between Muscovy and China, which accelerated in the 1690s. The state, as it began to organize the state caravan trade, recruited Merchant Hundred merchants to lead its state caravans. Of the fifteen state caravans dispatched between 1689 and 1719, Merchant Hundred merchants led several of these, but none were led by gosti.[5] Meanwhile, it left gosti such as the Filat'evs, Luzin, Nikitin, and Shorin to continue in their private affairs.

In some sense, it is disingenuous to talk of the Merchant Hundred as "the middle." After all, these traders had attained privileged status. Meanwhile, recall that privileged merchants did not even dominate the trade moving through Siberia: hundreds of traders who crossed the Urals never bore such status. According to Vilkov, nonprivileged merchants accounted for two-thirds of "Russian" goods brought to Siberia.[6] Since the "middle" was much broader than the categories of privileged merchants, this chapter begins by pausing on a long-lived merchant family that never attained privileged ranks.

Noritsyn Family

The Noritsyn family hailed from Lal'sk, a small town west of the Ural Mountains nestled in the forests of the Russian North. Lal'sk was located in Ustiug district about 50 kilometers dead east of the large town of Velikii Ustiug. It first appeared in the sixteenth century, allegedly established by Novgorodians who fled the horrors of Ivan IV's *Oprichnina*. Taking the commercial vibe

---

4. Golikova, PKK. Monahan, "Trade and Empire," chap. 5.

5. Aleksandrov, "Russko-kitaiskaia torgovlia," 427; Aleksandrov counts seven state caravans from 1689 to 1697. Kurts, *Gosudarstvennaia monopoliia*, details eight state caravans, six of which were dispatched before the 1728 Treaty of Kiakhta, four of which appear to have been led by Merchant Hundred merchants. Ides's and Lange's state caravans bring the number to fifteen.

6. Vilkov, "Tranzit 'russkikh' tovarov," 113–26. If this was generally true of Siberian trade for most of the seventeenth century, it was not true of the documented China trade in the 1690s where gosti dominated.

of Novgorod with them, the town became filled with artisans and petty merchants who made their livelihoods in craft production and trade. So thoroughly did these endeavors occupy the townspeople that Lal'sk was notable in the seventeenth century for not having much of an agricultural population. To an unusual degree for a premodern rural community, people bought foodstuffs with earnings from sales of goods that they made or traded. Lal'sk artisans produced many of the goods that merchants brought to supply the Siberian population in exchange for furs and fabrics. Some gosti sourced their agents from Lal'sk, prompting one historian to call it a "nest of agents."[7] For many, this tiny town—which consisted of just sixty-three households in 1654—was the launchpad for journeys of thousands of miles. Noritsyns lived there from at least 1609.[8]

From 1624 to 1744, at least twenty-nine different Noritsyn men traveled to Siberia to trade. The surprising ubiquity across time and space of this family reveals that people who never attained privileged status sustained themselves across generations on the Siberian trade, suggesting a certain vibrancy for the layers of commercial activity below the privileged strata. The Noritsyn family worked for privileged merchants across several generations, they had links to major elite traders of both gosti and boyar ranks, and they engaged in Siberian trade on their own accounts as well: at some moments they trafficked in horses. And yet, despite regularly brushing shoulders with the commercial elite, they never joined the privileged ranks themselves.

The Noritsyn family are first on record trading in Siberia when the Romanov dynasty had existed but for a decade and as Russian military brigades in tandem with hunters and trappers (*vatagi*) were doggedly moving eastward in search of furs. In their first Siberian ventures, they were in the employ of well-known and well-capitalized merchants. In 1624 Petr Stepanov Noritsyn brought 600 rubles worth of Russian goods to Tomsk as the agent of Andrei and Petr Stroganov.[9] At least four other Noritsyn men ventured into Siberia in the 1630s. Their numbers—in Lal'sk and in Siberia—grew as the century progressed. By midcentury in Lal'sk there were six different Noritsyn households, all related. In 1673/74 about ten different

7. Makarov, "Volostnye torzhki," 193–219.

8. I am deeply indebted to Yulia Strazdyn' of the Lal'sk Historical Museum for her generous help in obtaining information about the Noritsyn family. Via e-mail correspondence, she has shared information from Lal'sk property survey books (*perepisnye knigi*) printed in I. S. Ponomarëv's *Sbornik materialov po istorii goroda Lal'ska Vologodskoi gubernii*, 1897), the archive of Velikii Ustiug (Velikoustiuzhskii gosudarstvennii arkhiv, f. 27, op. 1, d. 9), and church record books (*Metricheskie knigi*) of Resurrection Church in Lal'sk, as well as her personal knowledge.

9. TKSG, vol. 2, 92.

Noritsyns passed through Verkhotur'e customs, typically in groups assisting one another. Not all of the Noritsyn men were merchants and their degree of wealth varied, but some did quite well: Ivan Semenovich's operations were sufficiently extensive that he had a "man" operating on his behalf in Tobol'sk in 1670. In 1674 he had an income of at least 900 rubles. Meanwhile, that same year his kinsman Ivan Grigorievich Noritsyn paid taxes on an income of 500 rubles. This family was not so wealthy that they built their own church in their hometown of Lal'sk, but they were wealthy enough that they donated significant funds for the construction of a local church.[10]

Other Noritsyns knew financial hard times. One strategy for weathering financial hardship was debt servitude. In 1640, Nikifor Semenov Noritsyn gave off his eldest son Stepan to Gerasim V. Bel'skii as an indentured servant in order to cover his debts amounting to several hundred rubles.[11] Bel'skii was a very wealthy Moscow merchant who remained in the tax-paying city population, never rising to privileged merchant rank, even though his wealth allegedly far exceeded that of the greatest merchants of the day; in other words, a valuable connection.[12] In the next year, however, S. N. Noritsyn—whom I am presuming in this case was Stepan Nikiforov—was in Eniseisk, not as a ward or employee of Bel'skii but in the capacity of agent for one Ivan Usov, a Merchant Hundred merchant. Noritsyn was headed to the Lena region to deliver honey and supplies to a camp where Usov's *promyshlenniki* were acquiring fur pelts.[13] One year later, in September 1642, he returned to Lal'sk looking to buy up new wares with the money he had earned selling products at the Kholmogory fair.[14] In the autumn of 1659 Stepan Nikiforov Noritsyn secured state contracts to deliver several hundred rubles worth of grain, malt, and horse-shaft bows (*duga*), illustrating that, even though they never joined the privileged corporations, lesser merchants did serve the state in commerce-related capacities.[15] By the 1670s he was an agent of Ostafii Filat'ev and brought several of his own relatives along to help on long trips into Siberia.[16] The path that took Stepan from indebted householder to agent of the wealthiest merchant of Siberia held another steep change in fortune, however. At some point after 1677/78, Stepan Nikiforov syn (the younger) Noritsyn found himself in financial straits. His

---

10. E-mail from Julia Strazdyn', February 10, 2015.
11. Makarov, "Volostnye torzhki," 212.
12. Golikova, PKK, 182, 192.
13. Aleksandrov, "Rol' krupnogo kupechestva," 183.
14. Makarov, "Volostnye torzhki," 206.
15. Ibid., 204.
16. TKSG, vol. 3, 100.

wife retained their property in Lal'sk while Stepan and a nephew moved to Moscow to live in the household of the gost' Ostafii Filat'ev. The Lal'sk survey book records the merchant's name as Evstafii Filip'ev.[17] But there is little doubt that this is a mistaken rendering of Ostafii Filat'ev's name, for it was not unusual for Ostafii to be written as Evstafii and at the time there was no such gost' by the name of Filip'ev.

Meanwhile, Mikifor Stepanov Noritsyn (the grandson of Petr Noritsyn who was the Stroganov's agent in the 1620s, mentioned above) became the agent of the Moscow merchant G. Bel'skii; he declared goods at Verkhotur'e customs on his behalf in 1673/74.[18] After Mikifor Stepanov's father died in the late 1670s, he and two of his brothers, Mitka and Fedka, moved into the Bel'skii household in Moscow to cover their father's debts. It is interesting that Mikifor's father, Stepan, had been registered as a landless peasant (*bobyl'*), not a merchant, but he engaged in trade nonetheless. In 1639/40, Stepan Petrov and his brother Semen Petrov departed for Siberia together for trade. Stepan may have missed the birth of his son Mitka while away, but he was back with his family in 1646. His brother, Semen, however, was listed in the property survey as having "fled" to Siberia. Indeed, Siberia held both opportunity for the able and refuge for the desperate. In 1665/66, the brother of Stepan Mikiforov (agent of Ostafii Filat'ev in the 1670s) became impoverished and "fled to Siberia" after his property burned.[19] Perhaps in that same fire of 1665/66, the property of Stepan's relative Fëdor Stepanov syn also burned and he relocated, not to Siberia but to the Archangel monastery in Velikii Ustiug.[20] These moments of indebtedness and fleeing, in a town with such a large extended family, call into question the nature and the limits of kinship. Certainly we see much family cooperation at the customs house and in the shared living conditions recorded in property records. Without more and different sources, a richer narrative eludes us. But perhaps we see members of the Noritsyn family resorting to debt servitude because it was not a stigmatized mark of ultimate failure but a strategy by which one could become solvent again while, if one worked for a merchant enterprise,

17. *Perepisnye knigi* of 1682, in Ponomarëv, *Sbornik materialov* via Julia Strazdyn', e-mail, February 10, 2015.

18. TKSG, vol. 3, 92, 100.

19. *Perepisnye knigi* of 1682, in Ponomarëv, *Sbornik materialov* via Julia Strazdyn', e-mail, February 10, 2015. The brother in question, confusedly, was named Stepan Mikiforov the Bigger. Since Russians typically named their children after the nearest Saint's day, children born at the same time of year could often end up with the same first name.

20. From *Perepisnye knigi* of 1682, in Ponomarëv, *Istoriia goroda Lal'ska Vologodskoi gubernii*, via Julia Strazdyn', e-mail, February 10, 2015.

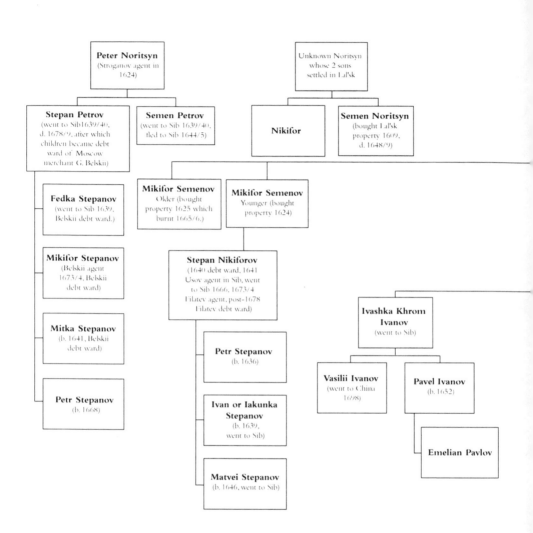

FIGURE 8.1 Noritsyn family tree. I have made certain tenuous assumptions to construct this figure. In some cases, no patronymic is provided, but I have assigned an individual a place in the genealogy based on similar chronology and/or proximity in the historical record. Also, the lexicon of names from which Russians drew was limited, often determined by the saint's day nearest to the day of birth. On top of that, certain family names tended to repeat. As a result the same name-patronymic combinations repeat in the Norisyn genealogy. For example, we encounter a Mikifor Semenov in the early seventeenth century and in the early eighteenth century. And there were two Petr Stepanovs from different branches of the family whose lifetimes probably overlapped. Without knowing an individual's lifespan or age when mentioned in the sources, it is impossible to be sure I have situated them generationally correctly, but I have made my best attempt. Ultimately, at the risk of depicting the Noritsyn family tree imperfectly, this visual conveys the breadth and longevity of this family and its members who did business in Siberia. In this figure Sib is short for Siberia.

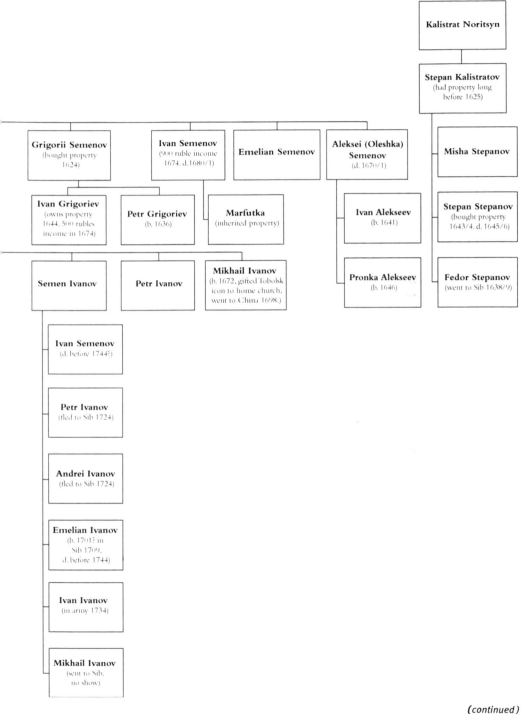

(continued)

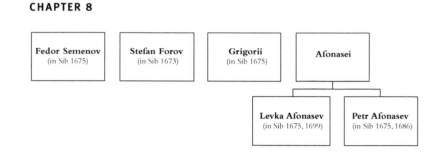

Figure 8.1   (continued)

simultaneously learning skills and gaining valuable experience to be profitably leveraged in future endeavors.

Just as kinship ties shaped elite merchant networks, they were a guiding principle in lower strata of early modern Russian commerce as well. Agents of gosti traveled with their brothers and nephews for help. Elite merchants would sometimes source their help from one family. Like privileged merchants, other Noritsyns besides Ivan Semenovich employed men to manage rented shop spaces and assist in moving consignments.[21] But the term for their auxiliary help is "man." Although it is not unheard of to see agents of agents (Filat'ev's and Shababin's agents had agents) in Siberian customs books, I have not encountered anyone specifically labeled a Noritsyn "agent."[22] Of course, agents were typically not family, and the Noritsyn family network was so deep that they sourced assistance among the family pool more often than not.

While some Noritsyns worked as hired help, others traded in Siberia on their own account. Some were likely engaged in a combination of support and independent trade as they took advantage of safety in numbers and comfort in kin company. Working for the Filat'evs may have provided a springboard to trade in China independently. In 1698/99 Mikhail Ivanov Noritsyn received permission for himself, his nephew Vasilii Ivanov, and six

---

21. RGADA, f. 1111, op. 2, d. 599, l. 26; RGADA, f. 214, kn. 892; TKSG, vol. 1, 45, 48, 63.
22. Vilkov, *Remeslo i torgovlia*, 252.

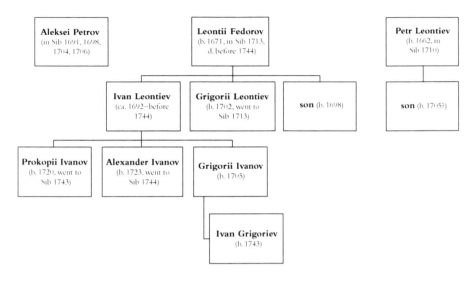

others to travel to China to trade goods of his making and furs.[23] Perhaps it was in anticipation of this trip, and the dangers entailed, that Mikhail gifted to his local church in Tobol'sk an icon of the Virgin Mary that he had commissioned—that is, copied—from the same icon in Tobol'sk that had been painted there in 1636. That icon is undergoing restoration as this book goes to print.[24]

The Noritsyns gained a reputation for their experience and expertise in Siberia. Very much connected to privileged merchant networks, they nonetheless maintained an identity set apart. For example, Aleksei Noritsyn, a fourth-generation (at least) Noritsyn involved in Siberian commerce, was appointed by the gost' Ushakov to handle the collection of his goods when Ushakov's agent died on the road short of Sol'vychegodsk on his way back from China in 1691.[25] This task bears great responsibility, yet Noritsyn was not specifically named as an agent of Ushakov. On a separate occasion, a Noritsyn man was called on to sort out the remaining merchandise of agents who died while in the field.[26] Aleksei Noritsyn had been trading actively in Siberia on his own account for the previous decade and would continue to do so. In 1697/98 Aleksei Noritsyn declared a small shipment of furs to the

23. RGADA, f. 1111, op. 2, d. 599, l. 26.
24. I thank Yulia Strazdyn' for this information.
25. RGADA, f. 159, op. 5, d. 290, l. 2.
26. RGADA, f. 214, op. 5, d. 290; f. 1111, op. 2, d. 599, ll. 7–8.

Siberian office.[27] In December 1704 Aleksei Petrov syn Noritsyn (in this customs book his patronymic was recorded; I surmise the records refer to one Aleksei) spent about a month in Tiumen' buying up nine horses from local state porters (*iamshchiki*), Cossacks, soldiers, and townsmen. He paid between 1.5 and 5 rubles for each horse, and transported them all back to Russian towns.[28] It may be that this was a niche that Aleksei developed for himself, or was a means to an end: Noritsyn merchants relied heavily on horses for transport. For example, they arrived at Verkhotur'e customs on separate occasions in 1673/74 with goods laden on twenty-eight and thirty-one horses.[29] Alternatively, a reason that remains out of view, such as fulfilling an order for a Boyar prince, may account for this spurt of horse purchasing.

The Noritsyn family adopted practices followed by privileged and non-privileged merchants alike. They borrowed and lent money close to home, as we have seen, and in the credit markets of Siberia. They also looked to the tsar in Moscow for advocacy on commercial matters. In Irkutsk in 1697/98 Levka Noritsyn lent 600 rubles to Ivan Stupin, who was about to embark for China. Stupin was in the employ of Andrei Nikitin, a nephew of the gost' Gavril R. Nikitin. They agreed that Stupin would repay the loan by June 29, 1699 in Nerchinsk. Six months before the loan was due, however, in January 1699, Levka appealed to the chancery in Verkhotur'e voicing concerns over recouping his debt. Ivan Stupin had not yet returned from China, but Gavril R. Nikitin had passed away in prison and his property was being impounded by the state. Levka asked the tsar to intervene by sending a letter to the Nerchinsk governor authorizing and directing him to allow Levka to collect his debt as arranged.[30] Even far from Moscow, Levka's access to knowledge networks and experience enabled him to act preemptively to protect his interests.

The Noritsyn family illustrates the strong regional ties between northern Russian towns and Siberia. Some historians, notably S. V. Bakhrushin, advised that Siberian economic history should be studied in conjunction with the northern towns of Russia.[31] They would be gratified to know that the Noritsyn family enterprises bear out that claim, and they are not alone. More than gosti, or even members of the Merchant Hundred, merchants from the northern Russian towns of Ustiug district are the ones who traveled

---

27. RGADA, f. 214, op. 5, d. 841, l. 3.
28. GBUTO GATO, f. 29, op. 1, d. 38, ll. 1–7. This was slightly below average prices, as Hellie ascertained in *Economy and Material Culture*, 40–46.
29. TKSG, vol. 3, 91, 100.
30. RGADA, f. 1111, op. 2, d. 599, l. 7.
31. Bakhrushin, "Torgovye krest'iane v XVII v.," in NT, 2: 118–34.

regularly to Siberia and returned with furs and fabrics to Ustiug, where their pelts advanced north to Arkhangel'sk or south to Moscow. Traders from Moscow rarely ventured to Siberia. Instead, they headed north by river to Sol'vychegodsk and Velikii Ustiug to meet parties returning from Siberia.

In all, records leave traces of at least twenty-nine different men from the Noritsyn family who engaged in Siberian commerce from 1624 to 1744. The Noritsyn family registered just over sixty transactions, which is roughly equivalent to one-third of the total number of Merchant Hundred transactions in Siberia encountered in this research. My sense is that there were other families like them—the Vorypaev family of the Bosov network is just one example. We can only speculate whether not entering the privileged corporations was a deliberate choice, or if attaining that rank was an aspiration unrealized, and if so, what the explanation is. Baron suggested that the gosti used their clout in ways that inhibited wealth accumulation of lower classes of merchants.[32] Although I accept that gosti understood the advantages of eliminating competition, Baron's implication that gosti are culpable for an underdeveloped middle class is unsubstantiated. Certainly this seems less demonstrable in Siberia, where one finds merchants like the Noritsyns commanding trade and establishing niches across generations. However fragmentary the data about their affairs, the Noritsyns' sustained and substantive engagement in Siberian commerce suggests the existence of a broad middling merchant corps.

We observe this family through its ups and downs across the seventeenth and eighteenth centuries. We see them in affluence and indebtedness. At certain moments, the Noritsyns seemed well positioned to attain privileged status but did not. One might take this fact, along with the examples of indebtedness we have encountered, as an example of the sort of "failed middle class" that marks this historiography. But the Noritsyn family, to my mind, more appropriately invites a much different interpretation. First, they owned substantial property and paid taxes—sometimes quite large amounts—in their hometown of Lal'sk. As agents, state contractors, and merchants of their own account, they were a family of some stature, albeit modest relative to the gosti elite. Finally, that this family endured is a mark of success. From roughly 1600 to 1750 I have encountered over sixty-five men of the Noritsyn family, twenty of whom traded in Siberia. They did not disappear from the merchant ranks. They remained among the ranks of guild merchants in the eighteenth century. In the nineteenth century a Noritsyn

---

32. Baron, "Weber Thesis," 335.

founded a paper factory, and to this day, descendants of the Noritsyn family continue to reside in Lal'sk.[33]

Anatomy of the Merchant Hundred

Men from such merchant families could, in principle, rise to the Merchant Hundred, the larger, less exclusive "feeder pool" of privileged merchants from which gosti were in turn drawn. As in any highly competitive environment, most members of the Merchant Hundred did not progress to that more select status up the commercial pyramid. Only a fraction did. Thanks to the work of S. V. Bakhrushin, G. R. Nikitin's career is a well-known case of seventeenth-century upward (and downward) mobility.[34] Meanwhile, even as most historians intuitively surmise that G. R. Nikitin was not a lone case of upward merchant mobility, other such trajectories remain poorly charted. Reconstructing the careers of Russian merchants of humble origins who progressed to the privileged ranks of the Merchant Hundred demonstrates concretely upward social mobility in early modern Russian. Andrei Gostev and his son Il'ia Gostev offer a portrait of two generations managing a family business. Spiridon Iakovlev Liangusov, who began his career in the Gostev family's employ, went on himself to become a Merchant Hundred member. These merchants, who hailed from northern European Russia, demonstrate the opportunities the Siberian frontier presented for commercial entrepreneurs in seventeenth- and early eighteenth-century Russia.

The Merchant Hundred corporation was not merely a feeder pool for gosti. It fulfilled important commercial functions. Where gosti were in charge of European Russia's major customs posts in Moscow and the border towns, Merchant Hundred merchants always accompanied them as assistants. Merchant Hundred merchants also served in various commerce-related capacities in the Siberian Office (and presumably other chanceries). Indeed, indicative of the overall growth of the Muscovite government in the seventeenth century, the archive of the Siberian Office reveals that an increasing number of Merchant Hundred merchants staffed the department across the seventeenth and early eighteenth century.[35]

When they were not serving the state—and sometimes when they were—Merchant Hundred merchants attended to their own commercial

---

33. E-mail correspondence with Yulia Strazdyn', March 3, 2015.
34. Bakhrushin, "Torgi gostia Nikitina," in NT, 3: 226–51; Monahan, "Gavril Romanov Nikitin," 47–56.
35. See Ogloblin, *Obozrenie* 3:195, 341–42; 4:61, 78–85, 87, 91, 95.

affairs. A sampling of records from the 1620s to 1728 found fifty-four merchants of the Merchant Hundred operating in Siberia. Many Merchant Hundred merchants operated at a complex enough scale that, like gosti, they often had agents trading on their behalf represent them at Siberian customs. But whereas gosti themselves did not venture to Siberia, Merchant Hundred merchants did. For example, the Merchant Hundred merchant Fëdor Gorokhov, who was sent to Siberia to buy up grain in order to pay soldiers' salaries in the winter of 1644, also traded in Siberia himself on his own account as well in that same decade.[36]

Like gosti, Merchant Hundred or other merchants might be assigned to lead trips, a practice that obtained throughout the corporation's existence. The incidence of Merchant Hundred merchants leading state trips intensified in the trade between Russia and China that emerged in the late seventeenth century. Although they were not exclusively used, Merchant Hundred merchants were critical in executing state affairs in the Middle Kingdom. To speculate why, perhaps rather than interfere in the affairs of the gosti known to be actively trading in China, the state looked to the ranks of Merchant Hundred merchants to help the state profit alongside the gosti who were dominating this emerging trade.

The Noritsyns and families like them were the building blocks on which greater trade houses were built. They should be kept in mind as we discuss merchants of the privileged ranks, the Gostevs and the Liangusovs. The Gostevs were Merchant Hundred merchants of a privileged but modest sort. Their agent, Spiridon Iakovlev Liangusov, went on to become a key merchant in the burgeoning China trade at the end of the century.

Gostev

Andrei Kuzmich Gostev was the first to rise to privileged merchant status from a family whose origins in the Russian North remain obscure.[37] Like so many northerners, he was of a commercial bent. He engaged in the Siberian trade and did quite well for himself, such that he had agents in his employ by midcentury. His "man," Luchka Andreev, declared sixty moose hides and five coats of rabbit fur for him in the 1640s.[38] Extant documents show Andrei Kuzmich Gostev as a member of the Merchant Hundred from at least 1658,

36. RGADA, f. 214, stb. 134, l. 51; RGADA, f. 1111, op. 2, d. 26, l. 26 (1644).
37. Iakovlev, *Tamozhennye knigi Moskovskogo gosudarstva XVII v.*, 1: 200.
38. SPbII RAN, f. 187, op. 1, d. 1, l. 1.

a rank he held until his death in 1664.[39] He seems to have retained modest methods, nonetheless. Gostev was out in the field with his agents, as likely to declare his own goods at customs as to have his men working for him. He appears twice in a customs book from Tiumen' for 1661/62 with different men in his employ each time. Meanwhile, Luchka Andreev appeared several more times on Gostev's behalf at Tiumen' customs in the early 1660s.[40]

The years 1661–63 were busy in Siberia for Andrei Gostev. On January 5, 1662 Gostev's agent Iakov Mikoforov with his son Spirka made a declaration (listed in the same entry as the gost' Semen Zadorin's agent and traders from Ustiug). Iakov paid the modest sum of 9 altyn, 2 dengi (almost one-third of a ruble) on a shipment he jointly declared with about half a dozen other merchants, including an agent of Zadorin.[41] Two days later Luchka Andreev declared goods on Gostev's behalf.[42] On August 18, Gostev's agent Kirill Ivanov arrived at Tobol'sk customs on his way back from Tomsk.[43] On February 2, 1663, Gostev's "man," Filka Kondratiev, arrived at Tiumen' from Verkhotur'e and paid portage tax at Tiumen' for one sled with a porter.[44] Less than two weeks later, on February 15, 1663, the agent Kirill Ivanov returned to Tiumen' from Tobol'sk with a shipment that was large enough to require the help of Gostev's men Misha Ondreev and Filka Kondratiev. Andrei Gostev was traveling with Iakov Parfanov from Lal'sk, the Noritsyns' hometown. Together they paid tax on five sleds and five porters.[45] Gostev's agents were going about their business amid illustrious-by-proxy company: within the month agents of the gosti Filat'evs, Shorin, Zadorin, and Gusel'nikov, and peasants of Boyar Boris Ivanovich Morozov and Fëdor Stroganov all passed through that same Tiumen' customs posts.[46] January was one of the busiest months at western Siberian customs, as many mobilized for the Irbit fair.

Andrei Kuzmich Gostev groomed his son to take over the family business, which he did when Andrei passed on. The transactions of this father and son team account for almost one-quarter of the total transactions recorded

39. Golikova, PKK, 314.
40. SPbII RAN, f. 187, op. 2, d. 20, l. 26 (1661/62); d. 21, ll. 1–21 (1662/63). Another potential kinsman was one Ivan Gostev from Bobrovskii, who, in the fall of 1635 at Ustiug customs, sold hops (xmel') and rye (rzhy) to the Ustiug tavern and Ignatii Kabakov.
41. SPbII RAN, f. 187, op. 2, d. 20, l. 26.
42. SPbII RAN, f. 187, op. 2, d. 20, l. 26.
43. Vilkov, "Tobol'sk—tsentr tamozhennoi sluzhby," 136.
44. GBUTO GATO, f. 47, op. 1, d. 381, l. 110.
45. Ibid.
46. SPbII RAN, f. 187, op. 2, d. 20, ll. 15 (Boyar B. I. Morozov's peasant passed through on December 12), 24, 25v, 26, 29.

by privileged merchants in the customs books studied.[47] Their numerous appearances together assure one that Il'ia was not a complete novice when the time came to assume responsibility for his father's dealings in Siberia. The 1663 entries are the last I found for Andrei Gostev in the customs books. That same year Il'ia Andreevich Gostev appeared at customs without his father. Not long after, in 1664, Andrei Gostev was no longer recorded among the ranks of the Merchant Hundred.

As observed in networks of gosti merchants, one finds kin networks within kin networks in the commercial operations of the Gostevs. In 1663 Il'ia appeared at customs with his agent, Spiridon Iakovlev (Liangusov). "Spirka," as he was first named in the customs books, was the son of Andrei Gostev's agent, Iakov Mikiforov. Spiridon, as he would be known in adulthood, accompanied his father on a trip in 1659 "for security," reads the customs book entry.[48] He grew up to be Il'ia's agent before moving on to even greater success and status. Ten years after appearing at the Tiumen' customs post helping his dad with security, Spiridon Iakovlev was a member of the Merchant Hundred and had his own agents doing his bidding in the markets of Siberia.

Whereas often a son would be awarded privileged status to replace his father upon passing, this was not the case with Il'ia Gostev. His father disappears from the record in 1664, yet Il'ia was not made a Merchant Hundred merchant for several years afterward. This was managed meritocracy, where candidates without connections had to work harder to prove their merit. For his part, Il'ia seems to have spent little time in Moscow trying to curry favor at the center. Throughout his career he is sometimes referred to as a Merchant Hundred member of Viatka. Indeed, he received the substantial grant payment of 80 rubles in Viatka.[49] This distinction was never noted for his father. Like the better-known Bosov and Ushakov merchants, Gostev also found it profitable to maintain a base in the Russian North from which to launch Siberian operations.

---

47. The customs books studied, which do not exhaust the extant sources, are, in chronological order: Golovachev, *Tiumen' v XVII stoletii*, kn. 97, kn. 170; SPbII RAN, f. 187, op. 1, d. 1, ll. 1–3; op. 2, d. 17, ll. 1–25; RGADA, f. 214, kn. 301, ll. 1–100; GBUTO GATO, f. 47, op. 1, d. 378, l. 1; SPbII RAN, f. 187, op. 2, d. 20, ll. 1–33; GBUTO GATO, f. 47, op. 1, d. 381, ll. 1–127; TKSG, 4 vols.; RGADA, f. 214, kn. 588, ll. 1–14; SPbII RAN, f. 187, op. 2, d. 52, ll. 1–8; RGADA, f. 1111, op. 1, d. 187, ll. 120–33; SPbII RAN, f. 187, op. 2, d. 80, ll. 1–8; RGADA, f. 214, kn. 1398, ll. 224–462; stb. 1376, ll. 1035–59; GBUTO GATO, f. 29, op. 1, d. 88, ll. 1–9; d. 139, ll. 1–23; d. 29, ll. 1–12; d. 36, 16 ll.; d. 37, ll. 1–10; d. 38, ll. 1–44; d. 39, ll. 1–9; d. 40, ll. 1–6; d. 134, ll. 1–38.

48. SPbII RAN, f. 187, op. 2, d. 20, l. 26.

49. Golikova, PKK, 446.

By the early 1670s, Il'ia Andreevich Gostev had proved his merit sufficiently to earn entrance into the Merchant Hundred corporation.[50] He
remained in the Merchant Hundred corporation for about three decades
until his death in 1704.[51] Il'ia Gostev appeared in western Siberia in the
second half of the seventeenth century more often than any other merchant
of the Merchant Hundred encountered in this research. He himself traveled
about Siberia on trade and had at least three agents in his employ: Spiridon
Iakovlev, Eleska Fëdorov, and Ivan Makarov. In one declaration Ivan Makarov
is listed as a shop manager (*sidelets*). Ofonka Kharitonov and Kuzka Kalmak
worked for him as shop managers, while additional people were recruited to
help protect and move larger shipments. This network cooperated with one
another in the field: for example, in one case the agent Ivan Makarov left
some goods behind with Spiridon Iakovlev.

Il'ia Gostev's activities are unique because he is the only privileged Russian merchant whom I observed explicitly cooperating with Bukharan merchants. In Tara in 1674/75 Il'ia Gostev's agent carried a shipment of goods
to Tobol'sk on behalf of a Bukharan merchant. It seems to have been more
than a one-off cooperation, because on another occasion that same year,
Il'ia Gostev's agent and a Bukharan jointly paid a warehousing fee in Tara.[52]
These rare examples of formal cooperation may have occurred more than
the historical record reflects.

On March 19, 1674, Il'ia Gostev's agent Spiridon Iakovlev passed through
Verkhotur'e on his way back from Tobol'sk. He had two shop managers, as
well as a Kalmyk slave girl named Sedeleika, helping him with a shipment
that occupied seventeen wares-laden horses. They paid warehouse charges
for three days before continuing on their way to Rus'.[53] Ten days later, brav-
ing mud season on what must have been an early spring, on March 29, 1674,
Il'ia Gostev's agent Sava Fëdorov arrived at Verkhotur'e from Solikamsk
with a shipment loaded on eleven horses. He was carrying all sorts of goods
invaluable for settlers in Siberia—pots, spoons, needles, European fabrics, as
well as—perhaps surprisingly, since he was heading east—"Eastern" products
such as silk and pepper. Customs officials valued the shipment at 810 rubles,
23 altyn, and 2 dengi. He had additional men with him for protection

50. TKSG, vol. 4: 50–51. Golikova recorded that he entered the corporation in 1676, but his
declaration in a Tiumen' customs book from 1672/73 already lists him as a Merchant Hundred
merchant.

51. Golikova, PKK, 331; TKSG, vol. 1, 83, 98; vol. 3, 72,106.

52. TKSG, vol. 1, 86.

53. TKSG, vol. 3, 73.

and help, including his nephew Malafeiko Prokop'ev.[54] Six years later, Sava Fëdorov again traveled to Siberia as Il'ia Gostev's agent, passing through Verkhotur'e with 1,003 rubles worth of declared merchandise in May 1680.[55]

Membership in the Merchant Hundred enhanced his fortunes. By the mid-1680s Il'ia Gostev had new agents working for his growing trade enterprise. Grigorii Ignatiev paid a cart tax as Il'ia Gostev's man, along with the trade stall manager Karpushka Fëdorov in October 1686.[56] Perhaps the agent Zotsei Grigoriev, who paid one-tenth tax on six thousand squirrel hides upon arriving to Tiumen' from Verkhotur'e on January 8, 1687, was the son of the agent Grigorii Ignatiev, revealing another father-son team amid the Gostev enterprises.[57] Yet Zotsei (or "Izotko," as it is rendered in another document) is not a typical Russian-sounding name; perhaps Zotsei was a non-Russian, baptized property of Grigorii Ignatiev. Grigorii Ignatiev declared furs purchased at various bazaars worth a total of 171 rubles in Tobol'sk later that winter on February 21, 1687. Il'ia Gostev's agent Ivan Kurtiev declared a shipment of wares worth 185 rubles, 18 altyn, and 2 dengi in Tobol'sk on March 15, 1687, which he sent with the trade stall manager Zotsei (Izotko) Grigoriev Plotnikov off to Tara.[58] Ivan Vasiliev Kurtiev rented two trading stalls on Il'ia Gostev's behalf in March 1687.[59] In March 1687, Il'ia Gostev's agent Ivan Kurtiev and the trade stall manager Izotko Plotnikov declared two sledges at Tobol'sk customs.[60] Kurtiev transported 788 rubles worth of goods to Tobol'sk customs in May 1687 for Gostev.[61] I have no evidence that Gostev himself traveled to China, but his transactions reveal that the emerging China trade had a gravitational pull even on Siberian merchants who did not travel there. In 1696 Gostev's shop manager in Nerchinsk sold a substantial amount of furs to agents of the Filat'evs, who were outfitting themselves to depart for Beijing.[62]

In all, Gostev or his agents appeared at Tobol'sk customs fifteen times in 1686 alone, declaring goods worth hundreds of rubles.[63] In the midst of this

---

54. TKSG, vol. 4, 106.

55. RGADA, f. 1111, op. 1, d. 187, l. 124.

56. RGADA, f. 214, kn. 892, l. 56v.

57. RGADA, f. 214, kn. 892, l. 82v.

58. RGADA, f. 214, kn. 892, l. 119v. Perhaps this is an alternate spelling for Zotsei Grigoriev, and this man worked for Il'ia Gostev in various capacities.

59. RGADA, f. 214, kn. 892, l. 129.

60. RGADA, f. 214, kn. 892, l. 131v.

61. RGADA, f. 214, kn. 892, l. 204.

62. Aleksandrov, "Russko-kitaiskaia torgovlia," 443.

63. My data do not provide a total value of these shipments.

activity, his agent Spiridon Iakovlev Liangusov disappeared from the ranks of the Gostev network. In 1686 when Il'ia Gostev's man Grigorii Ignatiev paid for renting a trading bench in Tobol'sk for September through April, Spiridon Iakovlev no longer worked for Il'ia Gostev.[64] He had himself become a member of the Merchant Hundred with his own agent network at work in Siberia.[65]

Spiridon Iakovlev Liangusov

Spiridon Iakovlev spent a lifetime engaged in Siberian trade. As indicated above, he first appeared at a Siberian customs post in 1659 as a boy accompanying his father, Iakov, who worked for Andrei Gostev. According to hometown survey records, "Spirka" was sixty years old in 1710, which means he was born at midcentury, and would have been about nine years old on that trip in 1659.[66] Spiridon Iakovlev hailed from the same region, but a different town than his Gostev bosses. The Gostevs seem to have been from the town of Viatka whereas Liangusov's native town was Khlynova (now Perm'), situated on a northern bank of the Kama River. This Viatka district, situated west of the Urals, has a long history with the early exploitation of Eurasian furs. Natives to what became the Perm' and Viatka districts of Muscovy paid tribute to Kazan, and sometimes Novgorod and Muscovy, before Muscovy finally asserted its authority over the area in the sixteenth century.

The Liangusovs were townsmen who lived on monastery lands. A 1678 survey records the residents in the household of "Spirka and Grishka, Iakovlev children of Liangusov." Along with Spirka and Grishka, there were two younger brothers, Petrushka, ten, and Zakharko, who was seven in 1678. The household also consisted of two purchased Kalmyk boys, five and fifteen years old.[67] Note that the Kalmyk girl, Sedeleiko, whom Spirka had purchased in 1674, was not counted among the household members. The number of Kalmyks that comprised the Liangusov household grew over the years. The household consisted of a total of seventeen people in the 1710 survey and continued to grow. All of the purchased Kalmyks of the household were baptized and given Christian names.[68]

---

64. RGADA, f. 1111, op. 1, d. 187, ll. 11, 49v, 67v, 77, 95, 109v.
65. TSKG, vol. 1, 98; vol. 3, 72; vol. 4, 27–75; SPbII RAN, f. 187, op. 2, d. 52, l. 4; RGADA, f. 214, kn. 892, ll. 67v, 88v; f. 1111, op. 2, d. 611, l. 52; AI, vol. 5, no. 268.
66. "Kupchina gostinoi sotni Spiridon Liangusov," 235.
67. Ibid., 234.
68. Ibid., 234–36.

Spiridon began his career tagging along with his father, and then independently in the employ of the Gostev merchants. Spiridon Iakovlev appears
on numerous occasions from 1672 to 1676 in Tiumen' and Verkhotur'e
as Gostev's agent. He traded with sufficient success that, in 1680, he was
initiated into the Merchant Hundred, a rank he would hold until his death
in 1713.[69] A decree dated February 15, 1680 admitted twelve men "from
Kadashevskii borough" into the Merchant Hundred and fifteen men into the
Woolen Clothiers' Hundred. Among those were men "of Viatka, Spiridon
Liagusov [sic] with brothers."[70] The Kadashevskii neighborhood was home
to many merchants and artisans. The language is vague, but being named
as both a Kadashevets and as a man of Viatka suggests that Spiridon was a
recent, previous, or dual resident of Moscow at the time of his admission to
the Merchant Hundred.[71]

He was admitted to the Merchant Hundred "along with his brothers."
This was typical of the less exclusive Merchant Hundred—some scholars
consider that Merchant Hundred status automatically extended to siblings
and children. Practically speaking, one wonders to what extent the twelve-
and nine-year-old Petr and Zakharko participated. That their old brother
had accompanied their father on trips to Siberia at nine years of age reveals
they were at an age to be capable of contributing, even if their capacity for
independent action or serving, for example, in the Siberian Office was likely
limited. In contrast to the Noritsyns, Spiridon Liangusov does not seem to
have had deep kin reserves to assist him in Siberia. In 1659, the same year
that he first appeared at Siberian customs, Ivan Ivanov Liangusov of Khlynov,
likely a relative, was kidnapped by Kalmyks and sold to Crimean Tatars. After
escaping captivity, a vision of two icons appeared to him in a dream. Miracu-
lously, he later came on the exact icons in Saratov. He acquired them both,
left one in Saratov, according to instructions of the angel in his vision, and
brought the icon of the Mother of God Odigitrii to Solovetskii lavra, where
it was received by Arkhimandrite Varfolomei in 1662.[72] If Ivan Ivanov Liangusov ever engaged in Siberian trade with Spiridon, it has slipped through
the records. Spiridon's other brother, Grigorii, did travel to Siberia with him

69. Aleksandrov, "Russko-kitaiskaia torgovlia," 438 fn.48. He cites f. 214, kn. 588. TKSG,
vols. 2, 3, 4. Golikova, PKK, 337. On 374 Golikova writes that Spiridon Liangusov, from the town
of Khlynov, was in the Merchant Hundred from 1682 to 1713. The historian Kurts called Spiridon
Liagusov [sic] a gost' in 1700, but Golikova's study does not report him as having reached that rank.
Kurts, Gosudarstvennaia monopoliia, 1.
70. Golikova, PKK, 338.
71. Ibid., 337.
72. Bychkov, Katalog sobraniia slaviano-russkikh rukopisei, 149–50.

in 1674. The two declared goods together at Turinsk customs, along with Grigorii's son, Misha, who, sadly, was not counted among the household four years later in 1678.[73]

Leaving Gostev's employ appears to have been amicable. As in the case of the Filat'evs and G. R. Nikitin (mentioned in chapter 6), customs data records continued cooperation between Liangusov and the Gostev network. For the months of September, October, and November 1686, Spiridon rented a Tobol'sk trading bench next to his former boss Il'ia Gostev.[74] Although Spiridon did not rent a trading stall in Tobol'sk in December 1686 and January 1687, his agent Ivan Aleksandrov Zverev was in Siberia trading on his behalf. Zverev declared bazaar purchases worth 211 rubles in Tobol'sk on January 29, 1687.[75] One month later on February 27, 1687, Ivan Zverev again declared 148 rubles worth of fur that "his people" had brought to Tobol'sk from Surgut.[76] Spiridon, atypically, employed a female shop manager. Akinfeika Vasileva paid tax on two sleds at Tobol'sk customs also in February 1687.[77] A son, Filat, was born to Spiridon in about 1686, but this did not prevent him from making the trek to Siberia in the winter of 1687.[78] The venture was major, for Spiridon Iakovlev Liangusov came from Russia (accompanied by other trading people who remained nameless in the customs entry) with a large amount of assorted Russian wares worth 359 rubles and paid rent for two trading stalls at the marketplace in February and March 1687.[79] In May 1687, Spiridon (or his agent) arrived at Tobol'sk with a Verkhotur'e visa and almost 800 rubles worth of merchandise, which included Russian wares and pearls.[80] In these endeavors, Spiridon was tapping into the local and regional needs of Siberia. There was money to be made (or fabrics and furs to be acquired) by supplying Siberia with Russian and "German" goods.

Spiridon Iakovlev Liangusov's horizons extended beyond Siberia-Rus' regional trade; he was instrumental in the emerging China trade. In the wake of the Treaty of Nerchinsk of 1689, officially sanctioned trade between Russia and China increased significantly. As merchants such as the Filat'evs, Shorins, Luzins, and Gavril Nikitin directed their energy to the China trade,

---

73. TKSG, vol. 2, 50; "Kupchina gostinoi sotni Spiridon Liangusov," 234.
74. RGADA, f. 214, kn. 892, l. 11.
75. RGADA, f. 214, kn. 892, l. 89.
76. RGADA, f. 214, kn. 892, l. 105.
77. RGADA, f. 214, kn. 892, l. 111. Sedeleika was the Kalmyk girl he bought in 1674, see above.
78. "Kupchina gostinoi sotni Spiridon Liangusov," 235.
79. RGADA, f. 214, kn. 892, ll. 99–101v, 110, 128v, 142.
80. RGADA, f. 214, kn. 892, l. 202v.

the state recruited other merchants to trade in China on its behalf. Such initiatives shaped the decade for Spiridon Liangusov.

In the summer of 1693, a caravan of 209 people, and many more horses and other livestock, left the small fortress town of Nerchinsk bound for Beijing, the capital of the Chinese Empire. Eberhard Ides, a Dutchman in the Russian service, led the state caravan. But it was not an exclusively state endeavor. In addition to the 23 state servitors, 26 agents of privileged merchants and about 160 support people headed eastward from the Siberian outpost. Among them was Spiridon Liangusov, carrying 3,667 rubles worth of goods consisting mostly of furs and Russian (or German) wares to trade in Beijing.[81] The China trade was growing fast; it would define the decade for Spiridon Liangusov, who would lead state caravans himself in the coming years, as the government in Moscow sought to partake in the profits Russian merchants were already reaping in the bourgeoning China trade. After dispatching his own goods with the caravan of Eberhard Ides in 1693, Spiridon traveled to China on the state's behalf—documents refer to him as a *kupchina*, or "state merchant"—for three or four consecutive years from 1694 to 1699.[82] Remarkably, a son was born to the forty-five-year-old Spiridon in 1695, prompting one to wonder if his wife accompanied him on his travels, as Bukharan wives sometimes did, or about the veracity of either the above-cited document or the conjugal fidelity in the Liangusov home.[83]

The experience he accrued on these trips put Liangusov in good stead to lead a state caravan. In February 1697 he departed from Moscow bound for China.[84] The caravan made its way along Russian rivers, across the Urals, and progressed slowly along rivers and portages of Siberia until it reached Irkutsk, where the caravan's final outfitting took place. In Irkutsk the governor was to issue Liangusov furs of sable, sable bellies, ermine, lynx, and squirrel from tribute collections and in-kind customs revenue. In addition, the caravan was fortified in Irkutsk with sixty servitors for security, two translators, and grants in money, grain, and salt.[85] Then the entire caravan was loaded onto two large flat-bottom boats (*doshchaniki*) that the Irkutsk governor had procured in order to cross Lake Baikal. Before departing, Liangusov received new orders altering his route itinerary. He had left Moscow in February 1697 with a directive to travel to China via Selengisk, south across the steppe,

81. Aleksandrov, "Russko-kitaiskaia torgovlia," 427, 439.
82. AI, vol. 5, no. 268, 499.
83. "Kupchina gostinoi sotni Spiridon Liangusov," 235.
84. Aleksandrov, "Russko-kitaiskaia torgovlia," 459.
85. DAI, vol. 10, no. 67, 284–85 (February 8 and 15, 1697).

along a new route the gost' G. R. Nikitin had pioneered in 1674. But in March 1697, one month after Liangusov had departed Moscow, the Kremlin dispatched to Irkutsk a fast courier with the new instructions, who reached Irkutsk in October 1697, before Liangusov's caravan. Because of fighting among Kalmyks, Mongols, and Chinese on the steppe, Liangusov was forbidden to travel via Selengisk. Instead, he should proceed to China from Nerchinsk.[86] Indeed, part of what drove the growth of Nerchinsk as the departure point for the China trade was the Dzhungar-Mongol-China war that had begun in 1688, which hampered the existing trade route to China along the Irtysh River via Lake Yamysh. All these logistics took considerable time, to say nothing of the arduous travel itself. Liangusov and his caravan departed from Nerchinsk—7,000 versts (4,640 miles) from Moscow—for China in July 1698.

As expected given the nature of steppe travel, these state caravans did not travel in isolation. The state was well aware that private merchants were fellow travelers with state caravans. One state memo regarding the caravan reads, "And with him [Liangusov] for his trade are gost' agents, and Merchant Hundred merchants, and merchants of various Moscow neighborhoods and other towns."[87] Indeed, on his final journey of the century to China, 477 merchants, agents of privileged merchants, state servitors, and auxiliary helpers, as well as the distinguished Grigorii Dmitrievich Stroganov, accompanied Liangusov.[88] One of the accompanying merchants was I. P. Savateev, a fellow Lal'sk merchant who progressed to the Merchant Hundred and himself led a state caravan to China in 1708.[89]

Nor did state agents trade only on the state's behalf on these missions. According to norms that seem to have been as fixed as they were intangible, a state merchant traded on his own account after "doing right by the sovereign's treasury." Those who have regarded state service as a suffocating vice on privileged merchants miss the tremendous opportunity that leading a state caravan created. In addition to the state funding the significant transportation costs—estimated, along with taxes and fees, to typically amount to about 75 percent of the value of the goods transported—the merchant enjoyed a significant tax break on his own goods that he was free to transport and trade after the tsar's business was completed. Spiridon Liangusov, for example, was

86. DAI, vol. 10, no. 67, 286 (March 23, 1697).
87. *Akty istoricheskie*, vol. 5, no. 268, 491.
88. Aleksandrov, "Russko-kitaiskaia torgovlia," 428; Ogloblin, *Obozrenie*, 2: 76.
89. Demidova and Miasnikov, *Russko-kitaiskie otnosheniia v XVIII v.*, vol. 1, no. 41, 590.

granted a tax waiver for up to 4,000 rubles worth of merchandise he brought with him on the state caravan he led in 1698.[90]

The caravan of 1698 paid over 2,000 rubles in taxes in Verkhotur'e before departing.[91] Since they did not pay taxes on the sovereign's items, presumably this indicates the volume of goods declared for private trade in the caravan. Predictably, this mix of private and state trade raised state concerns about the specter of smuggling. The Nerchinsk governor later wrote to the customs head in Verkhotur'e, intimating that the 2,000 rubles Verkhotur'e customs had collected struck him as too small; a previous state caravan led by the merchant Grigorii Bokov (who went on to become a gost') had generated double the revenue.[92] In typical Muscovite fashion, administrative directives warning to inspect thoroughly (*krepko*) and collect all necessary taxes flitted across Eurasian space in the scrolls of messengers racing from post to post.[93]

Just as Bukharan expatriates in the Russian Empire built mosques in Siberia, from Vilno to Beijing, the early modern Russian Orthodox built churches to observe their faith in distant places, in many cases with state support. Orthodox believers may have first appeared in Beijing in the 1650s. Following the razing of the Albazin fort in the Amur River valley, refugees from the razed fort resettled in Beijing, were they were allowed, in their special quarters, to found an Orthodox church.[94] A Russian Orthodox church was constructed in Beijing in 1683.[95] Commerce and confession indeed were fellow travelers: trade caravans in the 1690s helped support the Orthodox mission in Beijing by shuttling clergy and liturgical items such as "a tablecloth for the mass, myrrh, and some holy oils" across Eurasian space.[96] Ivan Savateev, a merchant from Lal'sk who went on to lead a state caravan to China himself, traveled with Liangusov's 1698 caravan. Upon returning to Nerchinsk in 1699 he reported on the meager Orthodox mission there:

> I had been for purposes of trade to the Chinese capital with the caravan of the merchant Spiridon Liangusov, and we were in the newly consecrated church more than once and heard the sacred liturgy; and

90. Aleksandrov, "Russko-kitaiskaia torgovlia," 428.

91. RGADA, f. 1111, op. 2, d. 457, l. 167.

92. RGADA, f. 1111, op. 2, d. 457, ll. 167–68. On November 27, 1699 the Verkhotur'e customs head Shyshelov brought the requested document to the Verkhotur'e governor. According to Golikova, Grigorii Timofeevich Bokov was in the Merchant Hundred from 1681 to 1713 but did not become a gost'. His brother, Savva Timofeevich Bokov, was a Merchant Hundred from 1681 to 1696 and was promoted to gost' in 1696. Golikova, PKK, 369.

93. RGADA, f. 1111, op. 2, d. 599, l. 76; AI, vol. 5, no. 268, 499.

94. Widmer, *Russian Ecclestastical [sic] Mission in Peking*, 31–32.

95. Ibid., 20.

96. Ibid., 25.

that newly consecrated church in China stood in the city of Peking, to the East, on the right-hand side at the corner of the town close to the wall, and next to that church was laid out a suburb for Russians dwelling in the Chinese capital, and that suburb communicates with the Chinese dwelling yards; and near the church are erected great earthen ramparts with facings 3 arshins high . . . and in them they maintain the tabun [herd] of Russian and Mongol caravan horses; and from the embassy compound to that church by measurement it would be about 2 versts. And in that church the liturgy is sung by the priest Maksim; and he says that it is impossible for him to do it [properly] on account of his great age and failing eyesight, and there are no deacons there with him, only his son has learned to read and helps him in the service; and the Church-warden is Dmitri Grigor'ev, who is not married, and he bakes the wafers, but is illiterate. Spiridon Liangusov had with him the priest Vasilii Aleksandrov, who said the liturgy more than once. And they send people to that church, to the service, from the embassy; and behind them go soldiers, 3 or 4. The soldiers when the singing takes place come into the porch and take off their caps and stare, and from outside few other natives ever come, and there is no jeering. But to what religion they are more inclined they cannot say, though it was said that many natives come daily to the Jesuit Church. . . . And of our Christian religion in China, counting men, women, and children there are 30 in all.[97]

The Orthodox Church in Beijing, which Liangusov's caravan found languishing—and evidently overshadowed by the Jesuits in the competition for native souls—was nonetheless an important and welcome bastion of the familiar for merchants and soldiers far from home. It is said that one of the men from his hometown who accompanied Spiridon to China returned home to Khlynov only to live out his days as a tonsured monk.[98]

Liangusov reached Nerchinsk from China in July 1699; the caravan may have made Moscow by the autumn of 1699 or by the Russian Christmas. Return travel generally went faster because merchants were not as occupied with buying up wares they would trade in China on their way across Siberia. Liangusov returned to Moscow with just over 55,134 rubles worth of Chinese goods, as well as 3,918 rubles worth of unsold goods. By the time Liangusov's caravan reached Beijing, the situation along the Irtysh had

97. Quoted in ibid., 31–32.
98. "Kupchina gostinoi sotni Spiridon Liangusov," 236.

stabilized, enabling a Bukharan caravan to arrive to Beijing via the Irtysh route shortly before Liangusov's. This created a glut in Russian goods that drove prices down and left Liangusov with unsold wares. Nevertheless, V. A. Aleksandrov calculated that Liangusov's caravan returned a profit margin of 14 percent.[99]

Trade documents recording Liangusov's involvement in Siberian trade span just over half a century, revealing impressive longevity.[100] But we know little of Liangusov's commercial activities in the first decade of the eighteenth century. On the personal front, the decade held personal joys for Liangusov. His older son married and began his family; Spiridon had three granddaughters by 1710. Sadly, none of those children was alive seven years later. Since Spiridon himself passed away in 1713, it is unknown if he lived through the heartbreak of losing grandchildren.[101] He did not live to see the birth of more grandchildren. In 1717, his son Filat was twenty-eight years old and, following in his father's footsteps, a member of the Merchant Hundred. He and his wife Katerina Kornilova lived in Khylnov with their three-year-old boy, Ivan, and a six-month-old girl, Anna. In 1721, Ivan was nine years old. His sister Anna had passed away but he had a new brother, Maksim. His father, Filat Spiridonich Liangusov, was absent when this census was taken, called by tsarist order and election of the Viatka *mir* to accompany a state caravan to China. Spiridon Liangusov's other son, Fedot, seems to have died at the age of thirty-seven before having children, but his sons Ivan and Maksim, Spiridon's grandchildren, were counted among the merchants of Khylnov in the second and third censuses (*revizii*) of 1747 and 1764.[102]

The Merchant Hundred and the State China Trade

In the late seventeenth century, the size of the Merchant Hundred corporation was expanding along with the volume of trade between Russia and China. So too was the number of Merchant Hundred merchants who traded in Siberia. After all, the signing of the Treaty of Nerchinsk in 1689 set terms

99. Aleksandrov, "Russko-kitaiskaia torgovlia," 458.

100. Such career longevity was not unique among elite merchants. See Monahan, "Trade and Empire," chap. 4, 387.

101. David Ransel argues that the merchant Tolchenov felt heartbreak at the passing of his daughter. See Ransel, *A Russian Merchant's Tale*, 128.

102. "Kupchina gostinoi sotni Spiridon Liangusov," 236. This report contains contradictory information: It says that Fëdot died in 1731 at age twenty-seven. But it also says that Fëdot was fifteen in 1710 and twenty-six in 1721. If the latter two fact are correct and Fëdot died in 1731, he would have been thirty-seven.

for increased trade between China and Russia, which the state and privileged and nonprivileged merchants all sought to take advantage of.

In the decades following the Treaty of Nerchinsk, private trade continued to operate with the state's approval. As the state moved to engage directly in the China trade, it did so in ways that complemented the existing trade. It relied on Merchant Hundred merchants, generally those with experience in the China trade, to lead several caravans to China. Absent at the head of these caravans were the gosti who were already involved in the China trade and continued to operate. Spiridon Liangusov was one of several Merchant Hundred merchants designated to lead state caravans. Ivan Prokofievich Savateev, a third-generation Merchant Hundred merchant (1692–1702), was another.[103] His father, Prokofii Iakovlev Savateev (Merchant Hundred 1683–86),[104] had been active in the Siberian trade, trading there on his own and the tsar's behalf.[105] Like Liangusov, he developed significant experience in the Siberian trade before being tapped to lead a state caravan in 1702.[106]

Privileged merchants dominated the documented Russian-China trade in the last decade of the seventeenth century. But as Peter's reign drew to a close, some of the largest shipments were carried by merchants of nonprivileged ranks. The Kursk merchant Mikhail Slepokovkin sent a massive shipment to China in 1728.[107] Grigorii Oskolkov, who led a state caravan to China, was not of privileged rank; he retained his peasant designation even while his kinsmen belonged to the Merchant and Woolen Clothiers' Hundreds.[108] The use of nonprivileged merchants and soldiers executing state commercial tasks may have been on the increase, but it was certainly not unprecedented.[109] Russian imperial administration suffered from a chronic lack of personnel. Throughout the seventeenth century one finds instances of military and administrative personnel being sent on buying trips—for example, to buy candles and paper for the chancery in Verkhotur'e. Military

---

103. Golikova, PKK, 389. For more on Ivan Prokof'evich see RKO, vol. 1; Suvorov, "Novootkrytye istoricheskie dokumenty," no. 4.

104. Golikova, PKK, 333, records him as a Merchant Hundred member from 1683 to 1684. A 1686 Tobol'sk customs book records him as a Merchant Hundred, extending his tenure. See RGADA, f. 214, kn. 892, l. 57v.

105. In 1686, 1687. RGADA, f. 214, kn. 892, ll. 57, 57v, 166, 166v; TKSG, vol. 4, 58; Golikova, PKK, 333.

106. Demidova and Miasnikov, *Russko-kitaiskie otnosheniia v XVIII v.*, vol. 1, no. 13, 58.

107. GBUTO GATO, f. 29, d. 139, l. 12. For more see Aleksandrov, "Russko-kitaiskaia torgovlia."

108. Golikova, PKK, 325.

109. RGADA, f. 214, op. 5, d. 1495, ll. 45–46. E.g., Semen Luliakov was sent on a state trip.

men always escorted state shipments as protection, yet there was still space
for private trade.

Private trade continued to go hand in hand with state trade following
the Treaty of Nerchinsk. The state, in typical fashion, continued to make
exceptions to decreed proscriptions against merchants traveling to China. It
did this with the Filat'evs in 1693.[110] It did this with the merchant Grigorii
Oskolkov in 1708 as well. In 1707 Grigorii Oskolkov made the following
appeal to Tsar Peter:

> Tsar, in past year we traded in Siberian towns various Russian and for-
> eign wares and by your decree for the sake of trade we were released
> with permission to the Chinese kingdom. But now, according to your
> decree, only those sent with state merchants (*s kupchami kazny*) can go
> to China. But in previous trade, we your slaves, and agents and shop
> managers, and those with Chinese wares, did not go anywhere with
> forbidden, undeclared, or secret wares, and always paid customs taxes as
> required. And besides Siberian and Chinese trade, we your slaves, have
> no experience in Russian towns and in previous years were never there.
> Besides Siberian trade, we have nothing . . . to pay to your treasury.
> And so I ask you, Your Merciful Highness, to allow me to buy non-
> forbidden wares in Russian towns and Arkhangel'sk and take them to
> Siberia for trade (*na Sibirskuiu ruku tovarov*) and grant me, my agents, my
> shop managers, and workers your decree so that we can pass through
> Russian and Siberian towns without delay. And I'll pay whatever taxes
> are required according to your order. Your low slave, Grigorii Oskolkov,
> June 10, 1707.[111]

As we see, in an empire of separate deals, exceptions were the rule. This petition is also important for indicating the contours of Oskolkov's portfolio.
If it is established that gosti like the Filat'evs or Sveteshnikov had diverse
commercial portfolios, Oskolkov makes the case that Siberian and Chinese
trade is his only livelihood. His remarks indicate that trade was sufficiently
vibrant to have generated a dedicated niche that precluded other endeavors. Even as we may regard Oskolkov's claims—that he and his employees
never smuggled, for example—with skepticism, his remark that he has no
endeavors beyond Siberian and China trade is noteworthy: true or not, he
considered such a rationale a credible stance. Critically, he links his request
to his ability to enrich the tsar's treasury by paying taxes. It was a strategy

110. AI, vol. 5, no. 217, 372–73.
111. RGADA, f. 214, op. 5, d. 1106, l. 1.

that worked. A note on the petition reads: "Give the order for tsarist decree that he is released to pass with his wares without delay."[112] A letter written January 15, 1708 granted him permission to travel through Russian towns for trade.[113] Curiously, the matter of China is skirted.

Siberia in the Empire: Not as Transit, but as Place

By now it is evident that fortunes were not exclusively made on long-distance China trade. Although it is true that soldiers were the majority Russian population and the Great Migration came only in the nineteenth century, Siberian towns were growing. With an increasing Siberian population, there was real money to be made in supplying everyday items to the Siberian territory. John Bell noted as much when he wrote that "many of [Siberian inhabitants] are merchants, and very rich, by the profitable trade they carry on to the borders of China, and many places in their own country."[114] In this chapter we encounter individuals, like the Ushakovs, who made their money on the quotidian. The Ushakov family built a fortune delivering commonplace goods and services such as grain, fish, and contracts on state pubs (*kabaky*). The expansion of their kabak endeavors, as demonstrated in the previous chapter, raised the ire of other prominent gosti, who worried that drunkenness impaired their profits. That is, the Ushakovs did not exclusively invest in furs and Eastern goods, the patterns of Siberian commerce we have thus far emphasized.[115]

So busy did Siberian engagements keep them that they voluntarily based their operations in or closer to Siberia. They saw advantage in relocating closer to Siberia not in exile, not as an escapist measure, but for economic opportunity. The Ushakovs were not the only family who moved its base more eastward. Recall the gost' Peter Mikliaev from chapter 6 who sought out Olearius to tutor his son in Latin and German and relocated to Kazan.[116] That son may have been Ivan Mikliaev, who was from Kazan, where he was well poised to cultivate connections in both Arkhangel'sk and Astrakhan. Ivan Mikliaev did not limit his focus to the Volga and Dvina river routes, however. In the 1690s he partnered with another merchant to send a

112. RGADA, f. 214, op. 5, d. 1106, ll. 2v–3. "*Dat veleti on Gdrv gramota shtoby emy propustit s tovare bez zaderzhanie.*"

113. RGADA, f. 214, op. 5, d. 1106, ll. 2v–3.

114. Bell, *Travels from St. Petersburg*, 1: 185.

115. Aleksandrov, "Sibirskie torgovye liudi Ushakovy."

116. Olearius, *Travels of Olearius*, 175.

shipment worth over 4,000 rubles to China.[117] Besides Ushakov and Mikliaev, Oskolkov, Shangin, and Zarovnianov were merchants of modest backgrounds who relocated to Siberia and became wealthy.[118]

A Siberia was emerging that was more than a military colony. Sparsely populated and yet diverse, a frontier society was evolving—one with its own specificities that simultaneously mimicked behaviors of the wealthy merchants of the metropole. For example, as did elites in Moscow, more modest Siberian merchants sought to solidify commercial relations and advantage through marriage. In 1757 a Tobol'sk townsman married his daughter to a merchant from Ustiug.[119] The Tomsk merchant Petr Petrovich Shikhov (presumably not a relation of the Shikhov dynasty of Tara Bukharans) married his son Vasilii to the daughter of another prominent Tomsk merchant.[120]

In Siberia (and throughout Russia) lesser merchants were striving to move goods for a profit in the same spaces that gosti operated. Although gosti invariably enjoyed better political connections with elites in the metropole, one never knows what advantages local connections might have afforded. In Siberian towns where the clerk (tseloval'nik) was typically imported from another northern Russian town, it is easy to imagine that the merchant from the same hometown (Yaroslavl', Vologda, Eranchin, Lal'sk, etc.) might have enjoyed favor. Of course, gosti may have been just as likely to benefit from connections with clerks from northern Russian towns since this was where they typically sourced support staff. To be sure, the state was always a formidable part of the equation. Details penned in the state record, fees and taxes levied, and the rigor with which inspections were conducted could be malleable variables. And let no one underestimate the state's ability to obstruct trade: impounding goods was a profit-sapper at best. Yet all such circumstances that constrained conditions of trade notwithstanding, once he cleared the "gates" of the state at the Siberian marketplace, the merchant faced just that: a marketplace. The decision to buy from a state servitor, the agent of an elite gost', a local trader, or a Bukharan merchant were made by the buyer. There was also a labor market: gost' agents who did not organize their own work crews (artely) competed with local and lesser merchants for the same pools of furs.

This was despite having to compete with other ranks of people, especially servitors. Servitors and Cossacks were the demographic majority in Siberia.

117. Aleksandrov, "Russko-kitaiskaia torgovlia," 439.
118. Ibid., 436–37.
119. GUTO GAT, f. 156, op. 1, d. 2345, ll. 1–5.
120. Boiko, "P. P. Shikhov," 34.

Their duties could make them mobile—they were dispatched to quell disorder, collect tribute, build churches, bridges, or roads, escort people to Moscow or convicts to all ends of Siberia, participate in diplomatic missions, salt expeditions, buying trips, or any of the like that got them moving around Siberia. Invariably, they would do some trading in their travels. Initially the state forbade such practices, but in 1693 acquiesced in decreeing that soldiers were allowed up to 50 rubles worth of trade tax-free.[121] They are the truly local level of traders below the middle level discussed here.

Reflections on Mobility

Although several details of these merchants' stories remain elusive, customs books and Siberian Office records permit reconstructions that nonetheless bring into view an unmistakable record of merchant life in pre-Petrine and Petrine Russia. Incomplete as they are, the portraits reveal certain salient features of privileged Muscovite merchant life, such as career longevity and the persistence of family as an organizing principle of commercial life, features that obtained as we move slightly down the pyramid of commercial privilege to examine merchants like the Gostevs and Spiridon Liangusov. The careers of the Gostevs and Liangusovs present a picture of upward mobility in Muscovy facilitated by commercial opportunities on the Siberian frontier. The repeat trips and expanding networks reflect the discrete cumulative successes conducting complicated trade operations that resulted in these individuals' rise in rank. Luck and patronage operated at the far-flung edges of empire too, but skills and experience made for elements of a meritocracy. In the Gostev family we witness two generations maintaining a family trade network that incubated the career of Spiridon Iakovlev Liangusov, yet another trader of modest means, who himself attained privileged status. These upwardly mobile merchants testify to opportunities present and realized in early modern Russia.

The stories of Andrei and Il'ia Gostev and Spiridon Liangusov are cases of upward mobility. This chapter could also have featured stories of downward mobility or, better put, entrepreneurs that never quite got off the ground. Certainly Siberian customs books abound with random trading people from (usually) northern towns and sometimes Moscow neighborhoods who do not reappear. Even more voluminous, and probably a better indicator, are the help in the networks of successful merchants. After all, existing

---

121. PSZ, vol. 3, no. 1474, 160–67 (August 30, 1693). On Cossack trade in Siberia: Nikitin, *Sluzhilye liudi v zapadnoi Sibiri*; Witzenrath, *Cossacks and the Russian Empire*.

entrepreneurial networks spawned the careers of Spiridon I. Liangusov and Gavril R. Nikitin. Stories of upward, downward, or static mobility are to be expected in any economy with a degree of dynamism and freedom of action. Malcolm Gladwell in *Outliers: The Story of Success* claimed that one-quarter of the world's richest men of all time emerged in the late-nineteenth-century industrializing United States of America, with another critical mass emerging in the baby-boom generation of America.[122] Gladwell's basic notion—that certain contexts lend themselves to greater opportunities for success—is compelling. If generalizations can be made about particular contexts, definitive conclusions can never be separated from the grit and circumstances of individuals that enriched themselves or did not in given "lucky" moments of opportunity. It is an interesting question to know how opportunities in Russia compared with those worldwide in the expanding early modern economy, a question this study can only ask, not answer.

Meanwhile, as the history of the Noritsyn family demonstrates, mobility is not the only story here. Here we have documentation of a family that is numerous, long-lived, and engaged in commercial activity that appears sustainable. Yet they did not rise up to the privileged ranks. To judge this family a failure ignores the historical contingency of cultural attitudes toward work, status, and wealth, imposing on early modern Russians a narrow standard of wealth accumulation and status-climbing that is intensely prevalent in affluent, postindustrial, capitalist society. Perhaps this family's history leaves us with a case to think on how the constellations of probability, challenge, success, and aspiration coalesced in this and other early modern settings. This investigation into career trajectories and social mobility afforded by commercial opportunities on the Siberian frontier helps deepen understanding of entrepreneurial culture in early modern Russia. Charting individual career mobility of the Merchant Hundred in Siberia reveals a dynamic commercial world in which opportunities and success could provide livelihood and even transform one's social station.

---

122. Gladwell, *Outliers*, 35–68.

Conclusion

Before Russia was a vast empire that spanned all of Eurasia, it was Muscovy. Muscovy was (in)famously located at the "edge of Europe," a construction whose gravitational pull increased over the course of our story.[1] Muscovy was likewise situated at the forested edge of the vast Eurasian steppe, what has been called the eastern half of the Afro-Eurasian ecumeme. Such a position placed it on the northern outskirts of trade routes that had been established by 2000 BCE. The local and regional circulation along these Silk Road trade routes was as significant as the peripatetic (transcivilizational) transmission from the Atlantic to the Indian Ocean and beyond.[2] Despite its fringe positioning relative to this vast system, Muscovy was nonetheless the most successful and sustained political successor of the Mongol hordes. An economic system of agriculture and trade supported the political system that strategically channeled these resources to emerge from a competitive geopolitical crucible as the most enduring state in the region. By the seventeenth century, the Russian economy was substantially integrated with Western trading partners who craved its maritime products and reexported Eastern goods.

---

1. Wallerstein, *The Modern World System*, vol. 1, 315.
2. Christian, "Silk Road or Steppe Roads," 10–14.

These historical circumstances would be plain enough with a bird's-eye view, were it not for the fact that Peter the Great, and the unrelated but far more consequential emergence of European hegemony in the modern period, have obscured Russia's past.[3] Peter's explicit recasting of Russia's orientation toward Europe amounted to a revolution that has shaped perceptions about Russia within and without Russia ever since. For Russians, Dostoevsky's poignant statement that "in Europe we were hangers on, in Asia we were masters" captures the inferiority complex that, in its negative manifestations, gave way to chauvinistic nationalism and a vein of toxic Eurasianism. From a Western European vantage point, Russia was an empire bent on expansion,[4] aggressive but illiterate, always bungling, ill equipped, impecunious, and late to the table of European civilization.

By situating Muscovy more firmly in Eurasian space and time and focusing on commercial life of merchants in early modern Siberia, this study has challenged that (barely caricatured) view. In seventeenth-century Siberia, where state and empire building overlapped, one finds a state whose acute awareness of its diversity, limited resources, and tenuous security resulted in practices often characterized by accommodation and pragmatism. Reconstructing commercial life on the Siberian frontier reveals that the Muscovite government under the first Romanov tsars was as interested in a "window on the West" as it was an "exit to the East." It sought not only to extract furs from the woodlands of Siberia but also to cultivate commercial ties beyond the taiga. Muscovy recognized in such a strategy opportunity to capitalize as middlemen in the Eastern trade and also supply its nascent Siberian settlements with needed goods. Thus the Muscovite state, simultaneously minimalist and activist, developed an instrumentalist approach to commerce.

Activist Commercial State in Eurasia

In studying Eurasian history, the fact that the Muscovite state sought to establish trade relations with its neighbors is obvious. During and before the seventeenth century Russia sent multiple missions to Central Asia, India, and the Middle and Far East. The desire for mutually beneficial trade relations was a standard part of the diplomatic message of these missions, which often

---

3. For a provocative elaboration of this notion see Poe, *Russian Moment in World History*.

4. For work refuting that conventional solecism see Martin, "Fur Trade and the Conquest of Sibir'," 67–79; Bassin, "Expansion and Colonialism on the Eastern Frontier," 3–21; Boeck, *Imperial Boundaries*; Winkler, "Another America," 27–51.

involved assisting or ransoming Russian merchants as well.[5] At the same time, this aspiration for trade relations had to compete with other priorities in a setting of limited resources. If the state recognized that trade generated wealth, and that territories that were safe to pass through facilitated trade, this did not mean it was in a position to create such circumstances promptly in Siberia. Security on the empire's southern steppe and western border posed more urgent challenges to state authority even as security remained an uphill struggle in Siberia well into the eighteenth century.[6] When Ides passed through Tiumen' in the 1690s, by which time a Russian military presence had existed there for over a century, he noted that the entire population feared Kalmyk attacks.[7]

Within this context, the state took measures to develop trade across Siberia. As the state confronted escalating military funding needs throughout the seventeenth century, and the Salt and Copper riots of 1648 and 1662 demonstrated the popular resistance to tax increases and currency adulteration, the desire for trade rose. The state became increasingly invested in managing commerce to maximize state revenue.[8] The New Trade Statute of 1667, which imposed protectionist measures that primarily affected Muscovy's western trading partners, generated between 100,000 and 200,000 rubles annually; allowing for a large degree of error, this may have amounted to somewhere between 6 and 14 percent of Muscovite revenue in the decades after its enactment.[9] Meanwhile, it is within this framework that we can best understand Muscovy's overtures to China in the middle of the seventeenth century (especially as political tensions kept Ottoman trade problematic). Russia sought to develop relations with China both for the profit potential of acting as a bridge for western-bound trade and as a market for Russian furs whose sales had begun to slacken in European markets.

International and domestic trade alike generated valuable revenue. Commerce, an essential prong of expansion, was likewise an essential facet of statehood. The state maintained a vision in which institutions served by

5. Kostomarov, *Ocherki torgovli*, 56; Ulianitskii, *Snosheniia Rossii s Sredneiu Azieiu*, 1–62; MIUTTSSR, vol. 3, pt. 1, 66, 157–59, 211, 226–28, 234–36, 262–68, 274–76, 319–24; RKO, vol. 1, no. 93, 228; Balkashina, "Torgovoe dvizhenie mezhdu zapadnoi Sibiri," 1–32; Dukes, "Russia on the Eurasian Frontier," 151; Druhe, *Russo-Indian Relations*, 24–30.

6. Malikov, "Formation of a Borderland Culture"; Fuller, *Strategy and Power*, chap. 1; Khodarkovsky, *Russia's Steppe Frontier*, chaps. 1, 3, 4; Sunderland, *Taming the Wild Field*.

7. Ides, *Three Years Travels*, 9.

8. Zaozerskaia, *Tsarskaia votchina*.

9. Kotilaine, "A Muscovite Economic Model," 24; Miliukov, *Gosudarstvennoe khoziaistvo*, 118.

loyal, honest administrators collected taxes justly from a vibrant merchant-ry.[10] It was not unheard of for the Moscow government to refund a merchant wrongly levied taxes.[11] "Having heard the petitions of merchants of various ranks from Russian and Siberian towns," began a 1698 decree that modified tax regulations in Siberia with the stated objective that "commercial enterprise would spread widely across Siberian towns so that the Sovereign's treasury would become full."[12] Even as the state recognized that it failed to eliminate official corruption,[13] it nonetheless continued to advance a vision that customs officials would collect taxes "in full and proper measure" (*merniuiu i udobnuiu*) so that merchants would pay taxes willingly and not smuggle or cooperate with provincial officials to cheat the tsar.[14]

Trade served another vital purpose, revealing what I call the state's instrumentalist approach to commerce: it was important for supplying vital provisions and equipment necessary to maintain permanent settlements, which are generally more effective than possession based on extractive models or even soldiers without settlers in securing territorial claims. As the state worked to establish infrastructure in newly claimed territories, it recognized that trade could reach where the state resources and infrastructure came up short.[15] Historiographical inertia has entrenched a picture of a shortsighted, greedy state that hindered merchants and economic development. The Russian state is seen to take interest in commerce only insofar as it helps advance military goals, or meet fiscal needs, a distinction somewhat dubious and not unique to Muscovy.[16] Contrary to a fiscal myopia, the state appreciated the importance of commercial activity and took significant measures to promote trade in its realm. This is especially apparent in Siberia. There, the state, trying to accomplish much with minimal resources, temporarily sacrificed revenue generation for the purpose of supplying goods and cultivating trade ties. It encouraged Muslim merchants to settle and trade there, as shown in chapter 7. The state recognized that these merchants could help provision the Siberian colony where the state could not.

10. PSZ, vol. 1, no. 107, 303 (October 25, 1653); no. 408, 677 (April 22, 1667); PSZ, vol. 2, no. 1015 (May 26, 1683); PSZ, vol. 3, no. 1594, 357 (September 1, 1697); no. 1654, 490–517 (November 12, 1698).

11. RGADA, f. 1111, op. 2, d. 191, l. 1. Burton, *Bukharans*, 482, 521.

12. PSZ, vol. 3, no. 1654, 494 (November 12, 1698).

13. PSZ, vol. 3, no. 1594, 359 (September 1, 1697); PSZ, vol. 13, no. 10,164, 947–53 (December 20, 1753).

14. PSZ, vol. 3, no. 1654, 492–94 (November 12, 1698).

15. On development in Volga region see: Romaniello, "Controlling the Frontier," 429–43; Romaniello, "Profit Motive," 663–85.

16. LeDonne, "Proconsular Ambitions," 53; Musgrave, *Early Modern European Economy*, 86–90.

Russia in the World

The early modern period brought important economic as well as political and religious reconfigurations. Just as the East-West orientation began to prevail in the mental geographies of intellectuals, northern Europe began a dramatic economic rise.[17] This was a long process, however; Francesca Trivellato has argued that the eighteenth-century Mediterranean remained an economic region with considerable vitality.[18] Even as economic hegemony shifted from south to north, it is important to recognize that European regions were already intricately interrelated. In the Netherlands' "first Golden Age, much of the capital and much of the knowledge and innovation upon which Dutch greatness was based was of southern origin."[19]

The Levant had been the major depot through which goods from the Far East made their way to Europe, the most wealthy and commercial parts of which had long been along the Mediterranean coast. In the early modern period, northern Europe became more of a destination for Far Eastern goods. Many of those goods arrived on ships of the East India Companies, not because the maritime companies had supplanted overland trade but because consumption in Europe was expanding significantly. As noted in chapter 1, perhaps one-fifth of the silk reaching Europe was traveling through Russia.[20] Goods could follow various routes through Russia: overland via Poland, although little can be concluded about this route quantitatively, through the Baltic ports, or via Arkhangel'sk. The Volga was a major route. Some goods traveled the entire course of the Volga River with an origin or termination point in Astrakhan. Others found their way to the Volga farther north, as overland routes via Siberia intersected the Volga River. Indeed, given the instability of the Volga steppe, some merchants may have seen Siberia as a more attractive alternative.

The reorientation that resulted from growth in northern European economies was reflected linguistically in the commercial lexicon. The word gost' in contemporary Russian means guest. This meaning is centuries old. Merchants that came to Kiev and later Muscovite principalities from distant places were guests, or gosti. In the late medieval period, the word encountered

---

17. Wolff, *Inventing Eastern Europe*, 13; De Vries, "Economic Crisis of the Seventeenth Century," 180–94.

18. Trivellato, *Familiarity of Strangers*, 6, ch. 4.

19. Musgrave, *Early Modern European Economy*, 139.

20. Israel, *Dutch Primacy in World Trade*, 153–54. Geopolitics (Russo-Iranian-Ottoman) and commercial circumstances (VOC v. Muscovy Co.; cost of shipping) affected flows of Persian silk to Europe.

in documents was often *surozhanye gosti*; Surozh was the location of the Genoese colony on the Black Sea in the late medieval period. The descriptor *surozhanye* eventually fell off, but the label *gosti* itself retained a southern association.[21] In other words, the merchants that initially came to Muscovy came from the south. Other linguistic developments further intimate the shift. By the end of the seventeenth century one encounters the word *iarmark* for "market" in Russia; this word came from the German *Jahrmarkt*. Previously, the words *torga* and the Turkic-based *bazaar* were more frequent.[22] By this reckoning, when Peter signaled his Western orientation by naming himself *imperator*, it was a ritualistic stamp on a transition that had been taking place in the previous century.[23] Linguistic transmissions continued apace. At the start of Peter's reign, the Muscovy Company had been reduced to a minor concern while Dutch was the language that may have held the greatest profit utility. Russian terms referring to trade and finance derived from Dutch, among them *bankroet* (bankruptcy), *beurs* (stock exchange), *dividend* (dividends), *kantoor* (office), *kwitantie* (receipt). The new Russian naval vocabulary was mainly Dutch, including *anker* (anchor), *konvooi* (convoy), *matroos* (sailor), *mast* (mast), *stuurboord* (starboard), and *zeil* (sailing). Of course, Dutch naval prowess was hardly coincidental to its commercial successes and Tsar Peter's fondness for things Dutch was more a consequence than cause of Dutch success. When the Scottish clergyman Gilbert Burnet met Peter the Great, "the language in which they conversed was Dutch."[24]

For Muscovy, a decisive reorientation came in the watershed sixteenth century. The arrival of the English—who came for the passage to the East but stayed for the maritime products—changed the scene dramatically. Without putting too fine a point on causation, an increase in and awareness of connectedness catalyzed more commercial overtures by the Russian state. The Volga trade became more visible, probably stimulated by the initiation of English contacts and their efforts to capitalize on transit to the East via Muscovy.[25] Just as Central Asian merchants attenuated direct trade between Russia and China by acting as middlemen, Russians and diaspora merchants acted as middlemen in the transfer of Eurasian goods to northern Europe. Other events also contributed significantly to realigning Muscovy's coordinates in the sixteenth-century world. There would be much contestation

21. Martin, "Muscovite Travelling Merchants," 24.
22. Mel'gunov, *Ocherki*, 220.
23. Bassin, "Geographies of Imperial Identity," 46.
24. Burke, *Towards a Social History of Early Modern Dutch*, 14 fn.29.
25. Romaniello, *Elusive Empire*, 88–90; Anisimov, *Reforms of Peter the Great*, 255.

between the Poles and the Russians before Smolensk was finally Russian territory, but Russia's conquest of Smolensk in 1514 facilitated overland trade via Poland that was for the most part sustained throughout subsequent wars.[26] Meanwhile, the conquest of Kazan and Astrakhan opened new avenues to the south. In 1563 the Russians signed a trade treaty with Shemakha, nestled between the west shores of the Caspian Sea and the Caucasus Mountains.[27] Ivan IV dispatched diplomatic embassies that fortified existing commercial traffic with Iran beginning in 1588.[28] But most significantly for our purposes, Ermak's routing of Kuchum in 1582 opened the door to Russia's "conquest" of Siberia in the sixteenth and seventeenth centuries.

Mel'gunov wrote that Russia transitioned from "Asiatic to Western life" in the early modern period.[29] Kotilaine, focusing specifically on economics, also argued that the trade orientation shifted from Asia to the West.[30] Yet even as Russia's trade with Western Europe was increasing, so too was its trade with Asia, increases Kotilaine attributed to Western demand.[31] At any rate, Russia was trading more than ever and it was trading Eastern products with the West. In the third quarter of the seventeenth century Muscovy began trading directly with China. The trade, notwithstanding some politically induced setbacks, grew robustly; by the mid-eighteenth century the volume of trade at Kiakhta on the Russia-Chinese border alone accounted for about 8 percent of Russia's foreign trade.[32] This was a boon for its trade with the West. Keep in mind, the fast depletion of the best and most accessible fur supplies drove the river-led expansion across Siberia. Accordingly, Russian forces had reached the Pacific Coast before the middle of the seventeenth century. By the time Peter I was tsar, as discussed below, Siberian furs did not play nearly the role they once had. Russia's domestic products—timber, hemp, potash, raw ingredients that maintained maritime navies and merchant ships, and leather—were also important, as were re-exported Asian goods. Any discussion of early modern Russia's place and orientation vis-à-vis East

---

26. Bakhrushin, "Russkoe prodvizhenie za Ural," in NT, 3: 140. In "Predposylki vserossiiskogo rynka v XVI v.," NT, 1: 46, Bakhrushin wrote: "the joining of Kazan and Astrakhan opened trade routes to the Caspian and Caucasus, to Shemakha and Iran. From the other end, Kazan was connected by the 'old Kazan road' across the steppe, beyond the Urals, with the Central Asian trading towns Bukhara and Urgench."

27. Bakhrushin, "Russkoe prodvizhenie za Ural," in NT, 3:140.

28. Janet Martin, "The Fur Trade and the Conquest of Siberia," 75; Kotilaine, *Russia's Foreign Trade*, 451.

29. Mel'gunov, *Ocherki po istorii russkoi torgovli*, 219.

30. Kotilaine, *Russia's Foreign Trade*, 505–9.

31. Kotilaine, *Russia's Foreign Trade*, 508.

32. Aksenov, et al., *Ekonomicheskaia istoriia Rossii*, 2:404.

and West necessarily invokes the legacy of Russia's great Westernizer, Peter I (1682–1725).

Peter I and Commerce

Few personalities loom larger in Russian history than that of Peter the Great. He was a man of action, of genius (of a sort). He embraced the West and the towering imperialism that naval strength symbolized. The meaning and legacy of Peter's reign have remained as important and contested in his wake as they were during his reign. In recent years, scholarship has focused on representations of empire—hunger for imperial glory that manifested itself cartographically in maps claiming big territory. Such cartographical representations stoked territorial aspirations, to which knowledge making (epitomized in the Great Northern Expedition, 1733–43) and cultural superiority were standard Enlightenment corollaries.[33] Between the sheer power of his tyrannically Westernizing personality and a historiographical deemphasis on political economy in recent decades, Peter's economic policies have been overshadowed by more celebrated aspects of his Westernizing reign, such as his love of boats.[34] Maritime and naval prowess were hallmarks of the contemporary empires Peter admired, but so too was commerce. As Anisimov observed, Peter's maritime fascinations were not limited to seagoing vessels. Peter wanted ports because they were conduits for trade. By means of ports, "this artery, the state's heart can be healthier and more profitable."[35]

For the most part, Peter plays a backstage role in the story told here. By the time he came to power, Siberian commerce was well established and had a significant inertia. Indeed, in a reign typically defined for its departures from tradition, it is important to recognize that Peter's frenetic reformist style has obscured deep continuities. His willingness to experiment with free trade and various tax-farm arrangements, his rulership style—long on decrees and short on implementation—have made it harder to see continuity in his commercial aims. In the main, Peter followed Romanov suit when it came to several aspects of commerce. Like his predecessors, he recognized that commerce had an important role to play in the maintenance of a robust state. Lindsey Hughes argued for the primacy of revenue collection in Peter's

---

33. See Sunderland, "Becoming Territorial." James Cracraft concluded that the cultural revolution Peter initiated was his most significant legacy. Cracraft, *Petrine Revolution in Russian Culture.*

34. For a call for more study of Petrine economic policy see Bushkovitch, "Legacy of Seventeenth-Century Reform in Petrine Times."

35. Anisimov, *Reforms of Peter the Great*, 251.

reign, also noting that this prioritization preceded Peter.[36] Ardent Westernizer to be sure, Peter was keen to develop trade relations with the West and East. Golikova's study of Astrakhan demonstrated that improving trade with the East was a high priority for Peter.[37] To the extent that domestic manufacture was promoted in Petrine Russia, this was standard mercantilist fare that received similar attention under his father, Tsar Aleksei Mikhailovich. As we saw in chapter 7, Peter followed his predecessors in encouraging Bukharan immigration. In a reign typically defined by departures, it is important to recognize this continuity.

Unsurprisingly for anyone who has studied this outsized personality, Peter brought his personal peculiarities to his pursuit of commercial ends. Facing more military commitments than any tsar since Ivan IV, not to mention the onset of the new style army, we see under Peter an intensification of specie focus, a typical mercantilistic priority. Indeed, Anisimov called Peter "a son of his time, a time when the concepts of mercantilism and protectionism dominated the statesmen's minds."[38] Contrary to one historian's assertions that "Peter the Great employed no fixed, consistent, or persistent economic philosophy or policy throughout his long reign. All historians of the period agree, to a greater or lesser degree, on the ad hoc character of his individual economic measures," one observes a familiar, elemental emphasis on commerce in Petrine Russia, even if Peter as a commercial strategist is hardly the picture typically presented.[39] It was not by accident that the volume of trade in Russia rose over Peter's reign (even if, for the first time in its recorded history, Russia had a negative trade balance).[40]

Perhaps as a result of being so enamored with Western ways, Peter displayed a heavy-handedness and bravado that marks a departure from the reticent savvy of the first Romanov tsars. True too, the devil is in the details, which may inform Kotilaine's judgment that "Peter made a bad system work better."[41] In his rush, Peter "missed the boat" in some respects. A great admirer of the Dutch, he did not follow their lead regarding the keeping of time. He converted Russia from the Orthodox to Julian calendar while almost all of the Netherlands (including the provinces Peter visited) had already abandoned the Julian for the Gregorian calendar. To be fair, in making the choice

36. Hughes, *Russia in the Age of Peter the Great*, 136.
37. Golikova, *Ocherki po istorii gorodov Rossii*.
38. Anisimov, *Reforms of Peter the Great*, 251.
39. Foust, *Muscovite and Mandarin*, 68. On Peter's commercial strategies: Anisimov, *Reforms of Peter the Great*, 244–68.
40. Mel'gunov, *Ocherki po istorii russkoi torgovli*, 248–53; Kahan, *Plow, the Hammer*.
41. Kotilaine, "A Muscovite Economic Model," 23.

he was in line with England, Sweden, and Hapsburg France, which retained the Julian calendar for some years to come. He wanted the formation of a trading company, at a moment when the trading company model had ceased to return impressive profit returns, as discussed in chapter 6.[42]

Peter's famous but unsuccessful battle against corruption provides one vivid illustration of how his style could amount to smoke and mirrors rather than substantive reform. Repeated orders and decrees offer a window to the unsuccessful struggle the state wielded trying to construct an administration of righteous servitors.[43] As Charles Halperin put it, by assigning governors in partnership in Siberia and keeping them on short rotations, the center in Moscow was essentially admitting defeat in its struggle to regulate the conduct of its provincial administration.[44] Peter I boldly resurrected the struggle. He styled himself an outspoken enemy of corruption and took several measures to combat corruption accordingly. In 1701, illustrative of his enthusiasm for administrative righteousness, an unlucky servitor (*stol'nik*) was executed for accepting a 5-ruble bribe, but it did not stop Peter's favorite, Alexander Danilovich Menshikov, from corruptly amassing one of the greatest fortunes in Russia. Peter created the *fiskaly*, a department devoted to rooting out corrupt servitors. In 1713 he decreed a whistle-blower law that would reward subjects who exposed "thieves of the people." In 1715, in the face of two years of overwhelming response, Peter revised his whistle-blower decree by narrowing his definition of what constituted corruption: the wording "thieves of the people" was replaced to specify "thefts from the tsar's treasury."[45] Despite such efforts, V. O. Kliuchevskii and D. O. Serov both deemed Peter's reign the most corrupt Russia had known.[46] The iconic role that corrupt officials occupy in nineteenth-century Russian literature gives the impression that little happened to improve the situation.

Ever enamored with Western ideologies and modes of imperialism, Peter yearned to capture trade routes via whatever means necessary. One version of Peter is that he proceeded with chauvinism and "gold hunger" into the depths of Central Asia. Although there is no denying a measure of bravado in the way in which these missions were carried out, his actions nonetheless can be seen as part of a consistent program focused on enlarging Russia's

42. PSZ, vol. 3, no. 1706 (1600). Peter prompted for a western trading company in 1699 and for an eastern one in 1711. See Baron, "Fate of the Gosti in the Reign of Peter the Great," in *Muscovite Russia*, 503.

43. Kollmann, *Crime and Punishment*, 194–96, 413.

44. Halperin, "Muscovy as a Hypertrophic State," 503.

45. Serov, *Prokuratora Petra I*, 13–18.

46. Kliuchevsky, *A Course in Russian History*, 140; Serov, *Prokuratora Petra I*, 13.

trade opportunities. Peter's "final testament" was a forgery.[47] He never issued a directive to: "penetrate as far as the Persian Gulf, if possible re-establish the former commerce with the Levant, advance as far as India which is the storehouse of the world. Having arrived at this point, we shall no longer be in need of English gold."[48] Yet there is a grain of truth to be salvaged here.

Over a century after the English began negotiating to secure overland transit to China, the French king dispatched Jesuits to find an overland alternative to the maritime routes to the Far East. The French Jesuit Philippe Avril's 1693 account asserted that the best routes to China went through Siberia.[49] Peter, like his predecessors and much of Europe, for that matter, had commercial aspirations that involved what would later be dubbed "the Orient." He was not blind to the competitive nature of commercial access and he understood that when state authority could supplant steppe banditry trade routes became safer and more profitable. Toward this end he initiated real efforts to secure the Russian position on the steppe.[50]

The importance of rivers as conduits to trade was well known to Peter. Thus when he heard reports that the Khivans had rerouted the Oxus River from its normal path into the Caspian Sea, he was interested in learning more. In 1714 he dispatched an expedition, led by a Muslim convert from the Caucasus, Prince Aleksandr Bekovich-Cherkasski, to the Caspian to study the hydrogeological situation. Peter's hope—undergirded by a hubris Soviet planners would emulate in spades—was to reroute the river into the Caspian, creating a water route from India to that landlocked sea.[51] In 1717, Bekovich-Cherkasski was dispatched on another mission this one gruesomely ill-fated. Whether the intention was to build one fort or conquer all of Central Asia, the Khivan khan ended the mission when he attacked the Russian contingent. Prince Bekovich-Cherkasski was beheaded and scalped. The Khivan khan allegedly had the prince's scalp made into a drum, which he gifted to the khan of Bukhara, who wanted no part in such transgressions and refused the gift.[52]

The Romanovs knew that peace was more conducive to commerce. At first blush, with several seventeenth-century wars on its western borders (where Muscovy was the aggressor to take Smolensk), and with persistent low-grade hostilities to the south, it can be a hard case to argue. But correspondence

47. Lehovich, "Testament of Peter the Great," 111–24.
48. Quoted in Sykes, A History of Persia, 2: 244.
49. Avril, Travels Into divers Parts, 142–46; Love, "A Passage to China," 86.
50. Mezhdunarodnye otnosheniia v Tsentral'noi Azii, no. 8, 180.
51. Bartol'd, Raboty po istoricheskoi geografii, 355–58; Pravilova, "Rivers of Empire," 7–8.
52. This is the account in Hopkirk, Great Game.

between Moscow and Siberia shows that the state understood friendly relations were more conducive to commerce, a lesson that European infatuation may have caused Peter to unlearn. The first Romanov tsar, Mikhail Fëdorovich, extended trade privileges to Kalmyks in western Siberia to entice them to cease their raids on Russian subjects in the 1620s. Similarly, he opted for peaceful trade over violent clashes with Mongols at Lake Yamysh in the 1630s.[53] The Muscovite government made the same choice with China, ceding territory to the Qing in exchange for peaceful commerce in the Treaty of Nerchinsk in 1689. After Peter's death, Anna Ioannovna's regime continued to make diplomatic agreements with Oriats to regularize trade.[54] The empresses Elizabeth and Catherine II allowed Kazakhs tax-free trade, while the state simultaneously devoted increasing resources to protecting caravans moving across the Eurasian steppes.[55] The development of the Irtysh line has been attributed to Peter's thirst for gold dust. To be sure, Peter is duly credited with knee-jerk initiatives that were regarded as unrealistic in their own time and to this day. Yet beneath the flurry of initiatives and revolutionary grandstanding, Peter's establishment of the Irtysh line, beginning in 1718 and proceeding into the 1730s, was part of a more sober state policy to develop trade routes to Central Asia.

Peter the Great has been credited with changing Russian imperialism dramatically. Ideas of civility and territoriality became increasingly important markers of empire and were cast with a deliberately Western orientation.[56] However, the onset of a self-consciously Western orientation must not be confused with Muscovy's long-established conception of itself as an empire.[57] From the fifteenth century, when the grand princes of Muscovy began to "gather the lands," the opening address of each state document painstakingly reminds the recipient of the many territories over which the grand prince was sovereign. By the seventeenth century Russian tsars saw themselves as the sovereign leaders of diverse peoples.[58] Tsar Aleksei Mikhailovich described his multiconfessional, multiethnic domains with pride to the Chinese emperor.[59] And yet Russian expansion across Siberia was pragmatic. Chronicle writers held forth on divine destiny, but Muscovite intrachancery correspondence is devoid

53. Perdue, *China Marches West*, 100, 107.

54. Frank, *Bukhara and the Muslims of Russia*, 58–59.

55. *Mezhdunarodnye otnosheniia v Tsentral'noi Azii*, no. 8, 180; Malikov, "Formation of a Borderland Culture," 286–91.

56. Slezkine, *Arctic Mirrors*, chaps. 1–2; Slezkine, "Naturalists v. Nations," 27–57; Sunderland, "Imperial Space."

57. Bassin, "Geographies of Imperial Identity," 46.

58. Kivelson, *Cartographies of Tsardom*, chap. 7.

59. RKO, vol. 1, no. 93, 228 (October 10, 1657).

of lofty imperial aims. Chancery documents speak of traveling a bit farther along the rivers to find more people to add to the registers of tribute (*iasak*) payers. Muscovy did not need the Enlightenment to tell it that taking names was essential to its imperial project, as the oldest document in the Tiumen' archive, a memo from Moscow, markedly illustrates.[60] The primary aspiration was to add people to the rolls of fur tribute payers. In the seventeenth century, the state was not after their souls. It was after fur, but not only that. The state also wanted to cultivate trade for the revenue it could generate and the quotidian function it could serve by supplying needed goods to the new territory. Indeed, the administrative subordination of the Office of Merchant Matters (established by 1631) to the Siberian Office and the establishment of an infrastructure of customs posts across Siberia testify to the association that Siberia had to trade in the state's view.[61]

Early Modern Economies

This book seeks to better incorporate Russia into a picture that is rapidly changing. As behavioral economics and information studies help us recognize that models of free markets are as tidy as they are fantastical—that far more fires the synapses of economic activity than supply, demand, and rational action—historians increasingly appreciate that early modern economies cannot be wholly comprehended by relying on neoclassical economic theory. Modern law, for example, has gone some distance in supplanting cultural norms as a restraining force. But law did not wholly govern the nature of exchange, for customs and culture remained (and remain) operative in sometime unpredictable ways. Scholars have observed this in many times and places. Richard White's seminal *The Middle Ground*, which explains that an Algonquian would steal from an enemy in order to fulfill a responsibility to a friend, is just one example demonstrating the added and inevitable complication of overlapping legal regimes in economies of empire.[62] To what extent canonical market forces like supply and demand governed early modern exchange is an area of rich inquiry.

Perhaps nothing undercuts the classical economic theory cornerstone of rational action as much as the nature of knowledge itself.[63] Rather than being an objective variable to input in economic equations, the problematical

---

60. GBUTO GATO, f. 47, op. 1, d. 28, l. 1.
61. Perkhavko, *Pervye kuptsy Rossiiskie*, 332.
62. White, *Middle Ground*, 98.
63. Hayek, "Use of Knowledge in Society," 519–30.

nature of knowledge has been demonstrated in our contemporary world. How much more so in the uneven informational landscape of the early modern world. Although the profit motive surely governed transactions to some degree, in a world where longer time horizons made liquidity a standard crux, trust was a consideration no less critical. Given the longer time horizon, deficiencies in cash, information, mobility, and, in many cases, political stability, it becomes clear that in premodern economies, a different calculus prevailed. In premodern peripheries the calculus was different still. Local residents were embedded in more complex relationships with exchange than out-of-towners encountered. Unschooled in local subtleties, we can imagine that nonlocals paid more in money and blunders than locals who understood operative currencies. Thus, if competition defines markets, merchants in Russia operated in a market setting, even if the competition took different forms than those neoclassical economic theory defines.

Revisiting Russian "Backwardness"

When it comes to explaining Russia's economic performance in its early modern context, two basic (undertheorized) truths seem particularly relevant. First, economies are rarely winner-takes-all scenarios.[64] As salespeople know, it does not matter how many rejections one meets, just that one achieves some sales. Beyond a certain minimum necessary for survival, great success can be achieved by securing far less than the total available share of the pie. A second obvious yet fundamental truth is that there is no absolute standard or bar in a competitive market setting. To win, one just has to be better than the competition. The flipside: to lose one just needs to be bested. Muscovy was on the losing end of this truth in the early modern era. In some scenarios (certain niches such as shipping, for example), though it may seem contradictory to the first basic truth, the vantage point of leadership affords advantages that enable one to diminish or eliminate competition. This dynamic, coupled with the disadvantages of lacking robust infrastructure to promote capital investment, explains why Muscovy never gained a substantial foothold in the export shipping business.[65] Further, the fierce competition for tonnage between the Dutch and British created a buyer's market that left Russians little incentive to develop shipping capacity. By the late sixteenth and early seventeenth century, Western Europeans had developed credit institutions and business organizations that were more vigorous, better funded, and

---

64. Levi raises this notion in "Ferghana Valley at the Crossroads," 213–32, esp. 217.
65. Preobrazhenskii and Perkhavko, *Kupechestvo Rusi*, 144.

therefore more capable of effecting entrepreneurial ventures than the ad hoc practices Russian merchants knew. This does not mean that Russians were deficient, but it did put them at an immediate disadvantage in competition with Dutch and English merchants. Taken together, these truths may help us understand the "triumph of the West" as well as explain why assessments of the Muscovite merchantry as a complete failure are wrong.

Russia, as did Europe and Asia, developed within a context, in relation to its neighbors. It encountered in uneven degrees other cultural and technological traditions, parts of which were more easily appropriated than others. The truth relevant to Russian development seems to be somewhere between two basic facts: that economic development is not necessarily a zero-sum game and that it is competitive. Call it a head start or an agenda: English and Dutch merchants' experience created competitive advantage. The size of Russia increased the costs of doing business and low population density created challenges not easily surmounted with available technologies. It is not patronizing to argue that Russians "held their own." The state sometimes defended its merchants' interests and sometimes undermined them in pursuit of specie, which Western merchants possessed in greater quantities.[66]

Anglo-Russian relations cannot be properly called quasi-colonial, despite some English intentions, because Muscovites pushed back effectively. Revealing its imperialistic stripes well before England emerged as a world power, Muscovy Company heads thought it the height of pretension that Muscovites would insist on reciprocal trade privileges.[67] During the Time of Troubles, rumors circulated that James I would annex northern Russia.[68] Correspondence between northern Russian towns in 1601 relayed the rumor that English ships with thousands of soldiers had landed at Kholmogory and were headed to Moscow.[69] Such ideas never gained real traction at the English court, but they were ideas in the minds of some Englishmen, revealing the condescending stance the English took toward Muscovy. Nonetheless, although the colonial attitude of some sixteenth-century English toward Muscovy did not permeate Russian soil, British accents and habits became standard fare on the Indian subcontinent. Some of the Dutch merchants involved in early explorations of the Russian northern coastline and trade with Muscovy, such as Isaac le Maire and Jacob van Heemskerk, went on to seek fortunes in other colonial endeavors, most notably the Dutch East

66. Childs, "Commerce and Trade," 154.
67. Baron, "Osip Nepea," in *Muscovite Russia*; LeDonne, *Russian Empire and the World*, 18.
68. Baron, "Thrust and Parry," in *Explorations in Muscovite History*, 28.
69. RIB, vol. 2, no. 98, 273.

India Company.[70] Russia did not become a colony of Western European states. From the perspective of self-preservation, then, the state did something right, even though travelers to Russia in the early modern period had already begun to emphasize what they thought the Russian state did wrong, a tradition that has persisted in modern historiography.[71] Recalling the gravestone epitaph that began this book, Muscovy proved resistant to penetration in an international arena of commercial imperialism.

Revising Russian Merchant Tropes

Hostile Western observers set the tone for most characterizations of Russian merchants. But it was not foreigners alone. Russians themselves helped consolidate tropes of dishonest, greedy merchants in all manner of literary representations and images.[72] Yet such characterizations are in no way specific to Russia. Classical and Judeo-Christian heritage alike had little respect (although much use) for individuals who merely moved goods instead of creating them, and worse, profited from it. The intellectual and cultural acceptance of profit making has a long history. And for most of that history the merchant's moral standing was ambivalent at best. Since negative tropes of merchants the world over are so ubiquitous, I see little purpose in addressing Russian merchants in this regard. I will, however, focus on dispensing of a few characterizations that were more particular to Russian merchants and that have had important implications for understanding Russian history. Taken together, this is the notion that Russian merchants by nature were backward and behaved in ways not conducive to progress or modernity. Indicators of their backwardness include their conservativeness, most prominently defined by aversion to risk and education; efforts to eliminate competition, often through currying political favor; and xenophobia and insularity.

Studying the dissident Kotoshikhin's hostile account immersed in Cold War ideologies was a recipe for seeing dysfunction in Muscovite commercial policy and mercantile culture. Even as he himself recognized the hostility of Kotoshikhin's and Kil'burger's accounts, Baron accepted Plekhanov's grim

---

70. Bushkovitch, *Merchants of Moscow*, 43–69; Israel, *Dutch Primacy in World Trade*, 44–47. I thank Paul Bushkovitch for bringing this to my attention.

71. Given the nasty methods the Dutch employed, the remarkable question is how they developed a reputation for honesty and forthrightness. See Kagarlitsky, *Empire of the Periphery*, 96. Poe, *"A People Born to Slavery"*; Kotilaine, "A Muscovite Economic Model."

72. Bernstein, "Russian Eighteenth-Century Merchant Portraits," 407–8.

pronouncements on Russian psychology.[73] To his credit, he was skeptical of ideologically driven interpretations and argued with himself throughout his work (he was left to argue with himself in part because few Western colleagues were talking about these things). Yet even as he recoiled at Pokrovsky's assigning of Russia to a universal—and at that moment, Western—development path, by accepting that Pokrovsky "greatly exaggerated [trade's] dimensions in Russia,"[74] Baron closed his mind to the possibility that seventeenth-century trade was significant and integrated with Western Europe, as Kotilaine has demonstrated.

Baron saw in Russia, first, an absence of characteristics of an early capitalist economy and second, that the blame for this lay with the Russian state or with the somehow deficient character of Russian merchants: conservative instead of innovative, risk averse instead of risk taking, and, perhaps most absurd, competition averse instead of free-market champions. Such a position depends on a platonic—platonic only in the sense of unreal; Plato had no love for profit seekers—ideal of competitor-capitalist that exists only in the fictional novels of Ayn Rand. The suggestion that Russian merchants' efforts to reduce competition disqualifies them from the ranks of proper capitalists is of course ludicrous. Historically and demonstrably, capitalists strive to eliminate competition. According to Braudel that is the definition of a capitalist.[75] Dating back to the early modern period, the rhetoric of free trade itself was invoked by the most progressive of capitalists to institutionalize privileged access.[76] Merchants with means to do so—British, Dutch, Russian, etc.—worked to leverage their influence in order to eliminate competition. The English Navigation Acts of 1651, with clauses banning foreign vessels from trading in colonial products, sought to eliminate competition.[77] Efforts to eliminate competition are often couched in nationalist rhetoric, but this is arguably drapery over economic motives. Merchants in a position to do

---

73. Baron, "Plekhanov on Russian Capitalism and the Peasant Commune"; "Plekhanov and the Origins of Russian Marxism"; "Plekhanov's Russia: The Impact of the West upon an 'Oriental' Society"; and "Fate of the Gosti in the Reign of Peter the Great," all in *Muscovite Russia*. See Baron, "Entrepreneurs and Entrepreneurship in Sixteenth/Seventeenth-Century Russia," in *Explorations in Muscovite History*.

74. Baron, "Ivan the Terrible, Giles Fletcher, and the Muscovite Merchantry," in *Muscovite Russia*, 564.

75. "Circuits et réseaux se trouvent dominés régulièrement par des groupes tenaces qui se les approprient et en interdisent l'exploitation aux autres, le case échéant." Circuits and networks are DOMINATED regularly by groups who tenaciously appropriate and prohibit the use to others, check any. Braudel, *Civilisation metériell économie et capitalisme*, 2: 165.

76. Pettigrew, "Free to Enslave," 3–38.

77. Bailyn, *New England Merchants*, 80–89.

so will no less readily maneuver to eliminate competition from their own countrymen.

The chartered English merchants worked as hard as anyone to limit competition and free-market conditions in Russia. This is part of what I mean in using the term "quasi-colonial." They worked not only to restrict Dutch and other access to the Russian market but also to keep other Englishmen from posing competition. "Their care was to make the Door of Entrance Strait and difficult," explained the charge against them. "Knowing that a few could better combine together, and agree upon Rates to put upon their Commodities than greater Numbers," the company men placed the entrance "fine" at 20 pounds, so high that from its implementation in 1666 until 1673 only eight men purchased the right to trade in Russia with the company. This was by design, as the "company men recognized that they could." When Parliament got involved and legislated a halved entrance fine of 40 shillings, fifty-six men joined in the next seven years.[78]

Another iteration of this same misinterpretation of what it means to be capitalist is that Russian merchants had misplaced priorities because they were occupied with currying favor among political figures rather than getting out there in markets and doing business. Such priorities reveal that they were neither progressive nor capitalist. Again, only in the pages of Ayn Rand's fiction do hero-capitalists spurn political favor. One need not take Braudel's prescient word for it. That capitalists seek favor can be readily measured in various ways, historical and contemporary. Two striking contemporary examples make the point. In the United States professional lobbying has grown to a $30 billion industry, an amount exceeding the GDP of half of the countries on earth; by far the largest investors in this industry are for-profit organizations or nonprofit organizations composed of corporate entities.[79] ALEC (American Legislative Exchange Council, euphemistically named to an Orwellian degree) is an organization funded by well-financed corporate leaders whereby industry lobbyists present "model legislation" to elected leaders being treated to a stay in resort locations on the corporate dime.[80] Baron, again, faulted the gosti because they petitioned the tsar not for greater

78. "Charge of Companies of Merchants," 139; Romaniello, "Captain John Elton and the Anglo-Russian Competition over Iran in the Eighteenth-Century."

79. IMF World Economic Outlook, "World GDP Ranking 2014," http://knoema.com/nwnfkne/world-gdp-ranking-2014-data-and-charts.

80. Hudai, "'Legislative Laundry'," http://dbapress.com/front-page/legislative-laundry-how-alec-funnels-millions-of-dollars-in-corporate-gifts-to-state-lawmakers-for-the-express-purpose-of-promoting-corporate-backed-legislation.

freedom but for greater favor.[81] Whether it goes by the label collusion, price fixing, insider trading, or monopolistic practices—charges readily familiar to twenty-first-century citizens of the industrialized capitalist world—these are all methods by which capitalists endeavor to limit or eliminate competition, unless, in theory, the law prohibits them, and sometimes not even then, as we have seen.

Xenophobia competes for pride of place among the most oft-repeated Muscovite stereotypes. Efforts of Moscow merchants to lobby for privilege against foreign merchants is attributed to xenophobia rather than rational economic interest. The charge repeats despite the fact that thousands of foreigners were invited to pursue their careers in Muscovy and did so.[82] There is a disconnect between Fletcher's screed against Muscovite xenophobia and Protestant churches in Muscovy, to say nothing of mosques.[83] "The Muscovite tolerate all sorts of Religions, and suffer all Nations to live among them," remarked Olearius, one of Muscovy's liveliest (if not always most reliable) reporters on Muscovite society.[84] Highlighting counterexamples such as Russian merchants hiring tutors and taking risks (how subjectively modern that risk taking becomes an indicator of progress) can go some of the distance in dismantling this historiographical stereotype. But broadening the context is even more demonstrative. Under a wider aperture, the charge as particular to Russians disintegrates. The restrictions surrounding liminal actors the world over in the premodern world shows that maintaining boundaries between groups was in no way a Moscow-specific practice. From Boston to Beijing, authorities placed restrictions on the movements and practices of merchants. English scholarship points out that English xenophobia was especially rampant in the late fourteenth century, at a time when unprecedented numbers of foreigners were in London.[85] In France, wrote De Vries, "the Crown was perfectly capable of laying siege to its own merchants (if they were Huguenots, as in La Rochelle in 1627/8), harassing foreign merchants into marginalization (the important resident Dutch merchant communities in midcentury Atlantic ports), or expelling them from French soil altogether (the Revocation of the Edict of Nantes of 1685)."[86]

---

81. Baron, "The Weber Thesis and the Failure of Capitalist Development," in *Muscovite Russia*, 335.

82. Olearius, *Voyages and Travells*, 107.

83. There was a Protestant church in Nizhni Novgorod in the seventeenth century. Hughes, "Attitudes towards Foreigners in Early Modern Russia," 3.

84. Olearius, *Voyages and Travells*, 107.

85. Beardwood, *Alien Merchants in England*; Lloyd, *Alien Merchants in England*; Archer, "Responses to Alien Immigrants in London," 755–74; Thrupp, "Aliens In and Around London," 251–72.

86. De Vries, "Economic Crisis of the Seventeenth Century," 187.

Francesca Trivellato has compellingly argued that "cross-cultural" trade
hardly embraced notions of cultural diversity, as diaspora communities tended
to minimize interface across cultures.[87] She called the insular, traditional
behaviors of Livorno merchants who operated at the pinnacles of early modern progress "cosmopolitan communitarianism." Thus Bukharans in Siberia
who traded with, but in practice seem to have minimally cooperated with
Russian merchants, fit the example Trivellato described in the early modern
Mediterranean. And the behavior fits with Benjamin Kaplan's argument,
eloquently paraphrased by David Frick, that early modern "toleration—the
nitty-gritty everyday practice of living with neighbors some may have considered benighted and destined for hell—had no necessary connection with
the ideals of tolerance espoused by a few precocious members of the early
modern elites; it was, in fact, often the opposite of tolerance."[88]

Russian backwardness is alleged in myriad other ways. Russian merchants
are alleged to have been education averse, as detailed in the introduction. Yet
though it is doubtful that any other merchant's collection rivaled the Stroganovs' library of nearly two thousand books, many merchants owned ten to
twenty books, according to Perkhavko. L. A. Timoshina found seventy-five
different merchant families who purchased books from the Printing Office
from the 1630s to the 1660s.[89] The merchant Peter Mikliaev, whom Adam
Olearius described as "intelligent and knowledgeable," asked Olearius to
tutor his son in German and Latin.[90] The merchant Grigorii Bokov enrolled
his son in the Slavic-Greek-Latin Academy that opened in 1687. Silvester
(Semen) Medvedev, the famous poet from the late seventeenth century, was
from a Kursk merchant family.[91] Bukharan merchants of the Russian Empire
were known for their fine schools and education. One imagines that Russians may have been among the merchant-students studying Persian and
Arabic in the Bukharan enclave in Astrakhan.[92]

A near fanatical adherence to religious and diplomatic protocol has been
attributed to Russians. Examples of superstitious (from the destruction of
the first printing press in 1564 to riots of the offended crowd when the
state decreed no kissing of the icon during an epidemic in 1771), violently
close-minded (execution for attempting to proselytize the Orthodox) acts
are regularly marshaled to distinguish Russian values from Western European

87. Trivellato, *Familiarity of Strangers*.
88. Frick, *Kith, Kin, and Neighbors*, 5.
89. Perkhavko, *Pervye kuptsy Rossiiskie*, 377–79.
90. Olearius, *The Travels of Adam Olearius*, 175.
91. Perkhavko, *Pervye kuptsy Rossiiskie*, 379.
92. Savich, "Iz istorii russko-nemetskikh kul'turnykh sviazei v XVII v.," 250.

norms. Such interpretations seem to rely on the delusion that the sanguine writings of Montesquieu negate the horrors of the Reformation. It is true that Muscovite courts executed a woman who treasonously dressed her chicken up as the tsar, but so too, in France in 1766, was a twenty-year-old boy executed for irreverence after failing to remove his hat during a religious procession.[93] It is often repeated that superstitious Muscovites drove the first printers out of Moscow in the sixteenth century, but seldom recalled that German Knights of the Teutonic Order would not allow—and even executed one of—a group of 123 artisans seeking to sail from Lubeck to Russia.[94] The point is not to flippantly suggest equivalencies; each of these cases has its own complicated story, but the point is that the "barbarity" of early modern Russia appears less of an outlier when juxtaposed alongside its contemporaries. To be sure, Muscovy bequeathed substantially less of a paper trail relative to Western Europe, a difference not to be dismissed. Consequently, however, the job of describing early modern Russia was left to others. We should not take Polish King Sigismund, who in 1569 called "the Muscovite, enemy to all liberty under the heavens," at his word.[95]

Another cliché about Russian merchants concerns their insularity. Peter Marperger felt obliged to include in his seventeenth-century phrasebook: "I don't love the sea. If I'm on land I don't need to worry about drowning," as language someone talking to a Russian merchant might find useful.[96] Russian merchants have been deemed inferior because they didn't travel internationally. Rather than crossing oceans, they passively stayed home. Russian gosti had permission to travel abroad but they rarely did so.[97] The remark is often repeated but little explored. First, regulations regarding travel require clarification. Gosti were permitted to travel abroad, but they still required documented permission to do so. Meanwhile, according to the Conciliar Law Code, other subjects could appeal to the state to receive documentation to travel abroad. Given these circumstances the significance of the oft-repeated privilege is in question. Nonetheless, this section seeks to take stock of Russians traveling abroad.

We might chuckle at the historical irony that the term "Russian" may derive from an Old Norse word, *ródskarlar*, which meant "men who row," whereas Europeans like Marperger proclaimed Russians inveterate

93. Dewey and Stevens, "Muscovites at Play," 189–203. Voltaire, *Relation de la mort du Chevalier de la Barre*, 1–20; Laqueur, "Lecture 12: Enlightenment," 44:07–44:40.

94. Volkonskii, *Pictures of Russian History and Russian Literature*, 79.

95. Bond, *Russia at the Close of the Sixteenth Century*, xvii.

96. Marpergers, *Moscowitischer Kauffmann das ist*, 150.

97. Dale, *Indian Merchants and Eurasian Trade*, 85; Baron, "Fate of the Gosti," 508.

landlubbers.[98] But to rest on that bemusement misses the point that Russians negotiated daunting distances. Russian merchants did travel abroad. In the early modern period they frequented the marketplaces of Bukhara, Istanbul, Iran, Poland, Sweden, and the Caucasus. They seemed to travel south and east more than westward in the fifteenth and sixteenth centuries, which makes sense since the south and east offered such dynamic trade centers at that time. Russians traveled southward to Astrakhan before it was Russian territory. Indeed, Janet Martin documented hundreds of Russians traveling to the Ottoman Empire.[99] Russians were heavily present in Sweden, a major early modern power.[100] In the seventeenth century Russian merchants began to travel to China. The Filat'evs were among the most visible of several merchants who made the trip to the markets of Beijing. In 1706 the English envoy in St. Petersburg, Whitworth, remarked, "The court here is turned quite merchant, and not content with ingrossing the best commodities of their own country . . . are now further incroaching on the foreign trade and buy up whatever they want abroad under the name of particular merchants, who are only payed for their commission, but the gain and the risk is the Czar's."[101]

Russian merchants traveling internationally were more frequently recorded as part of state-sponsored missions, but it is unknown if this reflects surviving documentation or past practices. "Smolianina" Timofei Smyvalov (participated in the Zmeskii sobor, 1566) in 1567 traveled with the gost' I. Afanas'ev to Antwerp to trade state wares with municipal officials.[102] In 1575 Russian merchants visited Dordrecht, on the Thure River in western Netherlands, with furs to trade.[103] If such trips seem rare in the sixteenth century, Russians regularly traveled to Western European courts from London to Spain in the seventeenth century.

If Russian merchants did not regularly travel to Europe independent of diplomatic embassies, the English and Dutch are in part to blame. Baron demonstrated that the Muscovy Company specifically maneuvered so that Russians would not travel to England.[104] The Dutch did the same. They were intensely focused on holding the carriage trade and employed questionable methods to obtain it. The Dutchman Olivier Brunel may have deceived the

98. Pritsak, "Origin of Rus'," 250.
99. Martin, "Muscovite Travelling Merchants," 25. *Opisi tsarskogo arkhiva XVI veka*, 98.
100. Kotilaine, "Russian Merchant Colonies in Seventeenth-Century Sweden," 85–101.
101. Baron, "Fate of the Gosti," 505.
102. Golikova, PKK, 67.
103. Houtte, *An Economic History of the Low Countries*, 194.
104. Baron, "Osip Nepea."

Stroganovs when they entrusted him to organize a sea expedition to search for a northeast passage.[105] Recall how the Dutch colluded in the 1640s to defeat Anton Lapt'ev's venture in portage, refusing to purchase the goods he brought to Holland, only to later buy said goods at Lapt'ev's asking price in Arkhangel'sk.[106] In 1668 Tsar Aleksei sent an embassy to France to establish direct trade relations. In 1669 Compagnie du Nord was established. But in the second half of the seventeenth century the Dutch remained the primary intermediaries of the Russo-French trade, suggesting their methods paid off.[107]

The early modern Dutch, sometimes called the first capitalists, pioneered cutthroat methods that have long since become illegal. The Dutch engaged in price-fixing, collusion, and fraud, releasing onto the market low-quality products with an English seal to undermine the reputation of the Muscovy Company.[108] According to Scotsman Samuel Collins, the Hollanders, whom he likened to locusts, innovated the smear campaign, "rendring the English cheap and ridiculous with their lying pictures, and libelling pamphlets." [sic][109] The Dutch gouged on the interstices and strategically gifted their way to victory in the Anglo-Dutch trade competition. In a unique twist on foreigner condescension that might make us wonder why it is the Russians who are accused of xenophobia, Collins, who was on the losing side of the Anglo-Dutch rivalry, even blamed Russian villainy on the Dutch: "the generality of them [Russians] are false, Truce-breakers, subtile Foxes, and ravenous Wolves, much altered, since their traffick with the Hollander, by whom they have much improv'd themselves in villany and deceit."[110]

Rather than xenophobic, obdurate conservatism, however, context and inertia better explain geographical limits on the movements of Russian gosti and their agents. First, channels of trade that brought goods to Muscovy were well established. Second, to state the obvious, the Russian Empire was already

105. Krizhanich, "History of Siberia," reports that the Dutch had explored the northern Arctic coast. See Dmytryshyn, Crownhart-Vaughan, and Vaughan, *Russia's Conquest of Siberia*, no. 113, 1: 433. Krizhanich may be referring to three unsuccessful attempts organized by the Dutch merchant prince Balthasar de Moucheron to find a northeast passage in 1594–96. See Israel, *Dutch Primacy in World Trade*, 48. Stephen Berrou (1556) and Barents (1596) also explored the north coast of Asia in the sixteenth century.

106. Solov'ev, "Moskovskie kuptsy v XVII v.," 515. On the Lapt'ev affair, see Hellie, "Muscovite-Western Commercial Relations," 63–91; Shakharov, et al., *Sbornik dokumentov*.

107. Kotilaine, *Russia's Foreign Trade*, 93.

108. Kotilaine, "When the Twain Did Meet," 33. According to English merchants Dutch misdeeds were by no means limited to Russian territory. They accused the Dutch of unjustly applying the tare fine to English cloth imports.

109. Collins, *Present State of Russia*, 129.

110. Ibid., 128.

quite extensive and many gosti had numerous agents at far ends of it. It was a greater logistical feat to get from Arkhangel'sk to Nerchinsk than from London to Venice. But rather than taking the indictment on its own terms and parsing gosti movements, we must ask the question: Why would a manager travel abroad when his enterprise depends on political clout and coordinating the movements of goods and people across a vast geography? When faced with multiple investment opportunities surely it made less sense to invest in shipping while carriage options existed, even if in hindsight this choice is accused of lacking vision. Crossing oceans was a monumental innovation that required intestinal fortitude and technological expertise (even if it took less technological expertise to cross the Atlantic than to round the African continent). Seagoing vessels acquired a symbolic import to which a whole genre of maritime painting testifies. Accordingly, the absence of this achievement has sometimes been seen as a deficit imbued with massive significance.

In some ways, Russian merchants cannot win. Alfred Rieber, for example, noted that merchants' children made up 7.5 percent of the school population in 1855, and about 5 percent of the urban population, where schools were located. In his interpretation, that merchant numbers "barely exceeded" their proportion of the population reflects an antieducation attitude.[111] Even revision-minded interpretations still conclude that merchants were ultimately inimical to the development of capitalism. If "not entirely passive," Russian privileged merchants were culpable for quashing the development of a middle class. Implicit in this thinking is that those undermiddle classes could have been the healthy bourgeoisie to nurture capitalism and freedom. For example, Wallace Daniel reversed the typical question of how the tsar oppressed the merchants, and instead considered the extent to which merchants in the eighteenth-century textile industry oppressed those beneath them. There, where competition for market share, materials, and labor were all fierce, merchants sought to curtail freedoms of peasants, who were sometimes their entrepreneurial competitors as well, in the name of securing labor supply. Daniel concludes, "the merchant-entrepreneurs, the group charged with promoting the entrepreneurial spirit, acted also to limit it."[112] Baron condemned the gosti for lobbying the state to protect themselves against foreign competition, thereby undermining employment opportunities for Russia's lesser townspeople and trading men.[113] Kotilaine, albeit less judgmentally, described how elite merchants lobbied the court to legislate against foreign

111. Rieber, *Merchants and Entrepreneurs in Imperial Russia*, 27.
112. Daniel, "Entrepreneurship and the Russian Textile Industry," 25.
113. Baron, "Fate of the Gosti" and "Who Were the Gosti?" in *Muscovite Russia*.

merchants employing Russians for their affairs. Eliminating competition—
that is exactly what capitalists seek to do. In these treatments, Russian merchants are not too passive, but they remain enemies of progress.

This book attempts to modify a historiography informed by ideological
chauvinism and based too strongly on the observations of hostile witnesses
(although it has relied on those sources too) by presenting a more grounded
sense of commercial life as it was experienced in early modern Russia. My
work only begins to uncover, let alone satisfactorily analyze, the intricacies of
Russian business practices. But the fact that G. R. Nikitin was mentored in
the Filat′ev network, just as Spiridon Liangusov was in the Gostev family, and
that Noritsyn merchants operated for nearly a century working at various
times for various merchants or for themselves, to say nothing of the myriad
instances of cooperation that emerge in the study of everyday Siberian trade,
suggests a world of Russian commerce not captured in the traditional historiography. To put it plainly, there was something of a "middle" and there
was upward mobility in early modern Russia. One can debate the depth and
the vibrancy (a subjective term) of Russian mercantile society, but those who
have considered the questions satisfactorily settled have underestimated the
gap between sources and scholarship on the matter.

AFTERWORD

Meanings of Siberia

The history of Russian expansion across Siberia is the story of an empire learning to function and evolving as it did so. By the early nineteenth century the Russian Empire under Tsar Nicholas I advertised an official self-identity of "Orthodoxy, Autocracy, Nationality," but in the seventeenth century such a formulation was still far off. Siberia helped shape the empire's evolution of what it would become. Yet in the process, perceptions about Siberia were cornered into meanings that betrayed its first centuries in the empire.[1] Siberia by the nineteenth century came to be conceived of as a wasteland—"a savage land of exile, a kingdom of frost inhabited only by bears and bandits" is how one nineteenth-century intellectual characterized popular perceptions of it.[2] Indeed, some dictionaries even reify the association metonymically, defining Siberia as a place of exile. Although Tsar Aleksei Mikhailovich's chosen-then-rejected bride-to-be, Euphemia Vsevolozhskaia (1647), and the famous religious dissident Avvakum (1653), not to mention some criminals, were exiled to Siberia in the seventeenth century, the systematic expulsion and exploitation of the empire's unwanted

---

1. Bassin, "Visions of the Russian East," 763–94.
2. Mikhail Bestuzhev, 1837, quoted in Bassin, "Visions of the Russian East," 778.

and dangerous en masse in Siberia came later.[3] Yet that an uneducated peasant in revolutionary France referred to his exile as "Siberia" begins to suggest the power of this mythic image of Siberia through time, space, and societal layers.

Like any imperial conquest, the pursuit of glory is among the usual suspects for motivation behind Siberian expansion. To take the Siberian chronicles at their word, the conquest of Siberia was about fulfilling God's glory.[4] But if earning God's glory consists in converting souls, Russia followed up with a lackluster missionary record.[5] Even the official rhetoric equivocated. For example, before an audience at the imperial center in Moscow, Tsar Fëdor in 1688 issued a statement that extolled the state's religious duty and its glory and priority in extending its hegemony into Siberia.[6] Yet in letters to foreign leaders, Tsar Aleksei Mikhailovich had celebrated the Christian and Muslim subjects of his realm.[7] Glory could be measured not only in souls. For an increasingly cartographically inclined political elite, broad swaths of possessed territory imparted imperial glory. Although Peter I vigorously adopted this aspect of Western ideology, patronizing explorations and cartographical sciences, the acquisition of territory for territory's sake does not seem to have been a major Muscovite motivator.[8]

---

3. On exile: Gentes, *Exile to Siberia, 1590–1822.* On Avvakum: "Life of Archpriest Avvakum By Himself." The story of Euphemia Vsevolozhskaia is reminiscent of Cinderella. Eligible maidens from the region were assembled in Moscow for the tsarevich's (son of the tsar) consideration. Unlike *Cinderella*, the tsarevich's choice was not autonomous. Semenova-Tian'-Shanskogo, *Rossiia,* 16: 383. On royal marriages: Martin, *A Bride for the Tsar.*

4. *Polnoe sobranie russkikh letopisei: Sibirskie letopisi.* See Yesipov and Remezov chronicles, especially. Kivelson analyzes the Remezov chronicle in *Cartographies of Tsardom,* 150–53.

5. Slezkine, *Arctic Mirrors.* Even Michael Khodarkovsky, who argues that religious conversion was important to the state "at all times," sees the seventeenth century as a period of "benign neglect." Khodarkovsky, "'Not By Word Alone,'" 268. Nor did the state heavily promote conversion in Kazan after the conquest. See Romaniello, *Elusive Empire,* chap. 4.

6. Shamin, *Kuranty XVII stoletiia,* 171 fn.71.

7. RKO, vol. 1, no. 72, 167 (February 11, 1654 letter from Tsar Aleksei Mikhailovich to Chinese emperor about Fedor Baikov's embassy)."*i velikie ikh gosudarstva rosiiskie ot goda v god rosprostranialos' i mnogie okrestnye velikie gosudari khristianskie i musul'manskie s nimi, velikimi gosudari, ssylalis'ia, a inye ot nikh, velikikh gosudarei pomoshchi iskali, i otets nash velikii gosudar' mnogim velikim gosudarem i ikh gosudarstvam sposobstvovali i pomoshch' podavali.*" Author's translation: ". . . and their great Russian imperial kingdoms grew year by year and many surrounding great Christians and Muslim kingdoms with their great sovereigns, went over [to Russia], and others of those great kingdoms sought help and they, Great Sovereign tsars and Grand Russian princes, and our father the Great Sovereign, supported and helped many great sovereigns and their kingdoms." This letter drew on language from previous diplomatic correspondence, Tsar Aleksei Mikhailovich's letter to the Indian shah in 1646. See V.A. Ulianitskii, "Snosheniia Rossii s Sredneiu Azieiu i Indieiu," 22.

8. Shaw, "Geographical Practice and Its Significance in Peter the Great's Russia," 160–76; Kivelson, *Cartographies of Tsardom,* 24. On lack of territoriality see Lantzeff and Pierce, *Eastward to Empire,* 223–24; Sunderland, "Becoming Territorial"; Sunderland, *Taming the Wild Field.*

If images of exile, emptiness, or imperial glory did not dominate the mental architecture of seventeenth-century Russians, what was Siberia to them? Moscow's notorious reticence on strategy and the general paucity of appropriate sources makes this a difficult question to answer. As Michael Khodarkovsky has observed, "Until the mid-eighteenth century one would search in vain for memoranda . . . articulat[ing] its attitudes and policies toward the peoples along the southern frontier."[9] As the example above regarding Orthodoxy demonstrates, if it was not entirely silent, the state could give a different line to different audiences. To the extent that Russians told themselves stories about Siberia, Siberia from the outset was about two things. In a very narrow sense, it was about geopolitical conquest. Conquering the khanate of Kuchum imparted the powerful cachet of God-sanctioned conquest depicted in the Siberian chronicles; after all, the khanate of Kuchum, like the khanate of Kazan, was descended from Muscovy's previous overlords. But the conquests of Kazan and Sibir' were different enterprises. Moscow was hardly innocent, but Kuchum pushed Muscovy's hand.[10] Moscow did not set eastward across Eurasia looking for battle-earned glory (just as it was hardly heroic wanderlust that prompted early moderns to cross the Urals and brave the Arctic Ocean).[11] In a more sustained way, the conquest of Siberia was motivated by the pursuit of wealth, an endeavor more effectively pursued in the absence of outright warfare.

From the earliest Siberian chronicles, why and how Siberia was claimed has been debated, and scholarship over the centuries has sustained a discussion on whether state or individual initiative drove Siberian expansion.[12] Along this spectrum of opinion, the unglamorous fact was that both were intricately, competitively, and symbiotically involved in this process and that neither can be properly excised from a good explanation of Russian expansion in Siberia. Lake Yamysh, a trade outpost on the Eurasian plain, and the subject of chapter 5, epitomized the point: it developed as a vibrant space for independent commerce, originally located beyond the bounds of state regulations—that is, a negative reaction against state regulation. And yet state

---

9. Khodarkovsky, *Russia's Steppe Frontier*, 40.

10. Kuchum rejected his predecessor's subordination to Moscow. For his part, Ivan IV encouraged the Stroganovs to seek defectors from Kuchum's khanate and authorized military engagement. See May 30, 1574 charter to the Stroganovs in Miller, *Istoriia Sibiri*, no. 5, 1: 332–34.

11. This interpretation, advanced by Johann Fischer in the eighteenth century, reached fever pitch among nineteenth-century nationalistic Russian historians. See Lantzeff and Pierce, *Eastward to Empire*, 226; Bassin, "Visions of the Russian East," 778–82.

12. See Armstrong, *Yermak's Campaign in Siberia*; Slezkine and Diment, "Introduction," in Diment and Slezkine, *Between Heaven and Hell*, 1–14; Shandor Sili, "Conceptions of the Conquest of Siberia in Russian and Soviet Historiography," 74–82.

trade came to account for a substantial proportion of trade flow there. The relationship at Yamysh, as elsewhere in Siberia, was not simply oppositional: state and private initiative coexisted. Commercial activity in Siberia was an essential aspect of Russian imperialism, albeit pragmatic imperialism. Commerce was an important feature of that pragmatic imperialism, not to be overshadowed by statist perspectives that see military forts instead of towns and state tribute collections and prohibitions on black sable trade instead of a revenue collected at customs posts from a wide range of people plying their wares in and through Siberian territory.

From the outset, the Muscovite government perceived Siberia as an entitlement to two kinds of wealth: wealth from furs (a story that in general terms is well known but in specifics may never be satisfactorily known) and wealth from trade with the East, a story that has been overshadowed by an emphasis on furs. The aspiration to exploit wealth from metals and minerals was present from the early seventeenth century, even if it was realized only in the eighteenth,[13] and oil was discovered in Siberia in the twentieth, but from its very first forays eastward Russians believed that the East held the promise of profitable commerce. To be sure, such calculations got a boost from ideology—vanquishing former overlords carried strong cachet with the Muscovites, and gaining territory became an explicit mark of imperial achievement under Peter the Great, even if these things were not the raison d'être of the early Russian Empire.

Trade with the East could mean trade with Persia, India, Central Asia, and China. Just as the term "Orient" for Westerners had amorphous geographical bounds (Russians didn't use the term "Orient"), the term "India" in early Russian sources could encompass an area much larger, including even China.[14] Thus the story of Siberia in the seventeenth and eighteenth century is one of Russia, long embedded in the political world of the steppe, becoming more connected to the Far East and more integrated into a world economy that was increasingly dynamic and increasingly penetrating in its own right.

Siberia was also a node in important trans-Eurasian trade routes. It was a place in which Russian and Central Asian merchants met to exchange furs, pots, pans, mirrors, needles, wax, and wool for myriad silks, Eastern fabrics, spices, roots, and livestock. The stories of Russian and non-Russian merchants who made their livelihoods on the Eurasian plains open up a new

13. Anika Stroganov was interested in mineral (iron ore, copper) exploitation; documents throughout the seventeenth century reveal efforts to find mineral deposits. Kurlaev and Mankova, *Osvoenie rudnykh mestorozhdenii*; Lantzeff and Pierce, *Eastward to Empire*, 83.

14. Kurts, *Russko-Kitaiskie snosheniia*, 10, 12 fn.3.

perspective on the Russian imperial experience by illustrating patterns of cross-cultural exchange as well as the dynamics of state regulation and private initiatives in a frontier setting. Simultaneously, these stories help integrate "remote" Siberia in the expanding early modern economy.

ACKNOWLEDGMENTS

It is a great pleasure to thank those who have helped me in the research and writing of *The Merchants of Siberia*. A Fulbright-Hays dissertation fellowship and support from the Stanford Center for Russian, East European, and Eurasian Studies enabled two years of archival work. At the Institute of History in St. Petersburg, Andrei P. Pavlov, Pavel V. Sedov, and Evgenii V. Anisimov were unimaginably generous. Michael Krom at European University provided a welcoming base. I am grateful to Evgenii Rychalovskii at RGADA. Beyond doing his job ably, his queries have improved my approach. A. I. Razdorskii and L. A. Timoshina shared their expertise about customs. I am deeply indebted to Vera Kliueva of Tiumen'. She took me in completely, introduced me to Bukharans in the archives, and gave me a place to stay. Cheerful archivists in Tiumen' and Tobol'sk made it a pleasure to work there. Yulia Strazdyn' of the Lal'sk Historical Museum generously shared her knowledge of the Noritsyn family.

It was a tremendous privilege to study at Stanford. I have learned much from Nancy Kollmann, Paula Findlen, Terence Emmons, Bob Crews, Philippe Buc, Brad Gregory (now at Notre Dame), and Richard White. Bob Crews's questions about the Irtysh inspired me to write a history of Lake Yamysh. Many fellow students, including Sebastian Barreveld, Ann Livschiz, Paul Stronsky, Jehangir Malegam, Suzanne Mariko Miller, Junko Takeda, Ian Reed, Corey Tazzara, Suzanne Sutherland, Chad Martin, and Matthew Booker made graduate life stimulating, supportive, and fun.

I am fortunate to have wonderful colleagues at the University of New Mexico, especially Melissa Bokovoy and Sam Truett. Opportunities to share my work have been tremendously rewarding. Money from the UNM history department's Shoemaker fund enabled me to participate in the Eighteenth-Century Russian Studies conference in Durham, England, in 2009, where Alexander Martin and William Butler asked hard questions. Gary Marker and Janet Hartley showed early faith that my dissertation would become a book. I thank Valerie Kivelson for her encouragement and sharp insights, and for inviting me to the University of Michigan History Workshop. I thank Walter Simons and John Kopper for inviting me to Dartmouth

College, and John Randolph for including me in the 2013 Fisher Forum at the University of Illinois. I am grateful to all of the participants of these forums. I thank Alfrid Bustanov, Ronald Suny, Scott Levi, Brian Boeck, Natalia V. Kozlova, Adrian Selin, Robert Jones, David Ransel, Kees Botterbloem, Steve Nafgizer, Clare Griffin, Rachel Koroloff, and Pey-yi Chu for commenting on portions of the manuscript. Sergei Plis' was always quick with translation help.

I completed the manuscript as a fellow at the Davis Center in 2013, an opportunity made possible with a subsidy from the UNM Dean of Arts & Sciences. At Harvard, presentations to the Early Slavists' Seminar, the Russian History Workshop, and the "Imperial Legacies and International Politics" seminar led by Tim Colton and Serhii Plokhy brought constructive feedback. I thank Kelly O'Neill, Michael Flier, Greg Afinogenov, Katya Khodzhaeva, and the seminar participants for their input. I especially thank Serhii Plokhy, John LeDonne, and Don Ostrowski, who read the entire manuscript and with whom conversations were as stimulating as they were helpful. Serhii Plokhy, with his enviable acumen, suggested the perfect title.

Paul Bushkovitch, a "patron saint" of many projects, has contributed to this one at critical turns. He is the reason I labored in Siberian archives, having alerted my adviser to the substantial seventeenth-century holdings there. After I finished the dissertation, his question, "How big a proportion of trade in Russia was Siberia?" helped shape the agenda for revisions, even as a satisfactory answer to this question remains elusive. I owe special thanks to Matthew Romaniello. From targeted bibliographic suggestions to big-picture thinking, his input has improved the book and made the process more fun. My greatest intellectual debt is to Nancy Kollmann, who has been a guide and inspiration on this project from its inception. Her enthusiasm for the past, unfailingly prompt and incisive feedback on many drafts, and the way in which she nudges one to a higher standard are models of how to teach and be.

John Ackerman took this manuscript into retirement, for which I am deeply grateful. Connecting with his editorial expertise felt like reaching shore. I thank Don Ostrowski and an anonymous reader for their insightful reports on the submitted manuscript. Roger Haydon and the staff at Cornell University Press piloted it to completion with expertise and professionalism. Cody Sinclair helped with proofreading. Any mistakes that remain are mine alone.

Friends have made the journey worthwhile. In Russia, Vladimir and Svetlana Kachkov, Tengis and Natasha Verulashvili, Aleksandr Lastochkin and Anya Guseva, Timur Akhmedanov, Natalia Mineeva, Konstantin Yaemurd, and Sabra Ayres helped in so many concrete and intangible ways.

The Siutkins in Siberia were gracious hosts and the Heermances in Palo Alto, California, became a second family. I thank Jim Herson not only for his work on the OCR (Optical Character Recognition) technology that has enabled electronic searching of digitized texts, but also for his rope gun skills, sense of humor, and inspiration. Mr. Wyllie was an inspiring history teacher. Eeva Latuso, Jaime Andersen, Jen Joliff, Linda Smith, Rachel Samuelson, Chris Clark, and Lindsey Flagstad (even though she always asks about my work on the uphills) helped more than they know.

Finally, I thank my parents and siblings, Jennifer, Brenden, and Susan, for their love, support, and trust that what I do must be worthwhile. My mother, Cathy Parker, cared for my son while I was in Cambridge. When she could not, my father, Tom Monahan, stepped in. This made it doable. The births of Kevin and Darby slowed progress, but I would not have it any other way. Without my husband, Seth Downs, *The Merchants of Siberia* would not have seen the light of day. I dedicate this book to him with all my love.

BIBLIOGRAPHY

Archives

GBUTO GATO   State Financed Institution of Tiumen' Oblast', State Archive of Tiumen' Oblast' (Gosudarstvennoe biudzhetnoe ucherezhdenie Tiumenskoi oblasti, Gosudarstvennii arkhiv Tiumenskoi oblasti)

    f. 29 Tiumen' customs administration

    f. 47 Tiumenskaia voevodskaia kantselariia

GUTO GAT   State Institution of Tiumen' Oblast', State Archive in Tobol'sk (Gosudarstvennoe ucherezhdenie Tiumenskoi oblasti, Gosudarstvennii arkhiv v gorode Tobol'ske)

    f. 156 Tobol'skaia Dukhovnaia Konsistoriia

Harvard University, Houghton Library, Bagrow Collection.

Godunov Map 1667. MS 71 (1).

Remezov, Semen Ul'ianovich (1642–ca. 1720), *Khorograficheskaia kniga* (cartographical sketchbook of Siberia, also referred to as *Khorograficheskaia chertezhnaia knigi* and *Chorographic Sketchbook*). MS Russ 72 (6).

SPbII RAN   Sankt-Peterburgskii insitut istorii Rossiiskoi akademii nauk (St. Petersburg Institute of History – Russian Academy of Sciences) St. Petersburg

    f. 28 Verkhoturskaia voevodskaia kantseliariia

    f. 187 Tiumenskaia voevodskaia kantseliariia

RGADA   Rossiiskii gosudarstvennii arkhiv drevnikh aktov (Russian State Archive of Ancient Acts)

    f. 159 Prikaznye dela novoi razborki

    f. 214 Siberian Office

    f. 1111 Verkhoturskaia Prikaznaia Izba

Published Primary Sources

Akishin, M. O. *Pribyl'nye dela Sibirskikh voevod i tamozhennykh golov XVII–nachala XVIII vv.* Novosibirsk, 2000.

Akty istoricheskie sobrannye i izdannye arkheograficheskoi komissieiu. 5 vols. St. Petersburg, 1841–42.

Alekseev, M. P., ed. *Sibir' v izvestiiakh zapadno-evropeiskikh puteshestvennikov i pisatelei: Vvedenie, teksty i kommentarii, XIII–XVII vv.* 2nd ed. Irkutsk, 1941.

Arkheograficheskaia komissiia. *Sibirskiia lietopisi.* St. Petersburg, 1907.

Armstrong, Terence, ed. *Yermak's Campaign in Siberia.* London, 1975.

Avril, Phillipe. *Travels Into divers Parts of Europe and Asia, Undertaken by the French King's Order to discover a new Way by Land into China.* London, 1693.

Bahadir, Ebülgâzî. *A General History of the Turks, Moguls, and Tatars, vulgarly called Tartars. Together with a description of the countries they inhabit.* 2 vols. London, 1730.

Barbaro, Giosofat, and Contarini, Ambrogio. *Travels to Tana and Persia, by Josafa Barbaro and Ambrogio Contarini.* London, 1873.

Bell, John. *Travels from St. Petersburg, in Russia, to diverse parts of Asia.* 2 vols. Glasgow, 1763.

Bond, Edward A., ed. *Russia at the Close of the Sixteenth Century, comprising the treatise "Of the Russe Common Wealth" by Dr. Giles Fletcher and "The Travels of Sir Jerome Horsey."* London, 1856.

Brand, Adam. *A Journal of the Embassy to China, 1693, 1694, 1695.* London, 1698.

Chardin, Sir John. *Travels in Persia, 1673–1677.* London, 1927. Reprint, New York, 1988.

"The Charge of Companies of Merchants More Equally Born by Impositions on Trade Than Fines for Admissions." n.p., 1690s. In *The Making of the Modern World,* http://www.gale.com/ModernEconomy/, http://galenet.galegroup.com/servlet/MOME?af=RN&ae=U100310938&srchtp=a&ste=14, http://ezproxy.library.tufts.edu/login?url=http://galenet.galegroup.com/servlet/MOME?af=RN&ae=U100310938&srchtp=a&ste=14&locID=mlin_m_tufts.

"The Course of the Tare of Cloth in Holland." 1627. http://gateway.proquest.com.ezp-prod1.hul.harvard.edu/openurl?ctx_ver=Z39.88-2003&res_id=xri:eebo&rft_id=xri:eebo:image:177900:2.

Davydov, M.B, et al., comps. *Russko-Shvedskie ekonomicheskie otnosheniia v XVII veke.* Moscow, 1960. http://www.vostlit.info/Texts/Dokumenty/Skandinav/Sweden/Russ_swed_ek_17.

Demidova, N. F., and V. S. Miasnikov. *Pervye Russkie diplomaty v Kitae ("Rospis'" I. Petlina i stateinii spisok F. I. Baikova).* Moscow, 1966.

———, comps. *Russko-Kitaiskie otnosheniia v XVII veke v dvukh tomakh.* 2 vols. Edited by S. L. Tikhvinskii. Moscow, 1969–72.

———, comps. *Russko-Kitaiskie otnosheniia v XVIII veke v dvukh tomakh.* 2 vols. Edited by S. L. Tikhvinskii. Moscow, 1978.

Dmytryshyn, Basil, E. A. P. Crownhart-Vaughan, and Thomas Vaughan, eds. and trans. *To Siberia and Russian America: Three Centuries of Russian Eastward Expansion,* vol. 1, *Russia's Conquest of Siberia, 1558–1700.* Portland, OR, 1985.

Dopolnenie k aktam istoricheskim. 12 vols. St. Petersburg, 1846–72.

Fedotov-Chekhovskii, A. A. *Akty otnosiashchiesia do grazhdanskoi raspravoi drevnei Rossii.* vol. 1. Kiev, 1860.

Fletcher, Giles. *Of the Russe Common Wealth.* In Bond, *Russia at the Close of the Sixteenth Century,* 1–152.

Frye, Richard N., trans. and ed. *The History of Bukhara.* Cambridge, MA, 1954.

———, trans. and ed. *Ibn Fadlan's Journey to Russia.* Princeton, NJ, 2005.

Georgi, Johann Gottlieb. *Russia: Or, a compleat historical account of All the Nations which compose that Empire.* 4 vols. London, 1780.

Golovachev, P. M. *Tiumen' v XVII stoletii: Sobranie materialov dlia istorii goroda.* Moscow, 1903. Reprinted with an introduction by Iu. L. Mandrika, Tiumen', 2004.

Guminskii, V. M., ed. *Remezovskaia letopis': Sluzhebnaia chertezhnaia kniga.* Tobol'sk, 2006.

Hellie, Richard, ed. "Muscovite-Western Commercial Relations." In *Readings in Russian Civilization*, 63–92. Chicago, IL, 1970.

Herberstein, Sigismund von. *Notes upon Russia*. London, 1851. Reprint, New York, n.d.

Iakovlev, I. A. *Tamozhennye knigi Moskovskogo gosudarstva XVII v.*, vol. 1, *Severnii rechnoi put': Ustiug Velikii, Sol'vychegodsk, Tot'ma v 1633–1636 gg*. Moscow, 1950.

Ides, Eberhard. *Three Years Travels from Moscow Overland to China thro' Great Ustiga, Siriania, Permia, Sibiria, Daour, Great Tartary, &c. to Peking*. London, 1706.

Kazakova, E. N., trans. *Litsevoi letopisnii svod XVI veka*, bk. 23, *1557–1567 gg*. Moscow, 2010.

Kozlova, N. V. *Gorodskaia sem'ia XVIII veka: Semeino-pravovye akty kuptsov i raznochintsev Moskvy*. Moscow, 2002.

Krizhanich, Yuri. "History of Siberia." In Alekseev, *Sibir' v izvestiiakh zapadnoevropeiskikh puteshestvennikov i pisatelei*, 552–68.

Kurts, B. G., ed. *Sochinenie Kil'burgera o russkoi torgovlie v tsarstvovanie Aleksieia Mikhailovicha*. Kiev, 1915.

Lapt'eva, T. A., and T. B. Solov'eva. *F. Lefort: Sbornik materialov i dokumentov*. Edited by E. E. Lykova. Moscow, 2006.

Lavrentsov, T. D., and K. A. Antonova, eds. *Russko-Indiiskie otnosheniia v XVII veke. Sbornik dokumentov*. Moscow, 1958. http://www.vostlit.info/Texts/Dokumenty/Indien/XVII/1600-1620/Russ_ind_17.

"The Life of Archpriest Avvakum by Himself." In *Medieval Russia's Epics, Chronicles, and Tales*, edited by Serge A. Zenkovsky, 320–70. New York, 1963.

Lipinskii, M.A. "Rospis' komu imianem i za kakuiu vinu kakoe nakazanie bylo s priezdu v Tobolesk voevod kniazia Petra Ivanovicha Pronskogo, da Fedora Ivanovicha Lovchikova, da d'iakov Ivana Trofimova da Ondreia Galkina." *Chteniia OIDR* (1883) bk. 1: 17–41.

Marpergers, P. J. *Moscowitischer Kauffmann das ist, ausfürliche Beschreibung der Commercien, welche in Moscau und andern. . . .* Lübeck, 1705.

Materialy po istorii Uzbekskoi, Tadzhikskoi i Turkmenskoi SSR, vyp. 3, pt. 1, *Torgovlia s Moskovskim gosudartsvom i mezhdunarodnoe polozhenie Srednei Azii v 16–17 v.* Edited by A. N. Samoilovich. Leningrad, 1932.

"The Method of Preparing Tar in Russia, with Remarks." *The Boston News-Letter*, February 15–22, 1720, 1.

Mezhdunarodnye otnosheniia v Tsentral'noi Azii XVII–XVIII vv.: Dokumenty i materialy. vol. 1. Edited by B. P. Gurevich and G. F. Kim. Moscow, 1989.

Milescu, Nicolae. *Puteshestvie chez Sibir' ot Tobol'ska do Nerchinska i granits Kitaia Russkago poslannika Nikolaiia Spafariia v 1675 godu: Dorozhnii dnevnik Spafariia s vedeniem i primechaniiami*. Zapiski Imperatorskago Russkago Geograficheskog Obshchestva. vol. 10, issue 1. St. Petersburg, 1882.

Miller, G. F. *Istoriia Sibiri*. 3 vols. 2nd ed. Moscow, 1999–2005.

———. "Izvestie o pesoshnom zolote v Bukharii, o chinennykh dlia onogo otpravleniiakh i o stroenii krepostei pri reke Irtyshe, kotorym imena: Omskaia, Zhelezenskaia, Yamyshevskaia, Semipalatnaia i Ust'-Kamenogorskaia." In *Sochineniiakh i perevodakh, k pol'ze i uveseleniiu sluzhashikh* (January, pp. 3–54; February, pp. 99–136). St. Petersburg, 1760. Reprinted in Chulkov, *Istoricheskoe opisanie*, 410–78.

———. *Opisanie o torgakh' Sibirskikh*. St. Petersburg, 1756.

Miller, G. F., and Peter Simon Pallas. *Conquest of Siberia by Chevalier Dillon, and the history of the transactions, wars, commerce &c. &c. carried on between Russian and China, from the earliest period.* 2nd ed. London, 1843.

Morgan, E. Delmar, and C. H. Coote, eds. *Early Voyages and Travels to Russia and Persia by Anthony Jenkinson and Other Englishmen.* 2 vols. London, 1886.

Müller, G. F. "Travels in Siberia." Translated by Victoria Joan Moessner. In Black and Buse, *G. F. Müller and Siberia,* 63–112.

"Nakaz Pazukhinym, poslannym v Bukharu, Balkh i Iurgench, 1669." In *Russkaia istoricheskaia biblioteka,* edited by A. N. Truborova, 15: 1–86. St. Petersburg, 1894.

"Neizvestnii." In Alekseev, *Sibir' v izvestiiakh zapadno-evropeiskikh puteshestvennikov i pisatelei,* 325–72.

Olearius, Adam. *The Travels of Olearius in 17th-Century Russia.* Translated and edited by Samuel H. Baron. Stanford, CA, 1967.

————. *Voyages and Travells of the Ambassadors sent by Frederick Duke of Holstein, to the Great Duke of Muscovy, and the King of Persia, begun in the year 1633 and finished in 1639.* Translated by John Davies. 2nd ed. corrected. London, 1669.

Opisi Tsarskogo arkhiva XVI veka i arkhiva Posol'skogo prikaza 1614 goda. Edited by S. O. Shmidt. Moscow, 1960.

Orlova, N. S., comp. *Otkrytiia russkikh zemleprokhodtsev i poliarnykh morekhodov XVII veka na severo-vostoke Azii: Sbornik dokumentov.* Edited by A. V. Efimov. Moscow, 1951.

Pamiatniki sibirskoi istorii XVIII veka. Bk. 1, *1700–1713.* Bk. 2, *1714–1724.* St. Petersburg, 1885. Reprinted by Slavistic Printings and Reprintings. Edited by S. H. Van Schooneveld. The Hague, 1969–70.

Parsamyan, V.A., ed. *Armiano-russkie otnosheniia v XVII veke.* Vol. 1. *Sbornik dokumentov.* Erevan, 1953. http://www.vostlit.info/Texts/Dokumenty/Kavkaz/XVII/1620-1640/Arm_russ_otn_17_v.

Pis'ma i bumagi Imperatora Petra Velikago. 12 vols. Edited by A. A. Preobrazhenskii. St. Petersburg, 1887–.

"Pistsovye knigi goroda Kazani, 1565–68 i 1646 g." In *Materialy po istorii Narodov SSSR,* vyp. 2, *Materialy po istorii Tatarskoi ASSR,* edited by S. G. Tomsinskii, 72–201. Leningrad, 1932.

Pokrovskii, N. N. *Aktovye istochniki po istorii Rossii i Sibiri XVI–XVIII vekov v fondakh G. F. Miller: Opisi kopiinykh knig (v dvukh tomakh).* vol. 1. Novosibirsk, 1993.

Polnoe sobranie russkikh letopisei: Sibirskie letopisi. vol. 36. Moscow, 1987.

Polnoe sobranie russkikh letopisei: Ustiuzhskie, Vologodskie letopis', 16–18 cc. vol. 36. Leningrad, 1982.

Polo, Marco. *The Book of Ser Marco Polo, the Venetian.* vol. 2. Edited and translated by Henry Yule. London, 1871.

Postlethwayt, Malachy. *The Universal Dictionary of Trade and Commerce.* 4th ed. New York, 1971.

Pouncy, Carolyn J., ed. and trans. *The "Domostroi": Rules for Russian Households in the Time of Ivan the Terrible.* Ithaca, NY, 1994.

Prodolzhenie drevnei rossiiskoi vivliofiki. vol. 1. St. Petersburg, 1786. Reprinted by Slavistic Printings and Reprintings, 251/1. Edited by C. H. Van Schooneveld. Paris, 1970.

Romodanovskaia, E. K., and O. D. Zhuravel'. *Literaturnye pamiatniki Tobol'skogo arkhiereiskogo doma XVII veka*. Novosibirsk, 2001.

Russkaia istoricheskaia biblioteka. vol. 2. St. Petersburg, 1875.

Lavrentsov, T. D. and K. A. Antonova, ed. *Russko-Indiiskie otnosheniia v XVII veke*. *Sbornik dokumentov*. Moscow, 1958. http://www.vostlit.info/Texts/Dokumenty/Indien/XVII/1600-1620/Russ_ind_17.

Shakharov, A. M., et al. *Sbornik dokumentov po istorii SSSR dlia seminarskikh i prakticheskikh zaniatii (period feodalizma)*, pt. 4, *XVII v*. Moscow, 1973. Slesarchuk, G. I., et al. *Russko-Mongol'skikh otnoshenii, 1607–1691*. 4 vols. Moscow, 1959–2000.

Smirnov, P. P. *Novoe chelobit'e Moskovskikh torgovykh liudei o vysylkie inozemtsev; iz obshchestvennykh nastroenii gorozhan XVII v*. Kiev, 1912.

Sobranie gosudarstvennykh gramot i dogovorov. 4 vols. Moscow, 1813–1826.

Solov'eva, T. B., and T. A. Lapt'eva. *Privilegirovannoe kupechestvo Rossii vo vtoroi polovine XVI–pervoi chetverti XVIII v.: Sbornik dokumentov*. Moscow, 2004.

Solov'eva, T. B., and D. M. Volodikhin. *Sostav privilegirovannogo kupechstva Rossii v pervoi polovine 17 veka (po materialam rospisei gostei, gostinnoi i sukonnoi soten)*. Moscow, 1996.

Spafarii, Nikolai. *Puteshestvie cherez Sibir' do granits Kitaia*. Chita, 2009.

Strahlenberg, Johan Philip. *An historico-geographical description of the north and eastern parts of Europe and Asia, but more particularly of Russia, Siberia, and Great Tartary; both in their ancient and modern state: together with an entire new polyglot-table of the dialects of 32 Tartarian nations, and a vocabulary of the Kalmuck-Mungalian tongue*. London, 1738.

Sukharov, I. P., comp. *Skazaniia Russkago naroda*. vol. 2. St. Petersburg, 1849.

Trofimova, O. V. *Pamiatniki Tiumenskoi delovoi pis'mennosti, 1762–1796*. Bk. 2. Tiumen', 2002.

———. *Tiumenskaia delovaia pis'mennost', 1762–1796 gg*. Bk. 1. Tiumen', 2001.

Volkov, M. Ia, ed. *Tamozhennaia kniga goroda Vologdy 1634–1635 gg*. 3 vols. Moscow, 1983.

Voltaire. "History." In *Philosophical Dictionary*. 2nd ed. Vol. 4, 48–74. London, 1824.

———. *Relation de la mort du Chevalier de la Barre*. n.p., 1766.

Witsen, Nicolaas. *Noord en Oost Tartarye*. Amsterdam, 1692. Reprint, 1705.

———. *Puteshestvie v Moskoviiu, 1664–1665: Dnevnik*. Translated by V. G. Trisman. St. Petersburg, 1996.

———. *Severnaia i vostochnaia Tatariia, vkliuchaiushchaia oblasti, raspolozhennye v severnoi i vostochnoi chastiakh Evropy i Azii*. 2 vols. Translated from Dutch by V. G. Trisman, et al. Amsterdam, 2010.

Secondary Sources

Abramov, A. "The Lake Nor-Zaisan and Its Neighbourhood." Translated by John Michell. *The Journal of the Royal Geographical Society* 35 (1865): 58–69.

Adams, Julia. *The Familial State: Ruling Families and Merchant Capitalism in Early Modern Europe*. Ithaca, NY, 2005.

Ageeva, O.G. "Kupechestvo i sotsial'naia prazdnichnaia kul'tura russkikh stolits petrovskogo vremeni." In *Mentalitet i kul'tura predprinimatelei Rossii XVII–XIX vv.*, edited by L.N. Pushkarev, et al., 24–42. Moscow, 1996.

Agzamova, G. A. *Sredneaziatskie tsentry torgovli i puti, sviazyvavshchie ikh s Rossiei (vto-raia polovina XVI–pervaia polovina XIX v.)*. Tashkent, 1990.

Akel'ev, Evgenii. *Povsednevnaia zhizn' vorovskogo mira Moskvy vo vremena Van'ki Kaina*. Moscow, 2012.

Akishin, M. O., and A. V. Remenev, eds. *Vlast' v Sibiri: XVI–nachala XX veka*. Novosibirsk, 2002.

Aksenov, A. I., et al., eds. *Ekonomicheskaia istoriia Rossii s drevneishikh vremen do 1917 g. Entsiklopediia*. 2 vols. Moscow, 2008–9.

———. *Genealogiia moskovskogo kupechestva. Iz istorii formirovniia russkoi burzhuazii*. Moscow, 1988.

Aleksandrov, V. A. "Narodnye vosstaniia v vostochnoi Sibiri vo vtoroi polovine XVII v." *Istoricheskie Zapiski* 59 (1955): 255–309.

———. "Rol' krupnogo kupechestva v organizatsii pushnykh promyslov i pushnoi torgovli na Enisee v 17 v." *Istoricheskie Zapiski* 71 (1962): 183.

———. "Russko-Kitaiskaia torgovlia i Nerchinskii torg v kontse XVII v." In *K voprosu o pervonachal'nom nakoplenii v Rossii XVII–XVIII vv.: Sbornik statei*, edited by L. G. Beskrovnii, 422–56. Moscow, 1958.

———. "Sibirskie torgovye liudi Ushakovy v XVII v." In *Russkoe gosudarstvo v XVII veke*, edited by N. V. Ustiugov, 131–50.

Aleksandrov, V. A., and E. V. Chistiakova. "K voprosu o tamozhennoi politike v Sibiri v period skladyvaniia vserossiiskogo rynka (vtoraia polovina XVII v.)." *Voprosy Istorii* 2 (1959): 137–38.

Aleksandrov, V. A., and N. N. Pokrovskii. *Vlast' i obshchestvo: Sibir' v XVII v.* Novosibirsk, 1991.

Andreev, A. I. "Trudy G. F. Millera o Sibiri." In Miller, *Istoriia Sibiri*, 1: 66–149.

Andreev, A. R., comp. *Moskva. Kupechestvo. Torgovlia: XV–nachalo XX veka*. Moscow, 2007.

Andrievich, V. K. *Sibir' v tsarstvovanie imperatritsy Ekateriny II (1762–1769)*. Pt. 2. Krasnoiarsk, 1889.

Anisimov, E. A. *The Reforms of Peter the Great: Progress through Coercion*. Armonk, NY, 1993.

Apollova, N. G. *Khoziaistvennoe osvoenie Priirtysh'ia v kontse XVI–pervoi polovine XIX v.* Moscow, 1976.

Arapov, D. Iu. *Islam v Rossiiskoi imperii (zakonodatelnye akty, opisaniia, statistika)*. Moscow, 2001.

Archer, Ian W. "Responses to Alien Immigrants in London, c. 1400–1650." In *Le migrazioni in Europa, secc. XIII–XVIII*, edited by Simonetta Cavaciocchi, 755–74. Florence, 1994.

Arel, Maria S. "The Arkhangel'sk Trade, Empty State Coffers, and the Drive to Modernize: State Monopolization of Russian Export Commodities under Mikhail Fedorovich." In Kotilaine and Poe, *Modernizing Muscovy*, 175–202.

———. "Masters in Their Own House: The Russian Merchant Elite and Complaints against the English in the First Half of the Seventeenth Century." *Slavic and East European Review* 77, no. 3 (1999): 401–47.

Arkhangel'skii, S. I. "Diplomaticheskie agenty Kromvelia i peregovorakh s Moskvoi." *Istoricheskie Zapiski* 5 (1935): 118–40.

Arshakuni, O.K. "Pamiatniki 3-ogo perioda razvitiia arkhitektury zhilykh zdanii XVII veka." In *Grazhdanskaia arkhitektura Pskova*. Leningrad, 1975. http://spegalsky.narod.ru/biblioteka/gr_arch_psk/period_3.html.

Arsiukhin, Evgenii. "Sibirskoe khanstvo: Tëmnaia istoriia," http://archeologia.narod.ru/tum/tum.htm.

Bagrow, Leo. "Semyon Remezov, Siberian Cartographer." *Imago Mundi* 11 (1954): 111–25.

Baikova, N.B. *Rol' Srednei Azii v Russko-Indiiskikh torgovykh sviaziakh*. Tashkent, 1964.

Bailyn, Bernard. *The Merchants of New England in the Seventeenth Century*. Cambridge, MA, 1955.

Bakhrushin, S. V. *Nauchnye trudy: Ocherki po istorii remesla, torgovli, i gorodov Russkogo tsentralizovannogo gosudarstva XVI–nachalo XVII v.* 4 vols. Moscow, 1952–59.

Bakieva, G. T., and Iu. N. Kvashnin. "Nekotorye osobennosti traditsionnoi kul'tury bukhartsev zapadnoi Sibiri." In *Chelovek: Ego biologicheskaia i sotsial'naia istoriia*, 225–29. Moscow-Odintsovo, 2010.

Baklanova, N. A. "Ian de-Gron, prozhektier v moskovskom gosudarstve XVII veka." *Istoricheskie Zapiski* 4 (1929): 109–22.

Balandin. "Nachal'no russkogo kamennogo stroitel'stva v Sibir'." In Vilkov, *Sibirskie goroda*, 174–98.

Balkashina, N. "Torgovoe dvizhenie mezhdu zapadnoi Sibiri, Sredeniu Azieiu, i Kitaiskimi vladeniiami." *Zapiski Zapadno-sibirskogo otdela Imperatorskogo russkogo geografichiskogo obshchestvo*, kn. 3 (1881): 1–32.

Barkey, Karen. *Empire of Difference: The Ottomans in Comparative Perspective*. New York, 2008.

Barnett, Vincent. "Tugan–Baranovsky, the Methodology of Political Economy, and the 'Russian Historical School.'" *History of Political Economy* 36, no. 1 (2004): 79–101.

Baron, Samuel H. *Explorations in Muscovite History*. Brookfield, England, 1991.

———. *Muscovite Russia: Collected Essays*. London, 1980.

Baron, Samuel H., and Nancy Shields Kollmann, eds. *Religion and Culture in Early Modern Russia and Ukraine*. DeKalb, IL, 1997.

Bartol'd, V. V. *Sochineniia*, vol. 3, *Raboty po istoricheskoi geografii*. Moscow, 1965.

Bashkatova, Z. V. "Gorod Tara i ego torgovlia v XVII v." In *Tamozhennye knigi Sibirskikh gorodov*, vol. 1, edited by D. Ia. Rezun, 67–72. Novosibirsk, 1997.

———. "Pushnaia torgovlia goroda Tary v seredine XVII v." In Vilkov, *Torgovlia gorodov Sibiri*, 86–99.

Bassin, Mark. "Expansion and Colonialism on the Eastern Frontier: Views of Siberia and the Far East in Pre-Petrine Russia." *Journal of Historical Geography* 14, no. 1 (1988): 3–21.

———. "Geographies of Imperial Identity." In *The Cambridge History of Russia*, vol. 2, *Imperial Russia, 1689–1917*, edited by Dominic Lieven, 45–63. Cambridge, UK, 2006.

———. "Visions of the Russian East in the Early Nineteenth Century." *American Historical Review* 96, no. 3 (1991): 763–94.

Bazilevich, K. V. "Elementy merkantilizma v ekonomicheskoi politike pravitel'stva Alekseia Mikhailovicha." *Uchenye zapiski Moskovskogo ordena Lenina gosudarst-vennogo universiteta im. M. V. Lomonosova* 41 (1940): 1–34.

———. "K voprosu ob izuchenii tamozhennykh knig XVII v." *Problemy istochniko-vedeniia.* Vyp. 2. Moscow–Leningrad, 1936.

———. *Krupnoe torgovoe predpriiatie v moskovskom gosudarstve 1600–1650.* Lenin-grad, 1933.

Beardwood, Alice. *Alien Merchants in England, 1350 to 1377: Their Legal and Economic Position.* Cambridge, MA, 1931.

Beckwith, Christopher. *Empires of the Silk Roads.* Princeton, NJ, 2009.

Bentley, Jerry H. *Old World Encounters: Cross-Cultural Contacts and Exchanges in Pre-Modern Times.* New York, 1993.

Bernstein, Lina. "Russian Eighteenth-Century Merchant Portraits in Words and Oil." *The Slavic and East European Journal* 49, no. 3 (2005): 407–29.

Black, J. L. and D. K. Buse. *G. F. Müller and Siberia, 1733–1743.* Fairbanks, AK 1989.

Blum, Jerome. *Lord and Peasant in Russia, from the Ninth to the Nineteenth Century.* Princeton, NJ, 1961.

Boeck, Brian J. "Containment vs. Colonization." In *Peopling the Periphery,* edited by Nicholas Breyfogle, Abby Schraeder, and Willard Sunderland, 41–60. New York, 2007.

———. *Imperial Boundaries: Cossack Communities and Empire-Building in the Age of Peter the Great.* New York, 2009.

Bogatyrev, Sergei, ed. *Russia Takes Shape: Patterns of Integration from the Middle Ages to the Present.* Helsinki, 2004.

Boiko, V. P. "P. P. Shikhov." In *Kratkaia Entsiklopediia po istorii kupechestva i kommertsii Sibiri,* edited by D. Ia. Rezun and D. M. Tereshkov. Novosibirsk, 1999.

Bondarenko, I. A., ed. *Slovar' arkhitektorov i masterov stroitel'nogo dela Moskvy XV–serediny XVIII v.* Moscow, 2008.

Bonney, Richard, ed., *The Rise of the Fiscal State in Europe, c. 1200–1815.* New York, 2000.

"Booze Blamed for Early Deaths of Young Men." *Moscow News,* June 15, 2007. Lexis/Nexis database, accessed August 27, 2007.

Boterbloem, Kees. *Moderniser of Russia, Andrei Vinius, 1641–1716.* New York, 2013.

Braddick, Michael J. *The Nerves of State: Taxation and the Financing of the English State, 1558–1714.* New York, 1996.

Braudel, Fernand. *Civilisation metériell économie et capitalisme XV–XVIIIᵉ siècle,* tome 2, *Les jeux de l'echange.* Edited by "Le Livre de Poche." Paris, 1979.

———. *The Wheels of Commerce,* vol. 2 of *Civilization and Capitalism, 15–18th Cen-tury.* Translated from French by Siân Reynolds. New York, 1982.

Brewer, John. "The Error of Our Ways: Historians and the Birth of Consumer Soci-ety." In *Cultures of Consumption,* Working Paper Series 8 (June 2004).

———. *The Sinews of Power: War, Money, and the English State, 1688–1783.* Bos-ton, 1989.

Brumfield, William C. *A History of Russian Architecture.* New York, 1993.

Brunelle, Gayle K. *The Merchants of Rouen, 1559–1630.* Kirksville, MO, 1991.

Bulatov, V. N., et. al. *Istoriia Arkhangel'skoi tamozhni XVI–XX vv.* Arkhangel'sk, 2001.

Bulgakov, M. B. "Torgovoe dvizhenie po Oksko-Moskovskoi rechnoi sisteme v sere-dine XVII v." In Preobrazhenskii, *Promyshlennost' i torgovlia v Rossii XVII–XVIII vv.*, 209.

Burbank, Jane, and Frederick Cooper. *Empires in World History: Power and the Politics of Difference*. Princeton, NJ, 2010.

Burke, Peter. *Towards a Social History of Early Modern Dutch*. Amsterdam, 2006.

Burton, Audrey. *Bukharan Trade, 1558–1718*. Bloomington, IN, 1993.

———. *The Bukharans: A Dynastic, Diplomatic, and Commercial History, 1550–1702*. Surrey, UK, 1997.

Bushkovitch, Paul. "The Legacy of Seventeenth-Century Reform in Petrine Times." In Kotilaine and Poe, *Modernizing Muscovy*, 447–61.

———. *The Merchants of Moscow, 1580–1650*. New York, 1980.

———. "Princes Cherkasskii or Circassian Murzas: The Kabardians in the Russian Boyar Elite, 1560–1700." *Cahiers du Monde Russe* 45, nos. 1–2 (2004): 9–30.

———. "Taxation, Tax Farming, and Merchants in Sixteenth-Century Russia." *Slavic Review* 37, no. 3 (1978): 381–98.

Bustanov, Alfrid K. *The Book Culture of Siberian Muslims*. Moscow, 2013.

———. "Notes on the Yasavīya and Naqshbandīya in Western Siberia in the 17th–Early 20th Centuries." In *Islam, Society, and States across the Qazaq Steppe (18th–Early 20th Centuries)*, edited by Niccolò Pianciola and Paolo Sartori, 69–94. Vienna, 2013.

———. "The Sacred Texts of Siberian Khwaja Families: The Descendants of Sayyid Ata." *Journal of Islamic Manuscripts* 2, no. 1 (2011): 70–99.

———. "Sufiiskie legendy ob islamizatsii Sibiri." In *Tjurkskie narody Evrazii v drevnosti i srednevekov'e: Tjurkologičeskij sbornik, 2009–2010*, edited by S. G. Kljaštornyj, T. I. Sultanov, and V. V. Trepavlov, 33–78. Moscow, 2011.

———. "Sviashchennye rodoslovnye I mezhregional'nye sviazi musulman Severnoi Evrazii: istoriia sem'I Shikhovykh v XVII–XX vv." ["Sacred Genealogies and Transnational Contacts of Muslims of Northern Eurasia: The History of the Shikhov Family in the 17th–20th Centuries."] Unpublished paper shared by author. January 2014.

Bustanov, A. K., and I. V. Belich. "Sviazi arkheologii i etnografii s gumanitarnymi i estestvennymi naukami." In *Integratsiia arkheologicheskikh i etnograficheskikh issle-dovanii*, edited by Kn. N. Tikhomirov, et al., 211–16. Omsk, 2010.

Bustanov, A. K., and S. N. Korusenko. "Famil'naia khronika sibirskikh saiidov, Shadzhara risalasi (tekst, perevod, kommentarii)." *Islam v Sovremennom Mire*, nos. 13–14 (2009): 45–61.

———. "Genealogy of the Siberian Bukharians: The Imyaminov Clan." *Archeology, Ethnology and Anthropology of Eurasia* 38, no. 2 (2010): 97–105.

Butsinskii, P. N. *Zaselenie Sibiri i byt pervykh ee nasel'nikov*. 2 vols. Kharkov, 1889. Reprint, Tiumen', 1999.

Bychkov, I. A. *Katalog sobraniia slaviano-russkikh rukopisei P. D. Bogdanova*. vol. 1. St. Petersburg, 1891–93.

"Celebrating the 450th Anniversary of the Printing of the 'Apostol' of Ivan Fedorov and Petr Mstislavets," Exhibit at the Russian State library, Moscow, Russia. March 13–April 1, 2014. http://www.rsl.ru/ru/s7/s381/2014/apostol.

Chartier, Roger. "Histoire des mentalités." In *The Columbia History of Twentieth-Century French Thought*, edited by Lawrence D. Kritzman and Brian J. Reilly, 54–58. New York, 2007.

Cherepnin, L. V. "I. V. Stalin o russkom feodalizme." *Uchenye zapiski Moskovskogo ordena Lenina gosudarstvennogo universiteta imeni M. V. Lomonosova*, yp. 156, 3–18. Moscow, 1952.

Chernyshov, A. V. *Staroobriadchestvo i staroobriadtsy zapadnoi Sibiri (XVII–XXI vv.): Annotirovannye bibliografiia istochnikovedcheskii obzor, dokumenty*. Tiumen, 2006.

Childs, Wendy. "Commerce and Trade." In *The New Cambridge Medieval History*, vol. 7, edited by Christopher Allmand, 145–60. Cambridge, UK, 1998.

Chimitdorzhiev, Sh. B. "Iz istorii Russko-Mongol'skikh ekonomicheskikh sviazei XVII v." *Istoriia SSSR* 3 (1964): 151–56.

———. *Rossiia i Mongolia*. Moscow, 1987.

Christian, David. "Silk Road or Steppe Roads?: The Silk Roads in World History." *Journal of World History* 11, no. 1 (2000): 1–26.

Chulkov, M. D. *Istoricheskoe opisanie rossiiskoi kommertsii pri vsiekh portakh i granitsakh ot drevnikh vremian do nynie nastoiashchago i vsiekh preimushchestvennykh uzakonenii po onoi Gosudaria Imperatora Petra Velikago i nynie blagopoluchno tsarstvuiushchei Gosudaryni Imperatritsy Ekateriny Velikiia*. vol. 3, part 1. St. Petersburg, 1785.

Chuloshnikov, A. "Torgovlia Moskovskogo gosudarstva s Srednei Aziei v XVI–XVII vekakh." In *MUITTSSR*, Pt. 1, *Torgovlia s Moskovskim gosudartsvom i mezhdunarodnoe polozhenie Srednei Azii v 16–17 v.*, edited by A. N. Samoilovich, 61–88. Leningrad, 1932.

Coleman, D. C. "Mercantilism Revisited." *Historical Journal* 23 (1980): 773–91.

Collins, David. "Subjugation and Settlement in Seventeenth- and Eighteenth-Century Siberia." In *The History of Siberia*, edited by Alan Wood, 36–56. New York, 1991.

Constable, Olivia Remie. *Housing the Stranger in the Mediterranean World: Lodging, Trade and Travel in Late Antiquity and the Middle Ages*. New York, 2003.

Cracraft, James. *The Petrine Revolution in Russian Culture*. Cambridge, MA, 2004.

Crean, J. F. "Hats and the Fur Trade." *Canadian Journal of Economics and Political Science* 28, no. 3 (1962): 373–86.

Crummey, Robert O. *The Formation of Muscovy, 1304–1613*. New York, 1987.

Curto, Diogo Ramada, and Anthony Molho. "Commercial Networks in the Early Modern World." EUI Working Paper HEC No. 2002/2. San Domenico, Italy, 2002. http://cadmus.eui.eu/bitstream/handle/1814/61/HEC02-02.pdf?sequence=1. Accessed April 27, 2011.

Dahl', V. I. *Tolkovii slovar' zhivogo velikorusskogo iazyka*. 4 vols. St. Petersburg, 1880.

Dahlmann, Dittmar. *Sibirien: Vom 16. Jahrhundert bis zur Gegenwart*. Munich, 2009.

Dale, Stephen. *Indian Merchants and Eurasian Trade, 1600–1750*. New York, 2002.

Daniel, Wallace. "Entrepreneurship and the Russian Textile Industry: From Peter the Great to Catherine the Great." *Russian Review* 54, no. 1 (1995): 1–25.

Darnton, Robert. *The Great Cat Massacre and Other Episodes in French Cultural History*. New York, 1984.

Davies, Brian L. "The Politics of Give and Take: Kormlenie as Service Remuneration and Generalized Exchange, 1488–1726." In *Culture and Identity in Muscovy,*

1359–1584, edited by Ann M. Kleimola and Gail Lenhoff, 39–67. Moscow, 1997.

———. *Warfare, State and Society on the Black Sea Steppe, 1500–1700.* London, 2007.

Davies, R. W. "Revisions in Economic History: XIV. Russia in the Early Middle Ages." *Economic History Review,* New Series 5, no. 1 (1952): 116–27.

Dechene, Louise. *Habitants and Merchants in Seventeenth-Century Montreal.* Translated by Liana Vardi. Montreal, 1992.

De Divitiis, Gigliola Pagano. *English Merchants in 17th c. Italy.* Translated by Stephen Parkin. Cambridge, UK, 1997.

Demidova, N. F. "Biurokratizatsii gosudarstvennogo apparata absoliutizma v XVII–XVIII v." In *Absoliutizm v Rossii (XVII–XVIII vv.),* 206–42. Moscow, 1964.

———. *Sluzhilaia biurokratiia v Rossii XVII v. i ee rol' v formirovanii absoliutizma.* Moscow, 1987.

Demkin, A. V. *Zapadnoevropeiskie kuptsy i ikh prikazchiki v Rossii v XVII veka.* Moscow, 1992.

———. *Zapadnoevropeiskie kuptsy i ikh tovary v Rossii XVII veka.* Moscow, 1992.

De Vries, Jan. "Connecting Europe and Asia: A Quantitative Analysis of the Cape Route Trade, 1497–1795." In *Global Connections and Monetary History, 1470–1800,* edited by Dennis Owen Flynn, 35–105. Burlington, VT, 2003.

———. "The Economic Crisis of the Seventeenth Century after 50 Years." *Journal of Interdisciplinary History* 40, no. 2 (2009): 151–94.

———. *The Economy of Europe in an Age of Crisis, 1600–1750.* New York, 1976.

———. "The Limits of Globalization in the Early Modern World." *Economic History Review* 63, no. 3 (2010): 710–33.

Dewey, Horace W., and Kira B. Stevens. "Muscovites at Play: Recreation in Pre-Petrine Russia." *Canadian–American Slavic Studies,* nos. 1–2 (1979): 189–203.

Diment, Galya, and Yuri Slezkine, eds. *Between Heaven and Hell: The Myth of Siberia in Russian Culture.* New York, 1993.

di Salvo, Maria. "The 'Italian' Nemetskaia Sloboda." *Slavonic and East European Review* 88, nos. 1–2 (2010): 96–109.

Donnelly, Alton. *The Russian Conquest of Bashkiria, 1552–1740.* New Haven, CT, 1968.

Dovnar-Zapol'skii, M. V., ed. *Russkaia istoriia v ocherkakh i stat'iakh.* Vol. 3. Kiev, 1912.

———. "Torgovlia i promyshlennost'." In Dovnar-Zapol'skii, *Russkaia istoriia v ocherkakh i statiakh,* 312–41.

Druhe, David N. *Russo-Indian Relations, 1466–1917.* New York, 1970.

Dukes, Paul. "Russia on the Eurasian Frontier and Early Modern Empire." In *The Place of Russia in Europe and Asia,* edited by Gyula Szvák, 13–24. Budapest, 2001.

Dunning, Chester. "James I, the Russian Company, and the Plan to Establish a Protectorate over North Russia." *Albion* 21 (1989): 206–26.

Duplessis, Robert S. "Review of *The Early Modern European Economy,* by Peter Musgrave." *Journal of Economic History* 60, no. 3 (2000): 877–78.

Eisendtadt S. N., and L. Roniger. *Patrons, Clients and Friends: Interpersonal Relations and the Structure of Trust in Society.* Cambridge, UK, 1984.

Emerson, Ralph Waldo. "Self-Reliance" (1841). In *Essays: First Series*. http://www.emersoncentral.com/selfreliance.htm.

Emmons, Terence. "Kliuchevsky and His Pupils." In *Modern Russian Historiography*, edited by Anatole G. Mazour, 118–45. Westport, CT, 1975.

Engels, Friedrich. *The Condition of the Working-Class in England in 1844*. London, 1892.

Enin, G. P. *Voevodskoe kormlenie v Rossii v XVII veke: Soderzhanie naseleniem uezda gosudarstvennogo organa vlasti*. St. Petersburg, 2000.

———. "Voevodskaia tamozhennaia poshlina v XVII v." In Pavlov, *Torgovlia, kupechestvo i tamozhennoe delo*, 248–55.

Esper, Thomas. "Russia and the Baltic, 1494–1558." *Slavic Review* 25, no. 3 (1966): 458–74.

Etkind, Alexander. "Barrels of Fur: Natural Resources and the State in the Long History of Russia." *Journal of Eurasian Studies* 2, no. 2 (2011): 164–71.

Evseev, E. N. "Tara v svoi pervye dva stoletiia." In Vilkov, *Sibirskie goroda*, 78–108.

"Ex Tempore: Orientalism and Russia." *Kritika* 1, no. 4 (2000): 691–728.

Fekhner, M. V. *Torgovlia russkogo gosudarstva so stranami vostoka v XVI veke*. Moscow, 1956.

Feshbach, Murray. "A Country on the Verge." *The New York Times*, May 31, 2006.

Filippov, A. M. "Novye dannye o posol'stve Seitkula Ablina." *Sovetskoe Kitaevedenie* 2 (1958): 135–37.

Findlay, Ronald, and Kevin H. O'Rourke. *Power and Plenty: Trade, War, and the World Economy in the Second Millenium*. Princeton, NJ, 2007.

Fisher, Raymond. *The Russian Fur Trade, 1550–1700*. Berkeley, CA, 1943.

Fletcher, Joseph. "The Mongols: Ecological and Social Perspectives." *Harvard Journal of Asiatic Studies* 46, no. 1 (1986): 11–50.

Floria, B. N. "Privilegirovannoe kupechestvo i gorodskaia obshchina v russkom gosudarstve (vtoraia polovina XV–nachalo XVII v.)." *Istoriia SSSR* 5 (1977): 145–61.

———. "Review of N. B. Golikova, *Privilegirovannye kupecheskie korporatsii Rossii XVI–pervoi chetverti XVIII v.*, vol. 1 (Moscow: Pamiatniki istoricheskoi mysli, 1998)." *Otechestvennaia Istoriia*, no. 2 (2001): 181.

Foltz, Richard C. *Religions of the Silk Road*. New York, 1999.

Forsyth, James. *A History of the Peoples of Siberia: Russia's North Asian Colony, 1581–1990*. New York, 1992.

Foust, Clifford. *Muscovite and Mandarin: Russia's Trade with China and Its Setting*. Chapel Hill, NC, 1969.

———. "Russian Expansion to the East through the Eighteenth Century." *Journal of Economic History* 21, no. 4 (1961): 469–82.

———. *Rhubarb: The Wondrous Drug*. Princeton, NJ, 1992.

Frank, Allen J. *Bukhara and the Muslims of Russia: Sufism, Education, and the Paradox of Islamic Prestige*. New York, 2013.

———. *Islamic Historiography and "Bulghar" Identity among the Tatars and Bashkirs of Russia*. Boston, 1998.

———. *The Siberian Chronicles and the Taybughid Biys of Sibir'*. Papers on Inner Asia 27. Bloomington, IN, 1994.

————. "Varieties of Islamicization in Inner Asia: The Case of the Baraba Tatars, 1740–1917." *Cahiers du Monde Russe* 41, nos. 2–3 (2000): 245–62.

————. "The Western Steppe: Volga-Ural Region, Siberia and the Crimea." In *Cambridge History of Inner Asia*, edited by Nicola DiCosmo, Allen J. Frank, and Peter B. Golden, 237–59. New York, 2009.

Frank, Andre Gunder. "ReOrient: From the Centrality of Central Asia to China's Middle Kingdom." In *Rethinking Central Asia: Non-Eurocentric Studies in History and Social Structure, and Identity*, edited by Korkut A. Erturk, 11–38. Reading, UK, 1999.

————. *ReOrient: Global Economy in the Asian Age*. Berkeley, CA, 1998.

Franklin, Simon, and Jonathan Shepard. *The Emergence of Rus'*. New York, 1996.

Frick, David. *Kith, Kin, and Neighbors: Communities and Confessions in 17c. Wilno*. Ithaca, NY, 2013.

Fuhrmann, Joseph T. *Origins of Capitalism in Russia*. Chicago, 1972.

Fuller, William C., Jr. *Strategy and Power in Russia, 1600–1914*. New York, 1992.

Fund, W. "West Siberian Broadleaf and Mixed Forests." *Encyclopedia of Earth*. 2014. http://www.eoearth.org/article/West_Siberian_broadleaf_and_mixed_forests.

Geiman, V. G. *Khoziaistvo krupnogo feodala-krepostnika XVII v*. 2 vols. Leningrad, 1933.

Gelder, M. van. *Library of Economic History*, vol. 1, *Trading Places: The Netherlandish Merchants in Early Modern Venice*. Boston, 2009.

Gentes, Andrew. *Exile to Siberia, 1590–1822*. New York, 2008.

Gerschenkron, Alexander. "Russia: Patterns and Problems of Economic Development, 1861–1958." In Gerschenkron, *Economic Backwardness in Historical Perspective: A Book of Essays*, 119–51. Cambridge, MA, 1962.

————. *Europe in the Russian Mirror: Four Lectures in Economic History*. Cambridge, 1970.

Gibson, James R. *Feeding the Russian Fur Trade: Provisionment of the Okhotsk Seaboard and the Kamchatka Peninsula*. Madison, WI, 1969.

Gladwell, Malcolm. *Outliers: The Story of Success*. New York, 2008

Glete, Jan. *War and the State in Early Modern Europe: Spain, the Dutch Republic and Sweden as Fiscal-Military States, 1500–1660*. New York, 2002.

Glinka, G. V. *Atlas Aziatskoi Rossii*. Vol. 1. St. Petersburg, 1914.

Goffmann, Daniel. *The Ottoman Empire and Early Modern Europe*. New York, 2002.

Golden, Peter B. *Central Asia in World History*. New York, 2011.

Goldstein, Darra. "Gastronomic Reforms under Peter the Great: Toward a Cultural History of Russian Food." *Jahrbücher für Geschichte Osteuropas, Neue Folge* 48, no. 4 (2000): 481–510.

Goldstone, Jack. "The Problem of the 'Early Modern' World." *Journal of the Economic and Social History of the Orient* 41, no. 3 (1998): 249–84.

Golikova, N. B. "Chislennost', sostav i istochniki popolneniia gostei v kontse XVI–pervoi chetverti XVIII v." In *Russkii gorod (issledovaniia i materialy)*, vol. 8, edited by V.L. Ianin and N.I. Nasonkin, 83–115. Moscow, 1986.

————. "Formy zamlevladeniia i zemlopol'zovaniia gostei i gostinoi sotni v kontse XVI–nachale XVIII v." In *Torgovlia i predprinimatel'stvo v feodal'noi Rossii. K iubileiu professora russkoi istorii Niny Borisovny Golikvoi*, edited by L. A. Timoshina et al., 26–45. Moscow, 1994.

————. *Ocherki po istorii gorodov Rossii: Kontsa XVII–nachala XVIII v.* Moscow, 1982.

————. *Privilegirovannye kupecheskie korporatsii Rossii XVI–pervoi chetverti XVIII v.* Vol. 1. Moscow, 1998.

————. *Privilegirovannoe kupechestvo v structure russkogo obshchestva v XVI–pervoi chetverti XVIII v.* Vol. 2. Moscow-St. Petersburg, 2012.

Golovachev, P. M. *Tiumen' v XVII veke.* Moscow, 1903.

————. *Tomsk v XVII veke.* Moscow, 1903.

Gommans, Jos. "The Horse Trade in Eighteenth-Century South Asia." *Journal of Economic and Social History of the Orient* 37, no. 3 (1994): 228–50.

Graham, Stephen. *Boris Godunof.* New Haven, CT, 1933.

Halperin, Charles. "Muscovy as a Hypertrophic State: A Critique." *Kritika: Explorations in Russian and Eurasian History* 3, no. 3 (2002): 501–7.

Hamamoto, Mami. "Conversion of Muslim Elites to Orthodoxy Christianity in Seventeenth-Century Russia." Paper presented at annual convention of the Association for Slavic, East European and Eurasian Studies (ASEEES), Los Angeles, CA, November 18–20, 2010.

Hansen, Valerie. *Silk Road: A New History.* New York, 2012.

Haugh, Alexandra M. "Indigenous Political Culture and Eurasian Empire: Russia in Siberia in the Seventeenth Century." PhD diss., University of California, Santa Cruz, 2005.

Hayek, F. A. "The Use of Knowledge in Society." *American Economic Review* 35, no. 4 (1945): 519–30.

Hellie, Richard. *The Economy and Material Culture of Muscovy, 1600–1725.* Chicago, IL, 1999.

————. "Great Wealth in Muscovy: The Case of V. V. Golitsyn and Prices of the 1600–1725 Period." *Harvard Ukrainian Studies* 19 (1995): 226–70.

Henshall, Nicholas. *The Myth of Absolutism: Change and Continuity in Early Modern European Monarchy.* New York, 1992.

Hirschman, Albert O. *The Passions and the Interests: Political Arguments for Capitalism before Its Triumph.* Princeton, NJ, 1997.

Hittle, Michael J. *The Service City: State and Townsmen in Russia, 1600–1800.* Cambridge, MA, 1979.

Hodai, Beau. "Legislative Laundry: How the American Legislative Exchange Council (ALEC) Funnels Millions of Dollars in Corporate Gifts to State Lawmakers for the Express Purpose of Promoting Corporate-Backed Legislation." http://dbapress.com/front-page/legislative-laundry-how-alec-funnels-millions-of-dollars-in-corporate-gifts-to-state-lawmakers-for-the-express-purpose-of-promoting-corporate-backed-legislation. 2011.

Hopkirk, Peter. *The Great Game: The Struggle for Empire in Central Asia.* New York, 1990.

Hosking, Geoffrey A. "Patronage and the Russian State." *Slavic and East European Review* 78, no. 2 (2000): 301–20.

————. *Russia: People and Empire, 1552–1917.* London, 1997.

Houtte, J. A. *An Economic History of the Low Countries, 800–1800.* World Economic History. Edited by Charles Wilson. London, 1977.

Howell, Martha C. *Commerce before Capitalism in Europe, 1300–1600.* New York, 2010.

Hughes, Lindsey. "Attitudes towards Foreigners in Early Modern Russia." In *Russia and the Wider World in Historical Perspective: Essays for Paul Dukes*, edited by Cathryn Brennan and Murray Frame, 1–23. Gordonsville, VA, 2000.

——. *Russia in the Age of Peter the Great*. New Haven, CT, 1998.

IMF World Economic Outlook. "World GDP Ranking 2014." http://knoema. com/nwnfkne/world-gdp-ranking-2014-data-and-charts.

Iskhakov, D. M., and I. L. Izmailov. *Etnopoliticheskaia istoriia Tatar*. Kazan, 2007.

Israel, Jonathan I. *Dutch Primacy in World Trade, 1585–1740*. New York, 1989.

Istoriia Moskvy. 6 vols. Moscow, 1952.

Iukht, A. I. "Russko-Vostochnaia torgovlia v XVII–XVIII vekakh i uchastie v nei indiiskogo kupechestva." *Istoriia SSSR* 6 (1978): 42–56.

Ivantsova, G. I., et al., *Tiumenskaia tamozhnia: Proshloe i nastoiashchee*. Tiumen', 1998.

Jones, Robert E. *Bread upon the Waters: The St. Petersburg Grain Trade and the Russian Economy, 1703–1811*. Pittsburgh, PA, 2013.

Jones, Ryan. "A 'Havoc Made among Them': Animals, Empire, and Extinction in the Russian North Pacific, 1741–1810." *Environmental History* 16, no. 4 (2011): 585–609.

Kabo, P. M. *Goroda zapadnoi Sibiri: Ocherki istoriko-ekonomicheskoi geografii (XVII–pervaia polovina XIX vv.)*. Moscow, 1949.

Kafengauz, B. B. *Ocherki vnutrennego rynka Rossii pervoi poloviny XVIII veka (po materialam vnutrennykh tamozhen)*. Moscow, 1958.

Kagarlitsky, Boris. *Empire of the Periphery: Russia and the World System*. Translated by Renfrey Clarke. Ann Arbor, MI, 2008.

Kahan, Arcadius. *The Plow, the Hammer and the Knout: An Economic History of Eighteenth-Century Russia*. Edited by Richard Hellie. Chicago, IL, 1985.

Kaiser, Daniel H. "Naming Cultures in Early Modern Russia." *Harvard Ukrainian Studies* 19 (1995): 276–83.

Kamenetskii, I. P., and D. Ia. Rezun. "Ozero Iamysh kak zona politicheskogo i khozia'stvennogo vzaimodei'stviia narodov v XVII v." *Gumanitarnye Nauki v Sibiri* 2 (2010): 32–35.

Kaplan, Stephen. *Provisioning Paris: Merchants and Millers in the Grain and Flour Trade during the Eighteenth Century*. Ithaca, NY, 1984.

Kaplun, I. I., D. I. Kopylov, and T. D. Rozhkova. *Tiumenskii uezd v XVII–XVIII vv. (Obzor fonda-kompleksa Tiumenskoi prikaznoi izby i voevodskoi kantseliarii)*. Tiumen', 1969.

Katanov, N. F. "O religioznykh voinakh uchenikov sheikha Bagauddina protiv inozemtsev zapadnoi Sibiri." *Ezhegodnik Tobol'skogo Gubernskogo Muzeiia* 15 (1904): 133–46.

Keenan, Edward L. "Muscovite Political Folkways." *Russian Review* 45, no. 2 (1986): 115–81.

Khazeni, Arash. "Through an Ocean of Sand: Pastoralism and the Equestrian Culture of the Eurasian Steppe." In *Water on Sand: Environmental Histories of the Middle East and North Africa*, edited by Alan Mikhail, 133–58. New York, 2013.

Khitrov, A. *K istorii Irbitskoe iarmarki*. n.p., 1872.

Khodarkovsky, Michael. *Bitter Choices*. Ithaca, NY, 2011.

————. "'Ignoble Savages and Unfaithful Subjects': Constructing Non-Christian Identities in Early Modern Russia." In *Russia's Orient: Imperial Borderlands and People, 1700–1917,* edited by Daniel R. Brower and Edward J. Lazzerini, 9–26. Bloomington, IN, 1997.

————. "'Not By Word Alone': Missionary Policies and Religious Conversion in Early Modern Russia." *Comparative Studies in Society and History* 38, no. 2 (1996): 267–93.

————. *Russia's Steppe Frontier: The Making of a Colonial Empire, 1500–1800.* Bloomington, IN, 2002.

————. *Where Two Worlds Met: The Russian State and the Kalmyk Nomads, 1600–1771.* Ithaca, NY, 1992.

Kilian, Janet Marie. "Allies and Adversaries: The Russian Conquest of the Kazakh Steppe." PhD diss., George Washington University, 2013.

Kirpichnikov, A. N. *Rossii v XVII v. v risunakh i opisanniiakh Gollandskogo puteshestvennika Nikolaasa Vitsena.* St. Petersburg, 1995.

Kivelson, Valerie A. *Autocracy in the Provinces: The Muscovite Gentry and Political Culture in the Seventeenth Century.* Stanford, CA, 1996.

————. "'Between All Parts of the Universe: Russian Cosmographies and Imperial Strategies in Early Modern Siberia and Ukraine." *Imago Mundi* 60, pt. 2 (2008): 166–81.

————. *Cartographies of Tsardom: The Land and Its Meanings in Seventeenth-Century Russia.* Ithaca, NY, 2006.

————. "Merciful Father, Impersonal State: Russian Autocracy in Comparative Perspective." In "The Eurasian Context of the Early Modern History of Mainland South East Asia, 1400–1800," special issue, *Modern Asian Studies* 31, no. 3 (1997): 635–63.

————. "Muscovite 'Citizenship': Rights without Freedom." *Journal of Modern History* 74 (2002): 465–89.

————. "On Words, Sources, Meanings: Which Truth about Muscovy?" *Kritika* 3, no. 3 (2002): 487–99.

Kliuchevsky, V. O. *A Course in Russian History: The Seventeenth Century.* Translated by Natalie Duddington with an introduction by Alfred J. Rieber. New York, 1994.

Kliuchevskii, V. O. *Kurs russkoi istorii.* Pt. 2. Moscow, 1937.

Kiueva, Vera P. "Bukhartsy v sisteme ekonomicheskikh otnoshenii sibirskogo goroda nachala XVIII veka." *Problemy Vzaimodeistviia Cheloveka i Prirodnoi Sredy* 2 (2001): 70–72.

————. "Ispol'zovanie genealogicheskikh dannykh pri izuchenii sotsial'noi istorii (na primere vyiavleniia rodstvennykh sviazei sibirskikh bukhartsev kon. XVII–nach. XVIII v.)." *Rodoslovnykh Chtenii* 2 (2001): n.p.

————. "Mekhanizm priniatiia rossiiskogo poddanstva vykhodtsami iz Srednei Azii (konets XVIII v.)." *Problemy Vzaimodeistviia Cheloveka i Prirodnoi Sredy* 3 (2002): 62–66.

Kollmann, Nancy Shields. *By Honor Bound: State and Society in Early Modern Russia.* Ithaca, NY, 1999.

————. "The Concept of Political Culture in Russian History." In *A Companion to Russian History*, edited by Abbott T. Gleason, 89–104. Oxford, UK, 2009.

————. *Crime and Punishment in Early Modern Russia*. New York, 2012.

————. *Kinship and Politics: The Making of the Muscovite Political System, 1345–1547*. Stanford, 1987.

————. "Muscovite Russia, 1450–1598." In *Russia: A History*, edited by Gregory L. Freeze, 27–54. New York, 1997.

Kopylov, A. N. "Domashnee i shkol'noe obrazovanie v Sibiri XVII–XVIII vv." *Izvestiia Sibirskogo Otdeleniia Akademiia Nauk SSSR*, no. 5, vyp. 2 (1966): 86–93.

————. "Tamozhennaia politika v Sibiri v XVII v." In *Russkoe gosudarstvo v XVII veke*, edited by N. V. Ustiugov, 330–70. Moscow, 1961.

Kopylova, S. "K datirovke kamennogo stroitel'stva v Tiumenskom troitskom mona-styre." In *Materialy nauchnoi konferentsii posviashchennoi 100-letiiu Tobol'skogo istoriko-arkhitekturnogo muzeia-zapovednika*, edited by I. N. Roshchevskii, 101–8. Sverdlovsk, 1975.

Korusenko, S. N. "Sibirskie Bukhartsy v XVII–XIX vv." In *Zapadnaia Sibir' i sopredel'nye territorii: Demograficheskie i sotsial'no-istoricheskie protsessy (XVIII–XX vv.)*, edited by V. A. Sal'nikov, et al., 88–97. Omsk, 2009.

————. "Sibirskie Bukhartsy: Dinamika, chislennosti, i rasselenie (XVII–XX vv.)." *Problemy istorii, filologii, kul'tury* 22 (2008): 485–91.

————. "Zemlevladenie i zemlepol'zovanie Bukhartsev v Sibiri: Genealogicheskii rakurs." In *Traditsionnye znaniia korennykh narodov Altae-Saian v oblasti prirodopol'zovaniia*, 39–45. Barnaul, 2009.

Kostomarov, N. I. *Ocherki torgovli Moskovskogo gosudarstva v XVI i XVII stoletiiakh*. St. Petersburg, 1862.

Kotilaine, Jarmo T. "Artisans: The Prokofiev Family." In Ostrowski and Poe, *Portraits of Old Russia*, 188–97.

————. "Competing Claims: Russian Foreign Trade via Arkhangel'sk and the East-ern Baltic Ports in the Seventeenth Century." *Kritika* 4, no. 2 (2003): 279–311.

————. "Mercantilism in Pre-Petrine Russia." In Kotilaine and Poe, *Modernizing Muscovy*, 137–66.

————. "A Muscovite Economic Model." NCEEER working paper. Washington, DC, 2004.

————. "Quantifying Arkhangel'sk's Exports in the 17th Century." *Journal of Euro-pean Economic History* 28, no. 2 (1999): 276–92.

————. "Review of *Tamozhennye knigi goroda Velikie Luki 1669–1676 gg.*, *Tamozhen-nye knigi sibirskikh gorodov XVII veka*." *Kritika: Explorations in Russian and Eur-asian History* 2, no. 3 (2001): 655–63. doi:10.1353/kri.2008.0076.

————. "Russian Merchant Colonies in Seventeenth-Century Sweden." In Zakha-rov, Harlaftis, and Katsiardi-Hering, *Merchant Colonies in the Early Modern Period*, 85–101.

————. *Russia's Foreign Trade and Economic Expansion in the Seventeenth Century: Win-dows on the World*. Boston, 2005.

————. "When the Twain Did Meet: Foreign Merchants and Russia's Economic Expansion in the Seventeenth Century." PhD diss., Harvard University, 2000.

Kotilaine, Jarmo, and Marshall Poe, eds. *Modernizing Muscovy: Reform and Social Change in 17c. Russia*. New York, 2004.

Kotkin, Stephen. *Armageddon Averted: The Soviet Collapse, 1970–2000*. New York, 2001.

―――. "Defining Territories and Empires: From Mongol Ulus to Russian Siberia, 1200–1800." Slavic Research Center, Sapporo, 1996. http://src-h.slav. hokudai.ac.jp/sympo/Proceed97/Kotkin3.html. Accessed September 24, 2012.

―――. "Mongol Commonwealth? Exchange and Governance across the Post-Mongol Space." *Kritika* 8, no. 3 (2007): 487–513.

Kozintseva, R. I. "Uchastie kazny vo vneshnei torgovle Rossii." *Istoricheskie zapiski* 91 (1973): 267–337.

Kozlova, N. V. "Dukhovnye gostei Mikhaila Shorina (1711 g.) i Alekseia Filat'eva (1731 g.)." In *Ocherki feodal'noi Rossii*, vyp. 5, edited by S. N. Kisterev, 188–204. Moscow, 2001.

―――. "'Na ch'ei opeke . . . dolzhny byt' vospitany . . .': Opeka i popechitel'stvo v srede Moskovskikh kuptsov v XVIII veke." In *Ot drevnei Rusi k Rossii novogo vremeni: Sbornik statei k 70-letiiu Anny Leonidovny Khoroshkevich*, compiled by E. L. Nazarova, 349–58. Moscow, 2003.

―――. *Rossiiskii absolutizm i kupechestvo v XVIII veke (20-e–nachalo 60-kh godov)*. Moscow, 1999.

Kraikovskii, A. V. "Torgovlia sol'iu na Russkom severe 1630-kh–1650-kh godakh." Dissertation. St. Petersburg, 2005,

"Kupchina gostinoi sotni Spiridon Liangusov." *Trudy arkhivnoi Viatskoi* (1905): 235.

Kurilov, V. N. "Uchastie sluzhilykh liudei v stanovlenii g. Tiumeni kak torgovo-promyshlennogo tsentra v XVII v." In Vilkov, *Goroda Sibiri*, 76–85.

Kurlaev, E. A., and I. L. Mankova. *Osvoenie rudnykh mestorozhdenii urala i Sibiri v XVII veke*. Moscow, 2005.

Kurts, B. G. "Gorod Verkhotur'e v XVII v." In *Iubileinii sbornik: Istoriko-geograficheskii kruzhkok pri Kievskom universitete*, edited by B. G. Kurts, n.p. Kiev, 1914.

―――. *Gosudarstvennaia monopoliia v torgovle Rossii s Kitaem v pervoi polovine XVIII v*. Kiev, 1929.

―――. *Russko-Kitaiskie snosheniia v XVI, XVII i XVIII stoletiiakh*. Kiev, 1929.

Kvetsinskaia, T. E. "Remesla Verkhotur'ia v XVII v." In Vilkov, *Istoriia gorodov Sibiri dosovetskogo perioda*, 104–16.

LaFraniere, Sharon. "The Cashless Society: Bartering Chokes Russian Economy." *Washington Post*, September 3, 1998, A1.

Lantzeff, George V. *Siberia in the Seventeenth Century*. Berkeley, CA, 1943.

Lantzeff, George V., and Richard A. Pierce. *Eastward to Empire: Exploration and Conquest on the Russian Open Frontier, to 1750*. Montreal, 1973.

Lapidus, Ira M. *A History of Islamic Societies*. 2nd ed. New York, 2002.

Laqueur, Thomas W. "The Enlightenment: Daring to Know and Its Difficulties." History 5 Lecture, ITunes audio, October 5, 2010, Berkeley, CA. https://itunes. apple.com/us/itunes-u/history-5-001-fall-2010-uc/id391536406?mt=10

LeDonne, John. "Building an Infrastructure of Empire in Russia's Eastern Theater, 1650s–1840s." *Cahiers du Monde Russe* 47, no. 3 (2006): 581–608.

————. "Proconsular Ambitions on the Chinese Border." *Cahiers du Monde Russe* 45, no. 1 (2004): 31–60.

————. *The Russian Empire and the World, 1700–1917: The Geopolitics of Expansion and Containment.* New York, 1997.

Lehovich, Dmitry V. "The Testament of Peter the Great." *American Slavic and East European Review* 7, no. 2 (1948): 111–24.

Lenhoff, Gail. "Rus-Tatar Princely Marriages in the Horde: The Literary Sources." *Russian History* 42 (2015): 16–31.

Lenhoff, Gail D., and Janet B. Martin. "Torgovo-khoziaistvennii i kul'turnii kontekst 'Khozheniia za tri moria' Afanasiia Nikitina." In *Trudy otdela drevnerusskoi literatury* XLVII, 95–126. St. Petersburg, 1993. This article was published first in English as "The Commercial and Cultural Context of *Journey Across Three Seas* of Afanasii Nikitin." *Jahrbücher für Geschichte Osteuropas* 37 (1989): 321–44.

Levi, Scott C. "The Ferghana Valley at the Crossroads of World History: The Rise of Khoqand, 1709–1822." *Journal of Global History* 2 (2007): 213–32.

————, ed. *India and Central Asia: Commerce and Culture, 1500–1800.* New York, 2007.

————. *The India Diaspora in Central Asia and Its Trade, 1550–1900.* Boston, 2002.

————. "India, Russia, and the Eighteenth-Century Transformation of the Central Asian Caravan Trade." *Journal of the Economic and Social History of the Orient* 42, no. 4 (1999): 519–48. Reprinted in Levi, *India and Central Asia*, 93–122.

Levin, Eve. "Plague deniers: The Challenge of Evidence of the Black Death from Russia." Paper presented at ASEEES, New Orleans, LA, November 15–18, 2012.

Lieberman, Victor B. *Beyond Binary Histories: Re-imagining Eurasia to c. 1830.* Ann Arbor, MI, 1999.

Liubavskii, M. K. *Obzor istorii russkoi kolonizatsii s drevneishikh vremen i do XX veka.* Edited by A. Ia. Degtiarev. Moscow, 1996.

Liubomirov, P. G. *Ocherki po istorii russkoi promyshlennosti XVII, XVIII i nachalo XIX veka.* Ogiz, 1947.

Lloyd, T. H. *Alien Merchants in England in the High Middle Ages.* Sussex, UK, 1982.

Longworth, Philip. *Alexis: Tsar of All the Russias.* London, 1984.

Love, Ronald S. "'A Passage to China': A French Jesuit's Perceptions of Siberia in the 1680s." *French Colonial History* 3 (2003): 85–100. doi:10.1353/fch.2003.0009.

Mahan, A. T. *The Influence of Sea Power on History, 1660–1783.* Boston, 1890.

Makarov, I. S. "Pushnoi rynok Soli Vychegodskoi v XVII v." *Istoricheskie zapiski* 14 (1945): 148–69.

————. "Volostnye torzhki v Sol'vychegodskom uezde v XVII v." *Istoricheskie zapiski* 1 (1937): 193–219.

Malikov, Yuri A. "Formation of a Borderland Culture: Myths and Realities of Cossack–Kazakh Relations in Northern Kazakhstan in the Eighteenth and Nineteenth Centuries." PhD diss., University of California, Santa Barbara, 2006.

Mancall, Mark. *Russia and China: Their Diplomatic Relations to 1728.* New York, 1971.

Mann, Charles C. *1491.* New York, 2005.

Marshall, P. J. "Europe and the Rest of the World." In *The Short Oxford History of Eighteenth-Century Europe, 1688–1815*, edited by T. C. W. Blanning, 218–46. New York, 2000.

Martin, Janet. "The Fur Trade and the Conquest of Sibir'." In *Sibérie II: Histoire, cultures, literature, questions Sibériennes*, 67–79. Paris, 1999.

———. "The Land of Darkness and the Golden Horde: The Fur Trade under the Mongols, 13th–14th Centuries." *Cahiers du Monde Russe et Soviétique* 19, no. 4 (1978): 401–21.

———. *Medieval Russia, 980–1584*. New York, 1995.

———. "Muscovite Frontier Policy: The Case of the Khanate of Kasimov." *Russian History* 19 no. 1 (1992): 169–79.

———. "Muscovy's Northeastern Expansion: The Context and a Cause." *Cahiers du Monde Russe et Soviétique* 24, no. 4 (1984): 459–70.

———. "Muscovite Travelling Merchants: The Trade with the Muslim East (15th and 16th cc.)." *Central Asian Survey* 4, no. 3 (1985): 21–38.

———. *Treasure in the Land of Darkness: The Fur Trade and Its Significance for Medieval Russia*. New York, 2004.

Martin, Russell. *A Bride for the Tsar: Bride Shows and Marriage Politics in Early Modern Russia*. DeKalb, IL, 2012.

Matthee, Rudolph. P. "Anti-Ottoman Politics and Transit Rights: The Seventeenth-Century Trade in Silk between Safavid Iran and Muscovy." *Cahiers du Monde Russe* 35, no. 4 (1994): 739–61.

———. *The Politics of Trade in Safavid Iran: Silk for Silver, 1600–1730*. New York, 1999.

Maxwell, Mary Jane. "Afanasii Nikitin: An Orthodox Russian's Spiritual Voyage in the Dār al-Islām, 1468–1475." *Journal of World History* 17, no. 3 (2006): 243–66.

McNeill, William H. *Europe's Steppe Frontier, 1500–1800*. Chicago, IL, 1964.

———. *The Rise of the West: A History of the Human Community*. Chicago, IL, 1963.

Mel'gunov, P. P. *Ocherki po istorii russkoi torgovli IX–XVIII vv*. Moscow, 1905.

Melikishvili, Alexander. "Genesis of the Anti-Plague System: The Tsarist Period." *Critical Reviews in Microbiology* 32 (2006): 19–31.

Merzon, A. Ts. *Tamozhennye knigi: Uchebnoe posobie o istochnikovedenii istorii SSSR*. Moscow, 1957.

Merzon, A. Ts., and Iu. A. Tikhonov. *Rynok Ustiuga Velikogo v period skladyvaniia vserossiiskogo rynka (XVII vek)*. Moscow, 1960.

Miliukov, P. N. *Gosudarstvennoe khoziaistvo Rossii v pervoi chetverti XVIII stoletiia i reforma Petra Velikago*. 2nd ed. St. Petersburg, 1905.

Mill, John Stuart. *The Principles of Political Economy, with some of their applications to social philosophy*. 7th ed. London, 1909. First published 1848. Bk. 5, chap. 2: "On the General Principles of Taxation," v.2.14, http://www.econlib.org/library/Mill/mlP64.html#d8.

Miller, David. "Monumental Building as an Indicator of Economic Trends in Northern Rus' in the Late Kievan and Mongol Periods, 1138–1462." *American Historical Review* 94 (1989): 360–90.

Mironov, B. N. *Vnutrennii rynok Rossii vo vtoroi polovine XVIII–pervoi polovine XIX v*. Leningrad, 1981.

Miroshchenko, E.A. "Kuptsy-staroobriadtsy v gorodakh Evropeiskoi Rossii v seredine XVIII veka (Iz istorii rossiiskogo predprinimatel'stva)." *Rossiiskaia istoriia* 5 (2006): 28–39.

Moiseev, V. V., ed. *Vlast' v Sibiri XVI– nachalo XX veka: Mezharkhivnii spravochnik.* Compiled by M. O. Akishin, A. V. Remnev, et al. Novosibirsk, 2002.

Monahan, Erika. "Gavril Romanov Nikitin: A Merchant Portrait." In *Russia's People of Empire: Life Stories from Eurasia, 1500–Present,* edited by Willard Sunderland and Stephen Norris, 47–56. Bloomington, IN, 2012.

———. "Locating Rhubarb: Early Modernity's Relevant Obscurity." In *Early Modern Things: Objects and Their Histories, 1500–1800,* edited by Paula Findlen, 227–51. London, 2013.

———. "Regulating Virtue and Vice: Controlling Commodities in Early Modern Siberia." In *Tobacco in Russian History and Culture,* edited by Matthew Romaniello and Tricia Starks, 61–82. New York, 2009.

———. "Trade and Empire: Merchant Networks, Frontier Commerce and the State in Western Siberia, 1644–1728." PhD diss., Stanford University, 2007.

———. "Uraisko Kaibulin: Bukharan in a Borderland." In Ostrowski and Poe, *Portraits of Old Russia,* 222–29.

Moon, David. *The Russian Peasantry, 1600–1930: The World the Peasants Made.* New York, 1999.

Morgan, David. *The Mongols.* New York, 1986.

Morrison, Alexander. "The Pleasures and Pitfalls of Colonial Comparisons." *Kritika* 13, no. 4 (2012): 918–20.

Muratova, S. R. "Na strazhe rubezhei Sibiri." *Natsional'nye Kul'tury Regiona* 16 (2007): 32–46. http://a-pesni.org/kazaki/sibir/a-nastraze.htm?q=a-pesni/kazaki/sibir/a-nastraze.htm.

Murchison, Roderick Impey. *The Geology of Russia in Europe and the Ural Mountains.* vol. 1. London, 1845.

Musgrave, Paul. *The Early Modern European Economy.* New York, 1999.

Naumov, Igor V. *The History of Siberia.* Edited by David N. Collins. New York, 2006.

Nikitin, N. I. *Sluzhilye liudi v zapadnoi Sibiri XVII veka.* Novosibirsk, 1988.

———. "Torgi i promysly sluzhilykh liudei zapadnoi Sibiri v XVII v." In Preobrazhenskii, *Promyshlennost' i torgovlia v Rossii XVII–XVIII vv.,* 7–20.

Noonan, Thomas S., and Roman K. Kovalev. "'The Furry 40s': Packaging Pelts in Medieval Northern Europe." In *States, Societies, Cultures East and West: Essays in Honor of Jaroslaw Pelenski,* edited by Janusz Duzinkiewicz, 653–82. New York, 2004.

Ogilvie, Sheilagh C. *Institutions and European Trade: Merchant Guilds, 1000–1800.* New York, 2011.

Ogloblin, N. N. "Bytovye cherty nachala XVIII veka: Razdache vetkhikh doshchanikov v zhalovan'e sluzhilym liudiam." *Chteniia OIDR* (1904), bk. 1, pt. 3: 1–21.

———. *Obozrenie stolbtsov i knig Sibirskago prikaza, 1592–1768.* 4 vols. Moscow, 1895–1901.

———. *Semen Dezhnev (1638–1671 gg.): (Noviia danniia i peresmotr starykh)* St. Petersburg, 1890.

Ohberg, Arne. "Russia and the World Market in the Seventeenth Century." *Scandinavian Economic History Review* 3, no. 2 (1955): 123–55.

Orekhov, A. M. "Tovarnoe proizvodstvo i naemnii trud v promyshlennosti po pererabotke zhivotnogo syr'ia v Nizhnem Novgorode XVII v." In Ustiugov, *Russkoe gosudarstvo v XVII veke,* 75–109.

Orlenko, S. P. *Vykhodtsy iz zapadnoi Evropy v Rossii XVII veka: Pravovoi status i real'noe polozhenie* Moscow, 2004.

Ostrowski, Donald. "The Façade of Legitimacy: Exchange of Power and Authority in Early Modern Russia." *Comparative Studies in Society and History* 44, no. 3 (2002): 534–63.

———. "Golden Horde." In *Encyclopedia of Russian History*, 2: 571–73. New York, 2004.

———. "Interconnections: Russia in World History, 1450–1800." Unpublished manuscript, 2013.

———. *Muscovy and the Mongols: Cross-Cultural Influences on the Steppe Frontier, 1304–1589.* Cambridge, UK, 1998.

———. "Toward the Integration of Early Modern Russia into World History." In *Eurasian Slavery, Ransom and Abolition in World History*, edited by Christoph Witzenrath. Aldershot, UK, 2015.

Ostrowski, Donald, and Marshall Poe, eds. *Portraits of Old Russia.* Armonk, NY, 2011.

"Ot Yamysheva—k slave." *Omskaia Pravda*, http://www.omskpravda.ru/?sid=4& id=2522. Accessed December 30, 2009.

Pavlov, A. P., ed. *Torgovlia, kupechestvo i tamozhennoe delo v Rossii v XVI–XVIII vv.* St. Petersburg, 2001.

Pavlov, A. P., ed. *Torgovlia Kurska v XVII veke.* St. Petersburg, 2001.

Pavlov, P. N. *Promyslovaia kolonizatsiia Sibiri v XVII v.* Krasnoiarsk, 1974.

———. *Pushnoi promysel v Sibiri XVII v.* Krasnoiarsk, 1972.

Pearson, M. N. *The Portuguese in India.* Cambridge, 1987.

Perdue, Peter. *China Marches West: The Qing Conquest of Central Eurasia.* Cambridge, MA, 2005.

Perkhavko, V. B. *Istoriia russkogo kupechestva.* Moscow, 2008.

———. "Kupchikhi depetrovskoi Rosii." *Voprosy Istorii* 1 (2009): 148–51.

———. *Pervye kuptsy Rossiiskie.* Moscow, 2004.

———. "Pervye moskovskie kuptsy." *Prepodavanie Istoriii v Shkole* 2 (1994): 4–6.

———. *Srednevekovoe russkoe kupechestvo.* Moscow, 2012.

———. *Torgovii mir srednevekovoi Rusi.* Moscow, 2006.

Perrie, Maureen. "Popular Revolts." In *The Cambridge History of Russia*, vol. 1, edited by Maureen Perrie, 600–617. New York, 2006.

Pettigrew, William A. "Free to Enslave: Politics and the Escalation of Britain's Transatlantic Slave Trade, 1688–1714." *William and Mary Quarterly* 64, no. 1 (2007): 3–38.

Pilkington, Hilary, and Galina Yemelianova, eds. *Islam in Post-Soviet Russia: Public and Private Faces.* New York, 2003.

Ping-ti, Ho. "The Salt Merchants of Yang-chou: A Study of Commercial Capitalism in Eighteenth-Century China." *Harvard Journal of Asiatic Studies* 17, nos. 1–2 (1954): 130–68.

Pipes, Richard. *Russia under the Old Regime.* New York, 1974.

Platonov, S. F. *Ocherki po istorii Smuty v Moskovskom gosudarstve XVI–XVII vv.* Moscow, 1937.

Plokhy, Serhii. *The Origins of the Slavic Nations.* New York, 2006.

Poe, Marshall. *"A People Born to Slavery": Russia in Early Modern European Ethnography, 1476–1748.* Ithaca, NY, 2000.

———. *The Russian Moment in World History.* Princeton, NJ, 2003.

———. "The Truth about Muscovy." *Kritika* 3, no. 3 (2002): 473–86.

———. "What Did Russians Mean When They Called Themselves 'Slaves of the Tsar'?" *Slavic Review* 57, no. 3 (1998): 585–608.

Pomeranz, Kenneth. *The Great Divergence: China, Europe, and the Making of the Modern World Economy.* Princeton, NJ, 2000.

———. "Social History and World History: From Daily Life to Patterns of Change." *Journal of World History* 18, no. 1 (2007): 69–98.

Ponomarëv, I. S. *Sbornik materialov po istoriia goroda Lal'ska Vologodskoi gubernii.* Velikii Ustiug, 1897.

Potanin, G. P. "O karavannoi torgovle s Dzhungarskoi Buxariei." *Chteniia* 14, no. 2 (1868): 21–113.

———. "Privoz i vyvoz tovarov g. Tomska v polovine XVII stoletiia." *Vestnik Russkogo Geograficheskogo Obshchestva* 27, no. 2 (1859): 125–44.

Potter, Cathy J. "Payment, Gift or Bribe? Exploring the Boundaries in Pre-Petrine Russia." In *Bribery and Blat in Russia: Negotiating Reciprocity from the Middle Ages to the 1990s,* edited by Stephen Lovell, Alena Bedeneva, and Andrei Rogachevskii, 20–34. New York, 2000.

Pozdeeva, I. V., et al. *Moskovskii pechatnii dvor—fakt i factor russkoi kul'tury.* In *Issledovaniia i publikatsii, 1652–1700.* vol. 2. Moscow, 2011.

Prak, Maarten, ed. *Early Modern Capitalism: Economic and Social Change in Europe, 1400–1800.* New York, 2001.

Pravilova, Ekaterina. "Rivers of Empire: Geopolitics, Irrigation, and the Amu Darya in the Late 19th Century." *Cahiers d'Asie Central* 17, no. 18 (2009): 255–87.

Preobrazhenskii, A. A., ed. *Promyshlennost' i torgovlia v Rossii XVII–XVIII vv.* Moscow, 1983.

Preobrazhenskii, A. A., and V. B. Perkhavko. *Kupechestvo Rusi IX–XVII veka.* Ekaterinburg, 1997.

Preobrazhenskii, A. A., and Iu. Tikhonov. "Itogi izucheniia nachal'nogo etapa skladyvaniia vserossiiskogo rynka." *Voprosy Istorii* 4 (1961): 80–109.

Price, Jacob M. "The Map of Commerce, 1683–1721." In *The New Cambridge Modern History,* edited by J. S. Bromley, 834–73. Cambridge, UK, 1970. doi:http://dx.doi.org/10.1017/CHOL9780521075244.

Pritsak, Omeljan. "The Origin of Rus'." *Russian Review* 36, no. 3 (1977): 249–73.

Puzanov, V. D. *Voennye faktory russkoi kolonizatsii zapadnoi Sibiri, konets XVI–XVII vv.* St. Petersburg, 2010.

Raffensberger, Christian. *Reimagining Europe: Kievan Rus' in the Medieval World.* Cambridge, MA, 2012.

Rakhimov, R. Kh. *Astana v istorii Sibirskikh Tatar: Mavzolei pervykh islamskikh missionerov kak pamiatniki istoriko-kul'turnogo naslediia.* Tiumen', 2006.

Ransel, David. *A Russian Merchant's Tale.* Bloomington, IN, 2008.

Razgon, V. N. *Sibirskoe kupechestvo v XVIII–pervoi polovine XIX v.: Regional'nii aspekt predprinimatel'stva traditsionnogo tipa.* Barnaul, 1999.

Reed, Bradly W. *Talons and Teeth: Country Clerks and Runners in the Qing Dynasty.* Stanford, CA, 2000.

Repin, N. N. "Torgovlia Rossii s evropeiskimi stranami na otechestvennykh sudakh (konets XVII–seredina 60-kh godov XVIII v.)." *Istoricheskie Zapiski* 112 (1985): 141–76.

Rezun, D. Ia. *Gorodskaia kul'tura Sibiri: Istoriia, pamiatniki, liudi.* Novosibirsk, 1994.

Rezun, D. Ia., and R. S. Vasilievskii. *Letopis' Sibirskikh gorodov.* Novosibirsk, 1989.

Rieber, Alfred. "The Comparative Ecology of Complex Frontiers." In *Imperial Rule,* edited by Alexei Miller and Alfred J. Rieber, 177–208. New York, 2005.

———. *Merchants and Entrepreneurs in Imperial Russia.* Charlotte, NC, 1982.

Risso, Patricia. *Merchants and Faith: Muslim Commerce and Culture in the Indian Ocean.* Boulder, CO, 1995.

Romaniello, Matthew P. "Captain John Elton and the Anglo-Russian Competition over Iran in the Eighteenth-Century." Unpublished paper presented at the University of New Mexico. Albuquerque, NM. March 26, 2015.

———. "Controlling the Frontier: Monasteries and Infrastructure in the Volga Region, 1552–1682." *Central Asian Survey* 19, nos. 3–4 (2000): 429–43.

———. *The Elusive Empire: Kazan and the Creation of the Russian Empire, 1552–1671.* Madison, WI, 2012.

———. "'In Friendship and Love': Russian Travels to Muslim Lands in the Early Modern Era." *Historical Yearbook* 6 (2009): 111–22.

———. "The Profit Motive: Regional Economic Development in Muscovy after the Conquest of Kazan'." *Journal of European Economic History* 33, no. 3 (2004): 663–85.

———. "Through the Filter of Tobacco: The Limits of Global Trade in the Early Modern World" *Comparative Studies in Society and History* 49:4 (2007): 914–37.

———. "Secular Conquests, Sacred Spaces: Transforming Orthodoxy on the Russian Frontier." Paper presented at the annual meeting of the American Historical Association (AHA), Boston, MA, January 6–9, 2011.

Rorlich, Azade-Ayse. *The Volga Tatars: A Profile in National Resilience.* Stanford, CA, 1986.

Rossabi, Morris. "The 'Decline' of the Central Asian Caravan Trade." In Tracy, *Rise of Merchant Empires,* 351–70.

Rostovtzeff, M. I. *The Social and Economic History of the Roman Empire.* Oxford, UK, 1926.

———. *The Social and Economic History of the Hellenistic World.* Oxford, UK, 1959.

Rothschild, Emma. "A Horrible Tragedy in the French Atlantic." *Past & Present* 192 (2006): 67–108.

Rowland, Daniel. "Architecture and Dynasty: Boris Godunov's Uses of Architecture, 1584–1605." In *Architectures of Russian Identity, 1500 to the Present,* edited by James Cracraft and Daniel Rowland, 34–47. Ithaca, NY, 2003.

———. "Did Muscovite Literary Ideology Place Limits on the Power of the Tsar (1540s–1660s)?" *The Russian Review* 49 (1990): 125–55.

Sanders, Thomas J. *Historiography of Imperial Russia.* New York, 1999.

Savich, N. G. "Iz istorii russko-nemetskikh kul'turnykh sviazei v XVII v. (nemetsko-russkii slovar' razgovornik G. Nevenburga 1629 g.)." *Istoricheskie Zapiski* 102 (1972): 246–86.

Schama, Simon. *The Embarrassment of Riches: An Interpretation of Dutch Culture in the Golden Age.* New York, 1997.

Sedov, P. V. "Podnosheniia v Moskovskikh prikazakh XVII v." *Otechestvennaia Istoriia* 1 (1996): 139–49.

Seleznev, A. G., et al. *Kul't sviatykh v sibirskom Islame: Spetsifika universal'nogo.* Moscow, 2009.

Semenova, A. V., ed. *Istoriia predprinimatel'stva v Rossii.* Bk. 1. Moscow, 2000.

Semenova-Tian'-Shanskogo. *Rossiia: Polnoe geograficheskoe opisanie nashego otechestva.* vol. 16. St. Petersburg, 1907.

Serov, D. O. *Prokuratora Petra I (1722–1725): Istoriko-pravovoi ocherk.* Novosibirsk, 2002.

———. *Stroiteli imperii: Ocherki gosudarstvennoi i kriminal'noi deiatel'nosti spodvizhnikov Petra I.* Novosibirsk, 1996.

Sevast'ianova, S. K. *Materialy k "Letopisi zhizni i literaturnoi deiatel'nosti patriarkha Nikona."* St. Petersburg, 2003.

Shakherov, V. P. "Gorodskie promysly i remeslo iuzhnoi chasti vostochnoi Sibiri v kontse XVII–nachale XIV v." In *Sovremennoe istoricheskoe sibirevedenie XVII–nachala XX vv.*, edited by Iu. M. Goncharov, 163–80. Barnaul, 2005.

Shakhova, A. D. "Dvory torgovykh liudei Pankrat'evykh i Filat'evykh v Moskve." In *Istoriografiia, istochnikovedenie, Istoriia Rossii X–XX vv. Sbornik statei v chest- Sergeia Nikolaevicha Kistereva*, compiled by L. A. Timoshina, 399–416. Moscow, 2008.

Shamin, S. M. *Kuranty XVII stoletiia: Evropeiskaia pressa v Rossi i vozniknovenie russkoi periodicheskoi pechati.* Moscow-St. Petersburg, 2011.

Shaw, Denis J. B. "Geographical Practice and Its Significance in Peter the Great's Russia." *Journal of Historical Geography* 22, no. 2 (1996): 160–76.

Shumilov, M. M. *Torgovlia i tamozhenoe delo v Rossii: Stanovlenie, osnovnye etapy razvitiia IX–XVII vv.* St. Petersburg, 2006.

Sili, Shandor. "Conceptions of the Conquest of Siberia in Russian and Soviet Historiography." In *New Directions and Results in International Russistics*, edited by Gyula Szvák, 74–82. Budapest, 2005.

Skalon, V. N. *Russkie zemleprokhodsty XVII veka v Sibiri.* 2nd ed. Novosibirsk, 2005.

Skrynnikov, R. G. *Sibirskie ekspeditsiia Ermaka.* Novosibirsk, 1982.

Sladkovskii, M. I. *History of Economic Relations between Russia and China.* Jerusalem, 1966. Reprint, New Brunswick, NJ, 2008.

Slezkine, Yuri. *Arctic Mirrors: Russia and the Small Peoples of the North.* Ithaca, NY, 1994.

———. *The Jewish Century.* Princeton, NJ, 2004.

———. "Naturalists v. Nations: Eighteenth-Century Russian Scholars Confront Ethnic Diversity." In *Russia's Orient: Imperial Borderlands and Peoples, 1700–1917*, edited by Daniel R. Brower and Edward J. Lazzerini, 27–57. Bloomington, IN, 1997.

———. "Savage Christians or Unorthodox Russians: The Missionary Dilemma in Siberia." In Diment and Slezine, *Between Heaven and Hell*, 15–32.

Slezkine, Yuri, and Galya Diment. "Introduction." In Diment and Slezkine, *Between Heaven and Hell*, 1–14.

Smirnov, P. P. "Ekonomicheskaia politika v XVII v." In Dovnar-Zapol'skii, 369–411.

———. *Goroda Moskovskogo gosudarstva v pervoi polovine Russkaia istoriia v ocherkakh i stat'iakh, XVII v.* Kiev, 1917.

————. "Posadskie liudi Moskovskago gosudarstva." In Dovnar-Zapol'skii, 85–111.

Smith, Adam. *An Inquiry into the Nature and Causes of the The Wealth of Nations.* Edited by Edwin Cannan. London, 1904. Original publication, 1776.

————. *The Theory of Moral Sentiments.* London, 1790. Original publication, 1759.

Smith, Lesley, and Geoffrey Parker, eds. *The General Crisis of the Seventeenth Century.* London, 1997.

Sokolovskii, I. R. "Reformirovanie v usloviiakh otsutstviia ratsional'noi politiki: Chem v deistvitel'nosti byli torgovye ustavy 1653 i 1667 gg." Paper presented at the conference "Fenomen reform v Evrope i Rossii nachala novogo vremeni (XVI–XVIII vv.)," European University, St. Petersburg, Russia, March 15–16, 2012.

————. *Sluzhilye "inozemtsy" v Sibiri XVII veka (Tomsk, Eniseisk, Krasnoiarsk).* Novosibirsk, 2004.

Solov'ev, S. M. "Moskovskie kuptsy v XVII v." In *Sochineniie v. 18 kn.,* kn. 20, *Dopolnitel'naia raboty raznykh let,* edited by I. D. Koval'chenko, 504–16. Moscow, 1996.

Soucek, Svat. *History of Inner Asia.* New York, 2000.

Spock, Jennifer. "The Parfiev Family: Northern Free Peasants." In Ostrowski and Poe, *Portraits of Old Russia,* 233–42.

Statisticheskii ezhegodnik. Moscow, 2009.

Steensgaard, Niels. *The Asian Trade Revolution of the Seventeenth Century.* Chicago, IL, 1974. Originally published as *Carracks, Caravans and Companies: The Structural Crisis in the European-Asian Trade in the Early 17th Century.* Copenhagen, 1973.

Stevens, Carol B. "Trade and Muscovite Economic Policy toward the Ukraine: The Movement of Cereal Grains during the Second Half of the 17c." In *Ukrainian Economic History: Interpretive Essays,* edited by I. S. Koropeckyj, 172–85. Cambridge, MA, 1991.

Struve, Karl, and Grigorii Potanin. "Poezdka po vostochnoomy Tarbagatiu, letom 1864 goda." *Zapiski Imperatorskago Russkago Geograficheskago Obshchestva* 1 (1867): 463–516.

Sunderland, Willard. "Imperial Space: Territorial Thought and Practice in the Eighteenth-Century." In *Russian Empire: Space, People, Power,* edited by Jane Burbank, Mark von Hagen, and Anatolyi Remnev, 33-66. Bloomington, IN, 2007.

————. "Empire in Boris Mironov's *Sotsial'naia Istoriia Rossii.*" *Slavic Review* 60, no. 3 (2001): 571–78.

————. *Taming the Wild Field: Colonization and Empire on the Russian Steppe.* Ithaca, NY, 2004.

Suvorov, N. "Novootkrytye istoricheskie dokumenty." *Vologodskie eparkhial'nye vedomosti* 4 (1872): n.p.

Sykes, Percy A. *A History of Persia.* vol. 2. London, 1915.

Syroechkovskii, V. E. *Gosti-Surozhane.* Moscow-Leningrad, 1935.

Sytin, P. V. *Iz istorii Moskovskikh ulits (ocherki).* 3rd ed. Moscow, 1958.

Szeftel, Marc. "The History of Suretyship in Old Russian Law." In *Russian Institutions and Culture up to Peter the Great,* 841–66. London, 1975.

Takeda, Junko. *Between Commerce and Crown: Marseille and the Early Modern Mediterranean.* Baltimore, MD, 2011.

Thrupp, Sylvia L. "Aliens in and around London in the Fifteenth Century." In *Studies in London History Presented to Philip Edmund Jones*, edited by A. E. J. Hollaender and William Kellaway, 251–72. London, 1969.

Tikhonov, Iu. A. "Problema formirovaniia vserossiiskogo rynka v sovremennoi sovetskoi istoriografii." In *Aktual'nye problemy istorii Rossii epokhi feodalizma*, edited by L. V. Cherepnin, 200–223. Moscow, 1970.

———. "Tamozhennaia politika russkogo gosudarstva v seredine XVI–do 60-kh godov XVII v." *Istoricheskie Zapiski* 53 (1959): 258–90.

Timoshina, L. A. *Arkhiv gostei Pankrat'evykh XVII–pervoi chet. XVIII vv.* vol. 1. Moscow, 2001.

———, ed. *Torgovlia i predprinimatel'stvo v feodal'noi Rossii: K iubileiu professora russkoi istorii Niny Borisovny Golikovoi.* Moscow, 1994.

———. "Voevodskoe i tamozhennoe upravlenie v pervoi polovine XVII v. (na primere gorodov Ustiuzhskoi chetverti)." In Pavlov, *Torgovlia, kupechestvo i tamozhennoe delo*, 255–61.

Tolmacheva, Maria. "The Early Russian Exploration and Mapping of the Chinese Frontier." *Cahiers du Monde Russe* 41, no. 1 (2001): 41–56.

Tolz, Vera. *Russia's Own Orient: The Politics of Identity and Oriental Studies in Late Imperial and Early Soviet Periods.* New York, 2011.

Tomilov, Nikolai A., and Allen J. Frank. "Ethnic Processes within the Turkic Population of the West Siberian Plain (Sixteenth–Twentieth Centuries)." *Cahiers du Monde Russe* 41, nos. 2–3 (2000): 221–32.

Tomsinskii, S. G., ed. *Khoziaistvo krupnogo feodala-krepostnika*, pt. 1, *Khoziaistvo Boiarina B. I. Morozova XVII v.* Leningrad, 1933.

Tracy, James, ed. *The Political Economy of Merchant Empires.* Cambridge, UK, 1991.

———. *The Rise of Merchant Empires: Long-Distance Trade in the Early Modern World, 1350–1750.* Cambridge, UK, 1990.

Trevor-Roper, Hugh. *The General Crisis of the Seventeenth Century: Religion, Reformation, and Social Change.* Indianapolis, IN, 1967.

Trivellato, Francesca. *The Familiarity of Strangers: The Sephardic Diaspora, Livorno, and Cross-Cultural Exchange in the Early Modern Period.* New Haven, CT, 2009.

Tsypushtanov, V. A. "Istoriia Levninskoi tserkvi." http://lenva.ru/istoriya-lenvenskoj-cerkvi.

Ulianitskii, V. A. "Snosheniia Rossii s Sredneiu Azieiu i Indieiu v XVI–XVII vv." *Chteniia v Imperatorskom Obshchestve Istorii i Drevnostei Rossiiskikh pri Moskovskom Universitete* 146, kn. 3 (July–September 1888): 1–62. Reprint, Moscow, 1889.

Unkovskaia, Maria V. *Brief Lives: A Handbook of Medical Practitioners in Muscovy, 1620–1701.* London, 1999.

Usmanov, M. A., and R. A. Shaikhiev. "Obraztsy tatarskikh narodno-kraevedcheskikh sochinenii po istorii zapadnoi i iuzhnoi Sibiri." In *Sibirskaia arkheografiia i istochnikovedenie*, 85–103. Novosibirsk, 1979.

Ustiugov, N. V. "Ekonomicheskoe razvitie russkogo gosudarstva v XVII v. i problema skladyvaniia vserossiiskogo rynka." In Ustiugov, *Nauchnoe nasledie*, 18–74.

———. *Nauchnoe nasledie.* Moscow, 1974.

———, ed. *Russkoe gosudarstvo v XVII veke.* Moscow, 1961.

———. *Solevarennaia promyshlennost' Soli Kamskoi v XVII veke.* Moscow, 1957.

V., I. "K istorii o Sabanake Kul'mameteve v 'Rodoslovnoi istorii o tatarakh,' Abu-l-Gazi." *Suleimanovskie chteniia.* Tiumen', 2012.

Valk, S. N. "Iina Ivanovna Liubimenko," *Voprosy ekonomiki i klassovykh otnoshenii russkom gosudarstve XII–XVII vekov.* Vol. 2, 483–93. Leningrad, 1960.

Veluwenkamp, Jan Willem, and Joost Veenstra. "Early Modern English Merchant Colonies: Contexts and Functions." In Zakharov, Harlaftis, and Katsiardi-Hering, *Merchant Colonies in the Early Modern Period,* 11–31.

Vershinin, E. V. *Voevodskoe upravlenie v Sibiri (XVII v.).* Ekaterinburg, 1998.

Veselovskii, N. I. *Pamiatniki diplomaticheskikh i torgovykh snoshenii Moskovskoi Rusi s Persiei.* vol. 3. St. Petersburg, 1898.

Veselovskii, S. B. *D'iaki i pod'iachie XV–XVII vv.* Moscow, 1975.

———. *Trudy po istochnikovedeniiu i istorii Rossii perioda feodalizma.* Moscow, 1978.

Vilkov, O. N. "O stroitel'stvo Tobol'ska." *Izvestiia SOANSSSR* 151, vyp. 1 (1969): 71–79.

———. "Pushnoi promysel v Sibiri." *Nauka v Sibiri* 45 (1999): n.p.

———. *Remeslo i torgovlia zapadnoi Sibiri v XVII v.* Moscow, 1967.

———. "Tobol'sk—tsentr tamozhennoi sluzhby Sibiri v XVII v." In Vilkov, *Goroda Sibiri,* 131–69.

———. "Torgovye pomeshcheniia gorodov Sibiri v XVII v." In Rezun, *Gorodskaia kul'tura Sibiri,* 8–24.

———. "Torgovye pomeshcheniia Tobol'ska v XVII veka." *Izvestiia SOANSSSR* 141, no. 6, vyp. 2 (1968): 91–97.

———. "Tranzit 'russkikh' tovarov cherez Tobol'sk v Sibir' XVII v." *Izvestiia Sibirskogo Otdeleniia Akademiia Nauk SSSR,* no. 9, vyp. 3 (1966): 113–26.

Vilkov, O. N., ed. *Goroda Sibiri (Ekonomika, upravlenie i kul'tura gorodov Sibri v dosovetskii period).* Novosibirsk, 1974

———. *Istoriia gorodov Sibiri dosovetskogo perioda (XVII–nach. XX vv.).* Novosibirsk, 1977.

———. *Ocherki sotsial'no-ekonomicheskogo razvitiia Sibiri kontsa XVI–nachala XVIII v.* Novosibirsk, 1990.

———. *Sibirskie goroda XVII–nachala XX veka.* Novosibirsk, 1981.

———. *Torgovlia gorodov Sibiri kontsa 16–nachala 20 v.* Novosibirsk, 1987.

Vinkovetsky, Ilya. *Russia America: An Overseas Colony of a Continental Empire, 1804–1867.* New York, 2011.

Vinogradoff, Paul. *Villainage in England: Essays in English Mediaeval History.* Oxford, 1892.

Volkonskii, Serge. *Pictures of Russian History and Russian Literature.* Boston, 1898.

Vvedenskii, A. A. *Dom Stroganovykh.* Moscow, 1962.

Wallace, Sir Donald Mackenzie. *Russia.* Illinois, 2006. Originally published in 1905.

———. *Russia on the Eve of Revolution.* New York, 1961.

Wallerstein, Immanuel. *The Modern World-Sytem I: Capitalist Agriculture and the Origins of the World-Economy in the Sixteenth Century.* New York, 1974; repr. Berkeley, 2011.

Werth, Paul W. "Coercion and Conversion: Violence and the Mass Baptism of the Volga Peoples, 1740–55." *Kritika* 4, no. 3 (2003): 543–69.

West, James L. and Iurii A. Petrov, eds. *Merchant Moscow: Images of Russia's Vanished Bourgeoisie.* Princeton, NJ, 1998.

White, Richard. *The Middle Ground: Indians, Empires, and Republics in the Great Lakes Region, 1650–1815.* New York, 1991.

Whittaker, Cynthia Hyla, ed. *Russia Engages the World, 1453–1825.* Cambridge, MA, 2003.

Widmer, Eric. *The Russian Ecclestastical [sic] Mission in Peking during the Eighteenth Century.* Cambridge, MA, 1976.

Willan, T. S. *The Early History of the Russia Company.* Manchester, UK, 1956.

———. *The Muscovy Merchants of 1555.* Manchester, UK, 1953.

Wills, John E., Jr. "European Consumption and Asian Production in the Seventeenth and Eighteenth Centuries." In *Consumption and the World of Goods,* edited by John Brewer and Roy Porter, 133–47. New York, 1993.

Wilson, C. H. "Trade, Society and the State." In *The Cambridge Economic History of Europe,* vol. 4, *The Economy of Expanding Europe in the Sixteenth and Seventeenth Centuries,* edited by E. E. Rich and C. H. Wilson, 487–576. Cambridge, UK, 1967.

Winkler, Martina. "Another America: Russian Mental Discoveries of the North-west Pacific Region in the Eighteenth and Early Nineteenth Centuries." *Journal of Global History* 7 (2012): 27–51.

Witzenrath, Christoph. *Cossacks and the Russian Empire, 1598–1725: Manipulation, Rebellion and Expansion into Siberia.* New York, 2007.

Wolff, Larry. *Inventing Eastern Europe: The Map of Civilization on the Mind of the Enlightenment.* Stanford, CA, 1994.

Woodruff, David. *Money Unmade: Barter and the Fate of Russian Capitalism.* Ithaca, NY, 1999.

Yakobson, S. "Early Anglo-Russian Relations (1553–1613)." *Slavonic and East European Review* 13, no. 39 (1935): 597–610.

Yi, Eunjeong. *Guild Dynamics in Seventeenth-Century Istanbul: Fluidity and Leverage.* Leiden, 2003.

Zabelin, I. E. *Istoriia goroda Moskvy: Neizdannye trudy.* Moscow, 2003.

Zakharov, V. N. "Torgovlia zapadnoevropeiskikh kuptsov v Rossii v kontse XVII–pervoi chetverti XVIII v." *Istoricheskie Zapiski* 112 (1985): 177–214.

Zakharov, V. N., Gelina Harlaftis, and Olga Katsiardi-Hering, eds. *Merchant Colonies in the Early Modern Period.* London, 2012.

Zaozerskaia, A. I. "Stat'i. Moskovskii posad pri Petre I." *Voprosy Istorii* 9 (1947): 19-35.

———. *Tsarskaia votchina XVII v.* 2nd ed. Moscow, 1937.

Ziiaev, *Ekonomicheskie sviazi Srednei Azii s Sibir'iu v XVI–XIX vv.* Tashkent, 1983.

———. *Uzbeki v Sibiri, XVI–XIX vv.* Tashkent, 1968.

INDEX

Nikitin, Afanasii, 39–40
Nikitin, Gavril Romanovich: arrested for criticizing the tsar, 231, 236; death of in prison, 312; employees of, 224; and Filat′ev family, 228, 236, 253, 333, 358; mentioned, 314; opens trade route to China through Gobi Desert, 55, 159, 223, 267, 324; service of to Russian state, 227; and trade with China, 159, 322; tries to curtail drinking of agents, 157, 222
Nikitnikov, G. L., 243
Nikitnikov, Nikita, 97, 209n2, 218
Nizhne Kolmysk, 89
Nizhni Novgorod: 42, 53, 64, 97–98, 101, 258n19, 352n83
Nogai khanate, 72, 75–76, 91, 112–13
Noritsyn family, 227, 234, 304–14
Noritsyn, Mikhail Ivanov, 309–10
Noritsyn, Mikifor Stepanov, 307–8
Noritsyn, Nikifor Semenov, 306, 308
Noritsyn, Petr Stepanov, 131, 305, 307–8
Noritsyn, Stepan Nikiforov, 306–8
Novgorod: conquest of, 39–40, 78, 97, 209n2; customs collections at, 53, 200; decline of as trading center, 108–9; fur trade at, xii, 28, 38, 78, 85, 211; and trade with Germany, 34, 36, 41, 78; growth of as trading center, 34, 36–38, 78, 108; Hansa league merchants evicted from, 34, 41; Ivan IV relocates *gosti* from to Moscow, 108; and trade with Kazan khanate, 97; Orthodox church at, 209n2, 212; tribute collection at, 80, 320

obrok (rent or tax), xi, 27–28, 97n27, 150, 280, 280, 288
Office of Merchant Matters, 90, 346
Office of New Convert Affairs, 292
Okhotsk, 119
Olearius, Adam, 95, 99, 105–8, 118–19, 146, 243, 246–48, 330, 352–53
Omsk, 113, 185, 203
one-tenth tax: Bukharans and, 139–40, 199n117, 280, 289; collection of in Siberia, 63n128, 64, 64n132, 133, 139, 195, 224, 319; inconsistencies and, 137, 140, 195, 199; payment of in kind, 133, 163; New Tax Statute of 1698 reforms, 140, 199; in Rus′, 134; smuggling and, 173
one-twentieth tax, 139, 195, 280
oprichnina, xi, 48, 304
Orenburg, 201–2, 299

Orthodox Church: and conquest of new territory, 79, 131; displays intolerance toward Bukharans, 269–70; historiography and, 25–27; is cautious about imposing Orthodoxy on frontier, 257, 261, 283; Ivan IV spreads into nearby khanates, 79; Mongols accommodate on steppes, 74; Prince Vladimir converts, 74; Muslim leader Uzbek accommodates, 75; and Old Belief, 257; penalty for attempting to convert individuals away from, 283; Russian state attempts to defuse tension regarding Bukharans, 280–81; Russian state conflicts with during plague, 218; Russian state derives legitimacy from, 300; sends missionaries to China, 223, 325–26; and storage of merchants′ goods, 150, 161, 210, 227
Ostiaks, 80, 84, 112, 123, 257, 283
Ottoman Empire, 21, 38, 40, 42, 44, 65–66, 101, 113, 122, 127n78, 154, 336, 338n20, 355
Ozbek/Uzbek (r. 1313–41), 74

Pankrat′ev, Danilo Grigorievich, 214, 232
Pankrat′ev family, 6n14, 214n17, 219n49, 227, 228n97, 232, 282n142
Pax Mongolica, 37
Pelym, 84n58, 131, 132n100, 133, 150
Perm′, 80, 81n48, 96, 118, 141n143, 320
Persia: Armenian migrants to, 69; Astrakhan exports goods to, 101; conflict of with Bukharan khanate, 100; England and Netherlands compete for trade with, 46; exports goods to Siberia, 113; Filat′ev family trades with, 234; Ivan IV seeks trade with, 44; merchants from and fur trade, 86; migration from to the steppes, 58; as rival of Ottoman Empire, 38, 40; Russia denies English transit to, 47; Russia merchants trade with, 56, 229; Russia′s negative trade balance with, 101; and tensions with China, 202. *See also* Iran; Safavid Empire.
Peter I. *See* Tsar Peter I.
Petrov, Semen, 307–8
Petrov, Stepan, 307–8
Petrovna, Elizaveta. *See* Empress Elizabeth.
plague, 72, 76, 215–16, 218–19, 248n211
polka (shelf), xi, 152, 156, 291
posad (merchant and artisan quarters), xi, 58, 209n2, 233, 259–60, 280
potash trade, 2, 53, 61, 87, 94, 340
prikazchik (agent), xi, 125n62

CPSIA information can be obtained at www.ICGtesting.com
Printed in the USA
BVOW05*1839210316

441179BV00001B/1/P